THE AMERICAN CONGRESS READER

The American Congress Reader provides a supplement to the popular and newly updated *American Congress* undergraduate textbook. Designed by the authors of the textbook, the *Reader* compiles the best relevant scholarship on party and committee systems, leadership, voting, and floor activity to broaden and illuminate the key features of the text.

Steven S. Smith is Kate M. Gregg Professor of Social Sciences and Director of the Weidenbaum Center at Washington University in St. Louis. He has authored or coauthored seven books and many articles on congressional politics, including *Call to Order: Floor Politics in the House and Senate, Party Influence in Congress*, and *Politics or Principle: Filibustering in the U.S. Senate*, and has coauthored several articles and a book on Russian parliamentary politics. He is a former Senior Fellow at the Brookings Institution and has taught at the University of Minnesota, Northwestern University, and George Washington University.

Jason M. Roberts is Assistant Professor of Political Science at the University of North Carolina at Chapel Hill. His research interests include American politics, the U.S. Congress, elections, and Supreme Court nominations. He has published articles in the *American Journal of Political Science*, the *Journal of Politics*, and *Congress and the Presidency*.

Ryan J. Vander Wielen is Assistant Professor of Political Science at Temple University. He was previously a Fellow in the Political Institutions and Public Choice program at Michigan State University and at the Weidenbaum Center at Washington University in St. Louis. He has recently been published in *Political Analysis* and *Loyola of Los Angeles Law Review*.

The American Congress Reader

Edited by

STEVEN S. SMITH
Washington University in St. Louis

JASON M. ROBERTS
University of North Carolina at Chapel Hill

RYAN J. VANDER WIELEN
Temple University

CAMBRIDGE
UNIVERSITY PRESS

CAMBRIDGE UNIVERSITY PRESS

Cambridge, New York, Melbourne, Madrid, Cape Town, Singapore, São Paulo, Delhi

Cambridge University Press
32 Avenue of the Americas, New York, NY 10013-2473, USA

www.cambridge.org
Information on this title: www.cambridge.org/9780521720199

First published 2009
Reprinted 2009

Printed in the United States of America

A catalog record for this publication is available from the British Library.

Library of Congress Cataloging in Publication Data

The American Congress reader / edited by Steven S. Smith, Jason M. Roberts, Ryan J. Vander Wielen.
    p. cm.
    ISBN 978-0-521-72019-9 (pbk.)
    1. United States. Congress.   2. United States. Congress – Evaluation.   3. United States –
Politics and government – 21st century – Public opinion.   4. Public opinion – United States.
    I. Smith, Steven S., 1953–   II. Roberts, Jason M.   III. Vander Wielen, Ryan J.   IV. Title.
                JK1041.A617   2009
            328.73–dc22   2008039660

ISBN 978-0-521-72019-9 paperback

Contents

PART XIII. FURTHER READINGS ON
CONGRESSIONAL POLITICS

THE AMERICAN CONGRESS READER

PART I. THE AMERICAN CONGRESS: MODERN TRENDS

CHAPTER ONE

What Is Wrong with the American Political System?

John Hibbing and Elizabeth Theiss-Morse

Hibbing and Theiss-Morse argue that the American public dislikes Congress, as it does other parts of government, because it dislikes the *processes* of government. Congress, in which conflict, partisanship, and bargaining is quite visible to the public, is disliked the most. It is Congress's transparency that makes it the least-liked among the major institutions of government.

The voices of citizens matter in a democracy, but understanding what these voices are truly saying is difficult. We know that the American public holds the political system, and the institutions composing it, in astonishingly low regard. We also know that people are especially disgusted with Congress. The reason for these negative feelings is much less clear. If we are to understand what citizens are saying, however, we must determine what lies behind their antipathy. We pursue this task in the pages that follow. Our primary thesis is that dissatisfaction with the political system and especially Congress is due in no small part to public perceptions of the *processes* involved. As will become apparent, some aspects of these allegedly flawed governing processes are of the sort that could be improved through the adoption of certain political reforms, but other aspects are endemic to open democratic government. That the people of the United States,

John Hibbing and Elizabeth Theiss-Morse. 1995. "What Is Wrong with the American Political System?" in John Hibbing and Elizabeth Theiss-Morse, *Congress As Public Enemy* (Cambridge University Press), 1–21. Reprinted with permission.

a country often viewed as the initiator of modern democratic government, have an aversion to democratic processes may sound absurd to many, and perhaps obvious to a few, but we ask for patience as we develop the evidence and logic behind this contention and as we append the necessary caveats and qualifications.

The public's negativity toward the political system and Congress has reached the saturation point. It pours forth with only the slightest provocation and has been duly recorded by countless political observers. In fact, these sentiments have been so much a part of the recent scene that only the briefest sampling is needed here. The title and first few paragraphs of a 1991 *Washington Post* article include these words and phrases: "an electorate ready to revolt," "anger," "frustration," "crisis of confidence," a political system "under indictment," "crisis of confidence" (again), "disaffection," "anxiety," "decline of confidence" (for variety), "disillusionment," "government off track," "frustrations," and "further frustrations" (for good measure).

While it is difficult to locate a portion of the political system currently held in high esteem, it is not difficult to locate the focal point of the alleged public unrest. It is, fittingly, the first branch of government, the U.S. Congress. The initial report of the joint American Enterprise Institute and Brookings Institution effort to renew Congress begins by stating simply: "Make no mistake about it: Congress is in trouble." We are told that people believe Congress is the broken branch, that it is an embattled institution, that its approval rating among the public is at an all-time low, that Congress faces "a wave of public criticism that is unprecedented in recent memory," and that "the public hates Congress."

It is now common practice, both for those retiring from Congress and for those staying, to complain about the hectic pace, the difficulty of passing legislation, the lack of comity among members, shrill demands from the people, the demanding interest groups, the intrusive media, and the byzantine, balkanized legislative process. Alas, House Republicans' 1995 success in eliminating three minor committees and a few dozen subcommittees was hardly sufficient to alter these perceptions. Perhaps the most jarring statement on the plight of Congress came when William Gray (D.-Penn.), who held one of the more powerful positions in the House as majority whip, explained his decision to leave Congress by noting that he wanted to make a difference in society. It used to be that people entered Congress because they wanted to make a difference; now it appears that some leave for the same reason.

So, virtually everyone - insiders and outsiders alike - seems to be upset with our national political institutions and particularly with Congress. The unrest may appear most intense outside the beltway, but many Washingtonians also are sincerely disappointed with the current functioning of the political system. Discontent seems ubiquitous.

When previous researchers have attempted to determine people's level of commitment to democratic values, the standard practice has been to focus on freedom of speech. This approach is not unreasonable, but a commitment to freedom of speech is hardly commensurate with a commitment to all democratic values, as many more elements of democratic values exist. More important, and as the research on commitment to freedom of speech indicates, a claimed commitment to certain values should not be equated with a commitment at the operational level. We may profess attachment to broad values but react negatively when these values are put into practice in specific instances.

The aspect of democratic values that concerns us most, and that has been largely ignored by previous research, is a commitment to basic democratic processes. We agree with Bernard Crick when he writes that the process of democratic politics involves compromise among competing interests, tolerance of diverse points of view, and "some recognition that government is . . . best conducted amid the open canvassing of rival interests." This means that democratic processes will not usually highlight certainty, agreement, and speed. Rather, they often reveal our lack of certainty, often remind us of our disagreements, and are seldom speedy.

In addition, the nature of modern democracy in a mass technocratic society is consistent with processes allowing for disagreements, debates, and decisions to be undertaken by *representatives* of various people, causes, and interests rather than by the people themselves. This leaves open the possibility that these representatives will be perceived to have been co-opted, leaving the ordinary people out of the process. Further, though it may not be absolute (and some people, such as the term-limit supporters, are trying to reverse the trend), there is a tendency in developed and differentiated societies for institutions to become complex, bounded, professionalized, and distinguished by unique norms, rules, standard operating procedures, and support structures.

So, true democratic processes in any realistic environment are bound to be slow, to be built on compromise, and to make apparent the absence of clean, certain answers to important questions of the day. Given the size, nature, and developmental stage of American society, our democratic processes are further characterized by visible agents (representatives of various concerns and people) and less visible principals (the people and concerns themselves), and by elaborate and ponderous governmental structures.

With these core features of democratic processes in mind, we turn to a brief preview of the public's process preferences. To put it simply, Americans tend to dislike virtually all of the democratic processes described above. They dislike compromise and bargaining, they dislike committees and bureaucracy, they dislike political parties and interest groups, they dislike big salaries and big staffs, they dislike slowness and multiple stages, and they dislike debate and publicly hashing things out, referring to such actions as haggling or bickering.

Americans want both procedural efficiency and procedural equity. What seems to escape many people is that democratic processes are practically by definition not procedurally efficient. The "haggling and bickering" so frequently decried by the people could very easily be termed informed discussion. And while eliminating interest groups and political parties might alleviate the sense that equity has been trashed by special interests, it would be impossible for democratic procedures to work in our kind of society without something like them. We need these groups to link the people and the governmental structures unless we want to try direct democracy (and the people do not).

In stressing Americans' distaste for open debate and methodical coalition building as well as their fondness for clear, quick decisions, we are not simply restating the point that most people have authoritarian streaks; the situation is more complicated than that. It is not so much that Americans are authoritarians in the sense that they crave a "man on a white horse." This would be easy to provide. What Americans want is much more difficult. They want stealth democracy.

They want opportunities for involvement, and they want to know that if they take the opportunity they will be taken seriously. At the same time, they do not really want to get involved. Not only that, they do not really want to have to see the political process being played out. They want democratic decision-making processes in which everyone can voice an opinion, but they do not prefer to see or to hear the debate resulting from the expression of these inevitably diverse opinions. To them, such debate is bickering, haggling, and all talk. They want openness in the sense that they want to know they or anybody else can exercise influence if they want to. They do not want key decisions to be made in private, but this does not mean people are likely to try to influence government or to want to see and hear every laborious step of the governing process. They only want to know that the opportunities exist. The American people want democratic procedures, but they do not want to see them in action.

Do not ever say that people will henceforth be denied the opportunity to observe a congressional committee meeting or that the position of dog catcher or weed commissioner will be turned into a nonelective office. Such proposals are usually opposed vigorously by a loud and substantial majority of Americans. But at the same time, do not infer from this opposition that the public likes to be involved – even in a passive way – in politics. It does not. The people simply do not want to be told that they *cannot* be involved. This desire should not obscure the basic fact that the American public dislikes many of the core features of democratic procedures.

Just as people want governmental services without the pain of taxes, they also want democratic procedures without the pain of witnessing what comes along with those procedures. Political observers have failed to understand this situation no doubt partly because many of us enjoy watching the give and take of politics. In this, we are quite different from ordinary people. They are put off by this same give and take; they do not want it. They want efficient, equitable decisions, and they want them reached in a fashion that does not force them to be exposed to the process. They also want to be confident nobody has been given an inside track or special, undeserved attention. Of course, the belief that politicians are always "haggling and bickering" is fueled by the perception that the process is dominated by special interests. A popular myth is that if members of Congress listened to the people rather than to the special interests, most disagreements would magically disappear. So while it is true that public dissatisfaction may be directed at what is felt to be a perversion of democracy rather than at democratic processes themselves, it is also true that popular assumptions about the cohesiveness of public opinion (and the detachment of special interests from that public opinion) are so unrealistic as to make this point inconsequential. People still wish to avoid the "open canvass" of diverse interests that is unavoidable with democracy.

None of this is to say that the public is displeased with the existing constitutional structure. Quite the contrary. The public still reacts negatively to proposals that would seriously disrupt the institutional relationships outlined in the Constitution even if some of the positions favored by the public seem consistent with a parliamentary structure. But the public draws a distinction between the constitutional outline and the way things are currently working or

not working. It believes portions of the original design have been subverted. The problem is not the Constitution; it is that we are not sticking closely enough to the Constitution.

If open debate is seen as bickering and haggling; if bargaining and compromise are seen as selling out on principle; if all support staff and division of labor are needless baggage; if carefully working through problems is sloth; and if all interests somehow become evil special interests, it is easy to see why the public is upset with the workings of the political system.

CHAPTER TWO

A Reassessment of Who's to Blame

A Positive Case for the Public Evaluation of Congress

David W. Brady and Sean M. Theriault

Brady and Theriault argue that there are things legislators do that bring public disapproval upon their institution. Legislators devise procedures to avoid accountability, engage in hyperbolic rhetoric, and blame their own institution. Moreover, extremists in Congress get disproportionate media coverage so that the public sees more conflict and partisanship than actually exists.

That Americans disapprove of Congress is generally as well accepted as any stylized fact in American politics. From 1974 (when Gallup first asked a congressional approval question) through 1997, congressional approval hovered around 30 percent. The average for 54 Gallup polls taken over the 23 years was 31 percent. At no point did a majority of Americans approve of the way Congress did its job – approval climaxed in 1974 at 48 percent amid the Watergate proceedings. Such bleak numbers led Glenn Parker to conclude, "Congress, like Prometheus, is inevitably doomed to suffer indignities." Sometimes, however, stylized facts turn out to be fiction. In 1998, Congress enjoyed widespread popular support, reaching a high of 63 percent in late September. Notwithstanding Congress' current popularity, the causes and consequences of the American public's

David W. Brady and Sean M. Theriault. 2001. "A Reassessment of Who's to Blame: A Positive Case for the Public Evaluation of Congress" in John R. Hibbing and Elizabeth Theiss-Morse, eds., *What Is It about Government That Americans Dislike?* (Cambridge University Press), 175–92. Reprinted with permission.

disapproval of Congress have been studied in classrooms.

The myriad opinions and explanations of low congressional approval can generally be broken down into two schools of thought. The first argues that the American public's disapproval of Congress is based on policy or conditions. Low congressional approval is an artifact of either a recessing economy or policies inconsistent with the public's preferences. Sometimes the latter is caused when Congress enacts policies that the public does not like; however, it is more likely caused when Congress does not respond to the public's demand for policy.

The second school of thought absolves Congress of its doggedly low approval in arguing that low approval stems from the Framers' institutional design. Fred Harris, a former member of Congress and chief defender of the institution, summarizes:

By its nature, Congress is conflictual, and sometimes confusingly, disturbingly, unattractively so. This is another reason for its seemingly perennial unpopularity. We say we like democracy, yet we hate conflict. But dealing with conflict, offering a forum for it and for its resolution – these are essential elements of democratic government.

Parker takes Harris' argument a step further by blaming the public: "The public often lacks the basic understanding of the legislative process that would lead to an appreciation of the significance of legislative actions." Although congressional defenders admittedly place some of the blame on members themselves, they generally conclude similarly to Harris: "The U.S. congress is today, perhaps more than ever, a place of largely well-motivated, well-prepared, and high-minded professional members."

Hibbing and Theiss-Morse provide an integrated explanation for low congressional approval. Their comprehensive and systematic argument consists of elements from both schools. They argue that "large staffs, mossback politicians, and oversized benefits packages" lead to congressional unpopularity. Additionally, they demonstrate how the American public unrealistically expects members to legislate without the democratic vulgarities defined as "diversity, mess, compromise, and a measured pace." For them high approval scores would result from both more responsible action by members of Congress and a more informed and understanding American public.

Even though the arguments summarized above represent a number of different explanations for low congressional approval, they each, either explicitly or implicitly, contain a comment element: low approval is at least partially the fault of the American public. Each explanation suggests that a more informed, educated American citizenry would not evaluate Congress as poorly as it does.

Before giving in fully to any of these explanations, we think that it is fair to ask if the American public legitimately holds the views that it does. In other words, do populist reasons exist for the public to view Congress negatively? Or, do members explicitly perpetuate the American public's cynical evaluation? We do not claim to have a definitive answer to these questions; rather we offer several speculative arguments that place the blame of low congressional approval squarely upon the members. We argue that it is *because of* the decisions made by the political elite that the American public disapproves of Congress. We present four practices members actively engage in that lead to congressional unpopularity. Each practice is briefly mentioned in this introduction before we present the more complete argument.

First, members of Congress avoid difficult votes by engaging in questionable legislative procedures. They employ these procedures to circumvent accountability. In this section, we examine the history of the congressional pay raise. We argue that individual members of Congress sacrifice the integrity of the institution so they can receive salary increases without paying a political price.

Second, members frequently engage in hyperbolic rhetoric. The hyperbolic rhetoric takes two forms. First, they employ Perot's quick-fix rhetoric in claiming to have easy solutions to hard problems. Unfortunately, the public hears the rhetoric and is left profoundly disappointed when their expectations are not realized. Second, and inversely, divergent proposals are not debated meaningfully; rather, the consequences are overblown and exaggerated in hopes of demonizing the proponents and killing the proposals. Members not only lose credibility when the consequences are not realized, but in the process the practice demeans the institution. We discuss the rhetoric used by Democrats during the Persian Gulf War debates and Republicans during Clinton's first budget as examples of this irresponsible rhetoric.

Third, members run for Congress by running against it. A popular campaign tactic in congressional elections is to bash the institution. Challengers try to tie incumbents to the "mess in Washington," as incumbents try to persuade the voters to send them back so an experienced voice can fight against the "Washington establishment." Congressional campaigns also intensify other activities disliked by the public such as negative campaigning. In this section, we show that as the elections get closer and more people pay more attention, the American public's approval of Congress decreases.

Last, and perhaps most important, the public face of Congress distorts the internal workings of the institution. While ideological extremists bash each other on television as well as in newspapers, the moderates are left to negotiate and legislate. We show, through a series of tests, that those who are most influential in passing legislation are least likely to show up in newspapers and television talk shows. Consequently, the public witnesses a higher proportion of fighting and combative rhetoric than actually exits.

Those aspects of Congress that Americans like least, according to Hibbing and Theiss-Morse, are those that they see most.

QUESTIONABLE LEGISLATIVE PROCEDURES

We argue that members often subvert the normal process to obtain outcomes that might not otherwise be realized. In doing so, members of Congress make the process appear even uglier than it already is. When the public witnesses a debasement of a process it already views skeptically, can we be surprised that they disapprove? David Dreier, a reform-minded member of the House, argues, "I don't think it's mere coincidence that the growing prevalence of restrictive floor procedures has coincided with the decline in public support for Congress." We show how the politics of congressional pay raises subverted the normal process. We speculate that both the subversion and the enactment of pay raises cause an already skeptical public to express disgust at Congress.

Congressional Pay Raises

Congressional pay raises are an explosive issue. Indeed, as James Madison noted over 200 years ago, "There is a seeming impropriety in leaving any set of men, without control, to put their hand into the public coffers, to take money to put in their pockets." Unfortunately for members of Congress, the Constitution reserves for them exclusively the duty to decide their pay. Controversies surrounding congressional pay are nearly as old as the republic itself.

Lest the American public think this controversy of increasing pay is a recent phenomenon, the congressional history is replete with stories surrounding congressional pay raises. In 1816, members changed their pay from a per diem basis to an annual salary. During the next election, many members lost their seats amid the public's rebellion, including nine who resigned even before the election. Perhaps the most audacious pay raise occurred in 1873. Just as the 42nd Congress was drawing to a close, members not only passed a 50 percent salary increase, but they made it retroactive for two years. Not surprising, the majority party paid dearly for this abuse of public authority. In the next election, 96 members of the Republican majority lost their seats.

The more recent history is also illustrious. In 1953, Congress established the Commission on Judicial and Congressional Salaries in hopes of delegating the duty of setting their pay to a commission. Two years later, upon the recommendation of the commission, Congress voted to increase their salaries from $12,500 to $22,500. In an attempt to keep pace with inflation, members again increased their salaries in 1964 to $30,000. Three years later, they modified the old commission, giving it a new name and new powers. The President's Commission on Executive, Legislative, and Judicial Salaries would meet every four years to make salary recommendations to the president. If the president included them in his budget, then they automatically became law unless either chamber passed a resolution to block them. In this way, members could increase their pay without having to risk public scorn by explicitly voting for it.

The commission was not raising their pay quickly enough, so Congress instituted additional devices. Following the inflationary early 1970s, Congress enacted a proposal that would "make members eligible for the same annual October cost-of-living increases given to other federal employees." It was not until 1981, when Congress rejected four consecutive cost-of-living increases, however, that the procedure became automatic. In 1985, Congress made it even more difficult to prohibit a pay raise increase. In response to a Supreme Court decision against the use of the legislative veto, Congress required both chambers and the president to disapprove of a pay raise within thirty days of the president's submission of his budget in order to stop the automatic increase. In exploiting their newly enhanced rules, members from both chambers passed a resolution to disapprove of the 1987 increase exactly one day after the thirty-day cutoff (which resulted in an almost 20% salary increase). Critics called this the "vote no and take the dough strategy."

The following year, the Senate passed the Grassley Amendment that "prohibit[ed] members from receiving a pay raise proposed by the president unless both the House and Senate explicitly voted for it." When the House failed to pass the same measure, Senate conferees on a 5–2 vote agreed to drop it from the conference report. In 1989, the commission recommended a 51 percent salary increase. The Senate voted to disapprove the pay raise in hopes that the House, where the agenda is more easily manipulated, would save the day. Unfortunately for them, one day before it would have automatically taken effect, Speaker Wright, already under intense scrutiny for his alleged ethics violations, buckled under public pressure and held a vote to kill the pay raise. Before caving in to the pressure, Wright strategized for the increase by both scheduling little legislative business prior to the thirty-day cutoff and trying to stiff-arm an adjournment vote as an increasing disapproval vote pended on the cutoff date.

Despite the public's rebuke early in the year, Congress was not ready to let their pay raise die. By tying the pay raise to a series of ethics provisions including a reduction in permissible honoraria, a restriction on the amount and kinds of gifts, and a prohibition on the conversion of campaign cash to personal income after retirement, members hoped that a pay increase would be more publicly palatable. These rule changes were coupled with a 10 percent immediate salary increase for Senators and an 8 percent immediate as well as a 25 percent future increase for Representatives. The measure passed in the waning days of the session. In 1991, the Senate brought its pay scale in line with the more progressive House scale so that their salaries were again the same at $125,000.

Since 1953, members of Congress have tried numerous attempts to increase their pay without politically paying for it. They have delegated the responsibility of setting their pay to a commission. They have linked it to inflation. They have delegated it to the president. They have made increases automatic. Finally, they have hidden it amongst a series of reforms.

Have any of these strategies been successful in isolating the members from a public that frowns upon congressional pay raises? No.

In each case, the pay raise became public. It invited criticism – not only because of the ends (increasing congressional pay), but also because of the means (perverse legislative procedures).

Fortunately for members, the public disapproves of the institution for these pay raise debacles. Except for 1816 and 1873, it appears that members have not been individually harmed. In this sense, the strategies devised for increasing their pay without repercussions have worked. A by-product of these questionable legislative procedures is an American public who lacks trust in Congress. Fortunately for members, broken trust in an institution does not typically have adverse electoral consequences for individuals.

EASY SOLUTIONS – DIRE PREDICTIONS

Through CSPAN members of Congress can speak directly to the American public. With this privilege comes a responsibility to lead, inform, and educate. Unfortunately, the hallowed chambers of Congress sometimes bear a striking resemblance to an elementary school playground. In this section, we argue that politicians engage in hyperbolic rhetoric to the detriment of the public's approval of political institutions, generally, and of Congress, specifically. The hyperbolic rhetoric of politicians is manifested in two ways. The first is the simplification of complex public policy problems. Instead of outlining the difficulty of rigorously and systematically solving complex problems, political actors frequently simplify the problems not so much to solve them but to gain politically. When the quick-fix solutions fail, the process is demeaned, and the American public reacts negatively. Second, politicians exaggerate policy implications in hopes of not only defeating the policy but also humiliating the policy's proponents in the process.

That politicians engage in hyperbolic rhetoric cannot be disputed. In this section we offer several case studies as proof. That this leads directly to public disapproval of Congress is speculation, albeit speculation with just cause. We submit that the hyperbolic rhetoric of politicians exacerbates negative feelings. Should we be surprised that the American public disapproves of an institution that it hears engaging in behavior that it purports to despise?

The Persian Gulf War

Members engaged in hyperbolic rhetoric in the Persian Gulf War debate. Instead of discussing the simplicity of the problem, they proffered drastic predictions. In what *The New York Times* (January 13, 1991, 1) described as "the plainest choice between war and peace since World War II," members could not refrain from exaggerating the consequences. Members who opposed President Bush's attempt at the "practical equivalent" of a declaration of war frequently debated the resolution on its merits, discussing the finer points of economic sanctions versus military action; however, more than a couple of members could not resist the temptation to humiliate their proponents by exaggerating the consequences of military action.

Even though *The Washington Post* (January 13, 1991, A1) characterized the debate as "the most intense, solemn, and emotional debate seen in the Capitol in many years," mean-spirited debate reared its ugly face. In addition to her "Armageddon" prediction if we went to war, Senator Barbara Mikulski (quoted in *The Washington Post*, September 8, 1998, A10) predicted that our declaration would "produce terrorism that would 'wreak havoc' on the United States." Senator Carl Levin (*Congressional Record*, January 11, 1991, S303) also predicted widespread terrorism: "The aftermath will be volcanic explosion of radicalism and fundamentalism which will engulf the region with an unpredictable outcome, and a reign of terrorism which will be felt worldwide." Representative Cardiss Collins's (*Congressional Record*, January 11, 1991) remarks in the House were even more draconian, "War is not just a word. In today's world it refers to massive death, destruction, and annihilation; hardship, food and medical shortages; economic disability, and countless other forms of disaster."

In comparison to these end-of-the-world prophesies, Representative Nancy Pelosi's prediction of environmental disaster seems understated:

Some of the consequences could be – according to the United Nations Environment Program – oil spills equal to a dozen *Exxon Valdez* spills coursing through gulf waters; oil fires raging for weeks and perhaps months; smoke and debris blocking sunlight, causing temperatures to drop and altering crop seasons which could result in widespread famine; toxic plumes ascending to the upper atmosphere and falling as acid rain; millions of fish, dolphins, sea birds and other marine life wash onto Gulf shores; chemical contamination of air, water, and vegetation; the Persian Gulf as a dead sea. [*The New York Times*, January 13, 1991, 10]

Lastly, members could not help but compare a potential Gulf War to Vietnam. Congressman Jim Traficant (*Congressional Record*, January 12, 1991, H401) made this parallel, "If Members think the gulf cannot turn into a Vietnam, let me tell Members something: Yitzhak Shamir and King Fahd are both singing 'Onward Christian Soldiers.' I assure Members that it can happen."

Hindsight, of course, is always perfect. Certainly, few military experts expected our victory in the Gulf War to be as clean and quick as it was. We do not doubt that these members believed in their dire predictions. Our argument, quite simply, is that when the American people hear these frightening predictions and then observe something different, it is not surprising that they loathe public debate and "bickering" and consequently evaluate Congress negatively.

RUNNING FOR CONGRESS BY RUNNING AGAINST IT

When Richard Fenno soaked and poked over twenty years ago, he stumbled across a phenomenon that has become one of the most universally accepted and recognized congressional campaigning tactics. He found:

The diversity of the House provides every member with plenty of collegial villains to flay before supportive constituents at home. Individual members do not take responsibility for the performance of Congress; rather each portrays himself as a fighter against its manifest shortcomings. Their willingness, at some point, to stand and defend their votes contrasts sharply with their disposition to run and hide when a defense of Congress is called for. Congress is not "we"; it is "they." And members of Congress run *for* Congress by running *against* Congress.

Although a new discovery for Fenno in the late 1970s, the ability of incumbents to win reelection by blasting the institution is unquestioned today. Congress has become the popular punching bag for politicians of both political parties and every ideology. Indeed, Senator William Proxmire lamented from the Senate floor, "No one and I mean nobody ever defends the Congress. In more than thirty years in this branch of the Congress, and in literally tens of thousands of conversations back in my State with people of every political persuasion I have yet to hear one kind word, one whisper of praise, one word of sympathy for the Congress as a whole." If members of Congress view their place of employment so negatively, why are we surprised that the American public also expresses negative attitudes about Congress? We submit that the relationship between members of Congress and Congress is one of the strangest relationships in employment history. When was the last time Bill Gates ridiculed Microsoft to keep his job?

Fenno found that the "villains" blamed by the seventeen members that he traveled with ranged from "the old chairmen" to "the inexperienced newcomers" and from "the tools of organized labor" to "the tools of big business." All the possible different characteristics of members were vilified by someone. Instead of attacking specific members through unflattering descriptions, members often focus their wrath upon the entire Washington system. An example of this strategy is when Barbara Mikulski, a twelve-year veteran of the Senate who is notoriously adept at using the rules to her advantage, "portrays Congress as an entrenched and wily enemy. Her speeches are laced with the gunpowder terms of combat: She is forever 'doing battle,' a 'scrapper' waging war along with other 'tough fighters'" (*The Washington Post*, September 8, 1998, A10).

This Congress bashing rhetoric is just one activity that intensifies during congressional campaigns. In addition to criticizing Congress, competing congressional candidates also engage in personal attacks, irresponsible rhetoric, and negative campaigning. How does the public react to these activities that we know they dislike?

We provide an answer by analyzing approval numbers. As congressional elections become more imminent, ignoring Congress becomes more difficult for the American public as news coverage and political ads become ubiquitous. What happens when the American mind is more focused on politics and when the political arena is intensified by elections? Using data from three different polling firms (Gallup, *New York Times*/CBS News, and *The Washington Post*/ABC News) over twenty four years, we analyze 114 different polls to hazard a guess. The dependent variable is the percentage of poll respondents who approve "of the way the U.S. Congress is doing its job." The independent variable of interest is the number of months before an election the poll is conducted. What happens to approval when elections near? With a simple specification of including only the independent variable of interest, we see that for each month away from an election Congress' approval increases by more than a quarter of a point.

Policy Is Centrist; Commentary Is Extreme

We believe that the strongest case for the people and against the political elite arises when the former are systematically and persistently presented with a skewed view of the legislative process. That is, policy is made via compromises wherein the major actors are ideologically moderate senators and representatives who reach agreements acceptable to majorities of the House and Senate. These individuals like Sam Nunn (D-GA) and Nancy Kassebaum (R-KS) are reasonable left-of-center and right-of-center senators whose policy views are well within the mainstream. Yet, in general it is not the moderates' voices that are heard discussing major policy issues; rather, the public hears the left and right. Clearly, this point is true when one thinks of shows such as *Crossfire* and *The McLaughin Group* where left and right are paid to yell at each other. If the informed public does not hear from the center but only the left and right then we could explain some of the Hibbing–Theiss-Morse thesis via an induced distortion of the legislative process. In order to test this thesis – policy is made in the center and the public hears the ideologues thus exaggerating the amount of bile in the system – we examine a couple of different dependent variables.

This reason for the public's condemnation of Congress is different from the previous three. In each of the first three, members alone engage in behavior that the American public dislikes. The display of political hollering that occurs on most political shows is caused by the member, the media, and even the public. We do not think that any one of the three is exempt from criticism; rather, the first two use each other to appeal to the third. Members use extreme rhetoric to gain the spotlight. The media offer the spotlight because they have concluded that the American public is more likely to watch a fight than it is a meaningful discussion of the issues.

Although the extremists get the coverage, the moderate's role in a legislative body is crucial. The winning side in the debate must make the necessary concessions to ascertain her vote. Given the primacy of the moderates in both enacting and interpreting legislation, it would not be unreasonable to expect their faces and their quotes to show up in the media's digest of legislative affairs. After all, they are the ones who ultimately decide the fate of legislation. The conventional wisdom of who gets news coverage, however, is exactly the opposite. Stephen Hess summarizes, "The consensus among journalists, senators, and scholars, then, is that the national media pay more and more attention to less and less important senators," which he defines as "the mavericks, the junior members, and the blow-dried but empty headed." It is in questioning this consensus that Hess conducts a study of "which senators get covered by the national news media, and why."

After examining thirty years of data from three different media outlets (Associated Press stories, national news magazines, and the network evening news programs), Hess concludes that the conventional wisdom is incorrect. He finds, "The coverage of the national news media from 1953 through 1983 has increasingly directed attention to the definable leaders at the expense of the nonleaders, mavericks, and others." These findings cast doubt upon the meaningfulness of the distinction between "outsiders" and "insiders" or "show horses" and "work horses." Rather, it suggests that the "insiders" and the "work horses" are the same as those getting media coverage.

To see if ideology influences media coverage in a more subtle way, we conducted our own tests that include not only variables that operationalize the findings of Hess, but also variables to test the conventional wisdom. Our dependent variable for the first test was the number of times *The New York Times* mentioned a senator's name from January 1, 1997, to June 5, 1998. To isolate particular systematic biases, we included a variety of control variables. First, we include three indicator variables for the senators from the states that immediately surround and include New York City (Connecticut, New Jersey, and New York) so that the results are not biased by local news stories. Second, we include institutional variables: whether the senator was a Democrat, was the majority or minority leader, or was a chair or ranking member of a committee. We decompose the last variable into the most and least important committees as defined by Hess. We also include the member's age and seniority in addition to a measure of his or her ideological extremity. For the last variable, we operationalize it as the distance between the member's ideology and the mean legislator's ideology, so that extreme liberals and extreme conservatives have the same score.

Table 2.1 shows the results from the multivariate regression. Being party leaders increases their *New York Times* mentions by over 250. Serving as chair of a major policy committee increases mentions by almost 80. When controlling for these measures, however, age and seniority have little influence upon press coverage. The results also support the conventional wisdom. For each point away from the median that a legislator is, she receives roughly one more mention in *The New York Times* even while controlling for institutional position. Mavericks, it seems, still get a disproportionate amount of coverage.

Table 2.1. *Who Gets Media Coverage? A Multivariate Regression Answer*

Coefficient	1997–8 *NYT* Mentions	Hess's Media Index (1983)
New York	318.15**	
	(42.12)	
New Jersey	88.73*	
	(40.55)	
Connecticut	61.68	
	(40.36)	
Ran for President		275.97**
		(27.38)
Democrat	−34.11**	−21.47*
	(11.83)	(10.92)
Party Leader	254.67**	182.28**
	(39.72)	(36.49)
"A" Committee Chairs	79.27**	37.95**
	(18.23)	(12.23)
"B" Committee Chairs	27.98	68.26**
	(17.36)	(16.68)
Age	−0.38	
	(0.50)	
Seniority	−0.13	
	(0.62)	
Ideology	0.98*	0.67*
	(0.50)	(0.36)
Constant	27.32	9.43
	(31.57)	(11.57)
Observations	100	100
R^2	0.62	0.65
F-value	14.44	28.73

Note: * $p < .05$. ** $p < .01$.

The results described above from the multivariate regression contradict the conclusions reached by Hess. Two possible explanations could account for this contradiction. First, the more sophisticated methodology of multivariate regression could detect an undercurrent of the media's preference for ideological members that Hess and Cook did not observe. Or, second, times might have changed. The media might now prefer to give coverage to mavericks whereas in the 1980s and before they sought comments from the leaders in the Senate. To test which of these explanations account for the difference between this study and the earlier studies, we perform a similar multivariate test on the data collected by Hess from the 98th Congress (1983–84).

The data from the earlier congress does show that position remains a good predictor of media coverage. In addition to position, the ideological extremity of the senators does indeed influence media coverage. For each ideological point away from the median member in the Senate, a senator receives two-thirds of a mention. Given that the media coverage index for the 98th Congress has a mean of forty-nine, this effect is quite substantial. In sum, this reanalysis of Hess's data shows, perhaps, that an undercurrent of media favoritism toward extreme senators was present afterall, at least in the latter part of Hess's study.

How do these results relate to our thesis that the public should not be blamed for disapproving of Congress? In concluding their study, Hibbing and Theiss-Morse argue, "People do not wish to see uncertainty, conflicting options, long debate, competing interests, confusion, bargaining, and compromised, imperfect solutions. They want government to do its job quietly and efficiently, sans conflict and sans fuss. In short, we submit, they often seek a patently unrealistic form of democracy." The results from the study would suggest that the media depict a realistic version of law making. Our results suggest that the public are subject to an overrepresentation of those things that they like least in the legislative process. They may be, in part, given the car wreck that they really want; however, the members and the media glorify the fight and downplay the meaningful debate. Is it surprising that the public disapproves of an institution that they see engaged in unnecessary and ideological bickering when it is this "messy debate" that they loathe the most?

CONCLUSION

In what for us is an unusually normative paper, we have attempted to redirect some of the criticism that has been placed at the feet of the Congress-disdaining American public. Scholars, journalists, and politicians have been making "if only the American public understood" arguments since the political process began opening up in the 1960s. We have suggested that the American public has in fact understood the cues, signals, and messages sent by members of Congress, the political elite, and the media. Indeed, they have understood them too well. In this chapter, we presented four arguments that restore some faith in the public's ability to reach rational evaluations of Congress.

First, the American public sees members of Congress avoiding difficult issues by placing them in perverse legislative procedures. We have shown that members have employed questionable legislative practices when it is in their interest. By doing so, the politicians escape accountability. We showed how the members of Congress have been willing to risk institutional approval to secure pay raises.

Second, the American public sees members of Congress engaged in hyperbolic, highly symbolic, and meaningless rhetoric in their debates. Politicians either promise easy solutions that are necessarily incapable of solving complex problems or engage in draconian predictions not only to defeat a proposal but to humiliate its proponents. These rhetorical practices debase the practice of debate. Consequently, the American public impugns what it sees as "bickering."

Third, the American public sees members of Congress bashing Congress. If those who make up the institution are unwilling to defend it, how can we expect the public to approve of it? Instead, each electoral cycle the public sees veteran legislators – many of whom have spent more of their life in Washington than they have in their district – running from the "Washington system." Not only do members run against Congress, but they also run negative campaigns and engage in the exact behavior that the American public loathes. We show that as elections near, the American public increasingly disapproves of Congress.

Fourth, the American public sees extremists talk, yell, and debate on television – unfortunately, they do not see moderates legislate. We have shown that when controlling for a variety of factors, ideologically extreme members are more likely to appear on television and in newspapers than their moderate counterparts.

Because ideologues are more resolute in their desire to be visible and the media are predisposed to cover conflict, the American public is rarely exposed to the moderate give-and-take that results in mainstream government policy.

We understand that Congress is faced with difficulties inherent within the Constitution. It mandates that representatives be popularly elected by the represented. Consequently, 435 members in the House are elected by 435 different constituencies and 100 senators are elected by 50 different constituencies. This electoral setup provides incentives for members of Congress to act with a keen eye toward their districts that at times can be detrimental to the nation.

In addition to the particularistic focus of members, we must recognize that the legislature is only one of three branches in the federal system established by the Constitution. This separation of powers system provides a number of veto points at which policy initiatives die. The system was designed to be slow, unresponsive, and lethargic. As such, the decisions made by members of Congress may be rational, but so too may be the evaluations made by the American public.

We also recognize that as parties have gotten stronger, the distribution of preferences in Congress has become more bimodal. This causes party leaders to be further left and further right, which bears directly upon our argument. Nevertheless, it has been our purpose to claim, even if not in the strongest sense, that the American public has legitimate reasons to hold Congress in low esteem not because of policy or the legislative process but because of the behavior of political elites.

We have not argued that the American public is absolved from all blame in perpetually poor approval ratings for political institutions, nor have we argued that members of Congress or the media should accept all the blame. Furthermore, we do not claim to have the definitive answer on why the American public disapproves of Congress. Rather, we have only suggested that a Congress-disapproving public is simply reacting to what it sees being played out by the political actors on the political stage.

CHAPTER THREE

Between the Campaigns

Public Approval and Disapproval of Government

James A. Stimson

Stimson observes that the public approval of Congress and legislators moves in tandem with approval of presidents and governors, along with trust in government generally and confidence in the economy. He infers that Congress's approval ratings are driven primarily by the public's judgment about whether things are going well in the country.

He had famously asked, "Are you better off than you were four years ago?" He had known the answer would be "no." He had said he could do better. Now, in April 1982, Ronald Reagan was in trouble. After a year of relatively good outcomes in 1981, the U.S. economy came full circle, from stagnation to modest growth, and now crashing into full-scale recession. Reagan's early approval ratings had been strong, often in the upper 60s. He had averaged upper 50s. Now as the economy started to slide, so, too, did Reagan's standing. It was low 50s in the fall of 1981 and dropped below fifty briefly in November. After one rebound, it went below 50 and stayed. By April he was at 43. It was not as low as he would go.

Ronald Reagan surely knew the insider's rule of thumb about approval and reelection: Below 50, you lose. Not precise and not based on many cases, the rule of thumb nonetheless had a perfect track record. Voters and consumers had been pessimistic in October 1980, when

James A. Stimson. 2004. "Between the Campaigns: Public Approval and Disapproval of Government" in James A. Stimson, *Tides of Consent* (Cambridge University Press), 137–57. Reprinted with permission.

Reagan had asked, "Are you better off?" Now their pessimism had sunk lower still. Production was declining. The number of unemployed had passed 10 million. After July of his first year in office, when the unemployment rate stood at 7.2 percent, it began to rise, continuing upward every single month. It was reaching near a modern high point at 9.3 in April, from which it would rise into unknown double-digit territory in September. Reagan's approval marched in counterstep. It reached a new low of 41 in July and August 1982. After a plateau, it fell further, to 37 in early January of 1983, to 35 in late January. Only two modern presidents had ever been that low: Richard Nixon, who soon thereafter resigned, and Jimmy Carter, whose low standing had helped Reagan assist him into early retirement.

Reagan's Democratic critics in the Senate had little reason to be gleeful over his troubles. They, too, were experiencing unkind reactions from the public. Not as severe as the president's and harder to see because the senators were rated by home state publics in polls that were not very frequent or very visible, nonetheless Democratic senators in the aggregate were in decline. Whatever their personal standing in the home state, most in 1982 were lower than they had been before. If they had hoped that Ronald Reagan's troubles would be their good fortune, they would be disappointed. As the economy went from warm to cool to grim, Republican senators, like their party leader in the White

House, saw their personal popularity back home decline. But the decline was almost the same for their colleagues across the aisle, the Democrats. Governors of the fifty states were also affected. The national recession meant state tax increases and painful budget cuts, both of which were much in evidence the next fiscal year. For a discontented public there seemed plenty of blame to go around. When asked how someone was doing his or her job, it didn't seem to matter much who that someone was and what in fact he or she had done.

Then, as is usually the case, signs of recovery began to appear even while unemployment was still rising. The last quarter of 1982 saw a return to growth, almost too small to measure. By early 1983 consumer confidence in the economy stopped its year-long decline. Just as Ronald Reagan was reaching bottom, people were, if not confident, at least beginning to doubt their most pessimistic assessments. The first quarter of 1983 produced a full point growth, about a 4 percent annual rate. It could be just an easy adjustment to an economy that had cooled too much or too fast. Or it could be the beginning of recovery.

Reagan approval turned upward, just a little, to about 40, still very low. But consumers and voters saw the turn in the economy this time. The gain in confidence by the second quarter was a real jump. Reagan, who had claimed that what was now called Reaganomics was responsible for the 1981 relatively good showing, had not been eager to attach his name to the recession that followed. By 1983 he was beginning again to claim credit.

By mid-1983 Reagan's approval numbers were in the middle 40s, up about 25 percent from the disastrous 35 of January. Reagan was the enemy of government. "Government isn't the solution," he said over and over again. "Government is the problem." When he had said that in 1982, the public had agreed. Trust in government was near an all-time low. Now in 1983, as Reagan began to recover, the public's esteem for government did, too. And it liked Congress a little better than it had before, and it notched up its approval of U.S. senators,

Reagan's friends on the Republican side and his Democratic foes alike. Governors, more victims of economic cycles than its causes, had suffered along with the president, but with a lag. The year 1983 was very bad for them.

The third quarter of 1983 produced a surge of growth. It was so substantial that it could not be anything but recovery. By mid-1983 the economy had made up the ground lost since 1981. By the end of that year it had moved solidly ahead. Then it was no longer in recovery; it was on its way to prosperity. By the last days of 1983 Ronald Reagan moved back into positive territory, reaching an approval of 54 percent. And as he did, Congress looked better, government regained trust, and senators and governors began to breathe easier. The dawn of election year 1984 produced a spirit of optimism. It would carry Reagan to easy victory over Walter Mondale, and times were good, too, for Reagan friends and foes in government, national and state.

Ronald Reagan made the transition from one of the least to one of the most approved presidents. And as he did, citizens began to approve everybody who governed, more than they had before. They began to like Congress better and to trust government more.

What was going on? Why did all those disparate things move together? What does it mean? We have worried about how much people trust government for thirty years or so. We worry because trust is seen as the cement of democracy. It has been lower in recent decades than when first measured. When it is low we ask why and look to alienation of a fundamental sort for explanation. Do people no longer believe in democratic institutions? What has government done to cause distrust? Is it too much scandal, too much regulation? Is it policies that fail, or something more fundamental, such as a loss of belief?

Approval we do not worry about. We think that presidents are approved when they are popular, personable, do popular things, and preside over good times. Declining approval, such as Reagan's in 1982, connotes simply that the public is not happy with outcomes. Its fix isn't a restoration of belief or faith, but simply better outcomes.

There is a vigorous debate among political observers about what role, if any, various parts of government play in regulating the economy. We debate in particular whether presidents are due either credit or blame for prosperity or recession when they are in the White House. Economists least of all believe that presidential policies have major influence for good or ill. The public, in contrast, seems to have no such doubts about efficacy. It credits presidents specifically for good times and blames them for bad times. Perhaps it is like baseball managers. They neither bat nor field, but are held responsible for their team's fortunes. The president is America's manager.

If presidential responsibility is problematic, what of Congress and its individual members? Congress has a role in taxing and spending and so, hypothetically, can be held responsible for economic outcomes. But it is very hypothetical. We expect economic leadership from the White House. The 535 individual members of House and Senate lack the leverage to lead. They can vote yes or no to proposals, but originating economic regulation is unlikely in our constitutional structure. Nonetheless, good times produce approval of Congress (the institution) and of its individual members.

Governors are not economic policymakers at all, not even hypothetically. They have no say in monetary policy, constitutionally reserved to the federal government, and their mandate to balance state budgets deprives them of any fiscal leverage as well. They respond to the economy but have no control of it. But when the Federal Reserve or the president or the unseen hand – take your choice – moves the economy into prosperity, governors are seen to be "handling their job" as governor. And that approval is withdrawn in bad times.

In this chapter I want to come to terms with what it means for citizens to approve or disapprove individual officeholders and government institutions, to trust or distrust "government" itself. My point of view is that all these things are more interconnected than the words of the questions would suggest and therefore

can't mean quite what we think they mean. I begin with the presidency, an office long evaluated and one for which much is known.

THE PRESIDENCY

Presidential approval is part of American culture. Along with the presidential horse race polls, it is grist for conversation by ordinary people. If someone on the street is asked what the president's approval rating is, the reading might not be accurate, but the question, also would not draw a dumbfounded stare. It is even evident in Hollywood, where ratings play a starring role in movies such as *The American President* and *Wag the Dog*.

Theories of what affects presidential approval are pretty well known, too. Often seen in political science journals, they are also common fare in news reports and commentaries. The ideas that new presidents have approval honeymoons or that approval surges in response to foreign crises won't be new to many readers of this book. They've worked their way out of regression analyses and into mainstream fare.

Because much is known and because I have been writing about the matter for a quarter of a century (since the Nixon administration), I don't want to belabor presidential approval here. Too important to omit, I restrict myself to laying out a little summary of where we stand and what we know, giving some emphasis to that which is not in movies or daily press reports. I begin with a description of the approval of three recent presidents (leaving out George W. Bush, the very most recent, because the record is too short as I write).

Three Recent Presidents

Presidential approval varies a lot, and that is within administrations, not among them. Although presidents are sometimes characterized as popular or not, the deeper reality is that almost all presidents experience striking variation within their terms. Approval given at one time in the presidency is withdrawn at others.

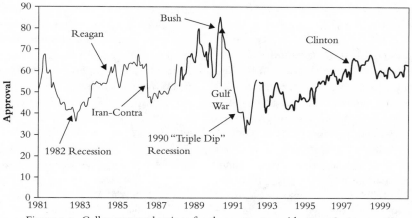

Figure 3.1. Gallup approval ratings for three recent presidents, 1981 to 2001.

Ronald Reagan's wild ride was not over with the exuberant 1983–84 recovery. His second term saw his approval plunge again in 1986 over the Iran-Contra scandal (see Figure 3.1). His vice president, George Bush, set new volatility records. His peak during the Gulf War was the highest ever achieved to that date (now surpassed by his son following the September 11 terrorism). It was followed by a steep plunge into percentages in the 30s as a sour economy overwhelmed memory of the war and left him vulnerable to defeat by Bill Clinton. Bill Clinton's ratings are the least volatile of the three (see Figure 3.2). His lows were not as low as Reagan or Bush and his highs were not as high. What is remarkable in Clinton's public standing is that it

increased while he weathered the storm of the Lewinsky scandal.

Some Basic Facts and Theories

If we look further, to the presidencies of the survey era, we can see that general patterns do emerge in most administrations and do not require a focus on particular events. I turn now to that more general accounting.

Equilibration

Underlying all the things that cause approval to be up sometimes and down at others, what operates in the background is equilibration. It

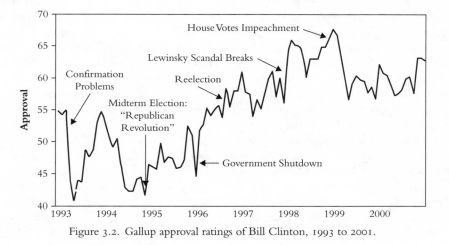

Figure 3.2. Gallup approval ratings of Bill Clinton, 1993 to 2001.

is the sort of "dark matter" in our theory, the unseen force that counterbalances that which we observe. The story is a simple one: When presidents are for some reason too high or too low in approval, and nothing happens but the passage of time, they tend to move back toward an equilibrium. Whatever it was that caused them to be too high or too low, that is, decays as time passes. This is important in a statistical sense, but also in politics. There is much speculation about the things presidents might do to draw attention and gain a few points in the polls. The theme of the movie *Wag the Dog*, but also a lot of serious writing about politics, it seems, is that presidents need only create some drama and they can repair damage to their standing whenever it is needed. From the president's point of view that seems too good to be true, and it is. What those accounts fail to factor in is that approval gains can decay just about as fast as they are created. And anything that depends on drama and novelty won't last. A president who perennially created drama to boost approval would be on a treadmill, always having to restore by new activity that which is constantly eroding.

Of the equilibrium we know two things. One is that it is close to 50 percent approval. Presidents above that in the polls tend to decline back toward it. Those below it tend to recover upward to it. That seems a sort of magic number, but this is probably coincidence. The second is that there is a lot less variation between presidents on this matter than press reports would imply. Although there are observable differences, they are small. It is not the case that we can label some of them popular and others unpopular and still do justice to the data.

Crises

Crises are the opposite force, dramatic events capable of moving approval away from – sometimes a long way from – equilibrium approval. In situations in which the nation is in peril against external threats, particularly, Americans "rally around the flag," coming to the support of the president, standing as the national symbol. It is hard to imagine that it could be otherwise. Normally the spokesperson for a political party allied against another party and half of the electorate that supports it, presidents can hardly expect approval to move far into the other side. Moments of crisis change that. Then there are no parties and no opposition, but only a single nation with a single leader. When the president acts for all, he or she can begin to expect approval for that action from all. It is very different from the "us and them" of normal politics.

Normalcy will always prevail in the long run. Thus the approval gained from crisis can never be expected to last. We are tempted always to regard each new crisis as different, *this time* redefining the nature of the polity. But the immediacy of crisis, the drama, is precisely what guarantees that it will not last. Crises get resolved, one way or another, and then they cease to be crises, cease to be dramatic, cease to have any effect on the president's public standing. Crises are punctuations, moments when the relentless return to equilibrium is halted. But the return will always take over.

We don't know about the really long term. Presidencies don't last long enough to know. Most episodes leave no further trace in the approval standings after about a year or so; smaller and sharper episodes can disappear more quickly. While there is often speculation that such temporary surges might be enough to carry a president through a reelection, there is no clear case where that has been so. Jimmy Carter's approval boosting crisis was the Iranian hostage situation. A year later the boost was all gone and the unresolved situation became a drag on Carter's standing. George Bush benefited from the Gulf War crisis as had no president before him. But like Carter, Bush's benefit deserted him before voters went to the polls.

The Honeymoon

The presidential honeymoon, a time of hope and expectation (with no tangible basis for disapproval), was a nice tradition. A kind of laying on of the hands of democracy, there was a nice symbolism to it. The people had spoken. The nation was one. The winner had a righteous claim to lead. It is easier to understand why it existed than why it appears to have gone. Millions of people, relatively independent of party, relatively neutral and moderate of viewpoint, have naturally adopted new presidents. They have acted as if public support was a right won by election, the president's to own until he did something to lose it. Brody points to a critical role for the media and the opposition party in this phenomenon. So long as the opposition does not criticize the new president, he writes, the media will not do so, either. Mostly commercial, media outlets need to minimize offending their listeners and subscribers if they are to be financially successful. And independent media attacks on the president, particularly a newly elected one, are potentially offensive. The constraint within which the media operate is that the parties effectively define the boundaries of what is legitimate and what is not. The space between them, between support and opposition, is legitimate ground for media commentary. Outside them, particularly being more critical than the opposition, is dangerous – and so editors and reporters do not go there. That effectively relegates the control of presidential criticism to the opposition; if it holds its fire, everybody holds back. If it attacks the president, then it can expect that the media will also engage in a less partisan form of presidential criticism. Brody's thesis then predicts the honeymoon as a natural consequence of a long tradition of withholding partisan criticism of presidents in their earliest months.

As American politics has become more polarized and conflictual, that tradition has disappeared. Party leaders on both sides now see it as their duty to rough up a new president of the other party lest he become too popular. Since the presidential honeymoon is as impermanent as the new marriage phenomenon for which it is named, I do not understand quite why this is the case. It would seem that the honeymoon would always fall of its own weight eventually in any case. When the president is no longer new, the factors that produced it lose force.

Perhaps we are dealing with exceptions here, that it is something about these particular presidents and these particular years that suppressed the tendency to honor the honeymoon. But Presidents Reagan, Bush, Clinton, and now George W. Bush constitute four exceptions in a row, spanning twenty years. That's a pretty big exception.

The National Economy

However much or little presidents have to do with regulating the economy, the economy definitely does regulate them. Movements in economic outcomes translate pretty directly into approval and disapproval. Not as dramatic as crises, economic effects are probably more important because they can be enduring. The approval gain from a recovery, for example, can grow strongly and steadily over time, changing the character of a presidency.

It is natural to see reaction to the economy as reward and punishment, tied to individual self-interest. In this "pocketbook" view, individuals approve when they and their families are prospering and take out anger for personal misfortune on the president. Although some such individual effects can be teased out of very complicated statistical analyses, most of the observable connection between economics and political response is what Kinder and Kiewiet call "sociotropic," evaluations based on the state of the national economy, not the personal pocketbook. This can be understood as resulting from the ease or difficulty of causal attribution. The connection between presidential action and individual economic situations is so distant that it is virtually impossible to assess it. (People do connect them, often with a partisan bias, but this isn't economic evaluation, but rather a rationalization for a view held for other reasons.) It is easier to hold the president responsible for the contours of the national economy, how things are going in general.

Another traditional view (that people first *experience* the economy and then evaluate the president) also does not hold. What the data say, in contrast, is that people evaluate the president on how they *expect* the economy to be months and years down the road. Optimism and pessimism are crucial ingredients of the political translation of economic views. When things are bad, but expected to get better, presidents do well. When they are good, but the public sees indicators of decline, approval will fall. This can be seen as a minor wrinkle in the economic picture. But it has a major consequence. It implies that governments cannot manufacture approval by trickery, by measures that might induce temporary surges of prosperity timed, for example, for elections. A public focused on the future does not fall for these tricks.

The view of presidential control we end with is in some sense hopeful. Presidents do affect their fates by achieving, or failing to achieve, the peace and prosperity the public desires. But when so much of politics is manipulation and spin, it appears to be the case that approval cannot be manufactured by the most sophisticated political trickery, cannot be bought by public relations. Modern presidents jawbone the economy from time to time, telling citizens that things are good, that presidential policies are due credit. The public, it appears, mimics the financial markets in this regard and makes up its own mind.

U.S. SENATORS

On thousands of occasions, surveys have asked respondents to evaluate one or both of their U.S. senators. It is not clear what ought to underlie such evaluations or what does. Mostly, the evaluations are assumed to tap individual skill at pleasing constituents and they are assumed to impinge on senators' reelection prospects. The purpose is to gauge state public opinion, usually on the assumption that state publics differ a good deal from one another.

I wish here to stand back from all those individual states and ask whether we can learn something about the nation from watching how fifty individual states respond to their senators. If you think about how Senator X is handling his or her job as senator, it is far from clear what standard one should invoke. Senators go to Washington, make speeches, sponsor legislation, and vote on bills. For an objective observer, it would seem quite difficult to know whether the senator is "handling" all those things well or badly. One can employ a partisan or ideological standard for what is a good or bad voting record, but the best that you can

summon for a neutral standard is whether or not the senator shows up for the votes.

In the absence of useful information for evaluating the senator's performance, we might expect more generic considerations to become important. Party is one of these. Respondents will usually know whether the senator is from their own party or an opponent, from the president's party or an opponent, and whether the two senators are on the same side of the party division. From this we might expect to see differential response to the parties. The action in Washington is often between presidents and the opposing party in Congress. From this we might expect tension between the president's standing and that of the opposition in Congress. When one is up, the other would be down, their two tracks over time negatively correlated.

The same absence of useful individual information might make respondents use general information, such as how things are going in the country, to evaluate their individual senators. We can't observe that senators have anything to do with, for example, the ebbs and flows of the national economy, but lacking any better standard, respondents might just credit everybody for good times and blame everybody for bad ones. Since this same process applies to the White House, we would expect positive correlations between the president's approval and that of all senators.

Thus our two expectations are in conflict. The negative evidence of expecting a seesaw between president and out party would conflict with the positive evidence of a world in which credit and blame go to all. Since it can't be both, a first step is to observe that correlation, to see how the standings of Democrats and Republicans move over time and to see whether they move together or opposite one another.

To do so I take all the approval readings for each party and solve for the average response that underlies them. The result is a national summary measure of the disparate responses of the state publics. What is unusual about the measure is that it taps response to an institution, the Senate, but by means of responses to individual senators. All the things that individual senators might do becomes a kind of noise

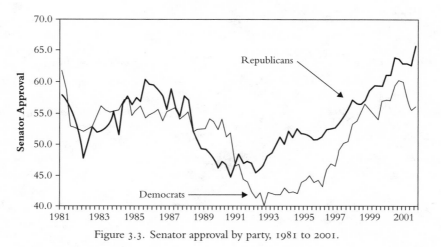

Figure 3.3. Senator approval by party, 1981 to 2001.

around a signal, which is the summary response to the whole Senate (or here to the parties in the Senate.)

The evidence of Figure 3.3 settles the issue. The standing of senators from the two parties tracks together, not opposite. And the "why" is not a mystery. One can clearly see the national economy in the background: a dip around the 1982 recession, a rise in the better times of 1984–89, down again with the 1990–92 triple dip, and a long upward movement with the economy through 2001. And all these things move both parties together. The correlation between the two series is a very high .67. Since the Senate parties are positively correlated and both move with the economic source of presidential approval, then both parties must also be positively correlated with presidential approval, support and opposition alike.

That the general state of things underlies senator approval is no shock. What is more surprising is how little the partisan game in Washington seems to matter. The president and opponents in Congress do battle, acting as if winning and losing really mattered in the ups and downs of the two parties. (And it does really matter for its policy consequences.) But all the posturing seems lost on the electorate, which sees the parties doing well or badly *together*. There is a cynical view around that many legislative contests are just empty debates, votes staged to win or to lose voters in the next election, not to decide policy. If that is true, then these data

begin to suggest that it is a wasted effort, and that voters don't much care who wins or loses, but just how things are going.

CONGRESS

In a totally different approach – national, not state, and institutional, not individual – respondents are asked what they think of Congress. Because it is the institution, "Congress," and not its individual members, it is less clear what we should expect. And it is a little unclear what this "Congress" is. Is it the House of Representatives, both bodies, some legislative abstraction? We begin with the expectation that Congress will be unpopular on average. A favorite whipping boy of all, including its own members, Congress takes a battering in public discourse. It has many critics and no friends. We thus expect it to be perennially unpopular.

Individual members, such as the U.S. senators we have already seen, have a more favorable situation. Much of what citizens know of them comes from their own activities, which are planned always to cast the member in a favorable light. Members are rarely criticized, except for two or three months before elections, and voters discount that for what it is. But the question we wish to pose for both is, "How do they move?"

Figure 3.4 provides a one-word answer to that question: "together." Whatever gulf divides

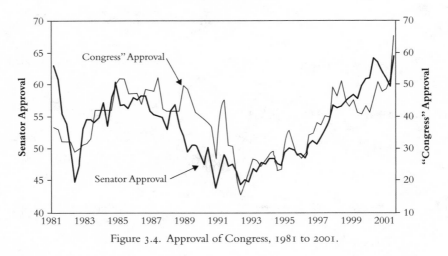

Figure 3.4. Approval of Congress, 1981 to 2001.

"Congress" from the hundreds of members who serve on its Senate side, the movement over time is two versions of the same story. The movements, correlated at .74, march to the same drummer. But the graphic device of scaling on two axes hides two important differences. Individual senators are much more approved on average (53%) than is Congress (38%). And the reaction to Congress, the institution, is much more varied, its lows dramatically lower than the senators and its highs about the same. Without a lot of confidence in the call, I suggest that the difference arises from a difference of knowledge. Voters really do know something about their senators. They have probably consciously decided to vote for or against them, for example. "Congress" is, in contrast, ephemeral, an image much more than a reality. Because that image is not rooted in much factual exposure, it is free to move with the times, free to change. The evidence that the image can change dramatically, as it did following the September 11 terrorism, for example, suggests that the perennial bad esteem for Congress is not deeply felt, just a casual prejudice, subject to change with each new piece of information.

and local taxation. For most citizens most of the time, this is more immediate than the influence of the federal government. From this we might infer that response to the governors is based on personal experience. If so, it would reflect the particular successes and failures of each state, the idiosyncrasies of state politics.

When we observe a net measure of the governors' standing, however, we see a restatement of the familiar national pattern. Figure 3.5 displays the average approval of governors by state samples with the previously estimated U.S. senator approval for reference. It bears saying that this result is partly inevitable, that a method that solves for average approval across states will discard much of the idiosyncratic variation. That is the intent. But the solution is very highly correlated with each of the individual governor's approval ratings, a fact that is inconsistent with the idea that state publics are different from one another, evaluating their governments on their own issues and politics. The governors, instead, rise and fall in unison with the factors that move response to national politics. All politics is not national, to paraphrase Tip O'Neill. But it is most definitely not local.

GOVERNORS

People have direct experience with state governors. Governors are responsible for things close to home, such as schools, highways, and state

TRUST IN GOVERNMENT

Trust in government, as noted in the introduction to this chapter, is widely seen to be fundamental. When it declines, it is regarded as

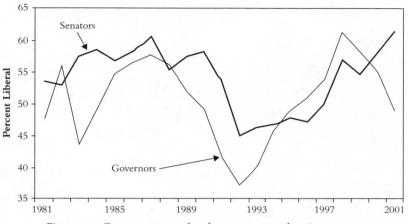

Figure 3.5. Governor approval and senator approval, 1981 to 2001.

pathological, not mere movement. Whether the explanation is declining trust in people on the whole, generalized to government, or declining trust produced by some kind of alienation and disaffection with government and its acts, decline is worrisome.

An alternative view, developed by Keele, holds that trust simply follows recent performance. Citizens trust government when it has performed well and withdraw trust when they are displeased with the state of things. As is usually the case, the national economy is the best indicator of performance. Keele shows that trust follows economic indicators and citizen responses such as presidential approval, which

themselves are moved by economic outcomes. Trust, in this story, loses its status as barometer of democracy and becomes part of a syndrome of citizen response to everything. It goes up as well as down, and its movements require explanation but not concern.

Figure 3.6, showing trust in government along with the congressional approval series of the earlier Figure 3.4, shows that the Keele view squares nicely with the data. The two different measures, derived from altogether different sources and measuring, in concept, quite different things, track closely together. This, of course, is a pattern now repeated several times. It suggests that something more general than

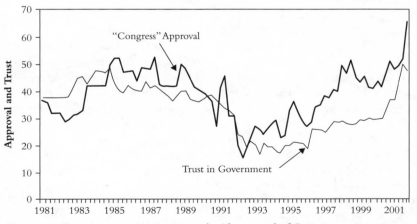

Figure 3.6. Trust in government compared with approval of Congress, 1981 to 2001.

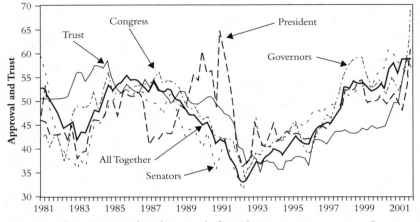

Figure 3.7. Generic approval, with approval of presidents, senators, governors, Congress, and trust in government.

each of these indicators lies beneath, a topic to which I now turn.

IS APPROVAL GENERIC?

It is by now obvious that we are dealing here with something different from what the survey questions seem to mean. When we ask how governors or senators or presidents are handling their jobs, we think the answers reflect on the individuals and institutions that are the focus of the questions. If President Bush is up or down a point or two, we ask what he has done recently and why the public is responding to him as it is. But now we see that it may not be responding to him at all. It may be expressing a generic satisfaction or dissatisfaction with government, for which he is merely beneficiary or victim.

What we are observing is generic approval and trust, a spirit that moves up and down over time and seems to respond to generalized satisfaction or dissatisfaction with the state of things. To express the idea, imagine that we can simply take all the approval and trust series, forget *whose* approval is being queried, and just estimate a generic approval over time. Figure 3.7 captures that generic approval for the twenty-one-year span where we have numerous measures of each. The figure, showing the estimate

of generic approval along with each of its components (standardized to squeeze them together in the space), shows the now familiar shape: declines in 1982, upturns in the mid-1980s, serious decline in 1990–92, followed by steady increases over the 1990s.

We can see some differences among the individual series. Presidential approval stands out from the others in 1986–87, when the Iran–Contra scandal lowered Ronald Reagan's standing but didn't affect that of others. And then George Bush stood out first in 1989, for a honeymoon not observable except in contrast to other trends, and then dramatically in 1991 at the time of the Gulf War. The low point of approval of Congress, just barely discernible, comes in 1992 with the House Banking Scandal. And the 1998–99 Lewinsky scandal period is interesting. We know that the scandal appeared to help Bill Clinton, so we would not expect to find much influence. But what is noticeable is a decline of trust in government during the scandal, accompanied by governors moving above the national government figures. The common pattern that would make sense of these movements is a joint disapproval of both Clinton and his opponents in Congress during the conflict.

The most important point, however, is that the lines are hard to pull apart and distinguish because they are pretty clearly measuring the same thing. Mainly what we see in Figure 3.7

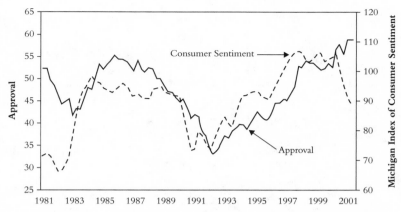

Figure 3.8. Generic approval and the Michigan Index of Consumer Sentiment (three-quarter moving average).

is mostly random variation around a common movement that applies to all these presumably different series. Approval and trust are generic, a syndrome of attitudes toward public affairs that only appears to be affected by and directed toward particular people and institutions.

A description of shared movements of Figure 3.7 will sound to readers a lot like a description of the U.S. economy: 1982 recession, followed by 1983–89 recovery, followed by the 1990 recession – becoming the triple dip downturn over 1990–92, followed by the steadily improving prosperity of the 1990s. It is evident that all those approval and trust measures tap some satisfaction and dissatisfaction with outcomes.

We can see more than a suggestion of that fact in Figure 3.8, which graphs the generic approval series against the University of Michigan consumer sentiment index, a generalized measure of citizen views of the economy. The two series have different measurement scales, with consumer sentiment normed around a neutral point of 100 (although the actual long-term average is considerably under 100). Thus, they are presented with separate scales on two axes. The pattern, however, is robust. Satisfied consumers are approving citizens. The two track quite closely together, with consumer sentiment leading approval by a quarter or two, sentiment tracking sharply with the twists and turns of the economy, while approval follows later.

Again, we can make some sense of discrepancies between the two. The 1991 Gulf War helped approval to stay high when confidence in the economy was falling. Perhaps it is mere accident or measurement issue, but it seems telling that economic confidence was consistently stronger during the Clinton presidency than was approval of all sorts. What we know about these years is that they mark intense partisan conflict, particularly 1994–2000, with the government shutdown in 1995–96 quickly followed by the Lewinsky scandal becoming an impeachment crisis in 1998–99. Conflict is unappealing to the public, likely to hurt the standing of all parties to it. So, for example, even if Bill Clinton may have been the *net* winner in the contest with the Republican Congress over the government shutdown (in my earlier interpretation), these data are consistent with an interpretation that conflict drags down public approval of government in general. (And we know from the previous figure that the state governors, not involved in that mess in Washington, became more approved than their national counterparts in this period.)

So what does it mean that citizens approve or trust? It appears to mean mainly that things are going well in the country. What is important about this pattern, and unexpected, is that the approval and trust are granted to those who have had no role in producing the outcomes.

PART II. REPRESENTATION AND LAWMAKING IN CONGRESS: THE CONSTITUTIONAL AND HISTORICAL CONTEXT

CHAPTER FOUR

U.S. Constitution, Articles I, II, III, and Amendments

Article I of the Constitution is devoted to Congress, leading many observers to call Congress the First Branch. Articles II and III concern the presidency and the courts, respectively.

ARTICLE I – THE LEGISLATIVE BRANCH

Section 1 – The Legislature

All legislative Powers herein granted shall be vested in a Congress of the United States, which shall consist of a Senate and House of Representatives.

Section 2 – The House

The House of Representatives shall be composed of Members chosen every second Year by the People of the several States, and the Electors in each State shall have the Qualifications requisite for Electors of the most numerous Branch of the State Legislature.

No Person shall be a Representative who shall not have attained to the Age of twenty five Years, and been seven Years a Citizen of the United States, and who shall not, when elected, be an Inhabitant of that State in which he shall be chosen.

(Representatives and direct Taxes shall be apportioned among the several States which may be included within this Union, according to their respective Numbers, which shall be determined by adding to the whole Number of free Persons, including those bound to Service for a Term of Years, and excluding Indians not taxed, three fifths of all other Persons.) [**The previous sentence in parentheses was modified by the 14th Amendment, section 2.**] The actual Enumeration shall be made within three Years after the first Meeting of the Congress of the United States, and within every subsequent Term of ten Years, in such Manner as they shall by Law direct. The Number of Representatives shall not exceed one for every thirty Thousand, but each State shall have at Least one Representative; and until such enumeration shall be made, the State of New Hampshire shall be entitled to chuse three, Massachusetts eight, Rhode Island and Providence Plantations one, Connecticut five, New York six, New Jersey four, Pennsylvania eight, Delaware one, Maryland six, Virginia ten, North Carolina five, South Carolina five and Georgia three.

When vacancies happen in the Representation from any State, the Executive Authority thereof shall issue Writs of Election to fill such Vacancies.

The House of Representatives shall chuse their Speaker and other Officers; and shall have the sole Power of Impeachment.

Section 3 – The Senate

The Senate of the United States shall be composed of two Senators from each State

(, chosen by the Legislature thereof,) **[The preceding words in parentheses superseded by 17th Amendment, section 1.]** for six Years; and each Senator shall have one Vote.

Immediately after they shall be assembled in Consequence of the first Election, they shall be divided as equally as may be into three Classes. The Seats of the Senators of the first Class shall be vacated at the Expiration of the second Year, of the second Class at the Expiration of the fourth Year, and of the third Class at the Expiration of the sixth Year, so that one third may be chosen every second Year; *(and if Vacancies happen by Resignation, or otherwise, during the Recess of the Legislature of any State, the Executive thereof may make temporary Appointments until the next Meeting of the Legislature, which shall then fill such Vacancies.)* **[The preceding words in parentheses were superseded by the 17th Amendment, section 2.]**

No person shall be a Senator who shall not have attained to the Age of thirty Years, and been nine Years a Citizen of the United States, and who shall not, when elected, be an Inhabitant of that State for which he shall be chosen.

The Vice President of the United States shall be President of the Senate, but shall have no Vote, unless they be equally divided.

The Senate shall chuse their other Officers, and also a President pro tempore, in the absence of the Vice President, or when he shall exercise the Office of President of the United States.

The Senate shall have the sole Power to try all Impeachments. When sitting for that Purpose, they shall be on Oath or Affirmation. When the President of the United States is tried, the Chief Justice shall preside: And no Person shall be convicted without the Concurrence of two thirds of the Members present.

Judgment in Cases of Impeachment shall not extend further than to removal from Office, and disqualification to hold and enjoy any Office of honor, Trust or Profit under the United States: but the Party convicted shall nevertheless be liable and subject to Indictment, Trial, Judgment and Punishment, according to Law.

Section 4 – Elections, Meetings

The Times, Places and Manner of holding Elections for Senators and Representatives, shall be prescribed in each State by the Legislature thereof; but the Congress may at any time by Law make or alter such Regulations, except as to the Place of Chusing Senators.

The Congress shall assemble at least once in every Year, and such Meeting shall *(be on the first Monday in December,)* **[The preceding words in parentheses were superseded by the 20th Amendment, section 2.]** unless they shall by Law appoint a different Day.

Section 5 – Membership, Rules, Journals, Adjournment

Each House shall be the Judge of the Elections, Returns and Qualifications of its own Members, and a Majority of each shall constitute a Quorum to do Business; but a smaller number may adjourn from day to day, and may be authorized to compel the Attendance of absent Members, in such Manner, and under such Penalties as each House may provide.

Each House may determine the Rules of its Proceedings, punish its Members for disorderly Behavior, and, with the Concurrence of two-thirds, expel a Member.

Each House shall keep a Journal of its Proceedings, and from time to time publish the same, excepting such Parts as may in their Judgment require Secrecy; and the Yeas and Nays of the Members of either House on any question shall, at the Desire of one fifth of those Present, be entered on the Journal.

Neither House, during the Session of Congress, shall, without the Consent of the other, adjourn for more than three days, nor to any other Place than that in which the two Houses shall be sitting.

Section 6 – Compensation

(The Senators and Representatives shall receive a Compensation for their Services, to be ascertained by Law, and paid out of the Treasury of the United States.)

[The preceding words in parentheses were modified by the 27th Amendment.] They shall in all Cases, except Treason, Felony and Breach of the Peace, be privileged from Arrest during their Attendance at the Session of their respective Houses, and in going to and returning from the same; and for any Speech or Debate in either House, they shall not be questioned in any other Place.

No Senator or Representative shall, during the Time for which he was elected, be appointed to any civil Office under the Authority of the United States which shall have been created, or the Emoluments whereof shall have been increased during such time; and no Person holding any Office under the United States, shall be a Member of either House during his Continuance in Office.

Section 7 – Revenue Bills, Legislative Process, Presidential Veto

All bills for raising Revenue shall originate in the House of Representatives; but the Senate may propose or concur with Amendments as on other Bills.

Every Bill which shall have passed the House of Representatives and the Senate, shall, before it become a Law, be presented to the President of the United States; If he approve he shall sign it, but if not he shall return it, with his Objections to that House in which it shall have originated, who shall enter the Objections at large on their Journal, and proceed to reconsider it. If after such Reconsideration two thirds of that House shall agree to pass the Bill, it shall be sent, together with the Objections, to the other House, by which it shall likewise be reconsidered, and if approved by two thirds of that House, it shall become a Law. But in all such Cases the Votes of both Houses shall be determined by Yeas and Nays, and the Names of the Persons voting for and against the Bill shall be entered on the Journal of each House respectively. If any Bill shall not be returned by the President within ten Days (Sundays excepted) after it shall have been presented to him, the Same shall be a Law, in like Manner as if he had signed it, unless the Congress by their Adjournment prevent its Return, in which Case it shall not be a Law.

Every Order, Resolution, or Vote to which the Concurrence of the Senate and House of Representatives may be necessary (except on a question of Adjournment) shall be presented to the President of the United States; and before the Same shall take Effect, shall be approved by him, or being disapproved by him, shall be repassed by two thirds of the Senate and House of Representatives, according to the Rules and Limitations prescribed in the Case of a Bill.

Section 8 – Powers of Congress

The Congress shall have Power To lay and collect Taxes, Duties, Imposts and Excises, to pay the Debts and provide for the common Defence and general Welfare of the United States; but all Duties, Imposts and Excises shall be uniform throughout the United States;

To borrow money on the credit of the United States;

To regulate Commerce with foreign Nations, and among the several States, and with the Indian Tribes;

To establish an uniform Rule of Naturalization, and uniform Laws on the subject of Bankruptcies throughout the United States;

To coin Money, regulate the Value thereof, and of foreign Coin, and fix the Standard of Weights and Measures;

To provide for the Punishment of counterfeiting the Securities and current Coin of the United States;

To establish Post Offices and Post Roads;

To promote the Progress of Science and useful Arts, by securing for limited Times to Authors and Inventors the exclusive Right to their respective Writings and Discoveries;

To constitute Tribunals inferior to the supreme Court;

To define and punish Piracies and Felonies committed on the high Seas, and Offenses against the Law of Nations;

To declare War, grant Letters of Marque and Reprisal, and make Rules concerning Captures on Land and Water;

To raise and support Armies, but no Appropriation of Money to that Use shall be for a longer Term than two Years;

To provide and maintain a Navy;

To make Rules for the Government and Regulation of the land and naval Forces;

To provide for calling forth the Militia to execute the Laws of the Union, suppress Insurrections and repel Invasions;

To provide for organizing, arming, and disciplining the Militia, and for governing such Part of them as may be employed in the Service of the United States, reserving to the States respectively, the Appointment of the Officers, and the Authority of training the Militia according to the discipline prescribed by Congress;

To exercise exclusive Legislation in all Cases whatsoever, over such District (not exceeding ten Miles square) as may, by Cession of particular States, and the acceptance of Congress, become the Seat of the Government of the United States, and to exercise like Authority over all Places purchased by the Consent of the Legislature of the State in which the Same shall be, for the Erection of Forts, Magazines, Arsenals, dock-Yards, and other needful Buildings; And

To make all Laws which shall be necessary and proper for carrying into Execution the foregoing Powers, and all other Powers vested by this Constitution in the Government of the United States, or in any Department or Officer thereof.

Section 9 – Limits on Congress

The Migration or Importation of such Persons as any of the States now existing shall think proper to admit, shall not be prohibited by the Congress prior to the Year one thousand eight hundred and eight, but a tax or duty may be imposed on such Importation, not exceeding ten dollars for each Person.

The privilege of the Writ of Habeas Corpus shall not be suspended, unless when in Cases of Rebellion or Invasion the public Safety may require it.

No Bill of Attainder or ex post facto Law shall be passed.

(No capitation, or other direct, Tax shall be laid, unless in Proportion to the Census or Enumeration herein before directed to be taken.) **[Section in parentheses clarified by the 16th Amendment.]**

No Tax or Duty shall be laid on Articles exported from any State.

No Preference shall be given by any Regulation of Commerce or Revenue to the Ports of one State over those of another: nor shall Vessels bound to, or from, one State, be obliged to enter, clear, or pay Duties in another.

No Money shall be drawn from the Treasury, but in Consequence of Appropriations made by Law; and a regular Statement and Account of the Receipts and Expenditures of all public Money shall be published from time to time.

No Title of Nobility shall be granted by the United States: And no Person holding any Office of Profit or Trust under them, shall, without the Consent of the Congress, accept of any present, Emolument, Office, or Title, of any kind whatever, from any King, Prince or foreign State.

Section 10 – Powers Prohibited of States

No State shall enter into any Treaty, Alliance, or Confederation; grant Letters of Marque and Reprisal; coin Money; emit Bills of Credit; make any Thing but gold and silver Coin a Tender in Payment of Debts; pass any Bill of Attainder, ex post facto Law, or Law impairing the Obligation of Contracts, or grant any Title of Nobility.

No State shall, without the Consent of Congress, lay any Imposts or Duties on Imports or Exports, except what may be absolutely necessary for executing it's inspection Laws: and the net Produce of all Duties and Imposts, laid by any State on Imports or Exports, shall be for the Use of the Treasury of the United States; and all such Laws shall be subject to the Revision and Controul of the Congress.

No State shall, without the Consent of Congress, lay any duty of Tonnage, keep Troops, or Ships of War in time of Peace, enter into any Agreement or Compact with another State, or with a foreign Power, or engage in War, unless actually invaded, or in such imminent Danger as will not admit of delay.

ARTICLE II — THE EXECUTIVE BRANCH

Section 1 – The President

The executive Power shall be vested in a President of the United States of America. He shall hold his Office during the Term of four Years, and, together with the Vice-President chosen for the same Term, be elected, as follows:

Each State shall appoint, in such Manner as the Legislature thereof may direct, a Number of Electors, equal to the whole Number of Senators and Representatives to which the State may be entitled in the Congress: but no Senator or Representative, or Person holding an Office of Trust or Profit under the United States, shall be appointed an Elector.

(The Electors shall meet in their respective States, and vote by Ballot for two persons, of whom one at least shall not lie an Inhabitant of the same State with themselves. And they shall make a List of all the Persons voted for, and of the Number of Votes for each; which List they shall sign and certify, and transmit sealed to the Seat of the Government of the United States, directed to the President of the Senate. The President of the Senate shall, in the Presence of the Senate and House of Representatives, open all the Certificates, and the Votes shall then be counted. The Person having the greatest Number of Votes shall be the President, if such Number be a Majority of the whole Number of Electors appointed; and if there be more than one who have such Majority, and have an equal Number of Votes, then the House of Representatives shall immediately chuse by Ballot one of them for President; and if no Person have a Majority, then from the five highest on the List the said House shall in like Manner chuse the President. But in chusing the President, the Votes shall be taken by States, the Representation from each State having one Vote; a quorum for this Purpose shall consist of a Member or Members from two-thirds of the States, and a Majority of all the States shall be necessary to a Choice. In every Case, after the Choice of the President, the Person having the greatest Number of Votes of the Electors shall be the Vice President. But if there should remain two or more who have equal Votes, the Senate shall chuse from them by Ballot the Vice-President.) **[This clause in parentheses was superseded by the 12th Amendment.]**

The Congress may determine the Time of chusing the Electors, and the Day on which they shall give their Votes; which Day shall be the same throughout the United States.

No person except a natural born Citizen, or a Citizen of the United States, at the time of the Adoption of this Constitution, shall be eligible to the Office of President; neither shall any Person be eligible to that Office who shall not have attained to the Age of thirty-five Years, and been fourteen Years a Resident within the United States.

(In Case of the Removal of the President from Office, or of his Death, Resignation, or Inability to discharge the Powers and Duties of the said Office, the same shall devolve on the Vice President, and the Congress may by Law provide for the Case of Removal, Death, Resignation or Inability, both of the President and Vice President, declaring what Officer shall then act as President, and such Officer shall act accordingly, until the Disability be removed, or a President shall be elected.) **[This clause in parentheses has been modified by the 20th and 25th Amendments.]**

The President shall, at stated Times, receive for his Services, a Compensation, which shall neither be increased nor diminished during the Period for which he shall have been elected, and he shall not receive within that Period any other Emolument from the United States, or any of them.

Before he enter on the Execution of his Office, he shall take the following Oath or Affirmation:

"I do solemnly swear (or affirm) that I will faithfully execute the Office of President of the United States, and will to the best of my Ability, preserve, protect and defend the Constitution of the United States."

Section 2 – Civilian Power over Military, Cabinet, Pardon Power, Appointments

The President shall be Commander in Chief of the Army and Navy of the United States, and of the Militia of the several States, when called into the actual Service of the United States; he may require the Opinion, in writing, of the principal Officer in each of the executive Departments, upon any subject relating to the Duties of their respective Offices, and he shall have Power to Grant Reprieves and Pardons for Offenses against the United States, except in Cases of Impeachment.

He shall have Power, by and with the Advice and Consent of the Senate, to make Treaties, provided two thirds of the Senators present concur; and he shall nominate, and by and with the Advice and Consent of the Senate, shall appoint Ambassadors, other public Ministers and Consuls, Judges of the supreme Court, and all other Officers of the United States, whose Appointments are not herein otherwise provided for, and which shall be established by Law: but the Congress may by Law vest the Appointment of such inferior Officers, as they think proper, in the President alone, in the Courts of Law, or in the Heads of Departments.

The President shall have Power to fill up all Vacancies that may happen during the Recess of the Senate, by granting Commissions which shall expire at the End of their next Session.

Section 3 – State of the Union, Convening Congress

He shall from time to time give to the Congress Information of the State of the Union, and recommend to their Consideration such Measures as he shall judge necessary and expedient; he may, on extraordinary Occasions, convene both Houses, or either of them, and in Case

of Disagreement between them, with Respect to the Time of Adjournment, he may adjourn them to such Time as he shall think proper; he shall receive Ambassadors and other public Ministers; he shall take Care that the Laws be faithfully executed, and shall Commission all the Officers of the United States.

Section 4 – Disqualification

The President, Vice President and all civil Officers of the United States, shall be removed from Office on Impeachment for, and Conviction of, Treason, Bribery, or other high Crimes and Misdemeanors.

ARTICLE III – THE JUDICIAL BRANCH

Section 1 – Judicial Powers

The judicial Power of the United States, shall be vested in one supreme Court, and in such inferior Courts as the Congress may from time to time ordain, and establish. The Judges, both of the supreme and inferior Courts, shall hold their Offices during good Behavior, and shall, at stated Times, receive for their Services a Compensation which shall not be diminished during their Continuance in Office.

Section 2 – Trial by Jury, Original Jurisdiction, Jury Trials

(The judicial Power shall extend to all Cases, in Law and Equity, arising under this Constitution, the Laws of the United States, and Treaties made, or which shall be made, under their Authority; to all Cases affecting Ambassadors, other public Ministers and Consuls; to all Cases of admiralty and maritime Jurisdiction: to Controversies to which the United States shall be a Party; to Controversies between two or more States: between a State and Citizens of another State; between Citizens of different States; between Citizens of the same State claiming Lands under Grants of different States, and between a State, or the Citizens thereof, and foreign States, Citizens

or Subjects.) [**This section in parentheses is modified by the 11th Amendment.**]

In all Cases affecting Ambassadors, other public Ministers and Consuls, and those in which a State shall be Party, the supreme Court shall have original Jurisdiction. In all the other Cases before mentioned, the supreme Court shall have appellate Jurisdiction, both as to Law and Fact, with such Exceptions, and under such Regulations as the Congress shall make.

The Trial of all Crimes, except in Cases of Impeachment, shall be by Jury; and such Trial shall be held in the State where the said Crimes shall have been committed; but when not committed within any State, the Trial shall be at such Place or Places as the Congress may by Law have directed.

Section 3 – Treason

Treason against the United States, shall consist only in levying War against them, or in adhering to their Enemies, giving them Aid and Comfort. No Person shall be convicted of Treason unless on the Testimony of two Witnesses to the same overt Act, or on Confession in open Court.

The Congress shall have power to declare the Punishment of Treason, but no Attainder of Treason shall work Corruption of Blood, or Forfeiture except during the Life of the Person attainted.

THE AMENDMENTS

The following are the Amendments to the Constitution. The first ten Amendments collectively are commonly known as the Bill of Rights.

Amendment 1 – Freedom of Religion, Press, Expression. Ratified December 15, 1791

Congress shall make no law respecting an establishment of religion, or prohibiting the free exercise thereof; or abridging the freedom of speech, or of the press; or the right of the people peaceably to assemble, and to petition the Government for a redress of grievances.

Amendment 2 – Right to Bear Arms. Ratified December 15, 1791

A well regulated Militia, being necessary to the security of a free State, the right of the people to keep and bear Arms, shall not be infringed.

Amendment 3 – Quartering of Soldiers. Ratified December 15, 1791

No Soldier shall, in time of peace be quartered in any house, without the consent of the Owner, nor in time of war, but in a manner to be prescribed by law.

Amendment 4 – Search and Seizure. Ratified December 15, 1791

The right of the people to be secure in their persons, houses, papers, and effects, against unreasonable searches and seizures, shall not be violated, and no Warrants shall issue, but upon probable cause, supported by Oath or affirmation, and particularly describing the place to be searched, and the persons or things to be seized.

Amendment 5 – Trial and Punishment, Compensation for Takings. Ratified December 15, 1791

No person shall be held to answer for a capital, or otherwise infamous crime, unless on a presentment or indictment of a Grand Jury, except in cases arising in the land or naval forces, or in the Militia, when in actual service in time of War or public danger; nor shall any person be subject for the same offense to be twice put in jeopardy of life or limb; nor shall be compelled in any criminal case to be a witness against himself, nor be deprived of life, liberty, or property, without due process of law; nor shall private property be taken for public use, without just compensation.

Amendment 6 – Right to Speedy Trial, Confrontation of Witnesses. Ratified December 15, 1791

In all criminal prosecutions, the accused shall enjoy the right to a speedy and public trial, by an impartial jury of the State and district wherein the crime shall have been committed, which district shall have been previously ascertained by law, and to be informed of the nature and cause of the accusation; to be confronted with the witnesses against him; to have compulsory process for obtaining witnesses in his favor, and to have the Assistance of Counsel for his defence.

Amendment 7 – Trial by Jury in Civil Cases. Ratified December 15, 1791

In Suits at common law, where the value in controversy shall exceed twenty dollars, the right of trial by jury shall be preserved, and no fact tried by a jury, shall be otherwise re-examined in any Court of the United States, than according to the rules of the common law.

Amendment 8 – Cruel and Unusual Punishment. Ratified December 15, 1791

Excessive bail shall not be required, nor excessive fines imposed, nor cruel and unusual punishments inflicted.

Amendment 9 – Construction of Constitution. Ratified December 15, 1791

The enumeration in the Constitution, of certain rights, shall not be construed to deny or disparage others retained by the people.

Amendment 10 – Powers of the States and People. Ratified December 15, 1791

The powers not delegated to the United States by the Constitution, nor prohibited by it to the States, are reserved to the States respectively, or to the people.

Amendment 11 – Judicial Limits. Ratified February 7, 1795

The Judicial power of the United States shall not be construed to extend to any suit in law or equity, commenced or prosecuted against one of the United States by Citizens of another State, or by Citizens or Subjects of any Foreign State.

Amendment 12 – Choosing the President, Vice-President. Ratified June 15, 1804

The Electors shall meet in their respective states, and vote by ballot for President and Vice-President, one of whom, at least, shall not be an inhabitant of the same state with themselves; they shall name in their ballots the person voted for as President, and in distinct ballots the person voted for as Vice-President, and they shall make distinct lists of all persons voted for as President, and of all persons voted for as Vice-President and of the number of votes for each, which lists they shall sign and certify, and transmit sealed to the seat of the government of the United States, directed to the President of the Senate;

The President of the Senate shall, in the presence of the Senate and House of Representatives, open all the certificates and the votes shall then be counted;

The person having the greatest Number of votes for President, shall be the President, if such number be a majority of the whole number of Electors appointed; and if no person have such majority, then from the persons having the highest numbers not exceeding three on the list of those voted for as President, the House of Representatives shall choose immediately, by ballot, the President. But in choosing the President, the votes shall be taken by states, the representation from each state having one vote; a quorum for this purpose shall consist of a member or members from two-thirds of the states, and a majority of all the states shall be necessary to a choice. And if the House of Representatives shall not choose a President whenever the right of choice shall devolve upon them, before the fourth day of March next following, then the Vice-President shall act as President, as in the case of the death or other constitutional disability of the President.

The person having the greatest number of votes as Vice-President, shall be the Vice-President, if such number be a majority of the whole number of Electors appointed, and if no person have a majority, then from the two highest numbers on the list, the Senate shall choose the Vice-President; a quorum for the purpose shall consist of two-thirds of the whole number of Senators, and a majority of the whole number shall be necessary to a choice. But no person constitutionally ineligible to the office of President shall be eligible to that of Vice-President of the United States.

Amendment 13 – Slavery Abolished.
Ratified December 6, 1865

1. Neither slavery nor involuntary servitude, except as a punishment for crime whereof the party shall have been duly convicted, shall exist within the United States, or any place subject to their jurisdiction.

2. Congress shall have power to enforce this article by appropriate legislation.

Amendment 14 – Citizenship Rights.
Ratified July 9, 1868

1. All persons born or naturalized in the United States, and subject to the jurisdiction thereof, are citizens of the United States and of the State wherein they reside. No State shall make or enforce any law which shall abridge the privileges or immunities of citizens of the United States; nor shall any State deprive any person of life, liberty, or property, without due process of law; nor deny to any person within its jurisdiction the equal protection of the laws.

2. Representatives shall be apportioned among the several States according to their respective numbers, counting the whole number of persons in each State, excluding Indians not taxed. But when the right to vote at any election for the choice of electors for President and Vice-President of the United States, Representatives in Congress, the Executive and Judicial officers of a State, or the members of the Legislature thereof, is denied to any of the male inhabitants of such State, being twenty-one years of age, and citizens of the United States, or in any way abridged, except for participation in rebellion, or other crime, the basis of representation therein shall be reduced in the proportion which the number of such male citizens shall bear to the whole number of male citizens twenty-one years of age in such State.

3. No person shall be a Senator or Representative in Congress, or elector of President and Vice-President, or hold any office, civil or military, under the United States, or under any State, who, having previously taken an oath, as a member of Congress, or as an officer of the United States, or as a member of any State legislature, or as an executive or judicial officer of any State, to support the Constitution of the United States, shall have engaged in insurrection or rebellion against the same, or given aid or comfort to the enemies thereof. But Congress may by a vote of two-thirds of each House, remove such disability.

4. The validity of the public debt of the United States, authorized by law, including debts incurred for payment of pensions and bounties for services in suppressing insurrection or rebellion, shall not be questioned. But neither the United States nor any State shall assume or pay any debt or obligation incurred in aid of insurrection or rebellion against the United States, or any claim for the loss or emancipation of any slave; but all such debts, obligations and claims shall be held illegal and void.

5. The Congress shall have power to enforce, by appropriate legislation, the provisions of this article.

Amendment 15 – Race No Bar to Vote. Ratified February 3, 1870

1. The right of citizens of the United States to vote shall not be denied or abridged by the United States or by any State on account of race, color, or previous condition of servitude.

2. The Congress shall have power to enforce this article by appropriate legislation.

Amendment 16 – Status of Income Tax Clarified. Ratified February 3, 1913

The Congress shall have power to lay and collect taxes on incomes, from whatever source derived, without apportionment among the several States, and without regard to any census or enumeration.

Amendment 17 – Senators Elected by Popular Vote. Ratified April 8, 1913

The Senate of the United States shall be composed of two Senators from each State, elected by the people thereof, for six years; and each Senator shall have one vote. The electors in each State shall have the qualifications requisite for electors of the most numerous branch of the State legislatures.

When vacancies happen in the representation of any State in the Senate, the executive authority of such State shall issue writs of election to fill such vacancies: Provided, That the legislature of any State may empower the executive thereof to make temporary appointments until the people fill the vacancies by election as the legislature may direct.

This amendment shall not be so construed as to affect the election or term of any Senator chosen before it becomes valid as part of the Constitution.

Amendment 18 – Liquor Abolished. Ratified January 16, 1919 Repealed by Amendment 21, December 5, 1933

1. After one year from the ratification of this article the manufacture, sale, or transportation of intoxicating liquors within, the importation thereof into, or the exportation thereof from the United States and all territory subject to the jurisdiction thereof for beverage purposes is hereby prohibited.

2. The Congress and the several States shall have concurrent power to enforce this article by appropriate legislation.

3 This article shall be inoperative unless it shall have been ratified as an amendment to the Constitution by the legislatures of the several States, as provided in the Constitution, within seven years from the date of the submission hereof to the States by the Congress.

Amendment 19 – Women's Suffrage. Ratified August 18, 1920

The right of citizens of the United States to vote shall not be denied or abridged by the United States or by any State on account of sex.

Congress shall have power to enforce this article by appropriate legislation.

Amendment 20 – Presidential, Congressional Terms. Ratified January 23, 1933

1. The terms of the President and Vice President shall end at noon on the 20th day of January, and the terms of Senators and Representatives at noon on the 3d day of January, of the years in which such terms would have ended if this article had not been ratified; and the terms of their successors shall then begin.

2. The Congress shall assemble at least once in every year, and such meeting shall begin at noon on the 3d day of January, unless they shall by law appoint a different day.

3. If, at the time fixed for the beginning of the term of the President, the President elect shall have died, the Vice President elect shall become President. If a President shall not have been chosen before the time fixed for the beginning of his term, or if the President elect shall have failed to qualify, then the Vice President elect shall act as President until a President shall have qualified; and the Congress may by law

provide for the case wherein neither a President elect nor a Vice President elect shall have qualified, declaring who shall then act as President, or the manner in which one who is to act shall be selected, and such person shall act accordingly until a President or Vice President shall have qualified.

4. The Congress may by law provide for the case of the death of any of the persons from whom the House of Representatives may choose a President whenever the right of choice shall have devolved upon them, and for the case of the death of any of the persons from whom the Senate may choose a Vice President whenever the right of choice shall have devolved upon them.

5. Sections 1 and 2 shall take effect on the 15th day of October following the ratification of this article.

6. This article shall be inoperative unless it shall have been ratified as an amendment to the Constitution by the legislatures of three-fourths of the several States within seven years from the date of its submission.

Amendment 21 – Amendment 18 Repealed. Ratified December 5, 1933

1. The eighteenth article of amendment to the Constitution of the United States is hereby repealed.

2. The transportation or importation into any State, Territory, or possession of the United States for delivery or use therein of intoxicating liquors, in violation of the laws thereof, is hereby prohibited.

3. The article shall be inoperative unless it shall have been ratified as an amendment to the Constitution by conventions in the several States, as provided in the Constitution, within seven years from the date of the submission hereof to the States by the Congress.

Amendment 22 – Presidential Term Limits. Ratified December 27, 1951

1. No person shall be elected to the office of the President more than twice, and no person who

has held the office of President, or acted as President, for more than two years of a term to which some other person was elected President shall be elected to the office of the President more than once. But this Article shall not apply to any person holding the office of President, when this Article was proposed by the Congress, and shall not prevent any person who may be holding the office of President, or acting as President, during the term within which this Article becomes operative from holding the office of President or acting as President during the remainder of such term.

2. This article shall be inoperative unless it shall have been ratified as an amendment to the Constitution by the legislatures of three-fourths of the several States within seven years from the date of its submission to the States by the Congress.

Amendment 23 – Presidential Vote for District of Columbia. Ratified March 29, 1961

1. The District constituting the seat of Government of the United States shall appoint in such manner as the Congress may direct: A number of electors of President and Vice President equal to the whole number of Senators and Representatives in Congress to which the District would be entitled if it were a State, but in no event more than the least populous State; they shall be in addition to those appointed by the States, but they shall be considered, for the purposes of the election of President and Vice President, to be electors appointed by a State; and they shall meet in the District and perform such duties as provided by the twelfth article of amendment.

2. The Congress shall have power to enforce this article by appropriate legislation.

Amendment 24 – Poll Tax Barred. Ratified January 23, 1964

1. The right of citizens of the United States to vote in any primary or other election for President or Vice President, for electors for President or Vice President, or for Senator or

Representative in Congress, shall not be denied or abridged by the United States or any State by reason of failure to pay any poll tax or other tax.

2. The Congress shall have power to enforce this article by appropriate legislation.

Amendment 25 – Presidential Disability and Succession. Ratified February 10, 1967

1. In case of the removal of the President from office or of his death or resignation, the Vice President shall become President.

2. Whenever there is a vacancy in the office of the Vice President, the President shall nominate a Vice President who shall take office upon confirmation by a majority vote of both Houses of Congress.

3. Whenever the President transmits to the President pro tempore of the Senate and the Speaker of the House of Representatives his written declaration that he is unable to discharge the powers and duties of his office, and until he transmits to them a written declaration to the contrary, such powers and duties shall be discharged by the Vice President as Acting President.

4. Whenever the Vice President and a majority of either the principal officers of the executive departments or of such other body as Congress may by law provide, transmit to the President pro tempore of the Senate and the Speaker of the House of Representatives their written declaration that the President is unable to discharge the powers and duties of his office, the Vice President shall immediately assume the powers and duties of the office as Acting President.

Thereafter, when the President transmits to the President pro tempore of the Senate and the Speaker of the House of Representatives his written declaration that no inability exists, he shall resume the powers and duties of his office unless the Vice President and a majority of either the principal officers of the executive department or of such other body as Congress may by law provide, transmit within four days to the President pro tempore of the Senate and the Speaker of the House of Representatives their written declaration that the President is unable to discharge the powers and duties of his office. Thereupon Congress shall decide the issue, assembling within forty eight hours for that purpose if not in session. If the Congress, within twenty one days after receipt of the latter written declaration, or, if Congress is not in session, within twenty one days after Congress is required to assemble, determines by two thirds vote of both Houses that the President is unable to discharge the powers and duties of his office, the Vice President shall continue to discharge the same as Acting President; otherwise, the President shall resume the powers and duties of his office.

Amendment 26 – Voting Age Set to 18 Years. Ratified July 1, 1971

1. The right of citizens of the United States, who are eighteen years of age or older, to vote shall not be denied or abridged by the United States or by any State on account of age.

2. The Congress shall have power to enforce this article by appropriate legislation.

Amendment 27 – Limiting Congressional Pay Increases. Ratified May 7, 1992

No law, varying the compensation for the services of the Senators and Representatives, shall take effect, until an election of Representatives shall have intervened.

CHAPTER FIVE

The *Federalist*, Nos. 10 and 51

James Madison

Federalist 10: James Madison begins perhaps the most famous of the *Federalist* papers by stating that one of the strongest arguments in favor of the Constitution is the fact that it establishes a government capable of controling the violence and damage caused by factions. Factions are both inevitable and often at odds with each other, and they frequently work against the public interest and infringe upon the rights of others. Majority factions are particularly dangerous and in need of being checked by the governmental institutions.

Federalist 51: The system of government that became known as separation of powers is explained by James Madison in *Federalist* 51. Separate institutions, comprising individuals selected by differing means, that share power is Madison's solution to the problem of both empowering government and preserving justice and liberty.

THE FEDERALIST NO. 10

The Utility of the Union as a Safeguard Against Domestic Faction and Insurrection (continued)

Daily Advertiser
Thursday, November 22, 1787
To the People of the State of New York:

Among the numerous advantages promised by a well constructed Union, none deserves to be more accurately developed than its tendency to break and control the violence of faction. The friend of popular governments never finds himself so much alarmed for their character and fate,

as when he contemplates their propensity to this dangerous vice. He will not fail, therefore, to set a due value on any plan which, without violating the principles to which he is attached, provides a proper cure for it. The instability, injustice, and confusion introduced into the public councils, have, in truth, been the mortal diseases under which popular governments have everywhere perished; as they continue to be the favorite and fruitful topics from which the adversaries to liberty derive their most specious declamations. The valuable improvements made by the American constitutions on the popular models, both ancient and modern, cannot certainly be too much admired; but it would be an unwarrantable partiality, to contend that they have as effectually obviated the danger on this side, as was wished and expected. Complaints are everywhere heard from our most considerate and virtuous citizens, equally the friends of public and private faith, and of public and personal liberty, that our governments are too unstable, that the public good is disregarded in the conflicts of rival parties, and that measures are too often decided, not according to the rules of justice and the rights of the minor party, but by the superior force of an interested and overbearing majority. However anxiously we may wish that these complaints had no foundation, the evidence, of known facts will not permit us to deny that they are in some degree true. It will be found, indeed, on a candid review of our situation, that some of the distresses under which we labor have been erroneously charged on the operation of our governments; but it will be found, at the same time, that other causes will not alone account for many of our heaviest misfortunes; and, particularly, for that prevailing and increasing distrust of public engagements, and alarm for private rights, which are echoed from one end of the continent to the other. These must be chiefly, if not wholly, effects of the unsteadiness and injustice with which a factious spirit has tainted our public administrations.

By a faction, I understand a number of citizens, whether amounting to a majority or a minority of the whole, who are united and actuated by some common impulse of passion, or of interest, adversed to the rights of other citizens, or to the permanent and aggregate interests of the community.

There are two methods of curing the mischiefs of faction: the one, by removing its causes; the other, by controlling its effects.

There are again two methods of removing the causes of faction: the one, by destroying the liberty which is essential to its existence; the other, by giving to every citizen the same opinions, the same passions, and the same interests.

It could never be more truly said than of the first remedy, that it was worse than the disease. Liberty is to faction what air is to fire, an aliment without which it instantly expires. But it could not be less folly to abolish liberty, which is essential to political life, because it nourishes faction, than it would be to wish the annihilation of air, which is essential to animal life, because it imparts to fire its destructive agency.

The second expedient is as impracticable as the first would be unwise. As long as the reason of man continues fallible, and he is at liberty to exercise it, different opinions will be formed. As long as the connection subsists between his reason and his self-love, his opinions and his passions will have a reciprocal influence on each other; and the former will be objects to which the latter will attach themselves. The diversity in the faculties of men, from which the rights of property originate, is not less an insuperable obstacle to a uniformity of interests. The protection of these faculties is the first object of government. From the protection of different and

unequal faculties of acquiring property, the possession of different degrees and kinds of property immediately results; and from the influence of these on the sentiments and views of the respective proprietors, ensues a division of the society into different interests and parties.

The latent causes of faction are thus sown in the nature of man; and we see them everywhere brought into different degrees of activity, according to the different circumstances of civil society. A zeal for different opinions concerning religion, concerning government, and many other points, as well of speculation as of practice; an attachment to different leaders ambitiously contending for pre-eminence and power; or to persons of other descriptions whose fortunes have been interesting to the human passions, have, in turn, divided mankind into parties, inflamed them with mutual animosity, and rendered them much more disposed to vex and oppress each other than to cooperate for their common good. So strong is this propensity of mankind to fall into mutual animosities, that where no substantial occasion presents itself, the most frivolous and fanciful distinctions have been sufficient to kindle their unfriendly passions and excite their most violent conflicts. But the most common and durable source of factions has been the various and unequal distribution of property. Those who hold and those who are without property have ever formed distinct interests in society. Those who are creditors, and those who are debtors, fall under a like discrimination. A landed interest, a manufacturing interest, a mercantile interest, a moneyed interest, with many lesser interests, grow up of necessity in civilized nations, and divide them into different classes, actuated by different sentiments and views. The regulation of these various and interfering interests forms the principal task of modern legislation, and involves the spirit of party and faction in the necessary and ordinary operations of the government.

No man is allowed to be a judge in his own cause, because his interest would certainly bias his judgment, and, not improbably, corrupt his integrity. With equal, nay with greater reason, a body of men are unfit to be both judges and parties at the same time; yet what are many of the most important acts of legislation, but so many judicial determinations, not indeed concerning the rights of single persons, but concerning the rights of large bodies of citizens? And what are the different classes of legislators but advocates and parties to the causes which they determine? Is a law proposed concerning private debts? It is a question to which the creditors are parties on one side and the debtors on the other. Justice ought to hold the balance between them. Yet the parties are, and must be, themselves the judges; and the most numerous party, or, in other words, the most powerful faction must be expected to prevail. Shall domestic manufactures be encouraged, and in what degree, by restrictions on foreign manufactures? are questions which would be differently decided by the landed and the manufacturing classes, and probably by neither with a sole regard to justice and the public good. The apportionment of taxes on the various descriptions of property is an act which seems to require the most exact impartiality; yet there is, perhaps, no legislative act in which greater opportunity and temptation are given to a predominant party to trample on the rules of justice. Every shilling with which they overburden the inferior number, is a shilling saved to their own pockets.

It is in vain to say that enlightened statesmen will be able to adjust these clashing interests, and render them all subservient to the public good. Enlightened statesmen will not always be at the helm. Nor, in many cases, can such an adjustment be made at all without taking into view indirect and remote considerations, which will rarely prevail over the immediate interest which one party may find in disregarding the rights of another or the good of the whole.

The inference to which we are brought is, that the *causes* of faction cannot be removed, and that relief is only to be sought in the means of controlling its *effects*.

If a faction consists of less than a majority, relief is supplied by the republican principle, which enables the majority to defeat its sinister views by regular vote. It may clog the administration, it may convulse the society; but it will be unable to execute and mask its violence under the forms of the Constitution. When a majority is included in a faction, the form of popular government, on the other hand, enables it to sacrifice to its ruling passion or interest both the public good and the rights of other citizens. To secure the public good and private rights against the danger of such a faction, and at the same time to preserve the spirit and the form of popular government, is then the great object to which our inquiries are directed. Let me add that it is the great desideratum by which this form of government can be rescued from the opprobrium under which it has so long labored, and be recommended to the esteem and adoption of mankind.

By what means is this object attainable? Evidently by one of two only. Either the existence of the same passion or interest in a majority at the same time must be prevented, or the majority, having such coexistent passion or interest, must be rendered, by their number and local situation, unable to concert and carry into effect schemes of oppression. If the impulse and the opportunity be suffered to coincide, we well know that neither moral nor religious motives can be relied on as an adequate control. They are not found to be such on the injustice and violence of individuals, and lose their efficacy in proportion to the number combined together, that is, in proportion as their efficacy becomes needful.

From this view of the subject it may be concluded that a pure democracy, by which I mean a society consisting of a small number of citizens, who assemble and administer the government in person, can admit of no cure for the mischiefs of faction. A common passion or interest will, in almost every case, be felt by a majority of the whole; a communication and concert result from the form of government itself; and there is nothing to check the inducements to sacrifice the weaker party or an obnoxious individual. Hence it is that such democracies have ever been spectacles of turbulence and contention; have ever been found incompatible with personal security or the rights of property; and have in general been as short in their lives as they have been violent in their deaths. Theoretic politicians, who have patronized this species of government, have erroneously supposed that by reducing mankind to a perfect equality in their political rights, they would, at the same time, be perfectly equalized and assimilated in their possessions, their opinions, and their passions.

A republic, by which I mean a government in which the scheme of representation takes place, opens a different prospect, and promises the cure for which we are seeking. Let us examine the points in which it varies from pure democracy, and we shall comprehend both the nature of the cure and the efficacy which it must derive from the Union.

The two great points of difference between a democracy and a republic are: first, the delegation of the government, in the latter, to a small number of citizens elected by the rest; secondly, the greater number of citizens, and greater sphere of country, over which the latter may be extended.

The effect of the first difference is, on the one hand, to refine and enlarge the public views, by passing them through the medium of a chosen body of citizens, whose wisdom may best discern the true interest of their country, and whose patriotism and love of justice will be least likely to sacrifice it to temporary or partial considerations. Under such a regulation, it may well happen that the public voice, pronounced by the representatives of the people, will be more consonant to the public good than if pronounced by the people themselves, convened for the purpose. On the other hand, the effect may be inverted. Men of factious tempers, of local prejudices, or of sinister designs, may, by intrigue, by corruption, or by other means, first obtain the suffrages, and then betray the interests, of the people. The question resulting is, whether small or extensive republics are more favorable to the election of proper guardians of the public weal; and it is clearly decided in favor of the latter by two obvious considerations:

In the first place, it is to be remarked that, however small the republic may be, the representatives must be raised to a certain number, in order to guard against the cabals of a few; and that, however large it may be, they must be limited to a certain number, in order to guard against the confusion of a multitude. Hence, the number of representatives in the two

cases not being in proportion to that of the two constituents, and being proportionally greater in the small republic, it follows that, if the proportion of fit characters be not less in the large than in the small republic, the former will present a greater option, and consequently a greater probability of a fit choice.

In the next place, as each representative will be chosen by a greater number of citizens in the large than in the small republic, it will be more difficult for unworthy candidates to practice with success the vicious arts by which elections are too often carried; and the suffrages of the people being more free, will be more likely to centre in men who possess the most attractive merit and the most diffusive and established characters.

It must be confessed that in this, as in most other cases, there is a mean, on both sides of which inconveniences will be found to lie. By enlarging too much the number of electors, you render the representatives too little acquainted with all their local circumstances and lesser interests; as by reducing it too much, you render him unduly attached to these, and too little fit to comprehend and pursue great and national objects. The federal Constitution forms a happy combination in this respect; the great and aggregate interests being referred to the national, the local and particular to the State legislatures.

The other point of difference is, the greater number of citizens and extent of territory which may be brought within the compass of republican than of democratic government; and it is this circumstance principally which renders factious combinations less to be dreaded in the former than in the latter. The smaller the society, the fewer probably will be the distinct parties and interests composing it; the fewer the distinct parties and interests, the more frequently will a majority be found of the same party; and the smaller the number of individuals composing a majority, and the smaller the compass within which they are placed, the more easily will they concert and execute their plans of oppression. Extend the sphere, and you take in a greater variety of parties and interests; you make it less probable that a majority of the whole will have a common motive to invade the rights of other citizens; or if such a common motive exists, it will be more difficult for all who feel it to discover their own strength, and to act in unison with each other. Besides other impediments, it may be remarked that, where there is a consciousness of unjust or dishonorable purposes, communication is always checked by distrust in proportion to the number whose concurrence is necessary. Hence, it clearly appears, that the same advantage which a republic has over a democracy, in controlling the effects of faction, is enjoyed by a large over a small republic, and is enjoyed by the Union over the States composing it. Does the advantage consist in the substitution of representatives whose enlightened views and virtuous sentiments render them superior to local prejudices and schemes of injustice? It will not be denied that the representation of the Union will be most likely to possess these requisite endowments. Does it consist in the greater security afforded by a greater variety of parties, against the event of any one party being able to outnumber and oppress the rest? In an equal degree does the increased variety of parties comprised within the Union, increase this security. Does it, in fine, consist in the greater obstacles opposed to the concert and accomplishment of the secret wishes of an unjust and interested majority? Here, again, the extent of the Union gives it the most palpable advantage.

The influence of factious leaders may kindle a flame within their particular States, but will be unable to spread a general conflagration through the other States. A religious sect may degenerate into a political faction in a part of the Confederacy; but the variety of sects dispersed over the entire face of it must secure the national councils against any danger from that source. A rage for paper money, for an abolition of debts, for an equal division of property, or for any other improper or wicked project, will be less apt to pervade the whole body of the Union than a particular member of it; in the same proportion as such a malady is more likely to taint a particular county or district, than an entire State.

In the extent and proper structure of the Union, therefore, we behold a republican remedy for the diseases most incident to republican government. And according to the degree of pleasure and pride we feel in being republicans, ought to be our zeal in cherishing the spirit and supporting the character of Federalists.

Publius

THE FEDERALIST NO. 51

The Structure of the Government Must Furnish the Proper Checks and Balances Between the Different Departments

Independent Journal
Wednesday, February 6, 1788
To the People of the State of New York:

To what expedient, then, shall we finally resort, for maintaining in practice the necessary partition of power among the several departments, as laid down in the Constitution? The only answer that can be given is, that as all these exterior provisions are found to be inadequate, the defect must be supplied, by so contriving the interior structure of the government as that its several constituent parts may, by their mutual relations, be the means of keeping each other in their proper places. Without presuming to undertake a full development of this important idea, I will hazard a few general observations, which may perhaps place it in a clearer light, and enable us to form a more correct judgment of the principles and structure of the government planned by the convention.

In order to lay a due foundation for that separate and distinct exercise of the different powers of government, which to a certain extent is admitted on all hands to be essential to the preservation of liberty, it is evident that each department should have a will of its own; and consequently should be so constituted that the members of each should have as little agency as possible in the appointment of the members of the others. Were this principle rigorously adhered to, it would require that all the appointments for the supreme executive, legislative, and judiciary magistracies should be drawn from the same fountain of authority, the people, through channels having no communication whatever with one another. Perhaps such a plan of constructing the several departments would be less difficult in practice than it may in contemplation appear. Some difficulties, however, and some additional expense would attend the execution of it. Some deviations, therefore, from the principle must be admitted. In the constitution of the judiciary department in particular, it might be inexpedient to insist rigorously on the principle: first, because peculiar qualifications being essential in the members, the primary consideration ought to be to select that mode of choice which best secures these qualifications; secondly, because the permanent tenure by which the appointments are held in that department, must soon destroy all sense of dependence on the authority conferring them.

It is equally evident, that the members of each department should be as little dependent as possible on those of the others, for the emoluments annexed to their offices. Were the executive magistrate, or the judges, not independent of the legislature in this particular, their independence in every other would be merely nominal.

But the great security against a gradual concentration of the several powers in the same department, consists in giving to those who administer each department the necessary constitutional means and personal motives to resist encroachments of the others. The provision for defense must in this, as in all other cases, be made commensurate to the danger of attack. Ambition must be made to counteract ambition. The interest of the man must be connected with the constitutional rights of the place. It may be a reflection on human nature, that such devices should be necessary to control the abuses of government. But what is government itself, but the greatest of all reflections on human nature? If men were angels, no government would be necessary. If angels were to govern men, neither external nor internal controls on government would be necessary. In framing a government which is to be administered by men over men, the great difficulty lies in this: you must first enable the government to control the governed; and in the next place oblige it to control itself. A dependence on the people is,

no doubt, the primary control on the government; but experience has taught mankind the necessity of auxiliary precautions.

This policy of supplying, by opposite and rival interests, the defect of better motives, might be traced through the whole system of human affairs, private as well as public. We see it particularly displayed in all the subordinate distributions of power, where the constant aim is to divide and arrange the several offices in such a manner as that each may be a check on the other – that the private interest of every individual may be a sentinel over the public rights. These inventions of prudence cannot be less requisite in the distribution of the supreme powers of the State.

But it is not possible to give to each department an equal power of self-defense. In republican government, the legislative authority necessarily predominates. The remedy for this inconveniency is to divide the legislature into different branches; and to render them, by different modes of election and different principles of action, as little connected with each other as the nature of their common functions and their common dependence on the society will admit. It may even be necessary to guard against dangerous encroachments by still further precautions. As the weight of the legislative authority requires that it should be thus divided, the weakness of the executive may require, on the other hand, that it should be fortified. An absolute negative on the legislature appears, at first view, to be the natural defense with which the executive magistrate should be armed. But perhaps it would be neither altogether safe nor alone sufficient. On ordinary occasions it might not be exerted with the requisite firmness, and on extraordinary occasions it might be perfidiously abused. May not this defect of an absolute negative be supplied by some qualified connection between this weaker department and the weaker branch of the stronger department, by which the latter may be led to support the constitutional rights of the former, without being too much detached from the rights of its own department?

If the principles on which these observations are founded be just, as I persuade myself they are, and they be applied as a criterion to the several State constitutions, and to the federal Constitution it will be found that if the latter does not perfectly correspond with them, the former are infinitely less able to bear such a test.

There are, moreover, two considerations particularly applicable to the federal system of America, which place that system in a very interesting point of view.

First. In a single republic, all the power surrendered by the people is submitted to the administration of a single government; and the usurpations are guarded against by a division of the government into distinct and separate departments. In the compound republic of America, the power surrendered by the people is first divided between two distinct governments, and then the portion allotted to each subdivided among distinct and separate departments. Hence a double security arises to the rights of the people. The different governments will control each other, at the same time that each will be controlled by itself.

Second. It is of great importance in a republic not only to guard the society against the oppression of its rulers, but to guard one part of the society against the injustice of the other part. Different interests necessarily exist in different classes of citizens. If a majority be united by a common interest, the rights of the minority will be insecure. There are but two methods of providing against this evil: the one by creating a will in the community independent of the majority – that is, of the society itself; the other, by comprehending in the society so many separate descriptions of citizens as will render an unjust combination of a majority of the whole very improbable, if not impracticable. The first method prevails in all governments possessing an hereditary or self-appointed authority. This, at best, is but a precarious security; because a power independent of the society may as well espouse the unjust views of the major, as the rightful interests of the minor party, and may possibly be turned against both parties. The second method will be exemplified in the federal republic of the United States. Whilst all authority in it will be derived from and dependent on the society, the society itself will be broken

into so many parts, interests, and classes of citizens, that the rights of individuals, or of the minority, will be in little danger from interested combinations of the majority. In a free government the security for civil rights must be the same as that for religious rights. It consists in the one case in the multiplicity of interests, and in the other in the multiplicity of sects. The degree of security in both cases will depend on the number of interests and sects; and this may be presumed to depend on the extent of country and number of people comprehended under the same government. This view of the subject must particularly recommend a proper federal system to all the sincere and considerate friends of republican government, since it shows that in exact proportion as the territory of the Union may be formed into more circumscribed Confederacies, or States oppressive combinations of a majority will be facilitated: the best security, under the republican forms, for the rights of every class of citizens, will be diminished: and consequently the stability and independence of some member of the government, the only other security, must be proportionately increased. Justice is the end of government. It is the end of civil society. It ever has been and ever will be pursued until it be obtained, or until liberty be lost in the pursuit. In a society under the forms of which the stronger faction can readily unite and oppress the weaker, anarchy may as truly be said to reign as in a state of nature, where the weaker individual is not secured against the violence of the stronger; and as, in the latter state, even the stronger individuals are prompted, by the uncertainty of their condition, to submit to a government which may protect the weak as well as themselves; so, in the former state, will the more powerful factions or parties be gradually induced, by a like motive, to wish for a government which will protect all parties, the weaker as well as the more powerful. It can be little doubted that if the State of Rhode Island was separated from the Confederacy and left to itself, the insecurity of rights under the popular form of government within such narrow limits would be displayed by such reiterated oppressions of factious majorities that some power altogether independent of the people would soon be called for by the voice of the very factions whose misrule had proved the necessity of it. In the extended republic of the United States, and among the great variety of interests, parties, and sects which it embraces, a coalition of a majority of the whole society could seldom take place on any other principles than those of justice and the general good; whilst there being thus less danger to a minor from the will of a major party, there must be less pretext, also, to provide for the security of the former, by introducing into the government a will not dependent on the latter, or, in other words, a will independent of the society itself. It is no less certain than it is important, notwithstanding the contrary opinions which have been entertained, that the larger the society, provided it lie within a practical sphere, the more duly capable it will be of self-government. And happily for the *republican cause*, the practicable sphere may be carried to a very great extent, by a judicious modification and mixture of the *federal principle*.

Publius

CHAPTER SIX

U.S. House Members in Their Constituencies

An Exploration

Richard F. Fenno, Jr.

Based on extensive travels with legislators in the districts, Fenno characterizes legislators' perceptions of their constituencies, reports legislators' varying attentiveness to their home constituencies, and observes different types of "home styles." The analysis highlights the variety of forms of representation that occur in Congress.

Despite a voluminous literature on the subject of representative–constituency relationships, one question central to that relationship remains underdeveloped. It is: what does an elected representative see when he or she sees a constituency? And, as a natural follow-up, what consequences do these perceptions have for his or her behavior? The key problem is that of perception. And the key assumption is that the constituency a representative reacts to is the constituency he or she sees. The corollary assumption is that the rest of us cannot understand the representative–constituency relationship until we can see the constituency through the eyes of the representative. These ideas are not new. Their importance has been widely acknowledged and frequently repeated ever since. But despite the acceptance and reiteration of Dexter's insights, we still have not developed much coherent knowledge about the perceptions members of Congress have of their constituencies.

Richard F. Fenno, Jr. 1977. "U.S. House Members in Their Constituencies: An Exploration" *American Political Science Review* 71: 883–917. Copyright © 1977 by the American Political Science Association. Reprinted with the permission of Cambridge University Press.

A major reason for this neglect is that most of our research on the representative–constituency linkage gets conducted at the wrong end of that linkage. Our interest in the constituency relations of U.S. senators and representatives has typically been a derivative interest, pursued for the light it sheds on some behavior – like roll call voting – in Washington. When we talk with our national legislators about their constituencies, we typically talk to them *in Washington* and, perforce, in the Washington context. But that is a context far removed from the one in which their constituency relationships are created, nurtured, and changed. And it is a context equally far removed from the one in which we might expect their perceptions of their constituencies to be shaped, sharpened, or altered. Asking constituency-related questions on Capitol Hill, when the House member is far from the constituency itself, could well produce a distortion of perspective. Researchers might tend to conceive of a separation between the representative "here in Washington" and his or her constituency "back home," whereas the representative may picture himself or herself as a part of the constituency – me *in* the constituency, rather than me *and* the constituency. As a research strategy, therefore, it makes some sense to study our representatives' perceptions of their constituencies while they are actually in their constituencies – at the constituency end of the linkage.

Since the fall of 1970, I have been traveling with some members of the House of

Representatives while they were in their districts, to see if I could figure out – by looking over their shoulders – what it is they see there. These expeditions, designed to continue through the 1976 elections, have been totally open-ended and exploratory. I have tried to observe and inquire into anything and everything the members do. Rather than assume that I already know what is interesting or what questions to ask, I have been prepared to find interesting questions emerging in the course of the experience. The same with data. The research method has been largely one of soaking and poking – or, just hanging around. This paper, therefore, conveys mostly an impressionistic feel for the subject – as befits the earliest stages of exploration and mapping.

As of June 1976, I had accompanied fourteen sitting House members, two House members-to-be and one House member-elect in their districts – for a minimum of two, a maximum of ten, and an average of five days each – sometimes at election time, sometimes not. In eleven cases I have accompanied the member on more than one trip; in six cases I have made only one trip. Since I am a stranger to each local context and to the constellation of people surrounding each member, my confidence in what I see and hear increases markedly when I can make similar observations at more than one point in time. In ten cases I have supplemented my trips to the district with a lengthy interview in Washington.

PERCEPTIONS OF THE CONSTITUENCY

The District: The Geographical Constituency

What then do House members see when they see a constituency? One way they perceive it – the way most helpful to me so far – is as a nest of concentric circles. The largest of these circles represents the congressman's broadest view of his constituency. This is "the district" or "my district." It is the entity to which, from which, and in which he travels. It is the entity whose boundaries have been fixed by state legislative enactment or by court decision. It includes the entire population within those boundaries. Because it is a legal entity, we could refer to it as the legal constituency. It captures more of what the congressman has in mind when he conjures up "my district"; however, if we label it the *geographical constituency*, we retain the idea that the district is a legally bounded space and emphasize that it is located in a particular place.

The Washington community is often described as a group of people all of whom come from somewhere else. The House of Representatives, by design, epitomizes this characteristic; and its members function with a heightened sense of their ties to place. There are, of course, constant reminders. The member's district is, after all, "the Tenth District of *California.*" Inside the chamber, he is "the gentleman from *California*"; outside the chamber he is Representative X (D. *California*). So, it is not surprising that when you ask a congressman, "What kind of district do you have?" the answer often begins with, and always includes, a geographical, space-and-place, perception. Thus, the district is seen as "the largest in the state, twenty-eight counties in the southeastern corner" or "three layers of suburbs to the west of the city, a square with the northwest corner cut out." If the boundaries have been changed by a recent redistricting, the geography of "the new district" will be compared to that of "the old district."

If one essential aspect of "the geographical constituency" is seen as its location and boundaries, another is its particular internal makeup. And House members describe their districts' internal makeup using political science's most familiar demographic and political variables – socioeconomic structure, ideology, ethnicity, residential patterns, religion, partisanship, stability, diversity, etc. Every congressman, in his mind's eye, sees his geographical constituency in terms of some special configuration of such variables. For example,

Geographically, it covers the northern one-third of the state, from the border of (state X) to the border of (state Y), along the Z river – twenty-two counties. The basic industry is agriculture – but it's a diverse district. The city makes up one-third of the population. It is dominated by the state government and education. It's an independent minded constituency, with a strong attachment to the work ethic. A good percentage is composed of people whose families emigrated from Germany, Scandinavia and Czechoslovakia. I don't exactly know the figures, but over one-half the district is German. And this goes back to the work ethic. They are a hardworking, independent people. They have a strong thought of "keeping the government off my back, we'll do all right here." That's especially true of my out-counties.

Some internal configurations are more complex than others. But, even at the broadest level, no congressman sees, within his district's boundaries, an undifferentiated glob. And we cannot talk about his relations with his "constituency" as if he did.

All of the demographic characteristics of the geographical constituency carry political implications. But as most Representatives make their first perceptual cut into "the district," political matters are usually left implicit. Sometimes, the question "what kind of district do you have?" turns up the answer "it's a Democratic district." But much more often, that comes later. It is as if they first want to sketch a prepolitical background against which they can later paint in the political refinements. We, of course, know – for many of the variables – just what those political refinements are likely to be. (Most political scientists would guess that the district just described is probably more Republican than Democratic – which it is.) There is no point to dwelling on the general political relevance of each variable. But one summary characterization does seem to have special usefulness as a background against which to understand political perceptions and their consequences. And that characteristic is the relative homogeneity or heterogeneity of the district.

As the following examples suggest, members of Congress do think in terms of the homogeneity or heterogeneity of their districts – though they may not always use the words.

It's geographically compact. It's all suburban – no big city in the accepted sense of the word and no rural area. It's all white. There are very few blacks, maybe 2 per cent. Spanish sur-named make up about 10 per cent. Traditionally, it's been a district with a high percentage of home ownership. . . . Economically, it's above the national average in employment . . . the people of the district are employed. It's not that it's very high income. Oh, I suppose there are a few places of some wealth, but nothing very wealthy. And no great pockets of poverty either. And it's not dominated by any one industry. The X County segment has a lot of small, clean, technical industries. I consider it very homogeneous. By almost any standard, it's homogeneous.

This district is a microcosm of the nation. We are geographically southern and politically northern. We have agriculture – mostly soy beans and corn. We have big business – like Union Carbide and General Electric. And we have unions. We have a city and we have small towns. We have some of the worst poverty in the country in A County. And we have some very wealthy sections, though not large. We have wealth in the city and some wealthy towns. We have urban poverty and rural poverty. Just about the only thing we don't have is a good sized ghetto. Otherwise, everything you can have, we've got it right here.

Because it is a summary variable, the perceived homogeneity–heterogeneity characteristic is particularly hard to measure; and no metric is proposed here. Intuitively, both the number and the compatibility of significant interests within the district would seem to be involved. The greater the number of significant interests – as opposed to one dominant interest – the more likely it is that the district will be seen as heterogeneous. But if the several significant interests were viewed as having a single lowest common denominator and, therefore, quite compatible, the district might still be viewed as homogeneous. One indicator, therefore, might be the ease with which the congressman finds a lowest common denominator of interests for some large proportion of his geographical constituency. The basis for the denominator could be any of the prepolitical variables. We do not think of it, however, as a political characteristic – as the equivalent, for instance, of party registration or political safeness. The proportion of people in the district who have to be included would be a subjective judgment – "enough" so that the congressman saw his geographical constituency as more homogeneous than heterogeneous, or vice versa. All we can say is that the less actual or potential conflict he sees among district interests, the more likely he is to see his district as homogeneous. Another indicator might be the extent to which the geographical constituency is congruent with a natural community. Districts that are purely artificial (sometimes purely political) creations of districting practices, and which pay no attention to preexisting communities of interest are more likely to be heterogeneous. Preexisting communities or natural communities are more likely to have such homogenizing ties as common sources of communication, common organizations, and common traditions.

The Supporters: The Reelection Constituency

Within his geographical constituency, each congressman perceives a smaller, explicitly political constituency. It is composed of the people he thinks vote for him. And we shall refer to it as his *reelection constituency.* As he moves about the district, a House member continually draws the distinction between those who vote for him and those who do not. "I do well here"; "I run poorly here." "This group supports me"; "this group does not." By distinguishing supporters from nonsupporters, he articulates his baseline political perception.

House members seem to use two starting points – one cross-sectional and the other longitudinal – in shaping this perception. First, by a process of inclusion and exclusion, they come to a rough approximation of the upper and lower ranges of the reelection constituency. That is to say, there are some votes a member believes he almost always gets; there are other votes he believes he almost never gets. One of the core elements of any such distinction is the perceived partisan component of the vote – party identification as revealed in registration or poll figures and party voting. "My district registers only 37 per cent Republican. They have no place else to go. My problem is, how can I get enough Democratic votes to win the general election." Another element is the political tendencies of various demographic groupings.

My supporters are Democrats, farmers, labor – a DFL operation – with some academic types. . . . My opposition tends to be the main street hardware dealer. I

look at that kind of guy in a stable town, where the newspaper runs the community – the typical school board member in the rural part of the district – that's the kind of guy I'll never get. At the opposite end of the scale is the country club set. I'll sure as hell never get them, either.

Starting with people he sees, very generally, as his supporters, and leaving aside people he sees, equally generally, as his nonsupporters, each congressman fashions a view of the people who give him his victories at the polls.

The second starting point for thinking about the reelection constituency is the congressman's idea of who voted for him "last time." Starting with that perception, he adds or subtracts incrementally on the basis of changes that will have taken place (or could be made by him to take place) between "last time" and "next time." It helps him to think about his reelection constituency this way because that is about the only certainty he operates with – he won last time. And the process by which his desire for reelection gets translated into his perception of a reelection constituency is filled with uncertainty. At least that is my strong impression. House members see reelection uncertainty where political scientists would fail to unearth a single objective indicator of it. For one thing, their perceptions of their supporters and nonsupporters are quite diffuse. They rarely feel certain just who did vote for them last time. And even if they do feel fairly sure about that, they may perceive population shifts that threaten established calculations. In the years of my travels, moreover, the threat of redistricting has added enormous uncertainty to the make-up of some reelection constituencies. In every district, too, there is the uncertainty that follows an unforeseen external event – recession, inflation, Watergate.

Of all the many sources of uncertainty, the most constant – and usually the greatest – involves the electoral challenger. For it is the challenger who holds the most potential for altering any calculation involving those who voted for the congressman "last time." "This time's" challenger may have very different sources of political strength from "last time's" challenger. Often, one of the major off-year uncertainties is whether or not the last challenger will try again. While it is true that House members campaign all the time, "the campaign" can be said to start only when the challenger is known. At that point, a redefinition of the reelection constituency may have to take place. If the challenger is chosen by primary, for example, the congressman may inherit support from the loser. A conservative southern Republican, waiting for the Democratic primary to determine whether his challenger would be a black or a white (both liberal), wondered about the shape of his reelection constituency.

It depends on my opponent. Last time, my opponent (a white moderate) and I split many groups. Many business people who might have supported me, split up. If I have a liberal opponent, all the business community will support me. . . . If the black man is my opponent, I should get more Democratic votes than I got before. He can't do any better there than the man I beat before. Except for a smattering of liberals and radicals around the colleges, I will do better than last time with the whites. . . . The black vote is 20 per cent and they vote right down the line Democratic. I have to concede the black vote. There's nothing I can do about it. . . . [But] against a white liberal, I would get some of the black vote.

The shaping of perceptions proceeds under conditions of considerable uncertainty.

The Strongest Supporters: The Primary Constituency

In thinking about their political condition, House members make distinctions within their reelection constituency – thus giving us a third, still smaller concentric circle. Having distinguished between their nonsupporters and their supporters, they further distinguish between their routine or temporary supporters and their very strongest supporters. Routine supporters only vote for them, often merely following party identification; but others will support them with a special degree of intensity. Temporary supporters back them as the best available alternative; but others will support them regardless of who the challenger may be. Within each reelection constituency are nested these

"others" – a constituency perceived as "my strongest supporters," "my hard core support," "my loyalists," "my true believers," "my political base." We shall think of these people as the ones each congressman believes would provide his best line of electoral defense in a primary contest, and label them *the primary constituency*. It will probably include the earliest of his supporters – those who recruited him and those who tendered identifiably strong support in his first campaign – thus, providing another reason for calculating on the basis of "last time." From its ranks will most likely come the bulk of his financial help and his volunteer workers. From its ranks will least likely come an electoral challenger.

A protected congressional seat is as much one protected from primary defeat as from general election defeat. And a primary constituency is something every congressman must have.

Everybody needs some group which is strongly for him – especially in a primary. You can win a primary with 25,000 zealots. . . . The most exquisite case I can give you was in the very early war years. I had very strong support from the anti-war people. They were my strongest supporters and they made up about 5 per cent of the district.

The primary constituency, I would guess, draws a special measure of a congressman's interest; and it should, therefore, draw a special measure of ours. But it is not easy to delineate – for us or for them. Asked to describe his "very strongest supporters," one member replied, "That's the hardest question anyone has to answer." The primary constituency is more subtly shaded than the reelection constituency, where voting provides an objective membership test. Loyalty is not the most predictable of political qualities. And all politicians resist drawing invidious distinctions among their various supporters, as if it were borrowing trouble to begin classifying people according to fidelity. House members who have worried about or fought a primary recently may find it somewhat easier. So, too may those with heterogeneous districts whose diverse elements invite differentiation. Despite some difficulty, most members – because it is politically prudent to do so – make some such distinction, in speech or in action or both. By talking to them and watching them, we can begin to understand what those distinctions are.

Here are two answers to the question, "who are your very strongest supporters?"

My strongest supporters are the working class – the blacks and labor, organized labor. And the people who were in my state legislative district, of course. The fifth ward is low-income, working class and is my base of support. I grew up there; I have my law office there; and I still live there. The white businessmen who are supporting me now are late converts – very late. They support me as the least of two evils. They are not a strong base of support. They know it and I know it.

I have a circle of strong labor supporters and another circle of strong business supporters. . . . They will 'fight, bleed and die' for me, but in different ways. Labor gives you the manpower and the workers up front. You need them just as much as you need the guy with the two-acre yard to hold a lawn party to raise money. The labor guy loses a day's pay on election day. The business guy gets his nice lawn tramped over and chewed up. Each makes a commitment to you in his own way. You need them both.

Each description reveals the working politician's penchant for inclusive thinking. Each tells us something about a primary constituency, but each leaves plenty of room for added refinements.

The best way to make such refinements is to observe the congressman as he comes in contact with the various elements of his reelection constituency. Both he and they act in ways that help delineate the "very strongest supporters." For example, the author of the second comment above drew a standing ovation when he was introduced at the Labor Temple. During his speech, he spoke directly to individuals in the audience. "Kenny, it's good to see you here. Ben, you be sure and keep in touch." Afterward, he lingered for an hour drinking beer and eating salami. At a businessman's annual Christmas luncheon the next day, he received neither an introduction nor applause when the main speaker acknowledged his presence, saying, "I see our congressman is here; and I use the term 'our' loosely." This congressman's "circle of strong labor supporters" appears to be

larger than his "circle of strong business supporters." And the congressman, for his part, seemed much more at home with the first group than he did with the second.

Like other observers of American politics, I have found this idea of "at homeness" a useful one in helping me to map the relationship between politicians and constituents – in this case the perception of a primary constituency. House members sometimes talk in this language about the groups they encounter.

I was born on the flat plains, and I feel a lot better in the plains area than in the mountain country. I don't know why it is. As much as I like Al [whom we had just lunched with in a mountain town], I'm still not comfortable with him. I'm no cowboy. But when I'm out there on that flat land with those ranchers and wheat farmers, standing around trading insults and jibes and telling stories, I feel better. That's the place where I click.

It is also the place where he wins elections – his primary constituency. "That's my strong area. I won by a big margin and offset my losses. If I win next time, that's where I'll win it – on the plains." Obviously, there is no one-to-one relationship between the groups with whom a congressman acts and feels most at home and his primary constituency. But it does provide a pretty good unobtrusive clue. So I found myself fashioning a highly subjective "at homeness index" to rank the degree to which each congressman seems to have support from and rapport with each group.

I recall, for example, watching a man whose constituency is dominantly Jewish participating in an afternoon installation-of-officers ceremony at a Young Men's Hebrew Association attended by about forty civic leaders of the local community. He drank some spiked punch, began the festivities by saying, "I'm probably the first tipsy installation officer you ever had," told an emotional story about his own dependence on the Jewish "Y," and traded banter with his friends in the audience throughout the proceedings. That evening as we prepared to meet with yet another and much larger (Democratic party) group, I asked where we were going. He said, "We're going to a shitty restaurant to have a shitty meal with a shitty organization and have a shitty time." And he did – from high to low on the "at homeness index." On the way home, after the meal, he talked about the group.

Ethnically, most of them are with me. But I don't always support the party candidate, and they can't stand that. . . . This group and half the other party groups in the district are against me. But they don't want to be against me too strongly for fear I might go into a primary and beat them. So self-preservation wins out. . . . They know they can't beat me.

Both groups are Jewish. The evening group was a part of his reelection constituency, but not his primary constituency. The afternoon group was a part of both.

The Intimates: The Personal Constituency

Within the primary constituency, each member perceives still a fourth, and final, concentric circle. These are the few individuals whose relationship with him is so personal and so intimate that their relevance to him cannot be captured by their inclusion in any description of "very strongest supporters." In some cases they are his closest political advisers and confidants. In other cases, they are people from whom he draws emotional sustenance for his political work. We shall think of these people as his *personal constituency*.

One Sunday afternoon, I sat in the living room of a congressman's chief district staff assistant watching an NFL football game – with the congressman, the district aide, the state assemblyman from the congressman's home county, and the district attorney of the same county. Between plays, at halftime and over beer and cheese, the four friends discussed every aspect of the congressman's campaign, listened to and commented on his taped radio spots, analyzed several newspaper reports, discussed local and national personalities, relived old political campaigns and hijinks, discussed their respective political ambitions. Ostensibly they were watching the football game; actually the congressman was exchanging political advice, information, and perspectives with three of his six or seven oldest and closest political associates.

Another congressman begins his weekends at home by having a Saturday morning 7:30 coffee and doughnut breakfast in a cafe on the main street of his hometown with a small group of old friends from the Rotary Club. The morning I was there, the congressman, a retired bank manager, a hardware store owner, a high school science teacher, a retired judge, and a past president of the city council gossiped and joked about local matters – the county historian, the library, the board of education, the churches and their lawns – for an hour. "I guess you can see what an institution this is," he said as we left. "You have no idea how invaluable these meetings are for me. They keep me in touch with my home base. If you don't keep your home base, you don't have anything."

The personal constituency is, doubtless, the most idiosyncratic of the several constituencies. Not all members will open it up to the outside observer. Nine of the seventeen did, however; and in doing so, he usually revealed a side of his personality not seen by the rest of his constituencies. "I'm really very reserved, and I don't feel at home with most groups – only with five or six friends," said the congressman after the football game. The relationship probably has both political and emotional dimensions. But beyond that, it is hard to generalize, except to say that the personal constituency needs to be identified if our understanding of the congressman's view of his constituency is to be complete.

In sum, my impression is that House members perceive four constituencies – geographical, reelection, primary, and personal – each one nesting within the previous one.

POLITICAL SUPPORT AND HOME STYLE

What, then, do these perceptions have to do with a House member's behavior? Our conventional paraphrase of this question would read: what do these perceptions have to do with behavior at the other end of the line – in Washington? But the concern that disciplines the perceptions we have been talking about is neither first nor foremost a Washington-oriented concern. It is a concern for political support at home. It is a concern for the scope of that support – which decreases as one moves from the geographical to the personal constituency. It is a concern for the stability of that support – which increases as one moves from the geographical to the personal constituency. And it ultimately issues in a concern for manipulating scopes and intensities in order to win and hold a sufficient amount of support to win elections. Representatives, and prospective representatives, think about their constituencies because they seek support there. They want to get nominated and elected, then renominated and reelected. For most members of Congress most of the time, this electoral goal is primary. It is the prerequisite for a congressional career and, hence, for the pursuit of other goals. And the electoral goal is achieved – first and last – not in Washington but at home.

Of course, House members do many things in Washington that affect their electoral support at home. Political scientists interpret a great deal of their behavior in Washington in exactly that way – particularly their roll call votes. Obviously, a congressman's perception of his several constituencies will affect such things as his roll-call voting, and we could, if we wished, study the effect. Indeed, that is the very direction in which our conditioned research reflexes would normally carry this investigation. But my experience has turned me in another – though not, as we shall see an unrelated – direction. I have been watching House members work to maintain or enlarge their political support at home, by going to the district and doing things there.

Our Washington-centered research has caused us systematically to underestimate the proportion of their working time House members spend in their districts. As a result, we have also underestimated its perceived importance to them. In all our studies of congressional time allocation, time spent outside of Washington is left out of the analysis. So, we end up analyzing "the average work week of a congressman" by comparing the amounts of time he spends in committee work, on the floor, doing research, handling constituent problems – but all of it in Washington. Nine of my members whose appointment and travel records I have checked carefully for the year 1973 – a nonelection year –

averaged 28 trips to the district and spent an average of 101 working (not traveling) days in their districts that year. A survey conducted in 419 House offices covering 1973, indicates that the average number of trips home (not counting recesses) was 35 and the number of days spent in the district during 1973 (counting recesses) was 138. No fewer than 131, nearly one-third, of the 419 members went home to their districts *every single weekend*. Obviously, the direct personal cultivation of their various constituencies takes a great deal of their time; and they must think it is worth it in terms of winning and holding political support. If it is worth *their* time to go home so much, it is worth *our* time to take a commensurate degree of interest in what they do there and why.

As they cultivate their constituencies, House members display what I shall call their *home style*. When they discuss the importance of what they are doing, they are discussing the importance of *home style* to the achievement of their electoral goal. At this stage of the research, the surest generalization one can make about home style is that there are as many varieties as there are members of Congress. "Each of us has his own formula – a truth that is true for him," said one. It will take a good deal more immersion and cogitation before I can improve upon that summary comment. At this point, however, three ingredients of home style appear to be worth looking at. They are: first, the congressman's allocation of his personal resources and those of his office; second, the congressman's presentation of self; and third, the congressman's explanation of his Washington activity. Every congressman allocates, presents, and explains. The amalgam of these three activities for any given representative constitutes (for now, at least) his home style. His home style, we expect, will be affected by his perception of his four constituencies.

HOME STYLE: ALLOCATION OF RESOURCES

Every representative must make a basic decision with regard to his home style: "How much and what kinds of attention shall I pay to home?" Or to put it another way: "Of all the resources available with which to help me do my job, which kinds and how much of each do I want to allocate directly to activity in the district?" There are, of course, many ways to allocate one's resources so that they affect the district. Our concern is with *resources allocated directly to the district*. Of these, we propose to look first, at the congressman's *time* and second, at the congressman's *staff*. The congressman's decision about how much time he should spend physically at home and his decision about how much of his staff he should place physically in the district are decisions which give shape to his home style.

Of all the resources available to the House member, the scarcest and most precious one, which dwarfs all others in posing critical allocative dilemmas, is his time. Time is at once what the member has least of and what he has the most control over. When a congressman divides up his time, he decides by that act what kind of congressman he wants to be. He must divide his time in Washington. He must divide his time at home. The decision we are concerned with here is the division of his time between Washington and home. When he is doing something at home, he must give up doing some things in Washington, and vice versa. So he chooses and he trades off; and congressmen make different allocative choices and different allocative trades. In this section, we shall focus on the frequency with which various congressmen returned to their districts in 1973.

"This is a business, and like any business you have to make time and motion studies," said one member. "All we have is time and ourselves, so we have to calculate carefully to use our time productively." It is not true, of course, that "all" the congressman has is time and himself. The office carries with it a large number of ancillary resources – a staff, office space, office expense allowances, free mailing privileges, personal expense allowances, etc. – all of which draw attention when the advantages of incumbency are detailed. Each congressman chooses how he will utilize these resources. The most important of these choices are choices about how to use his staff. And among the key choices about staff is how to allocate them between Washington and the district. In this section we shall focus particularly on one indicator of that decision – the percentage of his

total expenditures on staff salaries allocated by him to the salaries of his district staff.

The information on trips home and staff allocation was collected on Capitol Hill in June 1974. Six students, each of whom had just finished working for four months, full-time in a congressman's office, conducted a survey by visiting each member's office and talking to his or her administrative assistant or personal secretary. The question about trips home usually produced an educated estimate. The questions about staff yielded more precise answers. Each student presented the Clerk of the House's *Report* for 1973, with its list of each representative's staff members and their salaries; and the respondents simply designated which staff members were located in the district. A briefer, follow-up survey was conducted by four students with similar "Hill experience" in May 1975. This survey added to the store of information on those 1973 members who were still in Congress. For 1973, it should be noted, each member was allowed a maximum of sixteen staff members and a maximum payroll of $203,000. And for the two-year period 1973–74 (the 93rd Congress) each member was reimbursed for thirty-six round trips to his district. Members were not, of course, required to use any of these allowances to the maximum.

On the matter of trips home, there is evidence of personal attentiveness to the district and of variation in that attentiveness. The average number of 1973 trips per member was thirty-five, and the median was thirty. The range went from a low of four trips to a high of three hundred and sixty-five. One can ask: "for which kinds of House members is their frequent physical presence in the district an important part of their home style and for which kinds is it less so?" At this early stage, we can present only a few suggestive relationships. In order to do so, we have categorized the frequency of trips home into *low* (less than 24), medium (24–42), and high (more than 42). The categories are based on the responses to the question and to the appearance of reasonable cutting points in the data. These categories have been cross-tabulated with a number of variables that should be expected to correlate with the frequency of home visits.

Table 6.1. *Trips Home and Electoral Margin*

	Frequency of Trips Home (1973)			
Election Margin (1972)	Low (0–23)	Medium (24–42)	High (43+)	Total
Less than 55%	21 (29%)	28 (38%)	24 (33%)	73 (100%)
55–60%	18 (32%)	18 (32%)	20 (36%)	56 (100%)
61–65%	22 (27%)	17 (20%)	44 (53%)	83 (100%)
More than 65%	68 (33%)	66 (32%)	73 (35%)	207 (100%)
	129	129	161	419

Note: Gamma = −.03.

One standard supposition would be that representatives in electoral jeopardy will decide to spend more of their time at home than will representatives whose seats are well protected. As a generalization, however, this supposition receives no confirmation when our conventional measures of electoral safeness are used. As Table 6.1 shows, the frequency of trips home does not increase as electoral margins decrease. Indeed, there is just not much of a relationship at all. It might be noted, in this connection, that objective measures of marginality have not fared particularly well in producing consistent findings whenever they have been used. My own experience leads me to believe that only *subjective* measures of electoral safety are valid. House members feel more uncertainty about reelection than is captured by any arbitrary electoral margin figures. Furthermore, uncertainty about their primary election situation is totally untouched by such figures. The point is that subjective assessments of electoral safeness might be more strongly correlated with trips home.

A related hunch would be that the longer a congressman is in office, the less time he will spend at home. Part of the argument here overlaps with the previous one – the longer in office, the more secure the seat. But the more

important part of the reasoning would be that with seniority comes increased influence and responsibility in the House and, hence, the need to spend more time in Washington. These suppositions are supported by our data – but not as strongly and as consistently as we had imagined would be the case. A simple correlation between terms of service and number of trips home shows that as seniority increases, home visits decrease – as we would expect. But the correlation coefficient (Pearson's r) is an exceedingly weak −.235. When the data are grouped, however, the nature and strength of the relationship becomes clearer.

Table 6.2 pictures the relationship between the three categories of personal attentiveness and three levels of seniority. The summary statistics continue to be unimpressive, because for the middle levels of seniority no allocative pattern is evident. But looking at the lowest and highest levels of seniority, it is clear that the frequency of home visits is much greater for the low seniority group than it is for the high seniority group. The relationship between length of service and trips home, we conclude, is not a consistent, linear relationship. But for those at the beginning of their House careers and those farthest along in their House careers,

Table 6.2. *Trips Home and Seniority*

	Frequency of Trips Home			
Seniority	Low (0–23)	Medium (24–42)	High (43+)	Total
Low (1–3 terms)	34 (22%)	44 (28%)	78 (50%)	156 (100%)
Medium (4–7 terms)	43 (28%)	59 (38%)	52 (34%)	154 (100%)
High (8+ terms)	52 (48%)	26 (24%)	31 (28%)	189 (100%)
	129	129	161	419
Mean seniority	7.0 terms	5.0 terms	4.7 terms	

Note: Gamma = −.30.

Table 6.3. *Trips Home and Region*

Region	Frequency of Trips Home			Total
	Low (0–23)	Medium (24–42)	High (43+)	
East	5 (5%)	20 (20%)	76 (75%)	101 (100%)
South	36 (35%)	32 (30%)	36 (35%)	104 (100%)
Border	9 (26%)	10 (29%)	16 (45%)	35 (100%)
Midwest	29 (28%)	47 (44%)	30 (28%)	106 (100%)
Far West	50 (69%)	20 (27%)	3 (4%)	73 (100%)
	129	129	161	419

Regions:

East: Conn., Me., Mass., N.H., N.J., N.Y., Pa., R.I., Vt.

South: Ala., Ark., Fla., Ga., La., Miss., N.C., S.C., Tenn., Texas, Va.

Border: Del., Ky., Md., Mo., Okla., W.Va.

Midwest: Ill., Ind., Iowa, Kans., Mich., Minn., Neb., N.D., Ohio, S.D., Wisc.

Far West: Alaska, Ariz., Calif., Colo., Hawaii., Idaho, Mont., Nev., N.M., Oregon, Utah, Wash., Wyo.

their longevity is likely to be one determinant of their decisions on time allocation. Congressional newcomers appear to be more single-minded in pursuing the electoral goal than are the veterans of the institution.

A third reasonable guess would be that the more time-consuming and expensive it is to get to his district, the less frequently a congressman will make the trip. Leaving money aside (but recalling that for 1973–74, each member was provided with a "floor" of thirty-six trips), we would expect to find that as distance from Washington increases, the number of trips home decreases. It is not easy to get a measure of distance that captures each member's travelling time. For now, we shall use region as a surrogate for distance, on the theory that if any relationship is present, it will show up in a regional breakdown. And it does. Table 6.3 indicates that the members nearest Washington, DC. (East) spend a good deal more time at home than do the members who live farthest away from the Capitol (Far West). The less of his Washington time a member has to give up in order to get

home, the more likely he is to go home – at least at the extremes of distance. If distance is a factor for the other three regional groups, it does not show up here. Our guess is that the distance is a far more problematical factor in those cases. We shall, however, return to the regional variable shortly.

A persistent dilemma facing every member of Congress involves the division of time between work and family. And one of its earliest manifestations comes with the family decision whether to remain at home or move to Washington. If (for whatever reason) the family decides to remain in the district, we would expect the House member to go home more often than if the family moves to Washington. Table 6.4 shows that this is very much the case. Five times the percentage of representatives whose families remain at home fall into the high category of trips home as do representatives whose families are in Washington – 88 per cent to 17 per cent. To put the finding somewhat differently, the average number of 1973 trips for members with families in Washington was twenty-seven, for

Table 6.4. *Trips Home and Family Residence*

Family Residence	Frequency of Trips Home			Total
	Low (0–23)	Medium (24–42)	High (43+)	
Washington area	87 (41%)	89 (42%)	37 (17%)	213 (100%)
District	3 (4%)	6 (8%)	69 (88%)	78 (100%)
Unmarried	5 (14%)	12 (32%)	20 (54%)	37 (100%)
	95	107	126	328

Table 6.5. *Trips Home and District Staff Expenditures*

District Staff Expenditures	Frequency of Trips Home			Total
	Low (0–23)	Medium (24–42)	High (43+)	
Lowest 1/3	53 (39%)	42 (31%)	40 (30%)	135 (100%)
Middle 1/3	42 (30%)	55 (40%)	41 (30%)	138 (100%)
Highest 1/3	31 (23%)	32 (23%)	75 (54%)	138 (100%)
	126	129	156	411

Note: Gamma =.28.

members with families in the district it was fifty-two, and for unmarried members it was forty-four trips. Whether family decisions produce the home style or whether a home style decision produces the family decision remains an unanswered question. Either process seems perfectly plausible. It is clear, however, that some decisions about home style are family related decisions.

To sum up, a House member's decision on how to allocate his time between home and Washington is affected: (1) by his seniority, if it is very low or very high; (2) by the distance from Washington to home, if that distance is very long or very short; and (3) by the place where his family is located, whether his family moves to Washington or remains in the district. A congressman's electoral margin, objectively measured, has little effect on his time allocations. How, if at all, these factors are interrelated, and how strongly each factor contributes to the allocative pattern are matters for later analysis.

Members of Congress also decide what kind of staff presence they wish to establish in the district. Here, too, we find great variation. On the percentage of total staff expenditure allocated to district staff, the range, in 1973, went from

0 to 81 per cent. We might think that a member who decides to give a special degree of personal attention to "home" would also decide to give a special degree of staff attentiveness to "home." But the relationship between the two allocative decisions does not appear to be strong. Using percentage of total staff expenditure on district staff (as we shall throughout this section) as the measure of district staff strength, we find a very weak correlation (Pearson's $r = .20$) between a congressman's decision on that matter and the number of trips he takes home. Table 6.5 clusters and cross-tabulates the two allocative decisions. For our measure of district staff strength we have divided the percentage of expenditures on district staff into thirds. The lowest third ranges from 0–22.7 per cent; the middle third ranges from 22.8–33.5 per cent; the highest third ranges from 33.6–81 per cent. The cross-tabulation also shows a pretty weak overall relationship. For now, therefore, we shall treat the two decisions as if they were made independently of one another and, hence, are deserving of separate examination.

What kinds of members, then, emphasize the value of a large district staff operation? Once again, it turns out, they are not members in special electoral trouble. Table 6.6 displays the

Table 6.6. *District Staff Expenditures and Electoral Margin*

Electoral Margin 1972	District Staff Expenditures (1973)			Total
	Lowest 1/3	Middle 1/3	Highest 1/3	
Less than 55%	20 (27%)	28 (38%)	26 (35%)	74 (100%)
55–60%	20 (36%)	20 (36%)	16 (28%)	56 (100%)
61–65%	24 (29%)	29 (35%)	29 (35%)	82 (100%)
More than 65%	72 (36%)	61 (30%)	68 (34%)	201 (100%)
	136	138	139	413

Note: Gamma = −.04.

Table 6.7. *District Staff Expenditures and Seniority*

| Seniority | District Staff Expenditures | | | |
	Lowest 1/3	Middle 1/3	Highest 1/3	Total
Low (1–3 terms)	44 (29%)	54 (35%)	56 (36%)	155 (100%)
Medium (4–7 terms)	44 (29%)	56 (37%)	51 (34%)	151 (100%)
High (8+ terms)	47 (44%)	28 (26%)	32 (30%)	107 (100%)
	136	138	139	413

Note: Gamma = −.13.

total lack of any discernible impact of electoral situation (objectively measured) on district staff strength. Nor, as indicated in Table 6.7, does seniority make any difference in staff allocative decisions. That it does not adds strength to the idea that the relationship between seniority and home visits discovered earlier is accounted for – as we have suggested – by career-and-goal factors rather than by electoral factors.

The other variables discussed earlier – family residence and distance – do not have the obvious implications for staff allocation that they have for the member's own time dilemmas. It might be that if his family is in the district, and if he plans to be home a lot, a congressman might decide to have a big district staff operation to work with him there. That supposition receives some support in Table 6.8. Another possibility is that members might decide to use a strong district staff to compensate for their lack of personal attention via trips home. However, this idea is not supported in Table 6.8, nor in Table 6.9, which seeks to uncover regional and distance patternings of district staffs. Representatives who live nearest to Washington (East) and who tend to go home the most do tend to have large district staffs. But representatives who live farthest away and tend to go home the

least show only a slight tendency to compensate by allocating heavy expenditures to their district staffs.

Table 6.9, however, does reveal some regional allocation patterns that did not appear when we looked for regional patterns in home visits. Region, it appears, captures a good deal more than distance, particularly in relation to staff allocations. The southern and border regions emerge with distinctive patternings here. To a marked degree, House members from these two areas eschew large staff operations in their districts. Scanning our two regional tabulations (Tables 6.3 and 6.9), we note that every region save the Midwest reveals a noteworthy pattern of resource allocation. In the East we find a high frequency of home visits and large district staffs; in the Far West, we find a low frequency of home visits; in the southern and border regions, we find small district staffs. Again, the two types of allocative decisions appear to be quite distinct and independent. Region, we tentatively conclude, has a substantial affect on home style.

But regions are composites of several states; and while regional regularities often reflect state regularities, they can also hide them. Both situations have occurred in this instance. Figure 6.1 displays state-by-state allocation patterns – of

Table 6.8. *District Staff Expenditures and Family Residence*

| Family Residence | District Staff Expenditures | | | |
	Lowest 1/3	Middle 1/3	Highest 1/3	Total
Washington area	85 (40%)	77 (37%)	48 (23%)	210 (100%)
District	21 (28%)	17 (23%)	37 (49%)	75 (100%)
Unmarried	8 (22%)	10 (28%)	18 (50%)	36 (100%)
	114	104	103	321

Table 6.9. *District Staff Expenditures and Region*

Region	District Staff Expenditures			Total
	Lowest 1/3	Middle 1/3	Highest 1/3	
East	16 (16%)	31 (31%)	52 (53%)	99 (100%)
South	47 (46%)	36 (35%)	19 (19%)	102 (100%)
Border	18 (55%)	8 (24%)	7 (21%)	33 (100%)
Midwest	39 (37%)	34 (32%)	33 (31%)	106 (100%)
Far West	16 (22%)	29 (40%)	28 (38%)	73 (100%)
	136	138	139	413

Regions:
East: Conn., Me, Mass., N.H., N.J., N.Y., Pa., R.I., Vt.
South: Ala., Ark., Fla., Ga., La., Miss., N.C., S.C., Tenn., Texas, Va.
Border: Del., Ky., Md., Mo., Okla., W.Va.
Midwest: Ill., Ind., Iowa, Kans., Mich., Minn., Neb., N.D., Ohio, S.D., Wisc.
Far West: Alaska, Ariz., Calif., Colo., Hawaii, Idaho, Mont., Nev., N.M., Oregon, Utah, Wash., Wyo.

personal and district staff attentiveness. For each state delegation, we have computed the mean number of trips home made by its members in 1973; and we have divided the state delegations into those whose averages fell above and below the median number of trips for all House members, i.e., 30 trips, Also, for each state delegation, we computed an average of the percentage of staff expenditures allocated to the district staff by its members; and we have divided the state delegations into those whose averages fell above and below the median percentage for all House members, i.e., 29 per cent. The result is a crude fourfold classification of states according to their combined personal and staff resource allocations to "home." The underlined states fall strongly into their particular patterns; the others display weaker tendencies. Each state is identified, also, by its regional classification.

There are, as Figure 6.1 shows, distinctive state allocative patterns. Some were foreshadowed in the regional patterns discussed earlier. For example, the eastern states cluster in the high-trips home category; and the far western states cluster in the low-trips-home category. Southern and border states cluster in the weak-district staff category. Other state patterns, however, appear here for the first time. The large number of states clustering in the low-trips-home/small-district-staff category, for example were totally obscured in our regional data.

Explanations for these various state clusters are more difficult; and only a few guesses can be made here. The sharp separation between eastern and far western states in trips home is doubtless a function of distance. And – it now appears more strongly – some far western state representatives do compensate for the infrequency of their home visits by maintaining a relatively large staff presence in the district. Yet, if California members invest heavily in this compensatory allocative strategy, why don't the members from Washington and Oregon do likewise?

The decision of most southern and border state representatives to spend relatively little on their district staff operations may be explainable by a tradition of nonbureaucratized, highly personalized politics in those areas. Northeasterners may be accustomed to coping with bureaucrats – legislative or otherwise – whereas southern and border state residents would expect to deal directly with the elective officeholder. Yet, in terms of the amount of personal attentiveness to their districts, southern delegations vary widely. At first glance, that variation seems to be related to distance – with states in the near South receiving more attention than states in the far South. But the marked difference among, say, Kentucky, Tennessee, and Alabama would seem to require a more complex explanation. And, speaking of complexity, the similar disposition of resources by the unexpected mix of delegations in the low-trips-home/small-district-staff category (in the lower right hand corner of Figure 6.1) defies even an explanatory guess at this stage of our study.

Personal Attentiveness

District Staff Attentiveness	Above the Median in Trips Home	Below the Median in Trips Home
Above the Median in District Staff Expenditures	*Connecticut (E)* *Massachusetts (E)* *New York (E)* *Tennessee (S)* Illinois (MW) Maine (E) New Hampshire (E) Pennsylvania (E) Rhode Island (E) South Carolina (S) Vermont (E)	*California (FW)* Colorado (FW) Hawaii (FW) Idaho (FW) Iowa (MW) Kansas (MW) New Mexico (FW) Wyoming (FW)
Below the Median in District Staff Expenditures	*Kentucky (B)* *Maryland (B)* *North Carolina (S)* *Virginia (S)* *West Virginia (B)* Delaware (B) Indiana (MW) Montana (FW) Ohio (MW)	*Alabama (S)* *Arizona (FW)* *Florida (S)* *Louisiana (S)* *Minnesota (MW)* *Oklahoma (B)* *Oregon (FW)* *Washington (FW)* *Wisconsin (MW)* Arkansas (S) Michigan (MW) Nebraska (MW) South Dakota (MW) Texas (S) Utah (FW)

N.B. States that fall five trips or more above or below the median *and* whose district staff expenditures fall 5 per cent or more above or below the median are *italicized*. States not listed fall on the median in one or both instances. Regional classifications are in parentheses.

Figure 6.1. Allocation Patterns: By State

The allocative elements of home style vary across regions and among states within regions. The relevance of state delegations to patterns of resource allocation at home will come as no surprise to students of Congress. For there is virtually no aspect, formal or informal, of the legislative process on Capitol Hill that has not already revealed the importance of the state delegation. How much that importance is the product of extensive communication among delegation members and how much the product of similar expectations emanating from similar districts, has not been definitively answered. Nor can it be here. All we can say is that both are probably involved. State delegation members probably talk to one another about their allocative practices and follow one another's example and advice. Also, certain expectations and traditions probably develop within states, or sections of states, so that members feel constrained to make resource allocations that are not too far out of line with those expectations.

The ambiguity of this discussion raises one of the broadest questions concerning home style. Is a congressman's home style something he chooses and then imposes upon his district or is it something that is imposed upon him by the kind of district he represents? We shall worry that question and work our way toward an answer as we proceed. At this point it appears that either or both patterns can hold: for, while state regularities testify to district influences on home style, some states display no regularities; and all states display enough idiosyncratic behavior to testify to the presence of individual choice.

Home style is, then, partly a matter of place – i.e., it is affected by the nature of the congressman's geographical constituency. That constituency is, after all, the closest thing to a "given" in his nest of perceptions. But home style is also partly a matter of individual choice. And in this respect, it can be affected by his perception of his other three constituencies. That, indeed, is what we expect to find as we move to discuss the other elements of home style.

HOME STYLE: PRESENTATION OF SELF

Most House members spend a substantial proportion of their working time "at home." Even those we placed in the "low frequency" category return to their districts more often than we would have guessed – over half of them go home more than once (but less than twice) a month. What, then, do they do there? Much of what they do is captured by Erving Goffman's idea of *the presentation of self.* That is, they place themselves in "the immediate physical presence" of others and then "make a presentation of themselves to others." A description of all the settings in which I have watched members of Congress making such presentations, or "performances" as Goffman calls them, would triple the size of this article. But, surely, I have logged – during my thirty visits and ninety-three days in seventeen districts – nearly every circumstance concocted by the mind of man for bringing one person into the "immediate physical presence" of another.

In all such encounters, says Goffman, the performer will seek to control the response of others to him by expressing himself in ways that leave the correct impressions of himself with others. His expressions will be of two sorts – "the expression that he gives and the expression that he gives off." The first is mostly verbal; the second is mostly nonverbal. Goffman is particularly interested in the second kind of expression – "the more theatrical and contextual kind" – because he believes that the performer is more likely to be judged by others according to the nonverbal than the verbal elements of his presentation of self. Those who must do the judging, Goffman says, will think that the verbal expressions are more controlable and manipulable by the performer; and they will, therefore, read his nonverbal "signs" as a check, on the reliability of his verbal "signs." Basic to this reasoning is the idea that, of necessity, every presentation has a largely "promissory character" to it. Those who listen to and watch the

presentation cannot be sure what the relationship between them and the performer really is. So the relationship must be sustained, on the part of those watching, by inference. They "must accept the individual on faith." In this process of acceptance, they will rely heavily on the inferences they draw from his nonverbal expressions – the expressions "given off."

Goffman does not talk about politicians; but politicians know what Goffman is talking about. Goffman's dramaturgical analogues are appropriate to politics because politicians, like actors, perform before audiences and are legitimized by their audiences. The response politicians seek from others is *political support.* And the impressions they try to foster are those that will engender political support. House member politicians believe that a great deal of their support is won by the kind of individual self they present to others, i.e., to their constituents. More than most people, they believe that they can manipulate their "presentation of self." And more than most other people, they consciously try to manipulate it. Certainly, they believe that what they say, their verbal expression, is an integral part of their "self." But, like Goffman, they place special emphasis on the nonverbal, "contextual" aspects of their presentation. At least, the nonverbal elements must be consistent with the verbal ones. At most, the expressions "given off" will become the basis on which they are judged. Like Goffman, members of Congress are willing to emphasize the latter because, with him, they believe that their constituents will more readily discount what they say than how they say it or how they act in the context in which they say it. In the member's own language, constituents want to judge you "as a person." The comment I have heard most often from the constituents of my representatives is: "He's a good man," or "She's a good woman," unembossed by qualifiers of any sort. Constituents, say House members, want to "size you up" or "get the feel of you" "as a person," or "as a human being." And the largest part of what members mean when they say "as a person" is what Goffman means by "expressions given off."

So members of Congress go home to present themselves "as a person" – and to win the accolade, "He's a good man," "She's a good woman." With Goffman, they know there is a "promissory character" to the presentation. And their object is to present themselves "as a person" in such a way that the inferences drawn by those watching will be supportive ones. The representative's word for these supportive inferences is *trust*. It is a word they use a great deal. If a constituent trusts a House member, the constituent says something like: "I am willing to put myself in your hands temporarily; I know you will have opportunities to hurt me – though I may not know when those opportunities occur; I assume that you will not hurt me and I'm not going to worry about your doing so until it is proven beyond any doubt that you have betrayed that trust." The ultimate response members of Congress seek is political support; but the instrumental response they seek is trust. The presentation of self – what is "given" in words and "given off" as a person – will be calculated to win trust. "If people like you and trust you as an individual," members often say, "they will vote for you." So trust becomes central to the congressman–constituent relationship. Constituents, for their part – as Goffman would emphasize – must rely on trust. They must "accept on faith" that the congressman is what he says he is and will do what he says he will do. House members, for their part, are quite happy to emphasize trust. It helps to allay the uncertainties they feel about their support relationship with their various constituencies. If they are uncertain about how to work for support directly, they can always work indirectly to win a degree of personal trust that will increase the likelihood of support, or decrease the likelihood of opposition.

Trust is, however, a fragile relationship. It is not an overnight or a one-time thing. It is hard to win; and it must be constantly renewed and rewon. So it takes an enormous amount of time to build and maintain constituent trust. That is what House members believe. That is why they spend so much of their working time at home. Much of what I have observed in my travels can be explained as a continuous and continuing effort to win (for new members) and to maintain (for old members) the trust of their

various constituencies. Most of the communication I have heard and seen is not overtly political at all. It is, rather, part of a ceaseless effort to reinforce the underpinnings of trust in the congressman or congresswoman "as a person." Viewed from this perspective, the archetypical constituent question is not "what have you done for me lately" but "how have you looked to me lately." House members, then, make a strategic calculation that helps us understand why they go home so much. Presentation of self enhances trust; enhancing trust takes time; therefore, presentation of self takes time.

Of the "contextual" "expressions given off" in the effort to win and hold constituent trust, three seem particularly ubiquitous. First, the congressman conveys to his constituents a sense of his *qualification*. Contextually and verbally, he gives them the impression that "I am qualified to hold the office of United States Representative." "I understand the job and I have the experience necessary to do a good job." "I can hold my own – or better – in any competition inside the House." All members try to convey their qualifications. But it is particularly crucial that any nonincumbent convey this sense of being "qualified." For him, it is the threshold impression – without which he will not be taken seriously as a candidate for Congress. Qualification will not ensure trust, but it is at least a precondition.

Second, the congressman conveys a sense of *identification* with his constituents. Contextually and verbally he gives them the impression that "I am one of you." "I think the way you do and I care about the same things you do." "You can trust me because we are like one another." The third is a sense of *empathy* conveyed by the congressman to his constituents. Contextually and verbally, he gives them the impression that "I understand your situation and I care about it." "I can put myself in your shoes." "You can trust me because – although I am not one of you – I understand you." Qualification, identification, and empathy are all helpful in the building of constituent trust. To a large degree, these three impressions are conveyed by the very fact of regular personal contact at home. That is, "I prove to you that I am qualified," or "I prove to you that I am one of you," or "I prove to you that I understand you" by coming around frequently "to let you see me, to see you, and to meet with you." Contrariwise, "if I failed to come home to see and be seen, to talk and be talked to, then you would have some reason to worry about trusting me." Thus do decisions about the allocation of resources affect the frequency of and opportunity for the presentation of self.

Once he is home, what kind of a presentation does he make there? How does he decide what presentation to make? How does he allocate his time among his perceived constituencies? How does he present himself to these various constituencies? What proportion of competence, identification, or empathy (or other expressions) does he "give off"? In short, what kinds of home styles are presented; and how do they differ among House members? I shall work toward an answer to these questions by discussing the styles of two representatives.

Presentation of Self: A Person-to-Person Style

While it is probably true that the range of appropriate home styles in any given district is large, it is also probably true that in many geographical constituencies there are distinct limits to that range. Congressman A believes there is a good "fit" between his kind of district and his kind of home style. He thinks of his geographical constituency as a collection of counties in a particular section of his state – as southern, rural, and conservative. And he believes that certain presentations of self would not be acceptable there. "I remember once," he told a small group at dinner before a college lecture,

when I was sitting in the House gallery with a constituent listening to Congressman Dan Flood speak on the floor. Dan is a liberal from Wilkes Barre, Pennsylvania. He is a former Shakespearian actor and his wife is a former opera singer. Dan was wearing a purple shirt and a white suit; and he was sporting his little waxed moustache. My constituent turned to me and asked, "what chance do you think a man like that would have of getting elected in our district?" And I said, "exactly the same chance as I would have of getting elected in Wilkes Barre, Pennsylvania."

The expressions "given off" by a former actor with a purple shirt, a white suit, and a waxed moustache would be suicidal in Congressman A's district. Indeed, two days earlier as we got out of the car in one of his county seats, Congressman A said apprehensively, "see my brown shirt? This will be the first time that these people have ever seen me in anything but a white shirt." Brown – possibly; purple – never.

Congressman A sees his geographical constituency as a homogeneous, natural community. And he thinks of himself as totally at one with that community – a microcosm of it. Three generations of his family have lived there and served as its leaders and officeholders. He himself held two elective offices within the district before running for Congress. He has been steeped in the area he represents.

I should write a book about this district – starting with the Indians. It's a very historic district and a very cohesive district – except for Omega County. Nobody knows it like I do.

One thing that ties the district together is the dominance of the textile industry and the dependence of the people of the district – employer and employee – on the textile industry. . . . If I were hostile to the textile industry, it would be fatal. But that could never happen because I feel so close to the textile industry.

I represent a district in which my constituents and I have total mutual confidence, respect and trust – 95 per cent, nearly 100 per cent.

Congressman A feels a deep sense of identification with his constituents. It is this sense of identification that he conveys – verbally and nonverbally – when he presents himself to them.

"In my state," he says, "only a person-to-person campaign will work." So, when he goes home, he "beats the bushes," and "ploughs the ground," in search of face-to-face contact with the people of his district. From county to county, town to town, up and down main street, in and out of county courthouses, through places of business, into homes and backyards, over country roads and into country stores, from early morning till late at night: ("Anyone who hears a knock on the door after 11:00 p.m. knows it's me") he "mixes and mingles" conveying the impression that he is one of them.

In each encounter, he reaches (if the other person does not provide it) for some link between himself and the person he is talking with – and between that person and some other person. There is no conversation that does not involve an elaboration of an interpersonal web and of the ties that bind its members one to the other. In the forefront, always, are ties of family: Congressman A possesses an encyclopedic memory for the names and faces, dates and places of family relations, and for the life cycle events of family – birth, marriage, moving, sickness, and death. His memory and his interest serve him equally well in finding other common ground – be it rivers, plants and trees, farms, crops and businesses, hunting, fishing and football, land, buildings and automobiles, home, church, and country. He devours the district's history; on one trip he was absorbed in a county history and genealogy, on another the memoirs of U. S. Grant. He continually files, sorts, arranges and rearranges his catalogues of linkages – person-to-person, place to place, event to event, time to time.

The Congressman muses a lot about the keys to success in person to person relationships.

Do you remember Miss Sharp back in the post office? She had never met me before, but she called me Sam. That's the way people think of me. No person will ever vote against you if he's on a first name basis with you. Did you know that?

When I'm campaigning I sometimes stop in a country store and buy some salmon and crackers and share them with everyone there – and buy more if need be. Do you know that a man who eats salmon and crackers with you will vote for you? And if a man takes a bite of your chewing tobacco – or better still if he gives you a bite of his chewing tobacco – he'll not only vote for you, he'll fight for you.

People feel they can talk to me. When they are talking, they feel that I'm listening to what they have to say. Some people have the ability to make others feel that way and some don't. They feel that if they come to me with a problem, I'll do everything I can to help them.

The expression he tries to give off in all his person to person dealings is that he knows them, that they know him "as a person," that they are all part of the same community, and that his constituents, therefore, have every reason to make favorable inferences about him. "They know me," he says, "and they trust me."

Since he perceives his geographical constituency as a group of counties, it is natural to find him conveying this sense of identification in terms of counties. In three different counties – none of them his place of residence – he verbalized his relationship with the people who lived there as follows: Chatting with a group of businessmen riding to lunch after a meeting with the officials of Alpha County on water and sewer problems, he said,

Did you know that an Alpha County man saved my grandfather's life in the Civil War? In the battle of Williamsville, my grandfather was badly wounded and Lieutenant Henry from Henryville picked him up and carried him off the field – just a bloody uniform with pieces of bone sticking out. An orderly stopped him and said, 'What are you doing carrying that corpse?' Lieutenant Henry said, "That's no corpse; that's Captain McDonough; and so long as there's a spark of life in him, I'm going to try to save him." He did and my grandfather lived. My roots go deep in Alpha County.

Giving an after dinner speech to the Women's Business and Professional Club of Beta County, he said,

I feel as much at home in Beta County as I do any place on earth. I can't begin to describe to you the frustrations I feel when I see these crazy social experiments (in Washington). . . . These frustrations would make me a nervous wreck or worse if I could not come back home to be with you, my friends and neighbors, my supporters and my constituents. I come home to refresh my spirit and renew my strength, here in the heart of our district, where my family's roots go deep. To me, this truly is "holy ground."

Speaking to a sesquicentennial celebration in adjacent Gamma County, he began,

I have never recognized the artificial boundaries that separate our two counties. I have felt as much at home in Gamma County – our county – among my friends and neighbors as if I had been born here, raised here, and lived here every day of my life.

Later that evening, he reflected on his appearance at the sesquicentennial, which he ranked as the most important event of my four-day visit. "When Marvin introduced me today and said that there weren't five people out there, out of 4,000, who didn't know me, he was probably right. And those who don't know me think they do."

His repeated use of the term "at home" suggests that Congressman A perceives the people whom he meets as his primary constituency. When asked to describe "his very strongest supporters," he explained: "My strongest supporters are the people who know me and whom I have known and with whom I have communicated over the years . . . in my oldest counties, that means 30–40 years." He does not perceive his primary constituency in demographic terms but in terms of personal contacts. In a district seen as homogeneous there are few benchmarks for differentiation. And the one clear benchmark – race – is one he never mentions in public and only rarely in private. His primary constituents are the rural and small town whites who know him (or feel that they know him) personally. He seems to be, as he was once introduced, "equally at home with blue denim and blue serge, with rich folks and po' folks" – so long as the blue denim is nonunion. Standing around in a dusty, brown field swapping hunting jokes with a group of blue-collar friends and sitting in an antique-filled livingroom talking business with the president of a textile company rank equally high on his "at homeness" index. His primary constituency, as may be the case in homogeneous districts, is quite amorphous – as demographically amorphous as V. O. Key's classic "friends and neighbors" victory pattern. But it is sizeable enough and intense enough to have protected Congressman A, for a considerable number of terms, from any serious primary challenge.

Congressman A does not come home a lot, falling into our low-frequency category (0–23) of trips home. He spent eighty working days there in 1973. When he does, he spends most of his time where it is strategically profitable (and personally comfortable) – with his primary constituency. There, he reinforces his ties to the group of greatest importance to him in his traditionally one-party district. He explained, for example, why he took time out of a crowded Washington work week to fly home

to the installation of officers of a Boy Scout Council.

I wanted to make it because of who they were. They were Boy Scout leaders from six of my counties – the men who make scouting here a viable movement. They have given me some of my strongest support since I have been in politics. And they have never asked anything of me but to give them good government. So when they ask, I sure don't want to pass up the opportunity to meet with 90–100 of them. I knew about 90 per cent of them. And the other 10 per cent I know now. Some of those I hadn't met were sons of men I had known.

The scout leaders, of course, want more from him than "good government." They want his time and his personal attention. And he, believing these to be the essence of his home style, happily obliges.

When he mentioned that he had also left Washington once to speak at a high school graduation, I asked whether a high paid staff assistant in the district might relieve him of some of these obligations. (Some members in my group have just such an assistant who attends meetings "in the name of the congressman" when he cannot come.) Congressman A answered,

It wouldn't work. People want to see the congressman – me. At the high school commencement exercises, I could have sent the most scholarly person I could find, to make a more erudite, comprehensive and scholarly exposition than I made. If I had done so, the people there wouldn't have enjoyed one bit of anything he said. And they would never have forgiven me for not being there.

He has a small district staff – three people, one full-time office, and one half-time office – and when he is home, he is as apt to pick up someone's personal problems and jot them down on the back of an envelope as he tours around as he is to find out about these problems from his district aides. Congressman A, at home, is a virtual one-man band. His home style is one of the hardest to delegate to others; and he has no inclination to do so.

He allocates relatively little of his time to his larger reelection constituency. Omega County, singled out earlier as out of the district's mold, is not rural, is populated heavily by out-of-staters, and has experienced rapid population growth.

Congressman A admits he does not feel "at home" there. Yet he still gets a sizeable percentage of Omega County's votes – on grounds of party identification. He explained why he didn't spend time among these reelection constituents.

It is so heterogeneous, disorganized, and full of factions. . . . I don't spend very much time there. Some of my good friends criticize me and say I neglect it unduly. And they have a point. But I can get 50 per cent of the vote without campaigning there at all; and I couldn't get more than 75 per cent if I campaigned there all the time. If I did that, I would probably lose more votes than I gained, because I would become identified with one of the factions, and half the people would hate me. On top of that, I would lose a lot of my support elsewhere in the district by neglecting it. It's just not worth it.

There is another reason besides time costs and political benefits. It is that Congressman A's home style is totally inappropriate for Omega County, and he avoids the personal unpleasantness that would be involved in trying to campaign there. Strategically, Congressman A will accept any increment of support he can get beyond his primary constituency. ("The black people who know me know that I will help them with their problems.") But he allocates very little of his time to the effort.

Congressman A's presentation of self places very little emphasis on articulating issues. The Congressman's own abilities and inclinations run to cultivating personal, face-to-face relationships with individuals. The greater the social, psychological, and physical distance between himself and others, the less he is at home, regardless of the situation. And he was clearly least "at home" at a college, in a lecture-plus-question-and-answer format. He accepts invitations of this sort to discuss issues. But he does nothing to generate such engagements; nor does he go out of his way to raise issues in his dealings with others at home. On the single occasion when he broke this pattern, he tested out his potentially controversial position with his primary constituents (i.e., the American Legion post in his hometown), found it to be acceptable, and articulated it often thereafter. Congressman A's home style does,

however, take place *within an issue context*. There is widespread agreement in the district, and very strong agreement within his primary constituency, on the major issues of race, foreign aid, government spending and social conservatism. The district voted for George Wallace in 1968. Thus while Congressman A's home style is apparently issueless, it may depend for its very success on an underlying issue consensus.

There are, therefore, strategic reasons as well as personal reasons for Congressman A not to focus heavily on specific issues. To do so would be unnecessary and potentially divisive. Congressman A is protective of his existing constituency relations and will not want to risk alienating any of his support by introducing or escalating controversy of any kind. He is a stabilizer, a maintainer. And so, when asked to speak formally, he often responds with communitarian homilies. "I believe if ever there was a promised land, that land is America; and if ever there was a chosen people, those people are Americans." "If a man isn't proud of his heritage, he won't leave a heritage to be proud of. And that goes for his family, his community and his country." These utterances are not the secret of his success. But they do testify, again, to his continuing efforts to articulate a sense of community, to construct and reconstruct a web of enduring personal relationships and to present himself as totally a part of that web. If he gets into electoral difficulty, Congressman A will resort not to a discussion of "the issues," but to an increased reliance on his person-to-person home style. And, so long as his strategic perceptions are accurate, he will remain a congressman.

Presentation of Self: An Issue-Oriented Style

If Congressman B's geographical constituency places any constraints on an appropriate home style, he is not very aware of them. He sees his district as heterogeneous.

It is three worlds; three very different worlds. . . . It has a city – which is an urban disaster. It has suburbs – the fastest growing part of the district. . . . It has a rural area which is a place unto itself.

We spent all afternoon talking to the Teamsters in the city; and then we went to a cocktail party in a wealthy suburb. That's the kind of culture shock I get all the time in this district – bam! bam! bam!

The "three worlds" are not just different. They are also socially and psychologically separated from one another.

Actually the people in the three worlds don't know the others are even in the district. They are three separate worlds. In the city, they call it the city district; in the rural area, they call it their district. And both them are shocked when they are told that they each make up only one-quarter of the district.

The other half are the suburbs – which are, themselves, very disparate. A few suburbs are linked to the city; most are not. Some are blue-collar; others are affluent. Some are WASP; others are ethnic. The district is, then, perceived not only as diverse and artificial, but as segmented as well. The possibilities for an acceptable presentation of self would seem to be limitless.

Congressman B's past associations in the district do not incline him toward a style peculiar to any one of "the three worlds." His district ties are not deep; he is a young man who went to college, worked and got his political feet wet outside his district and his state. Nor are the ties strong; he grew up in a suburb in which he probably feels less "at home" ("We lost that stupid, friggin' town by 1,000 votes last time") than anywhere in the district. When he first thought about running, he knew nothing about the district. "I can remember sitting in the livingroom here, in 1963, looking at the map of the district, and saying to myself, 'X? Y? I didn't know there was a town called X in this district. Is there a town called Y?' I didn't know anything about the district." Furthermore, he didn't know any people there. "We started completely from scratch. I was about as little known in the district as anyone could be. In the city, I knew exactly two people. In the largest suburb, I didn't know a single person." He has (unlike Congressman A) absolutely no sense that "only a person like myself" can win in his district.

Indeed, he thinks the opponent he first defeated was better suited to the district and should have won the election. "If I were he, I'd have beaten me." In terms of a geographical constituency and an individual's immersion in it, it is hard to imagine two more different perceptions of me-in-the-constituency than those of Congressman A and Congressman B.

Congressman B has not been in office very long. Not only did he begin from scratch, but he has been scratching ever since. He lost his first race for Congress; he succeeded in his second; and he now represents an objectively (and subjectively) marginal district. His entire career has been spent reaching out for political support. As he has gone about identifying and building first a primary and then a reelection constituency, he has simultaneously been evolving a political "self" and methods of presenting that "self" to them.

His earliest campaign promises were promises about the allocation of resources. He pledged to return to the district every week and to open three district offices, one in each of the "three worlds." These commitments about home style were contextually appropriate, if not contextually determined. For a candidate who neither knew nor was known in the district, pledges of attentiveness would seem almost mandatory. Furthermore, they allowed him to differentiate his proposed style from that of the incumbent – who was not very visible in the district and who operated one office there staffed by two people. Also, these pledges allowed him to embroider his belief that "a sense of distance has developed between the people and the government," necessitating efforts to "humanize" the relationship. And finally, his pledges gave him a lowest common denominator appeal based on style to a district with palpably diverse substantive interests. In 1973, Congressman B made thirty trips home, spent 109 working days there, operated three district offices and assigned one-half of his total staff of fourteen to the district. Promises have turned into style. "We have given the impression of being hardworking – of having a magic carpet, of being all over the place. It's been backbreaking, but it's the impression of being accessible."

Congressman B's actual presentation of self, i.e., what he does when he goes home, has evolved out of his personal interests and talents. He was propelled into active politics by his opposition to the Vietnam War. And his political impulses have been strongly issue-based ever since. He is severely critical of most of what has gone on in American public life for the last ten years. And he espouses a series of programmatic remedies – mostly governmental – for our social ills. He is contemptuous of "old line" politicians who are uninterested in issues and who campaign "by putting on their straw hats and going to barbeques." Riding to a meeting at which he was to address one of his aging town committees, he shouted, "We don't want any old pols or town committees. Give me housewives who have never been in politics before." Whereupon, he rehearsed the opening lines of "the speech I'd like to give" to the town committee. "It will be a stirring speech. 'My fellow political hacks. We are gathered together to find every possible way to avoid talking about the issues.'" This comment, together with his running mimicry of the "old pols," exemplifies what Goffman calls a performance in the "back region," i.e., behind the scenes where the individual's behavior is sharply differentiated from, and serves to accent, his presentation of self to the audience in the "front region."

Congressman B presents himself in the "front region," i.e., in public, as a practitioner of an open, issue-based, and participatory politics. It was his antiwar stand particularly, and his issue-orientation generally, that attracted the largest element of his primary constituency. These were the antiwar activists – young housewives, graduate students, and professionals – who created, staffed, and manned the large volunteer organization that became his political backbone. In the end, his volunteers became skilled in the campaign arts – organizing, coordinating, polling, canvassing, targeting, mailing, fund raising, scheduling, advancing, leafleting – even "bumper-stickering." "We organized and ran a campaign the likes of which people in this district had never seen. Neither party had done anything like it." Lacking a natural community to tie into and lacking any widespread personal appeal (or basis for such), Congressman B turned to the only alternative basis for building support – an organization. The "strongest supporters" in his organization did not support him because they knew him or had had any previous connection with him. The bond was agreement on the central issues and on the importance of emphasizing the issues. That agreement was the only "qualification" for the office that mattered to them. Within this group, the sense of identification between candidate and supporters was nearly total. He was "one of them." They trusted him. And they, with some trade union help (especially financial), gave him a victory in his initial primary.

In reaching for broader electoral support, Congressman B has been guided, in addition to his commitment to "the issues," by a personal penchant for talking about them. That is, he is an exceptionally verbal person; and he has evolved a suitably verbal home style. He places special emphasis on articulating, explaining, discussing, and debating issues. In each campaign (whether he be challenger or incumbent) he has pressed for debates with his opponent; and his assessment of his opponents focuses on their issue positions and their verbal facility. ("He's very conservative and, I understand, more articulate than the last guy. I felt sorry for him; he was so slow.")

In his first two campaigns the main vehicle for presenting himself to his prospective election-reelection constituency was "the coffee." He would sit in a living room or a yard, morning, afternoon, and evening (sometimes as often as eight or ten times each day) with one or two dozen people, stating his issue positions, answering their questions, and engaging in give and take. At the verbal level, the subject was substantive problems. But Congressman B knew that expressions "given off" were equally important.

People don't make up their minds on the basis of reading all our position papers. We have twenty-six of them, because some people are interested. But most people get a gut feeling about the kind of human being they want to represent them.

Thus, his display of substantive knowledge and his mental agility at "the coffees" would help convey the impression that "as a human being" he was qualified for the office. And, not relying wholly on these expressions given off, he would remind his listeners, "No congressman can represent his people unless he's quick on his feet, because you have to deal with 434 other people – each of whom got there by being quick on his feet." Coffees were by no means the only way Congressman B presented himself. But it was his preferred method. "The coffees are a spectacular success. They are at the heart of the campaign." Strategically, they were particularly successful in the suburban swing area of the district. But he tried them everywhere – even in the city, where they were probably least appropriate.

Once in office, he evolved a natural extension of the campaign coffee – a new vehicle that allowed him to emphasize, still, his accessibility, his openness and his commitment to rational dialogue. It is "the open meeting," held twice a year, in every city and town in the district – nearly 200 in each session of Congress. Each postal patron gets an invitation to "come and 'have at' your congressman." And, before groups of 4 to 300, in town halls, schools, and community centers, he articulates the issues in a question–and–answer format. The exchanges are informative and wide-ranging; they are punctuated with enthusiasm and wit. The open meetings, like the coffees, allow Congressman B to play to his personal strengths – his issue interests and his verbal agility. In the coffees, he was concerned with conveying threshold impressions of qualification, and his knowledge and status reinforce that impression in the open meetings. But in the open meetings, he is reaching for some deeper underpinnings of constituent trust. He does this with a presentation of self that combines identification and empathy. "I am not exactly one of you," he seems to tell them, "but we have a lot in common, and I feel a lot like you do." He expresses this feeling in two ways.

One expression "given" and "given off" in the open meetings is the sense that the give-and-take format requires a special kind of congressman and a special kind of constituency and involves them, therefore, in a special kind of relationship. In each meeting I attended, his opening remarks included two such expressions.

One of the first pieces of advice I got from a senior member of my party was: 'Send out lots of newsletters, but don't mention any issues. The next thing you know, they'll want to know how you vote.' Well, I don't believe that.

My colleagues in Congress told me that the questionnaires I sent you were too long and too complicated and that you would never answer it. Well, 5000 have been filled out and returned already – before we've even sent them all out.

At the same time that he exhibits his own ability to tackle any question, explain any vote, and debate any difference of opinion, he massages the egos of his constituents by indicating how intelligent, aware, and concerned they are to engage with him in this new, open, rational style of politics. At the conclusion of an emotional debate with a group of right-to-lifers, whose views he steadfastly opposed, he summed up: "I don't want to pat myself on the back, but there aren't too many congressmen who would do what I am doing here today. Most of them dig a hole and crawl in. I respect your opinions and I hope you will respect mine." The "pat on the back" is for *them* as well as him. And the expression "given off" is that of a special stylistic relationship. From that relationship, he hopes, will flow an increasing measure of constituent trust.

A second, related, expression "given off" is the sense that Congressman B, though he is a politician, is more like his constituents than he is like other politicians. It is not easy for him to convey such an impression, because the only thing his potential reelection constituents know about him is that he is a politician. They do not know him from any prior involvement in a community life. So he works very hard to bind himself to his constituents by disassociating himself from "the government" and disavowing his politician's status. He presents himself as an antipolitician, giving off the feeling that, "I'm just as fed up with government and the people who run it as you are." Since he is a congressman-politician, he is unrelentingly harsh in his criticism of Congress and his fellow legislators.

As you know, I'm one of the greatest critics of Congress. It's an outrageous and outmoded institution.

All Congress has ever done since I've been in Congress is pass the buck to the president and then blame him for what goes wrong.... Congress is gutless beyond my power to describe to you.

Most members of Congress think that most people are clods.... Most of the guys down there are out of touch with their districts.... We aren't living in the 1930s anymore; of course some members of Congress are.... I could never understand the lack of congressional sensitivity to the problems of the elderly. There are so many of them there.

A politician seeking to convey the impression that he is not a politician, Congressman B hopes to build constituent trust by inviting them to blend their cynicism with his.

The presentation of self – an accessible, issue-oriented, communicative antipolitician – at the open meetings is a lowest common denominator presentation. It can win support in each of "the three worlds" without losing support in any. For it is the style, not the issue content, that counts most in the reelection constituency. Congressman B is completely comfortable in the setting. "That was fun," he says after each open meeting. And, occasionally, "it's more fun when there's some hostility." But it is the format more than the audience that makes him feel really "at home." He is not a person-to-person campaigner. "Two of my friends in Congress hold office hours and see people one at a time. That would be a horribly inefficient use of my time. I can see fifty at once. Besides, they don't want to get involved in a give and take." He, on the other hand, keeps his distance from the personal problems of his constituents, inviting them to talk with the staff members who accompany him to the open meetings. Of course, he meets people face-to-face – all the time. But he does not know or seek out much about them as individuals, not much that would build anything more than a strictly political connection. An aptitude for names and faces, a facility with tidbits of personal information and small talk, an easy informality in face-to-face relations – these are not his natural personal strengths. But they are not the keys to his success with his reelection constituency. He has evolved a home style

that does not call for person-to-person abilities in large supply.

The open meetings remain the centerpiece of his home style. "They are the most extraordinary thing we've ever done, and the most important." He sees them as vehicles which help him reach out to and expand his reelection constituency. For he remains a builder instead of a stabilizer in his constituency relations.

Politically, these open meetings are pure gold. Fifty may come, but everybody in town gets an invitation.... I do know that none of our loyalists come to the meetings. They know the meetings are nonpartisan. Maybe one or two of them will show up, but mostly they are new faces.

They have given him entree into the least supportive, rural areas of his district, where he recruits support and neutralizes the more intense opposition. At first, he says, "in some of these towns they didn't know what to say to a Democrat. They probably hadn't met one except for people who fixed their toilets." Yet at the open meetings, "we've had better turnouts, proportionately, in the rural area." "And we get a lot of letters from people there who say they disagree with us but respect our honesty and independence." In time – but only in time – interest and respect may turn into the supportive inferences that connote trust.

But as Congressman B spends more and more of his time at home cultivating an expanding reelection constituency, his oldest and strongest supporters have felt neglected. So Congressman B has a more complex strategic problem, in terms of allocating his time, than Congressman A.

When we began, we had the true believers working their hearts out. It was just like a family. But the more you gain in voters, and the more you broaden your constituency, the more the family feels hurt. Our true believers keep asking me, 'Why don't you drink with us?' "Why don't you talk to me personally anymore?' I have to keep talking to them about the need to build a larger majority. I have to keep telling them that politics is not exclusive; it is inclusive. It is not something that can be done in the living room.

The true believers are not threatening a total loss of support; but declining enthusiasm would

present a serious support problem. One way
Congressman B may deal with the problem is
to come home more, so that he can give the
necessary time to the true believers. He does
come home more than Congressman A, perhaps partly because his strategic problems at
home require it. Still, Congressman B emphasizes identifying and building support beyond
the primary constituency in "the three worlds."
And he finds the open meetings the most effective (and most comfortable) vehicle for him.
"What more could anyone ask," he says, "than
to have the congressman come to their town
personally?" His primary constituents do ask
something more. And, so long as he gives it to
them, he will remain a congressman.

Presentation of Self: Constituency Constraints and Constituency Careers

Our description of the person-to-person and
the issue-oriented styles is exemplary, not
exhaustive. Speculatively, however, presentation
of self would seem to be explainable by three
kinds of factors – *contextual, personal, and strategic.*
   Contextually, a representative thinks about
his constituency relations in terms of me-
in-the-constituency. That perception predates
his service in Washington and cannot be
understood by drawing inferences from his
Washington behavior. Part of the content of
that perception involves a sense of fit – a good
fit as in the case of Congressman A, a nonfit as
in the case of Congressman B, and a bad fit as in
the case of one congressman (not in my group)
who refers to his district as "outer Mongolia."
A congressman's sense of fit will, in turn, be
affected by whether he sees the district as homogeneous or heterogeneous. Good fits are more
likely in homogeneous districts. But the reverse
side of the coin is that home styles are more
likely to be imposed upon the congressman in
homogeneous districts. If Congressman A did
not represent his district, someone who performed similarly at home probably would. In a
heterogeneous district – Congressman B's case –
home style is much more a matter of individual
choice, and is more likely to be imposed by the
congressman on his district. Thus, upon further

analysis of the state-by-state resource allocation
data, we would expect to find the most idiosyncratic patterns appearing in the most heterogeneous districts. Homogeneous districts, in sum,
impose more stylistic constraints on a congressman than do heterogeneous districts.
   A second contextual impact on the presentation of self, however, may produce contrary
tendencies. Once a congressman has imposed a
particular presentational style upon his district,
his successors may feel constrained to continue
that style. That is, a congressman's home style
may be influenced by the previous congressman's home style. Congressman B deliberately
chose a style that contrasted with his predecessor's in order to help develop an identifiable political self. It is equally plausible (and it
happened in my group) that expectations about
style could be so strongly implanted in the district by a predecessor, that the new congressman
dare not change. Similarly, a choice of home
style by imitation or by contrast can occur with
reference to a neighboring congressman – if
the congressman choosing a style has reason to
believe that some of his constituents are likely
to compare him to that neighbor. Regardless of
district make-up, then, under certain conditions
one congressman's style may be shaped by the
style of another congressman, past or present.
   From the cases of representatives A and B, it
seems clear that the presentation of self is also
shaped by each individual's inclinations and talents. Every congressman has some latitude in
deciding how to present himself "as a person."
That is not to say that House members *like* to do
all the things they do at home. More members
than I would have expected described themselves as "shy," "reserved," or "not an extro-
vert." But they go home and present themselves anyway. And they try to do what they
are most comfortable doing and try not to do
that which they are most uncomfortable doing.
Congressman A seeks out person-to-person
relationships, but does not encourage issue-
oriented meetings. Congressman B seeks out
issue-oriented meetings, but does not encourage person-to-person relationships. Experience,
interest, abilities – all the personal attributes of a
congressman's self – help shape his presentation
of that self to others.

Strategically, each congressman must decide how he will allocate his time when he is at home. And it is of some help to think of this strategic problem in terms of his perceived constituencies. From our two cases, we might generalize that a man in a homogeneous district will spend most of his time with his primary constituency. Homogeneous districts are most likely to be perceived as protected in the general election, so that the strategic problem is to hold sufficient primary constituency support to ward off a primary challenger. By the same token, the primary constituency in a homogeneous district is probably more amorphous and less easily defined than it is in a heterogeneous district. Thus a concentration of effort in the primary constituency does not mean that any less time will be required to cultivate it.

By contrast, in a district perceived to be both heterogeneous and electorally unprotected, the congressman will spend relatively more time in his reelection constituency. But he faces a problem of balance. He will play "the politics of inclusion" by spending time expanding his reelection constituency, partly on the assumption that his strongest supporters have no inclination to go elsewhere. Yet he cannot neglect the primary constituency unduly, since their loyalty and intensity of commitment are necessary to sustain a predictably difficult election campaign. He may, of course, be able to allocate resources other than his time, i.e., votes, to keep his primary constituency content. But there is every evidence from my experience that the congressman's strongest supporters are more – not less – demanding of the congressman's time than his other constituencies.

A strategic problem in allocating time, alluded to briefly in discussing Congressman B, involves the presentation of self to one's strongest opponents – to the people each congressman believes he "will never get." House members handle the problem differently. But most of them will accept (and some will solicit) opportunities to present themselves before unfriendly constituents. The strategic hope is that displaying themselves "as a person" may reduce the intensity of the opposition, thus neutralizing their effect within the district. Intense opposition is what every congressman

wants least of. Any time spent cooling the ardor of the opposition is time usefully spent, for it may mean less intense support for the challenger. Functionally, the same accents used in presenting one's self to supporters apply to a presentation to opponents – the emphasis on qualification, the effort at identification, the projection of empathy. In other words, the process of allaying hostility differs little from the process of building trust. That makes it easier for House members to allocate some time – probably minor – to a strategy of neutralization.

Students of Congress are accustomed to thinking about a congressman's *career in the House* – his early adjustments, his rise in seniority, his placement on the ladders of committee and party, the accumulation of his responsibilities, the fluctuations of his personal "Dow Jones Average." But House members also pursue a *career in the constituency*. Congressman B's evolution from "scratch" to a concern with his primary constituency to a concern with his reelection constituency gives evidence of such a constituency career. He was as much a newcomer in the district as newcomers are (or were) purported to be in the House. He had to work out an appropriate home style there just the way each new House member adapts to the House as an institution. Congressman B has been, and is, in the expansionist phase of his career, continually reaching out for increments of support. Congressman A, by comparison, is in a more protectionist phase of his constituency career. He believes that he has, over a considerable period of time, won the trust of his constituents (i.e., his primary constituents). He is working mainly to reinforce that trust; to protect the support he already has. Congressman B does not talk about constituent trust; he never says, "my constituents trust me." His presentation of self is designed to build trust, but, as we have said, it takes time.

The idea of a career in the constituency helps to highlight an important fact about the congressman as an elective politician. As any textbook treatment of incumbency tells us, the congressman is a particularly long-lived political species. He has been making or will make presentations of self to his constituents *for a long time*. And they have been looking at or will look at him "as a person" for a long time. Relative to politicians with briefer constituency careers – like presidents – a congressman's political support will depend especially heavily upon his presentation of self. That, of course, is precisely what House members themselves tell us whenever we have asked. They tell us that their "personal record and standing" or their "personalities" are more important in explaining their election than "issues" or "party identification." They tell us, in other words, that their home style – especially their presentation of self – is the most important determinant of their political support. The idea of a lengthy constituency career helps us understand why this might be true. For it makes home style into a durable, consistent long term factor in congressional electoral politics. In any congressional electoral analyses patterned after our presidential electoral analyses, home style may have to be elevated to a scholarly status heretofore reserved only for party identification and issue voting.

HOME STYLE: EXPLANATION OF WASHINGTON ACTIVITY

When members of Congress are at home, they do something that is closely allied with, yet separable from, the presentation of self to their constituencies. They explain what they have done in Washington. For some House members, their Washington activities are central to their presentation of self. One congressman, for example, routinely began every speech before every district group as follows:

I have represented this district for the last twenty years. And I come to you to ask for a two-year renewal of my contract. I'm running because I have a twenty-year investment in my job and because I think you, as my constituents, have an investment in my seniority. In a body as large as the House of Representatives with 435 elected, coequal members, there has to be a structure if we're ever going to get anything done. And it takes a long time to learn that structure, to learn who has the power and to learn where to grease the skids to get something done. I think I know the structure and the people in the House better than any newcomer could. And

I believe I can accomplish things for you that no newcomer could.

He wants his constituents to see him "as a person" in terms of his importance in Washington. By contrast, neither Congressman A nor Congressman B makes his Washington activity central to his presentation of self. But whether or not his behavior in Washington is central to his presentation of self, every House member spends some time at home explaining and justifying his Washington behavior to his various constituencies. He tells them what he has done and why. What he says, how he says it, and to whom can be viewed as a distinctive aspect of his home style.

The objective of every congressman's explanations – our usage of *explanation* incorporates the idea of *justification* as well – is political support. And just as a congressman chooses, subject to constraints, a presentational style, so too does he choose, subject to constraints, an explanatory style. When most people think of explaining what goes on in Washington to constituents, they think of explaining votes. But we should conceptualize the activities subject to explanation more broadly than that. A House member will explain any part of his activity in Washington if he thinks that part of his activity is relevant to the winning and holding of support at home. Just what kinds of behavior he thinks his various constituencies want or need to have explained to them is an empirical matter; but one which bulks especially large among my representatives is their effectiveness (or lack of it) inside the House on behalf of their constituencies. Often this explanation of one's internal influence also entails a more general explanation of the workings of Congress.

In the case of our Congressman A, for example, press reports that he had lost a committee assignment of importance to the district because of his lack of power within the House posed a major explanatory problem.

Nothing is more damaging to a congressman in his district than to have his constituents believe that he doesn't have the power to get something he wants of that nature. . . . It might have been the only issue in the next campaign. . . . That would have been all that was needed – and only that – to defeat me. . . . No one in the world would believe my explanation, so I had to try for the next vacancy on the committee and I had to win. [Which he did, before the next election.]

For Congressman A, that is, explaining his internal House influence (or lack of it) might be more crucial to protecting his home support than explaining his votes. "I worked my head off to get that building," he said, as we drove by a new federal building in one of his county seats. "The people here were fixing to run someone against me if I hadn't produced it. People think you just have to wave a magic wand to get an appropriation, when most of it is just standing in line waiting your turn." Obviously, such an explanation of "how Congress really works" would not have satisfied his constituents in that county. So he had to produce.

The range of possible activities requiring a home explanation extends well beyond voting. Still, voting is the Washington activity we most easily recognize; and we can make most of our comments in that context. From John Kingdon's splendid discussion of "explaining," we know that, at the time they decide to vote, House members are very aware that they may be called upon to explain their vote to some of their constituents. Moreover, says Kingdon, the anticipated need to explain influences their decision on how to vote. They may cast a certain vote only if and when they are convinced that they have a satisfactory explanation in hand. Or they may cast a certain vote because it is the vote least likely to require an explanation. Kingdon is interested in finding out why members of Congress vote the way they do. But along the way, he helps make the case for finding out why members of Congress explain the way they do. For, if the anticipated need to explain has the effect on voting that Kingdon suggests – i.e., if it makes voting more complicated and more difficult than it otherwise would be – then the act of explaining must be as problematical for House members as the act of voting. House members believe that they can win and lose constituent support through their explanations as well as through their votes. To them, therefore, voting and explaining

are interrelated aspects of a single strategic problem. If that is the way House members see it, then it might be useful for political scientists to look at it that way, too – and to spend a little less of our time explaining votes and a little more of our time explaining *explanations.*

Members are, of course, called upon to vote much more often than they are called upon to explain. That is, they are never called upon to explain all their votes. Their uncertainty about which votes they will have to explain, however, leads them to prepare explanations for more votes than they need to, the need being enforced on them by dissatisfied constituents and, primarily, by the electoral challenger. The challenger, particularly, controls the explanatory agenda – or, better, tries to do so. All the uncertainty that the challenger produces for the perception of constituency, the challenger also brings to the problem of explanation.

Representatives will strike different postures regarding the need to explain. Some will explain their votes only when they feel hard pressed by constituents and/or challenger to do so. They will follow the congressional adage that "if you have to explain, you're in trouble." And their explanatory practices, if not their voting practices, will be calculated to keep them out of trouble. Other members bend over backward to explain every vote that any constituent might construe as controversial – sometimes well in advance of the vote. It is our hunch that the more issue-oriented a congressman's presentation of self, the more voluminous will be his explanations. Our Congressman B, for example, produces a heavy volume of explanation. "We have explained every difficult vote. Anyone who gives a twit about how I vote has the opportunity to know it. We have explained our votes on all the toughies." Given his presentational style, it is hard to see him adopting any other explanatory style. In both cases, the content of what he says is less important than the fact that he says it – i.e., than his style.

I shall resist the temptation to spell out all the possible relationships between the presentational and explanatory aspects of home style. But it seems obvious that they exist. We would, at the least, expect to find a "strain toward compatibility" operating between the two. And we would expect to find the presentation of self – as the centerpiece of home style – to be the more controlling aspect in the relationship. We would further expect both aspects of home style to be influenced by the same constituency constraints. For example, we would expect the broadest perception of me-in-the-constituency – the sense of fit the congressman has with his various constituencies – to underlie the choice of explanatory styles, just as it underlies the choice of presentational styles. A good illustration of this latter point lies outside my particular group of House members. It lies, instead, in the explanation of their historic impeachment vote by two members of the House Judiciary Committee.

In the face of extraordinary constituency interest, two Judiciary Committee Republicans took to statewide television and radio to explain their upcoming vote in favor of impeaching their own party's president. Representative Lawrence Hogan of Maryland cast his explanation heavily in terms of voting his individual conscience against the acknowledged wishes of many prospective constituencies – primary and reelection – in his announced try for the Maryland governorship. To accent his act of conscience, he acknowledged the grave risks to his career.

I know that many of my friends, in and out of Congress, will be very displeased with me. I know that some of my financial contributors (who have staunchly supported Richard Nixon and me) will no longer support me. I know that some of my long-time campaign workers will no longer campaign for me. But to those who were my campaign workers back in my first campaign, I want to remind you of something. Remember, I was running for Congress as a Republican in an area that was registered 3–1 Democratic, and in an effort to convince Democrats that they should vote for me, a Republican, I quoted John F. Kennedy who said: "Sometimes party loyalty demands too much." Remember that?

Well, those words have been coming back to haunt me in recent weeks. Clearly, this is an occasion when "party loyalty demands too much." To base this decision on politics would not only violate my own conscience, but would also be a breach of my own oath of office to uphold the Constitution of the United States. This vote may result not only in defeat in my

campaign for governor of Maryland, but may end my future political career. But that pales into insignificance when weighted against my historic duty to vote as my conscience dictates.

Representative William Cohen cast his explanation in terms of voting as the people of his state of Maine would vote if they were in his shoes. He did not say they were pressuring him to vote, but that he and they, as members of the same community, thought alike on fundamental matters.

I have tried to put all of these events into the context of a political system that I know well, that of the state of Maine. I have asked myself some questions.

What if the governor of Maine ordered his aides to keep a list of those people who supported his opponents? What if he tried to have the state treasurer's department conduct audits of those who voiced dissent? What if he ordered that state police to investigate those who were critical of his policies or speeches? What if he asked aides to lie before legislative committees and judicial bodies? What if he approved of burglaries in order to smear and destroy a man's credibility? What if he obtained information that was to be presented to a grand jury for the purpose of helping his advisors design a strategy for defense?

What would the people of Maine say? You and I both know that the people of Maine would not stand for such a situation, for it is inconsistent with our principles and our constitutional system of government.

Hogan and Cohen offered their listeners very different kinds of explanations for the same vote. It is our hunch that underlying the difference in their explanatory styles are different perceptions of me-in-the-constituency. Cohen sees himself, we would guess, as part of a fairly homogeneous reelection-plus-primary constituency. He identifies strongly with it; and he has a confortable sense of fit with this broad constituency. That being so, he would neither perceive nor explain his vote in terms that set his conscience against theirs. His explanation was, therefore, communitarian. "I am one of you, and the issue is our conscience as a community." Hogan, we would guess, perceives his geographical constituency to be heterogeneous, and has no strong sense of fit with any large or differentiable element of it. Almost surely he feels uncertainty about his prospective statewide constituency; but it seems that he feels uncertainty, even, about his relationships with the primary constituency in his district. It is hard, therefore, for him to find any communitarian bases for explanation. His explanation was individualistic. "I am following my conscience and disregarding the opinions of my constituents."

Neither explanation is inherently "better" than the other. Each had an element of strategic calculation to it. That is, each man chose his words deliberately; and, presumably, neither wanted to lose the next election by virtue of his explanation. That being the case, the acceptability of the two explanations by the Maryland and Maine constituencies becomes a question of some moment. We lack sufficient information to assess the actual impact of the two explanations on each man's political support. But we can try a more general answer. To the degree that Maryland voters already perceived Hogan to be "a man of conscience," and to the degree that Maine voters already perceived Cohen to be "one of us," their explanations probably would have been accepted. On the other hand, to the degree that Maryland voters had already come to view Hogan as a self-serving opportunist, and to the degree that Maine voters had already come to view Cohen as a spineless follower of the herd, their explanations probably would not have been accepted. That is, the credibility of any given explanation probably depends less on the content of the explanation itself than on its compatibility with some previously established perception of the explainer "as a person." "Issues," said one member, "are not as important as the treatment of issues."

Their reasoning goes something like this: There probably are, in every district, one or two issues on which the congressman is constrained in his voting by the views of his reelection constituency. (Whether he *feels* constrained – which depends on whether or not he agrees with those constituent views – is beside the point.) But on the vast majority of votes, a congressman can do as he wishes – provided only that he can, if and when he needs to, explain his vote to the satisfaction of interested constituents. The ability to get his explanations accepted at home is, then,

the essential underpinning of his voting leeway in Washington. Thus the question arises, how can the congressman act so as to increase the likelihood that his explanations will be accepted at home? And the answer the House members give is: he can win and hold constituent trust. The more your various constituencies trust you, House members reason, the less likely they are to require an explanation of your votes and the more likely they are to accept your explanation when they do require it. The winning of trust, we have said earlier, depends largely on the presentation of self. Presentation of self, then, not only helps win votes at election time; it also makes voting in Washington easier. So congressmen make a strategic calculation. Presentation of self enhances trust; trust enhances the acceptability of explanations; the acceptability of explanations enhances voting leeway; therefore, presentation of self enhances voting leeway.

When I asked Congressman C if he wasn't more liberal than his district, he said:

Hell, yes, but don't quote me on that. It's the biggest part of my problem – to keep people from thinking I'm a radical liberal. How do you explain to a group of Polish Catholics why you voted to abolish the House Internal Security Committee or why you voted against a bill to keep Jane Fonda from going to North Vietnam? How do you explain that? You can't.

When queried, later, on a TV interview to comment on his opponent's charge that he was "ten times more radical than George McGovern," Congressman C answered in terms of identification and trust. He said simply, "if he means by that that I'm some kind of wild-eyed radical, people around here know me better than that." Later still, he mused out loud about how he managed this problem.

It's a weird thing how you get a district to the point where you can vote the way you want to without getting scalped for doing it. I guess you do it in two ways. You come back here a lot and let people see you, so they get a feel for you. And, secondly, I go out of my way to disagree with people on specific issues. That way, they know you aren't trying to snow them. And when you vote against their views, they'll say, "Well, he's got his reasons." They'll trust you. I think that's it. If they trust you, you can vote the way you want to and it won't hurt.

A pair of examples from two different types of districts will illustrate variations on this theme.

Congressman D perceives his urban, predominantly black district to be homogeneous. His reelection constituency is "the whole black community"; and his primary constituency consists of the civic-minded, middle-class activists who have organized black politics in his city. As tends to be the case in homogeneous districts, the line between his reelection and his primary constituencies is not sharp. Congressman D, who was born, raised, and employed in his district, sees himself as a microcosm of both groups. Voting in Congress, therefore, is rarely problematical for him. "I don't have any trouble knowing what the black community thinks or wants. . . . I don't have any trouble voting. When I vote my conscience as a black man, I vote right for the district." Though he does not feel constrained, he, of course, is. "If I voted against civil rights legislation, my people would probably ask me why I did that. But I never would do it." On one occasion when it might have looked to them as though he had, he explained and they were satisfied.

When I come home, I go to the church groups and tell them what's been going on in Washington and explain to them why I voted as I did. For instance, I explained to them that I voted against the Voting Rights Bill (1970) because it was a fraud. Nixon wanted to get the fifty-seven Registrars working in the South out of there. After they heard me on the Voting Rights Bill, they went home mad. I know my people will agree with me.

Congressman D falls in the "medium frequency" category in trips home, having made thirty such trips in 1973. "I meet with church groups and other groups; and I let people see me just to let them know I haven't lost touch with them." The "other group" with which he meets most frequently (once a month formally and more often informally) is his district's political organization – "my political lifeline." "The more people see me working for them in our organization, the more popular I become, the more they trust me and are proud of me." From this presentation of self comes,

then, the essential condition for his voting leeway in Washington.

The fact is that I have the freedom to do almost anything I want to do in Congress and it won't affect me a bit back home. My constituents don't know how I vote, but they know *me* and they trust me. . . . They say to themselves, "Everything we know about him tells us he's up there doing a good job for us." It's a blind faith type of thing.

Congressman E describes his district as "heterogeneous – one-third urban, one-third suburban, one-third rural." His primary constituency is the rural area, where three generations of his family have lived. At the very moment we turned off a four-lane highway onto a back road on our way to a small town fair, he said,

It must be terrible to be without roots, without a place to call home. I have a profound sense of identification with these rural people. My wife still worries about me a little bit in this respect – that I'm too much of a country boy. But life's too short to play a role or strike a pose. This will be fun. I'm really going to enjoy myself.

Not only is he clearly most "at home" in the rural part of the district, but it casts a strategically disproportionate 40 per cent of his party's primary vote. "If these city people (in my party) with their slick city ways think they could go out to Mrs. O'Leary's cow pasture and get the farmers to throw out the local boy, they're crazy." His presentation of self is skewed toward his primary constituency. During his 35 trips and 100 working days at home in 1973, his scheduled appearances were allocated as follows: 41 in the urban area, 38 in the suburban area and 70 (or about 50 per cent) in the rural one-third of the district. His accessibility – especially to his primary constituency – is the essence of his presentational style and, hence, he believes, the basis for constituent trust.

Sometimes I do my talking to the same people over and over again. But they talk to others and they speak favorably about me. They tell others that "old George" is always available and accessible. And I get a reputation in that way. That's how I succeed in this kind of district. People think of me as a nice guy, one of the boys, and they make presumptions in my favor because I'm a nice guy.

It is sometimes argued that representatives from heterogeneous districts enjoy a special degree of voting leeway because no single constituency interest controls their electoral future. Congressman E makes this argument. When asked if any single vote could defeat him in his district, he replied, "No, not in my district. It's too diverse, not all urban ghetto or Idaho potato farmers. That gives me a chance to balance interests in my votes. There really aren't any dominant interests." The crucial extra ingredient in the argument – one usually left out – is this: The congressman must be able to explain his voting pattern to his constituencies and have that explanation accepted. And this is especially true as regards his primary constituency. Congressman E commented,

If I want to vote for an urban program, I can do it, and the people in the rural area will say, "He does have an urban constituency and he has to help them, too." And they will still vote for me so long as they think I'm a nice fella. But if I had no urban constituents – if I had all countryside – and I voted for an urban program, people in the rural areas would say, "He's running for governor, he's forgotten who his friends are." The same is true in the urban area. They know I'm a country boy and that I have a lot of rural area. So they say, "He gives us a vote once in a while; he's probably all right."

Congressman E is not unconstrained. He would, he admits, lose his primary constituency if he voted consistently for urban programs. He will also lose his primary constituency if they stop trusting him as "a nice fella" and no longer make "presumptions in my favor" when he explains his few urban votes. If we are to understand a congressman's voting patterns in Washington, it seems that we must also understand his presentational and explanatory patterns at home.

As a final note, two general patterns of explanation deserve mention. One I had expected to find but have not, and one I had not expected to find but have. Both invite further research. In view of the commonly held notion that elective politicians "talk out of both sides of their mouths" (which Goffman discusses in terms of performances before "segregated audiences"), I had expected to find members of Congress explaining their activity somewhat differently to their various constituencies. The likelihood seemed especially strong in heterogeneous districts, where the opportunity and temptation would be greatest. But I have found little trace of such explanatory chameleons in my travels. The House members I observed give the same explanations for their Washington activity before people who disagree with them as before people who agree with them – before nonsupporters as well as supporters, from one end to the other in the most segmented of districts. The lack of this kind of demagoguery, and the patient doggedness with which members explained their activities to unsympathetic audiences, surprised me. I do not mean they went out of their way to find disagreement (though such a practice is of central importance to the presentation of self in some cases – such as Congressman C). I only mean that when disagreement was present, members offered the same explanation for their vote that they offered under all other conditions. Their presentation of self may vary from group to group in the sense that the basis for demonstrating identification or empathy will have to differ from group to group. As they reach out to each group in a manner appropriate to that group, they may take on some local coloration; and they may tailor their subject matter to fit the interests of their audience. However, they rarely alter their explanations of their Washington activity in the process.

An explanatory pattern I had not expected to find was the degree to which the congressman at home explains his Washington activity by disassociating it from the activity of his colleagues and of Congress as a whole. I had assumed that home styles would be highly individualized. And I should not have been surprised, therefore, when I heard every one of my seventeen members introduced at home as "the best congressman in the United States." But I was not prepared to find each of them polishing this individual reputation at the expense of the institutional reputation of the Congress. In explaining what he was doing in Washington, every one of my House members took the opportunity to portray himself as "different from the others" – the others being "the old chairmen," "the inexperienced newcomers," "the tools of organized labor," "the tools of big business," "the fiscally irresponsible liberals," "the short-sighted conservatives," "the ineffective leadership," "the obstructionist minority," "those who put selfish concerns before country," and so on. The diversity of the House provides every member with plenty of collegial villains to flay before supportive constituents at home. Individual members do not take responsibility for the performance of Congress; rather each portrays himself as a fighter against its manifest shortcomings. Their willingness, at some point, to stand and defend their votes contrasts sharply with their disposition to run and hide when a defense of Congress is called for. Congress is not "we"; it is "they." And members of Congress run *for* Congress by running *against* Congress. Thus, individual explanations carry with them a heavy dosage of critical commentary on Congress.

CONCLUSION: POLITICAL SUPPORT, HOME
STYLE, AND REPRESENTATION

"A congressman has two constituencies," Speaker Sam Rayburn once said. "He has his constituents at home and he has his colleagues here in the House. To serve his constituents at home, he must serve his colleagues here in the House." For over twenty years, political scientists have been researching the "two constituencies." Following the thrust of Rayburn's comment, we have given lopsided attention to the collegial constituency on Capitol Hill. And we have neglected the constituency at home. Knowing less than we might about one of the two constituencies, we cannot know all that we should about the linkage between them. This paper argues for opening up the home constituency to more political science investigation than it has received. It suggests that students of Congress pay more attention to "home" as a research focus and a research site. No one can say what we might learn if the suggestion were heeded. But a few speculations will serve as a conclusion to this exploratory effort.

For one thing, it appears that a congressman's constituency is more complicated than our normal treatment of it in our literature suggests.

We have not, of course, obtained a constituent's-eye view of the constituency, having tried to keep the congressman's perceptions as our sole vantage point. But from that vantage point alone, it seems that we must be more precise about what we mean by "his (or her) constituents." If we are going to continue to talk in the language of role orientations – in which the "trustee's" votes are not determined by his constituents, and in which the "delegate" does follow the wishes of his constituents – we shall have to know just which "constituents" we (and he) are talking about. If we are going to continue to do survey research – in which we match the attitudes of the congressman with the attitudes of his constituents, or with his perceptions of the attitudes of his constituents – we shall, again, have to know just what "constituents" we (and he) are talking about. The abstraction "his (or her) constituents" is only slightly more useful as an analytical variable than the abstraction "the people." It may be that the distinctions attempted here are not the most useful ways of dividing up the home constituency for analytical purposes. But the days when our literature acknowledges the complexities of politics on Capitol Hill, while accepting the most simplistic surrogates for political reality at home, those days ought to be numbered.

While this article has not dwelled directly on the topic of representation, our exploration has implications for the family of questions, both descriptive and normative, raised by studies of representation. For people studying the conditions of electoral accountability, this study has something to say about the electoral accountability of members of Congress. They are not among Kenneth Prewitt's "volunteerists." House members work hard to get the job and work hard to keep it. In the course of that effort, they expend a great deal of time and effort keeping in touch with their various constituencies at home. Furthermore, they feel much more uncertain, insecure, and vulnerable electorally than our objective measures reveal. When a congressman describes his seat as "safe," he implicitly adds: "because, and so long as, I work actively to keep it so." And many a House retirement decision is made in anticipation of electoral difficulty. Surely, then, some of the necessary conditions for electoral accountability are present in Congress as they are not in certain other representative bodies in this country. But the existence of such conditions does not, by itself, tell us whether House members are as responsive to constituent desires as democratic theory may require. Our study can provide, however, some perspectives with which to pursue this normative inquiry.

For example, it appears that members of Congress feel a good bit more accountable – and, hence, I would guess, are more responsible – to some constituents than to others. House members feel more accountable to some constituents than to others because the support of some constituents is more important to them than the support of others. Thus, the process by which people become and remain representatives is closely related to their activity while they are representatives. In a representative democracy, the process is electoral; and the central problem for the representative is that of winning and holding voter support. From the viewpoint of this paper, problems of representation and problems of support are inseparable. It is precisely because a congressman's right to represent depends on his cultivation of electoral support that he develops such a complex and discriminating set of perceptions about his constituents. In a representative democracy, the representative learns who his, or her, various constituencies are by campaigning for support among them. The one deficiency in Hanna Pitkin's splendid book is the undifferentiated, uncomplicated idea of the constituency that she employs in her study of representation. And her monolithic view of "the constituency" remains viable only because she separates the process of running for office from the problems of representation. The traditional view of representation is somewhat more static and structural than the process–oriented view one gets by focusing on the cultivation of constituent support. To the congressman, the very word "political" connotes the ongoing problem of support. A "political vote" is one calculated to win (or to avoid losing) support. A "politically unwise move" is one that will lose support, etc. Focusing on the problem of support keeps the dynamism and the politics in the subject of representation. If politics is about "who gets what, when, and how," then the politics of representative democracy is about "who supports whom, when, and how – and how much." And, "what do various constituencies get in return for their support?"

A more inclusive, process-oriented view of representation has the effect of making it less exclusively a policy-centered subject. Traditionally, representation has been treated mostly as a structural relationship in which the congruence between the policy preferences of the represented and the policy decisions of the representative is the measure of good representation. The question we normally ask is: "How well does Representative X represent his or her district?" And we answer the question by matching and calibrating substantive policy agreement. But our view here is that there is an intertwining question: "How does Representative X carry his or her district?" To answer that question, we shall need to consider more than policy preferences and policy agreements. We shall need to consider the more encompassing subject of home style and the constituent trust generated by home style. We shall need to entertain the possibility that constituents may want good access as much as good policy from their representative. They may want "a good man" or "a good woman" whom they judge on the basis of home style and whom they trust to be a good representative in terms of policy. Indeed, the growing political science literature on voter behavior in congressional elections contains both evidence and speculation – usually under the rubric of the rising pro-incumbent vote – that voters are looking increasingly to just such candidate-centered bases for tendering electoral support. The point is not that policy preferences are not a crucial basis for the representational relationship. They are. The point is that we should not start our studies of representation by assuming they are the *only* basis for a representational relationship. They are not.

This last comment may be as valid normatively as it is empirically. What reason is there to believe that a relationship based on policy is superior to one based on homestyle – of which policy is, at most, only a part – as a normative standard for representative democracy? It may be objected that a search for support that stresses stylistic compatibilities between the representative and the represented easily degenerates into pure image-selling. And, of course, it may. But the search for support that emphasizes policy compatibilities between the representative and the represented easily degenerates into pure position taking. Position taking is just as misleading to constituents and as manipulative of their desires as image selling. Both representational bases, we conclude, may take a corrupt form. Appearing to do something about policy without a serious intention of, or demonstrable capacity for, doing so is no less a corruption of the representative relationship, no less an impediment to accountability and responsiveness, than is the feigning of a personal relationship without a serious intention of establishing one. They are equally corrupt, equally demagogic. They are substitutes for any real effort to help make a viable public policy or to establish genuine two-way communication and trust. At the least, normative theory ought to take account of both policy and extra-policy standards of good representation, and acknowledge their respective corruptions.

Our concentration on and our preference for the policy aspects of representation carries a related implication. For a people who profess an attachment to representative democracy, we have always seemed curiously uncomfortable when our representatives devote themselves to contact with their constituents. We tend to denigrate the home part of the representational process as mere "errand-running" or "fence-mending" and to assume that it takes the representative away from that which he, or she, really should be doing, i.e., making public policy in Washington. As one small example, we have always criticized, out of hand, the "Tuesday to Thursday Club" of House members who go home for long weekends – on the assumption, presumably, that going home was *ipso facto* bad. But we never inquired into what they did at home or what the consequences (other than their obvious dereliction of duty)

of their home activity might have been. Predictably, the home activities described in this paper will be regarded, by some, as further evidence that members of Congress spend too little of their time "on the job." But this paper asks that we entertain the alternate view that the Washington and the home activities can be mutually supportive. Time spent at home can be time spent developing leeway for activity undertaken in Washington. And it may be that leeway in Washington should be more valued than the sheer number of contact hours spent there. It may be, then, that the congressman's effectiveness in Washington is vitally influenced by the pattern of support he has developed at home and by the allocational, presentational, and explanatory styles he displays there. To put the point most strongly, perhaps we cannot understand his Washington activity without first understanding his perception of his constituencies and the home style he uses to cultivate their support.

No matter how supportive of one another their Washington and home activities may be, House members still face constant tension between them. Members cannot be in two places at once. They cannot achieve legislative competence and maintain constituency contact, both to an optimal degree. The tension is not likely to abate. The legislative workload and the demand for legislative expertise are growing. And the problems of maintaining meaningful contact with their several constituencies – which may make different demands upon them – are also growing. Years ago, House members returned home for months at a time to live with their supportive constituencies, soak up the home atmosphere, absorb local problems at first hand. Today, they race home for a day, a weekend, a week at a time. The citizen demand for access, for communication, for the establishment of trust is as great as ever. The political necessity and the representational desirability of going home is as great as ever. So members of Congress go home. But the quality of their contact has deteriorated. It is harder to sustain a genuine two-way relationship – of a policy or an extra-policy sort – than it once was. They worry about it and as they do, the strain and frustration of the job increases. Many cope; others retire.

Indeed, retirements from the House appear to be increasing. Political scientists do not know exactly why. But the research reported in this article points to the possibility that an inability or an unwillingness to improve the quality of the home relationship may be a contributing factor. Those who cannot stand the heat of the home relationship may be getting out of the House kitchen. If so, people prepared to be more attentive to home are likely to replace them. Thus, our focus on home activity may help us understand some changing characteristics of House members.

Our professional neglect of the home relationship has probably contributed to a more general neglect of the representational side of Congress's institutional capabilities. At least it does seem to be the case that the more one focuses on the home activities of its members, the more one comes to appreciate the representative strengths and possibilities of Congress. Congress *is* the most representative of our national political institutions. It mirrors much of our national diversity, and its members maintain contact with a variety of constituencies at home. While its representative strengths surely contribute to its deserved reputation as our slow institution, the same representative strengths give it the potential for acquiring a reputation as our fair institution. In a period of our national life when citizen sacrifice will be called for, what we shall be needing from our political institutions are not quick decisions, but fair decisions. Some of the recent internal congressional reforms have increased the potential for both representativeness and fairness. They have increased the equality of representation by distributing influence more broadly inside Congress. They have increased the visibility of representation by opening up congressional proceedings to public view. This is by no means all that is needed. But it is enough to place an added obligation on the members of Congress to educate their constituencies in the strengths as well as the weaknesses of the institution. Members should participate in consensus building in Washington; they should accept some responsibility for the collective performance of Congress; and they should explain to their constituents what an institution that is both collective and fair requires of its individual members.

The evidence of this study indicates that members have the leeway to educate their constituents if they have the will to do so. The evidence of this study also shows that they may not have that will. Instead, they often seek support and trust for themselves by encouraging a lack of support and trust in the Congress. By refusing to accept responsibility for an institutional performance, they simultaneously abdicate their responsibility to educate their constituents in the work of the institution. Instead of criticizing House members for going home so much, we should criticize them for any failure to put their leeway to a constructive purpose – during the legislative process in Washington and during the explanatory process at home. The trust of his, or her, supportive constituents should be viewed by a House member as his, or her, working capital – not just to be hoarded for individual benefit but to be drawn on, occasionally, for the benefit of the institution. So long as House members explain themselves but not the institution, they help sustain (wittingly or unwittingly) the gap between a 10 per cent approval level for Congress and a 90 per cent reelection record for themselves. If this imbalance seems unhealthy for both Congress and the Republic, we have yet another justification for an increased scholarly attentiveness to our House members at home.

CHAPTER SEVEN

Collective vs. Dyadic Representation in Congress

Robert Weissberg

We might measure the quality of representation in Congress by observing the congruence between the public's views and those in Congress. We could measure the congruence either between individual legislators' views and their districts' views (dyadic) or between the nation as a whole and Congress as a whole (collective). Weissberg observes that we are likely to have better collective than dyadic representation.

Legislative representation has long been a basic concern in political analysis. Particularly in the last 20 years a wide variety of theories, data, and methodologies have been employed to examine the question of whether legislators, in some sense, follow district opinion. The results of these studies are by no means conclusive and controversies abound on how one should analyze representation and what certain types of data actually indicate. Nevertheless, despite the sheer variety of analyses and debate, previous studies almost all share one fundamental perspective: they view representation in terms of a particular legislator and the constituency that elected that legislator. This dyadic perspective (i.e., one legislator and one constituency) is surely important, but it is not the only way of approaching representation. Specifically, a long and equally valid tradition exists that views representation in terms of *institutions* collectively

Robert Weissberg. 1978. "Collective vs. Dyadic Representation in Congress" *American Political Science Review* 72: 535–47. Copyright © 1978 by the American Political Science Association. Reprinted with the permission of Cambridge University Press.

representing a people. Within this tradition the central question would be whether Congress as an institution represented the American people, not whether each member of Congress represented his or her particular district.

This paper will explore both theoretically and empirically this notion of collective representation. In so doing we shall not only elaborate on an important (but frequently neglected) concept in the study of legislatures, but within the limits of our data we will attempt to show the following: (1) legislative representation of citizen opinion when viewed collectively is not nearly as poor as is indicated in most studies of legislator–constituency relationships; (2) at least some features of American politics typically associated with poor representation may in fact contribute to accurate representation; and (3) much of the public ignorance of legislative politics and opposition to disciplined parties is reasonable, given the operation of collective representation.

We shall first explicate the dyadic approach to the study of legislative–constituency opinion representation. This approach will then be contrasted with collective and virtual conceptions of representation. Second, nondyadic aspects of representation will be discussed and in part illustrated by data collected by Warren Miller and Donald Stokes. We shall see, for example, that a particular legislator's misrepresentation of constituency opinion can, under certain conditions, increase the overall level of opinion representation. We shall also show that partisan legislative voting discipline can likewise decrease opinion representation, despite claims to the contrary. Third, we will consider nondyadic representation in the context of democratic control of leaders through elections. We shall argue that there is no one-to-one relationship between accurate representation of citizen preferences and citizen electoral control over legislators. Indeed, random selection of legislators would maximize representation at the expense of citizen control. Finally, we shall examine certain citizen attitudes and behaviors in the light of different conceptions of representation and misrepresentation. We hope to show, for example, that ignorance of one's particular Congress member's voting record, political apathy, or even voting for unresponsive legislators are much more reasonable than previously claimed, given collective representation.

Before proceeding we should note two limitations. First, while we speak of legislators in general, our analysis will be of members of the U.S. Congress in particular. No doubt there are legislatures whose rules and functions would make our analysis irrelevant. Second, our data are the well-known Miller and Stokes data, a data set somewhat limited by small sample size in several districts. Nevertheless, both these problems are not serious since our effort is largely theoretical and illustrative. For such a purpose the Miller–Stokes data are perfectly adequate and restricting ourselves to the United States likewise poses no serious problem.

CONCEPTIONS OF CITIZEN–LEGISLATIVE REPRESENTATION

Perhaps due to our underlying democratic values, recent American research on legislative responsiveness has usually viewed representation in an electoral context. That is, citizens are (or are not) represented by an elected official they could have voted for or against. In this sense, a citizen could only be represented by one member of Congress, one governor, two senators, and one president, but not – say – a Supreme Court justice. Scholars have therefore asked: do elected officials represent those who

elected them (or who live in their districts)? Regardless of whether constituency opinion is measured by interviews or inferred from socio-economic or demographic data, the units of analysis have always been the legislator and the district, paired. Representation means a high correlation between constituency opinion and roll call voting on a pairwise basis.

It should be obvious, however, that the representation of an opinion (or interest) is theoretically independent of an electoral connection between the person with a preference and the person doing the representing. Much in the same way that individuals' economic interests can be advanced by organizations to which they do not belong (these are called "free riders"), their interests can be served in Congress among any one of 435 representatives and 100 senators. Moreover, it is quite likely that one's best representative could change over time and across issue areas. In fact, it is extremely unlikely that out of a pool of 435 legislators one's own legislator will represent one's particular opinion on an issue. An excellent illustration of such representation independent of an electoral relationship no doubt occurred when northern black and liberal white Congress members articulated the preferences of disenfranchised southern blacks during the 1950s and 1960s.

Though it is not customary to separate representation from a direct electoral relationship, any review of the various meanings of representation will show that representative institutions were never automatically equated with electoral institutions. Moreover, even when elections and representation were linked, dyadic representation was never the dominant historical model. In her analysis of the various meanings of representation, Pitkin describes an important school of thought that viewed legislatures as a group of individuals collectively representing the people *as a whole*. The purpose of the legislature is to create an accurate reflection of the community; misrepresentation occurs when the diverse interests and opinions of the political community are excluded from debate. A particular legislator, according to this view, was not a delegate for those particular people who chose him or her, but all the legislators taken collectively would act as if all the people themselves were acting since they were a reflection of the whole. This principle is quite similar to the principle of random sampling: a particular individual in a sample of 1,500 from a universe of 210 million does not personally represent 140,000 people, but the sample collectively is a close approximation of the 210,000,000 people.

The concept of virtual representation, particularly as employed by Edmund Burke, also separates the electoral association between two individuals from their representational relationship. As Burke put it, virtual representation occurs where "there is a communion of interest and sympathy in feelings and desires between those who act in the name of any descriptions of people and the people in whose name they act, though the trustees are not actually chosen by them." Hence, at least for Burke, the city of Birmingham is not automatically unrepresented merely because it has no delegate in Parliament. Because Bristol, which has the same commercial interests as Birmingham, does send members to Parliament, Birmingham is virtually represented. Indeed, Burke asserts that in many instances virtual representation is superior to actual representation (i.e., the representation of electors' interests by their elected officials) since virtual representation is based on common sentiment, not fallible attempts to advance interests one might not share. To be sure, Burke is not talking about constituency *opinions* when he speaks of "interest," but the basic thrust of his argument – that legislators "look out" for nonconstituency interests and thus represent them – is equally applicable to the analysis of opinion representation.

Moreover, many recent studies of legislative decision making have examined nondyadic representational relationships, though rarely has this type of relationship been deemed to be of special theoretical importance. For example, Wahlke, Eulau, Buchanan, and Ferguson in their study of four state legislatures find a significant number of legislators viewing themselves as representing state, as opposed to district, interests. Studies of interest group/legislative interaction have often noted that interest groups must of necessity cut across purely geographical division so that,

say, a New York industry wanting tariff protection may be "represented" by a member of Congress from California who happens to be on the relevant committee. Equally familiar are instances in which legislators will "broaden" their constituencies by becoming spokespersons for nongeographically based interests, e.g., automobile safety, withdrawal from Vietnam, or the fate of Soviet Jews. It is clear, then, that many researchers have dealt with nondyadic representation but this behavior has rarely been conceptually distinguished from purely district-oriented activity.

Finally, the concept of collective representation is even embedded in the idea of responsible party government despite this doctrine's emphasis on individual citizen policy voting. That is, citizens choose a party and the victorious party represents a national majority; members of the victorious party do not represent their district majority except insofar as district majorities are congruent with a national majority. Thus it is proper to speak only of national majorities being represented, not the relationship between particular voters and the legislators they actually selected. Indeed, one of the major purposes of party discipline is to eliminate purely dyadic representation.

In short, even if we require an electoral connection between citizens and their representatives, there is no historical or theoretical reason to limit analysis to dyadic representational relationships. To focus exclusively on such questions as "does Representative X follow the constituency's preferences on policies A, B, and C?" thus ignores several equally plausible ways of asking whether elected representatives represent.

REPRESENTATION WITHOUT CONTROL OR AGREEMENT

According to the dyadic model, the maximum possible degree of representation would occur if legislators followed the preferences of their constituents (somehow defined). It would therefore seem to follow that citizens would not be represented if (a) all members of Congress voted

Table 7.1A. *Perfect District-by-District Agreement, Perfect Aggregate Agreement*

Opinion/Roll Call Scores for	District			X All Districts
	1	2	3	
Constituency Preferences ($\overline{X}$)	1	2	3	2
Legislators (scale scores)	1	2	3	2
Differences in Preferences	0	0	0	

randomly or (b) all members of Congress – for any number of reasons – violated constituency preferences. We shall argue here that misrepresentation need not occur if Congress members voted randomly or otherwise chose to ignore constituency opinion. What makes such an argument possible is an acceptance of a collective perspective on representation which focuses on the representation of an opinion within an institution independent of an electoral relationship between opinion holder and legislator.

A different and somewhat broader way of viewing the amount of representation is to think of both constituency and legislative preferences (or votes) in terms of a continuum (or scale) as opposed to a yes/no voting dichotomy. In addition, with a sufficient distribution on a continuum we can examine the extent to which relatively small policy minorities are represented. In making this examination we make the same basic contention as in our previous discussion of representation; namely, that a certain degree of representation is likely though legislators may ignore or be oblivious to constituency opinion. Let us begin by considering the hypothetical data in Tables 7.1A and B, which depict a legislature of three constituencies.

Table 7.1A shows what might be considered perfect representation. Each district is represented by a legislator with the precise scale position as his or her constituency. Moreover, if we consider national opinion to be the sum total of individual legislator opinion (or behavior), the last column of Table 7.1A shows perfect representation. Table 7.1B, on the other hand, shows a situation in which two of the three districts are

substantially misrepresented (districts 1 and 3). Does this show that citizens in these districts go without adequate representation? In this particular example, it is evident that citizens in district 1 are represented by the legislator from district 3 and vice versa. Equally important, observe that the mean scale positions for both constituents and legislators in Table 7.1B are identical. Thus, on the whole, constituents are perfectly represented by legislators, though not necessarily on a dyadic basis. In the Burkean sense, representation is virtual, not actual.

What we have illustrated in Tables 7.1A and B is a general phenomenon. Specifically, by summing across both districts and legislators separately, then subtracting the grant totals, and dividing by the number of districts, we allow positive and negative district deviations to cancel each other out. Thus, as we see in Table 7.1B the scores for district 1 and 3, which show deviations of 2 and −2 scale positions from constituency means, cancel each other out when added together. Hence, citizens of district 1 are represented because legislators in both district 3 and district 1 misrepresent their constituents in precisely opposite ways. Statistically, this principle is:

$$\frac{\Sigma|d - R|}{N} \geq \frac{\Sigma d - \Sigma R}{N}$$

where

d = the mean district scale score
R = the representatives scale score
N = the number of pairs

In words, this formula can be stated thus: the average legislator–constituency difference on a

Table 7.1B. *Poor District-by-District Agreement, Perfect Aggregate Agreement*

Opinions/Roll Call Scores for	District			X All Districts
	1	2	3	
Constituency Preferences ($\overline{X}$)	1	2	3	2
Legislators (scale scores)	3	2	1	2
Differences in Preferences	−2	0	2	

Table 7.2. *Dyadic versus Collective Representation, by Issue Domain, 1958*
(District Majorities)

Issue Domain	X̄ Difference between Member of Congress and Partisan Constituents on Dyadic Basis	Difference between All Legislators and All Districts in the Aggregate	"Improvement" of Collective over Dyadic*
Social Welfare	3.26	2.45	24.8%
Civil Rights	2.92	2.41	17.5%
Foreign Affairs	4.34	2.62	39.6%

* Improvement is calculated by subtracting the aggregate from the dyadic scores and dividing the result by the dyadic score.

Source: Survey Research Center, University of Michigan.

dyadic basis is equal to or greater than the average difference between all legislators and all constituents. Moreover, for reasons that will be more fully discussed below, it will usually be the case that $\frac{\Sigma|d-R|}{N} > \frac{\Sigma d - \Sigma R}{N}$, so citizens as a whole are better represented by Congress than are citizens in each district by their particular legislators.

This principle can be illustrated with the Miller–Stokes data. Though an ideal illustration would require that both legislators and constituents be measured on the same scale, we shall make do with scales composed of different items and of different ranges. Table 7.2 shows both dyadic and aggregate (or virtual) representation on the issues relating to social welfare, civil rights, and foreign affairs. Observe that the mean district by district legislator–constituency difference (here measured by the mean of all those identifying with the legislator's party) ranges from 4.34 for foreign policy to 2.92 for civil rights. However, as the values in the second column indicate, this discrepancy is significantly reduced if viewed in terms of aggregate differences. For social welfare the overall legislator–constituency difference is reduced by about 25 percent of the average of dyadic differences, while on foreign affairs – which shows the largest amount of dyadic misrepresentation – representation is improved 40 percent in the aggregate. The latter finding is particularly important since the near-zero constituency – Congress members' correlation in foreign affairs reported by Miller and Stokes –

would lead us to expect extensive misrepresentation, when in fact Congress as an institution is doing a better job than suggested by the very low correlation. This is not to say that dyadic representation is poor; rather, whatever the degree of dyadic representation, collective representation is equal or better.

More generally, several politically important principles can be deduced from $\frac{\Sigma|d-R|}{N} > \frac{\Sigma d - \Sigma R}{N}$. First, as we have seen, extreme cases of dyadic misrepresentation (i.e., district mavericks) need not result in misrepresentation of any or all constituents. The quality of representation is in part dependent on the *distribution* of misrepresentation; the absolute level of dyadic misrepresentation is less important than how it is distributed. Imagine, for example, an extremely liberal district that happens to be represented by an extremely conservative member of Congress. If this were the only district in a political system these liberal citizens would indeed be misrepresented. But, if there also existed an extremely conservative district having an extremely liberal member of Congress, misrepresentation in the second district results in overall representation. It follows, then, that aggregate (or virtual) representation will be better than dyadic representation to the extent that dyadic misrepresentation is equally distributed on both sides of the overall constituency mean. Only if there is misrepresentation on both sides of the constituency mean can misrepresenting actions cancel each other out so if all legislators vote the same way or all violate constituency preferences in the same direction, dyadic and aggregate representation will be identical (this would be unlikely, of course, if legislators voted randomly).

This last point has important implications for the doctrine of responsible party government or, for that matter, any doctrine calling for greater legislative party cohesion. Specifically, in a legislature with two (or more) highly cohesive parties only two (or more) points in the distribution of citizen opinion will be *precisely* represented. To be sure, the point represented by the majority party may be the modal constituency issue position or the mean of all constituency issue position, but many issue positions are not literally represented in the legislature. On the other hand, let us imagine a situation consisting of two parties with different ideological centers of gravity but where some legislators can diverge substantially from the official "party line." If party deviates (i.e., those at odds with the official party position) are equally dispersed on the "right" and the "left," the mean legislative party positions may be the same as in the case of a cohesive party system. The obvious difference, however, between the two situations is that many more constituency opinions are *precisely* represented in the instance of decentralized parties. Thus, even if the legislative outcomes are identical in both instances, the less cohesive situation possesses the likely advantage of offering a greater variety of legislative spokespersons for various citizen positions.

Our arguments here are also relevant to the problem of representing minority interests in a system of single-member, first-past-the-post districts. On the long debate over the merits of proportional representation (PR) *vs.* single member districts (SMD), the representation of sizable interests without a majority in any particular district has usually been considered one of the advantages of PR and a democratic weakness of the SMD arrangement. This weakness can disappear, however, if some legislators (1) violate preferences of their own and all other constituency majorities and (2) if these violations are equally dispersed around the mean of all constituency majorities. Hence, so long as extreme misrepresentation in one

direction is balanced by equal misrepresentation in the opposite direction, extreme preferences not dominating any particular electoral district (e.g., the Klu Klux Klan race position) can be represented without overall constituency preferences being violated. We are *not* claiming that such balanced misrepresentation need result in PR-like equal representation of all public opinion in exact proportion to its popular strength; rather, in the aggregate, the violation of constituency preferences can produce a spokesperson for minority preferences, while not resulting in the legislature in general misrepresenting constituency majorities.

To assess the representation of district minorities via virtual representation, using the Miller–Stokes data we have computed the mean district-by-district difference between Congress members and members of the minority party and the overall difference between all district minorities and all members of Congress in the aggregate. These differences for the issues of social welfare, civil rights, and foreign policy are presented in Table 7.4. Not surprisingly, the mean pairwise gap between the Congress member and the mean of minority-party identifiers is larger than the gap for majority-party identifiers depicted in Table 7.3. This larger gap does not indicate, however, that district minorities receive poorer congressional representation than constituency majorities. Indeed, comparison of the aggregate legislator–minority constituency differences in Table 7.3 with the comparable figures in Table 7.2 shows that in civil rights and social welfare policy, the constituency minorities receive *better* overall representation than do majorities. For example, on civil rights issues and the mean aggregate difference for the majority is 2.41, while for the minority it is 2.20. In short, "minority representation" in a single-member district appears to be a problem only if viewed on a district-by-district basis. Viewing the legislature as an institution representing a collectivity does not mean, of course, that all minority preferences are, therefore, proportionately represented; rather, our analysis suggests that in the aggregate a district minority may receive no better representation than constituency majorities.

Table 7.3. *Dyadic versus Collective Representatives, by Issue Domain, 1958 (District Minorities)*

Issue Domain	X̄ Difference between Member of Congress and Opposing Partisan on Dyadic Basis	Difference between All Legislators and All Districts Minorities in the Aggregate	"Improvement" of Collective over Dyadic*
Social Welfare	3.41	2.38	30.2%
Civil Rights	3.21	2.20	31.5%
Foreign Affairs	4.79	2.70	43.6%

* See Table 7.2 for computation of "Improvement."
Source: SRC, University of Michigan.

The final point in our analysis of dyadic versus collective representation concerns the number of legislative districts. If all legislators perfectly followed district opinion the number of districts would, obviously, be irrelevant for the improvement of dyadic representation, i.e., $\frac{\Sigma|d-R|}{N}$ would always equal $\frac{\Sigma d - \Sigma R}{N}$. On the other hand, as legislators diverge from constituency preferences it seems clear that, assuming nonsystematic divergences, the larger the number of districts, the greater the likelihood that the distribution of extreme misrepresentation will be symmetrical, so the improvement due to the aggregating of opposing misrepresentation will likewise increase. In other words, the likelihood of, say, extreme liberal misrepresentation being canceled out by extreme conservative misrepresentation is greater in a large assembly than in one of, say, 5 or 10 members. To illustrate this principle we have computed the ratios of dyadic to collective representation for random samples of the districts in the Miller–Stokes study (Table 7.4). We should add that since Miller and Stokes do not collect data on

all Congress members, even the 1.00 sample is not the population of the House of Representatives; quite likely the full 435 cases as opposed to the 146 here would show even greater improvement of representation due to aggregation.

As expected, the greater the number of legislators, the more representative the institution as a whole. For the 1 of 10 sample (i.e., about 15 cases), dyadic and aggregate representations are nearly identical in social welfare and civil rights. Aggregate representation shows a sizable gain in the .5 sample (about 75 districts) where the figures are quite close to those for the entire set of districts. Though we cannot say with any certainty what the dyadic to aggregate ratio would be for all 435 cases, our figures here suggest that any improvement would likely be quite modest (though a very large assembly would likely give voice to many more points of view).

POLITICAL CONTROL AND REPRESENTATIVE GOVERNMENT

Representation, at least as considered in the context of elections, is usually viewed as a consequence of political control (i.e., the ability of citizens to remove undesirable officials). By means of popular, direct elections, the argument goes, citizens select officials, and this selection process will lead to or is necessary, though not sufficient for, the representation of citizen preferences (or interests) in policy making. Conversely, it is assumed that leaders free from citizen control (whether by being "safe" electorally or being appointed) will feel freer to ignore constituency demands. No doubt this

Table 7.4. *Legislatures Size and Improvement of Collective Representation by Issue by Issue Area, 1958*

Issue Domain	Sample		
	.10	.50	1.00
Social Welfare	.96*	.77	.75
Civil Rights	.98	.86	.82
Foreign Affairs	.86	.65	.60

* Entries are the ratios of collective to dyadic legislator-district differences; the lower the 'number, the greater the improvement due to collective representation.
Source: SRC, University of Michigan.

logic of political control encouraging representation accounts for the often-sought relationship between electoral competition (a supposed measure of control) and various policy responses that are viewed as responses to citizen preferences. There is, however, no *logical* interconnection between control of an official via the electoral capacity to terminate tenure and representatives. Perhaps the major reason why electoral control and representation appear so intimately linked is the plausibility of the connecting supposition, namely, that leaders will seek to please (i.e., represent) those who control their fate, and the clearer the control, the greater the effort to please.

We have seen, however, that representation of opinion can occur apart from an electoral control relationship. Indeed, it is *likely* that citizens will be best represented by someone with whom they have no electoral relationship, and even under random voting constituency majorities would frequently be followed. What we shall do here is explore the relationship between the representation of citizen opinion by legislators collectively and citizen electoral control of legislators. We shall show that if one accepts the notion of collective, as opposed to dyadic, representation, high levels of citizen control are not only unnecessary but may be in fact a hindrance to accurate representation.

If one's constitutional goal were simply the best institutional representation of mass opinions, the optimal solution is clearly a random sample of about 1,500 citizens who would thus accurately "represent" the population. Alternatively, the population could be subdivided into relatively homogeneous groups and citizens would be selected randomly from within each of these groups (as in quota samples). Neither of these random-sample solutions would, of course, allow citizen intervention through voting or geographically defined units such as states. Nevertheless, the model of a legislature by random sample need not be abandoned if we introduce the requirements of citizen choice and election districts defined by criteria other than homogeneity of opinion. It is possible to approximate a random sample while still maintaining existing constitutional requirements for the electoral system. The most obvious mechanism of approximation would be to increase the number of legislators. If we had a legislature of 42,000 members (i.e., each legislator represented 5,000 citizens) we would expect the legislature by virtue of its sheer size to be a much better microcosm of the population than where the ratio were, say, 1 to 500,000. One only has to compare the racial, ethnic, and sexual composition of the U.S. House of Representatives with that of the Senate to see how a large institution is a "better" sample than a small institution. Of course, each citizen has an electoral relationship, and thus a possibility of electoral control, with only 1 of 435 Congress members compared to 2 of 100 senators.

What if huge assemblies of citizens were unacceptable or impractical? On the basis of the random sample model we would suggest that collective representation would be increased if election districts were as homogeneous as possible in their preferences, despite geographical constraints. In actual practice this districting would have to be done not on the basis of opinion data, but on more apparent criteria such as economic base, income levels, racial and ethnic composition, or other characteristics associated with sets of predictable political preferences. Under such circumstances, the odds that each legislator is typical of the district would increase and, if such district homogeneity were general, the legislature would approximate a quota sample of the population. Needless to say, such criteria could very well lead to oddly shaped "gerrymandered" districts that would likely violate current reapportionment standards established by the federal courts.

A legislature composed of members chosen on the basis of quota-sample criteria for districting would provide representation on both a collective and a dyadic basis. That is, while citizens as a whole are more accurately represented by this legislature collectively than they would be if districts were diverse, it is also true that each citizen within the dominant district group probably receives the most accurate representation from his or her "own" legislator. Hence, at least at first glance, the relationship between the representation of one's opinions and the voting decision is restored. Nevertheless, it is also likely that where homogeneity of opinion prevails, the amount of electoral competition will be very low. It is difficult to imagine a well-developed two-party system and close elections where a strong consensus exists on policy preferences. Even if the legislator in such a homogeneous district did not share the district's opinion on the salient issues, it would seem unlikely that this legislator would openly advocate a contrary view in order to give voters a real choice. In short, if electoral control and representation are linked, the control is likely to be more nominal than threatening, given safe electoral margins and the lack of an organized opposition.

In making the argument that the dyadic electoral control relationship between citizen and legislator may not be all that important for policy representation, we are not claiming that such a relationship is inconsequential. To describe the nature of collective representation is not to devalue dyadic representation. Obviously, regardless of collective actions, a legislator is always electorally accountable to a constituency. This accountability may be imperfect, but its existence is not trivial politically. To appreciate this, one should consider the possibility of nonelected leaders who could not be removed regardless of popular objections. Clearly, such accountability is central to notions of democratic control of leaders by citizens as well as some degree of policy control. Moreover, apart from overall policy representation, purely dyadic representation may very well provide psychological benefits to citizens who may feel represented by their particular legislators regardless of the source of representation (or at least enjoy all the attention at election time).

IMPLICATIONS AND SPECULATIONS

Collective, as opposed to dyadic, representation is obviously both historically justifiable and politically possible. We have also suggested that citizen preferences can indeed be represented collectively even if particular legislators ignore their constituencies. What we do not know is whether citizens relate to legislators dyadically or as mere components of a collective body. Let us momentarily assume that citizens (unlike most political scientists) are less interested in dyadic legislature relationships than collective representation. If this were true, we would make the following predictions about citizen behavior.

First, given that voting for or against 1 of 435 legislators is unlikely to affect greatly the representation one receives, a lack of citizen concern and involvement in legislative elections is probably understandable (though citizens do not necessarily engage in the requisite calculus). After all, it could be argued that it makes little sense to get involved in improving one's representation when one cannot even vote on one's best representative and when one's vote, even if absolutely crucial in one's district, affects only a small fraction of the representative institution. Under such conditions, high involvement would be worthwhile only if legislative benefits could be gained from one's particular legislator (e.g., a private bill). If we assume that people are interested in what they can affect, we would also predict that citizen involvement would covary with the size of representative institutions. Specifically, the fewer the legislators, the greater the impact of each legislator on representation, so turnout should be greater in elections for small legislatures. The irony of this relationship is, of course, that low-involvement-generating large institutions are more likely to be representative of citizen preferences than the high-interest-generating smaller institutions.

A second set of predictions based on collective representation concerns citizen satisfaction with the performance of individual legislators. It has been commonplace to observe that, barring extreme misrepresentation on an especially salient issue (e.g., a southern member of Congress voting pro-civil rights during the 1950s and the 1960s), most legislators can get away with ignoring district opinion without electoral retribution. This absence of retribution might appear to be an odd situation until one realizes that legislator inattention does not necessarily mean that either the district majority or a particular individual's opinion goes unrepresented by the legislature as a whole.

Hence, we would guess that citizen satisfaction with legislators could very well be independent of satisfaction with policy outcomes in general. Overall legislative performance (even if the legislature itself were not highly evaluated) would thus "explain" the survival of legislators who do not perform particularly well in representing their districts. On the other hand, the same reasoning would account for why legislators doing a good job of representing constituency opinions sometimes meet defeat if things as a whole go badly.

Our analysis of collective representation would also predict a less obvious relationship between citizen satisfaction and powerlessness. Discussions of political power usually treat power as an instrumental value. We have argued – both in our discussion of random voting and the representation electoral control nexus – that citizens can receive benefits without holding much or any electoral power over legislators. Indeed, the absence of some coercive mechanisms, such as a strong two-party system, close elections may be associated with accurate representation. The fact that citizens still receive benefits (i.e., representation) under poor control situations, and even when they can affect only a very small portion of a legislature's composition, may make citizen toleration (if not satisfaction) with these "poor" conditions quite reasonable. This logic would seem particularly relevant for district and national minorities who would get "shut out" completely if legislators slavishly followed district majorities. No doubt notorious House iconoclasts like H. R. Gross or Vito Marcantonio represented significant numbers of otherwise unrepresented citizens while probably misrepresenting their district majority.

SUMMARY AND CONCLUSIONS

The major points of our discussion can be summarized as follows:

(1) If we define the worst possible conditions of representation as random legislative voting, under such conditions a majority of constituencies will still be represented about half the time, and even when this majority is violated, the legislative vote will usually be fairly close. Given citizens' ignorance of true majorities in the population and the use of broad estimates, citizens will probably perceive less blatant misrepresentation than is suggested by low correlations of the Miller–Stokes type.

(2) Collective representation will never be worse than dyadic representation. If individual legislators are "free" to deviate from district opinion it is likely that deviations will approach normality and the institution as a whole will be more representative of national opinion than the average legislator is representative of district opinion.

(3) Collective representation also appears to solve the troublesome theoretical problem of how minorities are to be represented in a system of single-member districts with first-past-the-post elections. As long as extreme deviations from district majorities are "canceled out" by opposing deviations, both the public generally and district minorities can be given representation.

(4) Electoral control is not a logical prerequisite to accurate representation. Indeed, it appears unlikely that one's "best" representation will come from the individual one votes for (or against). It also appears likely that by reducing the proportion of a legislature a citizen can choose by increasing the number of legislators, and by reducing electoral competition by creating homogeneous districts, the accuracy of representation will be improved.

(5) Finally, if we accept collective representation as meaningful for citizens, several somewhat puzzling attitudes and kinds of behavior become more understandable. Among these are citizen apathy towards legislative elections, willingness to tolerate unresponsive legislators from their districts, and a distaste for greater legislative party cohesion.

Lest our arguments be misunderstood, we should also add:

(1) We have *not* claimed that dyadic representation is unimportant. Obviously, as Mayhew and many others acknowledge, what Congress members do for their constituents is highly relevant for both their own careers and constituent voting. We are not trying to replace the study of dyadic representation with the study of collective representation; collective representation exists in addition to dyadic representation.

(2) We have *not* argued that collective representation is accurate representation. Our argument is that collective representation is likely to be *more* accurate, not perfectly accurate. Unfortunately, the Miller and Stokes data as we employ them do not allow statements about the absolute degree of representation.

(3) We do *not* state that elections lead to misrepresentation. We claim that it is possible, even quite likely, that representation of citizen preferences will occur independently of an electoral connection between member of Congress and a constituent. Elections are not irrelevant to the faithfulness of representation, but they are not the only determining factor.

Some final observations on the study of representation are appropriate. As we have previously indicated, the model of dyadic representation has completely dominated contemporary research. This is true whether the data are opinions or constituents or socio-economic characteristics of the district. Given both our constitutional order, which was never designed to make legislators into perfect mirrors of popular opinion, and the absence of unbiased communication channels between citizens and leaders, the search for extensive dyadic agreement may be the search for the impossible. It may be impossible for one legislator to represent 400,000 people with any degree of accuracy; it may, however, be possible for 435 legislators to represent more accurately the opinions of 220,000,000 citizens. To be sure, whether or not a particular legislator follows his or her constituency is an important question, but this question is not necessarily the most appropriate one if we ask, "Do representatives represent?"

PART III. CONGRESSIONAL ELECTIONS AND POLICY ALIGNMENTS

CHAPTER EIGHT

Elbridge Gerry's Salamander

The Electoral Consequences of the Reapportionment Revolution – Excerpts

Gary W. Cox and Jonathan N. Katz

Cox and Katz argue that the massive wave of redistricting that occurred post-1964 created an "incumbency advantage" in the U.S. House. They find that the political composition of the courts and state legislatures that redrew the districts are critical to understanding which party benefited from redistricting. On balance, they find that the redistricting created a larger advantage for Republican incumbents.

THE REAPPORTIONMENT REVOLUTION

A Sketch of the Reapportionment Revolution

The Court's Decisions

On March 26, 1962, the Supreme Court handed down its decision in the case of *Baker v. Carr*, thus initiating what has since been known as the *reapportionment revolution*. The suit was brought by urban plaintiffs in Tennessee, who challenged their state legislature's failure to reapportion despite widespread population shifts that had made urban districts vastly more populous than their rural counterparts. The ramifications of the case were clearly national, because urban and especially suburban Americans were significantly underrepresented in state legislatures

Gary W. Cox and Jonathan N. Katz. 2002. "The Reapportionment Revolution" and "Reassessing the Incumbency Advantage" in Gary W. Cox and Jonathan N. Katz, *Elbridge Gerry's Salamander: The Electoral Consequences of the Reapportionment Revolution* (Cambridge University Press), 12–27, 194–205. Reprinted with permission.

throughout the country. Thus, although the Court limited itself to declaring that state legislative reapportionment was justiciable, leaving more specific action in the case to the lower courts, its decision was immediately seen as a revolutionary step – one the Court had repeatedly declined to take.

The immediate consequence of *Baker* was more litigation. Indeed, within a year of the decision, all but 14 states were involved in reapportionment suits, and the Supreme Court used some of these cases to stake out a clearer substantive position. The Court had opined in *Baker* that inequalities in district populations – that is, malapportionment – might constitute a violation of the Fourteenth Amendment's guarantee of equal protection of the laws to all citizens. In *Gray v. Sanders*, handed down in 1963, the Court invalidated Georgia's unit-rule primary elections specifically on the grounds that they did not give all voters an equal voice and thus violated the Fourteenth Amendment. A year later the Court extended its "one person, one vote" principle to cover elections to both houses of all state legislatures and elections to the U.S. House of Representatives.

The initial reactions to *Reynolds* and *Wesberry* by the two parties were favorable, at least at the national level. The chairman of the Democratic National Committee praised the decisions as "something the Democratic party had long advocated and fought for and certainly welcomes," while the chairman of the Republican National Committee viewed the decisions as being "in the national interest and in the Republican party's interest."

The Republican reaction to *Wesberry* was presumably influenced by a memorandum written after the 1962 election that demonstrated that Republicans did best in the more populous – that is, the more underrepresented – congressional districts. The report showed that the Republicans had won 53 percent of the seats in districts with populations above 500,000, 42 percent of the districts with populations between 300,000 and 500,000, and only 27 percent of the districts with populations below 300,000. Even outside the South, the Republicans won 61 percent of the oversized districts (those 15% or more above average) and only 40 percent of the undersized districts (those 15% or more below average). In light of these figures, the national leadership might well have looked forward to the removal of congressional malapportionment.

The Nature of Congressional Malapportionment

In the 88th Congress (elected in 1962), 234 congressional districts deviated by at least 10 percent from the average district population in their respective states, with the maximum deviation being 118 percent. Looking only at the 324 districts in nonsouthern states with more than one district (thus excluding Alaska, Delaware, Nevada, Vermont, and Wyoming), one finds that 52 percent deviated by more than 10 percent from their respective averages, with a maximum deviation of 85 percent.

Previous analysis has shown that malapportionment prior to the reapportionment revolution hurt suburban areas the most, with inner-city areas being more or less properly apportioned and rural areas being overrepresented. If one looks at the relationship between a district's urbanness (measured by the percentage of its population living in urban areas) and underrepresentation (measured by its percentage deviation from the average population of congressional districts in its state) in the 11 nonsouthern states with 10 or more districts, one finds results consistent with this summary.

The next question is: who lost from malapportionment prior to the reapportionment rev-

olution in partisan terms? Consistent with the Republicans' assessment of the matter, the answer seems to be that malapportionment outside the South slightly hurt the Republicans. On average, districts won by Democrats in 1962 were slightly overrepresented (i.e., smaller), while districts won by Republicans were slightly underrepresented (i.e., larger). Moreover, controlling for the number of districts in each state and each district's urbanness, districts won by Democrats were significantly smaller than Republican-won districts – by about 6.7 percent relative to the state average.

Does this result mean that the Republicans were wise to welcome the Court's decisions? Not necessarily. What such a conclusion fails to recognize is that, although malapportionment may have benefited the Democrats, the distribution of votes in each state – the result of prior partisan gerrymandering – may have hurt them. Since removing malapportionment would necessarily entail a substantial redrawing of district lines, thus providing great opportunities for distributional artistry, the overall partisan effect of redistricting could turn out to be substantially to the Republicans' detriment – as we shall see that it was.

The Redistrictings

Having sketched the nature of the problem to which the courts demanded a solution, we can now turn to the redistricting actions themselves. In Table 8.1, we outline redistricting actions in each nonsouthern state from 1960 to 1970, identifying which party controlled the process.

How large were the changes wrought by all the redistricting outlined in Table 8.1? In order to address this question, we focus on one redistricting per state: the first redistricting occurring under court pressure in the decade. For a few states, this first court-pressured redistricting occurs in 1964. For most, it occurs later in the decade. To gauge how much each new district has been altered, we proceed as follows. First, we find the old district that was the single largest contributor of population to the new district (the "parent" district). Letting c denote the total population that the parent district had in common with the new district, p denote the total population in the *parent* district, and n denote

Table 8.1. *Partisan Control of Redistricting, 1960–1970 (Nonsouthern States)*

State	1960	1962	1964	1966	1968	1970
AZ		Democrat		Democrat[a]		Republican
CA		Democrat			Bipartisan	
CO			Republican			
CT			Bipartisan			
ID				Republican		
IA		Republican				
IL		Bipartisan		Bipartisan		
IN				Democrat	Bipartisan	
KS		Republican		Republican		
KY		Democrat		Democrat		
MA		Bipartisan			Bipartisan	
MD		Democrat		Democrat[a]		
ME		Republican				
MI		Bipartisan	Bipartisan			
MN		Bipartisan				
MO		Democrat		Democrat	Democrat	Democrat
MT				Bipartisan[a]		
NE		Bipartisan			Republican	
ND		Republican				
NH						Republican
NJ		Bipartisan		Democrat	Republican[b]	
NM	Democrat				Bipartisan	
NY		Republican			Bipartisan	Republican
OH		Bipartisan		Republican	Republican	
OK					Bipartisan	
OR				Bipartisan		
PA		Bipartisan		Bipartisan		
RI[c]						
SD				Republican		
UT				Democrat		
WA	Democrat				Democrat[d]	
WI			Bipartisan			
WV		Democrat			Democrat	

[a] Court-imposed plan.

[b] Democratic governor, but Republican supermajorities in both houses.

[c] Rhode Island had minuscule redistrictings in 1964 and 1966, which are not included here.

[d] Listed as a Democratic plan, despite a Republican governor, because the Democratic legislature forced the plan to a referendum – over the governor's objections – and won.

the total population in the *new* district, we compute a similarity index: $s = c/(p + n - c)$. The denominator in this fraction is the union of the parent and new districts (or, more precisely, the number of persons living in that union). Thus, s is simply the population living in the intersection of the parent district and new district divided by the population living in the union of these two districts.

If a new district is basically the same as its parent, having lost a few townships here and gained a few there, then s will be near unity. In some cases, however, the parent district is only faintly related to its offspring. In Arizona, for example, the 1966 redistricting created a new district 3. The largest single contributor to this district was the old district 1. But that district (Phoenix) had a 1960 population of 663,510. Thus, even though it gave 207,892 persons to the new district 3, more than the old district 3's contribution of 174,952, it also gave 455,618 to the new district 1. Thus, the overall similarity score between the old district 1 and the new district 3 was a bit less than 25 percent. Other low similarity scores arise when, for example, the parent district is very small and a lot is added to the new district from multiple sources.

The average similarity score in nonsouthern districts from states with at least five districts is 72.6 percent. That is, the population shared between parent and child districts averaged 72.6 percent percent of the union population in the larger northern states. Fully a quarter of the districts had similarity scores less than 58 percent. Clearly, a good proportion of districts underwent substantial alterations.

The size of the alterations, moreover, shows some systematic patterns. Given that the 1960s redistrictings' raison d'être was to remove malapportionment, it is no surprise that the biggest changes (lowest similarity scores) occur in those districts whose parents were farther from the average district population: these were the ones that needed to be added to or subtracted from in order to bring them into line. It also turns out that the average changes were smaller in states with more districts. In the smaller states, bringing a few districts into line typically entailed more or less substantial changes in every district, whereas in the larger states there could be relatively large subsets of districts that underwent relatively small changes. Finally, holding constant the parent district's deviation from the average population and the number of districts in the state, it turns out that *more urban districts were altered more substantially*. The effect here is substantively fairly large: as between two otherwise similar districts, one completely rural, one completely urban, the urban district's similarity score was on average 21.8 percent lower. The most thoroughgoing reworking of district lines, therefore, tended to occur in the more urban areas of each state.

Political Consequences of the Reapportionment Revolution

Most analyses of the political consequences of the reapportionment revolution have focused on its policy effects. The expectations were high. Removing malapportionment was sup-

posed to remove the veto power of intransigent rural legislators, opening the way for slum clearance, labor and welfare legislation, civil rights laws, and other items high on the liberal agenda. These expectations notwithstanding, scholars almost universally found few substantial policy changes traceable specifically to the reallocation of power from rural to suburban/urban areas. Here our focus is on two other literatures, one concerned with how 1960s redistrictings affected the electoral success of the two major parties, the other concerned with how it affected the relative success of incumbents and challengers.

In the United States during the 1960s, the boundaries of state legislative and congressional districts were established by state laws passed in the usual fashion. Thus, if one party controlled both houses of the state legislature and the governor's mansion, it could draw district lines to advantage its own candidates. In popular and academic jargon, redistricting plans that seek to maximize the gain of the redistricting party are known as *partisan gerrymanders*.

If neither party controls the redistricting process, partisan gerrymanders may give way to *incumbent-protecting gerrymanders*, in which a bipartisan alliance redraws district lines so as to preserve or enhance the electoral prospects of current officeholders. Even when one party does control redistricting, its incumbents may oppose a partisan gerrymander, because typically such gerrymanders transfer "excess" votes from districts the party already holds to districts it wishes to capture.

Reconsidering the Reapportionment Revolution

In our view, the wave of redistrictings sparked by the Supreme Court's reapportionment decisions was much more consequential than the previous literature would have it. Our basic point is that, although eradicating malapportionment might have favored the Republicans slightly outside the South, the political circumstances of the new redistrictings decisively favored the Democrats. We note three circumstances in particular.

Table 8.2. *Last Prerevolutionary and First Postrevolutionary Plans in 33 Nonsouthern States*

Prerevolutionary Plans	Postrevolutionary Plans				
	Partisan: Republican	Bipartisan: Republican	Bipartisan: Democratic	Partisan: Democratic	No New Plan Until 1972
Partisan: Republican	CO (4) KS (5) NH (2) SD (2)	MT (2) NY (41) OR (4) CT (6)	—	UT (2) IN (11)	IA (7) ME (2) ND (2) RI (2)
Mixed: Republican	OH (24)	MI (19) WI (10)	—	NJ (15)	—
Bipartisan: Republican	—	MA (12) NE (3) IL (24) PA (27)	—	—	MN (8)
Bipartisan: Democratic	—	—	—	—	—
Mixed: Democratic	—	—	—	—	—
Partisan: Democratic	ID (2)	—	AZ (3) CA (38) OK (6) MD (8) NM (2)	WV (3) KY (7) MO (10) WA (7)	—

Note: The number of districts in each state is indicated in parentheses. The terms *partisan, mixed,* and *bipartisan* are explained in the text.

First, traditional Republican dominance of the North meant that most redistricting actions in the 1960s overturned districting plans that were favorable to Republicans. Table 8.2 classifies the last prerevolutionary and first postrevolutionary districting plans in each of the 33 nonsouthern states that had more than one district and did not use multimember elections exclusively in the prerevolutionary period. Each districting plan falls into one of six categories: partisan Republican (i.e., a plan passed under unified Republican government); partisan Democratic; mixed Republican (i.e., a plan passed under divided government and an automatic conservative reversion favoring the Republicans); mixed Democratic; bipartisan Republican (i.e., a plan passed under divided government and an automatic radical reversion favoring the Republicans); and bipartisan Democratic.

As can be seen, 14 of the 33 plans in place when the reapportionment revolution arrived were Republican. Another nine were modifications of older Republican plans. Less than a third of the prerevolutionary plans were Democratic.

Even the accounting in Table 8.2 – by which over two-thirds of the prerevolutionary plans potentially favored Republicans – understates the degree of Republican dominance. California and Washington operated under Republican plans until 1961 and 1959, respectively, so that 75 percent of the total number of nonsouthern state elections between 1946 and 1966 were held under plans that potentially favored Republicans. Moreover, the Republicans dominated most of the larger states, so that over 80 percent of nonsouthern district elections in this period were contested under partisan Republican, mixed Republican, or bipartisan Republican plans.

Second, interacting with traditional Republican dominance in the North was Lyndon Baines Johnson's landslide victory over Barry Goldwater in 1964 – which meant that the Republicans found themselves at a low point in terms of their state legislative power just as the wave of court-mandated congressional redistricting peaked. One consequence of this electoral disaster was that the 1960s saw the replacement of mostly Republican plans with mostly bipartisan plans and partisan Democratic plans.

Third, the 1960s redistrictings were conducted under the threat of court action should the state legislature and governor not agree on a bill. Indeed, perhaps the single most important consequence of the Supreme Court's decision in *Wesberry* was to change the reversionary outcome of the congressional redistricting process (and the conditions under which it came into force).

Let us explain this last assertion. Since 1913, the U.S. House has had a fixed number (435) of seats (with minor variations in two Congresses). Since 1929, these seats have been automatically apportioned among the states according to population after each decennial census. It has then been up to each state to define the boundaries of its allotted number of districts. Typically, district boundaries have been established by the passage of a state law, with legislatures and governors bargaining within the confines of the ordinary statutory processes of their respective states. If the governor and state legislature could not agree on a new plan, then the next election was held under what we call the *reversionary plan* – a legally defined default.

Prior to the reapportionment revolution, the reversionary plan was usually the state's current plan. That is, if no new plan could be agreed upon, the current plan continued in force. The only exceptions to this rule arose when a state gained or lost seats pursuant to the decennial federal census. If a state had *gained* seats, the exception was minor: a state could simply elect the new members at large, preserving all the old districts. This was a relatively painless solution that incumbent members of Congress often found preferable to the disruption of their current districts. If a state had *lost* seats in the reapportionment, however, all members had to be elected at large, absent a new districting plan. This was a much less palatable reversionary plan, and its unpleasantness explains why the bulk of prerevolutionary redistricting action occurred in states that had lost representation in Congress.

When the current plan was also the reversionary plan (or was the main basis for that plan, as in cases where the state had gained seats), we say that the reversion was *conservative*. When the reversion was not conservative, we say that it was *radical*. In these terms, prior to the reapportionment revolution all states not losing seats had conservative reversions, while all states losing seats had radical reversions.

Now consider how the entry of the judiciary altered the strategic situation. The role of the courts in the 1960s varied from case to case, but often things played out as follows. First, a federal or state court would declare a state's current districting plan null and void. The court would then give the state a more or less clear and more or less constraining deadline; if the legislature and governor could not agree on a plan by the deadline, the court would impose a plan. Sometimes the plan that the court planned to impose was clear ex ante, sometimes not. But the court's plan was never the preexisting plan. Thus, *all redistricting action in the 1960s took place under the threat of a radical reversionary outcome of one kind or another.*

Another important point to note is that all reversions before the reapportionment revolution were *automatic*: a prespecified reversion was to be used when a prespecified condition was met. In contrast, reversions after the reapportionment revolution were *discretionary*: the conditions under which a reversion would be used, and the nature of the reversion itself, were at a court's discretion. Even when the state government produced a new districting plan, a court might decide that the plan produced was unconstitutional and impose its own. Moreover, the plan that a court imposed was restricted only by its interpretation of the relevant judicial criteria.

Some indication of the importance of automatic reversionary plans can be gained by considering a few examples. First, when the reversionary plan was conservative, the party favored by the current lines could simply refuse to agree to a new plan and preserve those lines. Missouri provides a case in point. As Short reports, "The Democratic party had a majority in both houses of the General Assembly in 1911; but, inasmuch as the number of Missouri's representatives in Congress was not changed by the reapportionment act of that year, and the existing districts were distinctly advantageous to that party, no serious attempt was made to formulate a redistricting measure which would meet with the approval of the Republican chief executive."

Second, when the reversionary plan was radical, the party favored under the reversion could be empowered. In Michigan, for example, the Republicans controlled both houses of the state legislature and the governorship when a three-judge federal court declared, on March 27, 1964, that the state's 1963 redistricting plan was unconstitutional in light of *Wesberry*. The state legislature was preoccupied with its own redistricting problem and, by the time it got around to congressional redistricting (about a month later, in early May), the strategic balance had tilted in favor of the Democrats. The court had clearly warned that all 19 House seats in Michigan would be filled at large if the legislature did not act before the 1964 election. This was a reversionary outcome that the Republicans found extremely distasteful in light of their estimates of the relative state-wide strengths of the two parties in the coming (Goldwater!) election. Moreover, state law required a 90-day waiting period before any new law became effective, a requirement that could be waived only by a two-thirds vote. Consequently, because the redistricting plan had to be in place before the primary election season began (in less than 90 days) and because the Republican advantage in the state House was only 58–52 (less than two-thirds), the federal court's firm deadline and clear reversionary plan meant that concessions had to be made to the Democrats. Indeed, Michigan was essentially operating under divided government during this redistricting.

The last anecdote suggests that the nature of the reversionary plan could sometimes be very important. In the next chapter, we look more systematically at the interaction between partisan control (unified or divided state government) and the nature of the reversion (automatic conservative or automatic radical).

Jurisprudentially, the Supreme Court's apportionment decisions in the period 1962–64 were soon described as "historical landmarks" and "certain to be as historic in American constitutional history as *Marbury v. Madison*." Structurally, they led to the (often substantial) redrawing of 301 of the 329 nonsouthern congressional districts during the years 1964–70. Yet, politically, the Court's decisions are depicted as having little overall impact, either on the struggle between Democrats and Republicans or on the struggle between incumbents and challengers. This contrast between large jurisprudential and structural effects and small political effects is the puzzle that the current literature presents.

REASSESSING THE INCUMBENCY ADVANTAGE

The Incumbency Advantage, the Vanishing Marginals, and Democratic Dominance of the House

The 1960s brought a remarkable complex of changes to House elections: a sudden increase in the incumbency advantage, a sudden decrease in the number of marginal districts, and a sudden eradication of pro-Republican bias outside the South. The dominant way of viewing these changes is still probably that suggested in the work of Erikson and Mayhew. In (one reconstruction of) their view, the causal sequence was as follows: (1) The incumbency advantage in House elections – a vote premium that accrued to incumbents per se – increased. (2) The incumbency advantage increased because one or more of the following events took place: (a) voters sharply dealigned from the parties during the turbulent 1960s, increasing the value of incumbency as a cue; (b) the staff and other resources of House members increased just as the expansion of the federal bureaucracy generated more opportunities to provide ombudsman services to constituents; (c) the importance of money in congressional elections and incumbents' advantages in raising money increased sharply in the 1960s. (3) The increased incumbency advantage led to a decrease in the proportion of marginal districts, and hence to a decrease in the swing ratio, or what we call *responsiveness*. (4) The permanently more sluggish response of congressional seat shares to congressional vote shares allowed the Democrats to retain their gains from the 1960s indefinitely. (5) The Democrats' good fortune to possess a majority of seats just when the incumbency advantage increased explains why pro-Republican bias disappeared.

Our work directly challenges points (1) (2) and (5) and bears on point (4) as well. Regarding point (1), by our estimates the real incumbency advantage has never been statistically discernible from zero for the Democrats. Hence, we deny the initial premise: there was no increase in the real incumbency advantage to lock in the Democrats' gains.

Regarding point (2), our results are inconsistent with any theory that sees the incumbency advantage growing larger primarily because the resources of office grew. One resource of office is the proportion of the electorate prepared to use incumbency as a voting cue. Other resources include staff and opportunities to provided casework. Still another resource is the ability to perform services for PACs in exchange for campaign contributions.

The first of these resource-based explanations suffers a unique difficulty, indicated in the following question. If the dealignment of the electorate in the 1960s produced more voters willing to use such a cue, why has the realignment of the electorate since the 1970s not produced fewer voters willing to use such a cue – and hence a decline in the incumbency advantage?

All three resource-based explanations share the following problems. First, there should be no difference in a party's losses in its voluntarily and involuntarily open seats, because the resources (whether the incumbency cue, the staff and casework opportunities, or the fundraising advantages) are lost in either case. Yet we know there is such a difference. Second, the majority party should not have a smaller incumbency advantage than the minority party, because majority-party members either have the same resource advantage (in the case of the incumbency cue or personal staff allocations) or a demonstrably larger resource advantage (in the case of committee staff allocations or the ability to raise PAC money). Yet we know

that the minority party tends to have the larger measured incumbency advantage after the mid-1960s. Third, the incumbency advantage should not vary with the size of the Democratic contingent in the House. Yet, we know that it does.

In our view, the causal sequence was much different than that articulated earlier. We see two main causal pathways. First, the Supreme Court's reapportionment decisions led immediately to a wave of court-supervised redistricting actions in the 1960s. These actions tended to undo preexisting Republican gerrymanders and also, in states under divided control, to be more favorable to incumbents – by padding their districts with their own partisans. Thus, redistricting led both to the eradication of pro-Republican bias outside the South and to a reduction in responsiveness.

Second, the Court's decisions also strengthened the redistricting-induced entry cycle, so that strong challengers and incumbents became better at avoiding one another's company. A side effect of this strategic avoidance was that the presence of an incumbent became a better indicator of a high vote share for the incumbent party, while the presence of a strong challenger became a better indicator of a high vote share for the challenging party.

The question that has dominated studies of congressional elections for the past 30 years is why the incumbency advantage increased. Previous scholars have taken it as established that most of the increase was real. Accordingly, their theories have concerned real resources that incumbents possess and that may plausibly have become more plentiful or valuable over time – primarily the incumbency cue, personal staff able to do casework favors for constituents, and personal and committee staff able to do legislative favors for PACs. Our emphasis, in contrast, has been on the reverse direction of causality. In explaining the correlation between the presence of an incumbent candidate and the incumbent party's vote share, we stress strategic exit – that is, the tendency for incumbents to retire in the face of poor vote prospects (which are then inherited by their replacements).

We believe that we have clearly established that a substantial portion of the incumbency advantage as conventionally measured is due to strategic exit. Thus, we feel justified in saying that the striking changes in strategic exit and entry that emerged in the 1960s are at least as much a puzzle worthy of explanation as is the increase in the real incumbency advantage. Put another way, an important puzzle to explain is the relatively sudden improvement in electoral coordination between incumbents and strong challengers.

Why Did Electoral Coordination Improve?

Our primary explanation of the improvement in electoral coordination – that is, strong challengers and incumbents getting better at avoiding one another – is that the reapportionment decisions increased the frequency and predictability of redistricting, thus strengthening the redistricting-induced cycle of entry/exit. The evidence in favor of this view starts with the sheer size of the macro change: the frequency of postcensus redistricting roughly doubled. After the reapportionment decisions, all candidates could count on virtually every district being redrawn after every census. That candidates did respond to this change in their environment is indicated in our analyses of voluntary exits by incumbents and entries by strong challengers: both were significantly influenced by the redistricting cycle – after but not before the reapportionment revolution.

Another sort of evidence that the redistricting cycle has been important in recent congressional elections concerns money. Contributions by PACs to challengers are relatively dispersed in the immediate aftermath of a redistricting (years ending in "2"), but they become steadily more concentrated as the redistricting cycle progresses toward its end. This pattern in contributions is visible only for the last three decades, as systematic data on campaign contributions have been collected only since 1972. Thus, we cannot say that money in congressional elections became *more* redistricting-related after the reapportionment revolution. However, we can say that the pattern of increasingly concentrated giving to challengers fits with the coordination theme that we have repeatedly sounded in this part of the book.

Why Did the Parties Differ?

In this section, we review several differences between the parties, along with our explanations for them. There are four key differences to explain. First, the Democrats fared significantly worse in their voluntarily than in their involuntarily open seats, especially after 1966; in contrast, the Republicans fared about the same in both sorts of open seat. Second, after *Wesberry* the Republicans' open-seat losses were larger when the Democrats' margin of control in Congress was larger, while the Democrats' open-seat losses were smaller. Third, the Republicans' vote loss in their involuntarily open seats increased significantly from before to after *Wesberry*, whereas the analogous figures for the Democrats did not increase significantly. Fourth, the Democrats' vote loss in involuntarily open seats is never statistically discernible from zero, whereas the analogous figure for the Republicans is (after *Wesberry*). Fifth, after *Wesberry* the Republicans suffered from a minority investment disadvantage, which made it systematically more difficult to (1) recruit candidates, (2) raise money, and hence (3), win.

To explain this quintet of party differences, we note that the reapportionment decisions led to the eradication of pro-Republican bias outside the South, which downshifted the Republicans' chances of securing a majority in the House. Because the value of a House seat was typically higher for the majority party, the *voluntary* retirement of a Democrat usually came about only in the face of particularly poor vote prospects. Thus, the Democrats tended to lose substantially more votes in seats that became open due to the voluntary as opposed to the involuntary withdrawal of the incumbent. In contrast, the value of a House seat was substantially lower for Republicans, and thus they more often abandoned such seats, even when they had good vote prospects. Thus, the

Republicans tended *not* to lose much more in voluntarily as opposed to involuntarily open seats (until 1996–1998, when, for the first time, they do).

A related argument explains why the two parties' open-seat losses responded in opposite fashion to a strengthening of the Democratic margin of control in Congress. When the Democratic margin increased, the expected value of a House seat for Republicans declined even further, making it even harder for them to recruit good candidates and defend their seats but easier for the Democrats. Thus, the Republicans suffered larger and larger open-seat losses as the Democrats' control of Congress strengthened, while the Democrats' losses became smaller and smaller.

Why did the Republicans' vote loss in involuntarily open seats increase substantially after *Wesberry?* Our explanation is that the party had increasing difficulties in recruiting high-quality candidates to defend those seats, because the expected value of a House seat was lower (due to the diminished probability of a Republican majority following the eradication of pro-Republican bias outside the South). In contrast, the Democrats had excellent prospects of retaining their majority and thus had little difficulty in recruiting strong candidates to defend their involuntarily open seats.

The same argument explains why the Democrats' vote loss in involuntarily open seats never differed statistically from their vote loss in seats defended by an incumbent Democrat. The high expected value of a House seat was sufficient to pull in a talented politician to defend the seat.

Finally, a few comments on the minority investment disadvantage. The syndrome of ailments afflicting the Republicans after *Wesberry* was typical of oppositions in dominant-party systems, though not as severe. In U.S. terms, the minority investment disadvantage extrapolates to southern politics. In the old days of the Solid South, the Republicans could not recruit any good candidates, as all serious would-be politicians entered the Democratic party. Presumably, they could also not raise any money from would-be favor-seekers. Finally, they won

seats only in a relatively few areas the Democrats were content to abandon.

The predicament of Republicans in the House of Representatives was never so dire as it had been for the Republican party of Alabama or Georgia. However, they did have well-known recruitment difficulties; they did have well-known frustrations with corporate PACs' tendency to give to the Democrats; and they did have trouble winning the open seats they needed to take or keep the House. Their problems might, in a more unitary system, have become self-reinforcing – leading to a one-party regime at the national level. In part due to our separated-powers system, the Republicans at the national level continued to compete, and all their problems decreased substantially after their stunning victory in the midterm elections of 1994 put paid to their status as the perennial minority.

Normative Consequences of the Increase in the Incumbency Advantage

The dominant explanations of why there is an incumbency advantage attribute it to resources intrinsic to incumbency. By one line of argument, the resources of office can be electorally beneficial – for example, staff can be located in the member's district and act as a perpetual campaign organization. By another line of argument, the relevant resource might simply be the right to have the word *incumbent* printed next to one's name on the ballot.

By either of these accounts, the incumbency advantage is potentially dangerous to democratic governance, because incumbents can win reelection for reasons other than the assiduity with which they serve the nation's or their constituents' interests. Prominent analysts have repeatedly viewed the increasing incumbency advantage as evidence of *dysfunction* in our body politic.

One argument sees incumbents as insulated from popular wrath and increasingly in bed with special interests. This belief has probably always existed. But it has certainly been a mainstay of op-ed essays on what ails the country over the last generation or so. Moreover, in the 1990s this belief, partly sustained by incumbents' fat margins of victory since the 1960s, was an important impetus behind the term limits movement in America. The logic seemed to be: if incumbents have an unfair advantage because they can use the (bloated) resources of their office as election subsidies, and if this unfair advantage frees them to ignore their constituents and serve special interests, then put a stop to it all by limiting the number of terms they can serve.

A second argument sees the increasing incumbency advantage primarily as evidence that members have succeeded in carving out a larger and larger "personal vote." Incumbents turn congressional resources, by dint of hard work, into a successful but very personal relationship with their constituents. They may be in bed with the special interests, but the real problem is that they have become ever more narrowly focused on their constituents' concerns to the detriment of national concerns. In a nutshell, the incumbency advantage allows members to ignore their parties in pursuit of the parochial interests of their constituents. As the parties are the primary agencies, along with the presidency, through which broad national goals are addressed, the result is a failure of collective responsibility in American politics.

A third argument sees the incumbency advantage as the reason that the Democrats succeeded in maintaining majorities in the House of Representatives throughout most of the postwar era, despite many Republican victories at the presidential level. Here, Democratic incumbents are able to support their party's benighted programs without paying the just price at the polls, because they have an unfair electoral bonus just for being in office.

Each of these arguments assumes that the increasing incumbency advantage was real. Incumbents were granted an increasingly valuable set of resources just for being incumbents, and this allowed them to pay less heed to some political actors (the good guys) in order to pay more heed to other political actors (the bad guys). What changes in the stories is the identity of the good guys and the bad guys. In story 1, incumbents ignore the virtuous citizenry in

their districts in order to pay more attention to evil but wealthy special interests. In story 2, incumbents ignore the virtuous parties in Congress in order to pay more attention to the greedy and shortsighted citizenry in their districts. In story 3, incumbents ignore the enlightened citizenry voting for Republican presidential candidates in order to pay more attention to the evil congressional empire, formerly known as the Democratic party.

The light touch with which we have exposited these arguments notwithstanding, they are all important. Indeed, the question of whom representatives of the people heed is central to democratic theory and practice. When incumbents adjust their role, paying less heed to X in order to pay more heed to Y, the consequences are potentially important, even if the adjustments are marginal. Moreover, exactly how much attention incumbents pay to party, constituents, and interest groups is constantly in flux, constantly contested by these groups and their champions. Thus, the logic of the stories previously told – that incumbents given a cushion of safety may redress the balance of forces on them in ways unhealthy for democratic governance – is perennial.

But what if the premise is false? What if incumbents did not acquire a cushion setting them free from electoral pressures? What if they only have the appearance of a cushion and not the reality?

If the cushion is more apparent than real, then the arguments just reviewed cannot get off the ground, logically speaking. Their conclusions may still be true. Maybe incumbents have paid relatively more attention to special interests and relatively less to their constituents. Maybe they have paid more attention to local yokels and less to parties. Maybe they have paid more attention to their parties and less to their constituents. Whatever the empirical merit of these competing conclusions, one cannot explain them by referring to an increasing incumbency advantage if there was no such increase.

We are not the first to suggest that incumbents' electoral safety did not increase. Jacobson has noted that, at the same time that incumbents' margins of victory increased on average, the size of their vote swings from election to election also increased on average, leading to almost no improvement in their probability of victory (until the late 1980s). But it is safety in the sense of a high probability of victory, not safety in the sense of winning big when you do win, that matters in all of the normative arguments given previously. Hence, Jacobson's work directly undermines the key premise of these arguments.

Note that Jacobson also conflicts with the conventional notion that incumbency confers a premium of so-and-so many percentage points. Logically, such a vote premium would also entail a premium in the probability of victory. If the vote premium grew, as conventionally asserted, then so should the probability-of-victory premium have grown. However, how could incumbents' probabilities of victory increasingly have outdistanced their nonincumbent replacements' chances, while at the same time incumbents have not become any more likely to win reelection when they seek it? One cannot both believe Jacobson and also believe the conventional wisdom on the vote-denominated incumbency advantage.

Our work provides further support for the Jacobsonian view and resolves the apparent conflict just noted. We deny that incumbency even confers a substantial vote premium (or, more modestly, assert that the evidence that it does is not compelling). There is thus no inconsistency between our view of the vote-denominated incumbency advantage (it increased little, if at all) and Jacobson's view of incumbents' probabilities of victory (they also increased little, if at all, until the late 1980s).

CHAPTER NINE

Strategic Politicians and the Dynamics of U.S. House Elections, 1946–1986

Gary C. Jacobson

Jacobson considers the role of challengers and national conditions in U.S. House elections. He finds that national conditions, such as the economy, scandal, and so on have little direct effect on congressional elections. He argues that national conditions play out through the entry/exit decisions of incumbents and challengers. Incumbents tend to retire when national conditions run against their party, whereas high-quality challengers run when conditions favor their party.

Free, competitive elections are supposed to encourage leaders to govern responsibly because voters can fire them if they do not. But the kind of accountability elections enforce depends on the structure of electoral politics. Where votes are cast to choose a governing party – and only incidently particular legislators, as in most parliamentary systems – enforcement of collective responsibility is unproblematic, and incentives for legislators to pursue successful national policies are unambiguous. Contests that revolve around local candidates and issues to the neglect of national parties and programs, like most present-day House elections, reward individual responsiveness at the expense of collective responsibility. They inspire far more sensitivity to the local implications of policies attacking national problems than to the national problems

Gary C. Jacobson. 1989. "Strategic Politicians and the Dynamics of U.S. House Elections, 1946–1986" *American Political Science Review* 83: 773–93. Copyright © 1989 by the American Political Science Association. Reprinted with the permission of Cambridge University Press.

created by aggressive pursuit of local interests. A national legislature composed of people who believe that when it comes to elections, "all politics is local" naturally finds it difficult to act responsibly.

For this reason, any feature of congressional election politics that does enforce some degree of collective accountability deserves special attention. The feature that has attracted the most scholarly attention is how a party's electoral fortunes rise and fall with the economy and the public's appraisal of the administration. The stronger the economy and the more widely approved the president's performance, the more congressional seats the president's party wins. The weaker the economy and the more dissatisfied people are with the administration, the more seats the president's party loses. Variations in the partisan division of congressional seats are thus the consequence of an electorate acting, in aggregate, like V. O. Key's "rational god of vengeance and reward."

Aggregate retribution implies individual retribution: voters might impose collective responsibility simply by voting their pocketbooks and opinions of the administration. But survey evidence makes it doubtful that the process is this simple. Individual analogs of national economic conditions (change in family income, experience with unemployment) appear to have little or no impact on voting for House candidates in general, though such results are somewhat stronger when analysis is restricted to districts held by incumbents of the president's party and to election years when the economy's performance was below par. More general economic assessments – of business conditions, of the administration's economic policies and performance, of party competence on economic matters – sometimes influence individual voting decisions; though, once again, few relationships remain stable across election years.

Evaluations of presidents and presidential candidates influence the House vote somewhat more consistently, but even here exceptions appear. For example, midterm assessments of Johnson and Reagan had a significant influence on House voters, while evaluations of Ford and Carter made little apparent difference. The impact of presidential coattails also varies considerably from one election to the next. Some studies have even concluded that Watergate did not have a major impact on voting decisions despite the heavy losses suffered by Republicans in 1974, though other analyses link the House vote to reactions to Ford's pardon of Nixon.

Some of the voters, some of the time, then, appear to treat the House election as a referendum on the administration and economy. But the survey findings are sufficiently spotty and inconsistent to leave grave doubts whether referendum voting is adequate to account for the observed aggregate patterns. Thus Samuel Kernell and I have proposed an alternative (though complimentary) explanation. We argue that strategic political elites play a pivotal role in translating national conditions into election results and therefore in holding members of Congress collectively accountable for the government's performance.

STRATEGIC POLITICIANS

Our explanation takes as its point of departure the same idiosyncratic features of U.S. elections that make the enforcement of collective responsibility problematic. The executive and legislature are elected separately. Electoral partisanship is muted; most citizens think that they should vote for the "better" person regardless of party. The same surveys that offer but limited

evidence of referendum voting offer abundant evidence of candidate-centered voting. What voters know and think of the particular pair of candidates running in the district has a major influence on their decision; and they evaluate House candidates far more often in terms of personal character and services than in terms of parties, policies, or national issues.

The choice offered locally between candidates is thus the main focus of electoral politics. In contests between House incumbents and challengers, the nature of the choice is shaped largely by the political talents and campaign resources of the challenger. Absent a strong challenge – the most common circumstances – the incumbent controls the campaign agenda, monopolizes media attention, and wins handily regardless of partisan trends. It takes a vigorous, well-funded challenge to offer voters the kind of alternative – a "qualified" candidate raising troublesome issues – that can threaten the incumbent with premature retirement.

Strong challenges do not emerge randomly; their occurrence varies with the prospects of victory. As a group, ambitious, experienced career politicians make the most formidable candidates for Congress. They have the most incentive and opportunity to develop the political skills and connections that produce effective candidacies. They also risk the most in trying to move to higher office, for defeat may retard or end a political career. Thus the best potential candidates will also be most sensitive to the odds on winning and so to conditions that affect the odds.

The availability of money for the campaign is certainly one crucial consideration. Astute career politicians will not enter contests without some promise of sufficient funds. People who control essential campaign resources also deploy them strategically. Regardless of their motives for contributing, they do not invest much in hopeless causes; better odds inspire more generous donations to nonincumbent House candidates with the appropriate view. Among the things potential donors consider is the quality of the candidate. Better candidates attract more money, just as the availability of money attracts better candidates.

Because electoral history teaches potential candidates and contributors that the national economy and the president's standing with the public affect election results, these things help shape perceptions of election odds and thus strategic decisions about running and contributing. When national conditions favor a party, more of its ambitious careerists decide that it is the year to go after a House seat. Promising candidates of the other party are more inclined to wait for a more propitious time. People who control campaign resources provide more to challengers when conditions are expected to help their preferred party, more to incumbents when conditions put it on the defensive. Because the effects of campaign spending are sharply asymmetrical – marginal returns on campaign spending are far higher for challengers than for incumbents in House elections – converging offensive and defensive strategies produce a net gain for challengers of the party favored by national conditions.

The collective result of individual strategic decisions is that the party expected to have a good year fields a superior crop of well-financed challengers, while the other party fields more than the usual number of under-financed amateurs. Strategic decisions skew the choice between pairs of candidates across House districts, so voters need only respond to the local alternatives to reflect, in their aggregate behavior, the national circumstances that shaped elite strategies. Personal economic experiences and evaluations of the president may still influence individual vote decisions, but a pervasive habit of referendum voting is not, in theory, necessary for voters to impose collective responsibility through the ballot box.

Taken to its logical extreme, the argument implies that prophecies about a party's electoral prospects could be purely self-fulfilling. But decisions based on illusion are hardly strategic; national conditions *must* have some independent effect on the outcome for the argument to make sense. And it is not difficult to imagine how national politics could affect voting even in a system of electoral politics dominated by local candidates and campaigns. National issues can be turned into local issues if a smart candidate has the resources to do it. Poor economic performance, for example, offers challengers representing the party out of power a wedge to separate the incumbent from his or her usual supporters. Whether the incumbent suffers real damage from the issue depends, however, on whether the challenger has the means and skill to exploit it. Thus a party will benefit more from advantageous national conditions, the better its challengers; and superior challengers will be more successful when national issues can be turned against incumbents. The interactive combination of exploitable national issues and vigorous challenges is what imposes a degree of collective accountability on members of Congress.

That, in brief, is the argument. For it to be valid – for strategic politicians pursuing their own careers to play an important, if unintentional, role in translating national conditions into aggregate election results – two basic conditions must hold. First, objectively superior candidates must be selective about when to try for the House. Empirically, the proportion of high-quality candidates should increase with the odds on winning; in particular, more high-quality challengers should appear when national conditions favor their party, fewer in contrary circumstances. Second, the presence of high-quality candidates must produce votes and victories beyond what can be explained by the conditions that enticed them to run; that is, experienced challengers must win significantly more votes and victories than inexperienced challengers in equivalent circumstances.

Richard Born has challenged the thesis on both counts. He argues that because many, if not all, challengers make their commitment to run for office well before the election year, most strategic career decisions cannot be influenced by national conditions during the election year. He also argues that other things being equal, high-quality challengers win no more votes than do inexperienced challengers and so cannot contribute to their party's aggregate performance. Insofar as he is correct on both points, one should find little or no relationship between the relative quality of a party's challengers and how well it does on election day.

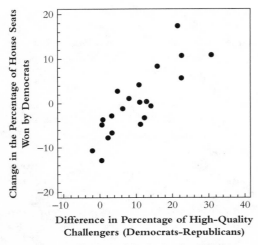

Figure 9.1. Difference of High-Quality Challengers and Change in Democratic House Seats.

To determine whether this is so, one needs to measure candidate quality. I use a simple dichotomous measure of quality – whether the candidate has ever held elective public office of any kind. Candidates who have held elective office are considered high-quality, experienced candidates; the others are not. More elaborate and nuanced measures of candidate quality have been developed, but I stick with this simple dichotomy for several reasons. First, it is objective and noncircular, removing any temptation to find some "quality" criterion that applies to all candidates who do well. Second, the measure's very crudity favors the null hypotheses and so offers a tough test of the Jacobson–Kernell thesis. If such a blunt instrument produces results consistent with that thesis, better measures should only strengthen the case. Finally, prior office is the background information pertaining to quality most reliably mentioned in the sources I draw on for data covering the first half of the postwar era. For this period, background information has to be gleaned primarily from newspapers archived at the Library of Congress and elsewhere; since the 1960s, much of this information has been available in *Congressional Quarterly Weekly Report's* special preelection reviews of all House races.

The scatterplots in Figures 9.1 and 9.2 are sufficient to show that Born is dead wrong on

one or both points. Figure 9.1 plots the proportion of House seats the Democrats gained or lost in postwar elections against their advantage in percentage of high-quality challengers. The relationship is striking: the correlation between the two variables is .85. Figure 9.2 takes a slightly different perspective, plotting the net difference in the number of successful challenges (Democrats minus Republicans) in these elections against the net difference in the number of experienced challengers. Again, a remarkably strong relationship emerges; these two variables are correlated at .88. Other formulations yield equivalent pictures; no matter how specified, the relative quality of a party's challengers is closely related to its aggregate electoral performance.

On this evidence, it would be perverse to argue that strategic candidacies are unrelated to election results. The remaining issue concerns the structure of the relationship. Born concedes that "political elites may well predicate personal strategy on their reading of the prevailing partisan winds" (though how they can do so if their decisions are made before the direction of the winds is known is not explained) but argues that "there is little reason to think that the collective consequences of such discrete actions make much difference on where these winds carry the parties on election day." At issue, then, is the degree to which high-quality candidates

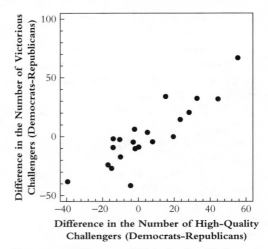

Figure 9.2. Difference of High-Quality Challengers and Difference in Challenger Victories.

Table 9.1. *The Probability of Victory and the Quality of Nonincumbent Candidates for the U.S. House of Representatives, 1946–1986*

Type of Race	Number of Cases	Winners (%)	Former Officeholders (%)
Open Seats			
No general election opponent	34	100.0	82.4
Held by candidate's party	821	75.0	62.6
Held by neither party	188	50.0	54.8
Held by opposite party	821	25.0	33.7
Challenges to Incumbents			
Incumbent's vote in last election (%)			
50.0–54.9	1,462	21.1	46.9
55.0–59.9	1,384	8.9	30.1
60.0–64.9	1,207	4.2	21.1
65.0–69.9	953	2.7	16.4
70.0 or more	1,213	.7	11.5

merely ride a favorable tide and the degree to which they contribute to the tide by attracting more support, and winning more victories, than would inexperienced candidates in the same circumstances. Before addressing this issue, however, the first task is to confirm that high-quality candidates follow rational career strategies in deciding when to try for the House.

STRATEGIC CAREER DECISIONS

The evidence that high-quality candidates make strategic career decisions based on the likelihood of advancement is overwhelming. The general point is made in striking fashion by the data in Table 9.1, which show how tightly the presence of high-quality candidates is linked to the odds on winning, given local circumstances at the time of the election. Open seats attract the largest share of experienced candidates, but within this category, it makes a great deal of difference which party holds the seat because this has such a large effect on the prospect of winning. Unopposed candidates for open seats naturally win every time, and high-quality candidates are most common in these races. Among challengers, the incumbent's margin of victory in the previous election is strongly related to the proportions of both victories and high-quality candidacies. Clearly, career politicians are highly sensitive to local conditions that affect electoral odds.

Experienced candidates are also sensitive to national conditions that shape electoral odds. The evidence for this is found in Tables 9.2 and 9.3. Table 9.2 presents probit equations estimating the probability that an experienced challenger opposed the incumbent, given local and national conditions, in more than six thousand postwar House elections. Local opportunities expected to influence career moves are measured by the percentage of votes won by the candidate of the challenger's party – and by whether the seat switched party hands – in the previous election. The economy and the president's level of popular approval measure the national conditions. A fifth variable, the party of the administration (scored 1 if Democratic, 0 if Republican), must be entered as a control because of the way some of the other independent variables are scored.

The state of the economy is measured as the percentage change in real disposable income per capita over the year ending in the second quarter of the election year. In using real income growth to proxy the economy, I follow a majority of scholars working in this area, who appear to have two principal reasons for adopting this measure. One is theoretical: it corresponds to the (dubious) assumption that economic voting is about personal finances. The other is that real income growth is usually more highly correlated with election results than any of the likely alternatives: GNP, inflation, and unemployment. In practice, it is a good summary

Table 9.2. *Estimates of the Probability That the House Challenger Has Held Elective Office, 1946–1986*

Variable	Democrats (1)	Republicans (2)
Intercept	−1.73***	−2.50***
	(.18)	(.17)
Party of administration	−.97***	.37*
	(.20)	(.22)
Change in party control of seat last election	.58***	.52***
	(.08)	(.08)
Votes won by challenger's party in last election (%)	.04***	.04***
	(.00)	(.00)
Change in real income per capita (2d quarter)	.04***	−.01
	(.01)	(.01)
Presidential approval (2d quarter)	.01***	−.00
	(.00)	(.00)
Log likelihood	−1,719	−1,548
Number of cases	3,084	3,123

Note: Coefficients are maximum likelihood estimates; standard errors are in parentheses.
* $p < .05$, one-tailed test.
*** $p < .001$, one-tailed test.

measure of economic performance on all of these dimensions. Because the administration's party (not just the Democratic party) is supposed to be rewarded or punished for its management of the economy, this variable is multiplied by −1 when a Republican sits in the White House (this is why the administration dummy is required).

Presidential approval is scored as the mean percentage of citizens approving of the president's performance in Gallup polls taken during the second quarter of the election year. Again,

Table 9.3. *Determinants of the Percentage of House Challengers Who Had Held Elective Office, 1946–1986*

Variable	Democrats (1)	Republicans (2)	Democrats-Republicans (3)
Intercept	54.78***	−10.30	65.09***
	(11.78)	(11.43)	(14.34)
Party of administration	−30.19***	10.63	−40.81***
	(8.28)	(8.05)	(10.10)
Seats won by Democrats last election (%)	−.22	.37*	−.58***
	(.17)	(.17)	(.21)
Change in real income per capita (2d quarter)	1.24**	.11	1.13*
	(.41)	(.41)	(.51)
Presidential approval (2d quarter)	.22*	−.10	.32**
	(.08)	(.08)	(.10)
Adjusted $R\pm$	.56	.10	.60
Standard error of residuals	4.52	4.38	5.50
Durbin–Watson	1.51	1.72	1.60
Number of cases	21	21	21

Note: The dependent variable is the percentage of challengers who have held elective office; standard errors of regression coefficients are in parentheses.
* $p < .05$, one-tailed test.
** $p < .01$, one-tailed test.
*** $p < .001$, one-tailed test.

this variable is multiplied by −1 under Republican administrations.

National conditions are measured in the second quarter (April–June) of the election year because this is the period during which most *final* decisions about candidacy must be made. Of course, decisions to run for Congress are sometimes taken months or even years earlier – though two-thirds of non-incumbent House candidates do not register with the Federal Election Commission until March of the election year or later. However, the crucial period is not when individuals decide to run for Congress but when they can no longer gracefully change their minds and decide *not* to run for Congress. Initial decisions to test the political waters may indeed be made right after the last election – if not earlier; final decisions to run or withdraw can be taken right up to the primary. Many potential candidates do decide against running after assessing the incumbent's vulnerability, the availability of funds, and the thrust of national economic and political trends.

Table 9.2, column 1 indicates that all of the local and national conditions significantly affect the probability that a high-quality Democratic candidate challenged the Republican incumbent. Republican challengers, in contrast, appear to be sensitive only to local circumstances (though the other coefficients show the appropriate signs, and presidential approval does not fall far short of the conventional level of statistical significance).

Aggregate data tell a similar story. In Table 9.3, the dependent variables are the percentages of Democratic and Republican challengers who have held elective office – and the difference between these two percentages – in postwar House elections. They are regressed on the economic and presidential approval variables, plus the current partisan division of House seats. This variable serves double duty in these equations. It acknowledges that the more seats a party holds, the greater the number of inviting targets it presents to the opposing party, regardless of other circumstances. But it also serves as a more general measure of opportunity; substantial gains by a party in one election are commonly followed by substantial losses in the next

(a majority of which do *not* consist of seats captured from the other party in the previous election), and strategic politicians should take this cycle of "surge and decline" into account. As before, the scoring of other independent variables makes it necessary to control for the party of the administration.

Again, economic conditions and the level of public approval of the president have a significant and substantial impact on the quality of Democratic challengers (Table 9.3, col. 1). Neither one matters for Republicans, who are sensitive only to the opportunities offered by the current level of Democratic strength in the House (col. 2). However, a composite variable measuring the relative quality of challengers is affected significantly by all of these variables (col. 3). And this is the key variable, because relative quality is what matters on election day (see Figures 9.1 and 9.2).

CANDIDATE QUALITY AND ELECTION OUTCOMES

Clearly, high-quality candidates run selectively, and their career strategies are sufficiently sensitive to national conditions – as well as other factors affecting their chance of winning – for patterns like those in Figures 9.1 and 9.2 to emerge. The remaining task is to show that high-quality candidates contribute to their party's success rather than merely taking shrewd advantage of favorable conditions that would benefit inexperienced candidates just as well.

A necessary, if not sufficient, condition for this to be true is that high-quality candidates win more victories and votes than inexperienced candidates. Table 9.4 demonstrates that this condition is met. Challengers and candidates for open House seats who have held elective office are much more likely to win. Experienced challengers are almost four times as likely as inexperienced challengers to defeat incumbents. They received an average of 42.2 percent of the two-party vote (compared to 34.7% for inexperienced challengers) in postwar elections. Candidates for open seats with prior office are also more likely to win, their chances depending

Table 9.4. *Political Experience and the Frequency of Victory in U.S. House Elections, 1946–1986*

Type of Race	Number of Cases	Winners (%)[a]
Open Seats		
Incumbent party candidate experienced	347	86.8
Neither candidate experienced	192	76.6
Both candidates experienced	199	65.3
Challenging party candidate experienced	95	49.5
Challenges to Incumbents		
Candidate experienced	1,714	17.7
Candidate not experienced	5,020	4.5

[a] For open seats, percentage of victories for party currently holding the seat.

also on whether their opponents are similarly experienced (as well, of course, as on which party already held the seat – see Table 9.1). For (new) open seats held by neither party, experienced candidates win four of five contests with candidates who have never held elective office ($N = 59$; data not shown).

The success enjoyed by high-quality candidates is not merely a consequence of more careful selection of targets, though such strategic behavior certainly contributes to it. They have a higher probability of winning and win a larger share of votes, even when local and national political circumstances are taken into account. And although high-quality candidates do better in part because they spend more money on the campaign, they receive significantly more votes and are significantly more likely to win even when campaign spending is taken into account. This is evident from results of analyses reported in Tables 9.5–9.7.

Table 9.5 presents probit estimates of the challenger's probability of winning the election, depending on whether the challenger has held elective office and other variables. Column 1, which covers the entire postwar era, shows that both local political circumstances (measured by the vote received by the challenger party's candidate in the previous election) and national tides (summarized by the change in the partisan distribution of the national vote from the previous election to the current one) strongly influence the challenger's probability of winning. It is also evident that high-quality challengers have a distinctly greater chance of winning than would

be expected from national and local political conditions alone.

An idea of how much difference the presence of a high-quality challenger makes is given by the lower half of the table. In probit analysis, the effect of any one variable depends on the level of probability established by all of the other variables. So, to interpret the results, the first column in the lower section of Table 9.5 lists an initial probability, and the subsequent columns show how this probability would differ with the addition of a high-quality challenger. The difference is notable. For example, conditions that would give an inexperienced challenger a .10 chance of winning would give a high-quality challenger a .20 probability of winning (compare the columns 1 and 2). The coefficients suggest that experience is worth as much as a 5-percentage-point reduction in the incumbent's previous vote margin ($.449/.089 = 5.0$) or a 2.6-percentage-point national vote swing to the challenger's party ($.449/.174 = 2.6$).

Table 9.5, column 2 shows a similar result for elections since 1972. Column 3 demonstrates that although some of the advantage superior challengers enjoy is attributable to better financing, experience itself continues to make an important independent contribution to the probability of winning. For example, an initial .10 probability of winning would rise to .17 with the addition of a high-quality challenger (compare columns 1 and 4).

In light of these results, it is hardly surprising to find that other things being equal, high-quality challengers also win a larger share of

Table 9.5. *Elective Office Experience and the Probability of a Successful Challenge in House Elections*

Variable	1946–1986 (1)	1972–1986 (2)	1972–1986 (3)
Intercept	−5.56***	−4.12***	−3.81***
	(.23)	(.28)	(.32)
Challenger's party's vote in last election	.09***	.06***	.03***
	(.01)	(.01)	(.01)
National shift in two-party vote	.17***	.14***	13***
	(.01)	(.02)	(.02)
Challenger experienced	.45***	.46***	.34***
	(.06)	(.10)	(.11)
Challenger's spending	–	–	.79***
			(.08)
Challenger's spending squared	–	–	−.06***
			(.01)
Incumbent's spending	–	–	−.15*
			(.08)
Incumbent's spending squared	–	–	.00
			(.01)
Log likelihood	−1,219	−433	−347
Number of cases	6,213	2,375	2,375

	Challenger Is Experienced		
Initial Probability			
.01	.03	.03	.02
.05	.12	.12	.10
.10	.20	.20	.17
.15	.28	.28	.24
.20	.35	.35	.31
.25	.41	.41	.37

Note: Coefficients are maximum likelihood estimates; campaign spending is in 100 thousand dollars, adjusted for inflation; standard errors are in parentheses.

   * $p < .05$, one-tailed test.
   *** $p < .001$, one-tailed test.

the vote. The evidence is in Table 9.6, which reports the regression of the challenger's share of the vote on the same independent variables. Taking local conditions and national trends into account, a high-quality challenger's vote share was, on average, 2.8 percentage points higher than that of an inexperienced challenger in postwar elections (col. 1). Controls for campaign spending in the elections since accurate spending data have become available reduce this figure to 2.4 percentage points. Note that without controls for spending (Table 9.5, col. 2), experience in elective public office was worth

more to challengers (4.4 percentage points) in the more recent period. The electoral value of prior office appears to have increased over these years. I shall return to this important point.

How do these district-level effects add up to aggregate changes in Congress? Some answers are suggested by Table 9.7. The dependent variable here is the change in the percentage of House seats won by the Democrats from the prior to the current election. I chose to examine changes in seats rather than votes – the other dependent variable commonly examined in this literature – because seats represent the electoral

Table 9.6. *Elective Office Experience and the Challenger's Vote in House Elections*

Variable	1946–86 (1)	1972–86 (2)	1972–86 (2)
Intercept	10.08*	12.14*	15.92*
	(.36)	(.58)	(.50)
Challenger's party's vote in last election	.69*	.59*	.41*
	(.01)	(.02)	(.02)
National shift in two-party vote	.94*	.88*	.71*
	(.02)	(.04)	(.04)
Challenger experienced	2.79*	4.44*	2.41*
	(.19)	(.35)	(.30)
Challenger's spending	–	–	4.62*
			(.16)
Challenger's spending squared	–	–	−.28*
			(.02)
Incumbent's spending	–	–	−.46*
			(.13)
Incumbent's spending squared	–	–	.01
			(.01)
R^2	.58	.49	.64
Number of cases	6,213	2,377	2,377

Note: The dependent variable is the challenger's share of the two-party vote; campaign spending is in 100 thousand dollars, adjusted for inflation; standard errors of regression coefficients are in parentheses.
* $p < .001$, one-tailed test.

Table 9.7. *National Forces, Strategic Politicians, and Interelection Seat Swings in House Elections, 1946–1986*

Variable	(1)	(2)	(3)	(4)
Intercept	71.31***	47.17**	18.97*	43.15**
	(12.17)	(14.17)	(8.25)	(13.27)
Party of administration	−38.48***	−23.05*	–	−21.28*
	(9.60)	(9.60)		(9.47)
Seats won by Democrats last election (%)	−.87***	−.60***	−.44**	−.62***
	(.16)	(.15)	(.13)	(.15)
Presidential approval	.31**	.20*	–	.19*
	(.10)	(.09)		(.09)
Change in real income per capita	.81*	.32	–	.20
	(.41)	(.41)		(.38)
Quality of Democratic challengers	–	.33***	–	–
		(.17)		
Quality of Republican challengers	–	−.52**	–	–
		(.18)		
Difference in quality of challengers	–	–	.62*	.42**
			(.09)	(.13)
Adjusted R^2	.73	.82	.80	.83
Standard error of residuals	3.91	3.16	3.33	3.14
Durbin–Watson	2.16	2.26	2.12	2.31
Number of cases	21	21	21	21

Note: The dependent variable is the change in the percentage of seats won by the Democrats from the previous election; standard errors of regression coefficients are in parentheses.
* $p < .05$, one-tailed test.
** $p < .01$, one-tailed test.
*** $p < .001$, one-tailed test.

bottom line; in any case, the results are not at all sensitive to this choice, because seat and vote swings are very highly correlated.

Two control variables are again included: the party of the administration (for the same reason as before), and the percentage of seats won by the Democrats last time (in recognition of the reality that the more seats a party already holds, the more difficult it is to win additional seats). The other variables are measured as before except that real income change is the average for the election year (this is the time period most commonly used in the literature) and presidential approval is taken from the last Gallup poll before the election. In several presidential election years, Gallup stopped polling as early as June, though most years have readings taken in August or later. This variable is thus measured less precisely than usual; but there is no alternative if we wish to analyze presidential and midterm elections together.

Table 9.7, column 1 represents the standard referendum model of House elections. As usual, both presidential approval and economic performance have a significant impact on party fortunes; together with the control variables, they explain 73 percent of the variance in interelection seat swings. Column 2 adds to the analysis the aggregate quality variable for each party's challengers. Both have a strong, statistically significant effect on seat swings in the expected direction, and the variance explained by the equation jumps to 82%. Note that the quality of Republican challengers is at least as strongly related to election results as the quality of Democratic challengers, even though high-quality Republican challengers appear to be less strategic in their behavior than high-quality Democrats. Note also that the effect of real income change is reduced by more than half and ceases to be statistically significant; presidential approval continues to have a significant influence, though it is reduced by a third.

A model that includes the relative quality variable but not income change and presidential approval (Table 9.7, col. 3) outperforms the model that does the opposite (col. 1). Indeed, fully 80 percent of the variance in postwar seat shifts can be explained by just two variables: the

relative quality of Democratic challengers and the current size of the Democratic contingent.

If, for a more complete specification, presidential approval and income growth are reintroduced (col. 4), the impact of relative candidate quality falls by about one-third but remains substantial. Its coefficient indicates that a 1-percentage-point difference in relative challenger quality is worth almost two House seats; a change of one standard deviation in this variable (8.73) translates into about 16 seats; the difference between its highest and lowest values (32.7) covers 59 seats. Presidential approval continues to make a statistically significant difference, but real income growth does not.

An estimate of the contribution strategic politicians make to interelection seat shifts in specific elections can be calculated by multiplying the regression coefficient in Table 9.7, column 4 by the difference between relative challenger quality for each election and its 1946–86 average, then dividing by the net share of seats that changed hands. For all postwar elections, an average of about 44 percent of the seat shifts can be attributed in this way to variations in the relative quality of challengers. In the elections with net shifts of 20 or more seats ($n = 11$), 42 percent of them could be attributed to strategic politicians. On this evidence, strategic politicians make a major contribution to partisan change in Congress and thus to the electoral enforcement of collective accountability.

Although these equations suggest that the economy has little direct effect on House election results once differences in the quality of challengers are taken into account, skepticism is warranted. Economic conditions must make some real difference, else it would be irrational for strategic politicians to care about the economy. At least, economic conditions should work interactively with relative candidate quality to influence election outcomes. A high-quality candidate should be better able to exploit favorable conditions to undermine the incumbent's support; a party should get more mileage out of favorable conditions with experienced candidates to exploit them. Table 9.8 presents data that test this possibility by allowing economic conditions and presidential approval

Table 9.8. *Interactive Models of National Forces, Strategic Politicians, and Interelection Seat Swings in House Elections*

Variable	(1)	(2)	(3)
Intercept	22.67**	26.95*	22.48**
	(8.44)	(14.76)	(7.09)
Party of administration	−5.31*	−9.79	6.51**
	(2.81)	(10.60)	(2.27)
Seats won by Democrats last election (%)	−.42**	−.47**	−.42***
	(.13)	(.16)	(.11)
Change in real income per capita	.04	–	–
	(.40)		
Difference in quality of challengers	.34*	.60***	.52**
	(.15)	(.13)	(.16)
Difference in quality of challengers × change in real income per capita	.09*	–	.04
	(.04)		(.04)
Presidential approval	–	.05	–
		(.11)	
Difference in quality of challengers × presidential approval	–	.004*	.003*
		(.00)	(.00)
Adjusted R^2	.82	.86	.86
Standard error of residuals	3.16	2.87	2.80
Durbin–Watson	2.35	2.04	2.09
Number of cases	21	21	21

Note: The dependent variable is the change in the percentage of seats won by the Democrats from the previous election; standard errors of regression coefficients are in parentheses.

  * $p < .05$, one-tailed test.
 ** $p < .01$, one-tailed test.
*** $p < .001$, one-tailed test.

levels to interact with aggregate candidate quality.

The results are positive. Real income change has no direct influence but works interactively with relative challenger quality to affect election results (Table 9.8, col. 1). The same holds for presidential approval levels (col. 2). If both interaction terms are included and the insignificant direct terms are dropped, presidential approval, interacting with candidate quality, continues to make a significant difference; but the interaction term for real income change shrinks to insignificance (col. 3). This evidence is consistent with the view that a party benefits from favorable national conditions only to the degree that superior challengers are available to take advantage of them and that high-quality challengers are more successful when they have favorable national conditions to exploit in their campaigns.

Additional evidence that high-quality challengers contribute significantly to their party's success comes from observing how aggregate interelection vote swings are translated into seat swings. This is commonly measured by the swing ratio, the change in percentage of seats a party wins for a given change in the percentage of the national House vote it wins. A standard way to estimate the swing ratio is to regress the seat swing on the vote swing over a series of election years; the regression coefficient gives the swing ratio. Table 9.9, column 1 estimates a swing ratio of 1.75 for postwar House elections. The fit is quite good (adjusted $R^2 = .89$), but not so good that it cannot be improved by including as independent variables the aggregate quality of each party's challengers (col. 2; adjusted $R^2 = .91$). Controlling for the aggregate vote swing, the better the party's contingent of challengers, the more seats it wins; that

Table 9.9. *Seat Swings as a Function of Vote Swings and the Quality of Challengers in House Elections*

Variable	(1)	(2)
Intercept	−.13	−1.01
	(.56)	(2.91)
Change in votes won by Democrats from previous election (%)	1.75***	1.31***
	(.14)	(.20)
Quality of Democratic challengers	–	.23*
		(.10)
Quality of Republican challengers	–	−.32*
		(.14)
Adjusted R^2	.89	.91
Standard error of residual	2.55	2.22
Durbin–Watson	2.19	2.67
Number of cases	21	21

Note: The dependent variable is the change in the percentage of House seats won by the Democrats from the previous election; standard errors of regression coefficients are in parentheses.

 * $p < .05$, one-tailed test.
*** $p < .001$, one-tailed test.

is, the better its challengers, the greater advantage a party can take of favorable national tides or the less damage it will suffer from contrary national tides.

CONCLUSION

Analysis of both aggregate time series and district-level election data from all 21 postwar House elections provides unambiguous support for the idea that strategic politicians have played an important part in translating national conditions into election results. Individual career (and contribution) strategies prompt decisions that enhance the electoral effect of national conditions; in adapting to expected partisan trends, politicians help to realize them.

As the focus of electoral politics has turned increasingly to local candidates and campaigns, the importance of strategic candidacies has, in some important respects, grown. Consequently, the electorate's ability to exercise democratic control by acting as a "rational god of vengeance and reward" has become more contingent and variable, depending to an increasing degree on elite decisions that are only partially determined by the economy and other systematic national forces. National conditions continue to create problems or opportunities for congressional candidates; but how they are handled or exploited makes more difference now than in the past, and this varies among candidates, between parties, and across election years. When a party does not field enough challengers with the resources and skills to take full advantage of the opportunities created by national conditions, partisan swings are dampened. The danger is that as enforcement becomes less automatic, incentives for collective responsibility – already underwhelming – will diminish further.

CHAPTER TEN

Congress

The Electoral Connection

David R. Mayhew

In this classic work, Mayhew argues that much of the behavior we observe from members of Congress can be explained by the fact that they are required to win reelection in order to retain their office. Viewing members as "single-minded seekers of reelection" leaves little about the individual and collective efforts of Congress unexplained.

The discussion to come will hinge on the assumption that U.S. congressmen are interested in getting reelected – indeed, in their role here as abstractions, interested in nothing else. Any such assumption necessarily does some violence to the facts, so it is important at the outset to root this one as firmly as possible in reality. A number of questions about that reality immediately arise.

First, is it true that the United States Congress is a place where members wish to stay once they get there? Clearly there are representative assemblies that do not hold their members for very long.

Yet in the modern Congress the "congressional career" is unmistakably upon us. Turnover figures show that over the past century increasing proportions of members in any given Congress have been holdovers from previous Congresses – members who have both sought reelection and won it. Membership turnover noticeably declined among southern senators

David R. Mayhew. 1975. "The Electoral Incentive" in David R. Mayhew, *Congress: The Electoral Connection* (Yale University Press), 13–77. Copyright © 1975 by Yale University Press. Reprinted with permission.

as early as the 1850s, among senators generally just after the Civil War. The House followed close behind, with turnover dipping in the late nineteenth century and continuing to decline throughout the twentieth. Average number of terms served has gone up and up, with the House in 1971 registering an all-time high of 20 percent of its members who had served at least ten terms. It seems fair to characterize the modern Congress as an assembly of professional politicians spinning out political careers. The jobs offer good pay and high prestige. There is no want of applicants for them. Successful pursuit of a career requires continual reelection.

A second question is this: even if congressmen seek reelection, does it make sense to attribute that goal to them to the exclusion of all other goals? Of course the answer is that a complete explanation of a congressman's or any one else's behavior would require attention to more than just one goal. There are even occasional congressmen who intentionally do things that make their own electoral survival difficult or impossible. The late President Kennedy wrote of congressional "profiles in courage." Former Senator Paul Douglas (D., Ill.) tells of how he tried to persuade Senator Frank Graham (D., N.C.) to tailor his issue positions in order to survive a 1950 primary. Graham, a liberal appointee to the office, refused to listen. He was a "saint," says Douglas. He lost his primary. There are not many saints. But surely it is common for congressmen to seek other ends alongside the electoral one and not necessarily incompatible with it. Some try to get rich in office, a quest that may or may not interfere with reelection. Fenno assigns three prime goals to congressmen – getting reelected but also achieving influence within Congress and making "good public policy." These latter two will be given attention further on in this discussion. Anyone can point to contemporary congressmen whose public activities are not obviously reducible to the electoral explanation; Senator J. William Fulbright (D., Ark.) comes to mind. Yet, saints aside, the electoral goal has an attractive universality to it. It has to be the *proximate* goal of everyone, the goal that must be achieved over and over if other ends are to be entertained. One former congressman writes, "All members of Congress have a primary interest in getting re-elected. Some members have no other interest." Reelection underlies everything else, as indeed it should if we are to expect that the relation between politicians and public will be one of accountability. What justifies a focus on the reelection goal is the juxtaposition of these two aspects of it – its putative empirical primacy and its importance as an accountability link. For analytic purposes, therefore, congressmen will be treated in the pages to come as if they were single-minded reelection seekers. Whatever else they may seek will be given passing attention, but the analysis will center on the electoral connection.

Yet another question arises. Even if congressmen are single-mindedly interested in reelection, are they in a position as individuals to do anything about it? If they are not, if they are inexorably shoved to and fro by forces in their political environments, then obviously it makes no sense to pay much attention to their individual activities. This question requires a complex answer, and it will be useful to begin reaching for one by pondering whether individual congressmen are the proper analytic units in an investigation of this sort. An important alternative view is that parties rather than lone politicians are the prime movers in electoral politics. The now classic account of what a competitive political universe will look like with parties as its analytic units is Downs's *Economic Theory of Democracy*. In the familiar Downsian world

parties are entirely selfish. They seek the rewards of office, but in order to achieve them they have to win office and keep it. They bid for favor before the public as highly cohesive point-source "teams." A party enjoys complete control over government during its term in office and uses its control solely to try to win the next election. In a two-party system a voter decides how to cast his ballot by examining the record and promises of the party in power and the previous record and current promises of the party out of power; he then calculates an "expected party differential" for the coming term, consults his own policy preferences, and votes accordingly. These are the essential lineaments of the theory. Legislative representatives appear only as modest "intermediaries." If of the governing party they gather information on grassroots preferences and relay it to the government, and they try to persuade constituents back home that the government is doing a worthy job.

How well a party model of this kind captures the reality of any given regime is an empirical question. One difficulty lies in the need for parties as cohesive teams (members whose "goals can be viewed as a simple, consistent preference-ordering").

But at the congressional level the teamsmanship model breaks down. To hark back to the discussion of Britain, the specified resource and incentive arrangements conducive to party unity among M.P.'s are absent in the congressional environment: First, the way in which congressional candidates win party nominations is not, to say the least, one that fosters party cohesion in Congress. For one thing, 435 House members and 98 senators (all but the Indiana pair) are now nominated by direct primary (or can be, in the few states with challenge primaries) rather than by caucus or convention. There is no reason to expect large primary electorates to honor party loyalty. (An introduction of the direct primary system in Britain might in itself destroy party cohesion in the Commons.) For another, even where party organizations are still strong enough to control congressional primaries, the parties are locally rather than nationally oriented; local party unity is vital to them, national party unity is not. Apparently it never has been.

Second, unlike the M.P. the typical American congressman has to mobilize his own resources initially to win a nomination and then to win election and reelection. He builds his own electoral coalition and sustains it. He raises and spends a great deal of money in doing so. He has at his command an elaborate set of electoral resources that the Congress bestows upon all its members. There will be more on these points later. The important point here is that a congressman can – indeed must – build a power base that is substantially independent of party. In the words of a House member quoted by Clapp, "If we depended on the party organization to get elected, none of us would be here."

Third, Congress does not have to sustain a cabinet and hence does not engage the ambitions of its members in cabinet formation in such a fashion as to induce party cohesion. It would be wrong to posit a general one-to-one relation here between party cohesion and cabinet sustenance. On the one hand, there is nothing preventing congressmen from building disciplined congressional parties anyway if they wanted to do so. On the other hand, as the records of the Third and Fourth French republics show, cabinet regimes can be anchored in relatively incohesive parties. Yet, to pose the proposition in statistical rather than deterministic form, the need for an assembly to sustain a cabinet probably raises the likelihood that it will spawn disciplined parties.

The fact is that no theoretical treatment of the United States Congress that posits parties as analytic units will go very far. So we are left with individual congressmen, with 535 men and women rather than two parties, as units to be examined in the discussion to come. The style of argument will be somewhat like that of Downs, but the reality more like that of Namier. Whether the choice of units is propitious can be shown only in the facts marshaled and the arguments embellished around them. With the units nailed down, still left unanswered is the question of whether congressmen in search of reelection are in a position to do anything about it.

Here it will be useful to deal first with the minority subset of congressmen who serve marginal districts or states – constituencies fairly evenly balanced between the parties. The reason for taking up the marginals separately is to consider whether their electoral precariousness ought to induce them to engage in distinctive electoral activities. Marginals have an obvious problem; to a substantial degree they are at the mercy of national partisan electoral swings. But general voter awareness of congressional legislative activities is low. Hence national swings in the congressional vote are normally judgments on what the president is doing (or is thought to be doing) rather than on what Congress is doing. In the familiar case where parties controlling the presidency lose House seats in the midterm, swings seem to be not judgments on anything at all but rather artifacts of the election cycle. More along a judgmental line, there has been an impressive relation over the years between partisan voting for the House and ups and downs in real income among voters. The national electorate rewards the congressional party of a president who reigns during economic prosperity and punishes the party of one who reigns during adversity. Rewards and penalties may be given by the same circuitous route for other states of affairs, including national involvement in wars. With voters behaving the way they do, it is in the electoral interest of a marginal congressman to help insure that a presidential administration of his own party is a popular success or that one of the opposite party is a failure. (Purely from the standpoint of electoral interest there is no reason why a congressman with a safe seat should care one way or another.)

But what can a marginal congressman do to affect the fortunes of a presidency? One shorthand course a marginal serving under a president of his own party can take is to support him diligently in roll call voting; there is ambiguous evidence that relevant marginals do behave disproportionately in this fashion. This strategy may not always be the best one. During the 1958 recession, for example, it may have been wise for marginal Republicans to support Democratic deficit-spending bills over the opposition of President Eisenhower; in the 1958 election Eisenhower's policies seem to have been ruinous for members of his own party. How about marginals of the opposition party? By the same logic it might be advantageous for opposition marginals to try to wreck the economy; if it were done unobtrusively the voters would probably blame the president, not them.

There are a number of intriguing theoretical possibilities here for marginal, of parties both in and out of power. Yet marginals seem not to pay much attention to strategies of this sort, whether ingenuous or ingenious. What we are pondering is whether individual marginals can realistically hope to do anything to affect the national component of the variance over time in congressional partisan election percentages. And the answer seems to be no – or at least extraordinarily little. Leaving aside the problem of generating collective congressional action, there is the root problem of knowing what to try to do. It is hard to point to an instance in recent decades in which any group of congressmen (marginals or not) has done something that has clearly changed the national congressional electoral percentage in a direction in which the group intended to change it (or to keep it stationary if that was the intention). There are too many imponderables. Most importantly, presidents follow their own logic. So do events. Not even economists can have a clear idea about what the effects of economic measures will be. The election cycle adds its own kind of perversity; the vigorous enactment of President Johnson's Great Society legislation (by all the survey evidence popular) was followed in 1966 by the largest Republican gain in House popular vote percentage of the last quarter century. Hence there is a lack of usable lore among congressmen on what legislative action will produce what national electoral effects.

And there is after all the problem of generating collective action – especially action among nonmarginal congressmen who can watch national election percentages oscillate and presidents come and go with relative equanimity. All in all the rational way for marginal congressmen

to deal with national trends is to ignore them, to treat them as acts of God over which they can exercise no control. It makes much more sense to devote resources to things over which they think they can have some control. There is evidence that marginals do think and act distinctively. House marginals are more likely than nonmarginals to turn up as "district-oriented" and "delegates" in role studies; they introduce more floor amendments; in general marginals of both houses display more frenzy in their election-oriented activities. But these activities are not directed toward affecting national election percentages. And although they may differ in intensity, they do not differ in kind from the activities engaged in by everybody else.

Are, then, congressmen in a position to do anything about getting reelected? If an answer is sought in their ability to affect national partisan percentages, the answer is no. But if an answer is sought in their ability to affect the percentages in their own primary and general elections, the answer is yes. Or at least so the case will be presented here. More specifically, it will be argued that they think that they can affect their own percentages, that in fact they can affect their own percentages, and furthermore that there is reason for them to try to do so. This last is obvious for the marginals, but perhaps not so obvious for the nonmarginals. Are they not, after all, occupants of "safe seats"? It is easy to form an image of congressmen who inherit lush party pastures and then graze their way through careers without ever having to worry about elections. But this image is misconceived, and it is important to show why.

First, when looked at from the standpoint of a career, congressional seats are not as safe as they may seem. Of House members serving in the Ninety-third Congress 58 percent had at least one time in their careers won general elections with less than 55 percent of the total vote, 77 percent with less than 60 percent of the vote. For senators the figures were 70 percent and 86 percent (the last figure including fifteen of the twenty-two southerners). And aside from these November results there is competition in the primaries. The fact is that the typical congressman at least occasionally has won a narrow victory.

Second – to look at the election figures from a different angle – in United States House elections only about a third of the variance in partisan percentages over time is attributable to national swings. About half the variance is local (or, more properly, residual, the variance not explained by national and state components). The local component is probably at least as high in Senate elections. Hence vote variation over which congressmen have reason to think they can exercise some control (i.e. the primary vote and the local component of the November vote) is substantial. What this comes down to in general elections is that district vote fluctuations beyond or in opposition to national trends can be quite striking. For example, between 1968 and 1970 the Republican share of the national House vote fell 3.3 percent, but the share of Congressman Chester L. Mize (R., Kans.) fell from 67.6 percent to 45.0 percent, and he lost his seat. It is hard for anyone to feel absolutely secure in an electoral environment of this sort. But the local vote component cuts two ways; if losses are possible, so presumably are gains. In particular, it seems to be possible for some incumbents to beef up their November percentages beyond normal party levels in their constituencies. In the House (but apparently not in the Senate) the overall electoral value of incumbency seems to have risen in the last decade – although of course some House incumbents still do lose their seats.

Third, there is a more basic point. The ultimate concern here is not how probable it is that legislators will lose their seats but whether there is a connection between what they do in office and their need to be reelected. It is possible to conceive of an assembly in which no member ever comes close to losing a seat but in which the need to be reelected is what inspires members' behavior. It would be an assembly with no saints or fools in it, an assembly packed with skilled politicians going about their business. When we say "Congressman Smith is unbeatable," we do not mean that there is nothing he could do that would lose him his seat. Rather we mean, "Congressman Smith is unbeatable as long as he continues to do the things he is doing." If

he stopped answering his mail, or stopped visiting his district, or began voting randomly on roll calls, or shifted his vote record eighty points on the ADA scale, he would bring on primary or November election troubles in a hurry. It is difficult to offer conclusive proof that this last statement is true, for there is no congressman willing to make the experiment. But normal political activity among politicians with healthy electoral margins should not be confused with inactivity. What characterizes "safe" congressmen is not that they are beyond electoral reach, but that their efforts are very likely to bring them uninterrupted electoral success.

Whether congressmen think their activities have electoral impact, and whether in fact they have impact, are of course two separate questions. Of the former there can be little doubt that the answer is yes. In fact in their own minds successful politicians probably overestimate the impact they are having. The actual impact of politicians' activities is more difficult to assess. The evidence on the point is soft and scattered. It is hard to find variance in activities undertaken, for there are no politicians who consciously try to lose. There is no doubt that the electorate's general awareness of what is going on in Congress is something less than robust. Yet the argument here will be that congressmen's activities in fact do have electoral impact.

The next step here is to offer a brief conceptual treatment of the relation between congressmen and their electorates. A congressman's attention must be devoted to what can be called an "expected incumbent differential." Let us define this "expected incumbent differential" as any difference perceived by a relevant political actor between what an incumbent congressman is likely to do if returned to office and what any possible challenger (in primary or general election) would be likely to do. And let us define "relevant political actor" here as anyone who has a resource that might be used in the election in question. At the ballot box the only usable resources are votes, but there are resources that can be translated into votes: money, the ability to make persuasive endorsements, organizational skills, and so on. By this definition a "relevant political actor" need not be a constituent; one of the most important resources, money, flows all over the country in congressional campaign years.

It must be emphasized that the average voter has only the haziest awareness of what an incumbent congressman is actually doing in office. But an incumbent has to be concerned about actors who do form impressions about him, and especially about actors who can marshal resources other than their own votes. Senator Robert C. Byrd (D., W.Va.) has a "little list" of 2,545 West Virginians he regularly keeps in touch with. A congressman's assistant interviewed for a Nader profile in 1972 refers to the "thought leadership" back in the district. Of campaign resources one of the most vital is money. An incumbent not only has to assure that his own election funds are adequate, he has to try to minimize the probability that actors will bankroll an expensive campaign against him. There is the story that during the first Nixon term Senator James B. Pearson (R., Kans.) was told he would face a well-financed opponent in his 1972 primary if he did not display more party regularity in his voting. Availability of money can affect strength of opposition candidacy in both primary and general elections.

Another resource of significance is organizational expertise, probably more important than money among labor union offerings. Simple ability to do electioneering footwork is a resource the invoking of which may give campaigns an interesting twist. Leuthold found in studying ten 1962 House elections in the San Francisco area that 50 percent of campaign workers held college degrees (as against 12% of the Bay area population), and that the workers were more issue oriented than the general population. The need to attract workers may induce candidates to traffic in issues more than they otherwise would. Former Congressman Allard K. Lowenstein (D., N.Y.) has as his key invokable resource a corps of student volunteers who will follow him from district to district, making him an unusually mobile candidate.

Still another highly important resource is the ability to make persuasive endorsements.

Manhattan candidates angle for the imprimatur of the *New York Times.* New Hampshire politics rotates around endorsements of the *Manchester Union Leader.* Labor union committees circulate their approved lists. Chicago Democratic politicians seek the endorsement of the mayor.

In all his calculations the congressman must keep in mind that he is serving two electorates rather than one – a November electorate and a primary electorate nested inside it but not a representative sample of it. From the standpoint of the politician a primary is just another election to be survived. A typical scientific poll of a constituency yields a congressman information on the public standing of possible challengers in the other party but also in his own party. A threat is a threat. For an incumbent with a firm "supporting coalition" of elite groups in his party the primary electorate is normally quiescent. But there can be sudden turbulence. And it sometimes happens that the median views of primary and November electorates are so divergent on salient issues that a congressman finds it difficult to hold both electorates at once.

A final conceptual point has to do with whether congressmen's behavior should be characterized as "maximizing" behavior. Does it make sense to visualize the congressman as a maximizer of vote percentage in elections – November or primary or, with some complex trade-off, both? For two reasons the answer is probably no. The first has to do with his goal itself, which is to stay in office rather than to win all the popular vote. More precisely his goal is to stay in office over a number of future elections, which does mean that "winning comfortably" in any one of them (except the last) is more desirable than winning by a narrow plurality. The logic here is that a narrow victory (in primary or general election) is a sign of weakness that can inspire hostile political actors to deploy resources intensively the next time around. By this reasoning the higher the election percentages the better. No doubt any congressman would engage in an act to raise his November figure from 80 percent to 90 percent if he could be absolutely sure that the act would accomplish the end (without affecting his primary percentage) and if it could be undertaken at low personal cost. But still, trying to "win comfortably" is not the same as trying to win all the popular vote. As the personal cost (e.g. expenditure of personal energy) of a hypothetical "sure gain" rises, the congressman at the 55 percent November level is more likely to be willing to pay it than his colleague at the 80 percent level.

The second and more decisive reason why a pure maximization model is inappropriate is that congressmen act in an environment of high uncertainty. An assumption of minimax behavior therefore gives a better fit. Behavior of an innovative sort can yield vote gains, but it can also bring disaster. For the most part it makes sense for congressmen to follow conservative strategies. Each member, after all, is a recent victor of two elections (primary and general), and it is only reasonable for him to believe that whatever it was that won for him the last time is good enough to win the next time. When a congressman has a contented primary electorate and a comfortable November percentage, it makes sense to sit tight, to try to keep the coalition together. Where November constituencies are polarized in the conventional fashion – labor and liberals on one side, business on the other – there is hardly any alternative. Yet, simply repeating the activities of the past is of course impossible, for the world changes. There are always new voters, new events, new issues. Congressmen therefore need conservative strategies for dealing with change. And they have some. For members with conventional supporting coalitions it can be useful to accept party cues in deciding how to cast roll call votes; a Republican House member from Indiana can hardly go wrong in following the party line (though for an Alabama Democrat or a Massachusetts Republican it would be madness to do so). It may be useful to build a voting record that blends in with the records of party colleagues in one's state delegation. It is surely useful to watch other members' primary and general elections to try to gain clues on voter temperament. But conservatism can be carried only so far. It requires a modest degree of venturesomeness just to hold an old coalition together. And for members in

great electoral danger it may on balance be wise to resort to ostentatious innovation.

Whether they are safe or marginal, cautious or audacious, congressmen must constantly engage in activities related to reelection. There will be differences in emphasis, but all members share the root need to do things – indeed, to do things day in and day out during their terms. The next step here is to present a typology, a short list of the *kinds* of activities congressmen find it electorally useful to engage in. The case will be that there are three basic kinds of activities.

One activity is *advertising*, defined here as any effort to disseminate one's name among constituents in such a fashion as to create a favorable image but in messages having little or no issue content. A successful congressman builds what amounts to a brand name, which may have a generalized electoral value for other politicians in the same family. The personal qualities to emphasize are experience, knowledge, responsiveness, concern, sincerity, independence, and the like. Just getting one's name across is difficult enough; only about half the electorate, if asked, can supply their House members' names. It helps a congressman to be known. "In the main, recognition carries a positive valence; to be perceived at all is to be perceived favorably." A vital advantage enjoyed by House incumbents is that they are much better known among voters than their November challengers. They are better known because they spend a great deal of time, energy, and money trying to make themselves better known. There are standard routines – frequent visits to the constituency, nonpolitical speeches to home audiences, the sending out of infant care booklets and letters of condolence and congratulation. Of 158 House members questioned in the mid-1960s, 121 said that they regularly sent newsletters to their constituents; 48 wrote separate news or opinion columns for newspapers; 82 regularly reported to their constituencies by radio or television; 89 regularly sent out mail questionnaires. Some routines are less standard. Congressman George E. Shipley (D., Ill.) claims to have met personally about half his constituents (i.e. some

200,000 people). For over twenty years Congressman Charles C. Diggs, Jr. (D., Mich.) has run a radio program featuring himself as a "combination disc jockey–commentator and minister." Congressman Daniel J. Flood (D., Pa.) is "famous for appearing unannounced and often uninvited at wedding anniversaries and other events." Anniversaries and other events aside, congressional advertising is done largely at public expense. Use of the franking privilege has mushroomed in recent years; in early 1973 one estimate predicted that House and Senate members would send out about 476 million pieces of mail in the year 1974, at a public cost of $38.1 million – or about 900,000 pieces per member with a subsidy of $70,000 per member. By far the heaviest mailroom traffic comes in Octobers of even-numbered years. There are some differences between House and Senate members in the ways they go about getting their names across. House members are free to blanket their constituencies with mailings for all boxholders; senators are not. But senators find it easier to appear on national television – for example, in short reaction statements on the nightly news shows. Advertising is a staple congressional activity, and there is no end to it. For each member there are always new voters to be apprised of his worthiness and old voters to be reminded of it.

A second activity may be called *credit claiming*, defined here as acting so as to generate a belief in a relevant political actor (or actors) that one is personally responsible for causing the government, or some unit thereof, to do something that the actor (or actors) considers desirable. The political logic of this, from the congressman's point of view, is that an actor who believes that a member can make pleasing things happen will no doubt wish to keep him in office so that he can make pleasing things happen in the future. The emphasis here is on individual accomplishment (rather than, say, party or governmental accomplishment) and on the congressman as doer (rather than as, say, expounder of constituency views). Credit claiming is highly important to congressmen, with the consequence that much of congres-

sional life is a relentless search for opportunities to engage in it.

Where can credit be found? If there were only one congressman rather than 535, the answer would in principle be simple enough. Credit (or blame) would attach in Downsian fashion to the doings of the government as a whole. But there are 535. Hence it becomes necessary for each congressman to try to peel off pieces of governmental accomplishment for which he can believably generate a sense of responsibility. For the average congressman the staple way of doing this is to traffic in what may be called "particularized benefits." Particularized governmental benefits, as the term will be used here, have two properties: (1) Each benefit is given out to a specific individual, group, or geographical constituency, the recipient unit being of a scale that allows a single congressman to be recognized (by relevant political actors and other congressmen) as the claimant for the benefit (other congressmen being perceived as indifferent or hostile). (2) Each benefit is given out in apparently ad hoc fashion (unlike, say, social security checks) with a congressman apparently having a hand in the allocation. A particularized benefit can normally be regarded as a member of a class. That is, a benefit given out to an individual, group, or constituency can normally be looked upon by congressmen as one of a class of similar benefits given out to sizable numbers of individuals, groups, or constituencies. Hence, the impression can arise that a congressman is getting "his share" of whatever it is the government is offering. (The classes may be vaguely defined. Some state legislatures deal in what their members call "local legislation.")

In sheer volume the bulk of particularized benefits come under the heading of "casework" – the thousands of favors congressional offices perform for supplicants in ways that normally do not require legislative action. High school students ask for essay materials, soldiers for emergency leaves, pensioners for location of missing checks, local governments for grant information, and on and on. Each office has skilled professionals who can play the bureaucracy like an organ – pushing the right pedals to produce the desired effects. But many benefits require new legislation, or at least they require important allocative decisions on matters covered by existent legislation. Here the congressman fills the traditional role of supplier of goods to the home district. It is a believable role; when a member claims credit for a benefit on the order of a dam, he may well receive it. Shiny construction projects seem especially useful. In the decades before 1934, tariff duties for local industries were a major commodity. In recent years awards given under grant-in-aid programs have become more useful as they have become more numerous. Some quests for credit are ingenious; in 1971 the story broke that congressmen had been earmarking foreign aid money for specific projects in Israel in order to win favor with home constituents. It should be said of constituency benefits that congressmen are quite capable of taking the initiative in drumming them up; that is, there can be no automatic assumption that a congressman's activity is the result of pressures brought to bear by organized interests.

A final point here has to do with geography. The examples given so far are all of benefits conferred upon home constituencies or recipients therein. But the properties of particularized benefits were carefully specified so as not to exclude the possibility that some benefits may be given to recipients outside the home constituencies. Some probably are. Narrowly drawn tax loopholes qualify as particularized benefits, and some of them are probably conferred upon recipients outside the home districts. Campaign contributions flow into districts from the outside, so it would not be surprising to find that benefits go where the resources are.

How much particularized benefits count for at the polls is extraordinarily difficult to say. But it would be hard to find a congressman who thinks he can afford to wait around until precise information is available. The lore is that they count – furthermore, given home expectations, that they must be supplied in regular quantities for a member to stay electorally even with the board. Awareness of favors may spread beyond their recipients, building for a member a general reputation as a good provider. "Rivers

Delivers." "He Can Do More For Massachusetts." A good example of Capitol Hill lore on electoral impact is given in this account of the activities of Congressman Frank Thompson, Jr. (D., N.J., 4th district):

> In 1966, the 4th was altered drastically by redistricting; it lost Burlington County and gained Hunterdon, Warren, and Sussex. Thompson's performance at the polls since 1966 is a case study of how an incumbent congressman, out of line with his district's ideological persuasions, can become unbeatable. In 1966, Thompson carried Mercer by 23,000 votes and lost the three new counties by 4,600, winning reelection with 56% of the votes. He then survived a district-wide drop in his vote two years later. In 1970, the Congressman carried Mercer County by 20,000 votes and the rest of the district by 6,000, finishing with 58%. The drop in Mercer resulted from the attempt of his hard-line conservative opponent to exploit the racial unrest which had developed in Trenton. But for four years Thompson had been making friends in Hunterdon, Warren, and Sussex, busy doing the kind of chores that congressmen do. In this case, Thompson concerned himself with the interests of dairy farmers at the Department of Agriculture. The results of his efforts were clear when the results came in from the 4th's northern counties.

So much for particularized benefits. But is credit available elsewhere? For governmental accomplishments beyond the scale of those already discussed? The general answer is that the prime mover role is a hard one to play on larger matters – at least before broad electorates. A claim, after all, has to be credible. If a congressman goes before an audience and says, "I am responsible for passing a bill to curb inflation," or "I am responsible for the highway program," hardly anyone will believe him. There are two reasons why people may be skeptical of such claims. First, there is a numbers problem. On an accomplishment of a sort that probably engaged the supportive interest of more than one member it is reasonable to suppose that credit should be apportioned among them. But second, there is an overwhelming problem of information costs. For typical voters Capitol Hill is a distant and mysterious place; few have anything like a working knowledge of its maneuverings. Hence there is no easy way of knowing whether a congressman is staking a valid claim or not. The odds are that the information problem cuts in different ways on different kinds of issues. On particularized benefits it may work in a congressman's favor; he may get credit for the dam he had nothing to do with building. Sprinkling a district with dams, after all, is something a congressman is supposed to be able to do. But on larger matters it may work against him. For a voter lacking an easy way to sort out valid from invalid claims the sensible recourse is skepticism. Hence it is unlikely that congressmen get much mileage out of credit claiming on larger matters before broad electorates.

The third activity congressmen engage in may be called *position taking*, defined here as the public enunciation of a judgmental statement on anything likely to be of interest to political actors. The statement may take the form of a roll call vote. The most important classes of judgmental statements are those prescribing American governmental ends (a vote cast against the war; a statement that "the war should be ended immediately") or governmental means (a statement that "the way to end the war is to take it to the United Nations"). The judgments may be implicit rather than explicit, as in: "I will support the president on this matter." But judgments may range far beyond these classes to take in implicit or explicit statements on what almost anybody should do or how he should do it: "The great Polish scientist Copernicus has been unjustly neglected"; "The way for Israel to achieve peace is to give up the Sinai." The congressman as position taker is a speaker rather than a doer. The electoral requirement is not that he make pleasing things happen but that he make pleasing judgmental statements. The position itself is the political commodity. Especially on matters where governmental responsibility is widely diffused it is not surprising that political actors should fall back on positions as tests of incumbent virtue. For voters ignorant of congressional processes the recourse is an easy one. The following comment by one of Clapp's House interviewees is highly revealing: "Recently, I went home and began to talk about the—act. I was pleased to have sponsored that bill, but it soon dawned on me that the point

wasn't getting through at all. What was getting through was that the act might be a help to people. I changed the emphasis: I didn't mention my role particularly, but stressed my support of the legislation."

The ways in which positions can be registered are numerous and often imaginative. There are floor addresses ranging from weighty orations to mass-produced "nationality day statements." There are speeches before home groups, television appearances, letters, newsletters, press releases, ghostwritten books, *Playboy* articles, even interviews with political scientists. On occasion congressmen generate what amount to petitions; whether or not to sign the 1956 Southern Manifesto defying school desegregation rulings was an important decision for southern members. Outside the roll call process the congressman is usually able to tailor his positions to suit his audiences. A solid consensus in the constituency calls for ringing declarations; for years the late Senator James K. Vardaman (D., Miss.) campaigned on a proposal to repeal the Fifteenth Amendment. Division or uncertainty in the constituency calls for waffling; in the late 1960s a congressman had to be a poor politician indeed not to be able to come up with an inoffensive statement on Vietnam ("We must have peace with honor at the earliest possible moment consistent with the national interest"). On a controversial issue a Capitol Hill office normally prepares two form letters to send out to constituent letter writers – one for the pros and one (not directly contradictory) for the antis.

Versatility is occasionally possible in roll call voting. For example a congressman may vote one way on recommittal and the other on final passage, leaving it unclear just how he stands on a bill. Members who cast identical votes on a measure may give different reasons for having done so. Yet it is on roll calls that the crunch comes; there is no way for a member to avoid making a record on hundreds of issues, some of which are controversial in the home constituencies. Of course, most roll call positions considered in isolation are not likely to cause much of a ripple at home. But broad voting patterns can and do; member "ratings" calculated by the Americans for Democratic Action, Americans for Constitutional Action, and other outfits are used as guidelines in the deploying of electoral resources. And particular issues often have their alert publics. Some national interest groups watch the votes of all congressmen on single issues and ostentatiously try to reward or punish members for their positions; over the years some notable examples of such interest groups have been the Anti-Saloon League, the early Farm Bureau, the American Legion, the American Medical Association and the National Rifle Association. On rare occasions single roll calls achieve a rather high salience among the public generally. This seems especially true of the Senate, which every now and then winds up for what might be called a "showdown vote," with pressures on all sides, presidential involvement, media attention given to individual senators' positions, and suspense about the outcome.

Probably the best position-taking strategy for most congressmen at most times is to be conservative – to cling to their own positions of the past where possible and to reach for new ones with great caution where necessary. Yet in an earlier discussion of strategy the suggestion was made that it might be rational for members in electoral danger to resort to innovation. The form of innovation available is entrepreneurial position taking, its logic being that for a member facing defeat with his old array of positions it makes good sense to gamble on some new ones. It may be that congressional marginals fulfill an important function here as issue pioneers – experimenters who test out new issues and thereby show other politicians which ones are usable.

The effect of position taking on electoral behavior is about as hard to measure as the effect of credit claiming. Once again there is a variance problem; congressmen do not differ very much among themselves in the methods they use or the skills they display in attuning themselves to their diverse constituencies. All of them, after all, are professional politicians.

There can be no doubt that congressmen believe positions make a difference. An important consequence of this belief is their custom of watching each other's elections to try to

figure out what positions are salable. Nothing is more important in Capitol Hill politics than the shared conviction that election returns have proven a point. Thus the 1950 returns were read not only as a rejection of health insurance but as a ratification of McCarthyism. When two North Carolina nonsigners of the 1956 Southern Manifesto immediately lost their primaries, the message was clear to southern members that there could be no straying from a hard line on the school desegregation issue. Any breath of life left in the cause of school bussing was squeezed out by House returns from the Detroit area in 1972. Senator Douglas gives an interesting report on the passage of the first minimum wage bill in the Seventy-fifth Congress. In 1937 the bill was tied up in the House Rules Committee, and there was an effort to get it to the floor through use of discharge petition. Then two primary elections broke the jam. Claude Pepper (D., Fla.) and Lister Hill (D., Ala.) won nominations to fill vacant Senate seats. "Both campaigned on behalf of the Wages and Hours bill, and both won smashing victories. . . . Immediately after the results of the Florida and Alabama primaries became known, there was a stampede to sign the petition, and the necessary 218 signatures were quickly obtained." The bill later passed. It may be useful to close this section on position taking with a piece of political lore on electoral impact that can stand beside the piece on the impact of credit claiming offered earlier. The discussion is of the pre-1972 sixth California House district:

Since 1952 the district's congressman has been Republican William S. Mailliard, a wealthy member of an old California family. For many years Mailliard had a generally liberal voting record. He had no trouble at the polls, winning elections by large majorities in what is, by a small margin at least, a Democratic district. More recently, Mailliard seems caught between the increasing conservatism of the state's Republican party and the increasing liberalism of his constituency.

After [Governor Ronald] Reagan's victory [in 1966], Mailliard's voting record became noticeably more conservative. Because of this, he has been spared the tough conservative primary opposition that Paul McCloskey has confronted in the 11th. But Mailliard's move to the right has not gone unnoticed in the 6th district. In 1968 he received 73% of the vote, but in 1970 he won only 53% – a highly unusual drop for an incumbent of such long standing. Much of the difference must be attributed to the war issue. San Francisco and Marin are both antiwar strongholds; but Mailliard, who is the ranking Republican on the House Foreign Affairs Committee, has supported the Nixon Administration's war policy. In the 6th district, at least, that position is a sure vote-loser.

These, then, are the three kinds of electorally oriented activities congressmen engage in – advertising, credit claiming, and position taking. It remains only to offer some brief comments on the emphases different members give to the different activities. No deterministic statements can be made; within limits each member has freedom to build his own electoral coalition and hence freedom to choose the means of doing it. Yet there are broad patterns. For one thing senators, with their access to the media, seem to put more emphasis on position taking than House members; probably House members rely more heavily on particularized benefits. But there are important differences among House members. Congressmen from the traditional parts of old machine cities rarely advertise and seldom take positions on anything (except on roll calls), but devote a great deal of time and energy to the distribution of benefits. In fact they use their office resources to plug themselves into their local party organizations.

Another kind of difference appears if the initial assumption of a reelection quest is relaxed to take into account the "progressive" ambitions of some members – the aspirations of some to move up to higher electoral offices rather than keep the ones they have. There are two important subsets of climbers in the Congress – House members who would like to be senators (over the years about a quarter of the senators have come up directly from the House), and senators who would like to be presidents or vice presidents (in the ninety third Congress about a quarter of the senators had at one time or another run for these offices or been seriously "mentioned" for them). In both cases higher aspirations seem to produce the same distinctive mix of activities. For one thing credit-claiming is all but useless. It does little good to talk about

the bacon you have brought back to a district you are trying to abandon. And, as Lyndon Johnson found in 1960, claiming credit on legislative maneuvers is no way to reach a new mass audience; it baffles rather than persuades. Office advancement seems to require a judicious mixture of advertising and position taking. Thus a House member aiming for the Senate heralds his quest with press releases; there must be a new "image," sometimes an ideological overhaul to make ready for the new constituency. Senators aiming for the White House do more or less the same thing – advertising to get the name across, position taking ("We can do better"). In recent years presidential aspirants have sought Foreign Relations Committee membership as a platform for making statements on foreign policy.

There are these distinctions, but it would be a mistake to elevate them over the commonalities. For most congressmen most of the time all three activities are essential. This closing vignette of Senator Strom Thurmond (R., S.C.) making his peace with universal suffrage is a good picture of what the electoral side of American legislative politics is all about. The senator was reacting in 1971 to a 1970 Democratic gubernatorial victory in his state in which black turnout was high:

Since then, the Republican Senator has done the following things:

- Hired Thomas Moss, a black political organizer who directed Negro voter registration efforts for the South Carolina Voter Education Project, for his staff in South Carolina, and a black secretary for his Washington office.
- Announced Federal grants for projects in black areas, including at least one occasion when he addressed a predominantly black audience to announce a rural water project and remained afterwards to shake hands.
- Issued moderate statements on racial issues.

In a statement to Ebony magazine that aides say Thurmond wrote himself, he said, "In most instances I am confident that we have more in common as Southerners than we have reason to oppose each other because of race. Equality of opportunity for all is a goal upon which blacks and Southern whites can agree."

PART IV. MEMBERS, GOALS, RESOURCES, AND STRATEGIES

CHAPTER ELEVEN

Senate Representation and Coalition Building in Distributive Politics

Frances E. Lee

Lee analyzes the implications of equal representation of states in the Senate on coalition building. The considerable variation in population across states means that some states need more federal funds than others. Given that each senator's vote counts equally in the chamber, Lee argues that the inclusion of large state senators in a coalition is more costly to coalition builders than the inclusion of small state senators.

Although all states are represented equally in the Senate, they differ widely in population. At the extremes, Wyoming has a population smaller than most congressional districts, whereas California is more populous than many nations. Such differences mean that states also vary greatly in their need for federal funds. The cost of governmental programs, after all, largely depends on the number of people served by them. Despite differences in need for federal funds, however, each state has equal representational power in the Senate. This article investigates how apportionment shapes the politics of distributive policymaking in the Senate.

Apportionment shapes Senate distributive policymaking for two reasons. First, senators representing small states have more to gain from procuring a given amount of federal dollars than do senators who represent large states. A federal grant of $5 million, for example, has a far greater effect in Wyoming than in California.

Francis E. Lee. 2000. "Senate Representation and Coalition Building in Distributive Politics" *American Political Science Review* 94: 59–72. Copyright © 2000 by the American Political Science Association. Reprinted with the permission of Cambridge University Press.

Such a grant yields greater electoral benefits for senators who represent small states, both in terms of their statewide visibility and the percentage of residents benefited. Senators representing large states, by contrast, have to procure substantially larger sums in order to obtain the same electoral benefits. All else being equal, procuring these larger amounts will be more difficult, especially in times of fiscal restraint. As a result, small-state senators are better positioned to benefit from distributive politics: Put simply, they need fewer federal dollars for their state but enjoy equal representational power. Second, Senate apportionment affects the incentives of coalition builders in distributive policymaking. The tremendous differences in state population create a unique coalition-building dynamic: All senators' votes are of equal value to the coalition builder, but they are not equal in price. Senators who attempt to build winning coalitions within budgetary constraints can accommodate the funding demands of small-state senators at a lower cost than those of large-state senators. As a result, coalition leaders have strong incentives to include senators representing small states in their coalitions.

To investigate the effects of Senate apportionment on coalition building in distributive policymaking, I examine the major surface transportation reauthorizations of the 1990s. In 1991 and 1998 Congress overhauled all transportation programs, devising formulas to distribute $151 billion and $216 billion, respectively, among the states. The primary issue at stake during these reauthorizations was distributional equity among the states. How did Senate coalition leaders build support for their proposals to distribute federal transportation funds? Which states emerged as the winners and losers? To answer these questions, I compare the compositions of the alternative coalitions developed in the Senate and assess which coalition-building efforts were most successful. The data strongly support the hypotheses advanced. I find that coalition leaders in the Senate build coalitions more efficiently by drawing on the support of small-state senators. These efficient coalitions are more successful. In 1991, the more efficient coalition won outright. In 1998, small states exercised a greater influence on the outcome of the legislation, with the final allocations more closely reflecting small-state senators' preferences than those of their large-state colleagues.

BUILDING COALITIONS IN THE SENATE

With very few exceptions, most of the scholarly work on legislative coalitions has been in formal theory. In game theoretic terms, the Senate politics of writing formulas to distribute federal funds is best conceptualized as a "divide-the-dollars" game, in which one state's gain is another state's loss.

Riker advanced the famous proposition that rational, utility-maximizing players in divide-the-dollars games will form only minimum-winning coalitions. If a given amount is to be divided among the players, then the larger the winning coalition, the smaller is each winner's share. Thus, a minimum-winning subset of any larger-than-minimum-winning coalition will always have incentives to eject superfluous members to maximize the payoff to themselves.

A key limitation of these formal models is that they do not address the ways in which Senate apportionment shapes coalition building. Formal approaches to coalition building have generally modeled divide-the-dollars games as symmetric, meaning that the value of a coalition is a function only of the number of players in it.

In symmetric games, the payoff that a coalition can provide to its members is dependent solely on the size of the coalition, not on the specific persons that make up the coalition. As discussed above, however, Senate apportionment means that senators from large and small states demand dramatically different amounts of federal funds. Senate coalition builders will thus find that small-state senators' demands can be accommodated at much lower cost to the coalition. The payoff a coalition can provide its members thus depends on the specific players included, not merely on the number.

A successful coalition builder must make the best offer to a large enough group of senators to ensure passage on the Senate floor. From the point of view of rational, utility-maximizing senators, the best offer is the one that allocates a share of the funds to their constituents greater than any other proposal.

To produce a winning formula a senator must distribute the funds so that at least a majority of senators will prefer that formula to the existing alternatives. In short, senators strategically choose formula factors (and weights to give them) so that at least a majority of states will receive a larger share of the funds than under the other formulas proposed.

In the Senate, moreover, coalition builders cannot use restrictive rules to protect their proposals from alternatives. Coalition leaders in the Senate usually cannot prevent dissatisfied senators from offering alternative proposals or using their individual prerogatives to obstruct. The successful coalition builder, then, must make the best offer to a very large group of senators. If there is strong opposition to the coalition leader's proposal, even from a small minority of senators, then the coalition will need at least 60 senators who will vote for cloture.

In the same vein, coalition builders will propose formulas that provide generous allocations to their own state. They want to form a successful coalition around a proposal that allocates the largest feasible percentage of funds to their own state. Given this goal, senators will seek to build winning coalitions at the lowest cost, leaving the maximum amount of funds for their own state. The smaller the coalition, the more benefits the winners can share among themselves. All else being equal, larger coalitions in distributive policy are indeed more expensive. But in the Senate, all else is never equal. One consequence of Senate apportionment is that it is simply more expensive to include some states in a distributive coalition than others.

In transportation policy, as in most federal programs, a state's need for funds correlates closely with state population. Senators who seek to meet these greater needs must procure greater amounts of funds in order to obtain the same electoral benefits for themselves that senators representing smaller states receive from procuring smaller amounts of funds. For example, if a senator from Wyoming were able to procure an additional $20 million in transportation funds in a formula fight, this would be an increase equivalent to nearly $40 additional per constituent, quite a windfall. In California, the $20 million increase would only mean an additional 62 cents per constituent. Such considerations make it less expensive for coalition builders to accommodate small-state senators' demands. As a result, smaller coalitions in the Senate are not necessarily less expensive for the coalition builder to construct, and larger coalitions are not necessarily more expensive. The cost of building a coalition depends on the specific states included, not merely on their number.

Rational coalition leaders who attempt to build coalitions at the lowest cost will thus seek out small-state senators' support. If multiple coalition leaders pursue this strategy, then there will be a "bidding war" for small-state senators. As long as these senators' states can be added to the coalition at a lower cost than others, these senators will continue to be more attractive to coalition builders. Rational coalition builders, however, will not compete to obtain the support of the senators who represent states that need more funds, such as California, New York, and Texas. Accommodating the demands of these senators would consume too much of the coalition leader's budgetary resources.

Members of Congress, however, have multiple goals, and making good public policy is one of them. Concern for good public policy constrains Senate coalition builders from exploiting

losing coalitions to the fullest extent imaginable. A transportation program that allocated no funds to twenty states, for example, would hardly be good public policy. Although the pursuit of reelection will lead senators to prefer formulas that distribute more to their state than less, their interest in good policy will check them from excluding the losers from any share of the funds.

In sum, senators are expected to support the proposals that offer their state the greatest share of funds. Coalition leaders will build support for their formula by making the best offer to a winning coalition of senators. In seeking to benefit their own state, coalition leaders will attempt to build winning coalitions "efficiently." Because of differences in state need for funds, the support of some senators can be gained at a lower cost to the program budget than that of others. Rational coalition builders will accordingly seek the votes of these senators. Thus, the following hypotheses will be tested:

HYPOTHESIS 1. *Successful coalition builders will seek out less costly members to increase the size of their coalition efficiently.*

HYPOTHESIS 2. *The final outcome of formula fights will more closely reflect the preferences of small-state senators than large-state senators.*

WHY TRANSPORTATION POLICY?

Surface transportation programs provide a good opportunity to study the dynamics of distributive policymaking. One reason is that Congress has jealously guarded its control over the distribution of transportation funds, which is done almost entirely by statutory formulas. Another is that demand for transportation funds is great across all areas of the country, unlike other programs, such as water projects and community development. Every state has roads, highways, and bridges, and thus all senators are concerned with the distribution of transportation dollars. Any differences in senators' success in procuring funds in this area are more likely to reflect differences in Senate influence than in state demand for funds.

A third reason is that the politics of transportation is intensely distributive, relatively uncomplicated by controversies over ideology or nondistributive issues. As Senator Trent Lott (R-MS) remarked during the 1991 fight over the transportation funding formula: "It's not a partisan issue. It is even hard to get a fix on how regional an issue it is. It really boils down to how well you do or how poorly you do under the formula." Finally, transportation policymaking provides a unique view into the dynamics of Senate coalition building because coalition leaders always indicate which states they seek to include. The funding formulas for transportation are very complex, with many "adjustments" that greatly affect the amounts states receive. This complexity enables senators to construct their coalitions strategically, targeting funds to particular states. Both because of the complexity and because senators are so concerned with geographic distribution when considering transportation programs, coalition leaders provide charts that explicitly indicate how much each state will receive under their proposed formula. Using these charts, I am able to reconstruct the composition of transportation formula coalitions better than in other areas for which information about winners and losers under various proposals is not so readily available.

OPERATIONAL DEFINITIONS

A coalition builder is a senator who offers a proposal. This concept is relatively easy to operationalize because bill sponsorship is a matter of public record. The composition of legislative coalitions is considerably more difficult to discern because most proposals introduced in Congress are never brought to a vote, and thus most senators never go on the record as supporters or opponents. Assuming that senators support the formula that is most generous to their state, however, a coalition can be defined as those senators whose state would receive more under one proposal than under any alternative offered.

To determine the composition of coalitions, I simply compare competing proposals. Sometimes coalition builders in formula fights will assume different amounts of money to be distributed with the formula. For comparison, I simply refer to the percentages allocated to each state under the proposals. It is clear from senators' comments that this approach is substantively sound. Percentage shares matter more to senators during formula fights than specific dollar amounts, as the latter are contingent on the final appropriation. During the 1998 transportation formula dispute, for example, senators Arlen Specter (R-PA) and Rick Santorum (R-PA) voted against the bill even though it would have greatly increased the amount of funds for Pennsylvania over the previous level. As Specter explained, "the pending bill would reduce Pennsylvania's share of the total highway formula from the 4.32 percent share under the original ISTEA law (FY 92–97) to 3.79." To address this concern, senators who propose a formula typically include on their charts each state's percentage share in addition to the dollar amount each would receive given a specific total to be distributed.

To determine the "efficiency" of coalitions, I compare the average amount of funds that coalition builders allocate to the states in their coalition: The more efficient is the coalition, the lower the cost of states in the coalition. Every formula, of course, is designed to allocate all the funds authorized for the program. During formula fights, however, each alternative redistributes only some portion of the funds by comparison to the other formulas proposed or in existence. From the perspective of coalition builders, the most efficient use of these funds is to build the least expensive winning coalition, leaving the most funds to concentrate on their own state.

THE 1991 TRANSPORTATION
REAUTHORIZATION

The 1991 Intermodal Surface Transportation and Efficiency Act (ISTEA) marked the last time the interstate highway construction program was reauthorized. Senators recognized that this legislation would define priorities and set precedents for federal highway policy in the postconstruction period. Senator Daniel Patrick Moynihan (D-NY), chair of the subcommittee with jurisdiction over highways, had a vision for the future of surface transportation policy. A critic of previous federal policy, Moynihan sought to emphasize urban planning, environmental protection, and mass transit. Under his leadership, the committee endorsed a proposal to consolidate federal highway categorical programs into a massive block grant, the Surface Transportation Program, which would enable states to spend highway funds on transportation programs of their own choosing, including mass transit.

Despite the sweeping policy changes at issue, the principal subject of contention during the 1991 reauthorization was the geographic distribution of funds. Both the Senate and the Environment and Public Works Committee approved without controversy the major program consolidations and policy changes that Moynihan favored. Deciding how to distribute federal funds, however, occupied both the committee and the Senate throughout the lengthy consideration of this legislation. Floor debate on the bill lasted for ten days, sometimes going late into the night. How did coalition leaders build support for their proposal? First, a comparison reveals that they constructed coalitions more efficiently by targeting funds to less populous states. Second, because small states' votes could be obtained at a lower cost, the outcome of the formula fight more closely reflected the preferences of small-state senators than large-state senators.

Composition of the 1991 Coalitions

Two coalition builders attempted to determine the distribution of federal transportation funds in 1991, Moynihan and John Warner (R-VA). Moynihan used two strategies. First, he opposed creation of the National Highway System (NHS), a key initiative of the Bush administration to prioritize maintenance of the nation's most heavily used roads and highways. This was a concession to less populous states. Senators from small states strongly opposed the NHS initiative because these states contained a very small proportion of this mileage. Second, Moynihan rejected efforts to change the funding formulas for highway programs, generally maintaining the apportionments states already received under the categorical grants for highways. Explaining his formula, Moynihan conceded: "We have no rationale for the allocation formula we adopt in this bill, save that it is the existing one. It is the one that is in place." This, too, was a concession to less populous states because they had long received back more in federal transportation dollars than they had paid in taxes to the Highway Trust Fund. In keeping these allocations, Moynihan maintained the existing highway coalition; he gained the support of all the members of the committee with the exception of four senators from states larger than average – Bob Graham (D-FL), Warner, Dave Durenberger (R-MN), and Howard M. Metzenbaum (D-OH) – who felt that their state was being shortchanged.

Warner expressed his intention to fight the formula "until we receive that degree of fairness and equity to which we think we are entitled in our respective states." When the Senate committee reported the bill on June 6, Warner objected to the motion to proceed and announced his intention to offer an amendment that based the funding formula on the FAST proposal introduced in the House of Representatives (HR 2950). The FAST proposal adopted the administration's NHS policy and proposed a formula to direct funds to states with high levels of highway use. As a consequence, the formula Warner favored would have increased the allocations to populous states and decreased those to less populous states. Invoking imagery of D-Day on its 47th anniversary, Warner addressed Moynihan: "Our forces have landed . . . and we have established a beachhead"; he urged him to "come to the peace table as quickly as possible."

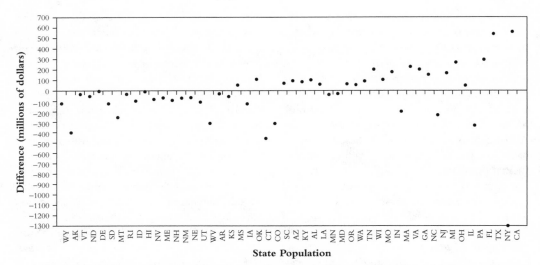

Figure 11.1. Difference between Allocations to States under Transportation Formulas Proposed by Warner (S. 1121) and Moynihan (S. 965), 1992–1996. *Note:* The difference is calculated by subtracting the amount for each state under S. 965 from that under S. 1121. When the point is above the zero line, the state receives more under Warner's formula; when below, it receives more under Moynihan's formula.

Figure 11.1 shows the difference between the Moynihan and Warner proposals in terms of the amount each state would receive. This difference was calculated by subtracting the amount allocated to each state under Moynihan's proposal from that allocated under Warner's proposal. When the point on the graph is above the zero line, the state would be better off under Warner's formula; when it is below the line, the state would be better off under Moynihan's proposal. This difference is plotted for each state in millions of dollars, with the states ranged on the x-axis from least to most populous.

The difference in the composition of the two coalitions is striking. Warner's bill would grant additional funds to nearly all the middle-sized and large states, compared to Moynihan's bill, while cutting funds to every state with fewer than five congressional districts. Of the 28 states with six or more congressional districts, 21 would have benefited from the Warner formula. Moynihan's bill combined benefits to a few populous states – Massachusetts, New Jersey, Pennsylvania, and New York – and to a couple of middle-sized states, Connecticut and Colorado, with benefits to all the least populous states.

With respect to Senate politics, however, the crucial difference between the two formulas illustrated in this figure is that there are more points below the zero line than above it. In other words, more states were better off under Moynihan's formula than under Warner's. Only 22 states would receive more dollars under Warner's formula, and twenty-seven would receive less.

Efficiency of Coalitions

Warner's formula would redistribute $4.9 billion of the total amount to be allocated under the program by comparison to Moynihan's formula. In redistributing these funds, however, the Warner formula was more generous to only 22 states, which was not sufficient to defeat the Moynihan formula. By comparison, Moynihan's bill distributed this $4.9 billion across more states, ensuring that 27 would receive more than under the alternative. He was able to do this because the members of his coalition were largely small-state senators and thus on average less expensive to include than the members of Warner's; coalition. As a result, the Moynihan coalition was more efficient, enabling the senator to garner a majority while reserving a substantial sum for New York. The mean state in Moynihan's coalition had a population of 2.5 million, considerably smaller than the average state (5 million). By including all the least populous states in his coalition, Moynihan added 23 of the 27 states in his group as beneficiaries at a cost of less than 2 percent of the program funds each. The mean state in Warner's coalition, by contrast, had a population of 7.6 million, considerably larger than the average state, and cost him 3.1 percent of the funds.

This coalition-building efficiency enabled Moynihan to grant 26 percent of the $4.9 billion redistributed funds to his own state. Under Warner's formula, by contrast, no state received a windfall of that magnitude. Virginia only received 6 percent of the redistributed dollars, an additional $233 million, under Warner's formula. In short, working with the same overall amount of dollars as Moynihan, the Warner coalition benefiting middle-sized and populous states at the expense of the least populous states was a political failure.

Outcome

Warner's formula, which later passed easily in the House, was not politically viable in the Senate. Although he supported Warner's bill, Senator Lloyd Bentsen (D-TX) recognized during floor debate that it did not have the votes to win: "There is a basic inequity there [in Moynihan's bill] that has to be corrected. I do not know that we have the votes. I understand how one could artfully put together a coalition where there are more winners than losers. . . . But at some point the question of equity has to come in." Bentsen recognized that to win on highway formulas, one must have more "winners" than "losers." In the Senate, of course, states and not numbers of constituents are the "players" in the game. This means that, at minimum, a coalition builder must ensure that a majority of states will not lose funds. Warner's formula did not meet even that low threshold.

It is clear from Warner's comments on the Senate floor that he had hoped to construct a successful alternative to the committee bill. When he first objected to consideration of the Moynihan bill, Warner explained that he currently represented a group of nine states and anticipated "it will grow to twice that number and perhaps three times that number." He sought to gain time by refusing to "relinquish one inch of ground, procedurally or otherwise." During the following ten days, however, Warner failed to gain the support he needed because his formula increased funding for populous states, which precluded coalition-building efficiency and made it impossible to create even a minimal majority coalition.

The Senate vote on the FAST formula took place on June 18, the day before the Senate passed the committee bill. Senators knew that the Warner alternative would not be adopted. Although the outcome was not in doubt, the votes show a strong correlation with states' interests. The FAST formula failed 41 to 57: 98 percent of the senators whose state would be better off under the Moynihan formula voted against FAST; 93 percent of those whose state would be better off under FAST voted for it.

Warner's failure and Moynihan's success support the hypothesis that coalition builders have incentives to benefit less populous states when writing formulas. At a very low cost to the program budget, Moynihan could build a majority coalition and still provide a windfall to his own state, along with generous allocations to a few others. By comparison, Warner made a highly inefficient attempt to build a Senate coalition. Adding the larger states to his coalition simply did not leave enough money to draw in a majority of states. Because of this dynamic, the outcome of the 1991 formula fight more closely reflected the preferences of small-state senators than those of their large-state colleagues. Nearly every small state was a member of Moynihan's winning coalition, and most of the large states were members of Warner's losing coalition. It is important to note that Moynihan's formula prevailed in conference with the House, which left most large-state senators dissatisfied and ready to revisit the funding formula issue at the next reauthorization of the program.

Just as in 1991, the key issue in the 1998 congressional debate over the transportation reauthorization – the Building Efficient Surface Transportation and Equity Act (BESTEA) – was the distribution of funds to states. The politics was more complex in 1998, however. Three members of the Senate Environment and Public Works Committee – Warner, chair of the Transportation and Infrastructure Subcommittee; Max Baucus (D-MT), ranking minority member of both the full committee and the subcommittee; and John Chafee (R-RI), chair of the full committee – each introduced distinct funding formulas and garnered substantial support among other members of the committee and in the chamber as a whole.

Warner once again backed a formula in the Senate (S. 335) that would have increased allocations to most of the populous states. By comparison, the Baucus formula (S. 532) would have allocated funds more equally across states, granting dramatic share increases to the less populous states in the Rocky Mountains and the Plains. With relatively minor changes, Chafee's bill – known simply as the ISTEA Reauthorization Act (S. 586) – would have continued the allocation patterns in the 1991 Moynihan formula.

Compared to the 1991 act, all three formulas proposed share increases for at least 33 states; under every formula at least 33 states would receive a larger percentage of the total allocation than they had received under ISTEA. Chafee's formula made the least extensive adjustment to existing legislation – redistributing a relatively small proportion of states' funding shares under ISTEA – whereas Baucus and Warner proposed more far-reaching changes. All three increased the shares for a supermajority of states relative to existing law by targeting a handful of populous states for the largest cuts: Warner and Baucus targeted Massachusetts (three percentage

share reduction), New York (two percentage share), and Pennsylvania (one percentage share); Chafee focused on Massachusetts (two percentage share), Georgia, Pennsylvania, and Texas (0.5 percentage share each). These reductions may appear small, but $216 billion was eventually authorized. Thus, a 1 percentage share cut is equivalent to a loss of $2.16 billion in a state's 1998–2003 funding level compared to what it would have received if the previous share had been maintained. All three coalition builders took the funds gained from targeting a few populous states and distributed them across many others, thus broadly conferring percentage share increases. As a result of these strategic choices, it appears that any of the formulas – if presented alone on the Senate floor – could have garnered a filibuster-proof majority to defeat the status quo.

Efficiency of Coalitions

Yet, no Senate majority preferred any one of these formulas to the other two. The Senate divided roughly into thirds: 26 senators (13 states) preferred the Warner formula; 44 senators (22 states) preferred the Baucus formula; and 30 senators (15 states) preferred the Chafee formula. Under Senate rules, regardless of which formula the committee reported, other coalition builders could offer their alternative.

Just as in 1991, gaining the votes of senators from populous states required a larger proportion of funds than gaining the votes of senators from less populous states. Efficiently constructed coalitions thus contained fewer large states and more small states.

The Warner coalition was the least efficient, that is, the average state in the coalition consumed a larger share of the program funds than the average state in either of the other two coalitions. The Warner group consisted of medium-sized and large states from the Midwest and South, and the average state had a population of 7.5 million and cost 3.1 percent of the funds. Relative to existing law, Warner proposed substantial funding increases for his coalition – a 15 percent increase in the average coalition state's share – and a 16 percent increase for Virginia. Given the high cost of the coalition's members, it is no surprise that the Warner group was also the smallest. Only 13 states preferred his formula to the others.

Like Moynihan's strategy for ISTEA, Chafee offered more funding for a few populous states – New Jersey, New York, and California – and for many small states. The average state in the Chafee coalition had a population of 5.3 million and cost 2.2 percent of the total funds. Accordingly, it was both more efficient and larger (15 states) than Warner's. There would be modest funding share hikes for the states in his coalition – 5 percent on average – and an 8 percent increase for Rhode Island. These relatively lower funding increases are the result of the less dramatic shifts that Chafee proposed in existing funding levels.

The Baucus coalition was both the largest and the most efficient. It consisted of about half the small states, several smaller-than-average southern states, and no state more populous than Illinois; the average member had a population of only 3.2 million and only cost 1.6 percent of the program funds. Although Baucus and Warner redistributed the same percentage of the funds – about 8 percent of ISTEA – Baucus constructed his coalition far more efficiently than Warner. Even though Baucus proposed the largest funding increase for his own constituents of any coalition builder – a 25 percent increase over the status quo – the coalition's efficiency enabled him to build the largest group (22 states) and even offer members the largest funding increases of any coalition builder, an average of 26 percent.

Outcome

Because no formula could command a majority, the three coalition leaders bargained in committee for seven months in an attempt to formulate a proposal that would prevail on the Senate floor. The same logic of coalition building continued to apply at this stage. Because of their lower funding demands, small-state senators remained more attractive as coalition members than other senators; they emerged as power brokers on the committee and strongly influenced the bill eventually reported. Baucus and three other small-state senators, Dirk Kempthorne (R-ID), Harry Reid (D-NV), and Craig Thomas (R-WY), were kingmakers in the committee, able to tilt the balance of power one way or the other. Kempthorne observed: "We've had lots of interest by different players . . . we're in a pretty good spot." Early in the bargaining process, Warner sought an alliance with Baucus. "I think there's a lot of mutuality," Warner said, "if we could get a merger, we have a very strong block of states."

Warner and Baucus did, in fact, ally around a new proposal. This required a substantial sacrifice from Warner, who had to abandon his plan to ensure that every state would receive back at least 95 percent of its contributions to the Highway Trust Fund, a longstanding goal of large-state senators that Warner had supported for years. Explaining this on the floor, Warner said: "It had been our hope to reach 95 cents [on the dollar] but we soon recognized that we could not do it if we were to build a successful coalition and to properly recognize the individual requirements of certain geographic regions of the United States, primarily the western states." The best that Warner could assure his large-state colleagues was a 90 percent return on their highway taxes.

After the Warner and Baucus coalitions converged, committee chair Chafee eventually gave them his support. Warner discussed the history of the alliance on the Senate floor: "As subcommittee chairman, I started out with a group called Step 21 [his initial formula] and then eventually we joined forces with a group headed by Senator Baucus – Stars 2000 is my recollection – and eventually our distinguished chairman joined us." In joining the coalition, Chafee obtained a modest funding share increase for Rhode Island and for most of the other small states in his coalition. Chafee's large-state members were the principal losers under the formula eventually reported. Eighty percent of the funding share cuts imposed in the committee bill were taken from large-state members of Chafee's coalition. The committee reported its bill to the Senate floor on October 1, 1997, by a vote of 18–0.

After trouble on the floor in 1997 and two weeks of debate in 1998 that focused on the distribution of funds to the states, the committee's formula was approved by the Senate on March 12, 1998, with a 96–4 vote. Before passage, some large-state senators – including Levin of Michigan and Specter of Pennsylvania – complained about the distribution of funds. No doubt, the large funding increases authorized which were 40 percent over the 1991–96 level, helped mollify the losers. Every state except Massachusetts received dollar increases over previous levels, even though 15 states had their funding shares reduced. It is clear that Warner was more pleased with the outcome in 1998 than in 1991. He had succeeded in raising the funding share for all the middle-sized southern states, particularly Virginia. In addition, he obtained small share hikes for the populous southern states, Florida and Texas. Warner could only secure these gains by increasing small states' shares above the 1991 formula level and by substantially cutting the shares for several populous states.

Warner's success suggests that he had learned some things since his defeat in 1991 about how to build successful Senate coalitions in funding formula politics. His 1997 strategy eventually mirrored that of Moynihan in 1991: Procure funding increases for one's own state by constructing an efficient Senate coalition. Doing so means securing small-state senators' votes using the funds gained by excluding some populous states from the coalition. By accepting smaller increases than he wanted for his own coalition members and by focusing share cuts on a few populous states, Warner was able to merge his group with Baucus's, thus building the supermajority coalition necessary to succeed in the Senate. As in 1991, the Senate's formula largely prevailed in conference with the House.

CONCLUSION

Equal representation of states in the Senate affects Senate politics in a crucial but long-ignored way. Senate apportionment creates a situation in which it is much less expensive to obtain some votes than others. In the context of funding formula controversies, it is clear that senators prefer the formula that will distribute the most funds to their state. Similarly, senators who build coalitions in support of formulas do so (at least in part) in order to increase funding to their own state. Because state need for federal funds corresponds closely with state population size, it is relatively inexpensive to provide funding increases for small states. As a result, coalition leaders who seek support for formulas that benefit their own state can both build winning coalitions and offer larger increases to their own states by including small-state senators and excluding their large-state counterparts. In sum, coalition leaders in the Senate have strong incentives to "strengthen the financial position" of less populous states.

The surface transportation battles of the 1990s clearly reveal these coalition-building dynamics. In both 1991 and 1997, the coalitions containing more small-state senators were less expensive to build, with the cost of the average vote being substantially lower in these coalitions than in those containing more large-state senators. Coalition-building efficiency gives senators two advantages. First, it enables them to provide more funds for their own constituents. In 1991 Moynihan both built a winning coalition and obtained a generous allocation for New York by devising a formula that all the small-state senators and a few large-state senators preferred to the alternative proposed. In 1997 Warner compromised his longstanding goal of increasing funding levels for all the large states and instead excluded a number of them from his coalition, using those funds to gain the support of small-state senators. In this way, he raised the funding share for his own state. Second, building coalitions efficiently enhances the chance of success. Efficiency means that more funds are available to spread across other states and thus garner additional votes. In 1991, the more efficient coalition won outright. In 1997, Warner merged with the highly efficient Baucus coalition to support a formula that could garner the supermajority needed to prevail.

Because they are so attractive to coalition builders, small-state senators have an advantage in funding formula disputes. They possess the votes needed to build efficient coalitions. For this reason, coalition leaders accommodate their demands to a greater extent than those of others. The bills passed by the Senate after both the 1991 and 1997 transportation formula fights more closely reflect the preferences of small-state senators than their large-state colleagues. In 1991, the formula preferred by small-state senators won outright. In 1998, the final bill gave larger funding increases to small states than to others.

These coalition-building dynamics have considerable consequences for understanding distributive policy in the United States. The overwhelming majority of all federal domestic assistance funds is allocated by congressionally mandated formulas. The longevity of funding formulas makes the small state's advantage in formula politics all the more significant. The distribution of committee and party power changes over time, but small states are always advantaged in the Senate. Regardless of when programs are created or reauthorized, small-state senators are always well positioned to benefit from their attractiveness to coalition builders.

CHAPTER TWELVE

Risk-Bearing and Progressive Ambition

The Case of Members of the United States House of Representatives

David W. Rohde

Rohde offers a theory of progressive ambition, the decision of political actors to seek higher elected office. He posits that actors employ a decision calculus in which they jointly consider the probability of winning office, the utility of office, and the costs of running. Actors will seek higher office when these factors are favorable for doing so. Rohde tests a series of hypotheses related to the decision calculus by examining the decisions of House members whether or not to run for Senate seats or governorships.

"Ambition lies at the heart of politics. Politics thrive on the hope of preferment and the drive for office." Since Joseph Schlesinger wrote those introductory lines to his superb study of career patterns in the United States, a substantial amount of research has been conducted on ambition and office-seeking behavior. Most of this research has, however, been primarily empirical in nature, and has not attempted to provide a more explicit theoretical framework for ambition analysis. In addition, most of this research has followed Schlesinger's example in selecting for analysis persons who actually achieved or tried for an office, and examining their career patterns and characteristics.

The present study departs from both of these trends. The theoretical focus is progressive ambition; the focus of the empirical analysis is on members of the U.S. House of

David W. Rohde, 1979. "Risk-Bearing and Progressive Ambition: The Case of Members of the United States House of Representatives" *American Journal of Political Science* 23: 1–26. Reprinted with permission.

Representatives between 1954 and 1974 and their decisions on whether or not to seek either a U.S. Senate seat or the governorship of their state. We begin by formulating a theory of progressive ambition and deriving a set of testable hypotheses from that theory. We then proceed to test those hypotheses on data on the office-seeking behavior of congressmen in relation to Senate seats and governorships. Instead, however, of analyzing the backgrounds of members of the House who sought those offices (analysis which has already been done), we will examine each member who had an opportunity to run for one of those offices and whether or not the opportunity was taken.

A THEORY OF PROGRESSIVE AMBITION

Schlesinger discusses three "directions" or types of ambition: discrete, static, and progressive. Briefly, discrete ambition relates to the politician who seeks an office for one term and then seeks neither reelection nor another office. Static ambition relates to the politician who seeks an office with the intent of attempting to retain it for as long as possible. Progressive ambition relates to the politician who holds an office and attempts to gain another regarded as more attractive.

Since Schlesinger's analysis considered people who behaved ambitiously, (i.e., sought certain offices), rather than (as in the present study) examining a selected set of politicians and predicting whether or not they would seek a given office, he did not address a certain conceptual question regarding the distinction between static and progressive ambition that we must consider. In discussing static ambition, he states: "How widespread such ambitions are we cannot tell, for the possibilities of making a career of one office are varied. Nevertheless, it is certainly a marked goal of many American congressmen and senators." Thus a retrospective analysis categorizes direction of ambition on the basis of manifest behavior, and (to use members of the House as an example) representatives who serve one term and leave voluntarily have discrete ambition, those who attempt to remain in the House have static ambition, and those who run for higher office have progressive ambition. A prospective analysis such as ours, however, cannot retain such a categorization. We believe, and here explicitly assume, that progressive ambition is held by almost all members of the House. That is, we assume that if a member of the House, on his first day of service, were offered a Senate seat or a governorship *without cost or risk*, he would take it. Thus static ambition is not something chosen a priori, but is a behavior pattern manifested by a member because of the risks of the particular opportunity structure he finds himself in, and his unwillingness to bear those risks.

Now we turn to some additional assumptions about the actors who are to be described by our theory. First, we assume that they are *rational*, in the sense of being maximizers of expected utility.

According to Author Goldberg:

Put most simply, being rational in a decision situation consists in examining the alternatives with which one is confronted, estimating and evaluating the likely consequences of each, and selecting that alternative which yields the most attractive set of expectations.

Whatever one's position on the usefulness or the range of applicability of rational choice models of politics, such models should be most useful in such calculated political choice situations as the choice between alternative offices.

Next we assume a particular calculus of decision making for the actors.

The expected value of running for office is a function of the probability of winning, the value of the office, and the costs of running; by our rationality assumption, an actor will run for higher office only if [the expected value of the higher office exceeds the expected value of the presently occupied office]. The higher the risks, the less likely is an actor to run [for higher office]. We will now proceed to apply these predictions to the specific situation of House members and the prospect of running for senator or governor, and to offer a series of hypotheses about the situation. At this point we will only discuss those hypotheses for which we offer empirical evidence. We will, therefore, confine our discussion here to the value of the higher office, the probability of winning the higher office, and the value of the House seat, all of which relate to the opportunity structure. After considering these factors, we will introduce one additional theoretical concept concerning the potential candidates themselves.

(1) *The value of the higher office.* We have assumed that (almost all) members of the House have progressive ambition. They would choose, if presented with a costless and riskless opportunity, to be senator or governor. It seems reasonable to begin our discussion by mentioning a few reasons why this should be so.

The attractiveness of a Senate seat relative to a House seat is fairly clear. One former member of the House who achieved a Senate seat summarized the situation this way:

I think at the time I first came to the Congress I really had my eye on the Senate. I like the pace of the Senate and I felt that there was an opportunity to make an impact as an individual in the Senate much more than in the House. Besides a Senator has a six-year term. The opportunity to make a mark in history just seemed to me much greater in the Senate.... It is a better job.

Another former representative emphasized the less hierarchical organization in the Senate.

I think one of the most basic differences between the House and the Senate is immediately in the Senate you have an opportunity to participate. In the House you have to wait your time and work your way up through the seniority system. The seniority system is much more constraining on individuals' activities in the House than it is in the Senate merely because of the numbers involved, 435 as opposed to 100. Here almost anybody can come into the Senate and – although you won't get your first committee choice – you'll be put in a position where there's so much to do and there's so much activity, so many problems, that you immediately get visibility that you sometimes never get in the House and you immediately have an impact upon legislation that you sometimes never get in the House.

The governorship, of course, has its own attractions, and one of the major ones is the more direct ability to control outcomes. A senator, who had been governor of his state, said:

The governor can make a decision and execute it. The constitution places vast power in the governor of —. As a senator, I make a decision and talk about it. There is a vast difference.

While there is certainly individual variation in the evaluation of the two offices, making a Senate seat more attractive to some and the governorship more attractive to others, there are also certain salient features of the opportunity structure of members of the House that affect the relative value of the two offices and make running for the Senate generally more attractive than seeking the governorship.

First, and probably foremost, is the six-year Senate term. The maximum term for a governor in the United States is four years, and a number of states even have two-year gubernatorial terms. A longer term permits an actor more time to enjoy the benefits of holding office instead of spending his time attempting to retain the office.

Second, there is the question of vulnerability. Recent research indicates that governors running for reelection are at least somewhat more vulnerable to defeat than are Senators in the same situation. Data for the period 1950–70 show that 85.5 percent of Senate incumbents running for reelection were successful. However, data on incumbent governors running for reelection in almost exactly the same period (1950–69) show that only 64.4 percent were successful. Certainly the likelihood of reelection to a prospective office will affect the value of that office to an individual.

Closely related to the prospects for reelection, and probably even more relevant to our discussion, is a third consideration: the prospects for a career in an office. Beyond a Senate seat and the governor's chair, the only major elective offices are the Presidency and Vice-Presidency – offices which few seek and even fewer attain. Thus, at this level, career considerations loom large. Nelson Rockefeller (R., N.Y.) holds at least the modern record for service as governor: 15 years. Indeed, Schlesinger shows that of the 151 governors serving during the decade 1950–59, only 30.5 percent served more than 4 years. However, by the time of Rockefeller's resignation from the governorship in December 1973, thirty-five members of the Senate had equalled or surpassed his length of tenure, and 60 percent had served more than four years.

A final consideration in this regard is one noted by Schlesinger:

The second manifest tie between offices is the similarity of functions. The legislative function requires similar skills and talents whether in the city council or the federal Senate. Different demands are made upon judges or executives. . . . Manifestly, the functional resemblance of offices is a condition which affects the course of political careers.

On all of these grounds – greater length of term, lower electoral vulnerability, greater career prospects, and similarity of functions – we would expect, in general, members of the House to place a higher value on a Senate seat than a governorship, and we are thus led to our first hypothesis.

H_1: *Among House members, the proportion of opportunities to run for the Senate that is taken will be greater than the proportion of opportunities taken to run for governor.*

While we argue that Senate seats are more attractive than governorships, it is clear that not all governorships are equally attractive. Governorships differ in the powers the occupant of the office has under the various state constitutions. We would expect that a House member from a state with a powerful governorship would find that office more attractive than would a member from a state with a weak governorship.

While we do not have data on governors' powers for the entire period under consideration, and therefore cannot test this expectation, there is one feature on which governorships differ and on which the data are readily available: length of term. We have already noted that an office with a longer term should be generally more attractive than an office with a shorter term, and that states vary in the length they set for their governor's term. A member of the House, who serves a two-year term, is going to find an alternative office which also has a two-year term less attractive, ceteris paribus, than an alternative office with a four-year term. Therefore, our second hypothesis is:

H₂: *Among House members, the proportion of opportunities to run for governorships with a four-year term that is taken will be greater than the proportion of opportunities taken to run for governorships with a two-year term.*

(2) *The probability of winning the higher office.* We assumed above that a member of the House would accept a Senate seat or governorship if they could get it without cost or risk. However, such circumstances are seldom, if ever, present. Members seeking higher office often have to bear substantial costs and risks. For many members the probability of winning the higher office will be relatively small, while for others it will be substantially larger.

One factor that will affect the probability of winning higher office is whether or not the office in question is held by an incumbent running for reelection. As we have seen incumbent Senators and governors have a substantially better than even chance of being reelected. Thus the risk of running against an incumbent is a good deal greater than the risk of running if there is no incumbent in the race. Indeed, for an actor who has decided to make a try for another office, such considerations can determine the timing of such an attempt. A former governor who decided to run for an open Senate seat rather than seek reelection said:

We were talking very realistically about the situation that would evolve if I were to run for reelection as governor. Then that term would have ended with—'s term in the Senate, and if I were then to try for the Senate I would be running against an incumbent who had been in office a couple of terms, and obviously if I wanted to be realistic it is a lot easier getting in if somebody is stepping out and you don't run against an incumbent in either party, and I couldn't do better than the chance that was afforded me.

Thus the third hypothesis is:

H₃: *Among House members, for both Senate and gubernatorial races, the proportion of opportunities to run for higher office that is taken in situations where no incumbent is seeking reelection will be greater than the proportion of opportunities taken in situations where an incumbent is seeking reelection.*

In addition to incumbency, another factor that will affect the probability of winning is the partisan bias of the electoral situation. Although party identification is no longer the dependable predictor of voting that it once was, there do remain some states (notably those in the deep South) which are relatively "safe" for one party or the other. If this is so, then obviously the likelihood of a candidate winning in a state which is "safe" for the other party is less than if the state is competitive or safe for his own party. Therefore:

H₄: *Among House members, for both Senate and gubernatorial races, the proportion of opportunities to run for higher office that is taken in states which are "safe" for the opposition party will be less than the proportion of opportunities taken in states which are competitive or "safe" for their own party.*

A final consideration which will affect the probability of winning relates to the base from which a candidate runs. It is fairly well known that name recognition is an important consideration in electoral situations. Potential candidates often poll their prospective constituency to determine how well known they are, and the results of such polls affect their decision on whether or not to run. Whether a candidate is known to a voter affects that voter's decision. One thing that will have a substantial impact on voter recognition is the degree of overlap between the constituency a prospective candidate presently represents and the constituency he would like to represent. For example, a randomly selected voter from Delaware is more likely to have heard of the single congressman from that state than is a randomly selected voter from California to have heard of any one of the state's 43 congressmen. A senator from a state with only one congressional seat, when asked why he gave up a safe House seat to run for the Senate, said:

Basically it was the same race . . . on the Senate side, of course, my predecessor was stepping down, so that in a way I was the person that was being challenged whether it was in the House or Senate.

Therefore, we argue that the greater the degree of overlap between a potential candidate's present constituency and his prospective constituency, the more likely he is to seek higher office.

Thus, in general, we would expect congressmen from small states to be more likely to run for higher office than congressmen from large states. There is, however, an additional factor affecting the value of the higher office which leads us to modify this expectation. While we would expect that there is little difference between the attractiveness of a Senate seat from a big state and one from a small state, such would not seem to be true in the case of governorships. First, and tautologically, a governor from a large state governs more people than one from a small state. He can have a substantial impact on the lives of a larger number of people, usually deals with a greater range of public policy matters, and is more likely to be observed by the national media. Second, there appears to be a relationship between the size of a state and the powers granted to its governor. Schlesinger has constructed an index of the powers of governors in 1969. If we divide the states by whether they are above or below the median state population and also divide them by whether they are above or below the median value of Schlesinger's index, it appears that in 1969 large states had relatively more powerful governors, and small states relatively weaker ones. Among the large states, 64 percent were above the median index value, while among the small states only 28 percent were above the median.

For governorships, then, something of an inverse relationship exists between the attractiveness of the office and the probability of winning. Thus there should be no clear effect from state size on House members seeking governorships, and so we restrict our next hypothesis to Senate candidacies:

H_5: *Among House members, for Senate races, the probability that a House member will run will be directly related to the proportion of the state's population, the population of his House constituency comprises.*

(3) *The value of the House seat.* It is commonplace to note that power in the House rests largely in its committees, and that the way to power in committees is through the seniority system. This is still largely true despite recent reforms designed to reduce the power of committee chairmen. Therefore, if we assume that a major motivation of members is to have power within the House (whether for its own sake, to increase their probability of winning reelection, or because they are concerned about policy outcomes), then the more senior a member is, the more power he will have, the higher will be the value of his seat to him, and the less likely he will be to seek higher office. Thus hypothesis six states:

H_6: *For both Senate and gubernatorial races, the probability that a House member will run will be inversely related to his seniority.*

(4) *Risk acceptance and progressive ambition.* To this point, our theory has outlined the impact of various situational factors (or the "opportunity structure") on the congressman's decision on whether to seek higher office. These situational factors determine the risks a potential candidate must face in trying to move up. The risks do not, however, tell the whole story. That is, if two candidates are faced with the same [probability of winning] and [cost of running], and each has an identical preference ordering in which [higher office] is preferred to [the current office] which is preferred to [holding no

office], it may still be the case that one will run and the other will not. This is because some people are more likely to select risky alternatives than are others. People with the same preference ordering will differ in the *intensity* of those preferences. One representative may find a Senate seat more desirable than his House seat, but only slightly so, while either is very strongly preferred to having no office. A second congressman may find the higher office enormously more attractive than his present one, which is only slightly preferable to returning to private life. The latter is the kind of person we conventionally refer to as ambitious, and he will accept far greater risks to achieve the higher office than will the former. Indeed, we believe that it is differences in intensity of preference, and thus willingness to take electoral risks in seeking offices, that distinguishes the ambitious politician from the nonambitious.

These considerations lead us to our next hypothesis:

H_7: *If two House members are presented with similar opportunities to seek higher office, and one is a "risk taker" and the other is not, then the "risk taker" will have a greater probability of running for higher office than the other.*

This concludes the discussion of hypotheses on which we will bring data to bear. We will discuss further consequences of our theory after presenting some empirical results.

THE DATA

The data used to test the hypotheses relate to all members of the U.S. House of Representatives who were presented with an opportunity to run for either a Senate seat or the governorship in elections between 1954 and 1974 inclusive. To test the hypotheses we require information on the length of governors' terms, whether an incumbent is running for reelection to the prospective higher office, the degree of interparty competitiveness of the state, the size of the state, and the seniority of each congressional incumbent.

We consider a member to have an opportunity to run for higher office if he is a member of Congress (subject to the exceptions discussed below) in a year when an election is held in his state for a Senate seat or the governorship, and the office in question is either held by an incumbent of the other party or has no incumbent seeking reelection. Thus for the present study we do not consider the possibility of a congressman opposing an incumbent of his own party. While we expect the nature of the calculations to be basically the same in such a case, the situations are quite different and require separate analyses.

We have already stated that we would exclude members with discrete ambition from our theoretical discussion and from our empirical analysis. Therefore, members who resign from the House or who announce their retirement at the end of a term are not considered to have had an opportunity to run for higher office. Second, since our consideration of progressive ambition is limited to the Senate and governorships, any House member who ran for any other office is excluded from the analysis. Third, since we have limited our discussion to situations where a congressman must give up his House seat to run for higher office, five states which elect their governors at times other than November of even numbered years are omitted from the analysis of members seeking governorships, as are members from other states who run in special elections held at times other than November of even numbered years. Finally, we exclude from our analysis of any given election all members who were elected to the House in special elections since the previous November election. Because of the necessity of planning ahead for a statewide race, such congressmen are almost precluded from running and, in fact, no such member did run.

Of course, to test hypothesis seven we need some indicator of which members of the House are risk takers. One possibility would be to develop a questionnaire which contains indicators of willingness to take risks, and administer the questionnaire to a set of potential candidates. The costs, however, would be great and such a course would be impossible with the timespan with which we are dealing. Instead, we assume that it is possible to employ previous behavior as an indicator of risk taking. Specifically, we examined the situation in which each member first sought election to the House. We classified situations in which (1) an incumbent was running for reelection, or (2) no incumbent was running, but the other party averaged 57 percent or more of the vote in the three previous elections as high risk situations and a member who first sought election in such a situation was classified as a risk taker. A race with no incumbent that did not fit (2) above was classified as low risk, and members who first sought election in such a situation are classified as "others."

This compilation yields a data set of 3,040 opportunities to run, of which 111 (or 3.7%) were taken.

TESTING THE HYPOTHESES

Table 12.1 presents the data on hypotheses one and two, relating to the relative value of the higher offices, controlling for whether or not the members are risk takers. Overall, House members are about three times more likely to run for senator than for a four-year governorship and about eleven times more than a two-year governorship. This pattern is true for both risk takers and for others. Again overall, risk takers are about two and one-half times more

Table 12.1. *Proportion of Members Running for Higher Office, Controlling for Risk Taking and Type of Office*

Office:	Member Is:		
	Risk Taker	Other	Total
Two-Year Governorship	0.6 (180)*	0.4 (252)	0.5 (432)
Four-Year Governorship	3.6 (522)	0.8 (623)	2.1 (1145)
Senate Seat	7.8 (715)	3.9 (748)	5.8 (1463)
TOTAL	5.4 (1417)	2.2 (1623)	3.7 (3040)

* Number of opportunities.

Table 12.2. *Proportion of Members Running for Higher Office, Controlling for Risk Taking and Probability of Winning*

Member is:	Percent of Opportunities Taken When Probability of Winning Was:		
	High	Low	Total
Risk Taker	6.0 (603)*	4.9 (814)	5.3 (1417)
Other	2.8 (795)	1.6 (828)	2.2 (1623)
TOTAL	4.1 (1398)	3.2 (1642)	3.7 (3040)

* Number of opportunities.

likely to run for higher office than are nonrisk takers.

In order to make the compilation of data manageable, we combined the test of hypotheses three and four. Members who faced an opportunity to run were placed in one of two categories: low probability of winning or high probability of winning. The former category included members who would have to face an incumbent, or who were in a state in which the other party averaged 57 percent or more of the vote for senator and governor over the previous four years; the latter category includes other members. Thus our combined prediction is that the proportion of members who run for higher office when the probability of winning is high will be greater than the proportion who run when the probability is low. Table 12.2 presents the relevant data.

While the results are in the predicted direction, the impact of probability of winning appears to be minimal. The reason for this apparent lack of relationship becomes clear, however, when we control for type of office (see Table 12.3). When we compare each cell in part A (the upper half) of Table 12.3 to the corresponding cell in part B, we almost always find a fairly substantial difference between the two proportions. The difference between the results here and those in Table 12.2 is due to the fact that Senate races offered mostly low probability opportunities while gubernatorial

Table 12.3. *Proportion of Members Running for Higher Office, Controlling for Risk Taking, Probability of Winning, and Type of Office*

A. PROBABILITY OF WINNING IS HIGH

	Member Is:		
Office	Risk Taker	Other	Total
Two-Year Governorship	1.1 (90)*	0.0 (124)	0.5 (214)
Four-Year Governorship	4.5 (309)	1.2 (410)	2.6 (719)
Senate Seat	10.3 (204)	6.5 (261)	8.2 (465)
TOTAL	6.0 (603)	2.8 (795)	4.1 (1398)

B. PROBABILITY OF WINNING IS LOW

	Member Is:		
Office	Risk Taker	Other	Total
Two-Year Governorship	0.0 (90)	0.8 (128)	0.5 (218)
Four-Year Governorship	2.3 (213)	0.0 (213)	1.2 (426)
Senate Seat	6.8 (511)	2.5 (487)	4.7 (998)
TOTAL	4.9 (814)	1.6 (828)	3.2 (1642)

* Number of opportunities.

races offered primarily high probability opportunities. (This is because incumbents are more likely to be involved in Senate races.)

The data in Table 12.3 offer a fairly strong test of the theory since the first four hypotheses plus hypothesis seven are all considered simultaneously. We can see that each of the elements that have been considered thus far have independent effects. If we look at the highest probability case from the point of view of the theory (risk takers with Senate opportunities and a high probability of winning), the proportion who run is more than one in ten, while in a number of low probability cases the proportion running is zero. The fact, however, that in the most attractive situation reflected in this table only one opportunity in ten is taken indicates how high the risks are even then. The situation is, again, only attractive relative to the others, not in absolute terms.

The reader will note that there is one cell in Table 12.3 that breaks the predicted pattern (nonrisk taker, two-year governorship, low probability of winning). This deviation is due to a single member seeking office, and as is often true the deviant case is instructive. In 1962, as a result of the 1960 census, Michigan gained one House seat. It was made an at-large seat, and Neil Staebler (a Democrat) won it. In 1964, the state was redistricted and the at-large seat was eliminated. Also in 1964, both a Senate seat and the governorship were up for election. The Senate seat was held by a popular Democrat, Philip Hart, who was seeking reelection. The governorship was held by Republican George Romney who was also first elected in 1962, defeating an incumbent Democrat with 51.4 percent of the vote, and who was running for a second term. Romney was the first Republican to win the governorship since 1946. Thus Staebler was presented with a number of alternatives. He could *not* run for reelection since his seat had disappeared, but he could (1) run for nothing (obviously unattractive); (2) run in one of the new open House districts (unattractive for someone who had already won a statewide race); or (3) run from his statewide base against an incumbent Republican governor who had won office with a smaller margin than he himself had received, in what appeared to be a superb year for a Democrat (obviously not an ideal alternative, but apparently the best of those available). Furthermore, while the governor's term was only two years, under the new Michigan Constitution the next election would be for a four-year term. Staebler chose the third option and was soundly trounced by Romney.

One alternative available to test hypothesis five would have been to ascertain the population of each congressional district, determine the proportion of the state's population contained within each district, and then rank the districts in terms of these proportions. Since, however, population figures on districts are based on census data and such figures become progressively more unreliable as the time since the census increases, we have followed the simpler course of determining the amount of overlap between

Table 12.4. *Proportion of Members Running for Senator, Controlling for Risk Taking and Number of Districts in State*

Number of Districts in State	Percent of Opportunities Taken When Member Is:		
	Risk Taker	Other	Total
1 or 2	45.9 (37)*	28.3 (46)	36.1 (83)
3–6	9.3 (86)	11.3 (53)	10.1 (139)
7–10	4.9 (182)	2.4 (124)	3.9 (306)
11–19	6.5 (124)	1.8 (163)	3.8 (287)
22 or more	4.9 (286)	1.1 (362)	2.8 (648)
TOTAL	7.8 (715)	3.9 (748)	5.8 (1463)

* Number of opportunities.

the district constituency and the statewide constituency by the number of congressional districts the state has. We then group the states into five categories: 1 or 2 districts, 3–6 districts, 7–10 districts, 11–19 districts, and 22 or more districts. These data are presented in Table 12.4

We see that the prediction is supported by the data. For both risk takers and others combined, the proportion of opportunities taken decreases monotonically as the number of districts in a state increases. Moreover, the relationship is clearly not linear. The likelihood of a House member seeking a Senate seat in a state with only one or two districts, where the constituency overlap is great, is more than one in three. This drops sharply to about one in ten for the next category, drops sharply again for the third, with the proportion of opportunities taken in the last three categories being about the same. Furthermore, in four of the five district categories, a comparison of the proportions for risk takers and for others shows that the former is substantially larger than the latter. Indeed, in the theoretically most attractive situation (risk takers, 1 or 2 districts) the proportion that runs approaches one in two, forty times larger than the least attractive situation.

We now turn to the last of our initial hypotheses. During the initial analysis for this paper, seniority data were not compiled. We were, therefore, going to test the seniority hypothesis in a future version of this analysis. However, some information bearing on the hypothesis can be presented, so it was decided to include it here, although it is largely retrospective data. The average number of consecutive terms in office served by House members between 1953 and 1969 was 5.22; the average number of terms served by the 111 members who ran for higher office was 3.52. Thus House members seeking higher office served about one and one-half terms less than the average House member. Furthermore, we find that the amount of seniority possessed by candidates varies with risk-taking category, type of office, and probability of winning (see Table 12.5). Among members who sought Senate seats, the only large difference is between members with the least attractive opportunity

Table 12.5. *Seniority of House Members Seeking Higher Office, Controlling for Risk Taking, Type of Office, and Probability of Winning*

A. SENATE SEAT

Member Is	Probability of Winning Was		
	High	Low	Total
Risk Taker	4.05 (21)	3.46 (35)	3.68 (56)
Other	3.88 (17)	2.58 (12)	3.34 (29)
TOTAL	3.97 (38)	3.23 (47)	3.56 (85)

B. GOVERNORSHIP

Member Is	Probability of Winning Was		
	High	Low	Total
Risk Taker	4.19 (16)	2.50 (4)	3.85 (20)
Other	2.00 (5)	1.00 (1)	1.83 (6)
TOTAL	3.67 (21)	2.20 (5)	3.38 (26)

Note: Cell entries give the mean consecutive terms served by members in the cell (number of members in cell in parentheses).

(nonrisk taker, low probability of winning) and all those in other cells. However, most of the other possible comparisons (e.g., among gubernatorial candidates) show more substantial differences. This is, of course, the least direct test of any of the hypotheses, and the results must be regarded as extremely tentative.

SUMMARY AND CONCLUSIONS

This study has differed from most other analyses of ambition in two ways: first, we have attempted to give a more concrete theoretical base to the study of progressive ambition, and second, our analysis has been prospective rather than retrospective. That is, we have attempted to predict which potential candidates would actually run for higher office, rather than analyze the career patterns of actors who ran.

We chose as the context of our analysis members of the U.S. House and the decision on whether or not to seek a Senate seat or a governorship. The period of analysis was 1954 to 1974. We assumed that progressive ambition was widespread among members of the House, that House members are maximizers of expected utility, and that the decision on seeking higher office is dependent on the probability of win-

ning, the value of an office, and the costs of running, with each of the three factors applied to both the House seat and the potential higher office.

We then offered a number of hypotheses about progressive ambition among House members. The data supported the following predictions: (1) congressmen are more likely to run for a Senate seat than for a governorship; (2) congressmen are more likely to run for governor if the term of office is four years rather than 2; (3) congressmen are more likely to seek higher office if the probability of winning is high rather than low (where low probability is indicated by an incumbent running for reelection or the state being safe for the opposition party); and (4) congressmen are more likely to run for the Senate in a small state than a large one. In addition, it appears that less senior congressmen are more likely to seek higher office than more senior congressmen.

We also introduced the concept of *risk taking*. We argued that risk takers were more likely to seek higher office than members who were not risk takers. We employed the situation in which a congressman first sought a House seat as an indicator of willingness to take risks. The data supported the prediction in almost all the situations that were examined.

CHAPTER THIRTEEN

Issue Politics in Congress – Excerpts

Tracy Sulkin

Sulkin argues who candidates that win congressional elections regularly and systematically assume their challengers priority issues from the preceding campaign and take legislative action on them while in office, a practice she terms "issue uptake." Campaign winners engage in uptake behavior, according to Sulkin, because they are motivated by reelection. Because challengers focus their criticism on incumbents weaknesses, the issues that challengers center on in campaigns send a valuable signal to winning legislators regarding issue areas they may have previously overlooked.

ELECTORAL CHALLENGES AND LEGISLATIVE RESPONSIVENESS

Going into his first reelection campaign in 1992, Senator Bob Graham was about as secure as any incumbent facing a challenge could hope to be. Though new to the Senate, he had a long history in Florida politics, including many years of service in the state legislature and two terms as governor. Endorsed by a host of newspapers and interest groups, he was described by many as the state's most popular politician, largely as the result of his reputation for action on environmental and economic issues of interest to his constituents. During his active and well-funded campaign, Graham further leveraged

Tracy Sulkin. 2005. "Electoral Challenges and Legislative Responsiveness" and "A Theory of Issue Uptake" in Tracy Sulkin, *Issue Politics in Congress* (Cambridge University Press), 1–42. Copyright © 2005. Reprinted with the permission of Cambridge University Press.

these strengths by highlighting his competence and interest in the economy, the environment, and the proper role of governmental regulation.

In contrast, his opponent, Republican representative Bill Grant, faced an even greater uphill battle than most challengers. Hurt by his record of overdrafts at the House bank and his recent switch from the Democratic to the Republican Party, Grant experienced considerable difficulty raising funds, eventually raising only $2,000,000 to Graham's $3 million. Characterized by *St. Petersburg Times* political reporter Bill Moss as having "drive, but no fuel," he nonetheless launched a spirited campaign against Graham, focusing on health care, economic issues, and the need for a balanced budget.

Not surprisingly, Graham won the race easily, netting nearly two-thirds of the vote. When he returned to Washington, he continued to pursue his interests in the environment and in general economic issues, introducing and cosponsoring legislation and serving on the Environment and Public Works and Banking, Housing, and Urban Affairs committees. More unexpectedly, perhaps, he also became much more active on Grant's priority issues from the campaign. In the term following the election, he introduced twenty-three bills, resolutions, and amendments relating to health issues (on topics ranging from public health and health education to ensuring emergency care and preventive health benefits to health maintenance organization enrollees to regulating the quality of hospitals), more than twice as many as he had introduced in the previous term. He also introduced thirteen measures on balancing the budget, more than four times as many as he had before.

Graham's attentiveness to Grant's issues is not a coincidence, nor is it unusual. To the contrary, it reflects a widespread yet largely unrecognized mode of responsiveness in the U.S. Congress. Winning legislators regularly take up their challengers' priority issues from the last campaign and act on them in office, a phenomenon I call "issue uptake." Congressional campaigns thus have a clear legacy in the content of legislators' agendas, influencing the areas in which they choose to be active and the intensity with which they pursue these activities. Moreover, as I will show, the extent of this legacy varies in a predictable way across individual representatives and senators, across legislative activities, across time, and across chambers of Congress. Understanding the factors leading to variation in uptake therefore offers fresh insight into some of the most important and enduring normative and empirical questions in American politics regarding the electoral connection in legislative behavior, the role of campaigns and elections, and the nature and quality of congressional responsiveness.

Legislators' motivation for engaging in uptake behavior is simple; they undertake it because they believe that doing so will help them to achieve their electoral goals. Because challengers focus their campaigns on the incumbent's weaknesses, their choices of campaign themes provide signals to winning legislators about important issues that they may have previously neglected. To the extent that legislators act on these signals, taking up salient issues and making them a part of their agendas, they can remedy any weaknesses, strengthening their records before the next campaign and inoculating themselves against possible attacks. Uptake thus has the potential to promote individual legislators' electoral goals as well as the health and legitimacy of the representative process, as legislators adjust their activity in office in response to electoral challenges. The central theme of this book is to explore these possibilities by investigating the dynamics of uptake, explaining

why it occurs, how it varies, what it reveals about legislators' motivations and decision making, and how it impacts the policymaking process.

Defining Uptake

By explicitly specifying the process through which legislators' activity in office is related to their campaign experiences, the study of uptake makes a significant advance in [improving or understanding of the linkages between electoral and legislative politics]. Though I focus on uptake as a mechanism for connecting campaigns to legislative behavior, it has its scholarly roots in other subfields of political science, particularly political communication and political theory. Scholars in these fields studying deliberation and discursive processes have been interested in determining the conditions under which ideas expressed by certain participants are incorporated into the arguments of others. If, for example, in a discussion about the merits of a particular tax policy, one discussant raises the issue of its impact on the budget deficit, do other discussants also address this point? To the extent that they do, uptake has occurred, and the deliberative process itself can be judged to be more successful, at least from a procedural standpoint.

In the congressional setting, uptake is conceived of in a slightly different way, going beyond language to focus on other types of behavior, in particular, participation in the legislative process, including legislators' sponsorship and cosponsorship of bills, resolutions, and amendments and their statements on the floor about pending legislation. If a challenger focuses her campaign on agriculture, defense, and education, uptake is measured as the amount of attention the winning legislator devotes to these issues in his legislative activity when he returns to Congress. Graham's introduction of measures on health care and the balanced budget is thus evidence of his uptake of Grant's themes.

At its roots, then, uptake is fundamentally about legislative responsiveness, as representatives and senators use their time in office to

respond to and address their previous challengers' critiques. Uptake levels provide an
indicator of this responsiveness, both for individual legislators and for Congress as a whole.
At the individual level, we can compare the rates
of uptake across legislators to place an individual
legislator's behavior in context. For example, we
can determine whether Graham's level of attention to his challenger's themes is relatively high,
relatively low, or somewhere in-between. Such
analyses also enable us to identify the factors
that distinguish those legislators who are highly
responsive to their challengers' critiques from
those who are less so and to predict uptake levels based on characteristics of a legislator or his
or her constituency. Similarly, aggregate uptake
patterns across all legislators allow us to assess the
strength of *institutional* responsiveness – the success of the institutions of representative democracy at transmitting issues from one stage of the
process to another as issues are introduced in
campaigns, incorporated into legislative activity, and translated into public policy. We can
investigate whether the legacy of campaigns is
stronger in certain types of activities than others, or at certain times within legislative terms,
and use these findings to estimate the longevity
of uptake effects. Although the opportunity to
study individual and institutional agenda-based
responsiveness is in some ways a side consequence of modeling the linkages between campaigns and legislative behavior, it is a critically
important one. By quantifying and measuring
uptake levels, we gain a new perspective on the
dynamics of the relationship between the electoral and legislative arenas as well as a more
nuanced understanding of the nature of legislative responsiveness.

As may be obvious, my approach is greatly
influenced by the agenda-setting tradition in
public policy, political communication, and
public opinion research. At the core of the
agenda-setting paradigm is a focus on issues:
how they arise, how they change, and how they
are communicated and acted on by different
actors in the political process. Within the public policy field, this tradition is exemplified by
the work of scholars who have studied agenda
formation and change at the national level.

In political communication research, the focus
has been on the microfoundations of agenda-
setting, examining in particular the relationship between the amount of media coverage
given to issues and the extent to which they are
perceived as important problems by the public.
Public opinion scholars have, in turn, attempted
to unite the insights of these two fields to focus
on the relationships between the governmental,
public, and media agendas.

The agenda-setting perspective is much less
familiar to scholars of legislative behavior, where
the focus has traditionally been not on legislators' relative attention to different issues, but on
the positions they take on roll call votes, which
are generally interpreted as manifestations of
their underlying ideological preferences. This
focus on preferences has informed nearly all of
the literature on legislative representation and
responsiveness. An agenda-based approach like
uptake thus constitutes a fundamentally different way of thinking about responsiveness.

AGENDAS, UPTAKE, AND LEGISLATIVE RESPONSIVENESS

An agenda-based approach to understanding
the linkages between campaigns and legislative
behavior reflects a clear theoretical departure
from previous research on Congress. Most fundamentally, it constitutes a major reconceptual-
ization and expansion of the concept of responsiveness: in legislative behavior, in campaigns,
and in congressional agenda-setting. By explicitly connecting all stages of the political process – legislators' experiences as candidates in
campaigns, their subsequent activities in office,
and the impact of these individual decisions on
the content of public policy outcomes – into
a single model, the uptake approach yields a
broader and more nuanced conception of individual and institutional responsiveness.

At the level of the individual legislator, it
shifts the expected locus of policy responsiveness, away from a sole focus on legislative voting decisions and toward the content
of agendas. Responsive legislators are those
who use their activity in office to demonstrate

attentiveness to salient issues they may have previously neglected. By linking legislators' experiences as candidates to their behavior as policy makers, uptake also highlights the *process* of responsiveness, as legislators learn about potential issue weaknesses in campaigns and then adjust their behavior in response to this new information.

At the institutional level, uptake provides an indicator of collective responsiveness: how attentive Congress as a whole is to the issues raised in campaigns. As a consequence, the study of uptake offers new lever age into understanding how information is processed and agendas are set in Congress. A perennial topic of interest in policy research has been the dynamics of agenda change – how it is that new issues reach individual legislators' agendas and the broader congressional agenda. [It has been] argued, for example, that agendas change when losers in the current status quo effectively introduce new cleavages and expand the scope of conflict. Although [this perspective views] minority parties or pressure groups as the agents of change, in my formulation challengers fulfill this role. In their efforts to unseat incumbents, they highlight their issue weaknesses, which are then picked up by the winners and incorporated into their agendas in order to avoid difficulties in future elections. In looking out for their own electoral interests, legislators contribute (albeit unintentionally) to the process of agenda change in Congress.

This point underscores the need for a reassessment of the importance of campaigns and elections in general and the role of challengers in particular. From the perspective of uptake, congressional campaigns matter not just because they may influence voters, but because they *clearly* influence winners, shaping the content of their agendas in the next Congress. Previous challengers' campaigns provide the target for uptake, and the threat of future challengers provides the motivation for responsiveness. This conception is in contrast to past research on challengers, which has generally focused on defining what it means to be a "quality" challenger and on explaining the emergence of such challengers. The basic argument in this literature is that challengers are important because of the role they can play in educating voters about differences between the candidates and because they occasionally upset incumbents, serving to promote accountability and possibly change the partisan composition of Congress. The uptake approach gives a new role to challengers – influencing the downstream policy agendas of winners. As such, it changes the location of incumbents' responsiveness to their challengers, away from the campaign and toward the floor of Congress. A growing literature in political communication focuses on dialogue and deliberation between candidates in campaigns. Theorists and pundits alike often lament the lack of discussion and debate on the issues as a sign of unresponsiveness. However, even if candidates do not engage in a back-and-forth dialogue on the issues, incumbents can still respond to their challengers in an arguably more meaningful way, through the content of their activity in office.

A THEORY OF ISSUE UPTAKE

The model of uptake requires that legislators recognize and act on their challengers' campaign issues. I proposed that engaging in this behavior is a strategic choice, undertaken by legislators who believe that it will promote their reelection goals. Presumably, all other things being equal, legislators would not choose to act on their challengers' themes, as paying attention to these issues diverts attention from other issues that may be of more intrinsic interest to them. However, to the extent that doing so helps them to accomplish their electoral goals, they have a clear incentive to look to their previous campaign experiences when formulating their agendas. Of course, reelection is not legislators' only goal; they may also want to make good public policy or to achieve influence in Congress. They may also wish to be good representatives, faithfully reflecting their constituency's interests, apart from any tangible benefit they may receive. Nonetheless, rational legislators should recognize that they cannot achieve these other goals unless they are able to remain in office, and so reelection is, for the majority, the most proximate goal.

This idea of the electoral connection, that, while in office, "congressmen must constantly engage in activities related to reelection," has become central to the study of legislative behavior. The possible mechanisms for this connection are numerous and are discussed in more detail later. In general, though, the lesson that comes from this literature is that the optimal legislative strategy for reelection-oriented representatives and senators is to use their time in Congress to build on their strengths and shore up their weaknesses. Uptake helps them to do the latter, and so has the potential to promote the reelection goal in several ways. Most simply, constituents may recognize and reward responsive behavior on the part of their legislators, forming more positive evaluations of their performance in office and increasing their likelihood of reelecting them. However, even if constituents don't directly recognize and reward responsiveness, it may still pay off indirectly. If a legislator's next challenger raises some of the same issues, a record of uptake may help him or her to counter these critiques more effectively. The criticism that a representative does not pay enough attention to an issue like education or agriculture or the budget loses much of its punch if the legislator can point to recent activity on the issue. Perhaps the best possible benefit of a record of responsiveness, however, is that it may prevent potentially strong challengers from deciding to run in the first place, thus increasing the probability that the incumbent will be reelected.

The purpose [here] is to explore these possibilities and develop a theory of uptake behavior at the individual level. This "strategic motivation" theory explains why challengers' campaign themes serve as a particularly important and effective signal to legislators about their relative issue weaknesses, why legislators should be motivated to take up these signals, how they make choices about when and where to demonstrate their responsiveness, and the mechanism through which this behavior pays off for them. In the process, it points to a number of predictions about variation in uptake that have

important implications for our assessments of the nature and quality of individual and institutional responsiveness.

Campaign Themes and Issue Salience

The general argument underlying my theory of uptake is that legislators stand to gain electorally by using their time in office to act on the "right" issues. Correctly identifying these issues is a critical task; because the size of their agendas is limited both by time and by resources, legislators simply can't be active in every realm of legislative activity or devote high levels of attention to every issue that might potentially be of interest to them or to their constituents. During the 1990s, for example, nearly 10,000 bills and resolutions were introduced in the House and Senate in each Congress on a myriad of issues, many more than an individual legislator could ever hope to address. When choosing their agenda priorities, legislators should therefore be very sensitive to signals about which issues have potentially high payoffs for them in future elections.

Although most research on the campaign as an information source focuses on voters, campaigns also constitute an important source of information for legislators. Observing their challengers' selection of campaign themes provides a signal to incumbents about their relative strengths and weaknesses in the district or state. We know from previous work on candidate behavior that challengers are particularly strategic in their choice of issues – they carefully select those that they believe best highlight the incumbent's weaknesses; [it has been argued], for example, that it is not necessary for voters to search their representatives' records to look for possible weaknesses because challengers are more than happy to do this for them.

Challengers' incentives for adopting this strategy are clear. Most obviously, highlighting incumbents' inadequacies may enable challengers to decrease voters' overall evaluations of their performance and ability. More indirectly, but perhaps more importantly, such efforts may constitute "heresthetical maneuvers," aimed at adjusting the agenda to create a more favorable decision environment. "A challenger cannot hope to win without reordering the campaign agenda." By focusing their campaign appeals on themes on which their opponents are weak, challengers may be able to accomplish this, increasing the salience of these issues in voters' minds and leading them to weigh them more heavily in their decisions.

Challengers' campaigns should therefore serve to focus legislators' attention on their weaknesses. If incumbent legislators are un-aware that they have neglected salient issues, their challengers will certainly inform them about this in their campaigns. If they suspect that these issues may be important, the campaign will confirm this for them. Of course, there may be other sources of these signals, like newspaper editorials, interactions with constituents and potential donors, opposition research funded by a candidate's own campaign organization, and so on, but the challenger's signals should be particularly effective in attracting the attention of a legislator. Emotion plays an impor-tant role in the processing of political infor-mation. In particular, anxiety and threat serve to stimulate learning and the search for new information. Campaigning is an anxious time for legislators – their records, their style, and even their character are being scrutinized, and their reelection prospects may seem threatened. In the presence of a threat, legislators should become acutely aware of their weaknesses and the need to remedy them. A challenge from an opposing candidate provides just such a threat, and so should motivate legislators to engage in uptake.

Moreover, all winning candidates, even those who do not appear particularly vulnerable in the current election, have the incentive to pick up and act on these signals. This is because legisla-tors are concerned not just with the present, but also with the future. In particular, they worry about their district's or state's "poten-tial preferences" – those latent interests that might not currently be of primary concern but, with time and diligent attention from the leg-islators' critics, could become highly salient. Indeed, in a situation in which constituents are not particularly attentive to their representatives' records, challengers may even be able to cre-ate the perception of weakness on issues simply by highlighting them in their campaigns. Even if a legislator wins an election fairly easily, in a future campaign a stronger challenger could pick up on a past challenger's issues and exploit them more successfully, beating the incumbent. Most legislators have faced at least one close election in their careers and are understand-ably eager to avoid another one. For instance, in the 100th Congress, over half of the members of the House of Representatives and approx-imately three-quarters of those in the Senate had won at least one election with a vote share of less than 55 percent. This bad experience no doubt lingers in their minds, informing their behavior in office well into the future, even when they may no longer be objectively vulnerable.

From this perspective, it would be a mis-take to assume that because a given challenger lost, his or her campaign themes were inher-ently "losing issues." Challengers lose most of the time for a variety of reasons beyond their choices of campaign themes. A weak candidate may still raise important issues, and voters may wish to see the winner address those issues in the next Congress. And, even if a set of issues does not resonate particularly strongly in a district or state at the present time, continued atten-tion to these themes by challengers and other opponents of the incumbent may lead them to become more salient in the future. Many times issues aren't viewed as particularly salient when they are first raised but, after a period of "soft-ening up," come to be seen as priorities. The incentive, then, is for winners to be sensitive to early signals about their potential issue weak-nesses and to act on them to take these issues off the table for future challengers looking for openings for their critiques.

Senator Daniel Patrick Moynihan's (D-NY) experiences in the 1988 election provide a good illustration of such behavior. His challenger, Robert McMillan, attacked him on environ-mental issues, running campaign ads accusing him of a lack of attention and action on coastal pollution. Although Moynihan had a good record on the environment, coastal pollution was an issue of increasing salience to his constituents and an area in which he had not been particularly active, introducing only two bills in the term preceding McMillan's challenge. Moynihan went on to beat McMillan by a comfortable margin but, rather than ignoring his critiques, appeared to respond to them, introducing nine more bills on the environment in his next term than he had in the previous term (from 14 to 25 introductions). More to the point, six of these introductions dealt explicitly with coastal pollution, a record of attentiveness that undoubtedly made it difficult for his next challenger to echo McMillan's criticism.

The idea that incumbents' behavior in office can deter strong challenges is not a new one and is, in fact, one of the general expectations underlying electoral connection theories of legislative behavior. It has been addressed most directly by scholars interested in incumbent–challenger dynamics in congressional races. For example, a number of studies have concluded that quality challengers are more likely to enter a race when they perceive that the incumbent has weaknesses that they can exploit, and, in races where the incumbent was defeated, voters were more likely to report that the challenger was better suited to handling pressing problems.

As such, there is considerable evidence that legislators' activity in office can have important consequences for their electoral prospects or, at the very least, that they believe it can. If incumbents can thwart strong challenges through their activity, then challengers may serve as enforcement mechanisms for representation. In such a situation, responsiveness occurs "less through voters and the election itself than by members avoiding behavior that would precipitate a viable challenger and by their actively pursuing endeavors that would block competition." In short, elections can promote responsiveness not just by serving as a mechanism through which constituents can replace poorly performing legislators, but also by providing an incentive for all legislators to adapt their behavior in office to avoid a challenge. As legislators exhibit this responsiveness to the issue priorities of their challengers, they also bring about institutional

responsiveness, as information from campaigns is carried over into legislative behavior and public policy.

Predicting Variation in Uptake

To summarize, the theory of uptake I develop here is, at its roots, a strategic motivation theory. Legislators' desire to be reelected leads them to demonstrate attention to salient issues they may have previously ignored. Challengers' campaigns serve as a source of information to legislators about these issues because challengers purposefully focus their campaigns on their opponents' weaknesses. To the extent that winning legislators subsequently act on these signals, taking up their challengers' issues in their legislative activity, they are both responsive to their constituencies and attentive to their own electoral interests. Being a faithful representative can thus pay off for legislators in ways both tangible and intangible.

The motivations behind legislators' uptake decisions have important consequences for the quality of legislative responsiveness and for the content of public policy outputs. If we assumed that uptake had no impact on reelection, then we might expect that few legislators would engage in it, since it requires that attention and resources be diverted away from other issues with potentially higher payoffs. If, on the other hand, we assume that the strategic motivation theory is accurate and that legislators take up their challengers' issues to promote their reelection goals, then we should expect that uptake would be fairly widespread. The theory also points to a number of important predictions about variation in uptake, including who should engage in it the most, where in the process it should be most prevalent, its dynamics over time, and the influence of differing institutional settings. [The hypotheses] are as follows:

H1: INDIVIDUAL VARIATION – *Legislators' uptake levels will vary with their electoral vulnerability.*

H2: LOCATION OF UPTAKE – *Uptake will occur across all types of legislative activities, though levels of uptake should vary in relation to the difficulty and potential payoff of different activities.*

H3: TIMING OF UPTAKE – *For senators, uptake levels will increase as the next election grows nearer. For members of the House of Representatives, with shorter terms, there will be no variation in uptake levels within their terms.*

H4: VARIATION ACROSS INSTITUTIONS – *Uptake levels will be higher in the Senate than in the House of Representatives. Institutional differences between the chambers will also result in differences in patterns of responsiveness.*

H5: ELECTORAL IMPACT OF UPTAKE – *Engaging in uptake will, all other things equal, increase legislators' vote shares in the next election.*

Electoral Vulnerability and Legislative Behavior

Electoral vulnerability is expected to play an important role in explaining why some legislators are highly responsive, while others exhibit lower levels of uptake. Models that posit a linkage between vulnerability and legislative behavior are common in the literature. The basic argument is that legislators' need to be reelected leads them to engage in activities that promote this goal. Scholars recognize that legislators' vote shares are not entirely within their control. The partisan inclinations of their constituents, the diversity of interests in their district or state, the quality of their copartisans running for other offices, and national political and economic conditions can all influence their prospects. Nonetheless, the depiction of legislators as reelection-driven suggests that they do exert some control over their own electoral fortunes. Exploring these linkages between legislators' behavior in office and their success in elections is thus central to the study of representation and responsiveness.

Most empirical studies of these linkages hypothesize that vulnerable legislators should be more likely to engage in activities that promote reelection. [However], the evidence that vulnerability influences legislative behavior is mixed at best; some find the predicted effect and some find an unexpected effect, but many find no effect at all.

Given these results, why do I propose that vulnerability should be important in explaining uptake levels? First, the content of legislative activity has a more direct theoretical connection to reelection prospects than the sheer volume of activity, so we should expect that any effect of vulnerability would be stronger for levels of uptake than for overall levels of activity. Second, a review of the literature on vulnerability and legislative behavior suggests that there may be more of a relationship than is commonly assumed, but that our ability to recognize these effects has been limited by our unidirectional focus. Many scholars assume that only a positive relationship between vulnerability and activity supports the predictions of the electoral connection theory when, in fact, there are other possibilities that are equally consistent with this theory.

Most studies of vulnerability and legislative activity have focused on the volume of this activity undertaken by legislators, with the expectation that legislative activities provide representatives with the opportunity to engage in position-taking, advertising, or credit-claiming, and so promote reelection. However, very few detail how the connection between activity levels and reelection might occur, a point that is crucial for establishing a theoretical justification for the vulnerability hypothesis. How, then, might this linkage happen? Perhaps, one might argue, legislative productivity itself is rewarded, either directly or indirectly, by increasing constituents' evaluations of the incumbent or by forestalling strong challengers. It might not particularly matter what issues legislators are position-taking or credit-claiming on, as long as they are doing so on something. However, there is little empirical evidence to support this hypothesis.

It is not surprising that our findings about the relationship between volume of activity and vulnerability have been mixed. There is very little evidence that quantity of activity is rewarded, and, while it may be correlated with the "quality" of behavior (i.e., whether it indicates responsiveness to salient issues), this correlation is far from perfect. I argue that any relationship that exists between vulnerability and legislative behavior will be made clearer if we focus more directly on the content of legislative activity rather than on its volume, since the theoretical connection to reelection prospects is much more direct for the former.

Reassessing Vulnerability

To fully assess the linkage between vulnerability and uptake, we also need to reevaluate our expectations about the direction the effect should take. As mentioned previously, the standard prediction derived from electoral connection theories is that vulnerable legislators, who have the greatest fear of losing the next election, should be the most motivated to increase their safety and so should display the highest rates of reelection-promoting behavior. In the case of uptake, this hypothesis, which I term the "inoculation hypothesis," predicts that vulnerability will be positively related to responsiveness, with the most vulnerable legislators engaging in the most uptake in the hope that this behavior will ensure their return to Congress after the next election. Safer legislators will be less concerned with reelection and will therefore exhibit lower levels of responsiveness.

While this hypothesis is certainly reasonable, it is important to ask whether it is the *only* reasonable prediction. If we find that safer legislators are more active or more responsive than their vulnerable colleagues, does this necessarily contradict the electoral connection theory? Some have argued that it does.

However, such conclusions are potentially shortsighted because they take only a static view of vulnerability and behavior. If we take a more dynamic approach to understanding the linkages between the two, asking what it is that makes legislators safe or vulnerable in the first place, the finding of a negative relationship between vulnerability and a reelection-promoting activity like uptake appears perfectly consistent with electoral connection theories. To assume otherwise oversimplifies the original arguments made about the nature of these connections.

Legislators' relative levels of electoral safety can be interpreted as reflections of the quality of their past behavior. Safe legislators are safe because they were responsive, while vulnerable legislators are vulnerable because they were not. If these legislators continue to engage in similar patterns of behavior in the current term, we should expect to see a *negative* cross-sectional relationship between vulnerability and uptake, with the safest legislators engaging in the most. I call this prediction the "electoral selection" hypothesis.

The inoculation and electoral selection hypotheses share a number of assumptions, most importantly that engaging in uptake will promote reelection, so that legislators who exhibit a high level of responsiveness in one Congress will do better in the next election. Where they differ is in their predictions about what should happen next. The theory underlying the inoculation hypothesis suggests that, having successfully achieved their goal of making themselves safer, legislators will then choose to decrease their uptake and turn their attention to matters of more interest. As such, only the most vulnerable legislators will actively work to promote their electoral prospects. The electoral selection hypothesis tells a very different story: that, having hit upon a useful strategy for making themselves secure, legislators will continue to pursue this activity to maintain their newly acquired safety.

Despite the intuitive appeal of the inoculation hypothesis, the predictions of the more dynamic electoral selection hypothesis accord equally well with our knowledge of how legislators actually behave. As should be clear, these alternative hypotheses about the relationship between vulnerability and responsiveness have very different normative implications for how we assess the role of elections in encouraging responsiveness. If the inoculation hypothesis is accurate and the most vulnerable engage in the most uptake, then maintaining competition in congressional elections is of utmost importance because the safer legislators are, the less responsive they will be to their constituents' interests. If, however, the results support the electoral selection hypothesis, then we might conclude that our concerns about incumbency advantage and the "vanishing marginals" in these elections are misplaced. Instead, the electoral security we observe for incumbents should be seen as a manifestation of past responsiveness, and the prospect of future elections provides the incentive to continue to be attentive to important issues. Of course, it is also possible that there is no relationship between vulnerability and uptake, a finding that would necessitate further reassessment of the relationship between elections and legislative responsiveness.

Location of Uptake

Regardless of these results, explaining variation across legislators provides only part of the uptake story. The strategic motivation theory also points to other important predictions – for instance, about the location of uptake in the political process. Investigating location is important for two reasons. First, it presents another opportunity to evaluate the validity of the theory. Second, the location of uptake has important implications for its impact on public policy. If uptake occurs at high levels on policy-relevant activities like bill and resolution introductions, this suggests that it can have a substantial downstream influence on the content of policy. If, on the other hand, evidence of uptake is most prevalent on an activity like floor statements which may be useful for credit-claiming but has few direct policy implications, then we might conclude that its impact on policy is negligible.

For which types of activities should we expect the highest levels of uptake? The answer is not immediately obvious, as there is a trade-off between the relative ease of the activity and its amenability to credit-claiming. All activities require some effort, a point that is made clear when we examine patterns of activity for the typical legislator. In the 105th Congress, for example, a total of 5,982 bills and resolutions were introduced in the House and 3,159 were introduced in the Senate. The average representative introduced about fourteen measures and the average senator introduced about thirty. Legislators in both chambers cosponsored 200–300 of these measures (∼5–10 percent of the total) and spoke on the floor about 1–2 percent of them.

It is clearly the case that legislators are selective in their choice of activities, taking formal action on only a small proportion of the total number of measures. However, differences in the frequency with which various types of activities are undertaken do allow us to infer their relative difficulty. The patterns suggest that introductions are the most difficult activity and cosponsorships the easiest, with floor statements falling in between but closer to introductions. This claim accords with intuitions about the amount of effort required for each activity. While introducing a measure involves devoting staff resources to writing it up and possibly shepherding it through the chamber and making a floor statement requires learning enough about the issue to speak about it, cosponsorship entails only officially signing on to an existing piece of legislation.

This might lead us to conclude that uptake rates would be relatively low on introductions. However, while they are clearly the most difficult of the three activities, they also provide legislators with the strongest opportunity to claim credit. Introducing a bill or resolution sends a clear signal that a given issue is important enough to the legislator that he or she is willing to devote a relatively high amount of attention to it and attach his or her name to it. This is important in a setting like Congress, where most outcomes are the result of collective action and it can be difficult to carve out an individual reputation.

Thus, there is potentially much to be gained by using introductions to demonstrate uptake. However, since legislators are juggling multiple goals and interests, they may not be able or willing to devote all of their relatively scarce introductions to their challengers' issues. Other activities like cosponsorships and floor statements should serve as important complements, allowing legislators to enjoy some of the credit-claiming benefits of introductions without all of the costs. From the point of view of legislators, the primary benefit of cosponsorships is that there are numerous opportunities to engage in them that require almost no time or effort, so they serve as an "inexpensive signal" to constituents. Their corresponding weakness, however, particularly in the case of uptake, is that they do not provide a very strong basis for claiming credit. Cosponsorship reflects participation in a collective effort, rather than an individual one, and so should have a smaller payoff. Multiple cosponsorships in a single area may signal considerable interest in and attention to that area, but a single cosponsorship is not likely to do a legislator much good in claiming credit. Thus, while we should not expect that legislators will concentrate all of their uptake on cosponsorships, given their low cost and the possibility of a credit-claiming benefit, we should still expect to see evidence of relatively high levels of uptake for them.

Of the three types of activities, floor statements are the most difficult to make predictions about because they have received the least scholarly attention, and so our understanding of their relative utility to legislators is weaker. It seems, though, that compared to introductions and even cosponsorships, floor statements are very hard to build a claim of credit on. Merely talking about an issue is unlikely to demonstrate much attentiveness to it. However, these statements do have the potential to be visible to audiences at home in the district or state. They provide easy material for hometown newspapers or television stations looking for a short quote or sound bite and can be used by legislators in their advertising. Moreover, combined with a record of introductions and/or cosponsorships on an issue, impassioned speeches on the floor may enhance the effort to credit-claim, and while they require some effort, they are not very taxing. To the extent, then, that floor statements are used as a supplement to introductions and cosponsorships, uptake rates for them should not be substantially lower.

Each type of activity thus offers distinct advantages and disadvantages in the quest to claim credit. Cosponsorships and floor statements are easier and are undertaken more frequently, so we might expect a higher raw number of these activities to be "challenger-themed." Introductions, while more difficult, offer a clearer claim to credit, so, compared to the other activities, we might expect that a relatively higher proportion of them would

be devoted to uptake. Of course, differences in circumstances (e.g., vulnerability or seniority) may lead different legislators to devote different levels of these activities to uptake. Investigating these patterns is therefore interesting from both an empirical and a normative perspective.

TIMING OF UPTAKE

The choice of legislative activities is not the only decision that legislators face when planning their uptake strategies. They also must address the issue of timing. Should they concentrate on it the most at the beginning of the term, when the issues of the last election are freshest in the minds of legislators, constituents, and other interested observers? Or should they increase their levels of uptake as the term progresses and the next election grows nearer? The answer depends, at least in part, on what chamber of Congress one is considering. Up to this point, I have generally referred to "legislators" in general, but there are important differences between the House of Representatives and the Senate that should be taken into account. In terms of the timing of uptake, the biggest factor is the length of terms. Given their two-year terms, House members do not have the luxury of putting off electoral considerations. In the first year they are planning their reelection bids, and in the second they are actively campaigning. Most potential challengers decide whether or not to run in the year before the election, so early uptake should be crucial for representatives. As such, there is no reason to expect that uptake levels should differ across the first and second years of representatives' terms.

The situation in the Senate is very different. A six-year term gives legislators much more time to attend to their various interests. While uptake should be relatively high immediately following the election, it seems likely that it would wane in the middle of the term, as it gets trumped by other, more pressing concerns. However, as senators enter their third congress and the next election grows nearer, they should become more focused on their reelection prospects and so should increase their uptake. This hypothesis is in line with other work on Senate behavior, which finds that senators tend to become more visibly reelection-oriented as their terms progress. Of course, for a solely reelection-driven senator, this may not be the best strategy – high uptake levels across all congresses in a term would seem to be more optimal. However, given senators' multiple goals and their limited ability to attend to all of these goals simultaneously, the expected pattern is that uptake should reach its highest levels in the third and final congress of their terms.

Institutional Comparisons

The presence of such institutional distinctions between the chambers opens up the possibility of more fundamental differences in uptake between the House and Senate, both in levels of responsiveness and in the factors explaining individual variation in that responsiveness. In thinking about how this might occur, we should consider differences in representatives' and senators' ability to engage in uptake and in their incentive to do so. This requires that we take into account variations in the nature of legislative work in the two chambers and in the competitiveness of the elections that send representatives and senators to Washington.

The conventional wisdom is that the House should be more responsive than the Senate. This, of course, was the plan of the framers of the Constitution, who designed the Senate to be more insulated from popular control. While House members were to face direct election every two years, senators were appointed by state legislatures for six-year terms. Even after the ratification of the Seventeenth Amendment, implementing direct election of senators, the greater frequency of elections in the House and the smaller constituencies that members there represent have often led scholars to conclude that members of that chamber should be more responsive.

Recently, this assumption has been called into question [by work suggesting] that the two chambers may be equally responsive, but that this responsiveness occurs by different mechanisms. For the Senate, they argue that "the most important channel for governmental representation is electoral replacement." The House of Representatives is responsive because "its members employ rational anticipation to produce a similarly effective public-policy response." Thus, they claim that the House of Representatives responds through adaptations in behavior, while the Senate remains responsive because unrepresentative senators lose their reelection bids, bringing in new members whose positions more closely approximate those of the public. Disaggregating from institutions to individuals, these findings suggest that individual House members are fairly responsive, while individual senators are less so.

However, these conclusions are based on a definition of responsiveness that relies on positions or preferences – in short, on the level of collective policy congruence. I argue that, when we move away from voting patterns toward an agenda-based measure of responsiveness like uptake, the prediction should be the opposite – senators should rate more highly than representatives.

First and foremost, uptake requires that legislators have the ability and willingness to be entrepreneurial, extending beyond their areas of current expertise or interest to address new issues. Of the two chambers, the Senate is simply more amenable to this. The Senate is less tightly organized than the House, enabling senators much greater leeway in their behavior. Consequently, the structure of the Senate allows members to be generalists, and, perhaps equally importantly, the norms of the chamber encourage this. The House and the Senate are expected to address the same issues, but with only 100 members, it is much more difficult for the Senate to cover them than it is for the House, with 435 members. Institutional imperatives simply don't allow senators to focus their activity in a single area, and, as such, they are less able to develop as much specialized knowledge of policy as their counterparts in the House. With this comparatively heavier workload comes greater freedom to choose issues and design their agendas. This feature of Senate life is, in fact, one of its attractions, and one that is frequently singled out by former House members who have become senators. This has potential advantages for senators both in terms of satisfying their personal policy interests and in having greater flexibility to engage in uptake.

Senators should also have more incentive to engage in uptake because they typically have more reason to be concerned about reelection. Compared to their House colleagues, they are more likely to face opposition, are challenged by more experienced opponents, are more likely to win by small margins, run more often in intense or hard-fought races, and are ultimately more likely to lose their reelection bids. From the perspective of uptake, we should expect that the memory of highly competitive elections in the past and the potential for more in the future should lead senators to display more uptake than representatives.

Finally, uptake may be easier for senators than for representatives because of differences in the nature of their campaigns. Senate challengers tend to highlight more issues in their campaigns, and these races tend to be more issue-oriented overall. These differences should provide more targets for responsiveness for winning legislators and so should increase the amount of uptake we observe.

All of these factors lead to the prediction that senators will be more responsive than representatives. They also point to another, more complicated, yet equally important, expectation – that the dynamics of the uptake decision may differ across the chambers. For example, it is possible that electoral vulnerability may influence representatives' and senators' behavior differently, or that senators and representatives may make different choices about when and where to engage in uptake.

Impact of Uptake

Exploring variation in uptake levels across individuals, across legislative activities, within a term, and across chambers can all provide indirect evidence for or against the strategic motivation theory. To the extent that vulnerability is related to uptake, that legislators engage in it at relatively high levels across activities, that individual levels vary with the proximity of the next election, and that senators exhibit more of it than representatives, the strategic motivation theory receives support. However, a more direct test is in order as well. Specifically, does engaging in uptake actually work to promote electoral security? If it does, high uptake levels in one term should, all other things being equal, increase vote shares in the next election. It could do so via a variety of mechanisms, perhaps increasing legislators' vote shares directly, reducing opposition at the primary or general election levels, or warding off potentially strong challengers.

These claims all highlight the broader point that uptake must be assessed in comparative settings. While we can make normative assessments of what a "good" uptake level should be, we can only evaluate whether a given legislator's level is high or low in relation to others. Approaching variation in uptake from many different perspectives is thus crucial for understanding the dynamics of responsiveness.

PART V. PARTIES AND LEADERS

CHAPTER FOURTEEN

Institutional Context and Leadership Style

The House from Cannon to Rayburn

Joseph Cooper and David W. Brady

Cooper and Brady argue that the homogeneity of legislative parties' electoral constituencies varies over time. The more homogeneous the electoral constituency of a party, the more cohesive the legislative party. A cohesive legislative party, in turn, concentrates power in the hands of central leaders and relies more on leaders to direct policymaking. The less homogeneous the electoral constituency and the less cohesive the legislative party, the more power will be dispersed and the more leadership will be oriented toward bargaining and maintaining good relations within the party.

Leadership is an aspect of social life that has been extensively studied in a variety of institutional or organizational settings. Yet, it remains a topic in which our intellectual grasp falls far short of our pragmatic sense of the impacts leaders have on organizational operations and performance.

This is as true, if not more true, of Congress than of other organizations. Here, too, analysts are perplexed by the difficulties of conceptualizing key variables, treating highly transient and idiosyncratic personal factors, and identifying relationships amidst a maze of interactive effects. Moreover, the task is rendered even more complex by the highly politicized character of the

Joseph Cooper and David W. Brady. 1981. "Institutional Context and Leadership Style: The House from Cannon to Rayburn" *American Political Science Review* 75(2): 411–25. Copyright © 1981 by the American Political Science Association. Reprinted with the permission of Cambridge University Press.

Congress as compared with most of the organizational contexts in which leadership has been studied.

This is not to say that knowledge and understanding of congressional leadership have remained static. Nonetheless, our grip on the topic is as yet not firm; we continue to lack a developed sense of what we should be looking at and how to proceed.

The purpose of this article is to aid in remedying this deficiency. It is premised on two key assumptions. First, the study of leadership requires comparative evidence regarding both behavior and contexts. Hence our use of history as a laboratory and our choice of Cannon and Rayburn as focal points of analysis. Second, the study of leadership requires abstract or analytical concepts to aid in formulating and testing important relationships. Hence our historical analysis relies on several broad concepts and relationships, drawn both from organization theory and from recent work on the operation of the Congress.

In sum, though this article deals with the transition from Cannon to Rayburn, its main objective is not to fill in the historical record. Its primary goals are rather to bring evidence and analysis to bear to improve our understanding of the key determinants and underlying dynamics of congressional leadership, and to suggest a set of propositions or hypotheses that can serve as a basis for more focused and elaborate forms of investigation and theory building.

The legacy the House of the nineteenth century left to that of the twentieth was a set of rules which placed the majority firmly in control of the House and centralized power in the hands of the Speaker as the agent of this majority. It was this legacy the House rejected when it revolted against the Speaker in 1910. In so doing it not only stripped the Speaker of many of his important powers, but also paved the way for a metamorphosis in the nature of the House as a political institution.

The Speaker and the House

It was with good reason that Speakers of the House in the years between 1890 and 1910 were often referred to as czars. The Speaker appointed the committees. He served as the chairman of and had unchallengeable control over the Rules Committee. He had great, though not unlimited, discretion over the recognition of members desiring to call business off the calendars, to make motions, or to address the House, and absolute discretion over the recognition of motions for unanimous consent and suspension of the rules.

These prerogatives gave the Speaker great power to control outcomes in the House. At the committee stage, those who had received prized assignments from the Speaker naturally felt a sense of gratitude and obligation to him. Those who desired a change in assignment knew full well that their chances of advancement depended on the good graces of the Speaker. Conversely, since in this age seniority was far from as sacrosanct as it is today, members were also aware that to alienate the Speaker was to risk loss of a chairmanship, an assignment, or rank on a committee.

Nor was the appointment power the Speaker's only source of leverage in controlling outcomes at the committee stage. Members of any particular committee were also disposed to cooperate with the Speaker because of the vast array of rewards and sanctions his position in the House bestowed on him. For example, the Speaker could provide access to the floor by granting a rule or recognizing a motion to suspend the rules; he could lend invaluable assistance in getting a project included in a bill or in getting a bill out of committee. Moreover, if all the rewards and sanctions at the disposal of the Speaker still proved to be insufficient, there was yet another factor that discouraged opposition at the committee stage. The plain fact was that to oppose the Speaker would in all probability be fruitless. If a committee refused to report a bill the Speaker wanted reported, the Speaker could pry the bill out of committee either through use of the Rules Committee or suspension of the rules. Similarly, if a committee reported a bill the Speaker opposed, the bill had little chance of reaching the floor. The power of the Speaker was such that he could obstruct the consideration of any bill he did not want considered. Given the various and potent types of leverage the Speaker possessed, it is not surprising that in this period committee chairmen took their cue from the Speaker regarding which bills they would report and that Speakers referred to the committee chairmen as their "cabinet."

As for action on the floor, here too the Speaker's prerogatives under the rules gave him great power. A number of factors combined to give him control over the agenda of the House. Through use of the Rules Committee and other privileged committees, he could interrupt the regular order of business either to give priority to a bill he wanted considered or to block a bill he opposed. He could use unanimous consent and suspension of the rules to give access to the floor to bills he favored and could deny the use of these procedures to bills he opposed. In addition, his discretion in the recognition of motions calling bills up for consideration was a source of leverage.

The Speaker's ability to control the agenda, however, stemmed not merely from his powers of repression, but also from the necessity of relying upon him if the House was to reach the bills it wanted to consider. The volume of legislation before the House made it exceedingly cumbersome to follow the involved order of business set forth in the rules. As a result, the House did not insist on following its regular order. Indeed, the points in the order where committee members could call business off the calendars were usually not reached. Instead, the House relied on the Speaker to bring bills up for its consideration and to determine the time of consideration through the use of privileged reports and special procedures, such as unanimous consent. In short, then, both because of the powers of the Speaker over the agenda and the unwieldiness of proceeding according to the regular order, the House gave the Speaker even more power over the agenda than his power under the rules bestowed on him.

A second aspect of the Speaker's power over floor decisions concerned his ability to control considerations on the floor. Here again, his command of the Rules Committee and his power as presiding officer gave him considerable leverage over floor debate and dilatory tactics. In addition, many of the same rewards and sanctions at the Speaker's disposal for controlling committee decisions could also be used to control floor decisions. Especially for members of the majority party, to oppose the Speaker was to risk the loss of his assistance in matters of vital importance to one's constituency and therefore also to impair one's chances of reelection. Moreover, through bestowing favors over a number of years, the Speaker could build up a substantial fund of credits, credits which could then be expended as needed to secure the cooperation of members in his debt. Thus, the ability of the Speaker to control decisions on the floor and in committee stemmed not only from the immediate impacts the exercise of his formal powers involved, but also from their long-run dividends.

The Speaker as Party Chief

To complement his prerogatives under the rules, the Speaker possessed another source of power that was equally significant. In placing a potent array of rewards and sanctions at his disposal, the rules did of course provide him with considerable leverage. However, the Speaker's ability to command majority support in committee and on the floor was materially aided by another factor: party discipline.

In an age when party regularity is far from an overriding consideration, it is difficult to appreciate how important party was in the House at the turn of the century. In this period the great majority of members in both parties subscribed to the doctrines of party government. Representative government was seen to depend on the existence of a responsible majority which had the power to rule and which, as a result, could be held accountable for performance. Only under such conditions, it was believed, could the people effect their wishes. The individual representative was thought to be elected on the basis of a party's platform and was therefore regarded to have an obligation to support party positions, even against personal convictions or desires.

The fact that members in this age thought and spoke in terms of the doctrines of party government had more than rhetorical importance. Party government served as the main justification for vesting great power in the Speaker and permitting him to play the role of Czar. Though the Democrats never fully accepted the proposition and ended by rejecting it, a cardinal tenet of Republican faith was that rule by a responsible majority party required centralizing organizational power in the Speaker.

The Speaker's position as head of his party thus also provided him with an important source of leverage. It is true, of course, that even in this period many issues were not treated as party issues. Nonetheless, most important issues were regarded as matters on which the party as a whole should stand together. In such a context the Speaker derived considerable power from his position as party chief. Initiative in the definition of party policies belonged to him. Moreover, if he could not win the support of all elements in the party, he had at his disposal a powerful mechanism for enforcing adherence to his wishes – the caucus. Through a binding vote in the caucus, he could oblige the opposition to support his policy positions out of party loyalty. In short, the Speaker could rule the House through the force of party discipline. As long as the bonds of party held taut, he had only to command the support of a majority of his party to command a majority in the House.

We may conclude, then, that the House of Reed and Cannon contained a highly centralized power structure with control resting

Table 14.1. *Czar Rule and Levels of Party Voting in the House (1881–1921)*

Congress	Year	Percentage Party Votes	Majority Party	Centralized Leadership
47	1881	16.6	Republican	No
48	1883	7.0	Democratic	No
49	1885	15.5	Democratic	No
50	1887	8.7	Democratic	No
51	1889	42.5	Republican	Yes
52	1891	4.2	Democratic	No
53	1893	6.1	Democratic	No
54	1895	24.8	Republican	Yes
55	1897	50.2	Republican	Yes
56	1899	49.8	Republican	Yes
57	1901	38.9	Republican	Yes
58	1903	64.4	Republican	Yes
59	1905	34.6	Republican	Yes
60	1907	26.3	Republican	Yes
61	1909	29.4	Republican	Yes/No
62	1911	23.0	Democratic	No
63	1913	19.9	Democratic	No
64	1915	21.7	Democratic	No
65	1917	9.4	Democratic	No
66	1919	14.9	Republican	No

essentially in the hands of the Speaker. The key to the Speaker's power lay not simply in his prerogatives under rules, nor in his position as party chief, but rather in the manner in which these two sources of leverage reinforced each other. The existence of a stable party majority insured the Speaker's ability to implement his formal powers and gave him a degree of maneuverability and control that the rules alone could not give him. Similarly, the rewards and sanctions the rules placed in the Speaker's hands gave party regularity a degree of priority it would not have possessed if it had rested merely on the extent of agreement among party members or their devotion to the doctrines of party government. Speakers could therefore quite appropriately refer to committee chairmen as their "cabinet." During this period the committee and party systems were blended to an extremely high degree. The Speaker was both the party leader and the chairman of the Rules Committee. The majority leader was the chairman of the Ways and Means or Appropriations Committee and, with the start of the whip system in 1897, the whip was chairman of Judiciary or a top member of Ways and Means. Unlike the contemporary House where party leaders and committee chairs are separate, committee and party leaders were one and the same. Tensions between the two systems were accordingly greatly reduced. Whereas in the contemporary House committee chairs often have low party support scores, such was not the case at the turn of the century. It was thus not a mere figure of speech to refer to committee chairs as a "cabinet." Both structurally and behaviorally, committee and party leaders were a cabinet.

The Bases of Czar Rule

We have argued that the interaction of the Speaker's formal powers and the strength of party resulted in a centralized form of leadership – Czar rule. This can be shown empirically. Data exist which strongly buttress the argument we have made deductively on the basis of the historical record.

First, if party strength functioned as a key ingredient of Czar rule, then levels of party voting should be markedly higher in congresses with centralized leadership. Table 14.1 presents data on party votes (90% of one party versus 90% of the other) for congresses from

1881–1921. It thus includes "Czar rule" congresses in which the Speaker possessed the formal powers described above and a ready ability to use the caucus, and congresses in which one or more of these sources of leverage was absent.

Table 14.1 shows a strong connection between centralized leadership power and levels of party voting. In the period from 1881 to 1899 party voting scores attained levels of 25 percent or more only in the three congresses in which centralized leadership power existed. In the period from 1899 to 1921 party voting did not drop below 25 percent until after the 1910 revolt against the Speaker, and then fell to below 10 percent in 1917 for the first time in a quarter-century. To further substantiate our argument, we ran a point bi-serial analysis of the data. This statistic is used when the data are dichotomous and is appropriate for Table 14.1, given a distinction between centralized and noncentralized leadership power. The point biserial for this data set was a striking .89, demonstrating the degree to which levels of party voting can be seen as associated with concentrated leadership power.

Second, if an interactive relationship exists between concentrated formal power and party strength, then party strength must have its own sources of determination and impact. Indeed, in our view the causal impact of party strength on the distribution of power in the House is of primary importance. For the Speaker to have the power involved in Czar rule, a majority of the House members had to agree to bestow such power. Since the House is organized on the basis of party and since during this period the Republicans were usually in the majority, it was their potential for group cohesion and loyalty that established the conditions for centralized leadership. In short, the vehicle through which centralized leadership developed was the congressional Republican party. The rationale underlying this development was that without party government the industrial gains of the late nineteenth century would have been negated by congressional Democrats.

However, to sustain the role and significance we have accorded party strength, we must be able to identify and demonstrate independent sources of determination. In this respect it may be noted that the development of strong party systems in Europe and Britain is associated with the rise of leftist-socialist parties and that in the United States those states where the parties represent polarized constituencies have high levels of party voting. Our argument is therefore that the fundamental bases of party strength at the turn of the century, as in all periods of our history, are largely external, that party strength is rooted in polarized constituency configurations.

In order to ascertain the constituency bases of the congressional parties as well as the differences between them, we calculated the degree to which each congressional party represented agricultural as opposed to industrial districts. For example, in the 55th House (1897–1899), 69 percent of the Democrats and 26 percent of the Republicans represented agricultural districts, that is, districts where the ratio of farms to industrial workers was at least three to one. Thus the difference between the parties was 43 percentage points. This differential was computed for the 47th through the 66th Houses (1881–1921) and serves as a measure of electoral polarization. The specific hypothesis is that there should be a strong relationship between polarization and party voting. Table 14.2 confirms the hypothesis. When polarization was high, so too was party voting. Conversely, in Houses where the differential was less than 20, that is, where the parties were less polarized, the proportion of party votes did not rise above 20 percent and dropped to as low as 4.2 percent. However, perhaps the best overall statistic is Pearson's r, which is .81 for the two variables presented in Table 14.2.

The data also show that during the period from the realignment of 1894–96 to approximately the election of Woodrow Wilson (the 54th through the 61st House), the parties remained polarized and levels of party voting remained high. On the other hand, during the "period of no decision" (47th through the 53rd Houses), the degree of polarization fluctuated, and levels of party voting varied accordingly. Similarly, after 1908 the congressional parties became less polarized as the Democratic party

Table 14.2. *Polarization of Parties and Party Voting in the House (1887–1921)*

Congress	Year	Differential	Party Votes
47	1881	36	16.6
48	1883	15	7.0
49	1885	25	15.5
50	1887	24	8.7
51	1889	41	42.5
52	1891	19	4.2
53	1893	22	6.1
54	1895	36	24.8
55	1897	43	50.2
56	1899	33	49.8
57	1901	35	38.9
58	1903	39	64.4
59	1905	41	34.6
60	1907	36	26.3
61	1909	31	29.4
62	1911	24	23.0
63	1913	12	19.9
64	1915	11	21.7
65	1917	14	9.4
66	1919	18	14.9

became more competitive in industrial districts, and party voting in the House again declined.

In sum, then, it is critical to note the correspondence between a polarized electoral system and a highly centralized leadership structure. Though the Speaker's formal powers reinforced party strength, the polarized electoral bases of the party system provided an indispensable platform for Czar rule. Thus, when electoral polarization began to decline, the centralized internal structure also began to come apart.

THE HOUSE FROM CANNON TO RAYBURN

Despite its power, the system of Czar rule could not maintain itself. It proved to be too rigid a system to accommodate the factional tendencies in the party system. During the early years of the twentieth century, economic and social ferment in the Midwest and West brought to Congress a group of young Republicans passionately devoted to enacting a whole series of reform measures. Cannon used his power as Speaker and party chief to contain and frustrate the desires of these members. In so doing, he

soon aroused their enmity not merely for his policies but also for the whole system of power then prevalent in the House.

The Revolt Against the Speaker

Though the number of Insurgent Republicans in the House was never large, by 1909 their strength in combination with the Democrats was sufficient to bring the revolt to a successful conclusion. The first step came in 1909 with the establishment of a Consent Calendar and a call of the committees every Wednesday to take up business on the House or Union Calendars. At this time more sweeping change was prevented by the defection of a group of conservative Democrats. The next year, however, the Insurgent Republican–Democratic coalition gained a decisive victory. On March 19, 1910, after a dramatic two-day fight, the House passed a resolution removing the Speaker from the Rules Committee, enlarging its membership, and providing for election of the committee by the House. This victory was followed two months later by the passage of a resolution, which established a procedure through which individual members could initiate the discharge of bills from committees. Finally, in 1911 the last major objective of the opponents of Czar rule was achieved. The House, now under Democratic control, amended its rules to provide for the election of all standing committees and their chairmen.

The immediate results of the revolt against the Speaker did not greatly impair the ability of the party leadership to lead the House on behalf of the party majority. In acting to weaken the Speaker, the Democrats had no intention of weakening the ability of the party majority to pass its program. Most Democrats believed as strongly in party government as most Republicans. Their objection was not to party government and party responsibility but to domination of the majority party and the House by the Speaker. Thus, when the Democrats gained control of the House in 1911, they set up an effective system of rule through the majority party. On the one hand, they made extensive use of the caucus and binding votes in caucus. On the other hand, they centralized power in the party by making the chairman of the Committee on Ways and Means, Oscar Underwood, both floor leader and chairman of the committee on committees. Under Underwood's leadership, the Democrats controlled the House as tightly as the Republicans had under Cannon. Indeed, it is fair to say that the Insurgent Republicans were no happier in the new "reformed" Democratic House than they had been in the old "tyrannical" Republican one. They had no greater liking for "King Caucus" than for "Czar rule."

The long-run results of the revolt, however, were quite different. If Czar rule was unable to maintain itself in the face of centrifugal pressures in the party system, caucus rule was even less fitted to do so. In the absence of the buttress the formal powers of the Speaker provided for party cohesion, increases in factional discord within the party alignments easily asserted themselves and led both to a disintegration of party control mechanisms and to a dispersion of power within the House.

The disintegration of party control mechanisms was gradual but extensive. The caucus was the first to go. Once the Democrats achieved the major items in their domestic program, the power of the caucus began to wane. From 1916 on, the divisions within the parties made it difficult to rely on the caucus and usage quickly declined. This is consistent with the data presented in Table 14.1 that shows party voting at less than 15 percent in the 1917–1921 period – a 22-year low. There were small upsurges in activity in the early 1920s and early 1930s during the initial years of party turnover in the presidency. However, its use for policy purposes soon became rare in the 1920s and simply disappeared in the late 1930s. Thus by the end of the 1930s the caucus was virtually moribund as a mechanism for determining party policy.

When the Republicans regained control of the House in 1919, they set up a steering committee and began to rely on it rather than the caucus. Though this committee from the first was less of a control device than the caucus and more of a coordinating and planning

mechanism, during the early 1920s it did serve to augment the leadership's power to direct its partisans. However, the same tendencies toward factionalism and bloc voting that reduced the caucus to marginal significance had a similar effect on the steering committee. By the late 1920s the party leadership had come to see the steering committee as a hindrance to their maneuverability and effectiveness. As a result, they abandoned the mechanism and began to rely instead on informal meetings among themselves, i.e., on an informal board of strategy composed of the Speaker, the floor leader, and a few trusted lieutenants. The situation did not change when the Democrats took control of the House in 1931. Though they too established a steering committee, their leadership operated in much the same fashion as the Republican leadership had in the late 1920s. In short, then, by the late 1920s reliance on party control mechanisms to coordinate action and enforce cohesion had largely passed from the scene. Instead, the majority party was reduced to operating primarily through a small coterie of men, gathered around the Speaker, who met to plan strategy and whose power of direction was much less than that of the caucus or even the steering committee in their heyday.

Nor were the caucus and the steering committee the only party control mechanisms to lose power and effectiveness in the period after 1916. The power of party mechanisms to control committee personnel also declined. Republican Speakers from 1890 to 1910 respected seniority, but they were quite prepared to violate it in the interests of party policy. The same is true of Underwood. By the 1920s the situation was substantially different. The decline of the caucus and, to a lesser extent, of the steering committee enhanced the power and independence of party factions. Their sheer willingness to stand together and cooperate with the leadership became more important than ever before. In addition, as the power and independence of party factions increased, the appointment mechanisms became more decentralized. Thus, by 1919 the Republicans had taken the power of appointment from the leader of the party and had vested it in a committee on committees, composed of nearly 40 members. Similarly, after 1923 the Democrats no longer combined the posts of floor leader and chairman of the committee on committees. In such a context seniority was transformed from an important consideration to a sovereign principle. It alone provided a standard in terms of which decentralized appointment mechanisms could distribute key committee positions among party factions without provoking disputes that would weaken the party. As a result, in contrast to earlier eras, departures from seniority were rare in the 1920s and even rarer thereafter.

From Hierarchy to Bargaining

Given the reductions in the formal powers of the Speaker between 1909 and 1911, the disintegration of party control mechanisms after 1916 produced a dispersion of power in the House. If in Cannon's day the Speaker's prerogatives as Speaker and as party chief combined to centralize power in the House, now the reduction in the formal powers of the Speaker and the disintegration of party control mechanisms combined to decentralize power in the House.

On the one hand, the rewards and sanctions which the rules placed in the hands of party leaders were reduced. The party leadership no longer had absolute control over committee appointment, the Rules Committee, or the consideration of minor business. On the other hand, the ability of party leaders to consolidate and maintain support in their own ranks was also reduced. If it is true that factionalism in the party system led to the decline of party control mechanisms, it is also true that the decline of these mechanisms had the further effect of allowing party factionalism greater expression. The result of these developments was to heighten the power and independence of the individual member and of key organizational units in the House. Denied the power they possessed over the individual member under Czar rule or caucus rule, party leaders began to function less as the commanders of a stable party majority and more as brokers trying to assemble particular majorities behind particular bills. Denied the power they possessed over the organizational

structure under Czar rule or caucus rule, party leaders began to function less as directors of the organizational units and more as bargainers for their support.

These tendencies intensified as time passed. During the 1920s the breakdown of the steering committee and the rise of seniority to predominance cast party leaders more firmly in the roles of brokers and bargainers than had been the case at the start of the decade. Similarly, events during the 1930s confirmed and strengthened these roles. If the level of party cohesion during the 1920s was not high enough to permit reliance on party control mechanisms, it was still of such proportions that in general the holders of key organizational positions were loyal to the leadership and willing to cooperate with it. Nor, despite the increases in factionalism and bloc voting, did party leaders during the 1920s confront any stable and comprehensive basis of division among their fellow partisans, any extensive and consistent split across a whole range of issues. By the late 1930s, however, the situation had changed in both these regards.

After a brief increase in party voting during the initial years of the New Deal, party strength again began to decline in a steady and substantial fashion. Moreover, this decline gave birth to a new and distinctive feature, the Conservative Coalition. Table 14.3 provides supportive data on both trends.

Thus, as the 1930s came to an end, party politics in the House began to display characteristics and configurations that were to become entrenched in the 1940s and to endure for several decades. These changes, however, made the task of the majority party leadership more, not less arduous. First, party divisions in the majority party now assumed a pronounced bifurcated form. In seeking to build majorities from issue to issue, the leadership accordingly was frequently threatened with the loss of support of a substantial portion of the southern wing of the party, a wing that from the late 1930s to late 1950s was roughly equal in size to the northern wing of the party. Second, the divisions within the majority party now began to be translated into the organizational structure in a manner that far exceeded previous experience. The party leadership's ability to use the machinery of

Table 14.3. *The Decline of Party Voting in the House and the Rise of the Conservative Coalition (1909–1953)*

Congress	Year	Percent Party Votes	Percent Coalition Activity	Percent Coalition Victories
61	1909	29.4	–	–
62	1911	23.0	–	–
63	1913	19.9	–	–
64	1915	21.7	–	–
65	1917	9.4	–	–
66	1919	14.9	–	–
67	1921	35.2	–	–
68	1923	13.4	–	–
69	1925	5.3	3.5	63.5
70	1927	5.6	1.4	100.0
71	1929	13.6	5.8	80.0
72	1931	13.8	4.9	62.0
73	1933	18.9	2.1	48.0
74	1935	14.2	4.3	56.0
75	1937	11.8	7.6	67.0
76	1939	17.6	9.3	95.0
77	1941	10.5	12.5	92.0
78	1943	9.6	21.8	96.0
79	1945	12.1	22.1	88.0
80	1947	12.7	19.6	100.0
81	1949	6.5	16.4	83.0
82	1951	4.9	24.9	86.0

the House to suit its own purposes accordingly declined. It began to encounter difficulty securing the support of particular committees and committee chairmen much more frequently. This was especially true of the one committee in the House on which the leadership was most dependent and which historically had always been regarded as falling within the province of the leadership – the Rules Committee. For the first time in history the leadership found itself confronted with a Rules Committee that regarded itself and acted as an independent agent, rather than as an arm of the leadership.

These developments further weakened the power and position of the leadership and in so doing further enhanced the independence of individual members and organizational units. Moreover, the impact was long-lasting, not transitory. A divided majority party was less amenable to leadership direction and control than an incohesive one. From the late 1930s on, the leadership was forced to place even more reliance on brokerage and bargaining than had been necessary in the early 1930s or 1920s.

THE RAYBURN HOUSE

The period from 1910 to 1940 may therefore be seen as a period of transition in the character of the House as a political institution. By 1940, the year Sam Rayburn assumed the Speakership, a new and distinctive type of House had emerged. It was a House that was destined to endure in most of its essential features until the reform of the Rules Committee in the early 1960s and in many of its essential features until the reemergence of the caucus in the late 1960s.

The House under Decentralized Rule

The Rayburn House was a far different body from the House of Cannon or Reed. Centralization of power and hierarchical control had given way to a diffusion of power and bargaining.

On the one hand, the majority party leadership could no longer command the organizational units due to the breakdown of party control mechanisms and the elimination of the Speaker's prerogatives over appointment and the Rules Committee. Rather, it had to seek to win their support and do so in a context in which divisions in the majority party had become so pronounced that they had begun to appear at key vantage points in the organizational structure. On the other hand, the majority party leadership could no longer command overwhelming support from the ranks of its partisans on the floor due both to the decline in party strength and the decline in the fund of rewards and sanctions at its disposal. Rather, it had to seek to build majorities from issue to issue and do so in a context in which a deep split existed in the ranks of the majority party and distaste for party discipline was intense and pervasive. Political scientists writing about the House in the 1940s and 1950s accordingly emphasized themes quite different from those emphasized in the initial decades of this century: the primacy and amount of catering to constituency, not party loyalty or discipline; the dispersed and kaleidoscopic character of power in the House, not the authority and responsibilities of party leaders; the role of committee chairmen as autonomous and autocratic chieftains, not their operation as loyal party lieutenants.

However, the fact that power became decentralized in the House does not mean that significant centers of power did not continue to exist. What occurred was a wider dispersal of power, not its fractionalization.

First, the party leadership retained substantial ability to influence and even control outcomes in the House. If party voting decreased, the party bond remained important both because of the degree of agreement still present and because of the interest most members had in establishing some kind of party record. Thus, though the leadership could no longer rule the House on the basis of votes drawn from its own party, it could still usually count on a large and stable reservoir of support from its fellow partisans. In addition, party leaders continued to derive leverage from other sources. The formal powers remaining to the Speaker aided their ability to control access to the floor and proceedings on the floor. The influence party leaders maintained over the party committee on committees enabled them to alter the political complexion of particular committees through the screening of new appointments. The power party leaders retained, due to their positions in the House and in the party, to dispense favors and build up credits augmented their capacity to secure the cooperation of ordinary members and holders of organizational positions. Finally, the leadership could rely on the president's influence to win the support of reluctant partisans both in committee and on the floor.

Second, committees and committee chairmen emerged as rival power centers of great importance. In a context in which House rules gave the committees immense power over the handling of legislation within their jurisdictions and committee rules and practice gave their chairmen immense power within their committees, the decline in leadership authority and power redounded to the advantage of the committees and their chairmen. Typically, committee opposition to legislation sealed its fate, even when favored by the leadership. Conversely, committees that operated in a unified fashion were accorded great deference on the floor and had high levels of success. Party leaders thus could not treat committees merely as instruments of their will nor chairmen simply as loyal lieutenants. Rather, they had to function largely as petitioners of committee support and floor managers of committee legislation.

In the Rayburn House the committees accordingly reemerged as the feudal baronies they had been in the decades immediately preceding Czar rule. And, indeed, to a significant degree the story of the Rayburn House is a story of conflict among northern majorities in the Democratic party, the majority party leadership, and southern-dominated committees in which northern pressure for action was continuing, leadership efforts sporadic, and committee obstruction very difficult to overcome. Ironically enough, then, the ultimate result of the revolt of 1910 was to redefine the problem of majority rule in the House, not to solve it. A new and equally serious difficulty, i.e., minority obstruction, simply replaced the difficulty that had aroused passions in the preceding era, i.e., autocratic leadership power.

Leadership Style in the Rayburn House

In sum, by 1940 the role and power of the party leadership in the House had been substantially altered. Though the leadership retained responsibility for and continued to provide overall guidance and direction in the conduct of the House's business, it now had to operate within a far harsher set of constraints than in 1910. At the floor stage, the leadership usually had no choice but to engage in the painful process of assembling shifting majorities behind particular bills through bargaining and maneuver. At the committee stage, the leadership was often forced to engage in intricate and prolonged negotiation with committees and committee chairmen. Indeed, the leadership was now placed in a position where inability to accommodate an organizational unit would mean failure to pass party legislation, unless it was able to organize a majority of such strength and intensity that it could force a vote on the floor through the pressure of opinion in the House or the use of a mechanism such as discharge. The result was that by 1940 the personal, political skills of the leadership, rather than its sources of institutional power, had become the critical determinant of the fate of party programs.

All this, in turn, led to the emergence of a leadership style that contrasted markedly with that of Cannon and Reed. The components of this new style emerged gradually in the 1920s and 1930s as power in the House decentralized. It crystallized under Rayburn and was fully applied by him. It represented his experienced and finely tuned sense of what made for effective leadership in a House in which the Speaker lacked the formal powers of a Czar, had to mobilize a majority party fairly evenly balanced between discordant northern and southern elements, confronted a set of committees and committee chairmen with great power and autonomy, and had to deal with individual members who rejected party discipline and prized their independence.

The main facets of the Rayburn style can be analyzed in terms of the following categories: personal friendship and loyalty, permissiveness, restrained partisanship and conflict reduction, informality, and risk avoidance.

Whereas Cannon and Reed relied on their authority and power as Speakers and party chiefs, Rayburn relied on personal friendship and loyalty. If the Speaker could no longer command the House, his vantage points in the formal and party systems as well as his personal prestige provided a variety of opportunities to do favors for members. Rayburn exploited these opportunities in a skillful and imaginative manner. He sought continually to bind members to him as a person on the basis of favors rendered to them as persons, favors that eased their lives in Washington, enhanced their sense of personal worth, and/or advanced their political careers. In contrast to Cannon and Reed, who emphasized policy goals over personal relationships, Rayburn sought to attain policy goals through personal relationships, through nurturing friendships and creating obligations.

Whereas Cannon and Reed were quite intolerant of party defection and quite amenable to employing punishments as well as rewards as means of inducement, Rayburn was very permissive. He explicitly legitimized party irregularity on the basis of policy disagreement or constituency pressure and was reluctant ever to punish or coerce a member. To be sure, he did withhold rewards or favors from those he felt failed to cooperate with him for light or insubstantial reasons. Nonetheless, his prevailing inclination was not to alienate members whose vote or help he might need on future occasions.

Whereas Cannon and Reed were highly partisan and accepted both intraparty and interparty conflict as necessary aspects of majority party leadership, Rayburn sought to temper partisanship in personal relationships and to restrain conflict generally. He saw party mechanisms, such as the caucus and steering committee, as mechanisms for exacerbating party divisions and studiously ignored them. He established friendly relations with minority party leaders receptive to his overtures and extended advice and favors to rank-and-file

minority members. He emphasized reciprocity
and compromise as the prime behavioral rules
for all members. Thus the guiding motif of his
regime was not "serve party policy goals," but
rather "to get along, go along," i.e., trade favors.

Whereas Cannon and Reed sought to
achieve party programs by mobilizing partisan majorities and working through a stable set
of partisan lieutenants, Rayburn's approach was
more informal and ad hoc. Bargaining needs and
opportunities determined his legislative strategies and personal contact served as his main
means of implementing these strategies. Thus,
on the whole, he worked through varying sets
of trusted friends who were loyal Democrats
and whom he had placed in key positions in
the committee system. However, he was not
averse when pressed at the committee stage to
appealing to powerful opponents, who were
nonetheless close friends, for help, men such as
the southern Democratic stalwart, Gene Cox,
or the Republican leader, Joe Martin. Similarly,
at the floor stage he customarily asked varying sets of members, who were close friends
and/or owed him favors, to insure his majority
by standing ready to vote for him if needed,
even against their policy preferences and/or
constituency interests.

Finally, whereas Cannon and Reed were
aggressive in the pursuit of party policy goals,
Rayburn was cautious. His inclination was to
avoid battles when the outcome was uncertain.
To be sure, in instances when a Democratic
president and/or large number of his fellow partisans pressed him, he would usually wage some
sort of fight. But both because he felt that defeat
undermined his influence and because he did
not like to expend his credits in losing causes, his
clear and decided preference was to refuse battle,
to wait until prospects for victory were favorable. Similarly, he shied away from challenging
any of the key facets of decentralized power in
the House, despite their restrictive impact on his
ability to lead. His inclination was to work with
what existed and endured, rather than to seek
basic change. Only when extremely provoked
did he contest the power of senior chairmen
or the prerogatives of the Rules Committee
and even then only indirectly. Thus he did not

discipline Graham Barden but rather took over
the Education and Labor Committee by filling
vacancies with liberal Democrats. Thus he did
not discipline Howard Smith or Bill Colmer
or limit the power of the Rules Committee. He
rather chose to expand its membership. In short,
then, Rayburn was far more inclined to accept
the defeat of party programs than to risk his
influence and prestige in battles to attain them.

The Bases of Personalized Leadership

Earlier we argued that Czar rule derived from
the interaction of the Speaker's formal powers and his leverage as party chief. We further
argued that party strength was the determining factor in this interaction and that it was
rooted primarily in the polarized constituency
bases of the two parties. The emergence by
1940 of a new type of House and a new leadership style, both of which we may identify with
Sam Rayburn, can be explained in terms of
the altered character and impact of these same
variables.

Confining ourselves simply to events in the
House, the interaction between formal power
and party strength again played a critical, though
quite different, role. As we have already suggested, the interaction of these variables now
worked to reduce leadership power. Party
strength could no longer support or justify high
concentrations of formal power in the leadership. Limited formal power, however, allowed
party divisions fuller expression and increases in
these divisions undermined party control mechanisms. The atrophy of these mechanisms, in
turn, augmented the power and independence
of party factions and transformed the leadership into bargainers and brokers, into middle-
men rather than commanders.

Evidence of the continuing decline in party
strength, which we interpret as both cause and
effect of the decentralization of power in the
House, has already been presented in Table 14.3.
To reinforce our tabular evidence we regressed
party voting against time for the whole period
from 1894–1952. The results are presented in
Figure 14.1. The slope of the line is negative

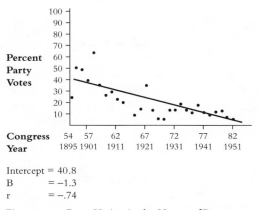

Intercept = 40.8
B   = −1.3
r   = −.74

Figure 14.1. Party Voting in the House of Representatives (1895–1953).

(B = −1.3) and the correlation between time and party voting −.74. Clearly, changes in party strength and changes in insitutional structure covary in a manner that is consistent with our argument.

Nonetheless, if we again would acknowledge the impact of the internal, interactive effect between formal power and party strength and accord party strength the determining role in this interaction, we again would also argue that levels of party strength are subject primarily to external determination. In short, though restricted formal power provided a context in which party divisions could be expressed and extended, the primary engine of increased divisiveness was increased disharmony in the constituency bases underlying the majority party coalition. Thus, as in the case of leadership

power and style during the period of Czar rule, the key to the Rayburn House and the Rayburn style lies in electoral alignment patterns.

Table 14.2 shows that from 1881 to 1921 party strength was high when the constituency bases of the parties were highly polarized and that it declined when these bases became less polarized. We have argued that increased factionalization in the party system was the primary source of the increased divisiveness that undermined the use of party control mechanisms in the 1920s. In order to show how constituency alignments are related to the further decline of party and the emergence of the Rayburn House, it is necessary to analyze the New Deal realignment and its aftermath.

The political revolution known as the New Deal was the product of the Great Depression. The voters providing the Democrats their majority came primarily from those groups most affected by the depression, farmers and low-income city dwellers, including blue-collar workers, ethnic groups, and blacks. Thus, the New Deal resulted in an increase in Democratic party allegiance across all constituent characteristics. Rather than recreating polarized congressional parties as in the period of Czar rule, the New Deal created a monolithic majority party which encompassed all types of constituencies. To the Democratic party's traditional base of support, the rural South, it added the urban Northeast and the urban and rural Midwest.

Table 14.4 illustrates and supports this point. It includes the following data, collected from the

Table 14.4. *Increases in Congressional Majority Party Composition during 1932 Realignment*

District Characteristic	Percent Democratic Congressmen			
	70th House (1927–29)	73rd House (1933–35)	Percentage Increase	Absolute Ratio Increase
Blue-Collar				
Low (Farm)	57	82	25	1.37
High (Labor)	32	64	32	1.97
Value Added				
Low (Non-Industrial)	54	81	27	1.40
High (Industrial)	34	67	33	1.89
Density				
Low (Rural)	53	77	24	1.38
High (Urban)	30	67	37	1.96

1930 census and mapped onto congressional districts: the number of blue-collar workers, value added by manufactures, and population density. Constituencies are ranked as high or low in relation to these characteristics in terms of the national mean and the percentage increase as well as the absolute ratio increase calculated for Democratic congressmen.

The monolithic majority party coalition created by the New Deal was formed around the basic issue of government aid to combat the effects of the Depression. Hoover and the Republican party favored voluntarism and nonintervention, whereas the Democrats favored active government involvement. As long as the issue of the role of government in combating the Depression remained the central and defining one, congressional Democrats had a broad basis for unity, despite their increased disparateness. And, indeed, in the 1930s there was a break in the long-term trend toward declining party voting (see Figure 14.1). However, as is now evident, the Roosevelt coalition could not maintain its cohesion across changing issue dimensions. As a monolithic rather than polarized coalition, it was particularly vulnerable to the emergence of issues that would divide its various components rather than unite them as the Depression had done.

In the late 1930s and early 1940s two factors combined to redefine the political climate and render it far less hospitable to majority party unity. The first was the alteration in the character and thrust of the New Deal, which focused attention and controversy on the federal government's general role as an agent of social welfare rather than its narrower role as an agent of economic recovery. The divisive potential of this development was signaled by the battle over New Deal legislation in the 75th Congress (1937–1939), a battle that in the eyes of many analysts marks the true emergence of the Conservative Coalition. The second was the worsening international situation, which finally led to the Second World War. This development focused attention and controversy not only on defense and foreign policy, but on the management of a war economy as well. In so doing, it also bypassed or submerged old bases of

Democratic unity and reinforced divisions along liberal–conservative lines.

The emergence and growth of the Conservative Coalition in the late 1930s and early 1940s, documented in Table 14.3, testifies to the impact of these factors in producing a new and enduring split in the congressional Democratic party that was rooted in differences between rural conservative southern constituencies and urban liberal northern ones. Nor is it surprising that as the dimensions of the split increased and finally stabilized, party voting declined. A comparison of the data in Table 14.3 broadly demonstrates the point; but to pin it down we calculated the correlation (Pearson's r) between Conservative Coalition activity and party voting for the period 1931–1953. The result is an impressive −.67.

In short, then, external factors are of primary importance in accounting for personalized rule as well as Czar rule. In a context in which the interaction of restricted formal power and declining party strength had already combined to disperse power, the emergence of a basic split in the majority party, rooted in constituency differences, further substantially undermined leadership power. Rayburn's highly personalized style was thus a reaction to his party situation, to the corps of independent and divided partisans he had to work with and lead. Indeed, his style is not only distinguishable in kind from that of Cannon and Reed, but even in degree from that of preceding Democratic Speakers, such as Garner and Rainey, who did not have to worry continually about southern support on key committees and the floor.

CONCLUSION

Our historical analysis of the transition from Cannon to Rayburn suggests several broad propositions or hypotheses that explain House leadership roles and behavior and have general import or significance for the analysis of legislative leadership. They are as follows.

First, institutional context rather than personal skill is the primary determinant of leadership power in the House. To be sure, leadership power, like other forms of power, is a combination of the fund of inducements available and the skill with which they are used. Nonetheless, skill cannot fully compensate for deficiencies in the quality or quantity of inducements. Indeed, the very skills required of leaders themselves vary in terms of the parameters and needs imposed by the character of the House as a political institution at particular points in its history. Thus, Rayburn was not and could not be as powerful a Speaker as Cannon or Reed. His sources of leverage in the formal and party systems were simply not comparable. Nor did Reed or Cannon require the same level of skill in building credits or bargaining as Rayburn to maximize their power. Similarly, it is doubtful that O'Neill can be as strong a Speaker as Rayburn whatever the level of skill he possesses, given the increased fractionalization in both the formal and party systems that has occurred in the past two decades.

Second, institutional context rather than personal traits primarily determines leadership style in the House. To be sure, style is affected by personal traits. Nonetheless, style is and must be responsive to and congruent with both the inducements available to leaders and member expectations regarding proper behavior. Indeed, the personal traits of leaders are themselves shaped by the character of the House as a political institution at particular points in time through the impact of socialization and selection processes that enforce prevailing norms. Thus, if Rayburn was a more permissive and consensual leader than Cannon or Reed, this is not because he was inherently a less tough or more affective person, but rather because of his weaker sources of leverage and the heightened individualism of members. If O'Neill's leadership style is far closer to that of Rayburn, McCormack, and Albert than to Cannon or Reed, this is not attributable to basic personality similarities and differences. It is rather attributable to the fact that the House he leads is far more like theirs than the House during the days of Czar rule. Similarly, though leaders remain distinct personalities (note, for example, O'Neill and Albert), range of tolerance for personal traits or predispositions that conflict with

prevailing norms is restricted. O'Neill therefore must and does curb the exercise of new sources of leverage gained since the revival of the majority caucus in 1969 to avoid even appearing like a Czar. In contrast, members who cannot eliminate or temper traits that run counter to prevailing norms are disadvantaged in the pursuit of leadership office. Witness Dick Bolling who would have been far more at home in the House of the 1890s. In a basic sense, then, the impact of context on leadership style has something of the character of a self-fulfilling hypothesis.

Third, there is no direct relationship between leadership style and effectiveness in the House. This is true whether effectiveness is interpreted relatively or absolutely. Interpreted relatively, effectiveness is a matter of the skill with which resources are used, not actual results. However, whereas style is primarily determined by the parameters and needs imposed by the political character of the House as an institution at certain points in his history, particular styles can be applied with varying degrees of skill. Note, for example, the differences between Rayburn, McCormack, and Albert. Similarly, if effectiveness is interpreted absolutely, i.e., in terms of actual results of achievements, there is still no direct or simple relationship between style and effectiveness. On the one hand, there is no one best "style"; the relationship between style and effectiveness is rather a highly contingent or situational variable. On the other hand, even when contexts dictate roughly similar styles, they do not necessarily accord them roughly equal chances of success. Thus, given his sources of leverage in the formal and party systems, O'Neill has little choice but to adopt a leadership style that in many key respects is similar to Rayburn's. Yet, the greater degree of fractionalization in both systems in the 1970s, as opposed to the 1940s, reduces his overall prospects for success in passing party programs. O'Neill therefore is likely to have far less success overall than Rayburn, even though he too leads in a highly personal, informal, permissive, and ad hoc manner.

Fourth, and last, the impact of institutional context on leadership power and style is determined primarily by party strength. To be sure, the degree of organizational elaboration substantially affects the intensity of the demands imposed on integrative capacity and is largely a product of factors other than party strength, e.g., size and workload. Nonetheless, integrative capacity derives or flows primarily from party strength. The higher the degree of party unity or cohesion the more power in both the formal and party systems can be concentrated in the hands of party leaders and the more leadership style will be oriented to command and task or goal attainment. The lower the degree of party unity or cohesion the more power in both the formal and party system will be dispersed and the more leadership style will be oriented to bargaining and the maintenance of good relations. The infrequency of eras of centralized power in the House is thus explicable in terms of the very high levels of party strength required to

support it, requirements which have increased as the organization itself has become more elaborate. Similarly, the degree of power dispersion now present is explicable in terms of present weaknesses in party unity or coherence both in absolute terms and relative to an organizational structure that has grown far more complex in the past two decades. Given the dependence of internal party strength on appropriate constituency alignments, all this, in turn, means that leadership power and style are ultimately tied to the state of the party system in the electorate, that external or environmental factors have a decisive bearing on the parameters and needs that institutional context imposes on leadership power and style. In short, then, to be understood Cannon and Reed must be seen in the context of an entire party system, and the same applies to Rayburn in the 1940s and 1950s, and to O'Neill today.

CHAPTER FIFTEEN

Setting the Agenda

Gary W. Cox and Mathew D. McCubbins

Cox and McCubbins argue that the majority party in the House behaves as a cartel. That is, members of the party cooperate to control the legislative agenda by delegating special agenda-setting powers to various offices – committee chairmanships, the speakership, and the Rules Committee – and by exercising party control over those offices. Effective use of these offices minimizes the number of defeats the majority party experiences on the floor of the House.

INTRODUCTION

For democracy in a large republic to succeed, many believe that responsible party government is needed, with each party offering voters a clear alternative vision regarding how the polity should be governed and then, if it wins the election, exerting sufficient discipline over its elected members to implement its vision. America was once thought to have disciplined and responsible parties. Indeed, students of nineteenth-century American politics saw parties as the principal means by which a continental nation had been brought together: "There is a sense in which our parties may be said to have been our real body politic. Not the authority of Congress, not the leadership of the President, but the discipline and zest of parties

has held us together, has made it possible for us to form and to carry out national programs."

Since early in the twentieth century, however, critics of American politics have often argued that congressional parties are largely moribund. Some contend that they have become nothing more than labels for like-minded politicians who act together when they agree but otherwise pursue their own agendas and careers. A chorus of critics depict members of Congress as dedicated to the pursuit of graft, campaign contributions, and the emoluments of office and as captured by interest groups who seek to turn public policy into private favors.

Even though Congress does suffer from many infirmities, we will argue that a hitherto unrecognized form of responsible party government has characterized U.S. politics since the late nineteenth century. As in the traditional view of responsible party government, our theory depicts congressional parties as electorally accountable and legislatively responsible, at least to an important degree. We differ from the traditional view, however, in at least two ways.

First, whereas traditional theories stress the majority party's ability to marshal a cohesive voting bloc as the source of its legislative power, our theory stresses the majority party's ability to set the agenda as the key to its success. The importance of this distinction can be suggested by recalling that the most prominent line of criticism of partisan theories focuses directly on the issue of voting cohesion.

Many prominent scholars view legislators' votes as driven primarily by their constituents' and their own opinions, with partisan considerations playing a distinctly secondary role. Building on such views, Krehbiel argues that the two parties' attempts to influence votes either are negligible or cancel each other out.

If, as these theories suggest, party pressures cancel out, however, then the majority party cannot marshal its troops effectively, as required by traditional theorists of responsible party governance. Instead of being driven toward the platform promises of the majority party by the force of its discipline, policies in Congress will be driven to the center of congressional opinion by the logic of the famous median voter theorem.

If one accepts the traditional view that parties are strong only to the extent that they can affect their members' behavior on substantive votes, and if one views congressional votes as positioning policy along a single left–right continuum, then Krehbiel's argument is persuasive. In particular, given these two assumptions, majority parties matter only if they can secure nonmedian policy outcomes, and, in order to do this, they must engage in the unenviable and unlikely to succeed task of regularly pressuring their centrist members to vote against their constituents' and/or their own opinions.

Our emphasis on agenda control deflects this canonical criticism of partisan theories in the following way. We do not model voting in Congress as if there were a single vote on a single dimension (per the standard unidimensional spatial model); rather, we envision a series of votes on different issues. This opens up the possibility that, even if the majority party were unable to secure a nonmedian outcome on any given issue considered in isolation – a debatable premise – it might nonetheless greatly affect the overall legislative outcome if it prevents some issues from being voted on at all.

To see how agenda-setting power can affect legislative outcomes, imagine a newly elected Congress and the set of existing government policies – label them $q_1, \ldots, q_n$ – that it faces. Each of these policies could, in principle, be adjusted, sliding them further to the left or right

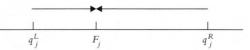

Figure 15.1. Illustration of leftward and rightward policy moves.

(e.g., less stringent or more stringent regulation of abortion). The newly elected members of the House have opinions regarding how each of the n policies should ideally be positioned along their respective left–right dimensions. Denote the center of congressional opinion (the median ideal position) regarding each policy by $F_1, \ldots, F_n$ for the n policies.

Note that one can divide the existing government policies into two main categories, depending on the relationship between the legislative median, F_j, and the status quo, q_j. In one category are policies that lie to the left of the current center of congressional opinion, $q_j < F_j$. If the House votes on a bill to change such a policy from the status quo (e.g., q_j^L in Figure 15.1) to the floor median, F_j, the result will be a *rightward* policy move. In the second main category are policies that lie to the right of the current center of congressional opinion, $q_j > F_j$. If the House votes on a bill to change such a policy from the status quo (e.g., q_j^R in Figure 15.1) to the floor median, F_j, the result will be a *leftward* policy move.

Now suppose in this simple example that Democratic majorities can block bills that propose rightward policy moves from reaching votes on the floor, thereby killing them without the necessity of a clear floor vote on the bill itself. The Democrats' blocking actions might take many forms, such as a chair refusing to schedule hearings, a committee voting not to report, the Rules Committee refusing to report a special rule, or the speaker delaying a particular bill. Each of these actions might in principle be appealed to the floor and reversed via a series of floor votes. It is a maintained assumption of our approach that the transaction costs involved in such appeals are typically so high that the majority's delaying tactics are effective in killing (or forcing changes in) the bills they target. To the extent that they are successful, the Democrats will produce a legislative agenda on which *every bill actually considered on the floor proposes to move policy leftward.* As a natural consequence, a majority of Democrats will support every bill.

This example, we hasten to add, overstates what our theory actually predicts (e.g., there are rightward policy moves that even the Democrats would like to make and, similarly, leftward policy moves that even the Republicans would support, when the status quo is extreme enough). Nonetheless, the discussion so far suffices to illustrate the potential power of a minimal form of agenda control (just the power to block) and makes clear that our theory sidesteps critiques that focus on the debility of party influence over floor votes (such as Krehbiel's). We can deny both the notion that parties must secure nonmedian outcomes issue by issue in order to matter and the notion that parties must exert discipline over how their members vote on bills in order to matter. Agenda control alone suffices – if it can be attained – to exert a tremendous influence over policy outcomes.

In sum, traditional theories of responsible party government see a Democratic (or Republican) majority as mattering because the majority can marshal its troops *on a given issue* and thereby attain policy outcomes that differ from those preferred by the median legislator *on that issue.* Aldrich and Rohde's theory of conditional party government shares this perspective: "most partisan theories would yield the expectation that the majority party would have sufficient influence . . . to skew outcomes away from the center of the whole floor and toward the policy center of [majority] party members." Such theories are vulnerable to Krehbiel's critique and its predecessors. In contrast, our theory sees a Democratic (respectively, Republican) majority as mattering because the majority can prevent reconsideration of status quo policies lying to the left (respectively, to the right) of the current median legislator on a given policy dimension – thereby filling the agenda mostly with bills proposing leftward (respectively, rightward) policy moves.

We should add that we do not view American parties as incapable of disciplining their troops. Indeed, we believe they regularly seek additional support on close votes, employing both carrots and sticks in the process. Such efforts can even lead to nonmedian outcomes on particular issues (typically via procedural maneuvers, such as closed rules, rather than by outvoting the opposition on the merits). However, the majority party's efforts on the floor are designed to *complement* whatever degree of agenda manipulation has already occurred by corralling a few votes on the margin, not to coerce moderate members to cast risky votes in order to maximize party cohesion. Picking which bills will be voted on at all – that is, which status quo policies will be at risk of change – is the primary technique; garnering enough votes to eke out a victory is important but secondary.

A second way in which our theory differs from traditional notions of responsible party government is that the latter stress the enactment of new policies – as promised in the party platforms – as the main normative criterion by which one should judge whether party government is operating successfully. In contrast, our theory stresses the avoidance of party-splitting issues, hence the preservation of some existing policies, as the key to the political survival of majority parties (whatever its normative merits).

We do not claim that parties cannot or do not compile positive records of accomplishment and are restricted merely to the preservation of portions of the status quo. Even the most heterogeneous majorities in congressional history, such as the Democrats of the 1950s, were able to agree on a number of new legislative goals and accomplish them. Thus, we have argued that control of the legislative agenda can also be translated into the enactment of some or all of the majority party's platform. However, the majority's success in changing policies, unlike its success in preserving policies, depends on its internal homogeneity.

Another way to frame this second difference is to say that we envision two stories in the edifice of party government, not just one. The first, or bedrock, story involves securing a superproportional share of offices for the party's senior members, imposing a minimal (primarily negative) fiduciary standard on those senior officeholders, and thereby ensuring that the party collectively is able to prevent items from appearing on the floor agenda. The second, or super-structural, story consists of enhancing the ability of the party's officeholders to push (as opposed to preventing) bills, imposing a more demanding fiduciary standard upon them (one requiring that they use their new powers for the collective benefit) and thereby enhancing the party's collective ability to push items onto the floor agenda.

By shifting the terms of debate from the majority party's ability to marshal its troops on a given issue to the majority party's ability to decide which issues are voted on to begin with, and from the majority party's ability to change policies to its ability to preserve policies, we seek to provide a new theoretical grounding for partisan theories of congressional organization – and to defend it empirically. In what follows, we will show that our theory explains important features of the postbellum history of the U.S. House of Representatives extremely well. To set the stage for that demonstration, in this chapter we provide a précis of our theory.

A PRÉCIS OF PROCEDURAL CARTEL THEORY

There are two main approaches in the literature on congressional organization. One view stresses how well congressional organization serves members' nonpartisan goals. For example, the House is declared well organized to (1) promote the reelection of its members; (2) make gains from legislative trade possible; (3) make specialization and the efficient generation of information possible; and (4) aid in bargaining with the other chamber or other branches of government. Political parties are explicitly denied a consequential role in these theories.

On the other hand, a new generation of partisan theories argues that the House is well organized to serve the collective interests of the majority party. One variant of partisan theory, known as the *conditional party government* model, focuses on how the majority party leadership's powers expand as the members they lead become more alike in political preference (and

more different from the opposition), leading ultimately to greater voting discipline and thus to greater success in legislating for the majority. Another variant, while accepting a version of the conditional party government thesis, focuses on an array of procedural advantages enjoyed by the majority party that are not conditional on its internal homogeneity. We call this variant "procedural cartel theory," the key aspect of which is the majority party's use of agenda control to achieve its desired outcomes.

Four key claims distinguish our approach. First, legislative parties arise, we believe, primarily to manage electoral externalities involved in running campaigns in mass electorates. Second, legislative parties are best analogized, we believe, to legal or accountancy partnerships, with various gradations of junior and senior partners. Third, legislative parties – especially in systems where floor voting discipline is costly to secure, as in the United States – specialize in controlling the agenda, rather than in controlling votes. That is, they seek to determine what is voted on to begin with, rather than to dictate their members' votes issue by issue (although they do regularly seek votes on the margin). Fourth, a legislative majority party allocates both negative (delay or veto) rights and positive (accelerating or proposal) rights among its senior partners (and groups thereof), but the mix of such rights changes with the degree of preference homogeneity among the party's members.

To explain the last point, note that there is a trade-off between increasing veto power (and suffering higher negotiation costs in order to do anything) and increasing proposal power (and suffering higher externalities from the decisions made by those with such power). The more *heterogeneous* the preferences within a given coalition, the more that coalition's partners will wish to limit the proposal rights of other partners, which necessarily entails strengthening their own and others' veto rights. The value of the coalition then comes more and more in keeping certain issues off the agenda and stabilizing the associated status quo policies. The more *homogeneous* the preferences within a given coalition, the more that coalition's partners will agree to expand each other's proposal rights,

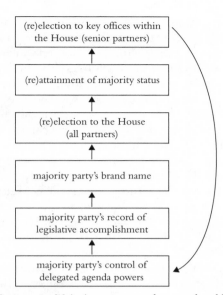

Figure 15.2. Majority-party agenda control and legislative success.

which necessarily entails weakening their own and others' veto rights. The value of the coalition then comes more and more in pushing certain issues onto the agenda with the hope of changing the associated status quo policies. Regardless of the coalition's homogeneity or lack thereof, regardless of whether its value stems more from stabilizing status quo policies or more from changing status quo policies, it will continue to seize the vast bulk of offices endowed with special agenda-setting rights and thus to cartelize agenda power. In this sense, *party government is not conditional* on the level of agreement within the party; rather, the nature of party government simply changes, from a more progressive vision (implicitly taken to be the only party government worth having in most of the previous literature) to a more conservative vision.

Having stated our inclinations on four important distinctions within the family of partisan theories, we can now diagram the elements of our theory (see Figure 15.2). Reading up from the bottom of the figure, we start with "majority party's control of delegated agenda powers," that is, with its control of the powers inherent in the various offices of the House endowed with such powers (e.g., the speakership and com-

mittee chairs). The better the majority party's control of such powers is, the more able will it be to fashion a favorable record of legislative accomplishment, although certainly other factors enter into this as well (such as the party of the president). The more favorable is the majority party's record of legislative accomplishment, the better its reputation or brand name will be, although again there are other factors that affect this, too (such as the president's actions). The better the majority party's brand name, the better will be the prospects for (re)election of its various candidates and the better will be the prospects for (re)attainment of majority status. The senior partners of the majority party care in particular about the latter because their ability to retain their chairs, speakerships, and other offices depends crucially on their party retaining its majority.

Reading the diagram top-down, instead of bottom-up, one starts with individual members of Congress assumed to care both about (re)election to the House and (re)election to offices within the House. They recognize that (re)election (especially to internal posts) depends crucially on majority status, which in turn depends on maintaining a favorable brand name for the party. Maintaining a favorable brand name, in turn, depends on the party's record of legislative accomplishment, hence on its ability to solve the various cooperation and coordination problems that arise within the legislative process. The party solves these problems primarily by delegating agenda power to its senior partners.

Because the element in this theory that we most wish to stress concerns agenda power, we turn now to a more extended consideration – albeit still abbreviated – of the cartel thesis. Chapter 16 provides a fuller elaboration of our theory.

THE PROCEDURAL CARTEL THESIS

The broadest thesis is that *agenda power in busy legislatures is almost always cartelized*. To put it another way, even though voting power in democratic legislatures is everywhere equal, proposal and veto power are everywhere unequal.

What do we mean by agenda power being cartelized in the specific case of the U.S. House? The agenda is cartelized when (1) special agenda-setting powers are formally delegated to various offices, such as committee chairs, the speakership, and the Rules Committee; (2) the majority party's members secure most of these offices, so that "agenda-setting services" can be procured only from members of the procedural cartel, just as certain kinds of economic services or goods can be procured only from the relevant economic cartel; and (3) the majority party's "senior partners," who hold these agenda-setting offices, act according to a minimal fiduciary standard – namely, that they do not use their official powers to push legislation that would pass on the floor against the wishes of most in their party.

Note that the features we have just listed also characterize most parliamentary governments: (1) Special agenda-setting powers are formally delegated to cabinet ministers, presiding officers, and directing boards (the analogs of the U.S. chairs, speaker, majority leader, and Rules Committee, respectively); (2) the governing coalition's members secure most, if not all of these offices; and (3) the governing coalition's "senior partners," who hold these agenda-setting offices, respect a norm according to which no bills are pushed that would split the governing coalition. It is often true that many parliamentary procedural cartels expect an even greater level of cooperation between their senior partners than would have been expected of U.S. committee chairs during the uneasy alliance of Northern and Southern Democrats in 1937–60. Nonetheless, the structural design of the most basic form of party government is similar across a wide range of systems: break the theoretical equality of legislators by creating a class of agenda-setting offices, ensure that the governing coalition's senior partners secure these offices, and deal with the consequent problems of agency loss and floor discipline, as best the local conditions permit.

The basic design of party government within legislatures admits a trade-off between two

costly methods of maintaining the power and advantages of these agenda-setting offices: procedural agenda control and voting discipline. Designing and maintaining rules that establish agenda control is costly; ensuring that members of the majority party vote with the party is also costly. Different legislatures, depending on their circumstances, choose different mixtures of these two costly mechanisms.

The question remains, why should agenda power be cartelized according to this basic recipe, in so many legislatures? Let us sketch out an answer to this question.

Although the details of legislative procedure differ widely across the world's democratic legislatures, one generalization holds universally: Important bills can only pass pursuant to motions formally stated and voted upon in the plenary session. The necessity of acting pursuant to formally stated motions means that every bill must consume at least some plenary time, if it is to have a chance at enactment. Simply put, plenary time is the sine qua non of legislation.

If all legislators have equal access to plenary time, then plenary time is a common pool resource, and rising demand for such time leads to various problems in the legislative process. Can a coalition restrict access to plenary time, enhancing its own members' abilities to propose and block, while diminishing those of the opposition? The majority is held together by the threat that failure to abide by certain norms of behavior will bring down the coalition, and with it each majority member's superior access to plenary time.

We suggest a somewhat more detailed and concrete recipe by which access to plenary time is restricted. A procedural cartel endows (or inherits) offices with agenda-setting powers, secures those offices for its senior partners, and ensures minimally fiduciary behavior by those senior partners.

How is it that such cartels stick together? In addition to the threat that the whole arrangement can come crashing down, depriving senior members of their offices or stripping those offices of their powers, we would add two additional reasons why access-hogging majorities, once formed, are stable. First, individual nonpivotal legislators in the majority have reason to fear punishment – such as lack of promotion, lack of aid for pet bills, demotion, and, ultimately, expulsion from the majority – should they violate crucial norms of behavior. Second, building up a mechanism by which to regulate access to plenary time (creating offices endowed with various special veto and proposal powers and ensuring that one's members secure those offices) entails large fixed costs and very low marginal costs on any particular policy or decision. The large fixed costs arise in creating and maintaining (1) the party's brand name and (2) the rules, procedure, precedent, and interpretation that establish and clarify the powers of agenda-setting offices. To the extent that the parties succeed in establishing themselves as the only viable route to the top offices, they can become very stable indeed.

Assuming that agenda-setting offices exist and that procedural cartels take most of them (but not all), why are senior partners subject to the minimal fiduciary standard we suggest, wherein they cannot use their official powers in such a way as to split their party? Note that, if this minimal standard is not imposed, one has a model similar to the committee government model in the United States or the ministerial government model in comparative politics. Agenda power is delegated to offices, and the governing coalition takes most of these offices;

however, the occupants of those offices are then free to act as they please. The result is that, if negotiations between chairs/ministers do not suffice to clinch a policy program supported by all, then the logical possibility exists that different chairs/ministers may push bills that a majority of their coalition would unsuccessfully oppose on the floor. We argue that, to avoid such events, the handiwork of chairs/ministers is subject to central screening – by the Rules Committee and majority floor leaders in the United States, and by the cabinet, directing board, and majority in the typical parliamentary system. The central screen helps ensure that chairs/ministers routinely foresee very low chances of success from using their official powers to push bills that would be (a) supported on the floor by most of the opposition and a swing group of the governing coalition and (b) opposed by a majority of their own party.

In our model, chairs/ministers remain free to use their official powers to *block* bills their partners wish to see passed. The only crime is using those powers to *push* bills that then pass despite the opposition of most of the governing coalition. If this crime of commission can be avoided, the majority coalition can determine which status quo policies will be preserved and which will run the risk of being overturned by bills allowed onto the floor.

CHAPTER SIXTEEN

Party Influence in Congress

Steven S. Smith

Smith provides an overview of legislators' motivations to create parties and the kinds of influence that parties might exercise once organized. In commenting on the sizable political science literature on these subjects, the author argues that party leaders are motivated by both policy and electoral goals and frequently must balance those goals. Leaders deploy a variety of resources to exercise both a positive and negative effect on legislative outcomes.

From observing many episodes of party and leadership action on Capitol Hill, I have found it useful to characterize congressional parties as seeking two collective goals – majority party status and policy. The goals are founded on the goals of individual legislators – reelection, good public policy, and power. For example, legislators seeking to enact certain policies are advantaged if their party wins majority control of Congress, its committees, and scheduling mechanisms. Legislators seeking reelection are advantaged if their party's record for policy achievement is viewed favorably by the public.

The collective electoral and policy goals of the congressional parties have the character of public goods. A public good is a benefit that is nonexcludable and jointly supplied. That is, achievement of a party goal benefits all party members whether or not they have contributed

Steven S. Smith. 2007. "The Microfoundations of Theories of Congressional Parties" and "The Types and Sources of Party Influence" in Steven S. Smith, *Party Influence in Congress* (Cambridge University Press), 25–54. Copyright © 2007. Reprinted with the permission of Cambridge University Press.

materially to the collective effort (nonexcludable) and is not exhausted for some members as other members benefit from it (jointly supplied). These features deserve a little discussion.

Congressional parties have the ability to determine their own membership so, in principle, the benefits of membership are excludable. In practice, the parties accept everyone elected under the party's label unless there is some specific and substantial grievance that their party has against them. The only exception in modern times occurred in 2001 when Democrats took the step of expelling James Traficant (D-OH) after he voted for the Republican candidate for speaker (Traficant was indicted a few months later on corruption charges and eventually expelled from the House). After the 1932 elections, when four Republican senators supported Franklin Roosevelt for president, a senior Republican proposed excluding the four from the Republican conference, but no action was taken. Going back a few more years, the endorsement of the presidential candidate of the opposite party led the Senate Republican caucus in 1872 to invite only those who supported the party's platform and candidates that year, thereby excluding Charles Sumner (R-MA). Plainly, exclusion from the caucus is seldom a threat and for several good reasons – the party prefers to have more rather than fewer members for the purpose of determining majority status, prefers more to fewer members for setting party ratios on committees and conference committees, and would rather minimize the number of new members required to gain majority status in the future.

While caucus membership is nonexcludable in practice, the benefits of caucus membership are not. Parties have the ability to favor some legislators over others in distributing the benefits of enacted policy and majority party status. Perhaps most notable, parties have denied committee chairmanships to legislators who, by virtue of the norm of seniority, expected them. After they gained a new majority in the 1994 elections, for example, House Republicans passed over the senior Republicans on three committees when filling chairmanships. The reasons for denying chairmanships to the senior party members have ranged from punishing someone for ethics transgressions, to lacking sufficient leadership skills, to being untrustworthy or disloyal on key policy issues. If chairmanships enhanced legislators' electoral prospects by giving them access to campaign donations or greater influence over policy important to them or their voters, as they might, denying chairmanships can be costly to the affected legislator. Thus, some of the benefits of party membership can be exclusive and exhausted for some members as others enjoy them. Consequently, parties have at least a few ways to motivate their members to support collective efforts by selectively manipulating incentives.

The use of selective incentives often is a controversial matter. When a move to strip legislators of committee chairmanships or assignments is contemplated, it usually is opposed by partisans who do not like the precedent or fear that the affected colleagues will switch parties or leave Congress. Examples from recent decades include unsuccessful efforts in 1995 to depose Sen. Mark Hatfield (R-OR) from the Appropriations Committee chairmanship after he voted against his party on a constitutional amendment requiring a balanced budget and to strip freshman Rep. Mark Neumann of his seat on the House Appropriations subcommittee for his stand against his party and committee chair on the adoption of a conference report on an appropriations bill. In Hatfield's case, the Republican leader, Bob Dole, is reported to have been very upset with Hatfield but worried that taking away the chairmanship would lead Hatfield to switch parties. Others expressed concern that Hatfield would be less motivated to run for reelection and put the seat at risk of being won by a Democrat. In Neumann's case, his fellow freshmen rallied to his defense and Neumann was promised a seat on the Budget Committee in addition to keeping his post on Appropriations! Republicans appeared to be particularly eager to punish disloyal colleagues in 1995 just after they gained new majorities in the House and Senate and were anxious to see their agenda enacted. Nevertheless, other considerations weighed heavily in the calculations of both leaders and rank-and-file members.

Leaders are far more likely to reward than to punish party colleagues. They may favor colleagues who have proven their willingness to take political risks for their party with campaign help, coveted committee assignments, seats on commissions and special committees, appointments to a variety of party positions – task forces, whip organisation posts, and so on. Some of these incentives hold only modest value, but major committee assignments and campaign assistance can be highly valued. None of these inducements is powerful enough to motivate a legislator to put his or her reelection at serious risk. Thus, for most legislators most of the time, support for the leadership can be useful in building a legislative career, but being *denied* caucus membership or *losing* valued benefits of caucus benefits unique to majority party status is not a serious threat.

Certain features of party membership – such as the party's reputation and policy outcomes – truly are nonexcludable and jointly supplied goods. A party's reputation for performing well or poorly in office is likely to have implications for all members of the party. This serves as a bond among fellow partisans, even across the House, Senate, and presidency. For this reason, legislators care about the public's evaluations of the president, the actions of partisans in the other house of Congress, and any events that are connected by voters to their party.

With respect to public policy, legislators vary in the policy domains that interest them, but there are policy domains (tax rates, overall spending, defense policy, and so on) that always attract the interest of all legislators. Legislation related to shared or similar preferences in salient policy domains serves as a public good. That is, once legislation is enacted, all legislators may benefit, and one legislator's benefit does not diminish another legislators' benefit.

Party efforts to acquire public goods – that is, to gain or maintain majority status or to enact or protect favored policies – are subject to collective action, coordination, and conflict-of-interest problems. The free rider problem arises because the successful achievement of party goals is not greatly influenced by the actions of any individual legislator. Consequently, the incentive for individuals to contribute a fair share to collective party efforts is small. For example, the ordinary legislator cannot expect to materially affect the reputation of his or her party and would reason that personal electoral prospects are more likely to be improved by campaigning at home than by participating in time-consuming efforts on Capitol Hill to enhance the party reputation. A legislator might even reasonably expect a net gain in votes from criticizing his or her own party.

Moreover, congressional parties, like other sizable groups, can suffer from the problems of coordination and transaction costs. The party's members must somehow coordinate their choices, or alternatively, create a mechanism that will choose one of the acceptable alternatives for them. Coordination is not a free commodity. The transactions required to coordinate the behavior of many people may be quite costly and even prohibitive. High transaction costs, relative to the expected gains from coordination, can prevent a collective choice and the realization of benefits from a public good.

Coordination among dispersed candidates for public office is a more daunting task than coordination among elected legislators who gather on Capitol Hill. It is not surprising, then, that coordination of national parties started among members of Congress. Still, transactions among legislators can be so time consuming that some collective decisions are not made. Meetings must be organized, responsibil-

ities delegated, information disseminated, and leaders held accountable – all of which may be viewed as costly to busy legislators. Organizational innovations that improve the efficiency of collective choice by reducing transaction costs can be expected whenever rising transaction costs (or rising benefits of collective action) increase the incentives for doing so.

Thus, while the collective goals require coordinated action to be achieved, we would expect legislators to contribute less than their fair share to the effort. Party goals certainly would be pursued inefficiently if legislators operated independently. To one degree or another, all congressional parties probably experience such inefficiency from time to time, but, at least in the long run, substantial inefficiency is likely to be addressed. Both inside and outside observers are quick to observe and comment on it. Competitive pressures from the other party encourage legislators to invent new ways of organizing their party for collective action and successful innovations in one party are readily adopted in the other.

Parties address the competitive challenges by organizing. Parties create committees, task forces, and leadership positions and assign responsibility for achieving collective party goals to the legislators appointed or elected to those posts. Legislators need to be motivated to pursue these efforts, but the same mix of goals that motivate others – an increment of influence over policy outcomes, visibility useful in the pursuit of reelection or higher office, satisfaction from involvement – may motivate at least a few legislators to attend to the collective interests of the party.

Legislators may not fully trust their leaders and committees. After all, power delegated to committees and leaders to pursue party interests might instead be used in pursuit of personal interests. Like all organizations, congressional parties address this threat – called the principal–agent problem, or simply the agency problem – in a variety of ways, such as by limiting the jurisdiction of committees and leaders, assigning some decisions to multimember committees or leadership groups rather than to individuals, subjecting top leaders to periodic election,

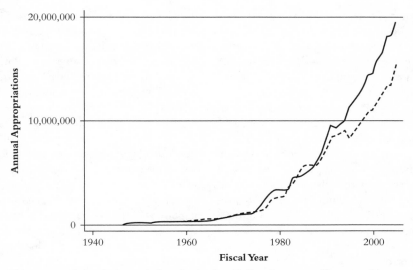

Figure 16.1. Annual appropriations in absolute dollars for party offices, 1946–2003: House (solid line) and Senate (dashed line). *Source:* Legislative Appropriations Bills.

and requiring leaders to justify their strategies at caucus or other party meetings.

Not all costs of collective action are paid by legislators. Often forgotten is the fact that certain collective party efforts can be provided without costing the rank-and-file party member anything. This is accomplished by appropriating public funds to supplement leaders' salaries, hire party staffs, and provide financial support of office operations and studio facilities. These appropriations became substantial after the 1946 Legislative Reorganization Act created party policy committees and continued a rapid rise over the following decades (Figure 16.1).

THE RELATIONSHIP BETWEEN ELECTORAL AND POLICY GOALS

Does it make any difference that I emphasize *both* electoral and policy goals? I have two answers to the question. First, yes, it does matter, and most major theoretical statements on congressional parties in the last 20 years either remain silent on the matter or, at least implicitly, agree with me. Second, by failing to come to terms with the relationship between electoral and policy goals, the existing theoretical accounts lack key ingredients that are required

to explain the creation and influence of congressional parties.

The Major Schools of Thought

One school of thought, I will call it the *electoral school*, follows in the footsteps of David Mayhew's book, *Congress: The Electoral Connection.* Mayhew explored the implications of an assumption about legislators' motivations – that legislators are single-minded seekers of reelection. Mayhew argued that reelection was the proximate goal of nearly all legislators, one that had to be achieved if they were going to achieve anything else. His book then explored the implications of the reelection goal for the behavior of individual legislators and for the organization of the policymaking process in the two houses. From this perspective, legislators do not have a personal or inherent interest in public policy or legislation. Rather, policy positions are advocated merely to serve the reelection goal, which entails a variety of nonlegislative strategies too.

An offspring of Mayhew's argument is the cartel theory of Cox and McCubbins. The congressional party, like a cartel, seeks to control factors that affect its success. A cartel, an organization of producers seeking a profit, limits competition and supply to allow the producers to fix prices and guarantee profits. Similarly, a congressional party seeks to control the legislative process to enhance the party's reputation and win elections. Gaining control over key features of the legislative process, such as the floor agenda, allows the congressional party, when in the majority, to keep off the floor matters that would divide the party or otherwise harm the party's image. Legislators who share a party label and therefore share a common fate have an incentive to manipulate the legislative process through the coordinated action of their party. The party, in turn, is driven by the goal of maintaining or enhancing the party reputation with the electorate.

A second school may be called the *policy school*. In this view, legislators seek policy outcomes as close to their own most preferred outcome as possible. Legislators may acquire policy preferences to appeal to home constituencies, to attract campaign contributions from special interests, to satisfy their personal preferences, or for other purposes, but, at least in their behavior as members of Congress, they behave as if minimizing the distance between their own preferences and the legislative outcome is the only consideration driving their choices as legislators. The most fully developed version of the policy school is spatial theory, which provides for a geometric characterization of the location of legislators and yields predictions of outcomes from the location of legislators' policy positions and the rules of the legislative process.

It is tempting to say that it does not matter which school of thought we favor because the two motivations – electoral and policy – are strongly correlated with each other. We might argue that the process of electing legislators matches candidates' policy dispositions to the policy positions of the local electorates. Liberal districts elect liberal candidates to Congress; conservative districts elect conservative candidates. For elected legislators, then, electoral and policy motivations are fully reinforcing and cannot be separated. Behavior that can be predicted from electoral motivations can be predicted from policy motivations, and vice versa.

This is the nature of representation. The schools are equivalent in all essentials, even if a little translation is required to see it.

I have noted that, as an empirical matter, I do not find this argument persuasive. Still, the distinct political motivations might predict identical behavior if the motivations are mutually reinforcing. Actually, most theorists say otherwise. Mayhew contends that the goal of reelection leads legislators to care little about mobilizing majorities for or against legislation, to give their attention to individualistic efforts to attract voters through position taking (announcing policy positions merely for home consumption), to ignore issues of general import and focusing on legislation with local benefits, to advertise themselves rather than engage meaningfully in the policymaking process, and to prefer individualistic activities over the teamwork of parties. In fact, Mayhew must allow for the existence of nonelectoral motivations – selective incentives – to explain why some legislators are willing to move beyond their own electoral needs to serve as party leaders. That is, nonelectoral motivations, such as additional influence or advantages in the policy process, must motivate at least some legislators (but not others). Mayhew plainly argues that the behavior generated by the goal of reelection is different from the behavior predicted by other goals.

Within the policy school, the spatial theorist assumes that *all* political forces that influence a legislator are captured by the concept of preferences, which is given a technical definition. A preference, in this view, is a legislator's most desired outcome at the moment of decision. The source of the preference is not relevant. The source could be personal policy commitments, campaign promises, interest group demands, or whatever, but the theorist focuses on the preference without concern about how it is formed. Party influence is not weighed against preference; rather, party influence, and any other political force, is incorporated in preference. With this definition, it is meaningless to speak of preferences versus other forces, such as partisan ones, because all direct influences on legislators' behavior are causally prior to preferences.

Strictly speaking, spatial theory posits that no other motivations are relevant once the preference is set. Preferences, along with the rules of the legislative game, determine legislators' behavior (strategies), but the theory simply does not address what forces are at work in determining preferences. Thus, spatial theory is silent on whether electoral considerations – or any other – are determinants of preferences.

Another variation within the policy school, which can be called the electoral coalition account, assumes a powerful connection between the electoral and legislative arenas but treats policy positions as the immediate cause of legislative behavior. In this set of studies, legislators' general policy positions are imported with elected legislators after each election and are assumed to be a product of the matching of electorates and legislators that occurs in the election process. Once legislators are in office, it is their policy positions, rather than prospective electoral considerations or other forces, which drive their behavior and determine the role of parties in the legislative arena.

THE INTERDEPENDENCE OF PARTY GOALS

My observation is that we must take this analysis a step farther. I have argued that legislators' electoral and career goals, their general policy attitudes, and their party labels are interdependent and important to Congress. Potential candidates for office choose a party and probably do so for both electoral and policy considerations. Furthermore, electoral success may reflect both policy and party considerations. And legislators' policy positions may reflect the influence of both electioneering and the need to appeal to fellow partisans. By the time a legislator arrives on Capitol Hill, these relationships – the triangulation of party, policy, and election – are established. Legislators do not choose their legislative party free of constraint in order to maximize utility in electoral or policy terms. Instead, the party label with which they ran for office dictates, with very few exceptions, the party with which they caucus in Congress. Thus, the most reasonable assumption appears to be

that a set of interdependent goals are imported to Congress that bind legislators to their parties.

Similarly, and less well understood, it seems, the electoral and policy goals of congressional parties are interdependent and often not fully compatible, at least in the short term. Winning elections helps create the sizable House and Senate coalitions necessary for passing or blocking legislation, and legislative success helps generate the desired reputation essential to winning elections. The responsibility of the party leaders is to further both party goals, while minimizing the severity of the tradeoffs that are required. This responsibility is manifested in the everyday activities of party leaders – managing the party organization, coordinating with the president or leaders of the other chamber, speaking on behalf of the party for the media and other audiences, managing floor activity, negotiating legislation within the chamber and with leaders of the other policymaking institutions, and even taking the lead in writing legislation and building majorities.

Fellow partisans may differ among themselves about the best choices to make. These differences are rooted in the variation in individuals' electoral and policy objectives and in judgments about collective and personal interests made under conditions of uncertainty. Intraparty conflict over the best collective strategic choices are reflected in arguments articulated in contests for leadership positions and the everyday meetings of the parties. As I illustrated in the Pelosi and Daschle episodes, this is the crux of intraparty politics on Capitol Hill.

Efforts to influence the voting behavior of legislators are a part, an important part, of a larger set of party activities intended to achieve collective goals. Leaders manipulate incentives (by using committee assignments, appointments for party posts, campaign contributions, and so on) to gain the votes of targeted legislators. The party creates and funds a campaign committee and leaders provide a variety of other services (radio and television studios; fund-raising activity; and staff support for research, publication, and other purposes) to enhance electoral prospects of partisans. Public relations activities and staff operations are designed to maintain or improve the party's reputation with the general public and to attract public support for the legislative objectives the party is pursuing.

Party goals are strongly implicated in floor activity. At the floor stage in the legislative process, legislators make policy choices for which they can be held accountable. Their actions are visible to their home electorates and often recorded for posterity. It is at this stage that it is most likely that a leader cannot simultaneously maximize the number of votes obtained, maximize the electoral value of the effort for party colleagues and candidates, and maximize the quality of the party's nationwide reputation. Choices are required and these choices motivate legislators to seek coordinated party strategies so that they do not work at cross purposes.

The complexities involved in pursuing electoral and policy goals are reflected in legislators' floor behavior. Policy goals are most obviously affected by the outcome of floor votes, although even floor votes do not always have much relevance to party goals. When a floor vote is relevant to a party's electoral or policy goals, party leaders may be involved in building majorities for and against legislation by structuring and influencing choices. Structuring choices is setting the agenda, while influencing choices once the agenda is set involves the manipulation of incentives to gain compliant behavior from individual legislators. Concern about majority party status and the party's reputation may alter the agenda-setting and direct-influence strategies that are chosen. For example, a legislator's electoral prospects may be harmed by voting with the party, which may force a party leader to choose between enhancing the chances of maintaining or gaining majority party status and winning a roll call vote. Or a party's reputation may be adversely affected by a loss and cause a leader to be more averse to risk in forcing a vote.

The strategic challenges motivate a collective response from party leaders. Party members demand it. Leaders are expected to create and use tools for minimizing the severity of the tradeoffs that they and their party colleagues

must make. In her account of majority party leaders' tasks, [political scientist Barbara] Sinclair emphasizes the structuring of choice – controlling the flow of legislation to the House floor and, by using special rules for major legislation to limit debate and amendments, manipulating the alternatives over which legislators are forced to make choices. By controlling the agenda, leaders can reduce the frequency with which they and their colleagues must choose between a preferred policy position and the position dictated by electoral concerns. They might be able to ensure that the opposition cannot offer an amendment that would split the party and create a public relations problem for the leadership. Parties may grant leaders other sources of influence that can be used to structure choices. Standing committee and conference committee members may be appointed for the purpose of generating policy proposals that suit the party's collective goals, which might be achieved by packaging legislation in certain ways. Thus, whether directly through floor scheduling or indirectly through the appointment of, or influence over, other agenda setters, control over agenda setting is expected to be a highly prized capacity of majority parties in Congress.

Sinclair's argument is an important one that is not fully incorporated in other discussions of agenda setting and parties. Agenda control by the majority party leadership not only helps the majority party establish a winning record that is useful for reelection, it also allows the majority party to diminish the severity of the tradeoffs it confronts when balancing electoral and policy objectives. These necessary tradeoffs are unlikely to be made in a satisfactory way unless skilled leaders give careful thought to them and are allowed to implement corresponding strategies.

The interdependence of parties' collective goals implies that even if party members are single-minded seekers of policy or reelection, as the single-goal theories assume, then fellow partisans share an interest in both collective goals. It appears that the assumption of multiple party goals is unavoidable, involves trade-offs between the goals at times, and serves as a realistic basis for developing expectations about the influence of parties in floor voting.

DIRECT AND INDIRECT INFLUENCE

Legislative party influence, direct or indirect, exists when the strategies of party leaders and rank-and-file members yield behavior on the part of at least some rank-and-file members that is more supportive of the party than it would be otherwise. As I have implied, direct influence corresponds to "pressure," "arm-twisting," and "leveraging" members. The subjects of direct influence are aware of the incentives to comply with requests to support the party or its leaders. Incentives might be tangible considerations, such as committee assignments and chairmanships, favorable scheduling of legislation, and campaign assistance, or less tangible considerations, such as the promise of continued convivial relations with party colleagues.

Direct influence usually is targeted at individuals. It is retail, custom-tailored politics – designed with the individual's interests and vulnerabilities in mind. From time to time, direct influence may be brought to bear on groups or factions of legislators, such as a state delegation that covets a committee assignment or piece of legislation. Direct influence also is implicated when committee chairs are informed by leaders and other colleagues that party loyalty is expected from them in their management of committee affairs and on major issues. Generally, direct influence involves an exchange, maybe an implicit one, between party leaders and individual legislators in which the individual legislators provide support for the party that they would not provide without the incentive provided by the party and its leadership. The match of parties' resources to legislators' interests determines the level of leaders' potential direct influence.

Indirect influence is simply all nondirect or nonpersonal forms of influence. The means for exercising indirect influence includes a somewhat disparate set of activities. These include, among other things, motivating other political actors to influence legislators on behalf of the legislative party, serving in a third-party role for deals arranged among fellow partisans, and setting the agenda in a way that favors certain policy outcomes. This is such a wide range of activities that it is difficult to generalize about. It is important to note that the indirect influence of leaders may not be obvious to members whose choices are constrained or altered by the action of party leaders. In fact, the source of indirect influence often is deliberately hidden from those legislators who are the targets of it. Indirect influence is frequently targeted at the House and Senate as a whole or at groups of legislators. Wholesale, rather than retail, politics is most frequently involved.

Party leaders seek to influence the electoral calculations of fellow legislators through public relations campaigns and appearances in the mass media. "Message" efforts, often organized with task forces or committees of legislators and sometimes organized for particularly important legislative battles, are now standard features of party efforts. Furthermore, leaders work with lobbyists, campaign contributors, presidents, local party officials, and others to orchestrate pressure on colleagues.

An important form of party leaders' indirect influence is to facilitate bargaining among fellow partisans in numerous ways, such as by

- arranging for meetings that would not occur otherwise,
- offering incentives for colleagues to work together,
- offering compromises or logrolls that otherwise would not have been proposed, or
- offering incentives to colleagues to adhere to agreements they have made with each other.

In more technical terms, leaders reduce or compensate for the transaction and opportunity costs associated with bargaining and enforce agreements (compromises and logrolls) among their colleagues.

Setting the agenda, the one kind of indirect influence that is given considerable attention by political scientists, may take several forms. The most commonly observed is manipulating the policy choices that are available for consideration on the floor by determining the bills to be considered and the rules under which bills are debated and amended. This form of influence over the agenda is most transparent in the House, where control over the Committee on Rules allows the majority leadership to determine the timing and content of special rules, resolutions that give legislation the right-of-way for floor consideration and set limits on debates and amendments. More indirect forms include inducing others, such as standing or conference committee members, to approve, block, or otherwise structure the agenda in a favorable way.

The distinction between direct and indirect influence is not without ambiguity. Party leaders frequently work with presidents and lobbyists to devise a common strategy for influencing the behavior of rank-and-file legislators. More important, some forms of indirect influence are built upon or coincident with direct influence. The Speaker's ability to control the floor agenda relies on his power to recognize legislators to make motions (without appeal) and his control over the Rules Committee. The right of recognition is important to controlling the floor agenda while also giving the Speaker the ability to do favors for legislators who seek to gain or avoid floor action on certain bills. In the case of the Rules Committee, the Speaker's ability to nominate the majority party members of the committee gives him a source of direct influence with those members who sit on the committee or seek appointment to it, an influence that serves as the foundation for setting the floor agenda on major legislation that passes through that committee. More generally, the manipulation of coveted committee assignments may be used as a source of leverage with individual legislators and as a way to affect the composition of committees so as to shape the form in which key legislation emerges and sets the floor agenda.

Plainly, the direct and indirect forms of influence do not operate in separate worlds. Having strong sources of one form of influence is likely to give party leaders influence of the other form, too. It seems likely that the strength of direct influence and the strength of indirect influence are positively correlated and, to some extent, interdependent. Each is sometimes put in the service of the other. If so, a theory of party strategy that focused on one form of influence to the exclusion of the other would be missing a central feature of the legislative world that party leaders inhabit.

Still, because the sources of direct and indirect influence are not identical, the two forms are not fully equivalent or interchangeable. Leaders' influence over committee assignments, which is a source of direct influence over individual legislators, comes from party rules governing the committee assignment process. Their influence over the floor agenda, which is a source of indirect influence, originates, in the case of the House, in chamber rules that create and empower the Committee on Rules to write resolutions governing floor debate and get the resolutions considered on the floor, in a chamber precedent that gives the Speaker the authority to recognize members on the floor to make motions, and in party rules that give the top party leaders the authority to nominate members to Rules. Plainly, it is possible to improve leaders' resources in one category without a large, immediate effect in the other category. If so, then direct influence and indirect influence are likely to be positively but not perfectly correlated with each other.

POSITIVE AND NEGATIVE INFLUENCE

Political scientists have noted the utility of distinguishing positive and negative forms of influence in the legislative arena. Negative power is the ability to defend the status quo in the face of a majority that favors change; positive power is the ability to change the status quo in the face of a majority that opposes change. Negative power usually involves preventing a decisive vote on a bill that would receive majority support. "Gatekeeping" is the term often applied to committees to reflect this form of indirect influence. It also may involve the application of direct influence to win votes against the passage of bills or amendments that would otherwise lead to a change in the policy status quo.

Table 16.1. *Types of Party Influence*

	Direct	Indirect
Positive	X	
Negative		X

Positive power includes the ability to force a vote on a particular proposal, as when a conference committee tucks new provisions into a bill that will not receive a separate vote later in either parent chamber. It includes the ability to protect bills from amendments, as when a bill is considered on the House floor under special rules limiting amendments or under suspension of the rules. Or it may simply involve buying votes by offering side payments (that is, special considerations unrelated to the policy at issue) to a few legislators to muster a majority in favor of a bill.

In principle, direct and indirect influence can be exercised for both negative and positive purposes. Four categories of influence are possible, as shown in Table 16.1, with most studies emphasizing either the direct, positive form (upper left) for majority party leaders or, more recently, the indirect, negative form (lower right), particularly agenda control. We must account for the full array of possibilities to accurately capture the nature of party influence on legislative outcomes.

Two stories illustrate the importance of considering the empty cells in Table 16.1. Direct influence may play a role in preventing a policy proposal from getting a vote on the floor of the House of Representatives (lower-left cell in Table 16.1). In 1994, the House majority leadership prevented a measure to change the House rules from coming to a vote. At stake was a budget deficit reduction bill called the "A-to-Z" bill after its chief sponsors, Robert Andrews (D-NJ) and Bill Zeliff (R-NH). Sponsored by a majority of the House, most minority party Republicans and some Democrats, the bill would guarantee every member the right to offer floor amendments that would reduce spending in any federal program. The leadership of the majority party Democrats opposed the bill because it would undermine their ability to set the floor agenda. The chief sponsors of the bill filed a discharge petition, which requires 218 signatures to force floor action on a bill, but were unable to persuade at least 33 of the cosponsors to sign the petition.

Press accounts, confirmed by subsequent systematic analysis, indicate that Democrats were persuaded by their leadership not to sign the petition. Leaders pursued extensive negotiations with key legislators and factions whose support of the leaders' position was in doubt. Only after agreeing to bring up a separate entitlement reform bill did the Democratic leadership persuade wayward party colleagues not to sign the discharge petition. The majority party leadership, it turned out, was compelled to bargain, make personal appeals and concessions, and use positive agenda-setting tools to prevent discharge. Direct influence and a promise to approve floor action on a new bill were required to prevent discharge of the A-to-Z bill.

An illustration of indirect influence enabling the enactment of legislation that otherwise would be killed (upper-right cell in Table 16.1) is the strategic use of packaging. An everyday strategy on Capitol Hill is to package into larger bills provisions that would not gain approval by both houses or the president as stand-alone measures. In the House, a packaged measure can be protected by a special rule, written under the direction of the leadership, which bars or limits floor amendments related to the unpopular provisions as long as a majority of the House supports the special rule. In the Senate, packaging provisions in reconciliation bills, which are considered under time limits set in law, protects the measures from filibusters that might otherwise arise. And a president, who cannot veto individual provisions in bills, may be persuaded to sign a large bill that includes provisions he dislikes.

PART VI. THE STANDING COMMITTEES

CHAPTER SEVENTEEN

Distributive and Partisan Issues in Agriculture Policy in the 104th House

Mark S. Hurwitz, Roger J. Moiles, and David W. Rohde

The authors test the competing theories of legislative organization – distributive, informational, and partisan – by examining the decisions and policies of the House Agriculture Committee. They argue that under certain conditions each of the theories offers some insight into committee behavior. Specifically, they find that the committee's policy space is multidimensional and that there are instances of both partisan and distributive considerations. Moreover, there are circumstances in which the committee acts in accordance with chamber preferences as well as instances in which high demanders on the committee take policy stances that are inconsistent with the floor.

There has been substantial debate among students of Congress concerning the theoretical and empirical applicability of various theories of legislative behavior and organization. Some scholars contend that one perspective is a sufficient explanation of legislative organization and decision making, but others argue that various theories apply at varying times and under differing circumstances. "Rather than seek a single, universal account of congressional politics – whether distributive, informational, partisan, or anything else – we should recognize that all of these considerations operate in varying degrees

Mark S. Hurwitz, Roger J. Moiles, and David W. Rohde. 2001. "Distributive and Partisan Issues in Agriculture Policy in the 104th House" *American Political Science Review* 95(4): 911–22. Copyright © 2001 by the American Political Science Association. Reprinted with the permission of Cambridge University Press.

and that the variation is systematic and predictable." This study is an effort to extend and apply the latter view.

We want to assist in the effort to see that these varying legislative theories are "knitted together." To that end, we analyze agriculture policymaking in the 104th House. The House Agriculture Committee is considered a classic constituency committee. Assignments to it are dominated by constituency interests, and its policies fit the distributive politics mold. With a new Republican majority for the first time in 40 years, however, the 104th House exhibited some of the most partisan behavior in this century. Moreover, a number of legislative initiatives, generally supported by the new House leadership, sought to eliminate certain entrenched agriculture programs, which posed a potential conflict between the partisan and distributive inclinations of some members.

We use a number of roll call votes on agriculture policy in the 104th Congress to analyze the behavior of members of both the House Agriculture Committee and the Agriculture and Rural Development Subcommittee of the House Appropriations Committee in comparison to the remainder of the House. Our purpose is not to support one theoretical view over another. Rather, evidence indicates that various perspectives apply simultaneously, and each perspective does not account for some empirical patterns.

THEORIES OF LEGISLATIVE BEHAVIOR AND ORGANIZATION

The three theories of legislative behavior and organization of interest here are addressed in detail elsewhere, and we will discuss them only briefly. The distributive perspective posits that legislative gains from trade result from exchange of votes and influence across multiple jurisdictions. This process is reinforced by the committee system, both because of differing preferences between committees and the floor and through the use of conference committees.

Krehbiel contends that instead of logrolling to maximize distributive gains, legislators act in order to obtain and distribute information. According to informational theory, committees generally are representative of the parent body and provide it with information on the merits of legislation within the committee's jurisdiction. From this perspective, "legislative choices in salient policy domains are median choices."

Partisan theories contend that parties can exert an independent influence on behavior and outcomes. Rohde's "conditional party government" theory argues that a changing environment in the electorate resulted in greater homogeneity within the parties in the House, and when certain issues exhibit strong party congruence, members of the majority party will provide the leadership with authority to exert influence to ensure desired partisan results. The theory is labeled "conditional" because it applies only in specified circumstances. Moreover, Rohde contends that each of these perspectives on legislative organization has applicability:

The complex environment I have been discussing cannot be captured by any single-motivation, universal perspective, and we should not seek to demonstrate that one of the rationales above is superior to the others across all congressional activity. Our challenge, as students of congressional politics, is instead to specify the conditions under which each rationale is relevant to behavior and outcomes of interest, and in particular the ways in which the sets of multiple motivations interact to affect results.

We share with informational theory the view that the median floor preference is a powerful force in majority-rule institutions such as the House. Yet, under some conditions, either distributive or partisan influences can move the legislative outcome away from the center of the floor. That is, House members may desire committees to provide information regarding legislation within their jurisdiction, but that is not necessarily the only thing that parties and members want from committees, so it is not the only structuring influence.

Under what conditions would we expect the legislative outcome to shift from the median House preference? From a distributive viewpoint, when certain issues within the jurisdiction of a particular committee are of great import to its members but not to the rest of the House, the committee will use its influence in various ways to ensure that the outcome on the floor accords with its policy preferences. Preferences on these distributive issues will cut across party lines on the basis of geographic or economic interests, and the committee may be able to affect the legislative outcome if the preferences of its members are both sufficiently strong and homogeneous. This condition includes the traditional notion of a committee, such as House Agriculture, as a supplier of "private goods" to its constituents. We discuss this perspective in greater detail in the section on preference outliers.

From a partisan viewpoint, member preferences on partisan issues will be shaped by conflicts along party lines among rank-and-file voters or among party activists. When the majority party is relatively (but not perfectly) homogeneous in its beliefs on an issue salient to its members, and those beliefs are different from the floor median, the majority will use its influence over the rules and structures of the body to attempt to steer the outcome away from the center of the floor and toward the median of the majority party. For example, the majority party may populate certain committees with party loyalists and offer positive or negative incentives to influence the preferences of some House members, or through rules and in other ways it may set the agenda of the House.

In general, when an issue is not highly salient to a constituency committee or the majority party, or when the membership of either is not sufficiently homogeneous on a salient issue, we would expect no distributive or partisan influence. Instead, the preference of the median member should dictate the outcome, as informational theory posits. We do not imply that distributive issues have no partisan content or vice versa. Certainly, these analytic categories have real-world overlap, and we classify them on the basis of their predominant character. Some issues will provoke partisan divisions, others will involve distributive concerns, some others will involve both, and still others neither. For convenience, we will describe the set of distributive issue dimensions as the distributive domain and the set of partisan issues as the partisan domain.

COMMITTEE OUTLIERS AND JURISDICTION

The issue of committees as preference outliers is related to the debate on the number and type of policy dimensions within the House. Essentially, a committee is an outlier if the preferences of its members systematically differ from those of the legislature as a whole. The members "more or less homogeneously demand high levels of benefits from policies that fall into their committees' jurisdictions."

Because we expect committees to be outliers on some (e.g., distributive) issue dimensions but not on others (e.g., those salient to parties), the relevant measurement issue concerns the appropriate level of analysis. To determine whether the committee is representative of the floor, we believe it is necessary to examine committee member and nonmember behavior on particular roll calls. Accordingly, we compare the floor votes of Agriculture Committee members and nonmembers on matters specific to the committee's jurisdiction. This allows us to analyze whether (and when) members of a committee have preferences that are different from those of the parent chamber, whether the committee is an outlier, and under what circumstances. Moreover, if the committee is an outlier, we can then explore whether this translates into committee power, as demons-

trated by legislative outcomes that are clearly affected by the preferences of the committee members.

AGRICULTURE POLICY AND COMMITTEES IN THE 104TH HOUSE

With "jurisdiction over programs that have concentrated benefits (for one's constituents) but widely dispersed costs," the House Agriculture Committee is considered one of the "constituency committees" from which classic distributive policies generally flow. In addition, while the Appropriations Committee is regarded as one of the chamber's "prestige committees," its Agriculture and Rural Development Subcommittee (hereafter, agriculture appropriations subcommittee) exists in a similar environment to the Agriculture Committee, as it determines spending allocations for agriculture policy each fiscal year. We chose to study both in our comparison of committee member behavior to that of the full House.

One consequence of the 1994 elections was that agriculture policy in the 104th House broke with tradition because of the partisan dimension injected into an otherwise distributive context. At least since the Eisenhower years, most of the GOP had been staunch defenders of farm price supports, but in 1995 the Agriculture Committee held hearings on the so-called Freedom to Farm bill (HR 2195), which was strongly supported by the new Republican leadership. In addition to reauthorizing farm programs, the primary purposes of the bill were to cut program budgets in general by about $16 billion over seven years and to eliminate and/or phase out specific farm subsidies. As originally drafted, the bill "threatened to shatter GOP unity." In fact, after it held hearings, the Agriculture Committee rejected Freedom to Farm when four southern Republicans joined all the Democrats in opposition. It was apparent that partisan and distributive motivations were in conflict for some committee members.

Another version of the bill was introduced by Chairman Pat Roberts (R-KS) in 1996

(HR 2854). Although the committee approved this draft with greater GOP support, dissension among committee Republicans reappeared on the floor when various amendments designed to phase out price supports, such as peanut and sugar programs, were offered. Our analysis concerns a number of roll calls from this version of Freedom to Farm (HR 2854). Comparable votes are chosen from the agriculture appropriations bills for fiscal 1996 (HR 1976) and 1997 (HR 3603).

The agriculture policy issue offers a particularly useful context within which to test the competing perspectives. The separate initiatives to eliminate specific farm programs provide a distinctive opportunity to separate distributive preferences from partisan or other motivations. Because distributive programs ordinarily pass by consensus, either by voice vote or nearly unanimous roll calls, variations in preferences usually are not revealed. Nevertheless, when the era of expanding government effectively ended with the indexing of tax brackets in 1981 and ballooning budget deficits, competition increased among members for dispensing pork to their constituencies. Thus, if the floor seeks to cut substantially or eliminate a distributive program that is salient to a constituency committee, an opportunity arises to examine conflict in distributive policy.

Let us summarize the theoretical expectations that will be judged against the evidence. We expect that multiple issue dimensions will be revealed in the voting on agriculture policy. More specifically, some issues will divide members along party lines. Others will cut across party lines based on constituency interests. Members from farm districts will be highly supportive of distributive agriculture policies, and those from nonagricultural districts will be much less supportive. These patterns will be reinforced by committee membership: Members of the two agriculture committees will exhibit greater support for distributive policies than other members, ceteris paribus. This means that we expect the agriculture committees to be high demanders of benefits and unrepresentative of the House on distributive matters, in contrast to the predictions of

Krehbiel's informational theory. Note, however, that this expectation applies only to distributive issues; we expect the committee to be more representative of the chamber on partisan issues.

DATA AND METHODS

In addition to the 1996 farm bill, the 104th Congress passed two agriculture appropriations bills, one for fiscal 1996 (hereafter, FY96) and one for fiscal 1997 (hereafter, FY97). Although these involved less conflict than Freedom to Farm, there were partisan and distributive aspects that shed light on the multiple interests of committee members. In floor action on these three bills there were thirty-seven roll calls, twelve on the farm bill, nineteen on FY96, and six on FY97. In order to draw the clearest comparisons for issue types, we selected all roll calls that we could identify a priori as either distributive or partisan. In particular, these roll calls allow us to compare member behavior on distributive and partisan dimensions in the same bill.

Distributive issues [fall under] the jurisdiction of a constituency committee, which address programs with broadly dispersed costs and concentrated benefits. All the roll calls we identify a priori as distributive were proposals either to eliminate a program altogether or to reduce substantially its funding level. On these votes, which would likely produce conflict, we expect legislators whose constituencies would be detrimentally affected to vote against the amendment. Thus, distributive behavior is revealed, a pattern not discernible when distributive legislation is passed by consensus.

Issues are considered partisan when they invoke the interests of competing partisan electoral coalitions or of respective groups of party activists. Examples are social welfare or environmental policy and questions regarding the appropriate (or inappropriate) scope of federal action. If an issue ordinarily divides the parties and leaders in their endeavor to move public policy in their preferred direction, we deem such a roll call to be partisan.

Table 17.1. *Vote on Selected Farm Bill Amendments by Member Status*

	Total[a]	Republicans	Democrats
Distributive Amendment to Phase Out Peanut Price Support Program, Roll Call 2034			
All members	209–212 (49.6%)	125–108 (53.6%)	84–104 (44.7%)
Agriculture Committee	6–42 (12.5%)	2–25 (7.4%)	4–17 (19.0%)
Appropriations subcommittee	2–9 (18.2%)	1–6 (14.3%)	1–3 (25.0%)
Noncommittee members[b]	201–161 (55.5%)	122–77 (61.3%)	79–83 (48.8%)
Partisan Democratic Substitute Amendment, Roll Call 2040			
All members	163–258 (38.7%)	1–233 (0.4%)	162–25 (86.6%)
Agriculture Committee	19–27 (41.3%)	0–27 (0.0%)	19–0 (100.0%)
Appropriations subcommittee	4–7 (36.4%)	0–7 (0.0%)	4–0 (100.0%)
Noncommittee members[b]	140–224 (38.5%)	1–199 (0.5%)	139–25 (84.8%)
Summary Statistics			
Distributive Peanut Amendment (Roll Call 2034)			
Committee vs. Noncommittee members[b]	$\chi^2(1) = 31.38$**	$\chi^2(1) = 27.89$**	$\chi^2(1) = 6.50$*
Subcommittee vs. Noncommittee members[b]	$\chi^2(1) = 6.00$*	$\chi^2(1) = 6.22$*	$\chi^2(1) = 0.86$
Partisan Democratic Substitute (Roll Call 2040)			
Committee vs. Noncommittee members[b]	$\chi^2(1) = 0.14$	$\chi^2(1) = 0.14$	$\chi^2(1) = 3.36$
Subcommittee vs. Noncommittee members[b]	$\chi^2(1) = 0.02$	$\chi^2(1) = 0.04$	$\chi^2(1) = 0.72$

[a] The pairs are yea–nay vote; the percentage voting yea is in parentheses.
[b] Representatives who are not members of either the Agriculture Committee or the agriculture appropriations subcommittee.
* $p \leq .05$.
** $p \leq .01$.

RESULTS AND DISCUSSION

For the selected roll calls we make direct comparisons of the committee and subcommittee members' floor votes relative to the rest of the chamber, controlling for party. We also address the manner in which district characteristics influence committee membership and voting behavior.

DISTRIBUTIVE AND PARTISAN VOTES ON AGRICULTURE POLICY

Table 17.1 reports on two amendments to the farm bill, one classified a priori as distributive, the other as partisan. The distributive vote was on roll call 2034, an amendment that would phase out over seven years federal support to peanut farmers. This is clearly a distributive issue. It is striking that this amendment failed, even if by only three votes, given its strong support from noncommittee members. Yet, there

was a clear consensus among members of both the Agriculture Committee and the agriculture appropriations subcommittee against ending the program, and they overcame a forty-vote deficit among the noncommittee members to preserve it. If the committee preferences had mirrored the rest of the chamber even a little more closely, the amendment would have passed. This is a clear example of outlier behavior by the committees, behavior that reversed the outcome preferred by the rest of the House.

Examination of the partisan patterns yields further interesting results. Although the roll call to terminate the distributive peanut program could be classified as a party-unity vote – a small GOP majority favored the amendment, while the Democrats opposed it – both parties on the floor showed substantial internal division. Within the committee and subcommittee, however, clear majorities of both parties staunchly opposed the amendment. This bipartisan resistance on the committees enabled them

Table 17.2. *Mean Absolute Differences in Percentage Voting Yea between Committee/Subcommittee and Noncommittee Members*

Roll Call	Noncommittee Members[a] versus	Total	Republicans	Democrats
All Distributive Votes	Committee	37.0	40.0	34.4
	Subcommittee	35.9	40.1	30.6
All Partisan Votes	Committee	0.3	3.3	4.8
	Subcommittee	12.0	18.7	4.1

[a] Representatives who are not members of either the Agriculture Committee or the agriculture appropriations subcommittee.

to overturn the preferences of the noncommittee members on this distributive issue.

Table 17.1 also shows the vote on Rep. Charles Stenholm's (D-TX) amendment to the farm bill, roll call 2040. The Democrats' substitute amendment, which proposed an alternative to the GOP's policy, clearly is a partisan issue. It supported greater federal involvement in agriculture, in contrast to the Republican leaders' phase out. As we would expect, the committee voting pattern was nearly identical to that of the noncommittee floor in a strong party-unity result. In fact, there were no partisan defectors in either committee. As predicted, committee member behavior is substantially different when faced with a partisan roll call than when a distributive vote is at issue.

The analysis of these two roll calls shows that both distributive and partisan dimensions were present in the farm bill. That is, multidimensionality exists in the legislative environment, even within a single bill. These roll calls are not unique, however. They are representative of the outcome and voting patterns for the other roll calls on the three bills. On every distributive roll call, an overwhelming majority of Agriculture Committee members voted in opposition to a majority of nonmembers on the floor. The same was true of the subcommittee on nearly all votes; its members voted consistently with the Agriculture Committee, not the rest of the House. In fact, committee and subcommittee behavior on the distributive votes had a profound effect on the outcome; in five of the roll calls the amendment's failure was a direct result of committee member divergence from nonmembers. Yet, on partisan votes the decisions

of committee members rather closely resembled those of their party colleagues.

Further evidence of multidimensionality, as well as the representativeness of the roll calls presented above, is found in Table 17.2. Here we present the mean absolute percentage differences in the percentage voting "yea" on all relevant roll calls between the committee or subcommittee compared to the rest of the House. These results confirm the divergence of both panels from the rest of the House on distributive issues. Across distributive roll calls, the mean absolute difference between both the committee and subcommittee and other representatives was more than 35 percent. This is in stark contrast to the absolute differences on partisan votes of 0.3 percent and 12 percent for committee and subcommittee, respectively. (Comparable values are obtained for each party separately.) These findings illustrate that when committee members were confronted with threats to distributive programs salient to their constituents, their behavior clearly differed from that of the chamber. Yet, when partisan issues were at stake, committee members act in concert with the House. The relatively high deviation between committee Republicans and GOP colleagues on the floor on distributive (but not partisan) votes implies a conflict in their distributive and partisan motivations.

THE EFFECT OF DISTRICT CHARACTERISTICS
ON VOTING BEHAVIOR

The discussion has focused primarily on the contrasting voting patterns of committee

Table 17.3. *Voting Behavior on Amendment to FY96 Bill to Prohibit Funds for Tobacco Program, Roll Call 1544, by Level of District Characteristics*

District Level[a]	Farm Employment			Rural Population		
	Number Voting		% Yea	Number Voting		% Yea
	Yea	Nay		Yea	Nay	
All Members						
Low	94	36	72.9	95	41	69.9
Middle	62	90	40.8	70	74	48.6
High	43	97	30.7	34	108	23.9
Agriculture Committee						
Low	–	–	–	1	0	100.0
Middle	2	9	18.2	2	13	13.3
High	6	30	16.7	5	26	16.1
Appropriations Subcommittee						
Low	–	–	–	–	–	–
Middle	1	3	25.0	2	5	28.6
High	2	5	28.6	1	3	25.0
Noncommittee Members[b]						
Low	94	36	72.3	94	41	69.6
Middle	59	78	43.1	66	56	54.1
High	35	62	36.1	28	79	26.2

[a] Division into approximately equal thirds is based upon the values obtained for the farm employment and rural population variables. See Appendix B for data sources.

[b] Representatives who are not members of either the Agriculture Committee or the agriculture appropriations subcommittee.

members and other representatives. It also is important to consider the effect, if any, of district characteristics on the voting behavior of these groups. Two indicators are relevant for agriculture policy. The first is *Farm Employment* as a percentage of district employment. The second is *Rural Population* as a percentage of district population. For each variable, the House membership is divided into thirds, representing low, middle, and high levels of both district farm employment and rural population.

To demonstrate a connection between constituency characteristics and roll call voting, we apply these district classifications to votes on roll call 1544, a failed (distributive) amendment to limit various tobacco support programs in the FY96 spending bill. The results in Table 17.3 indicate that House members from districts with high farm and rural proportions who serve on the two committees were most likely to oppose the amendment. Furthermore, noncommittee members from such districts were much

more likely to vote against it, in contrast to noncommittee members from the low categories of each variable, who voted overwhelmingly to cut these funds. Similar results were obtained in other distributive votes. The mean percentage of House members who voted to reduce distributive tobacco programs was more than twice as high for the low category than for the high category. On the partisan votes a majority of both parties at each level of farm and rural characteristics supported the party position. The highest mean absolute percentage differences among Republicans for these levels of farm and rural district characteristics are only 11.3 percent and 9 percent, respectively, while for Democrats they are 1.4 percent and 0.9 percent.

This analysis is consistent with the self-selection hypothesis, that is, high demanders of benefits attempt to secure a seat on committees with a direct connection to district concerns. On partisan matters, differences between committee members and nonmembers are negligible. Thus, the Agriculture Committee is both representative and unrepresentative of the House membership, depending on the type of issue involved.

Two further points can be made. First, the two committees are largely different from the rest of the House in terms of district characteristics as well as interest in agriculture policy. Rather than being a heterogeneous mix, they are drawn primarily from districts that are substantially more oriented toward agricultural concerns than the rest of the House and, therefore, are likely to be high demanders of agricultural benefits for their constituents. Second, members of these committees behave most similarly to the subset of noncommittee members who are elected from heavily rural and farm-oriented districts.

CONCLUSION

The results of the empirical analysis provide support for all the main points of our theoretical argument. We expected that multiple issue dimensions would be revealed in the roll calls, and that some of those dimensions would be characterized by partisan voting, whereas others would reflect distributive interests. The two roll calls on the farm bill that we examined in detail demonstrate exactly this pattern, and the results on all the other partisan and distributive amendments are consistent with those results. We also expected to observe a specific pattern in the voting related to committee membership: As high demanders, members of the agriculture committees should be much more supportive of distributive policies than nonmembers. On these issues, the committee would be unrepresentative of the House. This expectation was also supported. On all the individual distributive amendments, and in the aggregate, members of the two agriculture committees were substantially more supportive of the programs

than were nonmembers. Also as expected, on partisan issues there was no similar difference in the vote choices of committee members and nonmembers.

This study indicates that all three of the theoretical perspectives we discuss can explain some aspects of congressional behavior and organization, but none offers a complete account by itself. Partisan theory is not always applicable because not all issues invoke partisan interests. Similarly, distributive theory does not speak to all aspects of legislative politics because only some issues are primarily distributive, and the analysis regarding gains from exchange across jurisdictions does not seem to apply to all policy questions. Finally, some of the results we present are inconsistent with the majoritarian expectations of informational theory. On distributive issues, members of the agriculture committees are unrepresentative of the House and are high demanders of benefits. But they are representative of the House on other issues, as Krehbiel's theory predicts. Moreover, on some distributive roll calls the committee members voted in the direction opposite to a majority of the chamber, which produced an outcome different from that preferred by the rest of the House. In addition, there were multiple issue dimensions with different preference patterns for each of three bills analyzed, contrary to a unidimensional perspective.

We do not offer here a new general theory of legislative behavior, and that was not our purpose. Instead, we suggest the direction that future theorizing should take and provide some evidence in support of that suggestion. The results of this study seem consistent with the view that a multifaceted combination of the various theories of legislative organization, which specifies for each the locus and range of its applicability, promises a richer explanation of congressional behavior than any one of those theories alone.

CHAPTER EIGHTEEN

Principals, Goals, Dimensionality, and Congressional Committees

Forrest Maltzman and Steven S. Smith

The authors contend that committees are best viewed as agents of multiple principals. That is, committee members take direction from constituents, the parent chamber, and their party. The relative importance of these principals varies across committees and over time. The authors explore the influence of three factors – issue salience, partisanship, and dimensionality – on the relationship of committees to the principals.

Three issues distinguish recent positive theories of congressional institutions from each other. The first issue is the identity of the principals for whom standing committee members serve as agents. (The focus on committees and their members is natural because committees occupy a special place in the decision-making process.) The possible principals include district constituents, the parent chamber, and the parent parties (or at least the median voter within each party).

The second issue is motivation or goals. Reasonable motivations for the various principals have been proposed. Constituents seek federal benefits, the typical member in the parent chamber seeks to reduce uncertainty about policy outcomes, and party leaders seek to protect or enhance the reputation of the party. Committee members seek reelection, policy choices, or policy outcomes.

Forrest Maltzman and Steven S. Smith. 1994. "Principals, Goals, Dimensionality, and Congressional Committees," *Legislative Studies Quarterly* XIX (August): 457–76. Reprinted with permission.

The third issue is political dimensionality. The complexity of the issues and the presence of cross-cutting majorities are problems for any set of principals – constituents, chamber colleagues, or party colleagues. Problems that beset collective action by these groups are compounded by problems of majority-rule cycling whenever the political space is characterized by two or more dimensions.

We wish to draw attention back to the sources of variation in relations between committees, parties, and the parent chambers. After noting important sources of variation across committees and the theoretical difficulties those sources create, we outline several propositions about these sources of variation and report some new evidence that lends support to the propositions. We conclude by [discussing the] problems in the evolving theory of congressional institutions and suggest subjects to be addressed in the future.

REVISITING SOME PROPOSITIONS ABOUT CONGRESSIONAL COMMITTEES

Only two decades ago, it seems fair to say, most congressional scholars would have agreed on three propositions: members have multiple goals; committees operate in complex environments, in which their members have multiple principals; and the policy space within which Congress and committees operate is multidimensional. On balance, subsequent research appears to have reinforced the validity of these generalizations. The proposition of multidimensionality has been attacked with meaningful data, but the case for a strictly unidimensional interpretation of congressional politics remains weak.

Nevertheless, nearly all recent positive theories assume that one or more of these basic propositions is wrong or irrelevant. Such assumptions may account for much of the resistance to these new arguments among more traditional political scientists. The complications of multiple goals, multiple principals, and multiple dimensions threaten the viability of the principal–agent theories offered so far.

Consider multiple goals. Two goals – good public policy and reelection – appear to be widely held. In fact, in certain kinds of legislative activity, they are pursued jointly and are viewed as compatible. Yet, the presence of multiple goals greatly affects the viability of the existing theories. In the party theory, the reelection goal motivates members to be concerned about party reputation and to license leaders to take actions to preserve or enhance party reputation. Just how much members would condition this license if they disagreed with the policy stances of their leaders is left indeterminant. Similarly, information theory turns critically on the assumption that members care about policy outcomes. According to this theory, uncertainty about policy outcomes may lead legislators to prefer information about numerous policy options from the diverse membership of a committee. But uncertainty about reelection prospects may lead legislators to prefer a less diverse committee that keeps politically dangerous issues off the floor. The net effect of outcome-oriented and reelection-oriented strategies on committee composition is indeterminant.

Multiple sets of principals create similar theoretical problems. First, let us note how tempting it is to identify an ultimate principal for congressional committees. All rules governing the House are established by floor majorities, so it is natural to conclude that committees are created, their jurisdictions and powers set, and their products crafted to meet the needs of the parent chamber. And yet committees are composed of members who are subject to influences that, at least in the short or medium term, are not manipulated by the parent chamber – home constituencies, congressional parties, and so on. If committee members may be required to balance competing demands, their behavior cannot be predicted on the basis of the expectations of any one set of principals. Variation across committees and across time in the mix of goal-relevant demands further undermines simple models.

Finally, multidimensionality greatly complicates principal–agent relations. Multidimensional policy spaces make it highly unlikely that a single member or group will hold a median position in the parent chamber or within either party. Without such a median member or group, there is no clear majority preference about institutional arrangements, policies, or policy outcomes for a chamber or party. And without a predictable majority preference, the expectations of the principal cannot be defined, at least not narrowly.

Multidimensionality complicates matters in other ways as well. Most obviously, multidimensionality infects committee deliberations just as it does the deliberations of the parent chambers and parties. If more than one dimension is subject to legislation from a committee, even the committee's behavior is unstable. Why would any principal license agents whose behavior is so unpredictable? Why would committee members be motivated to specialize or to seek any gains from trade when their own committee's policy choices are so unpredictable?

SOURCES OF VARIATION

It may by now seem unlikely that a coherent principal–agent theory of congressional committees could capture their variation and their complexity in goals, principals, and dimensionality. But Congress may not exhibit all the variation and complexity that is possible. We must begin by developing and testing theories about that variation and complexity.

What causes potential principals to vary in importance for committee members? The relevant considerations include the character of the issue agenda, the alignment of policy preferences among members, and the inherited institutional arrangements. Some discussion of these sources is in order.

Over its history as Congress enlarged its policy agenda it continuously elaborated its committee systems, the basic means for dividing labor and increasing its capacity to process legislation. New issues have sometimes been sufficiently distinctive that their jurisdiction could be assigned to a single committee in each house. But, particularly with the increasing integration of national and international society in the twentieth century, new issues have not always fallen neatly within established jurisdictions, creating conflict among committees, sometimes producing slow and incoherent policymaking, and generating interest in reform.

Furthermore, the dimensionality and partisanship of policy alignments have varied. Highly partisan alignments have followed dramatic shifts in the coalitions supporting the two major parties, shifts that have been labeled realignments. The realignments have been associated with a change in the dimensionality of political divisions as well. The timing of these realignments – in the Civil War years, the 1890s, and the 1930s – has given congressional partisanship a cyclical cast that contrasts sharply with the consistent increases in the size and complexity of the congressional agenda. Thus, a pattern of periodically centralized party leadership appears to overlay a more linear trend toward more elaborate committee systems.

While the House and Senate have been subject to similar changes in the agenda and policy alignments, they have evolved different decision rules that affect the ability of each chamber to change its institutional arrangements. In the Senate, where there is more tolerance of individual initiative and obstructionism and more resistance to committee-imposed or party-imposed policy choices, the decision rules make change in institutional arrangements more difficult than do the decision rules of the House.

This brief discussion suggests that the relative importance of the various principals – home constituencies, party, the parent chamber – is likely to differ across committees and vary over time. Theorists seeking to account for such things as floor procedures, the power of party leaders, and committee assignment processes and outcomes must confront this variation. We suspect that the principal–agent relations shaping each committee's behavior varies in predictable ways.

In this preliminary effort, we restrict our attention to the House and to the effects of just three factors – issue salience, partisanship, and dimensionality – from among the many properties of issue agendas and preference alignments that are likely to influence each committee's relations with its parent chamber and parties. Issue salience affects the identity of the members who care to influence policy choices or outcomes. Partisanship affects the willingness of members to draw upon party organs to control committees. Dimensionality affects the ability of the parent parties and chamber to exercise control over committees.

Specifically, we test two hypotheses. First, when issues are unidimensional and are salient to most members but partisanship is low, the chamber–committee relationship dominates and chamber–committee congruence in expressed preferences is especially high. Second, when issues are multidimensional and are not salient to most members, committees are relatively autonomous and congruences in expressed preferences between chamber and committee and between party and committee are low.

We look for confirming and disconfirming data for these hypotheses in the roll call record on legislation from three House committees: Agriculture, Appropriations, and Energy and Commerce. Agriculture has jurisdiction over issues that lack broad salience, so its members should exhibit less congruity with the parent chamber and parties. Appropriations has a diverse jurisdiction that is not likely to produce unidimensional alignments; we expect low congruity on some of those dimensions. Energy and Commerce is the major authorizing committee of the House, with jurisdiction over issues that are usually salient to most members; its members should be largely congruent with the expressed preferences of their parent parties and chamber. We view the analysis of these three committees as a weak basis for generalization to all House committees.

DATA

We turn to the roll-call record to explore the degree of congruity in expressed policy preferences suggested by our hypotheses.

We limit ourselves to contested amendments from the 94th, 96th, 98th, and 100th Congresses, with a subset of amendments for the legislation associated with each House committee. We use two measures of congruence in expressed preferences. The disagreement measure is the frequency with which the chamber majority and committee majority disagree. The divergence measure is the average difference in the percentage of committee members and chamber members voting yea on each vote. The disagreement measure taps differences in median positions; the divergence measure taps differences in mean positions.

To supplement the congruence measures and explore dimensionality, we identify issue-specific scales for each committee. For each scale, we devise a qualitative characterization of the alignment of committee, party, and chamber positions and offer an additional test of committee–chamber congruence for single dimensions. Median scale scores are determined for the committee, for each party's committee contingent, for the chamber as a whole (excluding committee members), and for each party caucus (excluding committee members). In contrast to the divergence and disagreement scores, which capture central tendency and relative variance, the scales permit us to show the direction of any bias in committee or committee contingent positions.

To evaluate the observed differences between committee, party, and chamber medians, we used a difference of medians test. While the test enables us to determine whether the distribution that occurs could have occurred randomly, it does not indicate whether the differences are meaningful. Meaningfulness is determined in part by the distances between the various medians within a distribution. To assess these distances, we calculated the percentage of members whose scores on a particular issue dimension were situated at the chamber median or between the chamber and committee's median.

The assumption is that, the more members fall within this gap, the greater the distance between the committee and the chamber.

FINDINGS

Disagreement and divergence scores are reported in Table 18.1. Consider Agriculture Committee votes. The disagreement score shows that the Agriculture Committee and chamber majorities voted differently 11.9 percent of the time. That is, on five of the forty-two contested amendment votes, the majority of the committee did not support the decision eventually made by the full chamber. The divergence between Agriculture Committee members and all other members on these votes is 9.6 percent. That is, the difference between the percentage of committee members voting yea and the percentage of all other members voting yea averaged 9.6.

Two features of Table 18.1 should be noted. First, the committee–floor divergence scores are statistically significant for the Agriculture and Appropriations committees but not for Energy and Commerce. That is, the average difference between the committee and chamber in the percentage voting yea is larger than that expected by chance for Agriculture and Appropriations. Second, the committee–floor disagreement score is not statistically significant for any of three committees, although the score for Agriculture comes closer to statistical significance than do the scores for the other two committees. For these committees, then, committee majorities do not vote differently from chamber majorities more often than for randomly selected committees, even where the political

Table 18.1. *Committee–Chamber Divergence and Disagreement Scores*

Committee	Votes	Divergence Score	Disagreement Score
Agriculture	42	.0963*	.1190
Appropriations	346	.1122*	.0232
Energy and Commerce	146	.0788	.0959

* $p \leq .05$. See Appendix.

balance on two of the three committees is measurably different. In fact, for Appropriations and for Energy and Commerce the disagreement scores were so low that we can conclude that these committees concur with the majority of the floor more than a randomly drawn committee.

The scores indicate that Appropriations and Energy and Commerce express preferences more congruent with chamber preferences than does Agriculture. Such a finding is consistent with our predictions. The jurisdiction of Agriculture is less salient to most members than is the jurisdiction of either Appropriations or Energy and Commerce. The differences that exist between Energy and Commerce and Appropriations are not so clear, as their high salience might suggest. The disagreement and divergence scores indicate that the Appropriations Committee majority more often takes positions congruent with the floor majority, while the overall political balance on the Energy and Commerce Committee is more similar to the floor's.

The results of the dimensional analysis are illustrated in Figure 18.1, where the alignment of committee, party, and chamber medians is indicated for each recovered dimension. We have placed the floor's position in the middle of the scale and plotted the distance and direction between the floor (F) and the party caucuses (D for the Democratic caucus and R for the Republican caucus), committee contingents (Dc or Rc), and committee median (C). We use a set of tentative standards to characterize the relationship between the committee and the chamber and between the party contingents and their respective caucuses.

To characterize the relationship of the committee to the chamber, we use the terms *outlier* and *aligned*. To be classified as an outlier, the committee must satisfy two criteria. First, the committee distribution must significantly differ from the floor distribution. Second, at least 10 percent of all members must be situated at the floor median or between the floor and committee median. If these criteria are not both satisfied, the relation between the committee and chamber is characterized as aligned.

To summarize the relationship between each party's committee contingent and its caucus, we describe the contingent as either more extreme than, more moderate than, or aligned with its caucus. For a contingent to be labeled extreme, three conditions must be satisfied. First, the party contingent must be farther than its caucus from the chamber median. Second, the contingent median must be on the same side of the floor median as the caucus. Third, either the difference in caucus–contingent medians must be statistically significant or at least 10 percent of the caucus members must be at the caucus median or between the contingent and caucus medians. If either of the criteria in the third condition is met and if one of the first two conditions is met, we categorize the contingent as moderate. If a contingent is neither extreme nor moderate, we characterize the relationship as aligned.

To characterize the relationship between each dimension that we recovered and the liberal–conservative dimension, we use the terms *aligned* and *cross-cutting*. If the correlation between each member's score on a dimension and his or her average ADA rating for the 94th, 96th, 98th, and 100th Congress is greater than 0.75, we label the dimension as aligned. If the correlation is 0.75 or less, we classify the dimension as cross-cutting.

Only one dimension was recovered for Energy and Commerce. This dimension is aligned with the left–right ideological spectrum that is captured by ADA ratings. In contrast, both the Agriculture and the Appropriations committees have more than one dimension, some of which cross the dominant left–right spectrum. The Agriculture Committee has two distinct dimensions, one aligned with ADA ratings and pertaining to social welfare issues such as food stamps and another that crosses the first dimension, pertaining to agribusiness issues such as commodity price supports.

By our tentative standard, the committees are aligned with the full chamber on five of the eight recovered dimensions. Indeed, in the most common alignment the chamber median divides the caucuses and committee contingents of the two parties. Furthermore, on most

Agriculture Committee, Social Welfare Dimension (e.g., food stamps)
  Committee-chamber relation: aligned
  Caucus-contingent relation: extreme majority, aligned minority
  Relation to left-rigtit dimension: aligned
  Committee-party-chamber scale:

```
        |  |      | |                    |  |
————————————————————————————————————————————————
        Dc D      C/F                    Rc R
```

Agriculture Committee, Agribusiness Dimension (e.g., commodity price targets)
  Committee-chamber relation: outlier
  Caucus-contingent relation: extreme majority, moderate minority
  Relation to left-right dimension: cross-cutting
  Committee-party-chamber scale:

```
    |       |       |       ||       |
————————————————————————————————————————————————
    Dc      C       Rc      F/D      R
```

Appropriations Committee, Distributive Projects Dimension (e.g., water projects)
  Committee-chamber relation: outlier (Democratic bias)
  Caucus-contingent relation: extreme majority, moderate minority
  Relation to left-right dimension: cross-cutting
  Committee-party-chamber scale:

```
        |       |       | | | |
————————————————————————————————————————————————
        Dc      C       D Rc F R
```

Appropriations Committee, Government Management Dimension (e.g.,
appropriation for Department of Education)
  Committee-chamber relation: aligned (no bias)
  Caucus-contingent relation: aligned majority, moderate minority
  Relation to left-right dimension: aligned
  Committee-party-chamber scale:

```
        ||        |       |        |   |
————————————————————————————————————————————————
        Dc/D      C       F        Rc  R
```

Appropriations Committee, Size of Government Dimension (e.g., across-the-board
cuts)
  Committee-chamber relation: aligned (no bias)
  Caucus-contingent relation: aligned majority, moderate minority
  Relation to left-right dimension: aligned
  Committee-party-chamber scale:

```
    ||        |       |       |        |
————————————————————————————————————————————————
    Dc/D      C       F       Rc       R
```

Appropriations Committee, Defense Policy Dimension (e.g., funding for MX missile)
  Committee-chamber relation: outlier (Republican bias)
  Caucus-contingent relation: moderate majority, extreme minority
  Relation to left-right dimension: aligned
  Committee-party-chamber scale:

```
        | |        |    |   |
————————————————————————————————————————————————
        D  F\Dc    C    R   Rc
```

Appropriations Committee, Social Policy Dimension (e.g., funding for abortions)
  Committee-chamber relation: aligned (no bias)
  Caucus-contingent relation: aligned majority, aligned minority
  Relation to left-right dimension: aligned
  Committee-party-chamber scale:

```
    |  |        | |        |  |
————————————————————————————————————————————————
    D  Dc       F\C        R  Rc
```

Energy and Commerce Committee (single dimension identified)
  Committee-chamber relation: aligned
  Caucus-contingent relation: extreme majority, aligned minority
  Relation to left-right dimension: aligned
  Committee-party-chamber scale:

```
    |   |       |   |               ||
————————————————————————————————————————————————
    Dc  D       C   F               R/Rc
```

Note: F = floor median;
        D = Democratic caucus median:
        R = Republican caucus median;
        C = committee median;
        Dc = the median position of the Democratic contingent on the committee;
        Rc = the median position of the Republican contingent on the committee.

Figure 18.1. Alignment of Committee, Party, and Chamber Medians for Three
House Committees, by Policy Dimension.

dimensions, the parties' committee contingents are either aligned with or more extreme than the caucus and the committee is aligned with the chamber.

The one dimension for Energy and Commerce has an insignificant difference between the committee median and the chamber median. Of Appropriations' five dimensions, two – one that includes spending on water projects and one that primarily includes defense programs – have significant differences between committee and chamber medians. Of Agriculture's two dimensions, one – the agricultural subsidy dimension – has a significant difference. The other Agriculture and Appropriations dimensions are more strongly correlated with the left–right dimension and exhibit more committee–chamber congruence. It is reasonable to surmise that the more constituency-oriented or parochial dimensions are associated with less committee–chamber congruence and that dimensions more aligned with the liberal-conservative dimension are associated with more committee–chamber congruence. This surmise is consistent with our propositions about the effects of broad salience.

ADDITIONAL ISSUES IN THE POSITIVE THEORY
OF CONGRESSIONAL INSTITUTIONS

Our interpretation of the data presented here is preliminary. Nevertheless, we believe that the evidence demonstrates predictable variation across committees in their relation to the parent parties and chamber. The evidence is also consistent with our propositions about the influence of salience and dimensionality on the observed congruity of expressed preferences. Before concluding, we would like to raise five additional issues that must be addressed in future efforts to build a theory of congressional institutions.

The Evolution of Principal–Agent Relations

We must distinguish accounts of the origins of certain institutional arrangements from ac-

counts of the operative political relationships in later periods. Existing positive theories assume continuity in the relationships between chambers, parties, and committees rather than accounting for change. Reciprocity arrangements, uncertainty-reducing mechanisms, and collective-action solutions are assumed to be enduring. And the evidence supporting arguments about origins often involves little more than scattered historical examples.

We do not propose a dynamic theory here or insist that all efforts be devoted to developing a useful dynamic theory. For well-understood reasons, the relationship between conditions and institutions is complex and not easily predicted. Institutional arrangements tend to be sticky once established, and how they might change is unpredictable under fairly common conditions. But we must be suspicious of analyses that draw freely from different historical periods without taking into account the possibility that the context might have changed in crucial ways. More effort should be devoted to specifying the contextual conditions under which certain models are applicable.

Alternative Institutional Arrangements

To date, models have been developed that yield predictions consistent with certain general characteristics of congressional institutions. The models do not predict institutional arrangements in much detail, and existing studies do not identify the possible alternatives over which choices are made. We are left with only vague explanations about the particular arrangements chosen – say, standing committees, a strict germaneness rule, and limited debate.

For example, information theorists explain the delegation of power to committees as a strategy for motivating some members to gather and digest information for the rest of the chamber. Yet, they fail to mention other means of gathering and digesting information, many of which Congress has tried and continues to use – support agencies, holding tanks for specialized staffs (e.g., the Joint Economic Committee), party staffs, faction and issue caucus staffs, personal staffs, consultants, and so on. Why does Congress use committees in some cases and staff units of various kinds in other cases?

In party-based models, the majority party is the chief principal of important committees, and its goal is to enhance the party's reputation. Why should the majority party rely on standing committees composed of members of both parties? Partisan theorists set aside the possibility that the majority party wants to limit criticism that it is unfair to the minority party. Instead, they note that bipartisan committees may better predict what will happen on the floor. And yet in recent years the House majority party has relied more heavily on intraparty task forces to generate policy proposals.

Agents and Incentives

We find it puzzling that researchers have not studied the conditions under which committee members are motivated to perform functions important to their principals. Theory alone cannot tell us how much it costs to motivate committee members to perform the duties expected of them by their constituents, parent parties, or parent chambers. It is reasonable to assume that some incentives are necessary, but there is no basis for arguing that the allocation of certain special parliamentary rights is necessary or sufficient for this purpose. Indeed, if committee members are merely agents on behalf of the chamber, special rights that empower committees are themselves public goods that will not encourage individuals to incur the costs associated with committee specialization. Instead, we might want to account for the observation that members have multiple motivations. Such an observation leads to the possibility that many members are motivated to pursue issues within a jurisdiction for reasons other than the ounce of leverage gained from special rights allocated in rules. And, of course, we must anticipate the possibility that the mix of incentives important to committee members varies over time. In short, too little attention has been given to committee members' side of the equation.

The Conceptualization of Party

We have not developed here some obvious propositions about the role of party. For example, a highly partisan alignment of preferences would enable the majority party and its leaders to exercise control over committees.

Two other views of party have emerged in recent principal–agent theories. The first view gives little emphasis to variation in partisanship. Instead, [it is argued] that the shared party label creates a bond among fellow partisans: fellow partisans realize that their individual electoral prospects are influenced by the party's record. They therefore empower party leaders to look out for their common interests, including maintaining control over committees with jurisdictions relevant to the party record. In this view, then, party organization, leadership, and control over committee contingents represent a solution to a collective-action problem for party members.

The second view is critical of the position that parties operate as distinct principals of committees. This perspective argues that parties are coalitions based upon the similarity of their members' policy preferences – partisanship is nothing but preferenceship. Once the effects of preferences are controlled, partisanship has no remaining influence on the institution or policy choices. It is parties' status as policy coalitions, rather than their identity as organizations, that is important. Consequently, parties do not have an effect on the role or character of committees independent of the effect of the desires of the chamber majority. They merely happen to be the most frequently appearing coalitions.

In our view, neither perspective has supplanted the more conventional view that party strength shapes party–committee relations. The former does not directly address change and so does not offer an alternative to the conventional view. Perhaps it could do so by accounting for the effects of change in the relevance of the party record to members' electoral fortunes.

The latter is ahistorical. Having overcome collective-action problems that beset any new coalition, parties are likely to be distinctly advantaged over other coalitional groups that might form. Moreover, parties have acquired substantial institutional advantages over competing coalitional groups. In the House, these advantages appear to give the majority party an edge that allows it to move policy choices away from the chamber's median position and toward the party's median position. Why would majority party members close to the chamber median tolerate such a thing? Perhaps because they benefit from being tolerant in ways that have nothing to do with policy choices and outcomes.

And What About the Senate?

The Senate has received very little attention from positive theorists of congressional institutions. The absence of a general germaneness rule or limitation on debate, the ease with which legislation is held on the floor and not referred to committee, the unstructured amending process on the floor, the complexities of Rule XXII, majority party leaders' prerogatives, and several other features of the Senate distinguish it in crucially important ways from the House. Are we to conclude that senators care less than representatives do about enforcing reciprocity across committees? Might we conclude, following information theorists' logic, that senators need fewer incentives than representatives to generate the information their colleagues require? And, following partisan theorists' reasoning, should we infer that senators have less at stake than representatives in the reputations of their parties?

The consequences of neglecting the Senate are obvious. We should ask why the Senate fails to protect the handiwork of some of its committees. Presumably, motivating Senate committee members to specialize should be as difficult as motivating House committee members. Surely differences in the character of legislation affect the nature of information problems just as much in the Senate as in the House. And yet the Senate offers virtually no procedural safeguards to any of its committees.

According to partisan theorists, we expect parties to exercise special care in making assignments to those top committees whose policy jurisdiction is most relevant to party reputations. In the House, therefore, Appropriations, Budget, Rules, and Ways and Means are given special treatment by both parties. But what of the Senate? Senate Republicans allocate committee assignments on the basis of seniority. And both Senate parties informally guarantee every member an assignment on one of the four top committees – Appropriations, Armed Services, Finance, and Foreign Relations. Why don't Senate parties manage committee assignments as House parties do?

Clearly, something about the context of the Senate – its size, jurisdiction, terms of office, constituencies, inherited rules – shapes its institutional arrangements in critical ways. In future work, we should remember the Senate.

CONCLUSION

We are sympathetic to recent efforts to develop positive theories of congressional institutions. The basic thrust of the arguments – that institutional arrangements are the products of collective choice by goal-oriented legislators – is promising. We also believe that principal–agent models are consistent with how legislators see the relationship between committees and the parent parties and chambers. And we find many useful insights about congressional institutions in recent studies that seek to explore the implications of fairly simple models.

Yet it is plain to us that no single principal–agent relation, no single goal, and no single dimension of conflict dominates congressional politics, at least not for long. This has led us to doubt the viability of theories that fail to account for variation in principal–agent relations, goals, and dimensionality. Unless we are aiming for a theory of a small number of House committees in the late twentieth century, we must move to a larger developmental theory that accounts for the diversity, as well as the central tendency, of congressional institutions.

CHAPTER NINETEEN

Nonlegislative Hearings and Policy Change in Congress

Jeffery C. Talbert, Bryan D. Jones, and Frank R. Baumgartner

The authors suggest that committees use nonlegislative hearings, or oversight hearings, as a means of expanding their own jurisdictions. Because nonlegislative hearings afford committees considerable flexibility, they use these hearings in the hope of redefining an issue. Using nonlegislative hearings, committees will attempt to convince others that a given issue has multiple dimensions and that they have some claim to a component of the issue. The authors find that nonlegislative hearings have a significant influence on the evolution of committee jurisdictions over time.

NONLEGISLATIVE HEARINGS
AND POLICY CHANGE

When Senator Edward Kennedy assumed the chair of the Administrative Practices and Procedure Subcommittee of the Judiciary Committee in 1969, he inherited a weak unit with little legislative clout or public visibility. Within five years he changed the direction of federal policy in a dramatic way, however, even without expanding the legislative mandate of his subcommittee. While the "Ad Prac" subcommittee had statutory jurisdiction over only a limited number of topics, it had an extremely broad mandate for administrative oversight and investigation. With virtually the entire federal bureaucracy open to his investigation, Kennedy

Jeffery C. Talbert, Bryan D. Jones, and Frank R. Baumgartner. 1995. "Nonlegislative Hearings and Policy Change in Congress" *American Journal of Political Science* 39(2): 383–406. Reprinted with permission.

searched for areas where he could make a mark. After a few years of issue-jumping, he enlisted the assistance of Harvard Law Professor Stephen Breyer in 1974 to help the subcommittee focus on a specific issue area. After a year of planning and research, the Ad Prac Subcommittee held oversight hearings on deregulation of the airline industry. The resulting attention to the idea eventually forced Congress to act. When President Carter signed the Airline Deregulation Act of 1978, he asserted that "for the first time in decades, we have actually deregulated a major industry." The net result of these oversight hearings and subcommittee investigations was not only the deregulation of the airline industry but indeed a wave of deregulations of a variety of industries, constituting one of the greatest changes in federal practices in decades.

This case hints at the dynamics between policy and committee jurisdictions and at the role of investigative and oversight hearings in this process. The standard view of committee jurisdictions is that they are stable, with areas of specialization compartmentalized, allowing congressional "barons" to establish "fiefdoms." Bills are referred to substantive committees according to their established jurisdictions, and committees are proscribed from initiating bill hearings where they lack jurisdiction. This system, it is often alleged, hampers meaningful change by granting agenda control to those with a vested interest in the continuation of the status quo. This standard view of congressional jurisdictions has an important element of truth.

Committee jurisdictions are important. However, they are not immune from change. Further, entrepreneurial members of Congress know that to make their mark they must often stretch the limits of their statutory authorities, or use the committees where they do have influence to force action within the committees where they do not have such sway. In our example, Kennedy used oversight hearings where he had scant jurisdictional claim. Nonetheless, his pressure led to action in another committee and eventually by Congress as a whole.

Leaders of congressional committees and subcommittees use nonlegislative hearings for two important purposes: to justify future claims for jurisdiction over legislation and to force rival committees to act on matters that they might prefer to avoid. Legislative hearings are those that consider bill referrals. All others, including oversight and investigative, are considered nonlegislative. Nonlegislative hearings are important in jurisdiction-grabbing because there are few restrictions on the topics that any subcommittee may investigate. Committee leaders are adept at using nonlegislative hearings in order to claim future legislative referrals. This threat is often enough to cause rival committees to act to protect their own jurisdictional claims. Nonlegislative hearings have a greater effect on the legislative process than has been recognized in the literature.

Our example of Senator Kennedy and the Ad Prac Subcommittee provides a further illustration of this point. One of the most important aspects of the subcommittee's investigation of the Civil Aeronautics Board (CAB) involved gaining jurisdiction from the Commerce Committee. In fact, the Commerce Committee and its Subcommittee on Aviation strongly objected to Ad Prac plans to hold hearings. Senator Magnuson and Senator Cannon sent Kennedy a memo arguing that "the issues which have been raised by your staff are properly within the jurisdiction of the Committee on Commerce." While Kennedy responded to the letter by delaying the hearing, the Ad Prac Subcommittee continued its plans for the full investigation, which established the Ad Prac Subcommittee as an authority in the area and formalized

its claim to more jurisdiction. These jurisdictional battles are sometimes controversial, and sometimes go unnoticed, but they are a constant part of congressional life.

Public and official definitions of policy issues often change over time. Changes in these issue-definitions are often closely related to jurisdictional change in Congress. When issues come to be understood in new ways, different committees are able to claim new areas of jurisdiction. For example, regulation of pesticides was long the exclusive domain of the agriculture committees in the House and the Senate, as the chemicals were considered simply as the tools of farmers. However, during the 1960s and 1970s the environmental aspects of the industry became more salient publicly and a new set of congressional committees took an interest in these matters. The dual processes of issue-definition and jurisdictional change often combine in an interactive manner to reinforce rapid changes in public-policy outcomes.

In this article we show that nonlegislative hearings often play a central role in issue-definition, and therefore have a great impact on the policies eventually produced by Congress. Committees may begin with nonlegislative hearings on a particular element of an issue well established within the jurisdiction of another committee. If they are able to convince others that the issue actually has several dimensions, and that they have a jurisdictional claim to one of them, they may be able to claim some future jurisdiction. Activities by challenger committees may also force those committees faced with losing jurisdiction to act in order to forestall greater losses, as in the case of Kennedy and the CAB. Oversight hearings, which are not so tightly controlled by the Office of the Parliamentarian, by the party leadership, nor by strict rules of precedence, are often used by committees to claim new areas of jurisdiction or force rival committees to act.

In the pages that follow, we first discuss how oversight hearings are used by congressional committees to influence jurisdictional boundaries. Second, we examine empirical evidence using four diverse issues to demonstrate this process. Our evidence comes from examining all

congressional hearings on the topics of pesticides, smoking, drug abuse, and nuclear power
from 1945 to 1986, and from personal interviews conducted with members of congressional committee staffs. We also make use of
extensive coding of witnesses appearing in hearings on the topics of smoking and pesticides
during the same period. Finally, we place our
findings in the broader context of the literature on oversight and agenda studies, posing
new questions about how congressional oversight may be used as a tool in the policy process.

COMMITTEES AND JURISDICTIONS

The organization of the workload through a
specialized committee structure is one of the
most important elements of how Congress
works, and it has been one of the most often
studied aspects of that institution. These jurisdictions are neither automatically enforced nor
straightforward to determine. In fact, turf battles have long been a part of the congressional
process. These battles are not simple personality
conflicts among ambitious politicians, but they
have important policy consequences as well.

While cable television regulation had a foundation in the Energy and Commerce Committee, it was eventually referred to the Judiciary Committee as antitrust legislation. A staff
member from the House Judiciary Committee explained this referral by emphasizing the
power of the chair, not previous jurisdictional
control. "Our chair wanted that bill [Cable
Television Regulation Bill of 1992] because it
was an important issue. Since he is powerful and intimidating, he usually gets what he
wants." President Clinton's health-care-reform
effort involved turf wars between the House
Ways and Means Committee, the House Energy
and Commerce Committee, and the House
Education and Labor Committee, with similar
conflicts in the Senate. Battles for jurisdictional
control have long been an important element of
the legislative process.

Claims of specialized information and established expertise play an important role in the
referral of legislation to committees. This rela-

tionship was confirmed by a staff member from
the Senate Labor and Human Resources Committee, who reported that the more specialized information the committee possessed on
new issues, the greater their chances to claim
future jurisdictions. For example, when asked
about the new health reform, the staff member
responded, "we are the experts on this issue,
our chair has been pushing it for years, we
have to get the referral." Shortly after the Clinton health-care-reform package was released,
the House Education and Labor Committee
released a report detailing their claims to relevant portions of the plan. In addition to the
report, the committee also announced plans to
hold investigative hearings, or as one staff member said, to "flex their muscles." A staff member
for a House committee chair commented that
hearings are often useful to gauge the positions
of other committees. "The hearings are basically
for show, but they allow us to flex our muscles,
and provide a record of our position. Then we
can find out who is with us, and who is against
us." After such position taking, the committee usually receives communication from other
committees expressing their concerns and interests in the problem. This record allows the committee to know their competition and claims to
the issue any other committees may have. It also
provides a useful argument for future discussions
with the parliamentarian over which committee
should be granted jurisdiction over which legislation. Nonlegislative hearings are used to claim
future legislative authority. Committee leaders
and their staffs establish their records as experts
in the area so that future legislation is more
likely to be referred to them.

Hearings have been labeled a two-edged
instrument, in that they may promote some
problem or seek to remove it from public
debate. "Booster" hearings are often held to
focus on the seriousness of some public problem
and to build government support. On the other
hand, in "critical" hearings, executive policies
and programs are attacked. Most often oversight hearings are of the booster variety, and are
held in a context of policy advocacy. "Hearings
may provide the opportunity for representation
of different interests, although chairs have been

known to 'pack' the hearings with spokesmen for one point of view." Clearly, hearings are held with strategic purposes in mind. From the topics chosen to investigate to the list of witnesses invited to testify, nonlegislative hearings are always held in the context of future legislation.

A staff member for a Republican member of the House Energy and Commerce Committee restated this point, complaining that "hearings are not much use to us because the chairman is from the other party, and the hearings are usually stacked against us." In order to get a witness put on the list to testify at hearings, the staff member responded that "it was possible, but it would expend considerable resources, of which we have very little." As a general rule, the hearing process serves to frame a debate from the perspective of the committee that holds them. Thus, stacking is a common practice to allow the committee to control the hearings and to encourage a particular definition of the problem. If this reframing process is successful the committee may be able to claim control of legislation in the area in the future.

RESEARCH DESIGN, DATA, AND RESULTS

We expect to show two simple, related facts concerning nonlegislative hearings: they are an important means by which entrepreneurial chairs frame issues in new ways favorable to future jurisdictional claims; they help dismantle previously established jurisdictional monopolies enjoyed by others.

We have coded each of nearly 3,000 congressional hearings that appeared in the *CIS Index to Congressional Hearings* from 1945 to 1986 for each of four issues: pesticides, smoking, drug abuse, and civilian nuclear power. First, the hearings were coded according to which committees and subcommittees held them. This allows us to determine which committees have jurisdiction, and whether or not this jurisdiction is dominated by a small number of committees or shared by several. Further, we distinguish between those hearings scheduled to review a bill and all others. These nonlegislative hearings may be investigatory or oversight

in nature. The rules of jurisdictional assignment that apply to bill-referral hearings do not apply when there is no legislation, so our simple distinction between "legislative" and "nonlegislative" hearings corresponds to an important element in the jurisdiction game. Finally, we group the committees and subcommittees into jurisdictional blocks or venues for each issue. These are groups of committees or subcommittees that might share a policy view or orientation. From this venue measure we create an index of jurisdictional monopoly, which is simply the percentage of all hearings in a given year held in one of two rival venues. This measure of jurisdictional monopoly allows us to distinguish between issues firmly within the jurisdictional control of a single committee or a group of like-minded committees and those subject to serious jurisdictional disputes between hostile groups of committee entrepreneurs with different attitudes towards the policy in question.

For the cases of smoking and pesticides, we have also coded every witness who appeared at the hearings. For each of these two issues, we distinguish among those witnesses representing a specific group or professional interest: agricultural, environmental and health, or other and uncodeable. Agricultural witnesses are those that come from agricultural backgrounds such as farmers, USDA employees, pesticide manufacturers. Environmental and health witnesses are those that represent the medical profession, health officials, EPA employees or representatives, and others likely from their professional affiliation to focus on health and environment issues. Over 6,000 witnesses appeared in 386 hearings on pesticides matters during this period; 3,625 witnesses spoke before Congress in 313 hearings on smoking and tobacco matters.

Who Testifies Before Which Committees?

In both nonlegislative hearings and those scheduled to review a bill, the planning for witness testimony tends to be rigidly controlled, usually under the direction of the committee chair. For the air transportation example,

Table 19.1. *Congressional Testimony on Smoking/Tobacco before Agriculture Committees versus Testimony before Health and Taxation Committees, 1945–1988*

A. BILL-REFERRAL HEARINGS

Venue of Hearings	Type of Witnesses Testifying			
	Agriculture and Trade	Health	Taxation	Total
Agriculture and trade committees	91	4	4	100.0 (1141)
Health committees	34	66	0	100.0 (472)
Taxation committees	20	21	58	100.0 (221)
TOTAL	68	22	10	100.0 (1834)

Gamma = .83; tau-*b* = .61; Chi-squared (4 d.f.) = 1322.2 (*p* < .001).

B. NONLEGISLATIVE HEARINGS

Venue of Hearings	Type of Witnesses Testifying			
	Agriculture and Trade	Health	Taxation	Total
Agriculture and trade committees	98	2	0	100 (1378)
Health committees	21	79	0	100 (357)
Taxation committees	27	0	73	100 (56)
TOTAL	81	17	2	100 (1791)

Gamma = .97; tau-*b* = .81; Chi-squared (4 d.f.) = 2509.1 (*p* < .001).

Note: N's reported in this table refer to witnesses, not hearings. There were 144 bill-referral hearings and 169 nonlegislative hearings on smoking during this period.

Senator Kennedy planned the oversight hearings for over a year, down to the smallest detail. Each witness was carefully selected and reviewed in order to best make the point that Kennedy wanted the hearings to emphasize.

Table 19.1 and Table 19.2 show which types of witnesses are invited to testify before which committees, for both bill-referral and nonlegislative hearings. If our expectations are correct, the nonlegislative hearings would be home to a greater degree of bias than the referral hearings, and indeed this is the case. Based on nearly 10,000 witnesses coded for the two issues, nonlegislative hearings appear typically to show a greater bias than bill referral hearings, although neither could be seen as anything approaching neutral.

Table 19.1 shows that 91 percent of the witnesses invited to testify before an agriculture-venue committee considering legislation on smoking or tobacco were themselves from the agriculture industry. For nonlegislative hearings, the degree of bias is even greater: 98 percent of the witnesses before agriculture committees are from the industry. In the rival committee-venue, we see a similar, but less marked, tendency to invite those with whom one already agrees: 66% of those testifying before health or environmental committees considering legislation on smoking were themselves health experts. In nonlegislative hearings before the health-related committees, 79 percent of the witnesses were from the "home venue." We can note two important lessons here. First, committees neither seek nor receive complete information. Rather, they seek to promote certain views of their issues to bolster their abilities to produce favorable legislation. Second, bill-referral hearings tend to be slightly more balanced than nonlegislative hearings. There is probably greater pressure to allow dissenters to speak in hearings considering actual legislation. Nonlegislative hearings appear not only to allow greater jurisdictional freedom, but also to be the forum to preach to the converted.

Table 19.2 shows a similar, though slightly less pronounced, pattern in the case of pesticides. Health or environmental witnesses comprise 70 percent of all witnesses testifying before health

Table 19.2. *Congressional Testimony on Pesticides before Agriculture Committees in Congress versus Testimony before Health or Environmental Committees, 1945–1988*

A. BILL-REFERRAL HEARINGS

Venue of Hearings	Type of Witnesses Testifying		
	Agriculture and Industry Representatives	Health and Environment Representatives	Total (N)
Agriculture and related committees	70	30	100 (1396)
Health, environment, and related committees	30	70	100 (977)
Other committees	48	52	100 (325)
TOTAL	53	47	100 (2698)

Gamma $= .69$; tau-$b = .39$; Chi-squared (1 d.f.) $= 375.6$ ($p < .001$).

B. NONLEGISLATIVE HEARINGS

Venue of Hearings	Type of Witnesses Testifying		
	Agriculture and Industry Representatives	Health and Environment Representatives	Total (N)
Agriculture and related committees	74	26	100 (766)
Health, environment, and related committees	27	73	100 (2089)
Other committees	41	59	100 (466)
TOTAL	40	60	100 (3321)

Gamma $= .77$; tau-$b = .43$; Chi-squared (1 d.f.) $= 523.2$ ($p < .001$).

Note: N's reported in this table refer to witnesses, not hearings. There were 134 bill-referral hearings and 252 nonlegislative hearings on pesticides during this period.

or environmental committees considering bill referrals, and 70 percent of those testifying on similar issues before agriculture committees are from agriculture or industry themselves. Slightly higher for nonlegislative hearings, these percentages are 73 percent for health committees, and 74 percent for agriculture.

There is clearly extensive stacking of witnesses in hearings, but the practice seems more prevalent in nonlegislative hearings. The tactic seems to have been particularly important in the case of smoking policies. This pattern may be strongest where two fundamentally opposing dimensions of a single issue are home to powerful protective venues in Congress. The smoking case is remarkable in that two powerful and well-established sets of committees have clearly established jurisdictions over different parts of the same issue. Agriculture committees discuss tobacco; health committees discuss cancer and other health effects. Each invites those with a

similar perspective to speak, and each attempts to promote broader acceptance of their conception of the issue.

These findings should make clear the pitfalls inherent in any analysis of committee jurisdictions that does not consider the actions of rival committees. Smoking and tobacco policy is made neither by the agriculture committees acting in isolation nor by the health committees alone. Rather, both sets of committees are involved, and the policies eventually chosen by Congress are the net result of these shared jurisdictions. Many analyses of jurisdictional control or "government by subgovernment" may be misleading if the evidence comes from the patterns surrounding any single committee or allied set of committees. In many cases, a firmly entrenched interest with cozy relations to a set of congressional allies may still be opposed by a rival group hostile to its interests. This would only be evident if the analysis, like that presented here, were based on the issue and not the committee. By following an issue rather than a committee, we allow for the possibility of split jurisdictional control, and we can observe its importance.

Jurisdictional Control over Time

If the redefinition of issues occurs more easily through the oversight process than in legislative hearings, we would expect that jurisdictional dominance, the extent to which an issue is controlled within one committee's jurisdiction, would be more affected by the former. We expect nonlegislative hearings to provide a better arena for staking out new jurisdictional claims than bill-referral hearings. In particular, nonlegislative hearings would be more useful vehicles than referral hearings for breaking up issue monopolies.

Jurisdictional dominance is the extent to which hearings in an issue area are scheduled by a single committee, or a group of related committees that share a common view on the topic. There are good reasons for expecting related committees to hold similar views on an issue because of the tendency of issues and the coalitions that form around the issues to bifurcate. Since reversals of dominance are possible in which one side of an issue, previously not dominant, becomes dominant, jurisdictional dominance is calculated to have a maximum score when there is no conflict and a minimum score when there is even competition between two rival venues. This is done by calculating the percentage of hearings held in the dominant venue in a given year (ranging from 0% to 100%), subtracting 50, and reporting the absolute value of the result. This resulting variable has a maximum score of 50, indicating complete jurisdictional control by one set of committees, and a minimum of 0, indicating an even split in control.

Finally, we base the analysis on the number of distinct bodies (full committees or different subcommittees) holding hearings each year, rather than on the raw number of hearings. The number of distinct congressional bodies

is a more critical indicator of jurisdictional control.

If our model is correct, we would expect nonlegislative hearings to be at least as important as bill-referral hearings in accounting for any declines in jurisdictional dominance. If a committee or subcommittee wanted to investigate some aspect of nuclear power, for example, but lacked statutory jurisdiction, it could still hold oversight hearings on the topic in an attempt to define the issue from this new perspective. If its efforts were successful, future hearings to consider legislation would more likely be taken away from the previously dominant set of committees. One of the most powerful and secretive committees in the postwar Congress, the Joint Committee on Atomic Energy, was undone by precisely this kind of issue-redefinition. The Joint Committee was designed and used to limit jurisdictional control. However when the issue became understood as one of environmental degradation and consumerism rather than one of national security and economic growth, rival congressmen from other committees insisted on a change in the rules. The committee was abolished as a result, its jurisdiction split between several previous rivals.

Model and Results

In each of the four cases we have studied the jurisdictional dominance of particular committee-venues declines over time. Further, this decline is associated with increases in the number of hearings conducted and in the number of different bodies holding the hearings, as we have reported before. The relative roles of nonlegislative and referral hearings have not previously been reported, but these also conform to our expectations. Increases in oversight hearings can lead to increases in referral hearings, as proponents of the status quo fight attempted issue-redefinitions and to avoid subsequent losses in jurisdiction. Nevertheless, we expect that increases in nonlegislative hearings by hostile committees and subcommittees will be related to later declines in the percent of hearings held in the rival venue, even when we control for referral hearings.

We estimate a model to explain venue or jurisdictional dominance by accounting for the number of bodies (committees or subcommittees) holding nonlegislative hearings in a given year, the number of bodies holding referral hearings in that year, and the jurisdictional-dominance in the previous year. We include a measure of committee and subcommittee activity on bill–referral hearings in order to assess the uncontaminated effects of each type of hearing. Again, we expect that increases in *either type* of hearing will lead to declines in jurisdictional dominance, but that nonlegislative hearings will be more important in bringing about the decline of jurisdictional monopolies. We expect, first, that both referral and oversight hearings will decrease jurisdictional dominance; and, second, that the number of bodies holding oversight hearings will have a larger negative effect than the number of bodies holding referral hearings. If our results are robust, they should stand even after controlling for previous levels of jurisdictional control.

In three out of four cases, the model predicts as hypothesized. When appropriate controls are instituted, referral hearings do not contribute significantly (in a statistical sense) to the decline of jurisictional dominance. Nonlegislative hearings, on the other hand, are significant. For all of our policy areas except for drug abuse, the number of bodies holding oversight hearings is significantly related to declines in jurisdictional dominance. For three of the four policy areas, referral hearings are negatively related to dominance, as expected (but the results are insignificant), while in the case of pesticides, referral hearings are positively (but again insignificantly) related to dominance. Our expectations are met in almost every case. Most importantly, the data show that nonlegislative hearings appear to play a particularly important role in breaking apart policy monopolies.

The case of drug abuse represents an interesting deviation from the patterns observed in the other three areas. We have examined graphs of each of the variables in this study, and for the cases of pesticides, smoking, and nuclear power,

we observed sustained declines in monopoly jurisdictional controls within reasonably short time spans. For drug-abuse policy, however, the jurisdictional monopoly collapsed within a single year (1968). Throughout the period 1945 through 1967, the nation's drug policy was dominated by an enforcement mentality, and those policy efforts that were mounted at the national level were exclusively directed toward control and interdiction. Then, as the drug problem reached the national agenda, the number of hearings dramatically rose (from three in 1967 to eight in 1968 and 39 in 1969). The hearings focused both on enforcement-interdiction and on education-treatment, causing a breakup of policy monopoly of the enforcement agencies. After the dramatic collapse of the enforcement monopoly, numerous hearings were held in both venues, but oversight hearings increased as budgetary outlays in both areas increased. Moreover, to some degree the enforcement venue reasserted itself during the Reagan years. So while nonlegislative hearings were intimately bound up with the initial collapse of the enforcement monopoly during the late 1960s, they performed a different role thereafter. This problem of dual roles explains the lack of significance for *either* kind of hearing.

This suggests a modification to our theory of jurisdictional change. When jurisdictional monopolies become fully competitive, then nonlegislative hearings may shift roles, moving from devices for the strategic claiming of jurisdictional "turf" to the more traditional device of overseeing the bureaucracy (and perhaps making symbolic statements). They are no longer as useful as devices for attacking the status quo. We might see a jurisdictional struggle as involving three stages, each characterized by a different use of nonlegislative hearings. In the first stage, actors within a particular policy venue use nonlegislative hearings as devices to oversee the bureaucracies under their jurisdiction. This is the traditional view of the oversight function. In the second stage, "poaching" committees may use nonlegislative hearings to raise new aspects of the policy, thereby claiming part of the turf. If the turf battle is won, the new structure may become competitive or the competing committees may reach an accommodation on the division of the jurisdictional spoils. In such a case, both sides may use nonlegislative hearings as oversight devices once again. This appears to have been the pattern in the case of drug abuse policy. What had once been a single area dominated by enforcement concerns has become two distinct areas: one still concerned with enforcement, another powerful group concerned with education and treatment. Considering the tremendous increases in federal funding in this area, there seems room for both, whereas in the past there was greater competition.

Nonlegislative hearings are more closely linked to changes in jurisdictional control than are referral hearings for three of the four cases we studied. While oversight and referral hearings are undoubtedly related (that is, the factors that stimulate more oversight hearings also seem to stimulate more referral hearings), the changes in oversight appear to have a greater impact on jurisdictional stability. Referral hearings are not as likely to bring a reduction in the jurisdictional control of the issue. First, there is wider variability in oversight hearings, because they are easier to schedule by an entrepreneurial committee or subcommittee chair. If the issue is of great interest, an entrepreneurial congressman can schedule hearings. If it is of low interest, oversight hearings are less likely to be scheduled, thereby leaving the field to those with the established jurisdiction. Second, often referral hearings occur in response to breaches in jurisdictional monopolies forged through the strategic use of oversight hearings, so their occurrence is stimulated by oversight activities. Hence the most radical declines in jurisdictional dominance tend to occur with upsurges in oversight hearings.

CONCLUSIONS

Oversight has traditionally been viewed as a process in which elected members of government watch over the administration of public policy. Given the complicated nature of this task, Congress generally seems to fall short of the goal of effective and consistent oversight. Our study proposes a new way to look at oversight and investigatory hearings in Congress. When these actions are considered as part of the broader legislative context in which rival congressional bodies search for ways to have a policy impact, they appear to play an important substantive role. Nonlegislative hearings are an important part of a process through which issues are raised, redefined, and put on the table for serious consideration. In fact, we concluded that models of oversight behavior by Congress must also include consideration of the indirect uses of the oversight function. Often, the justification of oversight is to claim future jurisdictional control from a rival committee which may have a vested interest in the maintenance of the status quo. The importance of this strategic use of the oversight function will escape any analyst, assuming clear jurisdictional control rather than relying on a broader empirical observation that allows for competing congressional overseers.

We have examined these questions in several different ways by using data from four diverse policy issues over the last 40 years. Our evidence suggests that nonlegislative hearings are tremendously biased. Even more than in the case of bill-referral hearings, committee leaders stack the list of witnesses in nonlegislative hearings to insure that a certain viewpoint is heard. This witness stacking makes sense if we consider one of the main purposes of nonlegislative hearings: to focus on those aspects of a given policy that justify future claims to jurisdictional control by the committee. Second, we have argued that nonlegislative hearings are an attractive tool for committee entrepreneurs hoping to widen their jurisdictional boundaries. Referral hearings are subject to rules of precedence, and rival committees jealously guard their turf. One of the only ways to establish expertise in a new area is to begin with nonlegislative hearings focusing on a new element of an old issue. This indirect strategy may either force a rival committee to act in ways that it would not have done independently, or it may provide the justification for a future referral when legislation is being considered.

Finally, we have argued elsewhere that jurisdictional change in Congress often follows a punctuated pattern, with stable periods interrupted by rapid change. These periods of change are dominated by the extensive use of oversight hearings to encroach on established jurisdictional boundaries. Oversight hearings allow committees to investigate new issue areas and to build an increased base of information in these areas. As more oversight hearings are held in rival congressional venues, those committees that are put in the defensive posture must also increasingly hold hearings or risk their jurisdiction. Thus, oversight hearings can force reviews of current policy in a way that the more structured bill-referral process can not. Committee oversight is not only a check on the administrative agencies, but also a check on other committees. A derelict committee may be prodded into action by challenger committees seeking a piece of its jurisdiction. Once the jurisdictional claim is established, a new group has agenda-setting powers, and the resulting legislation may differ accordingly.

These jurisdictional dynamics conform to the notion of accountability through competition. Challenger committees will only be interested in other jurisdictions if they perceive a payoff. Therefore, members of the challenger committees must perceive public and political benefits from increased attention to the issue. In all the cases we have reviewed, this appears to be the case. Challenger committees expanded their jurisdictions because the committees in control of the issues failed to act despite important changes in the public understanding of the underlying policies. While our discussion of these challenges emphasizes their successful occurrence, we should point out that such effective challenges are probably rare. Stability in jurisdictions appears to be the norm, but such periods of punctuation can occur, usually through the use of oversight hearings. When they do occur, they can have long-lasting policy consequences.

Our study also points to the importance of something that those in Congress know only too well: in order to maintain control, a committee must jealously guard its jurisdictional turf. Even though Congress is ruled by a number of parliamentary procedures and norms, these rules are not so strict, nor their application so obvious, as to be automatic. As analysts, we ignore at our peril the leeway that changing issue-dimensions give to jurisdiction-seeking members. We must question where Congress fits on [a continuum of order]. We suspect that there is enough flexibility in the definition of issues to push even the highly structured process of congressional hearings closer toward the anarchical side than analysts have often allowed.

PART VII. THE RULES OF THE LEGISLATIVE GAME

CHAPTER TWENTY

Sample of a Special Rule

Special rules from the House Committee on Rules are the primary means through which nontrivial legislation reaches the House floor. Special rules typically specify the length of floor debate, who controls the debate time, and which, if any, amendments can be considered.

H. RES. 636: SPECIAL RULE FOR H.R. 1908 – PATENT REFORM ACT OF 2007

Resolved, That at any time after the adoption of this resolution the Speaker may, pursuant to clause 2(b) of rule XVIII, declare the House resolved into the Committee of the Whole House on the state of the Union for consideration of the bill (H.R. 1908) to amend title 35, United States Code, to provide for patent reform. The first reading of the bill shall be dispensed with. All points of order against consideration of the bill are waived except those arising under clause 9 or 10 of rule XXI. General debate shall be confined to the bill and shall not exceed one hour equally divided and controlled by the chairman and ranking minority member of the Committee on the Judiciary. After general debate the bill shall be considered for amendment under the five-minute rule. It shall be in order to consider as an original bill for the purpose of amendment under the five-minute rule the amendment in the nature of a substitute recommended by the Committee on the Judiciary now printed in the bill. The committee amendment in the nature of a substitute shall be considered as read. All points of order against the committee amendment in the nature of a substitute are waived except those arising under clause 10 of rule XXI. Notwithstanding clause 11 of rule XVIII, no amendment to the committee amendment in the nature of a substitute shall be in order except those printed in the report of the Committee on Rules accompanying this resolution. Each such amendment may be offered only in the order printed in the report, may be offered only by a Member designated in the report, shall be considered as read, shall be debatable for the time specified in the report equally divided and controlled by the proponent and an opponent, shall not be subject to amendment, and shall not be subject to a demand for division of the question in the House or in the Committee of the Whole. All points of order against such amendments are waived except those arising under clause 9 or 10 of rule XXI. At the conclusion of consideration of the bill for amendment the Committee shall rise and report the bill to the House with such amendments as may have been adopted. Any Member may demand a separate vote in the House on any amendment adopted in the Committee of the Whole to the bill or to the committee amendment in the nature of a substitute. The previous question shall be considered as ordered on the bill and amendments thereto to final passage without intervening motion except one motion to recommit with or without instructions.

Sec. 2. During consideration in the House of H.R. 1908 pursuant to this resolution, notwithstanding the operation of the previous question, the Chair may postpone further consideration of the bill to such time as may be designated by the Speaker.

SUMMARY AND TEXT OF AMENDMENTS
MADE IN ORDER

1. **Conyers (MI)/Smith (TX)/Berman (CA)/Coble (NC): Manager's amendment**. The amendment incorporates a number of revisions. They include revisions to the sections on damages, willful infringement, prior user rights, post-grant review, venue, inequitable conduct, applicant disclosure information, inventor's oath requirements, among others. **(20 minutes)**

2. *Issa (CA):* The bill eliminates provisions in the law permitting certain applicants to delay or prevent publication of their applications. This amendment would strike that provision and permit applicants to delay publication until the later of (1) three months after a second PTO deci-

sion or (2) 18 months after the filing date. **(10 minutes)**

3. *Issa (CA):* Amends the section relating to United States Patent and Trademark Office regulatory authority by adding the requirement that Congress be provided 60 days to review regulations before they take effect. Congress may bar implementation of the regulation by enactment of a joint resolution of disapproval. **(10 minutes)**

4. *Jackson-Lee (TX):* This amendment requires the Director of the United States Patent and Trademark Office to conduct a study of patent damage awards in cases from at least 1990 to the present where such awards have been based on a reasonable royalty under Section 284 of Title 35 of the United States Code. The Director of the PTO would be required to submit the findings to Congress no later than one year after the Act's enactment. **(10 minutes)**

5. *Pence (IN):* Amends the provisions governing post-grant review proceedings to prohibit a post-grant review from being instituted based upon the best mode requirement of patent law. **(10 minutes)**

CHAPTER TWENTY-ONE

Sample of a Unanimous Consent Agreement

Unlike the House, the Senate does not use special rules to bring up legislation. Rather, the majority leader tries to coax senators to agree by unanimous consent to limit the time for debate or number of amendments that will be allowed for a particular bill.

UNANIMOUS-CONSENT AGREEMENT — S. 214

Mr. REID. Mr. President, I ask unanimous consent that on Monday, March 19, at 2 p.m., the Senate proceed to the consideration of Calendar No. 24, S. 214, a bill to preserve the independence of U.S. attorneys; that when the Senate considers the bill, it be considered under the following limitations: that there be 6 hours of general debate on the bill, with the time equally divided and controlled between Senators LEAHY and SPECTER or their designees; that once the bill is reported, the Committee-reported amendment be agreed to and the motion to reconsider be laid upon the table; that the only other amendments in order be the following: the Kyl amendment regarding the nomination and confirmation of U.S. attorneys; the Sessions amendment regarding appropriate qualifications for interim U.S. attorneys; that debate on each amendment be limited to 3 hours equally divided and controlled in the usual form; that the amendments have to be offered and debated during Monday's session, except as noted below; that on Tuesday, the Senate resume consideration of the bill immediately after the opening proceedings and there be 90 minutes of additional debate time on the bill and the amendments are to run concurrently with the time equally divided and controlled between the two leaders or their designees; that upon the use or yielding back of time, but not later than 11:30 a.m., without further intervening action or debate, the Senate proceed to vote in relation to the Kyl amendment, to be followed by a vote in relation to the Sessions amendment; that upon disposition of the amendments, the bill be read a third time, and the Senate proceed to vote on passage of the bill, as amended; that the text of these amendments be printed in the RECORD once this consent is granted.

The PRESIDING OFFICER. Is there objection? Without objection, it is so ordered.

CHAPTER TWENTY–TWO

On the Effects of Legislative Rules

Gary W. Cox

In this essay, Cox demonstrates how the rules of the legislative game can and do have profound impacts on legislative outcomes. Cox concludes that understanding how the rules operate and who controls changes in the rules is critical to understanding how a legislature operates.

In this essay, I consider how a legislature's rules of procedure can affect both the process and the outcome of legislation. By legislative rules of procedure I mean both the standing orders the legislature may establish for itself and those statutory or constitutional provisions that materially affect the legislature's processing of bills. The discussion is divided into two main parts.

First, I consider whether or not rules of procedure should have any effects at all, given that they can often be changed by simple majorities of legislators. One way that this concern can be expressed is in terms of policy instability. In multidimensional spatial models of legislative decision making under pure majority rule, the *generic* result is instability – that is, there almost never exists a policy that cannot be defeated in a pairwise majority vote by some other policy. Riker has argued that rules are valued primarily for their anticipated effect on policy outcomes, so that generically there will be no stability in the choice of rules, just as there is none in the choice of policies. By this argument,

Gary W. Cox. 2000. "On the Effects of Legislative Rules" *Legislative Studies Quarterly* XXV(2): 169–92. Reprinted with permission.

one cannot point to the rules as playing any systematic role in determining legislative outcomes. Here, I do not consider Riker's "inherited instability" argument based on the multidimensional spatial model but instead focus on a related argument based on the unidimensional spatial model.

The second part of the essay classifies the effects that rules have. Rules can change the set of bills that plenary sessions of the legislature consider; they can change the menu of amendments to any given bill considered in the plenary; they can affect how members vote; and – putting the first three effects together – they can affect which bills pass. I review evidence that rules do in fact have the suspected effects.

CAN LEGISLATIVE RULES HAVE ANY EFFECTS, IF THEY CAN BE CHANGED BY THE ASSEMBLY?

In studying how rules of procedure affect legislative outcomes, we must make an important initial distinction between exogenous rules and endogenous rules. Exogenous rules are those that cannot legally be changed by the legislature itself; changes require the assent of some other actors separate from or external to the legislature. Endogenous rules, in contrast, are those that can legally be changed by the legislature itself.

Most studies of the effects of legislative rules take them to be exogenous. For example, in the

1970s and 1980s, much of the literature stressing the importance of committees in the U.S. Congress assumed, either implicitly or explicitly, that the committees' jurisdictions were stable and that the seniority norm was essentially inviolable. Studying the effects of rules by assuming that they are exogenous is a useful endeavor, but it can be analogous to studying presidential vetoes in the U.S. under the assumption that vetoes cannot be overridden. When rules can be overturned by the very actors whose behavior is supposedly constrained by the rules, doubts are legitimately raised about how effective those rules can be.

Suppose, for example, that the current rules of procedure in some legislature promote a particular policy choice, X, but that a majority exists in the legislature that would prefer a different policy, Y. In this case, the majority preferring Y could replace the current rules with ones consistent with passing Y, and then pass Y. Knowing this, any agents empowered under the current rules might acquiesce in Y's passage rather than obstructing it or amending it, as they would be able to do were the rules exogenous. Thus, one might argue that stable rules of procedure must either be inherently neutral as far as policy choice is concerned or they must be consistent with the equilibrium policy choice under majority rule. For example, in the case of a unidimensional policy space, the equilibrium policy choice under majority rule is the median voter's ideal point. It should not be possible to maintain rules that potentially interfere with the selection of the median voter's ideal policy unless that potential is never actualized.

Although scholars used to take the effectiveness of rules of procedure for granted, arguments such as the one just given have suggested that rules might have no independent causal force, at least when they can be changed by a simple majority of those subject to the rules. Reacting against this sort of argument, scholars have suggested a variety of ways in which the causal impact of rules, which continues to be widely accepted as an empirical matter, can be theoretically explained. I consider three such arguments next.

The Rules Are in the Constitution (or Otherwise Entrenched)

A first possibility is that the legislature's internal rules of procedure are stable because they are stipulated in the constitution and the constitution cannot be amended by a simple majority of the assembly. If some legislative rules are entrenched in the constitution, and they lead to a policy choice, X, will that be stable? If a coalition (of legislators and nonlegislators) existed that was large enough to amend the constitution, preferred Y to X, and could find a set of rules that yielded Y, then X would not be stable and neither would the rules leading to it. But, if one continues to assume a unidimensional policy space, then constitutionally entrenched rules will enable the stabilization of nonmedian policy outcomes. For example, if the constitution requires a three-fourths majority of the assembly to amend, then the range of stable policies expands from the median to the interquartile range; if the constitution requires another body to concur by majority, then anything between the medians of the two bodies would be stable, and so forth.

Empirical examples of entrenched rules of procedure include both constitutional stipulations such as the *vote bloqué* in France or the urgency procedure in Brazil and Chile and nonconstitutional stipulations such as the U.S. Senate's filibuster and cloture provisions. More generally, of 16 countries covered in a multiauthor study of Western European legislatures, 6 required supermajorities to change the legislative rules of procedure, while Cox and Morgenstern report that in 7 Latin American countries the president has entrenched agenda-setting powers of one sort or another.

The Rules Suit the Majority Party and It Can Protect Them

If party leaders can expel members from legislative caucuses, deny them renomination, or deny them future office opportunities, then the majority party (or coalition) may be able externally to enforce a given set of rules. Cox and McCubbins tell such a story for the U.S. House of Representatives. Whatever one thinks of their story in the U.S. case, something like it seems plausible in countries such as Costa Rica, the United Kingdom, Venezuela, and Taiwan.

The Legislators Are Too Busy to Change the Rules

Legislation is more like research and development than it is like choice among already known alternatives. Members of most major legislatures are thus constantly strapped for time.

But overriding any legislative decision made pursuant to the rules takes time and effort, and overturning the rules themselves takes even more time and effort. The costs entailed in overturning rule-based decisions and rules are thus *largely exogenous*: they are the costs in terms of time and effort needed to construct a strategy for overturning the decision and to assemble the required coalition in support of change. If one believes these claims – that it is costly to overturn rule-based decisions and more costly to overturn rules, and that the costs entailed are largely exogenous opportunity costs – then one must also believe that rules have consequences.

Consider, for example, the ability to "veto" bills that U.S. committees are routinely alleged to possess. As bills can be discharged, one might argue that committee vetoes can be overridden whenever a floor majority wishes. But suppose a member files a discharge petition on a particular bill. She now tries to get other members to sign her petition but finds that hardly anyone knows what the bill is about. They are too busy with their own issues. When asked to sign, the other members face a choice. They can take the petitioner's word that it is in their interests to sign. They can take the committee's word that it is in their interests not to sign. Or, they can allocate scarce resources to investigate the matter for themselves. Unless the petitioner can find enough members who either already know about the issue at stake and agree with her or are willing to take her cue over the committee's,

the petition may stall because the other potential signatories are too busy to investigate the matter.

Suppose that the petitioner thinks she might get enough signatures from members who already know their preferences or are willing to take her cue. She now faces another hurdle. There is not enough time on the floor to pass every bill on the calendars, much less every bill in committee. Does a majority of the House prefer that the to-be-discharged bill take an increment of time on the floor, at the cost of not being able to proceed with some other bill (or bills) in the queue? Which other bill(s) will be sacrificed? Unless these issues can be negotiated as well, the petition will still fail, even if in a world of complete information (all members costlessly know their operative political preferences) and zero transaction costs (no time budget constraint on the floor) it would pass.

For important enough bills, the two costs suggested above will be lower: more members will already know about the bill and have clear preferences, and more will be willing to bump something else off the floor in order to proceed with it. But for less important bills, the costs can be prohibitive. Thus, even when vetoes can be overridden by a simple majority, and even when the bill vetoed would improve policy for some majority on the floor, the veto can stand. If one wishes to reject this conclusion, one must believe that every bill that would improve the status quo policy for some majority is identified and passed in each Congress.

The general point is this: Even "suspensory vetoes" are important and consequential in an assembly in which time is short. As I shall argue below, positive agenda power – the ability to initiate the next step in a bill's progress toward passage, at a given time – is even more important and harder to overturn.

If Rules Have Effects...

Suppose that one believes that rule-based decisions are costly to overturn and that the rules themselves are even more costly to overturn. This is enough to motivate a belief that rules will have causal effects but not enough to say much about what those effects might be. In the next sections, I consider some of the effects that rules have.

Rules can have proximal, intermediate, and final effects. The proximal effects of rules are to distribute resources (e.g., staff) and agenda power (e.g., a suspensory veto subject to discharge). The distribution of resources and agenda power stipulated by the rules in turn affects the menu of policy choices with which members are faced and how members vote on any given policy choice (intermediate effects). Finally, the ability to set the menu of policy choices and to affect voting behavior may lead to an impact on the policy actually chosen.

The proximal effects of rules are the easiest to describe, although even here there is a wide range of specific techniques. In the next two sections, I will consider the intermediate effects – how rules affect the menu of choices and voting behavior.

HOW RULES AFFECT THE MENU OF CHOICES

Agenda powers can be classified in two broad categories:

1. The power to put bills on or keep them off the floor agenda (thereby determining whether or not the floor has the chance to alter policy along a given dimension);
2. The power to protect bills from amendment on the floor.

Each of these species of agenda power is differently allocated in different assemblies. In each case, the question is whether the rules that allocate agenda power produce *agendas* that are consequentially different from those that would have been constructed by floor majorities (whether or not these agendas then lead to different policy outcomes is considered later).

Setting the Floor Agenda

In considering how the plenary agenda is set, I shall build on the work of Shepsle and Cox

and McCubbins. Shepsle's model begins with two main elements: a set of w issues, or policy dimensions, that the legislature must decide, and a set of n legislators, each with strictly quasiconcave preferences defined over the policy space. The issues are partitioned into a number of jurisdictions. The members are divided into a number of committees (with membership on more than one committee possible), each with its own jurisdiction. Committees are given the exclusive right to propose bills in their jurisdictions, but a committee's jurisdiction may itself be the union of smaller subjurisdictions (possibly, though not necessarily, attached to subcommittees). A committee with a complex jurisdiction may propose a separate bill for each of its subjurisdictions, but it cannot propose one omnibus bill dealing with all at once.

The sequence of events in Shepsle's model is (1) the committees propose bills: i.e., put them on the plenary agenda; (2) the plenary amends each of the bills put on its agenda by the committees, as its members see fit; and (3) each bill, as amended, is put to a final up or down vote. Although this particular sequence is not followed in all legislatures, something like it is followed in many.

Cox and McCubbins alter Shepsle's model in three main ways. First, they consider fully strategic actors instead of "sincere" legislators. Second, they divide Shepsle's committee stage into separate agenda-setting, amendment, and final passage substages. Just as the floor legislative process can be divided into these stages, so the committee legislative process can, too. Third, they consider two polar distributions of agenda power – the floor agenda model and the partisan agenda model.

In the first model, the floor agenda is determined as if by majority vote in the plenary session. One way to interpret this model is literally. In some cases, much of the plenary agenda is decided by the plenary itself. Shepsle's model can formally accommodate such cases by assuming that there is just one committee – a committee of the whole. Another way to interpret the floor agenda model is to say that there are in fact a number of distinct committees but that the floor can extract bills from any committee it chooses; thus, the committees cannot bottle up bills that a floor majority wishes to consider.

In the second model, the floor agenda is determined as if by majority vote in the majority party caucus. Again one might interpret this literally – as a model of those few periods in the U.S. House's experience when the majority party caucus seemed to rule the roost – or indirectly – as a model of committees which must anticipate the reaction of control committees or majority party leaders.

A key consideration in the model is the location of the status quo point on each dimension. Normalizing, one can take F_j, the location of the median legislator on the floor on the jth dimension, to be $F_j = F = 0$. That is, we locate the zero point on each dimension at the floor median on that dimension. This is done without loss of generality since the scale is arbitrary. The location of the status quo point, SQ_j, varies with j. Positive values of SQ_j indicate right-of-center status quo points, while negative values indicate left-of-center status quo points.

Now consider how the plenary agenda is set. Suppose first that there is a separate floor vote on whether or not to consider each of the w dimensions of policy. Suppose also that every member votes his or her own constituents' interests (or his or her personal beliefs) rather than following the party line. If the motion to consider dimension j is passed, the ultimate consequence will be that policy on dimension j is moved from SQ_j to F. If the motion fails, then policy will remain at SQ_j. Thus, a member will vote to consider dimension j if and only if she prefers F to SQ_j. An agenda formed by a sequence of floor votes on what to consider next would thus produce an agenda that consisted of all dimensions with status quo points not equal to F.

Nota bene that constructing agendas by pure majority vote in the plenary does not offer any inherent advantage to the majority party or coalition. Suppose that a majority party exists and is left-leaning, so that most of its members are to the left of F, while most of the minority party's members are to the right of F. The bills that the median legislator decides to proceed with concern the dimensions with status quo points not equal to F. These status

quo points can be put in four basic categories. First, "far left" status quo points are so far left that even a majority of the left-leaning majority party prefers F to the status quo (as does a majority of the minority party). Second, "near left" status quo points are such that a majority of the majority prefers the status quo to F (with a majority of the minority preferring the reverse). Third, "near right" status quo points are such that a majority of the majority prefers F to the status quo, but a majority of the minority party prefers the status quo to F. Finally, "far right" status quo points are such that majorities of both parties prefer F to the status quo.

From these four possible locations for the status quo emerge three possible voting patterns. If the status quo is either far left or far right, then majorities of both parties will support placing a bill on the agenda. If the status quo is near left, then a majority of the majority party will oppose placing the bill on the agenda, but lose. If the status quo is near right, then a majority of the minority party will oppose placing the bill on the agenda, but lose. *Thus, in the floor agenda model, whether the majority party does better or worse than the minority in terms of setting the agenda for plenary action depends entirely on the location of the status quo points on the various dimensions.*

An alternative model of how the plenary agenda is set, the partisan agenda model, assumes that the majority party has a veto over the placement of any issue on the floor agenda. More specifically, if a majority of the majority party opposes placing a particular bill on the agenda, it can prevent its appearance. I shall be less concerned with how such an agenda selection mechanism might arise than with what the consequences would be, were it to exist. The most obvious consequence would be that no status quo preferred by a majority of the majority party to the floor median – no near-left status quo in the example above – could gain a place on the floor agenda. Thus, under this model, one should never observe the majority party unsuccessfully opposing the placement of a bill on the plenary agenda.

Comparing Point Estimates
Cox and McCubbins pose two questions to assess the success of the majority party in

controlling the floor agenda. First, how frequently is the majority party *rolled* on agenda-setting votes? A roll is counted when a majority of the majority party opposes the placement of a bill on the floor agenda, but loses. If the majority can veto agenda items, then its agenda-setting roll rate should be zero. Second, how frequently does a majority of the majority coalition oppose the final passage of a bill, but lose? If the only issues that were placed on the agenda by a left-of-center party were those on which the status quo was right-of-median, then the worst that could happen to these bills would be that they were amended to the floor median, in which case the median legislator and all to her left would still prefer passing the bill to rejecting it. Thus, the majority's final passage roll rate should also be near zero.

To address the first question, Cox and McCubbins examined all 5,789 bills that originated in the House in eight selected congresses and were reported out of committee. They found that in only four of these cases (or 0.07%) did a majority of the majority party's committee members dissent from the committee report. Indeed, majority dissent of any magnitude was quite rare. Thus, in the House at least, the majority's record of avoiding issues that produce serious splits on initial report was nearly perfect.

What about the majority coalition's final passage roll rate? In the 45th to 99th Congresses, Cox and McCubbins find that the modal roll rate for the majority party on final passage votes is *zero*, with an average of 3 percent.

The majority's low roll rates – 0.07 percent at the agenda-setting and 3 percent at the final passage stage – contrast with rather higher figures for the minority: about 5 percent at the agenda-setting and 25 percent at the final passage stage. Thus, in the U.S. case, the preliminary evidence tends to reject the floor model in favor of the partisan (or "cartel") model.

Regulating Debate and Amendment on the Floor

But what happens if exogenous events force an issue onto the agenda? What happens if the Senate is held by the other party, which does its best to force issues onto the agenda? What happens, in other words, if the majority coalition in a particular chamber cannot perfectly control its plenary agenda and ensure that only unidimensional bills of a coalition-friendly sort appear on the agenda?

In these cases, controlling the flow of amendments on the floor may be especially important. The reaction of the majority to an unavoidable but unpleasant issue may be to package it with several other issues to create an omnibus that is at least palatable to the majority. But then the majority will need to ensure that the package is not picked apart on the floor, which will entail restricting the range and nature of amendments offered.

Do majority parties or coalitions actually have the ability to restrict amendments on the floor in ways that the median voter (on some particular dimension) might not agree with? It seems clear enough that the French government has such an ability via the package vote, that the U.K. government has such an ability via the guillotine, and that several Latin American presidents have a similar ability. Even in the U.S. House, where there are not constitutionally entrenched agenda-setting powers, there is a wide array of case-study evidence that the majority party uses restrictive procedures on the floor to protect majority party legislation.

HOW RULES AFFECT VOTING BEHAVIOR

Rules affecting the distribution of resources and agenda power can affect the voting behavior of members in two broad ways: (1) by allowing agenda setters to manipulate who can monitor votes, and (2) by providing the wherewithal to make side payments. Let us consider each of these points in turn.

One way to view legislators' voting behavior is as the net result of various different considerations that can be divided into three main categories: constituents' preferences, personal preferences, and party preferences. If a legislator's constituents' interests, his or her personal beliefs, and his or her party's desires coincide, voting decisions are easy. If these considerations conflict, however, then manipulating the observability of members' actions becomes particularly important. Governing or majority coalitions with agenda control can frame issues in ways that protect their members from the scrutiny of their constituents or expose them to the scrutiny of their party leaders.

An example of protection from constituents, or "providing cover," is an omnibus bill that includes a controversial provision or two, along with many popular or necessary provisions. Members can vote for the whole and justify their votes as ways to secure the (locally) popular bits, while decrying or disowning the (locally) unpopular bits. Restrictive procedures can be used to ensure that the members are never faced with an amendment that proposes to remove just the unpopular parts. Another example of protection from constituents is a vote of confidence. In the unlikely event that she is challenged, a member can apologetically explain that the vote was really about the continuation in office of the government, so that she was not at liberty to vote simply on the merits of the issue (on which, of course, she is 100% in accord with her aggrieved constituents).

An example of exposure to party leaders' scrutiny is Willy Brandt's "stay in your seat" confidence vote. Worried that some of his backbenchers might support the no-confidence motion confronting his government if allowed to vote anonymously, Brandt ordered his troops to stay in their seats and took advantage of the German requirement that an absolute majority of legislators must support the no-confidence motion in order to bring the government down.

Agenda power and other resources (e.g., staff) distributed by rules can also provide the wherewithal to make side payments to members. For example, if party leaders control assignment to committees or portfolios, desired assignments can be held out as inducements to good behavior. In the United States, Cox and McCubbins provide and review evidence showing how parties use party assignments to shore up loyalty on the margin.

Two further points about side payments ought to be made. First, side payments are often used to clinch deals or clear legislative hurdles. Particularistic benefits may be ends in themselves for the ordinary member, but for party leaders they are also means to the accomplishment of broader goals. Second, positive and negative side payments intended to influence members' voting behavior are a *part* of any healthy legislative leviathan, but they are of quite variable importance. In electoral systems that foster personal votes, it is not even in the party's best interest to "force" their members to vote in particular ways, since this substantially reduces their probabilities of reelection, thus damaging the party's prospect of attaining or retaining majority status. In the United States, the typical procedure is for majority party leaders to "buy" no more votes than they must in order to secure a legislative victory.

The bottom-line question, of course, is whether or not attempts by parties to manipulate who can monitor members' votes and to distribute side payments do in fact influence members' voting behavior. In parliamentary systems, the ability of parties to control their members' voting behavior by making issues matters of confidence is widely accepted (although questions have been raised about the credibility of government threats to resign). In contrast, legislative parties in presidential systems do not have the big gun of confidence to enforce discipline at the voting stage. Strong correlations still typically exist between voting behavior and partisan affiliation in such systems, but it is hard to say whether these correlations arise simply because members join parties with which they tend to agree or whether there is also some party influence above and beyond what would be expected on the basis of members' preferences.

So, how can one detect the influence of party on roll call voting? Some headway has recently been made in solving this methodological problem. If House members vote with their parties only when the party position is congenial to their constituents and/or to their personal ideologies, then (1) their voting behavior should not change when they switch parties (unless their constituency or ideology changed when they switched); (2) there should be no systematic relationship between members' reelection success and how frequently they vote with their party on key party votes (by assumption, no one is casting "tough" – i.e., electorally costly – votes for their party; thus, if one member is more loyal to the party than another on key votes, this can only be because his or her constituency is more in tune with the party's position, and such members will be no more likely to suffer larger-than-average vote drops or actual defeat than less loyal members); and (3) members should be no more likely to support their party than would be expected on the basis of the positions they advocate in elections.

HOW RULES AFFECT FINAL POLICY CHOICES

In this section, I consider how rules might affect final policy choices. I first consider how the rules enable the majority party or coalition to get what it wants, then how they can simplify legislative negotiations.

Helping the Majority "Get Its Way"

Rules can empower the majority party or coalition, when there is one, at three broad stages of the legislative process: at the agenda-setting stage, at the amendment stage, and at the voting stage. I shall consider each of these stages, in reverse order. In each case, the question addressed is how power at a particular stage can lead to final policy outcomes favored by the majority.

The Whip Model

Perhaps the most frequently mentioned way in which a majority party or coalition can get its way is by exerting discipline over its members when they vote. While this technique may be important in parliamentary systems with strong parties, in some of the presidential systems of Latin America and the United States, this technique is important only on the margins. Rather than insisting on a solid block of party votes to ensure passage of their legislation, parties in some presidential systems allow their members to dissent more often but still seek to corral a

few pivotal votes when needed. The evidence that parties can actually pressure their members into voting has already been reviewed. Are the votes in fact pivotal, so that they make the difference between winning and losing?

The evidence here is largely anecdotal, but there are a lot of anecdotes, at least for the United States. The standard operating procedure for Speakers in the U.S. House on close votes is to have a certain number of "vest pocket" or "just-in-case" votes lined up in advance. If the bill appears ready to fail, the Speaker then calls in as many of these votes as are needed to ensure victory, in some cases even stopping the clock to provide time to find the needed votes.

The Restrictive Rule Model

One step earlier in the legislative process than votes on final passage are votes on amendments to bills. And before the actual amendments come, decisions must be made about which amendments will be in order. In cases where the government has the power to prevent all amendments and hence present members with take-it-or-leave-it choices, it can clearly affect the final outcome.

Theoretically, the impact of this sort of power on the legislative outcome is captured in the widely known setter model. In the United States, the partisan effect of restrictive rules on outcomes is contested. But there is certainly evidence that the majority party uses restrictive rules on partisan issues and that the minority complains about it. More compellingly, members' voting behavior on (rule/bill) pairs is what one would expect on the hypothesis that *members* believe that the rule will have an effect on the outcome.

To explain this last point, due to Sinclair, we must remember that under House procedure a "special rule" is sometimes adopted to regulate plenary debate and amendment activity on a particular bill. Members vote first on the issue of whether to accept the rule, then on the substance of the bill. Suppose the majority party fashions the proposed rules in order to prevent amendments that the minority would like to move and that all members know this.

Suppose further that the electoral consequences of votes on rules are murky: members can always talk about fairness or efficient transaction of business or minority stalling and majority bullying to shield themselves from any claim that a vote for a rule, R, which facilitates passage of a bill, B, is really a vote for B, or that a vote against R is really a vote against B. Suppose finally that all members believe that R will *in fact* facilitate passage of B and that both parties are pressuring their members to support the party position.

Given these three assumptions, one expects the following patterns in voting behavior on (rule/bill) pairs. Some majority party members will have constituencies that support the substance of the bill. They will vote both for the rule and for the bill. Other majority party members will have constituencies that oppose the substance of the bill. These members are likely to vote against the bill because to do otherwise incurs electoral risk. Put another way, it will be relatively expensive for the party to buy these members' votes on the bill. In contrast, it may be considerably cheaper to buy their votes on the rule, depending on how securely shielded from electoral retribution they feel. The party need offer no side payment at all to members who personally favor the bill. Members who are personally indifferent or mildly opposed can be bought by compensating them just for their personal distaste; they need not be compensated for electoral risk (or, at least, the electoral risk is reduced and hence the needed compensation).

All told then, one expects majority party members whose constituents oppose the bill either to vote against both the rule and the bill or to vote for the rule but against the bill (with only a few voting for both). A similar argument leads one to expect minority party members to fall mostly into two camps: those voting against both rule and bill, and those voting against the rule but for the bill. Sinclair shows that these opposed expectations about majority and minority voting on (rule/bill) pairs do obtain, suggesting support for the underlying assumption that members believe rules to have causal force. At present, this is probably the best statistical evidence we have that rules affect outcomes.

The Partisan Agenda Model

Before a bill gets to the stage at which permissible amendments on the floor are decided, it has to get out of committee. The power to decide which bills make it to the floor is arguably the least appreciated but most fundamental power in terms of influencing final outcomes.

Recall that under the partisan or cartel agenda model, the majority coalition monopolizes the plenary agenda, in the sense that it is able to prevent the appearance on the floor agenda of any bill with which a majority of the majority would prefer not to deal. With this sort of agenda selection power, the issues that actually make it to the plenary will all have status quo points that are either to the minority's side of the floor median or so far to the majority party's side that a majority of the party would prefer pulling them back to the median. Thus, even if every separate decision taken by the House is unidimensional and ends up at the floor median, the policy location in the multidimensional space in which the whole sequence of decisions takes place will be substantially biased from what it would have been under a neutral agenda structure. If the majority is left-leaning, movements will be made leftward on a good number of dimensions with relatively fewer rightward movements (and those only to correct "far left" status quo points). Few rightward movements from the "near left" are passed because no resources are devoted to finding such moves, and if they do crop up, considerable resources are deployed against them. The net result is that policy will be more leftist than would have been the case under a neutral agenda.

CONCLUSION

Legislative rules have effects because they distribute real resources whose effects cannot be undone without incurring real costs in time and effort, because they confer benefits that parties find worth preserving through extralegislative means, and because they are sometimes entrenched legally. In a world in which time is short, the power to delay or expedite can be crucial, even if decisions to decelerate or accelerate a particular bill can be appealed to the plenary. In a world in which the effects of rules on final outcomes are obscure to voters, members fear electoral retribution from their constituents less than they would on straightforward votes on substance. Moreover, the obscurity of procedural rules' effects makes it easier for parties to maintain control of procedural votes than to maintain control of substantive votes.

The actual effects rules have are sorted here into three categories: effects on the menu of choices (which bills are considered on the floor? which amendments are allowed?), effects on voting behavior, and effects on the final legislative outcome (which bills pass?). Evidence of such effects is visible in most of the legislatures that have actually been studied, although the quality of the evidence varies widely, since it is difficult to make the necessary counterfactual comparisons (e.g., what would the agenda have been had the rules been different?) cleanly.

Typically, the effect of rules is most visible in conjunction with a majority party or coalition's efforts to push through its legislative agenda against opposition. If one ordered the world's legislative parties from those with the greatest incentives to push through their legislative agendas to those with the fewest incentives, the ordering would put parliamentary parties at the top (the government falls if its program fails); proactive congressional parties, such as those in the United States, next (where the legislative parties are sometimes viewed as having electoral incentives to prosecute agendas); and reactive congressional parties, as in Latin America, last (where the party label means less and, relatedly, there are fewer incentives to prosecute a party agenda).

It is interesting to examine the structure of agenda power across these three levels of incentive. Control of the agenda is firmest in the parliamentary regimes, especially the more Westminsterian ones. It is lodged, moreover, in the hands of legislative party leaders (who typically assume executive office). Control of the agenda is next firmest in the United States. It is again lodged in the hands of legislative party leaders (who, due to the separation of powers, do not assume executive office). Control of the agenda is weakest in Latin America. It is lodged partly in the hands of the president, an executive official who often attempts to be "above parties," and partly in the hands of the *mesa directiva*, typically composed of legislative party leaders.

It is interesting to note also that the meaningfulness of party labels, in terms of the policies that each party is likely to pursue, is ordered roughly the same way as are the incentives to legislate: European parliamentary democracies first, U.S. presidential systems second, and Latin American presidential systems last. There appears, in other words, to be a positive correlation between (1) legislative parties' incentives to legislate (and the frequency with which they actually do legislate); and (2) the extent to which agenda power is centralized in the hands of legislative party leaders of the majority coalition; and (3) the electoral meaningfulness of the party label in policy terms.

CHAPTER TWENTY-THREE

The Partisan Basis of Procedural Choice

Allocating Parliamentary Rights in the House, 1789–1990

Sarah A. Binder

Binder explores the history of rules changes in the U.S. House. She finds that majority parties typically change the rules to limit the power of legislative minorities for short-term partisan gain. Concerns about workload or institutional capacity have little effect on rules changes.

Compiling a manual of parliamentary practice in 1801, Thomas Jefferson emphatically recognized the importance of procedure in securing the rights of minority party members in the U.S. Congress. In a democratic political institution, majority parties would achieve their favored outcomes by taking advantage of their superior size, and minority parties would resist by availing themselves of protective rules to amend, delay, or obstruct the majority's agenda. Yet, the portrait of congressional rules as stable guarantors of the minority's right to participate meaningfully in the legislative process is deceptive. Far from rigidly securing the rights of the opposition, congressional rules are themselves the object of choice. Just as policy outcomes are contested by coalitions within each chamber, so too are the formal rules of the legislative game.

What leads members of Congress – in theory entitled to full and equal participation as members of a democratic legislature – to alter

Sarah A. Binder. 1996. "The Partisan Basis of Procedural Choice: Allocating Parliamentary Rights in the House, 1789–1990" *American Political Science Review* 90(1): 8–20. Copyright © 1996 by the American Political Science Association. Reprinted with the permission of Cambridge University Press.

the procedural rights afforded members of the minority party? I shall articulate and test several competing explanations to account for formal changes in the rules of the House of Representatives that have created or suppressed minority rights from 1789 to 1990. The results suggest the power of a partisan theory of procedural choice to explain the timing and direction of formal change in House rules. The distribution of parliamentary rights in the House is conditional on the shape of partisan forces in the chamber. In allocating rights to the minority, partisan advantage rather than collective institutional concerns drives members' procedural choices.

EXTERNAL DEMANDS AND PROCEDURAL CHOICE

The macro perspective on institutional change – linking external pressures and internal change – is not new to the study of Congress. The logic of the argument is relatively simple: The rapid early growth of the House and its leading role in the new national government led to the swift introduction of limits on individual rights. Institutional strains, in short, are said to have made "legislative egalitarianism impossible." Because every member's ability to achieve his or her political goals is in theory equally and adversely affected by expansion of the chamber's agenda, it would be in the collective interest of members under conditions of increasing House size and legislative activity to support new rules aimed at better management of chamber activity. Such procedural changes would increase the likelihood that both majority and minority party coalitions would gain the time necessary to pursue legislative goals important to their respective coalitions, increasing individual members' support for such change.

Of course, because rules changes in the House are adopted by simple majority vote, majority party leaders in practice only need to convince their own party members of the need for such restrictive procedural change. Thus, a workload/size theory of procedural change leads to the following expectation:

WORKLOAD HYPOTHESIS (SUPPRESSION). *The majority party is more likely to suppress minority rights when increases in the level of demands on the chamber increase the value of time for the majority.*

A second expectation drawn from such an institutional logic would connect changes in workload and size to efforts to reinforce minority rights. If increases in the size and workload of the chamber lead to restrictions on minority rights, then lessening of external demands ought to increase members' incentives to expand minority rights. On those occasions on which majority parties have responded to minority party demands for new procedural rights, we would expect to find a relationship between workload and procedural rights again:

WORKLOAD HYPOTHESIS (CREATION). *The majority party is more likely to create minority rights when workload and resulting time pressures on the chamber decrease.*

PARTY COMPETITION AND PROCEDURAL CHOICE

In assessing the modern House – in which minority rights to offer amendments are routinely limited by the majority party and many committees are disproportionately stacked in the majority party's favor – many observers have speculated about the impact of the near-permanent Democratic majority and near-permanent Republican minority on procedural choice. Because the majority often limited

minority party rights when the Democrats controlled the House from 1955 to 1994 – the longest period of uninterrupted party control of either chamber in American history – many scholars have argued that the majority was simply incapable of understanding what it was like to be in the minority. Without a doubt, they concluded with more frequent party turnover in the House, each side would develop an institutional memory of life in both positions.

An implication of this perspective is that members choose procedural arrangements based on their calculations about future parliamentary needs. Recognizing the partisan impact of procedural rights, majority party members seek those procedural rights that would best serve their longer-term partisan interests. Assuming that both majority and minority party members can make a reasonable calculation about their future status in the institution, each side would make procedural choices about minority party rights accordingly. Majority parties anticipating defeat in the coming election would create minority rights to prepare for their parliamentary future; majority parties anticipating continued control of the chamber would suppress minority rights knowing that such changes would make it easier for them to control the House agenda in the future. Linking longer-term electoral calculations with short-term preferences about rules leads to two testable propositions:

PARTY COMPETITION HYPOTHESIS (SUPPRESSION). *The majority party is more likely to suppress minority rights when it discounts its chances of losing majority control.*

PARTY COMPETITION HYPOTHESIS (CREATION). *The majority party is more likely to create minority rights when it anticipates losing control of the chamber.*

A scenario at the close of the Forty-Third Congress in 1875, however, raises questions about the relevance of future parliamentary needs to procedural choice. In 1875, majority party Republicans brought the House back into a lame-duck session, the November 1874 elections having cost them control of the coming Congress for the first time in nearly 20 years.

Facing persistent obstructionism by the Democratic minority and anxious to ensure passage of what would be the last Reconstruction-era civil rights bill before losing control of the House, Republicans changed the rules to limit minority obstructionism. Instead of expanding minority rights to prepare for their impending minority status, the majority altered chamber rules to secure its immediate policy goals. The 1875 case suggests that short-term, rather than long-term, partisan calculations might motivate members' procedural choices – a possibility I explore next.

PARTISAN PREFERENCES AND PROCEDURAL CHOICE

Large and cohesive majorities can set legislative agendas, assemble policy coalitions, and secure legislative victories with relative ease. Unlikely to face factional disputes among their members, such majorities can also easily defeat most minority obstructionism. Given a strong enough coalition, such majorities will rarely be constrained by decision rules requiring either a bare majority or supermajority vote for passage. Indeed, when a majority party so dominates the chamber, there should be little debate over the set of chamber rules: Given the similarity of members' views, nearly any set of rules would produce similar legislative results.

It is fairly unusual, however, for the majority party to enjoy such unchallenged power within Congress. As majority party strength declines, it becomes tougher for a majority to successfully pursue its policy agenda. Given the difficulties of assembling and maintaining a majority coalition under such conditions, the advantages and disadvantages conferred by existing rules become far more salient to members. Because legislative rules determine, for example, which proposals may be advanced, who may propose them, and how the proposals will be pitted against each other, chamber rules have a much larger effect in determining the winning legislative coalition when party members' preferences begin to diverge.

It follows then that members' procedural choices should closely reflect their views about policy. Indeed, as suggested by the 1875 case,

majority parties are likely to try to change the rules in their favor if they believe such changes will increase their chances of legislative success. Unless such changes are deemed necessary for securing policy goals, a majority party would not necessarily invest in efforts to alter chamber rules in its interests. Instead, efforts to change House rules are more likely when the achievement of majority party legislative goals is hampered by minority obstructionism. Thus linking partisan preferences to procedural choice yields an expectation about the partisan conditions leading to suppression:

PARTISAN NEEDS HYPOTHESIS (SUPPRESSION). *The higher the level of minority obstructionism, the more likely the majority party will suppress minority rights.*

Partisan need alone, however, is arguably insufficient to produce restrictive procedural change. Instead, a majority party must also be sufficiently stronger than the minority to succeed in its procedural effort. Because suppressing minority rights, by definition, limits the minority's ability to amend, debate, or obstruct the majority's agenda, we should expect the minority party to oppose any effort to limit its parliamentary rights. Further, because rules protecting the minority party rarely preclude dissident majority party members from taking advantage of the rule, the majority party must be sufficiently united over its legislative goals in order successfully to limit minority rights. Minority obstructionism is unlikely to impel support for restrictions on minority rights if the majority party itself is factionalized over policy. Thus sufficient partisan capacity, as well as partisan need, is necessary for suppressing minority rights, which leads to the following expectation:

PARTISAN CAPACITY HYPOTHESIS (SUPPRESSION). *The stronger the majority party relative to the minority party, the more likely the majority party will suppress minority rights.*

A reverse logic holds for the creation of minority rights. The weaker the majority party, the more likely a faction of the majority will join a cross-party coalition in favor of expanding minority rights. Under such conditions,

Table 23.1. *Conditions Fostering Suppression of Minority Rights, 1789–1894*

Hypothesis	Variable	Mean Suppression Congresses (n = 10)	Nonsuppression Congresses (n = 41)	Difference
Partisan capacity	Difference in majority and minority party strength	15.45	8.70	6.75[**]
Partisan need	% obstructive floor motions (lagged)	13.30	6.10[a]	7.20[***]
Workload	Workload factor score	.70	−.20	.90[***]
Party competition	Change in party control in following Congress	.50	.25[b]	.25

[a] n = 40 (excludes 1st Congress).
[b] n = 40 (excludes 18th Congress due to discontinuity in chamber parties).
[**] $p < .01$, one-tailed test.
[***] $p < .001$, one-tailed test.

extending minority rights would serve the policy interests of both minority party members and those majority party members desiring to challenge the majority party's control of the agenda. If cross-party coalitions are necessary to extract procedural rights from the majority, then strong minority parties are essential to the creation of new rights: the stronger the minority party, the fewer the number of majority party defectors necessary to form a winning coalition in favor of extending minority rights. Thus the alignment of partisan policy preferences also leads to a testable proposition:

PARTISAN CAPACITY HYPOTHESIS (CREATION). *The weaker the majority party relative to the minority party, the more likely a cross-party coalition will create new minority rights.*

Immediate short-term policy preferences, rather than longer-term calculations about party control or broader institutional concerns about managing the legislative agenda, would thus motivate members either to suppress or to create minority party rights.

Preference alignments, external demands, and party competition, of course, might vary independently. Variation across all three factors might influence the probability of changes in House minority rights. My goal is to assess the relative influence of each of these variables in explaining the suppression and creation of minority rights across the history of the House. Contrary to conventional expectations about

the impact of workload and changing party control on procedural change, the findings here will suggest the influence of partisan alignments and inherited rules in structuring change in procedural rights.

PATTERNS OF SUPPRESSION IN THE HOUSE

Looking first at simple bivariate relationships during the first period (1789–1894), the conditions fostering suppression of rights lend initial support for both workload and partisan preference hypotheses (Table 23.1). Minority rights are more likely to be suppressed under conditions of higher workload, higher majority party advantage in strength over the minority, and higher levels of minority party obstructionism. Contrary to the party competition hypothesis, however, subsequent change in party control does not dampen the suppression of minority rights. In fact, although the difference is statistically insignificant, minority rights are more likely to be suppressed prior to a switch in party control than when the majority retains its control of the chamber. Thus, a rise in legislative activity, as well as increases in the majority party's perceived need and actual capacity for procedural change, appear to have statistically significant effects on the likelihood of suppression.

Judging from bivariate tests, suppression in the second period appears to occur under slightly different conditions (Table 23.2). High

Table 23.2. *Conditions Fostering Suppression of Minority Rights, 1895–1990*

Hypothesis	Variable	Suppression Congresses (n = 9)	Nonsuppression Congresses (n = 37)	Difference
		Mean		
Partisan capacity	Difference in majority and minority party strength	19.50	13.00	6.50*
Partisan need	Number of recorded votes (lagged)	656.00	290.00	366.00*
	Discharge motions filed (lagged)	37.00	17.00[a]	20.00
	Newly acquired minority right	.44	.08	.36*
Workload	Workload factor score	.22	−.10	.32
Party competition	Change in party control in following Congress	0.00	.19	.19**

[a] n = 36 (missing data for 101st Congress).

 * $p < .05$, one-tailed test.
 ** $p < .01$, one-tailed test.

partisan capacity and partisan need are still strongly related to the suppression of minority rights. The relationship between legislative activity and suppression, however, is weaker than in the first period: workload is not statistically higher in Congresses with restrictive rules changes than in those without. There is, however, some support for the party competition hypothesis: majority parties retaining control of the chamber in the second period are more likely to suppress minority rights. To make sense of the relative influence of these partisan

and nonpartisan factors on rules changes in both periods, I turn to multivariate tests of the politics of rights suppression.

PREDICTING SUPPRESSION, 1789–1894

A maximum likelihood logit model of suppression in the eighteenth and nineteenth centuries confirms the importance of partisan need and capacity in shaping procedural choice (Table 23.3). In a model assessing the impact

Table 23.3. *Minority Rights Suppression, 1789–1894 (Maximum Likelihood Logit Models)*

Hypothesis	Variable	Coefficient	Change in X (from, to)	Impact (%)
Partisan capacity	Difference in majority and minority party strength	.16* (.07)	(1.95, 18.09)	26
Partisan need	% obstructive motions (lagged)	23.46* (11.33)	(.02, .14)	31
Workload	Workload factor score	.04 (.59)	(−1.03, .97)	1
Party competition	Change in party control in following Congress	1.06 (1.14)	(0, 1)	12
	Constant	−5.92*** (1.9)	—	—

Note: Entries are unstandardized coefficients (standard errors in parentheses). −2 log likelihood = 30.68; model chi-squared 18.9, $p < .001$; correctly predicted = 90%; reduction in error = 50%; N = 49.

 * $p < .05$.
 * $p < .001$.

of minority obstructionism, the difference in majority and minority party strength, subsequent change in party control of the chamber, and levels of legislative activity, the coefficients for lagged obstruction and party strength difference are both significant and in the predicted (positive) direction. Overall, the model correctly classifies 90 percent of the cases and reduces error by 50 percent.

Contrary to the conventional wisdom, increases in workload do not increase the probability of suppression. In fact, increased legislative activity has virtually no effect on the choice of restrictive rules. Instead, suppression is 31 percent more likely when obstructionism increases from 2 percent to 14 percent of all floor motions and 26 percent more likely when the majority party's advantage in strength over the minority climbs sixfold. Although the party competition hypothesis predicts that suppression is more likely when the majority anticipates retaining control of the House, the results suggest that suppression is actually more likely (but only nominally so) when the majority party loses control.

PREDICTING SUPPRESSION, 1895–1990

By 1894, when Reed's rules had been readopted by the majority party, the role of party had been formalized in House rules, granting the majority party almost unfettered control over the floor agenda. Under this different procedural context, however, minority parties still devised procedural strategies intended to limit the majority's control of the agenda. Unlike the earlier period, however, there has been no single form of minority obstructionism in the latter period. Thus, in modeling the pattern of suppression after 1895, I try several alternatives to tap the procedural difficulties encountered by majority parties.

One method of capturing the increased incidence of minority obstructionism is to use a variable that indicates whether a minority right was created in the previous Congress. By extending new rights to the minority, the majority party potentially makes itself vulnerable to nettlesome activity by the minority. Testing for the effects of changes in party strength difference, workload, party control of the chamber, and newly created minority rights, the first model in Table 23.4 suggests moderate support for the partisan preference hypotheses. The coefficient for a newly created minority right is statistically significant and in the predicted (positive) direction. The coefficients for the difference in party strength and workload variables are also significant in the predicted (positive) direction. As expected, the coefficient for the change in party control variable is not. The model, however, provides only a 25 percent reduction in error over the modal category.

As noted, however, changes in the discharge process and floor voting rules opened the majority party to periodic procedural threats from the minority party. The second model in Table 23.4 begins to test for the effects of these rules changes by adding a variable to tap the number of recorded votes cast in the previous Congress. Nearly doubling the model's reduction in error, the addition of the variable lends further support for the partisan preference and workload hypotheses. Majority parties are more likely to suppress minority rights when their perceived capacity and need for change increases and when legislative activity is increasing as well. The expectation of retaining control of the House, in contrast, does not have a measurable effect on the likelihood of suppression.

In the third model in Table 23.4, I add a variable to tap the introduction and use of the discharge rule – a rule change that provides minority members a chance to shape the legislative agenda. Although the discharge variable does not reach statistical significance, its introduction improves the overall fit of the model, increasing the reduction in error to 56 percent. All three models suggest that accounting for levels of partisan capacity and partisan need, as well as the level of workload, is essential for predicting patterns of rights suppression, even after implementation of Reed's rules. Moreover, in the most robust of the three models, change in party control is unrelated to the probability of suppression.

Table 23.4. *Minority Rights Suppression, 1895–1990 (Maximum Likelihood Logit Models)*

Hypothesis	Variable	Model			Change in X (from, to)	Impact (%) (model 3)
		1	2	3		
Partisan capacity	Difference in majority and minority party strength	.13* (.07)	.240* (.120)	.320* (.150)	(5.45, 23.11)	2
Partisan need	Number of recorded votes (lagged)	–	.005* (.002)	.006* (.003)	(12, 740)	1
	Discharge motions filed (lagged)	–	–	.030 (.030)	(0, 57)	0
	Newly acquired minority right	4.40** (1.80)	9.430* (4.400)	9.800** (4.400)	(0, 1)	79
Workload	Workload factor score	1.80* (.95)	3.900* (2.100)	4.400* (2.100)	(−1.04, .97)	7
Party competition	Change in party control in following Congress	−8.80 (53.80)	−8.600 (52.200)	−8.400 (48.800)	(0, 1)	0
	Constant	−4.80** (1.60)	−11.100** (4.900)	−14.500** (6.300)	–	–
−2 Log likelihood		27.47	19.030	16.310	–	–
Model chi-squared		18.01**	26.000***	28.720***	–	–
Correctly predicted (%)		84.80	88.900	90.100	–	–
Reduction in error (%)		25.00	45.000	56.000	–	–
N		46.00	45.000	44.000	–	–

Note: Entries are unstandardized coefficients (standard errors in parentheses).

   * $p < .05$, one-tailed test.

  ** $p < .01$, one-tailed test.

*** $p < .001$, one-tailed test.

Assessing the impact of each variable from the third model (Table 23.4, column 5), partisan need again has the largest influence on the likelihood of suppression, with newly created minority rights all but certain to be suppressed in the following Congress. In contrast, a switch in party control has no effect on restrictive procedural change. The rest of the findings, however, show some interesting changes in the post-Reed era. First, an increase in workload has a very weak but positive effect on the likelihood of suppression. Second, although an increase in partisan capacity bolsters the probability of suppression, the relative impact is highly diminished in comparison to the earlier period. Such a finding is consistent with the general change in House politics after the adoption of Reed's rules. Because of rules changes secured in the nineteenth century, the role of the majority party in structuring the chamber agenda was formalized in House rules by the end of the 1890s. By ensuring the power of a simple majority to control the content of the agenda, as well as floor debate and amending opportunities, nineteenth-century rules changes endowed twentieth-century majority parties with an inherent advantage over the minority. That development appears to have reduced the majority party's reliance on coalition strength to suppress new minority obstructionism in the modern House.

PATTERNS OF CREATION IN THE HOUSE

The politics of suppression suggests that immediate partisan goals have historically motivated majority parties to alter the distribution of minority rights. The politics of creation leads to a similar conclusion.

Table 23.5. *Conditions Fostering Creation of Minority Rights, 1789–1990*

Hypothesis	Variable	Mean		Difference
		Creation Congresses (n = 7)	Noncreation Congresses (n = 89)	
Partisan capacity	Difference in majority and minority party strength	6.72	12.39	5.67*
	Minority party strength	31.47	24.47	7.00***
Workload	Workload factor score	.05	−.03	.08
Party competition	Change in party control in following Congress	.43	.23	.20

* $p < .05$.
*** $p < .001$.

The size of the majority party's advantage in strength over the minority is smaller in Congresses when rights are created than in Congresses with no new minority rights (Table 23.5). Thus, as suggested in the partisan capacity hypothesis, the weaker the majority party relative to the minority, the more likely a right will be created. Indeed, minority parties gaining new rights are statistically stronger than minority parties that fail to procure new rights. Under these conditions, a cross-party coalition in favor of extending minority rights is most likely to form. With such a strong minority, only a few majority defectors are necessary to form a winning coalition in favor of reallocating parliamentary rights. In contrast, there is no evidence that declining workload or anticipation of minority status leads majority parties to extend minority rights.

The requirement of a cross-party coalition to procure new rights is consistent with historical circumstances under which rights have been created. The extension of new minority rights has historically occurred when a faction of the majority party agrees with members of a strong minority party that reinforcing minority rights would serve both coalitions' interests. Cross-party coalitions of Progressive "insurgent" Republicans and minority party Democrats in 1910, 1924, and 1931 were driving forces behind the extension of new minority rights. For example, a coalition of Progressive Republicans and minority Democrats in 1924 forced the Republican leadership to alter

the discharge rule in its favor, earning the right for 150 members to call up a discharge motion on the floor and defeating an effort to increase the required number to 218. In the 1970s as well, cross-party coalitions were responsible for procuring new minority rights. For example, Democrats offered increases in minority staff and a ban on proxy voting to entice Republican support for broader institutional reforms, many opposed by senior majority party Democrats.

DISCUSSION AND CONCLUSIONS

Contrary to conventional themes about the development of the House, the emergence of a partisan, majoritarian institution was not inevitable. Far from being the inescapable consequence of secular trends, restrictive procedural choices in the House appear to reflect short-term partisan goals of the majority party, rather than longer-term partisan considerations or broader collective concerns about increasing efficiency of the chamber. When increased partisan capacity and need for procedural change coincide, majority parties have been most successful in limiting minority rights and moving the House toward a more partisan and majoritarian chamber. But when minority parties strengthen and attract the support of a majority faction, the process stalls and minority rights are reinforced. There is, in other words, a partisan basis to procedural choice in the House. Across the history of the House, crucial procedural choices have been shaped not by members' collective concerns about the institution, but by narrow calculations about partisan advantage.

To be sure, students of congressional development recognize that rules battles have at times been fought along a partisan dimension. In fact, most studies of congressional change highlight the role of Speaker Reed in silencing minority party obstructionism in 1890. Reed's innovations are generally cited as a significant turning point in House procedure, because the majority party claimed the right to strictly limit the procedural role of the minority in making policy. By taking a longer-term perspective, however, this study suggests that Reed's actions were but part of a more gradual course of institutional change. Indeed, rules changes in the 1890s both followed and preceded a century of strategic partisan calculations by the majority party about favored policy outcomes and the rules necessary to achieve them.

Such an emphasis on the evolution of minority rights, rather than simply on major institutional reforms such as Reed's rules, arguably provides a unique theoretical route to explaining institutional change. As suggested by Aldrich, "the dynamic path, that is to say, the political history, is the central object of our theoretical inquiry." What the historical path of House minority rights suggests is that both partisan preferences and inherited rules shape future institutional choices. The influence of members' goals on institutional choice is seen clearly in the relationship of party strength and change in minority rights. As the electoral strength of the major parties shifts over time, so, too, does the distribution of parliamentary rights: stronger *majority* parties succeed in limiting minority rights, and stronger *minority* parties attract majority party defectors to reinforce minority rights.

Still, the evolution of minority rights suggests that members' goals are themselves both shaped and constrained by the inherited institutional context. First, members' procedural choices depend in large part on existing rules. When minority parties devise new ways of obstructing the majority, the preferences of the majority party about desired institutional arrangements shift as well. If inherited rules did not affect procedural choice, then change in partisan capacity alone would account for most of the variation in minority rights – which it does not. Instead, minority exploitation of inherited rules has a substantial impact on change in minority rights, as majority parties realize a partisan need for changing the rules of the game.

Second, and relatedly, members' procedural choices depend on past procedural choices. Once majority rule is firmly entrenched at the end of the nineteenth century, there should be little reason for subsequent majority parties newly to suppress minority rights. But when minority parties procure and then exploit parliamentary rights after 1900, majority parties once again perceive that their party goals are threatened, and they proceed to adjust the procedural score accordingly. Changes in the political landscape, in conclusion, often make past decisions about procedural arrangements untenable. As goal-seeking actors, politicians will continue to try to alter institutional arrangements in response to a shifting historical context.

CHAPTER TWENTY-FOUR

The Evolution of Agenda-Setting Institutions in Congress

Path Dependency in House and Senate Institutional Development

Jason M. Roberts and Steven S. Smith

Roberts and Smith recount the origin and history of the two primary agenda-setting mechanisms in the U.S. Congress – special rules in the House and unanimous consent agreements in the Senate. They argue that the lack of an effective means of cutting off debate in the Senate put the Senate on a path of inefficiency, whereas the House was able to develop an efficient means of agenda control.

INTRODUCTION

Scheduling legislation is one of the most vexing collective-action problems faced by a legislative body. When the combination of must-pass legislation and legislation wanted by individual members exceeds the available time and resources, choices among alternatives must be made. These choices about the form and content of the legislative agenda create winners and losers, so it is important that we understand how these agenda-setting institutions emerge and develop. We focus on the two most important agenda-setting institutions in the U.S. Congress – special rules in the House and unanimous-consent agreements (UCAs) in the Senate.

Jason M. Roberts and Steven S. Smith. 2007. "The Evolution of Agenda-Setting Institutions in Congress" in David W. Brady and Matthew McCubbins, eds., *Party, Process, and Political Change: Further New Perspectives on the History of Congress* (Stanford University Press), 182–204. Copyright © 2007 by the Board of Trustees of the Leland Stanford Jr. University. All rights reserved. Used with permission of Stanford University Press, www.sup.org.

THE MOTION ON THE PREVIOUS QUESTION AND PATH DEPENDENCY

A potentially strong path dependency exists in the development of congressional agenda-setting mechanisms. This path-dependent process is stronger than those usually encountered in processes of institutional change. Pierson describes path-dependent processes that are a product of the increasing returns of an institutional arrangement. In fact, increasing returns are a common, maybe the most common, form of path-dependent processes. With little difficulty, we can see this form operating in Congress, too. But what we see in the contrasting paths of House and Senate development is a stronger form.

Both the House and the Senate rules contained a previous-question motion from the First Congress; however, the motion had not yet been transformed into a tool to end debate. The question took the form of "shall the main question be now put," which was the traditional parliamentary means of putting off discussion on a controversial measure. If the motion failed, discussion was put off; if it passed, discussion continued. The early Senate rarely invoked the motion, and eliminated it from its rules in 1806. The House overturned a ruling of the Speaker in 1807 that a successful previous-question motion ended debate on a bill before reversing this precedent in the face of obstruction in 1811. Thus, from 1811 forward, the House had an effective means for a majority to end debate on a bill or proposed rule change, while the Senate, bound by its lack of a previous-question motion, has never been able to develop an efficient means of ending debate.

Our working hypothesis is that the presence or absence of a motion for the previous question played a pivotal role in the development of House and Senate rules. House majority parties have regularly modified and elaborated on their chamber's rules, while Senate majority parties seldom seek, let alone achieve, a change in their chamber's rules. As a consequence, modern House rules are several times as long as Senate rules. When the House and Senate have determined that some limitation on debate is desirable, as for budget measures and trade agreements, special provisions have been written for the Senate to guarantee that debate could be closed. But this has happened only when supermajorities favor the change and often has happened as a part of a much larger legislative package.

The Senate's history appears to share features of increasing-returns processes. The initial event (dropping the little-used previous-question motion from the rules) seemed unimportant at the time but had lasting effects. The long-term effects were unpredictable because they depended on so many other unpredictable events, the procedural change proved very difficult to reverse (and has not been fully reversed), and the long-term consequence was inefficiency for an institution in which the constitutionally specified decision-making process was no different than that of the House. Because reform of debate-closing rules can be filibustered, this feature of Senate procedural history surely is a self-reinforcing process that can be characterized as path dependent.

Nevertheless, the story of path dependency in Senate procedure is special. Many of the factors — collective-action hurdles, transaction costs, vested interests, accumulated social capital, and so on — that contribute to institutional persistency are not the primary forces underlying the path dependency of Senate procedure. In contrast to the increasing-returns process, the Senate's basic decision rule has not been changed even under conditions of dramatically *decreasing* returns for the majority of senators. On only rare occasions have the costs of the inherited rules proved so high for a large enough number of senators to produce reform that reduced the threshold for cloture, itself an unwieldy procedure in comparison to House mechanisms for limiting debate, and even then the reforms have been modest. This is the product of the threshold itself and the infrequency with which large majorities arise that may find their enduring interests subverted by the threshold.

Recognition of potentially path-dependent features of congressional procedure is essential to a comparison of House and Senate agenda-setting mechanisms and their implications for the development of legislative parties. House rules have been adopted, modified, or eliminated many times with little or no support from minority-party legislators; Senate rules seldom have. The consequence is a different blend of procedures and parties in the two houses and a different dynamic to the changing role in policymaking of the parties of the two houses.

EFFORTS TO MODIFY THE ORDER OF BUSINESS

In the late nineteenth century, the House and Senate faced similar, although certainly not identical, logistical problems in the decades following the Civil War. By the 1880s, both houses faced serious obstacles to the completion of even routine legislative business. Our hypothesis is that two problems — an expanding legislative workload and renewed, sharp partisan conflict — were the mutually reinforcing motivations for change. A large legislative workload reflected an expanding nation, new demands for federal programs, and an increasingly complicated tariff code. The revival of the Democratic Party as Reconstruction ended generated intense competition for control of Congress and eventually yielded very polarized parties, particularly at the turn of the century. Minority obstructionism, made more damaging by the time pressures of a large workload, became a serious problem in both houses.

Before inventing more flexible agenda-setting devices of special rules and UCAs, both houses of Congress addressed the challenges of scheduling with changes in the order of business provided in their standing rules. Over the course of the nineteenth century, both chambers created special times and days for the transaction of particular kinds of legislative business and identified classes of legislation that could be reported and considered at any time (privileged measures). The daily schedule and classification of legislation were changed frequently, sometimes in response to abusive practices of the membership and sometimes in response to the burden of legislative business.

The challenges were not identical in both houses. The size of House grew far more rapidly than the Senate as the nation's population grew faster than states that were added to Union. The House was quicker to elaborate a complex order of business and create a set of floor calendars. For example, the House went further than the Senate in limiting certain kinds of motions to specified times or days and eliminating the requirement of gaining recognition on the floor to submit petitions, bills, and reports. In 1890 the regular tinkering with the order of business was overcome by a sweeping set of changes proposed, and later imposed, by Speaker Thomas Brackett Reed (R-Maine). The rules assigned to the Speaker several powers previously reserved for the House (referring bills to committee and disposing of business on the Speaker's table such as executive messages). More important, the Reed rules made it easy for a House majority to continue deliberating on a measure in the "morning hour," which could be stretched to any length, thus undermining a common source of obstructionism in the House.

Ultimately, changes in the formal order of business proved inadequate to the challenge of scheduling important legislation for floor consideration. In both chambers, debates about what to consider next and ad hoc motions from bill managers or sponsors to create special orders were common, often generating confusion about the schedule as well as tension within and between the parties. As we detail in the following sections, the struggle to solve this problem was addressed in fundamentally different ways in the two houses.

THE HOUSE OF REPRESENTATIVES AND SPECIAL RULES

The House Committee on Rules first gained power to report to the House at all times in 1841, but it would take decades for the committee to begin to play a major role in shaping the agenda and floor debate in the chamber through the use of what we now refer to as special rules. The Committee on Rules quickly moved from reporting "special orders," which provided that measures be considered on the floor outside the regular order, to "special rules," which added limitations on debate or amendments. By the time of the revolt against Speaker Joseph Cannon during the 61st Congress, the House had almost completely discontinued use of special orders in favor of special rules, and it had developed many of the components of modern-day special rules, including amending restrictions, waivers of points of order, and self-executing provisions.

FIRST USES OF SPECIAL ORDER: RESOLUTIONS FROM THE COMMITTEE ON RULES

The first documented instance of the Committee on Rules attempting to alter the rules for consideration of a specific bill occurred in the 47th Congress during consideration of the Tariff Act of 1883. The original bill sought to lower the sales tax on tobacco, matches, and medicine and easily passed the House in mid-1882. The Senate took up the bill in early 1883 and made radical changes, striking out all but the enacting clause and transforming the measure into a general tariff-reduction bill. The Senate bill was not wholly acceptable to the Republican leaders in the Senate, but Senators Morrill (R-Vt.), Sherman (R-Ohio), and Aldrich (R-R.I.) allowed the bill to pass with the understanding that they would be able to alter it in conference. Simultaneously, the House was trying to pass a tariff bill, but a sharply divided Republican caucus was unable to come to agreement on a bill. The result was a House bill with the same title as the Senate measure but one that dealt only with internal taxes, in contrast to the exclusive focus on tariffs in the Senate version. The House Republicans caucused on this issue and voted to disagree with the Senate amendments and request a conference. However, close to 40 members of the Republican caucus were absent from the meeting and presumably would have voted to accept the Senate bill if given the opportunity.

Republican leaders of both chambers sought to pass a bill with significantly higher tariffs than the bill passed by the Senate and decided that the best approach was to get the bill to a conference committee where the provisions of the bill could be amended to provide for higher tariff rates. The House leadership could bring up a motion to disagree with the Senate amendments and go to conference, but under House rules a motion to agree with the Senate amendments would have taken precedence and likely would have passed. An alternative approach was to consider a motion to disagree and request a conference under suspension of the rules, which would require a two-thirds vote of the chamber — a margin that was likely unattainable. A third approach was taken. Representative Reed, who had recently become a member of the Committee on Rules and became Speaker a few years later, authored the following resolution, which was reported from the committee:

Resolved, That during the remainder of the session it shall be in order at any time to move to suspend the rules, which motion shall be decided by a majority vote, to take from the Speaker's table House Bill Number 5538, with Senate amendment thereto, entitled "A bill to reduce internal-revenue taxation," and to declare a disagreement with the Senate amendments to the same and to ask for a committee of conference thereon, to be composed of five members on the part of the House. If such motion shall fail, the bill shall remain upon the Speaker's table unaffected by the decision of the House upon such motion.

The resolution was adopted. It is the first known instance of the adoption of a special order to supplant or supplement the standing rules by a simple majority rather than a two-thirds majority. The episode also demonstrated the potential of the Committee on Rules to augment the power of House majorities by limiting the House to a vote to disagree with the Senate amendments. The rule did not provide for a motion to agree with the Senate amendments, thus forcing a vote between going to conference or not passing a tariff bill. This use of the Rules Committee to shape the agenda allowed majority-party Republicans to ensure that their preferred outcome – a bill with higher tariffs – was adopted while also preventing a vote on the Senate bill, which was preferred by most Democrats and moderate Republicans.

The House was slow to repeat this use of the Committee on Rules. The resolution providing for consideration of the tariff bill was the only one reported by the committee during the 47th Congress; none were reported during the 48th Congress. When interjections into the order of business by the Committee on Rules reappeared during the 49th Congress, they all took the form of special orders – they provided for the consideration of a particular bill or bills from a committee but did not alter the procedures by which the bills were considered. Although the wording of these special orders was not consistent, the following order from the 49th Congress (1885–1887) is typical:

Resolved, That on Tuesday, February 1, 1887, the House will take a recess at 5 o'clock p.m. until half past 7 p.m., and that the evening session shall be devoted exclusively to the consideration of such measures as may be presented by the Committee on Military Affairs.

Special orders were not new features of House procedures, but the ability to change the order of business through a majority rather than supermajority vote was an innovation. The debate on these orders suggests that special orders were not particularly partisan in effect. Minority members still held all parliamentary rights under the "regular order," including the right to offer amendments and dilatory motions. With the burgeoning workload, the House simply needed a more efficient means of reaching bills that were unlikely to be reached by taking bills off the calendar in order. Special orders served this role quite well, often designating days for multiple bills or committees in the same order.

THE EARLY SPECIAL RULES

The transformation of special orders into special rules began in the 51st Congress (1889–1891), the first with Reed as Speaker. Traditional special orders were still employed, but 7 of the 11 interjections into the regular order by the Committee on Rules in that Congress were special rules. All 7 limited the time for either general debate or amendments under the 5-minute rule, while two of the rules barred all amendments – the first "closed" rules.

The 51st Congress also marked a shift to partisan debate over the content of reports from the Committee on Rules. During debate on the rule for considering the currency bill, a minority party legislator, Representative James Blount (D-Ga.), called attention to the power of special rules to restrict policy alternatives and provide political cover for the majority party:

If it was permissible for me to state what occurred in the Republican caucus last night, I could show an infinite amount of division; I could show just such a division on the other side of the House as makes it necessary to put the whip of this order upon them to save them from such a record as would be terrible to them. . . . Your Republican platform declared for silver coinage. In your secret councils many of you have recognized the importance of some sort of coinage of silver, yet here is an order changing the rules of this House to escape that issue in the Congress of the United States. (*Congressional Record*, June 5, 1890, p. 5646)

The use of special rules to prevent cross-party coalitions from amending or even overturning the legislation of a majority of the majority party has come to be recognized as a vital source of influence for majority-party leaders.

By the 54th Congress (1895–1897), Reed was back in the Speaker's chair and legislators referred to reports from the Committee on Rules as "rules." The use of special rules began to grow and the rules became increasingly restrictive of amending activity. Some began to stream-

line activity by including "self-executing" previous-question orders in special rules that had the effect of closing or restricting amending opportunities in the House under the hour rule, such as in this rule:

Resolved, That immediately after the adoption of this resolution it shall be in order in the House to call up for debate, the previous question being considered as ordered, a bill reported by the Ways and Means, entitled "A bill to temporarily increase revenue to meet the expenses of Government and provide against a deficiency;" that at 5 o'clock, without delay or other motion, the vote shall be taken. General leave to print is hereby granted for ten days. (*Congressional Record*, December 26, 1895, p. 305)

This rule eliminated amending opportunities by embedding the previous-question motion in the rule, limited the time for general debate to less than 1 day, and precluded "other motions," such as the motion to recommit.

Thus, over the course of only a few Congresses, the House moved from a body that had a difficult time transacting any business to a body with the means to dispose of major legislation in less than a day. Commenting on this transformation, Representative Bailey (D-Tex.) warned, "It was foolish, I grant you, to debate without deciding; but it is dangerous to decide without debating. . . . This error, sir, is more mischievous than the one which we have abandoned". The phrase was borrowed from Senator Henry Cabot Lodge, who had used a different version to criticize the Senate filibuster.

Innovations in special rules were not always restrictive in nature. During consideration of an appropriations bill, members discovered that many of the salaries funded in the bill had not been authorized and were subject to successful points of order raised by minority-party members. The Committee on Rules responded by reporting a rule that read,

Resolved, That hereafter, in consideration of the bill [HR 16472] making appropriations for the legislative, executive, and judicial expenses of the Government, and for other purposes, in the Committee of the Whole House on the state of the Union, it shall be in order to consider, without intervention of a point of order, any section of the bill as reported, except section 8; and upon motion authorized by the Committee on Appropriations it shall be in order to insert in any part of the bill any provision reported as part of the bill and heretofore ruled out on a point of order.

The 1906 special rule appears to have been one of the first rules to waive points of order. This waiver did not have profound policy consequences, but the incident was important for two reasons. First, the rule expanded the repertoire of special rules to supplant a new class of standing rules. Rather than merely limiting debate or amendments, the rule showed that a House majority also could set aside any restriction in the standing rules, which eventually would include germaneness and many other important restrictions. Second, the rule was adopted in response to unanticipated developments on the floor, which in the future would limit the effectiveness of innovative minority tactics.

The ability of majorities to streamline floor action on legislation is one of the defining characteristics of the modern House of Representatives. However, this has not always been the case. Before the development of the special order and the institution of the Reed rules, the House was chaotic with members regularly obstructing business and arguing over the order of business. The special order and later the special rule developed as means for the House to legislate efficiently and for majority parties to gain control of the agenda. These developments would have been much more difficult, if not impossible, without a previous-question motion. The previous-question motion not only provided a means for the House to close debate on substantive legislation but it also allowed a majority to close debate and prevent amendments to special orders and special rules. In less than two decades the House developed many of the features of modernday special rules, including debate and amendment restrictions, waivers, and self-executing provisions, and often used them for partisan purposes, especially on tariff legislation. Despite the development and innovation of special rules in the late nineteenth and early twentieth centuries, the use of this new procedural tool was limited. It would be decades before the House permitted the Committee on

Rules to be the primary agenda-setter in the House.

THE SENATE AND UNANIMOUS-CONSENT AGREEMENTS

The term *complex* has sometimes been applied to the important class of UCAs that interests us – those that limit debate or amendments in some way. In the modern Senate, most complex UCAs are negotiated by, or under the supervision of, the majority leader and are offered by him, but the floor leaders' responsibility for agreements took decades to emerge after UCAs became a regular feature of floor action.

PRE-1914 PERIOD

Although the Senate has always been less formal and more leisurely than the House in floor procedure, the first, and somewhat isolated, use of a unanimous-consent request to limit debate or amendments occurred in 1846. Not surprisingly, the 1846 agreement was raised in a most casual way. A senator observed that the debate on the Oregon resolutions seemed to be winding down after more than 2 months and that "it would be an accommodation to many Senators to have an understanding as to the exact day" the Senate would vote. The agreement was quite informal – merely to vote on the resolutions in 3 days. A senator noted that the chamber could not be sure that debate on amendments would end by then; another assured him that the remaining debate would be brief. Notably, one senator said that he "had not the slightest objection to fixing upon some day for terminating the debate, provided it was not to be regarded as establishing a precedent." On the appointed day, the debate lasted longer than some senators had expected, but they brought the resolutions to a vote.

Identifying complex UCAs in the mid-nineteenth century is difficult. As informal agreements, UCAs were not reported or indexed in the *Senate Journal* or other official publications. Perusal of the *Congressional Globe*, which does not provide reliable coverage of all procedural action, indicates that by 1870 UCAs were being used with some frequency. As many are today, the UCAs were time-limitation agreements that provided for disposal of a measure by a specified time. The typical UCA provided for a vote on a bill by a certain time, usually 4 or 5 o'clock, 1 or 2 days in the future. The presiding officer usually repeated the agreement once offered so that senators could hear and understand it.

As early as 1870 the Senate found itself bound by an interpretation of the parliamentary status of UCAs that made them difficult to enforce. On Saturday July 4, 1870, with many senators losing patience as their summer stay in Washington was extended, the hour for a final vote on a naturalization bill under a UCA passed, with opponents continuing to press amendments and debate the bill. Senators observed that the debate continued in violation of the UCA. John Sherman, in fact, complained that it was the first violation of a UCA in the history of the practice. When a point of order was raised by another senator, the president pro tempore, Henry Anthony, stated that the chair did not have the power to enforce the agreement. "The agreement under which the Senate came to an understanding to vote at five o'clock on Saturday was by unanimous consent," Anthony declared. "It was not an order entered on the *Journal*, but merely an understanding among Senators. The Chair has no power and no right to enforce an agreement of that kind". Anthony's repeated rulings established a precedent that UCAs could not be enforced by the presiding officer, a precedent that led to much confusion over the next four decades.

Anthony's interpretation appeared to be based on the casual nature of UCAs in the years before the Civil War, when UCAs were viewed as mere gentlemen's agreements. The argument was based on two premises – that UCAs were not recognized in the Senate's rules and that the presiding officer had no authority except that granted explicitly by the rules or an order of the Senate. After Anthony left the Senate, Henry Cabot Lodge (R–Mass.) became the Senate's

unofficial parliamentarian-in-residence and frequently articulated this rationale.

In practice, presiding officers after Anthony were not entirely consistent in their approach to UCAs in the late nineteenth century. Most presiding officers contributed to the implementation of UCAs by noting that the time had arrived to call up or vote on a measure subject to a UCA. But senators varied in their understanding of the role of the presiding officer, and the role of presiding officers in facilitating the UCA process was not settled before the century ended. Most presiding officers routinely refused to enforce UCAs, but others chose to go their own way and their colleagues tolerated their choices. In 1888 Senator John Ingalls (R–Kans.), then president pro tempore, interrupted a senator who exceeded the 5-minute limit for a speech under a UCA and asked if there was objection to allowing the senator to continue. Ingalls was not alone in enforcing the UCA limits on speeches. President Pro Tempore William Frye (R–Maine) once took the initiative to note that debate was not in order under a UCA and ruled on a point of order raised against amendments based on provisions of the same UCA. And Vice Presidents Charles Fairbanks and James Sherman were not timid about enforcing UCAs at times.

Responsibility for negotiating UCAs appears to have rested primarily on the shoulders of bill managers until the second decade of the twentieth century. The *Congressional Record* is replete with long exchanges among senators about a bill manager's unanimous-consent request. Confusion about the provisions of UCAs was common, with senators sometimes quoting the *Record* to prove a point. Senators sometimes complained that they were not present when unanimous consent was granted.

Further complicating the use of UCAs after the turn of the century was the thesis that UCAs could not be modified, even by unanimous consent. Lodge made this argument in 1907 and consistently maintained the position along with the view that the presiding officer could not enforce UCAs. Lodge's theory was that a UCA, as a gentlemen's agreement, created an obligation that could not be violated at a later time by senators who happened to be on the floor and were seeking a modification. Lodge argued, as Sherman had maintained in 1870, that modifications in UCAs, even by unanimous consent, would eventually undermine confidence in UCAs. Although presiding officers were not consistent on this matter, the Lodge thesis was the prevailing interpretation during the first decade of the twentieth century.

Agreements that provided for a vote on a bill and pending amendments at a certain time were a regular part of floor-management practice at the turn of the century. Although compliance with UCAs was generally good, critical features of modern floor practice were not in place. No formal party floor leaders were present to orchestrate agreements and oversee their implementation. The thesis that UCAs could not be modified by unanimous consent made them inflexible tools for scheduling. Presiding officers enforced agreements sporadically, whether because of the ignorance of precedent or the forbearance of senators.

In the first years of the twentieth century, the Senate adopted practices that reduced confusion about UCAs. Senators began to submit unanimous-consent requests in writing to the desk. UCAs were often read by the secretary at the request of the presiding officer. UCAs that were intended to govern the conduct of business on subsequent days were printed on the title page of the daily Calendar of Business as long as they were operative. And the secretary appears to have reworded numerous agreements so that they would conform to what had become the "usual form," as some senators noted on the floor. These innovations occurred without any official recognition of the UCAs in the standing rules of the Senate.

Arguments about the twisted logic in Senate precedents on UCAs came to a head in January 1913. After having failed in previous days to gain unanimous consent for consideration and a vote on a prohibition bill, Newell Sanders (R-Tenn.) asked for unanimous consent once again and, probably, much to his surprise, received it. Reed Smoot (R-Utah) quickly inquired, "Was there a unanimous consent agreement just entered?" When the substitute presiding officer indicated that there was, Smoot immediately asked that it be reconsidered, to which the presiding officer responded that "it is beyond the power of the Senate to change or interfere with a unanimous consent agreement after it is made." Several senators insisted that they had not heard the request and that previous practice in such cases was to have the request submitted to the Senate again. Others, including Lodge, had to confess that a UCA must be observed. One senator, Joseph Bristow (R-Kans.), proclaimed that he was free to violate the UCA. The next day, Smoot suggested that the request be resubmitted to the Senate. Over the strong protest of another Republican, New Hampshire's Jacob Gallinger, President Pro Tempore Augustus Bacon (D-Ga.), now back in the chair, indicated that he had no power to rule on the matter and allowed the issue to be decided by the Senate. A large majority voted to have the request resubmitted, which it was, and Smoot promptly objected to the request. Gallinger then restated the request – with a different date for action on the measure – and it was accepted.

By the beginning of the next session, a committee recommended the adoption of a new rule, an additional paragraph for Rule 12. The rule provided that

no request by a Senator for unanimous consent for the taking of a final vote on a specified date upon the passage of a bill or joint resolution shall be submitted to the Senate for agreement thereto until, upon a roll call ordered for the purpose by the presiding officer, it shall be disclosed that a quorum of the Senate is present; and when unanimous consent is thus given, the same shall operate as the order of the Senate, but any unanimous consent may be revoked by another unanimous consent granted in the manner prescribed above upon one day's notice. (Rule 12 [4])

The requirement for a quorum call was not controversial. Even the provision for UCAs to be considered orders of the Senate, enabling the presiding officer to enforce them, received little discussion. Lodge and Smoot complained about the ability to modify UCAs by unanimous consent but appeared to accept the logic once the proponents of the rule accepted an amendment that required 1 day's notice of a request to modify such a UCA (one providing for a final vote). Later rulings would allow the 1-day notice requirement to be waived by unanimous consent. A bipartisan majority supported the proposal, as amended.

POST-1914 PERIOD

With the new rule, UCAs became formally recognized as orders of the Senate. As such, a UCA supersedes Senate rules and precedents that are contrary to its provisions. Presiding officers began to exhibit consistency in their interpretation of the parliamentary status of UCAs and their power to implement them. They would enforce UCAs as all other orders of the Senate and, over time, a large body of precedent accumulated in support of the proposition that presiding officers were obligated to take the initiative in enforcing the provisions of UCAs.

By the early 1920s, central features of modern Senate floor practice were in place. As orders of the Senate, UCAs began to be reported faithfully in the *Journal*. It took a few years for floor leaders to assume primary responsibility for negotiating UCAs and managing their approval on the floor. By 1921 party leaders were actively engaged in the process. In the 1910s and 1920s, as party leaders assumed control of the Senate floor, the presiding officer's role as neutral arbiter and enforcer of UCAs was settled.

Practices surrounding UCAs were not entirely settled in the mid-twentieth century. In the last half of the twentieth century, the majority leader became more inventive in designing agreements to limit debate and amendments. Just as the House majority leadership began to craft limits on debate and amendments in special rules to the political situation of each bill, Senate majority leaders acquired a larger repertoire of UCA provisions. This process took place in stages.

For more than 30 years, nearly all UCAs propounded were of a standard form. The form is recorded in former Senate parliamentarian Floyd Riddick's *Senate Procedure*:

Ordered, by unanimous consent, that on the calendar day of _____, 19 _____, at not later than _____ o'clock p.m. the Senate will proceed to vote, without further debate, upon any amendment that may be pending, any amendment that may be offered, and upon the bill (*bill number and name*) through the regular parliamentary stages to its final disposition; and that after the hour of _____ o'clock p.m., on said calendar day, no Senator shall speak more than once or longer than _____ minutes upon the bill, or more than once or longer than _____ minutes upon any amendment thereto.

The purpose of these UCAs was to gain final disposition of a bill, including any action on amendments, by a certain time and to divide time for debate equitably in the meantime.

To see how the content of UCAs evolved since the 1930s, we have coded the provisions of UCAs for selected Congresses. Nearly all complex UCAs were offered by the majority leader so we can safely characterize UCA provisions by leader. The percentages in the table refer to the percentage of all complex UCAs – those that limit debate or amendments in some way – adopted under each leader.

Under Joseph Robinson (D-Ark.), who Gamm and Smith characterize as the first modern floor leader, and Albin Barkley (D-Ky.), UCAs remained of the traditional form. Their successors, Ernest McFarland (D-Ariz.), Robert Taft (R-Ohio), and William Knowland (R-Calif.), were not particularly innovative but occasionally singled out one or more amendments for special debate limits. For the most part, these leaders offered time limitation agreements after debate on a measure had consumed considerable time and as their colleagues came to recognize the importance of moving on to other legislation.

Robinson is noteworthy for another reason vital to the modern use of UCAs. During his tenure, with a friendly vice president presiding, the precedent was established that, when more than one senator seeks recognition, priority of recognition is given to the majority leader. This precedent allows the majority leader to gain recognition to address the Senate, make a motion before another, or ask for unanimous consent. With the right of first recognition, the majority leader is given an opportunity to propound UCAs.

Lyndon Johnson (D-Tex.) has been given credit for great innovation in Senate leadership, including his use of UCAs. More frequently than his predecessors, Johnson successfully propounded time-limitation agreements before the motion to proceed on a measure was offered. Then, much more frequently than earlier UCAs, Johnson's UCAs divided control of time for general debate on a bill between the floor leaders, giving Johnson more control over the flow of debate and an opportunity to offer amendments of his own in a timely way. Moreover, Johnson sought to keep the Senate focused on the bill at hand by barring nongermane amendments when he could. Finally, Johnson's UCAs were more likely to provide for special treatment of one or more amendments than were his predecessors' UCAs.

Mike Mansfield (D-Mont.) was far less aggressive than Johnson, but at least at first, the mix of provisions changed little under Mansfield. This did not last long. As senators became more assertive and amending activity expanded, a more tactical, flexible approach to setting the floor agenda was required. This flexibility wasn't always a matter of choice. Under Mansfield, senators often objected to unanimous-consent requests that required amendments to be germane and the use of germaneness provisions dropped.

Robert Byrd (D-W.Va.), who took over routine floor duties for Mansfield in the late 1960s and early 1970s, instituted innovations in UCA practice. Most obviously, Byrd frequently offered multiple UCAs during the course of debate on a single measure. UCAs became far less comprehensive and frequently dealt with a single amendment or short period of time. To be sure, UCAs providing for time agreements on a bill were offered before the debate on the measure began, but they were regularly supplemented during the course of debate. The lower relative frequency of certain kinds of UCA provisions was due to the limited or tactical purpose of many of Byrd's UCAs.

Bryd's successors were not quite so quick to offer UCAs, but they did continue to use the full array of UCA provisions. Omnibus measures – particularly budget measures, which were debated under time limitations established by statute – reduced the number of UCAs propounded by leaders. Beginning in the mid-1980s, UCAs providing for the consideration of a single amendment were more common. The greater frequency of provisions barring second-degree amendments reflected the leaders' efforts to more fully structure the floor agenda when possible. Such provisions were almost always accompanied by provisions barring other motions, appeals, and points of order. At times, although for only a small fraction of bills, amendments to certain sections of bills were barred by UCAs.

Modern UCAs come in all sizes, big and small. While UCAs are often tailored to individual measures and often to brief periods of debate and a single amendment, they also have been used to establish a comprehensive floor agenda for a measure, or even a set of measures, in delicate legislative situations. UCAs have the virtue of being difficult to modify (only by unanimous consent, of course) so they provide a particularly useful means for cementing arrangements intended to guarantee votes on certain measures or amendments or preclude votes on others.

A STILL UNSETTLED PRACTICE

The Senate remains a legislative body with inherent inconsistencies in its rules. Unanimous-consent, supermajority requirements for cloture and other motions, and the constitutional requirement of a simple majority for approving legislation live side by side. On occasion, these inconsistencies surface and senators are confronted with difficult parliamentary choices.

For example, among the issues raised but still not resolved is whether the Senate should, by majority vote, overturn rulings of the presiding officer based on UCAs. A common situation is one in which the presiding officer rules that an amendment is out of order because it violates a UCA that requires amendments to be germane. Should the Senate majority overturn a ruling that an amendment is out of order?

The power to appeal a ruling to the Senate may undermine senators' confidence that a UCA will be observed and threaten the entire practice of operating by unanimous consent. But to back away from appeals when proceeding under a UCA hands to the presiding officer a source of influence over outcomes that the Senate has not been explicitly granted.

LESSONS FROM THE HISTORY OF HOUSE SPECIAL RULES AND SENATE UCAS

The remarkable parliamentary ingenuity that is reflected in modern House special rules and Senate UCAs reflects the common purposes of these agenda-setting mechanisms. In both chambers, majority-party leaders seek to structure debate and amending activity to improve legislative efficiency and to the advantage of their parties. Yet the differences in the tools available to set the agenda are one of the most prominent and visible differences between the contemporary House and Senate. The House is often considered a model of legislative efficiency, while legislating in the Senate is often an arduous, if not impossible, task. That these differences persist over time is quite remarkable, given that both chambers respond to similar external forces that shape the public agenda and that the chambers themselves determine their floor procedures. Differences in their decision rules (simple majorities vs. unanimous consent) and the inherited body of floor procedures, themselves in part a product of the longstanding decision rules, have generated different paths of development in agenda setting and a different repertoire of strategies for floor leaders.

PATH DEPENDENCY: THE PREVIOUS-QUESTION MOTION AND AGENDA SETTING

The presence or absence of a motion for the previous question has played a pivotal role in the development of House and Senate rules. Reducing opportunities to speak, offer legislation or amendments, and obstruct action is the essence of efforts to improve efficiency in legislative agenda setting and related decision-making processes. Such efforts generally serve the interest of the majority more than the minority. Consequently, the minority often argues that efficiency-improving changes undermine a fair, deliberative process and opposes the changes. In the House, majority support for a previous-question motion allows the majority party to get a vote on a rules change and impose its will on the minority. In the Senate, organized minority-party opposition is generally enough to prevent a vote on a rules change. The consequence is that the House has a body of rules and precedents that allow a simple majority to set its agenda. The Senate never has, even though Senate majorities have sometimes expressed an interest in efficiency-improving reforms.

PATH DEPENDENCY: INSTITUTIONAL CONSTRAINTS ON PARTY DEVELOPMENT

While agenda-setting mechanisms reflect early procedural choices of the two houses, legislative party development is influenced by development of agenda-setting institutions. In the House, with its effective means of agenda control – perhaps most important, the ability to bring a matter to a vote – the incentive exists to devise the means to coordinate party strategy in setting the agenda and enhancing the ability of leaders to induce cooperation for fellow partisans. In the Senate, the majority party can do little to structure the agenda and get votes without the cooperation of the minority. As a consequence, strong central leadership serves less purpose and may even be more dangerous. Majority-party senators would be suspicious of a leader who can impose discipline on them while making necessary concessions to the minority to acquire unanimous consent or supermajorities to limit debate and amending activity.

In our view, legislative parties are both electoral coalitions and policy coalitions. Resolving conflict between electoral and policy objectives is the everyday burden of parties and their leaders. In fact, we would assert that balancing collective electoral and policy goals is a public good for legislative parties that leaders are asked to provide in the form of legislative strategies.

Both perspectives appear to be essential to understanding legislative parties. On the one hand, the history of House special rules and Senate UCAs indicates that majority parties consistently seek to *create* procedural tools to manage the agenda in their interest and that a certain minimum level of support for efforts to set the agenda are expected of rank-and-file members. Legislative parties surely are, in major part, procedural cartels. On the other hand, the *use* of procedural tools may reflect the extent of agreement about the policy purposes to which partisans hope that they are put. This would be reflected more in the timing and content of special rules and UCAs than in their frequency or, in the case of special rules, the vote margins by which they were adopted.

DIFFERENT RESPONSES TO SIMILAR CONDITIONS

The late nineteenth century proved to be a critical period for both House and Senate parliamentary practice. Developments common to the two houses – a sizable increase in the legislative workload and the renewal of sharp partisan conflict – led to nearly continuous conflict about the floor agenda and a search for new rules to allow the majority party to get action on its legislation. Modifications of the formal order of business and competing special-order motions were typical of both House and Senate sessions.

We have observed that a critical difference in initial conditions – the presence of a motion for the previous question in the House and the absence of such a motion in the Senate – has been responsible for major differences in procedural development between the two houses since the late nineteenth century. These institutional features pre-date the modern party system and are clearly rooted in the nature of the two bodies in their formative years. They created a procedural status quo that was impossible to dislodge. In the House, majorities have no incentive to give up the motion for the previous question because it is the means by which a majority is able to get a decisive vote on a pending question. In the Senate, minorities have no incentive to reinstate a previous-question motion and have managed to retain supermajority rules for closing debate.

PART VIII. THE FLOOR AND VOTING

CHAPTER TWENTY-FIVE

Greasing the Wheels

Using Pork Barrel Projects to Build Majority Coalitions in Congress – Excerpt

Diana Evans

In this excerpt, Evans considers the nature of coalition building for individualistic or "pork barrel" projects in Congress. She argues that party leaders use pork projects to gain votes on other general interest legislation.

[My] argument is that one important strategy by which policy coalition leaders create legislative majorities for controversial general interest legislation is to buy legislators' votes, one by one, favor by favor. Doing so not only helps leaders to unite their party, but it also can draw members of the other party away from their own caucus. Where attainment of a secure majority on the merits seems doubtful, distributive benefits provide the extra margin of support to compensate for pressures that otherwise might persuade members not to vote for such a bill. This strategy is particularly interesting for its use of the sort of policy that is most reviled by observers of Congress – pork barrel policy – to pass the type that is most admired – general interest policy.

Before proceeding to a discussion of the process of acquiring votes with distributive benefits, it is worthwhile to elaborate on the definition of general interest legislation. I define such legislation as broad-based measures that affect the whole nation or a large segment thereof. This

Diana Evans. 2004. "Pork Barrel Politics and General Interest Legislation" in Diana Evans, *Greasing the Wheels: Using Pork Barrel Projects to Build Majority Coalitions in Congress* (Cambridge University Press), 29–56. Copyright © 2004. Reprinted with the permission of Cambridge University Press.

definition of general interest legislation is somewhat similar to Douglas Arnold's definition of general benefits. Arnold requires that in order to be general in their impact, policies must "fall uniformly on members of society." Subsumed by this definition is breadth of impact: Such policies obviously affect everyone. But aside from pure public goods, most policies do not have a truly uniform impact; even Arnold's examples, which include economic growth and stable prices, are unlikely to be truly uniform in their effects on all socioeconomic levels. Therefore, I prefer to stress the breadth, rather than the uniformity, of a policy's effects. As this implies, there is a great deal of territory between the extremes of pork barrel and general interest legislation, and policy coalition leaders can use pork to gain votes just as easily for policies in that middle range as for general interest policy. However, the legislative challenge with which this book is concerned is the collective action dilemma faced by Congress in passing general interest legislation, not policies in the middle range of impacts.

Winning support for general interest legislation with pork barrel benefits is a strategy that can be used by any leader of a policy coalition: committee and subcommittee chairs, party leaders in each house of Congress, and the president. Clearly, the need to buy votes depends on the size and unity of a party's caucus. If the caucus has a large majority and is tightly unified on most matters, vote buying with pork is likely to be unnecessary. If, on the other hand, the party is heterogeneous and fragmented or in the minority, vote buying becomes more necessary in order for party leaders' preferences on general interest legislation to prevail. Even as congressional party leaders' powers have grown over the past twenty years, there are still advantages to using the carrot of pork barrel benefits rather than the stick of party discipline to gain compliance with leaders' policy goals. In that manner, leaders can pass general interest policies that they believe will redound to the party's overall benefit in subsequent elections. It should be noted, however, that this is a strategy most available to the majority, as it is more likely to control distributive benefits.

Committee leaders can use pork for the same purpose, but their goals may differ from those of their party leaders. Committee leaders may not be in tune with their own party leadership on a given issue within their jurisdiction; if they can distribute pork, they are more able to pursue an independent course, defying their leadership in order to attain their own policy preferences. Of course, the more sanctions the leadership possesses to use against rebellious committee chairs, the less likely such a strategy is. But to the extent that chairs hold their positions independent of caucus leaders, they can use this strategy more freely, without fear of the ultimate sanction, loss of the chairmanship. When chairs are elected by caucus, they can actually gain independence from their leaders by distributing pork. No wonder the Republican leadership, having just attained the majority in the House in 1995, sought to weaken committee chairs by imposing six-year term limits and initially banning the distribution of pork by appropriations subcommittee chairs.

THE CONDITIONS FOR USING PORK TO BUILD MAJORITY COALITIONS

Regardless of who the policy coalition leaders are, I assume that four conditions must exist in order for them to pursue this coalition-building strategy. First, they must have access to sufficient distributive benefits to trade for members' support for their favored legislation. For committee leaders, some jurisdictions are more useful than others in this regard. For example, the House committees on International Relations and the Judiciary have less opportunity to distribute pork than the Transportation and Infrastructure (formerly Public Works and Transportation) Committee and the Appropriations Committee, due to the nature of the matters under their jurisdictions.

A second necessary condition for implementing the vote-buying strategy is that leaders must be willing to use it. This circumstance should not be taken for granted, despite the obvious appeal of pork barrel benefits. An example of one who was not so willing was Representative Norman Mineta (D-Calif.), when he took over the chairmanship of the Aviation Subcommittee of the Public Works and Transportation Committee in 1989. That subcommittee previously had been known for its generous distribution of pork barrel projects; however, Mineta, who was known to oppose such projects, held fast against their inclusion in the bills reported under his leadership.

Third, I assume that rank-and-file members who sell their votes on general interest legislation for a pork barrel project are motivated by the reelection goal. If they otherwise would oppose the bill but agree to trade their vote for a project, they must care more about the project and its impact on their reelection than about the general interest provisions of the bill to which the project is attached.

Fourth, policy coalition leaders who use this strategy are not driven by their own electoral goals to pass the underlying general interest legislation. Instead, they are motivated by the other two commonly recognized goals, making good public policy or achieving internal influence.

The third and fourth conditions deserve some elaboration. Restating them together, when leaders buy votes with pork barrel benefits, they take advantage of rank-and-file members' electoral goals to pass bills that the leaders favor; however, the leaders themselves are motivated by other goals. The idea that leaders use members' desire for reelection is not new. The assumption that underlies this hypothesis, that legislators desire reelection, has been central to much of the theory concerning congressional behavior for several decades, not only among distributive theorists, but also among those who acknowledge other goals in addition to reelection. Much of the plausibility of the reelection assumption rests on the fact that in legislative institutions where power and influence increase with seniority, successive electoral victories are necessary in order for legislators to achieve any of their other goals.

Whether pork barrel benefits confer an electoral advantage is a matter of scholarly controversy. For example, there is evidence that federal spending in a member's district has no significant impact on reelection outcomes. But in individual-level analysis, there is evidence that distributive projects have both direct and indirect effects on voters' choices. The indirect effect operates through an increase in voter awareness of new grants, which results in an increase in an incumbent's popularity, which in turn positively affects the incumbent's share of the vote. Additionally, there is evidence that members who narrowly won open seat elections enjoyed more new distributive benefits in the first four months of their terms than other members; those high levels of new awards early in their terms in turn reduced their chances of facing high-quality challengers in the next election. However, there is some indication that the electoral advantage conferred by pork barrel benefits accrues more to Democrats than to Republicans, perhaps because it is expected more of Democrats. Similarly, there is disagreement about the impact of district service, including distributive benefits, but members of Congress themselves clearly believe that district service is helpful in building their reputations. For this belief, there is persuasive evidence. Thus, consistent with both theoretical scholarship and much of the empirical literature on pork barrel politics, I assume that members of Congress seek distributive benefits as a way to aid their constituents and thereby boost their own reelection chances.

However, a persistent puzzle is posed by reelection-based theories of congressional behavior: What motivates potential policy coalition leaders to devote resources to pass

general interest legislation that will not disproportionately benefit their districts? Presumably, their constituents will not particularly thank them for such efforts, compared with their gratitude for distributive benefits. Both informational and partisan theories deal with this problem in part by allowing party leaders or committee members to receive distributive benefits for devoting time to the legislative enterprise, as such benefits reduce the opportunity costs of building coalitions to pass broad-based legislation. In those theories, the solution to the dilemma, like its source, is reelection-based.

However, even that solution begs the question of the source of the original motivation to make good public policy. I agree with Mayhew that there is little direct electoral payoff to individual members for time devoted to passing collective benefit bills. That is not to say that their constituents necessarily are indifferent to national problems. However, members can make points with their constituents as easily by simply taking positions on national issues as by working on solving them behind the scenes, as typical constituents (unlike attentive elites) lack the Washington-insider information that they would need to discover whether or not there was action behind the talk. It can therefore be argued that it is irrational for reelection-driven members to engage in legislative work on issues that do not offer concentrated benefits to constituents or to interest groups.

Nevertheless, it makes sense to assume that members have other goals in addition to reelection; by serving in Congress, they wish to accomplish something. Their other goals may consist of a number of things, but as Richard Fenno persuasively demonstrates, internal influence or power and the desire to make good public policy certainly are among them. Likewise, Lawrence Dodd argues that members want to "make a mark" in a policy area, which can be seen as a combination of Fenno's good public policy and influence goals. Arnold identifies a similar motivation, altruism, meaning among other things that policy coalition leaders care about a particular public policy area.

Thus, we arrive at the fourth condition: that leaders' efforts to pass general interest legislation must be motivated by their goals of good public policy or power and influence rather than reelection; reelection itself is taken care of by other, perhaps related, activities. Although leaders may compensate themselves for the opportunity costs of their efforts to pass general interest legislation by inserting into the bill special benefits, perhaps disproportionate ones, targeted to their own districts, this possibility does not negate the role of nonelectoral motives in their efforts to pass broad-based legislation. After all, there are simpler ways to gain constituency benefits than by doing the spade work needed to pass major legislation, ways that leave more time for other reelection-enhancing activities. Thus, it is reasonable, even necessary, to assume that goals other than reelection, such as making good public policy and gaining influence in the House or Senate, motivate the extensive behind-the-scenes work needed to make national policy. It is not necessary to specify whether the good public policy and influence goals operate together or alone on any one legislative effort; all that matters here is that policy leaders' goals in working to pass general interest legislation are primarily nonelectoral.

Nevertheless, here again, the motivation for party leaders may differ in degree, at least, from those for other policy coalition leaders, such as committee chairs. Party leaders seek to pass general interest legislation to improve the party's public record in a way that will result in the reelection of its incumbents and help to capture some seats currently held by the other party. By doing so, they increase their own chances of retaining their leadership positions and, if they are not in the majority, gaining control of the chamber itself. Thus, for leaders themselves, the motive for mobilizing to pass general interest legislation is not their own reelection; rather, it is some combination of power and good public policy (the latter, in this case, in the eyes of the electorate).

How do these motives work for other policy coalition leaders, especially committee chairs? To the extent that committee and subcommittee chairs are chosen for their adherence to their caucus's policy preferences, as they are to some extent in both parties in the House, the motivation to promote the preferences of the majority of the caucus is the same as that of the party leaders themselves. That is, if they deviate too far from caucus preferences, they risk losing their leadership positions. On the other hand, they are not as responsible individually for the public record of their party as the top leaders, so they are likely to face greater temptation to seek public policy that conforms to their own policy preferences, as long as it falls within the boundaries of what the caucus is willing to tolerate. The exceptions are likely to be the chairs of the committees whose jurisdictions encompass those issues that define the differences between the parties and thus its public record, such as Appropriations, Budget, and the tax-writing committees (Ways and Means in the House and Finance in the Senate) and, of course, the Rules Committee in the House. The chairs of those committees and their subcommittees probably have less freedom to deviate from caucus preferences than others because they are responsible for the matters that largely comprise the party's identity. For other committee chairs, the balance between party goals and their own policy preferences may be tilted to a greater degree in favor of their own preferences. In any case, they, like party leaders, also are motivated by nonelectoral goals.

The president is the exception to the condition that policy coalition leaders are motivated by nonelectoral goals. He is the one figure who is held responsible by the public for collective benefits, especially the condition of the economy and (when events bring it to the forefront) national security; in other words, the president is held responsible for results. Therefore, for presidents the motive for using pork barrel benefits to pass such legislation is, at least in part, electoral.

To summarize the discussion of the third and fourth conditions for using pork barrel benefits to buy votes for general interest legislation: When leaders use the vote-buying strategy, they take advantage of the electoral goals of the members to whom they give benefits. However, except for the president, leaders themselves are motivated not by their own reelection, which they can provide for much more efficiently by other means, but by some combination of the power and good public policy goals. Returning to my broader argument, pork barrel benefits help leaders to unify fractious caucuses around their position and to undermine the unity of the opposing party. This is especially true for majority party leaders and chairs, who are more likely to have benefits to give.

Types of Benefits

For leaders committed to certain public policy positions, vote buying has a major advantage over another type of legislative mobilization: It allows a bill's sponsors to pass the measure without altering its central provisions, whereas they otherwise might be forced to compromise on the bill's content to gain support for it. Therefore, because vote buying with pork allows policy coalition leaders to protect the bill's provisions, it gives them more freedom to craft it as they see fit. Of course, in reality, both vote buying and substantive modification of the bill are likely to be used. That is, in the interest of gaining important allies, some alterations usually are made in the central provisions of the bill; but to avoid changes beyond a certain point, projects for individual members may be added to buy those members' votes. Such outright vote buying is especially useful when further changes in the substance of the bill would make it unacceptable to the very coalition leaders who are working for its passage. Moreover, as noted earlier, the strategy is particularly important when other ways of inducing loyalty to leadership desires, such as party rewards and sanctions, are weak or absent altogether. Indeed, vote buying with distributive benefits can enable leaders to cross party boundaries to win votes on both sides of the aisle.

Of course, other sorts of individual favors, often in the form of IOUs, might be used by a coalition leader who does not have ready access to distributive benefits: a promise to appear at a district fund-raiser, a committee chair's pledge to hold a hearing in a member's district, the president's commitment to support a member's favorite legislative proposal in the future, or even

a tacit understanding that the leader owes the member a favor. However, such trades are difficult to document and therefore are usually not amenable to systematic empirical analysis. The most observable currency consists of distributive benefits attached to the bill under consideration. Because such distributive benefits lend themselves to clear quid pro quo deals on a specific piece of legislation and because they are of a type believed to directly aid members' reelection bids to a degree that, for example, a hearing in the district might not, distributive benefits may be the most effective resource. Thus, benefits explicitly attached to the bill or the accompanying committee report are the main focus of this chapter.

In addition, the focus here is on pork barrel benefits given to identifiable geographic areas, specifically, members' own districts (or states, in the case of senators), even though such benefits also may be targeted to individuals and interest groups outside the districts of the members who requested them. Beneficiaries of the latter sort may aid members' reelection, typically by making campaign contributions. The discussion of beneficiaries in this chapter is restricted to geographic districts because it is impractical reliably to document benefits given to entities that are not geographically defined.

The remainder of this chapter lays out the vote-buying strategy from the coalition leaders' point of view; it also considers the reactions of the leaders' targets, the legislators whose support they seek.

LEADERS' STRATEGY: FORMING THE COALITION

The key figure in forming supporting coalitions for legislative initiatives is typically a member of Congress in a formal leadership position, who by virtue of that position has access to more of the political resources needed to pass legislation than rank-and-file members. Although policy entrepreneurs are not necessarily restricted to members holding formal leadership positions, in order to use distributive side payments to gain votes on general benefit legislation, a legislator must have the capacity to link such benefits with the bill in question. As the preceding discussion suggests, the people with the greatest ability to do this are committee and subcommittee chairs as well as the parties' top House and Senate leaders and the president himself. Therefore, for discussion purposes, the person who is in a position to use distributive benefits to form a majority coalition is referred to as the policy coalition leader or simply the leader. Although that person is likely to hold a formal leadership position, the term is sufficiently generic to include anyone who spearheads the effort to pass a particular bill.

In any public policy area, proposed legislation may originate in one or more of several places. The following brief discussion is not intended to be comprehensive on that score but is meant to illustrate the reasons that coalition leaders might wish to protect a bill's general interest provisions by buying votes with pork barrel add-ons.

Potential policy coalition leaders may begin with their own most-preferred policy. However, it is very unlikely that major legislation modeled strictly on the policy views of one leader could gain a majority on the merits. Instead, the leader most likely must incorporate provisions into the initial version of the bill in response to the demands of desired coalition members. If the leader is a committee chair, he or she may need to respond to party leaders, the ranking minority member of the committee, rank-and-file committee members, or chairs of other key committees. At some point in the process of modifying the bill, the leader may deem further changes unacceptable; from then on, if the bill lacks a majority, the leader must seek a way to gain the votes of more members without doing violence to the bill's provisions. By adding pork barrel benefits targeted to individual legislators, the leader can preserve the bill's central policy provisions, thus simultaneously serving his or her good public policy and influence goals. Because of their divisibility, such benefits can be targeted to the districts of members whose support is needed but might otherwise not be forthcoming.

Additionally, party leaders as well as committee chairs may be expected to pass legislation on behalf of a president of their party; in those cases, their ability to craft the policy to their own liking is probably severely constrained; but they may be under strong pressure to protect key substantive provisions of the bill as ardently as they would if the bill were their own. Similarly, when different parties control the presidency and one or both chambers of Congress, policy coalition leaders may be responsible for passing alternatives to the president's legislative initiatives. In either case, the incentives to add distributive benefits to gain votes for the bill are equally strong.

However, leaders are unlikely to give projects to just anyone who opposes the bill. Rather, they must answer two questions in order to determine to whom to give distributive benefits in return for votes. The first question relates to the overall coalition strategy: how large a supporting coalition do they need, and thus to how many members must they give projects? The second question concerns the allocation strategy: Exactly which members should they target? Should they give benefits to members on the fence or to opponents, to members of their own committees or to key leaders? I argue here that the coalition and allocation strategies are related; that is, the size of the coalition depends at least in part on who controls the allocation process – the leaders or the members who seek benefits, which depends in turn on the availability of full information to the leaders.

Coalition Size

The issue of how many members leaders must help in order to construct a majority coalition becomes rather complicated, as this discussion shows. There are two options for coalition size: First, leaders can grant projects to a minority of members sufficient to form a bare majority coalition for the bill when combined with those who support it on its merits. This is likely to be the result when leaders exert tight control on the distribution of projects, minimizing the number that they give. Alternatively, leaders can try to maximize support for the bill, giving to anyone who asks, in which case the tendency would be toward a universalistic or at least a supermajority coalition of project recipients, far more than needed to pass the bill. This is likely to occur when control of project allocation is more diffuse, residing to a greater degree with rank-and-file members, who demand a project in return for votes that most of them would have cast for the bill without a project. These two options are analogous, but not identical, to the well-known alternatives for coalition size in the literature on distributive politics – minimal winning and universalistic coalitions.

The empirical literature on distributive politics, like the formal literature, has produced conflicting findings concerning the extent of distribution of pork barrel benefits, although on balance, when Congress distributes benefits to itself, the evidence for oversized (rather than bare majority or minimal winning) coalitions is strong. On one hand, there is evidence that, in the distribution of funds by the federal government (most of it not specifically earmarked by Congress), spending within specific programs does not cover even a near-majority of districts. However, an examination of the *discretionary* distributional decisions made by bureaucrats shows that, to secure their budgets, bureaucrats distribute grants widely to legislators' districts. Because they know they must ask for congressional support repeatedly, they make project grants so as to maximize that support, although even here, a blanket statement that distribution is universalistic is unwarranted. Finally, research on the decisions that are most analogous to those examined here – how congressional committees distribute benefits across congressional districts – has found allocation to oversized majorities in such areas as public works, appropriations, public lands and tax policy.

In contrast, in the situation analyzed in this book, where leaders need to increase support for a general interest bill, they may find it unnecessary to distribute benefits universally in order to accomplish their goals. In fact, they may not even need to give benefits to a simple majority. This is true when members reveal their true preferences for the bill and demonstrate that there is a base of support on the merits. In that

case, leaders may choose to target projects only to the minority of members needed to round up the bill's support to a majority. Here, the decision as to who receives a project is not entirely with rank-and-file members as it is under the simplest assumptions of the formal literature; instead, the leaders determine the size of the coalition.

However, a leader is likely to get only one chance to engage in the sort of efficient and highly targeted vote buying that produces small distributive coalitions. The dynamic of a game changes if players know that it is to be repeated indefinitely; and a minimal winning strategy is not likely to be stable over a series of bills. Thus, even if a committee's leaders followed a minimal winning strategy for one bill, they probably could not sustain it over a subsequent stream of similar bills, because minimal winning coalitions tend, in repeated play, to give way to universalistic coalitions. Because legislation is not decided in isolation, the condition of repeated play typically is met. That is, legislative leaders (as well as presidents) produce a continuous stream of legislative proposals. In so doing, they reveal their own strategies for passing bills; thus, leaders have the advantage of surprise only the first time they try to buy votes with pork barrel benefits. The first time they use this approach, they may well succeed in buying votes for a bill using a minimal number of pork barrel benefits. But on subsequent bills, members who did not get a project in return for their votes the first time feel like fools for having "given away" their votes on the earlier bill. Those members now have an incentive to try to take control of project distribution away from the leaders; they do so by concealing their true policy preferences and bargaining for a project regardless of their support for the merits of the second bill, in effect holding up the leaders for a project in return for their votes.

It then becomes increasingly difficult for leaders to obtain accurate information about members' true preferences; and members' concealment of their voting intentions is therefore an effective strategy for getting a pork barrel project. On the second and subsequent bills, a majority of members is likely to bargain for projects, and they will most likely be granted them, as leaders now cannot be certain who would support the bill without one. In fact, an incentive now exists for all who conceivably could support the bill to bargain for a project in return for their votes. From the leaders' point of view, giving projects to these members secures their votes and avoids the risk of alienating them, as members now know that projects are rather freely given in return for votes. Thus, the first time leaders use the vote-buying strategy is their last, best opportunity to give projects to less than a majority of the membership. After that, the number is bound to balloon as the number of *apparent* fence-sitters increases as a result of members' concealing their true opinions about the bill itself and demanding projects. In that situation, leaders have an incentive to play it safe and give projects even to members who they think are bluffing about the possibility of voting against the overall bill without a project.

Moreover, leaders want more than a simple affirmative vote on the bill. In addition, they want it to pass with as few hostile amendments as possible; they want any presidential veto to be overridden; and they want to be able to break a filibuster in the Senate. If amendments do not threaten the provisions that rank-and-file members care about, those members may either support the amendments on the merits or attempt to use their votes on them as bargaining chips with committee leaders. In such cases, the members could promise to vote with the leaders on the bill overall but threaten to vote with the opposition on amendments that do not endanger benefits for their districts or policies that they prefer. In fact, while it may be difficult for most members to conceal their general preferences on recurring legislation on which they already have a voting history, they can much more easily conceal their preferences on individual amendments and credibly threaten to deprive leaders of important victories unless they are given a distributive benefit. Thus, by giving benefits to a supermajority of members, leaders guarantee themselves an extra margin of protection. That is not to say that they grant every single request from every member; to do

so would quickly break the bank. However, in the interest of good will, leaders have an incentive to give something to every member who asks. As accurate nose counting becomes impossible, bet hedging seems increasingly wise.

Nevertheless, when distributive benefits are attached to a general interest bill, a truly universalistic coalition, as opposed to an oversized, supermajority coalition, is unlikely. That is because the nondistributive provisions of the bill are likely to require some members to oppose it on ideological or constituency grounds, regardless of whether the member receives a project. And a pork barrel benefit that goes only to part of the district may not be sufficient compensation for a member's taking an ideologically dissonant position or one that is opposed by the majority of the district. For such actions, the net electoral impact, even with a project, could be negative. Indeed, such members may not even seek a project, as they cannot promise to support the bill in return. In turn, failure to support the bill could doom the project, as leaders might well retaliate against them by eliminating it in conference.

In summary, the number of members to whom leaders give pork barrel benefits depends on the degree to which rank-and-file members conceal their true preferences for the bill or hostile amendments to it. The first time leaders use the vote-buying strategy, the sequence of events is likely to help them to minimize the number of projects. That time, leaders have an opportunity to ascertain members' opinions on the bill without complicating matters with the promise of projects. Once an accurate headcount is achieved, leaders can then reveal a vote-buying strategy to remedy any deficit of support. But however small the number of project recipients on the first bill, there will be strong pressures toward universalism on the second and subsequent bills, as control of the allocation process slips from the hands of the leaders and shifts to rank-and-file members.

Why do similar universalistic pressures not develop on the first bill on which leaders attempt to buy votes? It does seem possible that once word gets out that leaders are distributing pork, a large majority of members would seek to bargain for a project from the beginning. From the perspective of committee leaders, the fact that they must come before the chamber repeatedly to pass legislation suggests some risk in ever following a minimal allocation strategy. That is, members who did not receive a project might conceivably retaliate on this bill or on subsequent legislation. Thus, even on the first bill in a sequence of distributive projects, one might expect that leaders have an incentive to give projects to far more members than needed to form a majority for the bill.

However, time is a factor limiting the pressure toward universalism during the passage of only one bill. That is, before the word gets out that votes are being bought, there is likely to be a core of members willing to commit early to the leaders' most cherished policy proposals. Those members are poorly positioned to bargain later, when they realize that they might have done so. Additionally, it takes time for members to get a feel for how freely leaders are willing to give out projects, especially when there is a leadership change, such as a new committee chair, or when the majority changes to the other party, as it did in the 104th Congress. Often, legislators see who got projects only after the committee reports the bill. Only then will many realize that projects were given not just to the usual leaders but also to rank-and-file members, perhaps extending even to freshmen. But by then it is too late to deal, especially if the bill comes to the floor under a restrictive rule (in the House) that the committee now has a majority to pass. Additionally, distributive benefits often are not listed in legislative language anyway, presumably because they are too easy for pork barrel opponents to trace. Rather, they may appear only in committee reports as directives to the agency that will administer the law. Thus, even without a restrictive rule there may be little opportunity to add individual projects by floor amendment. Even if it were practical, such amendments appear even more blatantly self-serving than having such projects tucked into report language earlier in the process. For these reasons, opportunities for anyone other than the leaders themselves to add projects at the postcommittee stage are limited. The upshot of all of this is that the first time leaders give out distributive benefits to buy votes, they are likely to need to give them only to a minority of members; on subsequent bills, however, the pressures toward supermajority pork barrel coalitions are likely to be irresistible.

Allocation Strategy

In addition to deciding how many members to whom they should give pork barrel benefits to win votes for their policy preferences, leaders must decide how to allocate projects to individual members of Congress. That is, to which members do leaders give projects? As with the closely related question of the number of projects, the choice of allocation strategy is dependent at least in part on the availability of accurate information on member preferences on the bill; the more information leaders have about members' likely support for the bill, the more precisely they can target the benefits. If leaders have such information and initially find that they lack majority support for the bill, they must begin giving benefits to some nonsupporters. Rather than giving projects to firm opponents, vote buyers are likely to look first to members who are most persuadable: those on the fence. For those who are truly indifferent or conflicted about the bill, a project can serve to convert the calculated benefit of supporting the bill from zero to a net positive.

However, a strategy of giving only to fence-sitters is not likely to be feasible; leaders may also have to give projects to some supporters. As noted earlier, support, particularly on a large, complex bill, is many-faceted. Some members who strongly favor the bill's basic policy provisions on the merits may need inducements to support the coalition leaders' positions on some particulars; otherwise, they may believe that amendments that leaders themselves see as hostile are innocuous or even marginally positive. Indeed, some amendments might actually be attractive to less avid supporters of the bill, especially amendments that weaken controversial provisions and thereby provide political cover from potential criticism at home. Thus, leaders are likely to give projects to weaker supporters whose backing they calculate to be at risk on certain issues, in addition to fence-sitters. The purpose is to extract their loyalty on all votes related to the bill.

Such an approach is not unique: Giving to likely supporters is a strategy typically followed by political action committees (PACs) in their allocation decisions, despite the seeming inefficiency of contributing to those who already generally favor their positions. As Hall and Wayman have shown, such a strategy is more rational than it seems at first blush, for such contributions buy friendly legislators' active efforts to obtain favorable legislative treatment for the PAC, when they might otherwise use their limited time to pursue other priorities. Moreover, giving to members who regularly support them is a strategy for helping to ensure that their friends stay in office where they can continue to help their contributors. A similar rationale may apply when leaders use pork barrel projects to buy support on legislation.

An additional, seemingly obvious means to build a majority coalition would be to attempt to convert opponents of the policy proposal by giving them projects. However, that strategy is both naive and fraught with risk. First, such an approach can work only with members who are not initially so opposed to the bill that they will in any case vote against it or try to undermine it with amendments. Therefore, the number of opponents whom this strategy can convert is limited. Second, giving a project to members who are likely to vote against the bill anyway could tempt other, less opposed members to betray their benefactor as well. For this reason, it does not make sense to give projects to opponents simply to mute their vocal opposition, as some scholars have suggested. If district benefits are to be effective as an incentive for loyalty, they cannot be given to those who are sure to vote against the leader's position, even if they do it quietly. After all, there must be some threat of punishment of shirkers, but giving projects to members who are likely to oppose the bill suggests to everyone that the ultimate punishment − withdrawal of projects − is unlikely to be imposed. Such a message fundamentally undermines the purpose for which the projects are given in the first place.

Therefore, the most fruitful allocation strategy for leaders is to give projects to fence-sitters and supporters of the general interest legislation. Clearly, full information about member preferences is necessary for leaders to exercise this degree of targeting of project awards. Thus, when leaders are most likely to have full information about members' stands (i.e., on the first bill on which vote buying is used), we can expect to see one of two possible relationships between members' expected overall support for the bill ex ante and leaders' decision to award them a project. To the degree that leaders attempt to be as efficient as possible in their project awards, the relationship will be curvilinear. That is, as members become more committed to the bill, their support is more secure without a project; as their support becomes less firm, leaders are more likely to see them as responsive to a project; as they become more opposed, giving them a project is futile and even counterproductive. Alternatively, to the extent that leaders seek to buy firm support on all possible votes related to the bill, especially on hostile amendments that even the bill's supporters might be tempted to endorse, the relationship between members' expected support for the bill and the receipt of a project will be positive. As is true with the previous alternative, as members become more opposed, there is less reason for leaders to try to buy their support with a project.

However, on the second and subsequent go-rounds of legislation from the same leader, the relationship between members' probable support for the bill without a project and the award of a project is likely to be weak or nonexistent. That is because, as noted earlier, once leaders have revealed a willingness to bargain for votes by giving out benefits, increasing numbers of members, now including strong supporters as well as weak ones and fence-sitters, realize that there is a payoff for strategically concealing their true preferences on the bill. Thus, on the second and later bills, the leaders' safest strategy is to take a more reactive, less systematic approach to allocating projects, waiting for the inevitable flood of requests for projects and granting something to everyone with the clear mutual understanding that there is a quid pro quo: Recipients are expected to support their benefactors on all important votes on the bill. By the time this happens, the rank-and-file members have the whip hand; giving them distributive benefits is the only feasible way to protect the bill.

In devising their allocation strategy, leaders face other considerations in addition to members' likely support for the legislation; a number of other variables influence project distribution. They are partisanship, membership on the committee with jurisdiction over the bill, leadership positions on other important committees and in the chamber as a whole, and electoral vulnerability.

First among these variables is partisanship, specifically, the possibility of partisan bias in the allocation of benefits. If partisan theories are correct, projects should go to members of the majority party. There is also evidence of linkage between committee membership and partisan advantage, with majority party members on the committee of jurisdiction receiving a disproportionate share. However, it is well established that the degree of partisanship varies among committees; thus we might expect concurrent variation in the degree to which partisanship affects the distribution of pork barrel benefits.

The Senate Appropriations Committee, one which once was renowned for its bipartisanship along with its House counterpart, is today increasingly partisan. Accordingly, Balla, Lawrence, Maltzman, and Sigelman have found evidence for a much more subtle form of partisan bias in earmarking funds to higher education by that committee than previously had been recognized. In a process that they call "partisan blame avoidance," Balla et al. found that the Appropriations Committee majority gives earmarks to senators of both parties. However, when it comes to the actual dollar amounts of those earmarks, majority party members were significantly more generous to their own. The rationale was not exactly one of universalism. Rather, it was the inoculation of members of the majority party against charges of wasteful spending by making the minority complicit in

the earmarking process. At the same time, giving higher dollar amounts to their own members allowed the majority to have its cake and eat it too, the cake being an extra measure of any electoral benefits that flow from such spending.

However, the extent to which there is likely to be a partisan bias depends on the reason for which projects are given out. When leaders distribute projects to buy members' votes for general interest legislation, there is no reason to expect a partisan bias. On the contrary, such awards provide leaders with a means to overcome partisan differences on public policy, giving members of the opposite party a reason to vote for the bill. They will also, of course, give to their own party members, as failure to do so while giving to the other party's members would be likely to provoke resentment in their own caucus, tempting some of the latter to vote against the committee on some matters. Thus, leaders are likely not only to give to members of their own party to overcome disagreement, as Cox and McCubbins argue; they are likely to give to members of the other party for the same reason. Thus, vote buying can shore up the unity of the party of the vote buyers, but it offers the additional advantage of undermining the cohesiveness of the other party.

In addition to using project awards to overcome the strictures of partisanship, leaders need to seek the support of members who can be especially helpful to the bill's chances of passage. If the coalition leaders are committee or subcommittee chairs, it is important for them to have their committee members behind them on the floor. A united front, particularly a bipartisan one, is extremely helpful on the floor of the House or Senate, in part because noncommittee members take voting cues from their own party's members on the committee. If both parties on the committee can be united, potential opponents outside the committee have less credibility in their efforts to build an opposition coalition. Thus, we can expect committee and subcommittee leaders especially to favor members of their own subcommittee and committee with project awards.

This rationale for a procommittee bias in project awards differs from, but is reinforced by, that found in much of the literature, where it has been argued widely that committees give a disproportionate share of benefits to their own members because the committees themselves tend to be composed of those with a high demand for the policies within their jurisdictions.

Whether or not committees are composed of high-demanders, committee chairs are likely to award projects to their members in order to provide the members with greater incentive to give solid, bipartisan support for passing the leaders' favored legislation, thus smoothing the path on the floor of the House or Senate. To the extent that committees are composed of high-demanders, that tendency is reinforced by the members themselves, as they are likely to request larger numbers of projects.

If the purpose of including such benefits is to buy the support needed to pass the committee's version of the bill, the help of other key leaders is needed, especially that of chamber leaders who not only control floor consideration of a committee's bill but also increasingly preside over postcommittee adjustments to its provisions. Additionally, leaders of other committees and subcommittees important to the bill's success are likely to be favored. In particular, overlapping jurisdictional claims on the legislation, even if they do not result in its referral to committees other than the coalition leader's own, can pose risks on the floor. While it may be necessary to mollify other committee chairs by changing the content of the bill, giving them distributive benefits could help to reduce their objections and the need to change key provisions. Previous research suggests that chamber and committee leaders are indeed advantaged in the allocation of benefits in distributive policy.

Finally, leaders may find a particular opportunity to buy the votes of members who are electorally vulnerable. As noted earlier in this chapter, the evidence concerning the electoral impact of federal spending in a member's district is mixed, but members themselves evidently believe that it is helpful; otherwise, they would not seek distributive benefits so assiduously. Consistent with members' own

apparent assumption that pork barrel projects help to protect their seats, it is likely that the smaller a member's winning margin in the previous election, the more likely leaders are to target them with a project in return for their vote.

Thus, the coalition and allocation strategies taken together result in two closely linked models of vote buying. The first time policy coalition leaders use the vote-buying strategy, they have the most control that they will ever have over project awards, and they are likely to give projects to less than a majority of members as they seek to round up support over and above that which they have already ascertained exists. To the extent that they have enough information about member preferences to follow an active strategy of selecting project recipients, they can be expected to give projects to the following legislators: those whose support is strategically essential, that is, members of the committee of jurisdiction and top leaders of other key committees, as well as floor leaders, members who are on the fence, supporters, especially weak supporters, and if needed, weak opponents, as well as electorally marginal members.

On the other hand, when leaders choose to follow the less risky strategy of responding to all of those who come to them for a project, as they must do on bills subsequent to the first one on which they use the vote-buying strategy, members' views on the bill will have little bearing on their chances of getting a project. That is because members now have an incentive strategically to conceal their true preferences in order to bargain for a project. However, the other variables, especially committee membership and leadership position, are all still likely to play a role in some form, as coalition leaders target those who may be especially helpful to their efforts to pass their favored version of the bill. While key members may be no more likely to get a pork barrel benefit, they may nevertheless get a larger number or more valuable benefits than members whose support is less likely to have a multiplier effect. When leaders follow this more passive strategy, the coalition of project recipients is likely to grow quickly to a supermajority from the first to second bill.

CONCLUSIONS

The vote-buying approach to passing general benefit legislation is not inconsistent with recent theories that address the collective action dilemma. However, it is in some respects a more flexible technique, as the pork barrel offers currency with a bipartisan appeal. Although Republicans have more ideological reason than Democrats to oppose such benefits and may receive less electoral advantage from providing them, there is journalistic evidence, along with my own findings, that they energetically pursue such benefits. Cox and McCubbins argue that distributive benefits provide a method for papering over intraparty divisions and hence increase the party leaders' control and make party government more possible. It is my argument that distributive benefits allow leaders to do more; they can in fact transcend party splits by buying the votes of members of the other party for the leaders' favored legislation, especially when those votes are more easily acquired than those of members of their own party.

An example of such a party-splitting issue is the North American Free Trade Agreement (NAFTA), where President Clinton, leading the policy coalition, joined Republicans and conservative Democrats in pushing the treaty in opposition to members of the House Democratic leadership. On the other hand, if liberal Democrats had allowed their votes to be bought for a special benefit for their districts, many of them would have risked electoral support at home, especially from unions.

Thus, the vote-buying approach can just as easily undermine as shore up party unity. Moreover, it gives considerable freedom to leaders who have access to particularized benefits. Indeed, the only limitation on this freedom is the increased tendency of party caucuses (in the case of Democrats) and their leadership (especially the Republicans in the 104th and later Congresses) to pass over members who stray too far or too often from the party's center of gravity when choosing committee chairs. Nevertheless, the infrequency with which that is done suggests that although committee chairs must be mindful of the party, they generally have a good deal of leeway to use a pork barrel strategy to craft deals that lure members of the other party from their own fold, possibly compensating for losses of support from their own caucuses.

CHAPTER TWENTY–SIX

Models of Legislative Voting

John W. Kingdon

Kingdon explores why members of Congress make the voting decisions they do. He finds that many members employ cues from their party, members of their state delegation, and relevant interest groups in deciding how to vote on bills.

THE MODELS

Identifying and describing models of legislative voting is not an easy task, as it turns out. There is actually quite a large number of constructs and arguments abroad in the literature which could be considered to be implicit or explicit models of voting. Our first task is to identify a set of models that do purport to be representations of decision processes involved in legislative voting and to summarize their major features. It is impossible in these pages to go into sufficient detail to do full justice to their richness and complexity. Nor is it my purpose to enter into a detailed critique of each model. But I will briefly state the major approach of each model without, I hope, doing violence to its intent.

Cue-Taking

Best exemplified by the Matthews–Stimson model, cue-taking starts with the assumption that legislators must somehow cut their great information costs in order to reach decisions

John W. Kingdon. 1977. "Models of Legislative Voting" *Journal of Politics* 39(3): 563–95. Copyright © 1977 Southern Political Science Association. Reprinted with the permission of Cambridge University Press.

that will further their goals. The dominant strategy for accomplishing this is turning to their colleagues within the legislative body for cues which they follow in voting. These cues may come from individual legislators or from such groups of them as the state party delegation, the party, or even the whole body. Matthews and Stimson operationalize these fundamental tenets through the use of a computer simulation.

Cue-taking is actually a family of models. The genesis of the ideas is to be found far back in the literature, in the notion of specialization among legislators. A well-developed committee system is supposed to allow them to specialize in a few areas, and then for the areas in which they are not specialists, to rely on each others' judgments.

Policy Dimensions

Set forth early in the work of MacRae, policy dimensions have been most recently explored by Clausen, who argues that they constitute a theory of voting decisions. According to Clausen, a congressman starts with some notion of the policy content of the issue before him, and thinks of it in terms of a dimension (e.g., more or less government management of the economy). He places himself on that dimension, and compares his position to the position of the legislation, choosing the alternative presented which comes closest to his position. One way in which he may accomplish this matching is by picking the cues on which he will rely according to the degree to which the cue agrees with his own policy position. The cues on which he relies also differ from one policy dimension to another, so that, for instance, constituency is important on civil liberties and party on government management of the economy.

Predisposition-Communication

A predisposition-communication model is presented in the work of Cherryholmes and Shapiro. They argue that a congressman first assesses the strength of his predisposition for or against a bill. He does so by taking account of his own past behavior, the House party position, and the effects the bill would have on his constituency and region. If these factors predispose him strongly one way or the other, he simply votes on the basis of this predisposition. If his predisposition is not sufficiently strong, he enters an elaborate communication process among colleagues and with the President, the outcome of which determines his position. The actual model in this case is a computer simulation.

Consensus

In my own work on congressmen's voting decisions, I have presented a consensus decision model. According to this model, a congressman implicitly asks whether there is any controversy over the issue in the environment. If not, his decision rule is simple: he votes with the consensus in that environment. If there is controversy, he subsets the environment, and asks if there is any controversy in the field of forces that would affect his own decision, and if he finds none, he votes with that field. He can also use this mode of decision if there is a degree of conflict in his field, so long as the conflict is not substantial and so long as a dominant consensus can be discerned. The set of preconsensus processes which affects the degree of consensus present in congressmen's fields is as important as the final consensus rule. These processes include simple agreement in the congressional environment on a course of action, contrived consensus among the major reference groups, and the structuring of the fields according to the congressman's personal policy attitudes, his past voting history, or his weighting of potentially intense actors such as constituency.

Past Behavior

In the budgetary process, Wildavsky argues that legislative decisions on agency budgets are structured in large part by past decisions affecting these agencies. The incremental method as an aid to calculation bases this year's budget on last year's budget, with a narrow range of increases or decreases.

Goals

Many decision models in other contexts portray decision-makers as being goal-seeking. The first step in such an argument, therefore, is to specify the goals which the decision-makers seek to maximize. Some recent works on congressmen, while not purporting to be complete models of voting decisions, are nevertheless highly relevant. Fiorina constructs a very instructive formal model of constituency-representative relations based on a congressman's goal of reelection. Mayhew argues that reelection structures a congressman's behavior to a considerable degree, and that treating this goal as the congressman's primary preoccupation helps us to understand many features of the legislative process. Fenno's comparative committee study expands the list of goals. In differentiating among congressional committees, he finds it useful to characterize them as primarily serving one of three goals for committee members: reelection, influence within the House, and good public policy. An integrative model of legislative voting decisions might build in this goal-seeking feature and even these particular goals.

Given this array of models, one might be tempted to treat them as alternatives, and to attempt to discriminate among them in some fashion. One would achieve this discrimination, presumably, according to several criteria: the models' ability to account statistically for decision outcomes, the empirical plausibility of the models, their logical features, or some combination of these criteria. One would then choose the best of the models and discard the others as not satisfying these criteria as well as the chosen one does.

Another approach, the one which I take in this paper, is to treat each of these models as

having a grasp on an important part of reality. In this view, then, we do not have a case
of incompatible, competing models. Instead,
there are several compatible models which are in
need of a persuasive means of integrating them.
Let us turn to a way in which this might be
done.

CONSTRUCTING AN INTEGRATIVE MODEL

In constructing a model which has a potential
for weaving together threads of previous work,
we should first keep in mind several features
which we would ideally want such a model to
exhibit. We would obviously want a persuasive
model to be able to account for outcomes statistically. In addition to that conventional consideration, the model should be plausible, in the
sense that it should be an accurate representation of legislators' decision-making processes
which is intuitively realistic. As such, it should
not be too complex or elaborate, picturing a
deciding legislator as engaging in an extended
search for information or proceeding through
an impossibly involved set of steps. It should also
be politically sensible, allowing full play for such
important political forces as constituency considerations and interaction within the legislative
chamber. Finally, it should be comprehensive,
including all the relevant forces that might have
an important bearing on the decision.

Keeping these considerations in mind, we
start the task of developing an integrative
model by noticing that most of the previous
work on legislative voting begins with similar assumptions about information processing,
search behavior, and decision-making capacity. These assumptions, entirely familiar to
readers of Herbert Simon and other students
of decision-making, posit that legislators, like
other decision-makers but perhaps even more
than most, must make a large volume of complex decisions, while constrained by limits on
time and cognitive capacity to do so without
extensive study of each issue. Taking account
of this decisional overload, the previous models
and our integrative model all largely agree on

the need for decision-making procedures that
cut legislators' information costs and simplify
their choices. They also agree that legislative
voting is a repetitive problem-solving situation,
which calls for standard ways of making voting
decisions that can be applied vote after vote. Lest
this appear to be an obvious point, one could
argue just as plausibly that legislators' simplification of decisions may not be the inexorable
result of an impossible set of demands on their
time, but rather due to their simple lack of inclination to devote a great deal of time and energy
to substantive policymaking, particularly on the
floor. In either case, however, from the perspective of describing their behavior, legislators
are realistically portrayed as adopting decision
rules, which drastically simplify their choices,
whether or not they have an inescapable need
to do so.

In building an integrative model, we also
begin with an assumption that is not particularly emphasized in many previous models of
legislative voting, namely, that legislators are
goal-seekers. Their behavior is purposive, and is
not simply reaction to external forces. A natural
preliminary step in dealing with that behavior is
to identify the goals which seem to affect most
legislators most of the time. For the purposes of
this paper, I find it useful to work with adaptations of the goals that Fenno specifies. His formulations – the goals of reelection, influence
within the House, and good public policy –
are restated here so as to make them somewhat
more comprehensive. Thus the primary goals of
legislators are as follows:

(1) Satisfying Constituents
It could be that constituency considerations
come back ultimately to an interest in reelection. But one observes congressmen taking
account of constituency reaction long before
and much more frequently than they worry
explicitly about gain or loss of votes in the next
election.

(2) Intra-Washington Influence
Another set of considerations in voting has
to do with satisfying a set of actors within

Washington, who are not necessarily closely connected to the constituency. These include going along with one's party leadership, favor-trading among fellow legislators, and following the lead of the administration, particularly if the President is of the deciding legislator's party. One takes these into account, presumably, in order to build influence within the government, a set wider than the House itself. The same concept, retitled, could be used for state or foreign capitals.

(3) Good Public Policy

Most legislators have their conception of good public policy, and act partly to carry that conception into being. Their policy attitudes, their ideology (if it can be called that), decidedly affect their behavior. Their previous pattern of behavior, their voting history, enters here as well, since that pattern represents their traditional policy position on the issue currently confronting them.

These appear to be the goals which most legislators seek most of the time. I will shortly present ways of introducing them into an integrative model of legislative voting and of operationalizing and using them empirically.

An Integrative Model

We are now in a position to present a model which attempts to integrate the various models in a fashion which incorporates the features just discussed. That model is displayed in Figure 26.1.

The first two steps are the same as the first two in the consensus mode of decision, which I have presented elsewhere. If there is no controversy in the environment at all, the congressman's choice is simple: he votes with that environment and is done with it. On many bills, for instance, a unified committee reports the bill and nobody opposes the committee position in any particular. If there is some controversy, he subsets the environment, considering only the actors that are most critical to him – his own constituency, his party leadership, his trusted associates in the

House, his own policy attitude, etc. – which I call the "field of forces," which bear on his decision. If there is no conflict among those actors, he votes with his field. I assume, as a legislator does, that if there appears to be no consideration that would prompt him to vote in a way different from that toward which he is impelled by every factor in his field of vision, then there is no reason to think twice. And as I have argued above, this is a beginning to an integrative model, which is common to a number of the previous works on legislative voting.

If there is some conflict among the congressman's relevant actors, he then proceeds to consider his goals, which I conceive for the purposes of this paper as being the three discussed above – constituency, intra-Washington influence, and public policy. But a goal is not brought to bear on the decision if it seems unimportant to him on this issue. It must pass what I have labelled a critical threshold of importance in order to be evoked and relevant to the decision. For example, a congressman's constituency may have a vague and largely unarticulated opposition to foreign aid. In that case, he would say that there was a constituency opinion on the issue, but that it was not intense enough to bother taking account of. The same could apply to the other goals. In the next section of this paper, I present some operationalizations of these thresholds and use them to deal with data on voting decisions.

If none of the goals is important enough to the congressman in the given decision to be relevant, he then proceeds to follow trusted colleagues within the House. He chooses colleagues who are on the committee that considered the bill and who agree with him in general philosophical, policy terms. If one or more goals are important enough, he asks if there is conflict among the goals which have been evoked. If there is none, the choice is then clear: to vote with the evoked goal or goals (Step C1). It could be in this case that only one of them is relevant to the decision, or that two or even all three are, but that they all point him in the same direction. For example, it could be that the policy goal on a given issue is the only one which passes

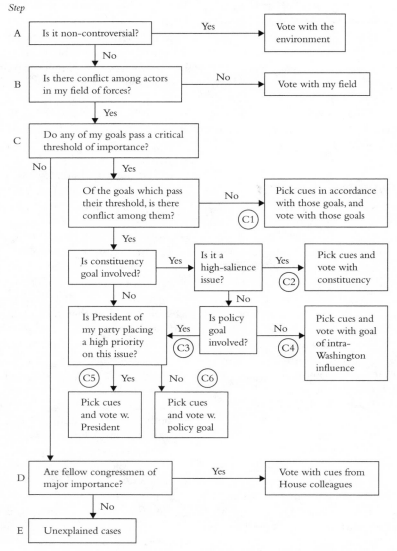

Figure 26.1. An Integrative Model of Legislative Voting Decisions.

its critical threshold, and the other two, while either opposed to, favorable to, or neutral concerning his conception of good public policy, are not in any event important enough to him on that issue to be potentially controlling. He votes in that case according to his conception of good public policy. As the model specifies, part of this decision may well be picking cues within the House to reinforce his policy goal, as a means to that end, in the fashion discussed above. Other examples of no conflict among evoked goals could be given, but this one will perhaps suffice.

If there is some conflict among the goals which the legislator considers relevant to his decision, he proceeds implicitly to some decision rules, which help him sort out the conflicts and make a satisfactory choice. It might be helpful at this point in the argument to present all the logically possible combinations of

Table 26.1. *All Possible Combinations of Conflicts among Goals, and the Resultant Outcomes*

Combinations	Outcomes,[a] Expected and Actual		Totals
	High-Salience Issues[b]	Low- or Medium-Salience Issues[b]	
Policy and constituency *vs* Intra-Washington	Constituency (C2) 1/2[a]	Policy or Pres.[c] (C3) 2/2	3/4
Policy and intra-Wash. *vs* Constituency	Constituency (C2) 0/0	Policy (C3) 3/3	3/3
Constituency and intra-Wash. *vs* Policy	Constituency (C2) 0/0	Policy or Pres.[c] (C3) 0/0	0/0
Policy *vs* Constituency	Constituency (C2) 1/2	Policy (C3) 6/6	7/8
Constituency *vs* Intra-Washington	Constituency (C2) 0/0	Intra-Wash. (C4) 3/4	3/4
Policy *vs* Intra-Washington	President[b] (C5) 3/5	Policy[b] (C6) 3/3	6/8
TOTALS	5/9	17/18	22/27

[a] The goal stated in each cell is the expected outcome, the goal which the model would predict would dominate the decision. The notation in parentheses refers to the appropriate step in Figure 26.1. The actual performance is captured in the numbers in each cell. The first is the number of cases in which the outcome is as predicted by the model, the second is the total number for that cell. For instance, in the case of a conflict between the constituency and intra-Washington influence goals, on low- or medium-salience issues, the model would predict that the representative would vote according to the intra-Washington consideration. Of the four cases in which there was such a conflict on such an issue, the congressman voted as the model expects in three.

[b] In the case of the conflict between Policy and Intra-Washington, "high-salience" refers to the presidential involvement specified in Figure 26.1, Step C5, low-salience to noninvolvement (Step C6). In the others, the salience of the issue refers to the general visibility of the issue in the press, in the public, and among participants. See *Congressmen's Voting Decisions*, 292–293, for the coding particulars.

[c] In these cases, since the congressman cycles through Steps C5 and C6, there is a chance that the President's request may overturn the policy consideration, and it did in fact happen in one case. Thus that case is coded as accounted for by the model, even though policy did not control, because the model predicted the outcome correctly. In the other case, the President's priority is not involved, so the congressman votes according to his policy position. See the text for further explanation.

conflict among the three goals, which is done in Table 26.1. In the first column, the possible combinations are listed, and the second and third columns contain the outcomes which the model would predict for each of the combinations. The numbers are relevant to the operationalization, which is explained in the next section of this paper.

There are a variety of ways in which the decision rules could be stated in this part of the model. I hypothesize that the congressman considers the constituency interest first. He may not end up voting with the constituency, but he always considers it when it is above the minimal level of importance. Placing this goal first is in keeping with the fact that the congressman owes his tenure in office to his constituency, and

as Fiorina and Mayhew argue, reelection is of critical importance to him.

If the constituency is not involved, the only logically possible conflict among the three goals left is between policy and intra-Washington influence. In that case, I hypothesize that the congressman has a disposition to vote with his policy goals, unless he is of the same party as the President and the President places a high priority on the issue. Intra-Washington considerations other than that one, such as party leadership requests or favor-trading, would not, I would argue, be enough to overcome a really strong policy predisposition. But a high-priority request from a president of his party would. The results in Steps C5 and C6 of the model reflect this reasoning.

If the constituency goal is involved, the congressman weighs that consideration against policy and/or intra-Washington influence. I have set forth elsewhere an account of that sort of balancing. The key here is that there is a filter for the salience of the issue – the general visibility of the issue in the press, in the attentive public, and among the participants in the legislative process. If the issue is of high salience, and if constituency is a relevant consideration, the model postulates that in view of the likelihood that important constituents will notice and disapprove of a vote out of keeping with their interests, the constituency consideration will dominate the others (Step C2). If the issue is of lower salience, however, the congressman has more freedom to allow his policy views or intra-Washington considerations to control the choice.

In the case of low- or medium-salience issues, if the policy goal is relevant to the issue, the congressman is disposed once again to favor it. He must check the possibility, however, that the intra-Washington goal would be involved and would center on a priority request from a President of his party which conflicts with his policy goal. He therefore (at Step C3) cycles through the presidential step described above, but in most cases ends up voting in accordance with his policy views (Step C6). If the policy goal is not relevant, the only logically possible conflict (Step C4) is between constituency and intra-Washington influence. Since it involves a low- or medium-salience issue at that point, I hypothesize that the congressman decides in favor of the intra-Washington consideration, in line with the argument presented above.

I have now discussed a framework by which, I would argue, the various models of legislative voting might be persuasively fit together into a general theory of legislative voting decisions which is at once comprehensive, parsimonious, and plausible. I have detailed, both verbally and through the integrative model, the ways in which a set of decision processes may be tied together. It remains now to present ways of operationalizing the key concepts and applying them to a set of data on congressmen's voting decisions.

ANOTHER LOOK AT THE DATA

In this section, I apply the concepts discussed above to my interview data, which are described at length in *Congressmen's Voting Decisions*. Briefly, I repeatedly interviewed a sample of Members of the U.S. House of Representatives in 1969, concerning their sources of information and voting cues, their decision rules, and the importance of various political actors in their decisions. Each of the interviews, in contrast to a survey type of instrument, concentrated on one decision which they had recently made. Generalizations are thus based on my cumulation of these decision histories over the course of the entire session, and the unit of analysis is the decision ($n = 222$).

I should make clear at the outset that, strictly speaking, the theory which I have presented above is not to be completely tested in the pages to follow. The model was generated from the previous literature and from the data set used in my own previous study. Hence, a complete validation would have to rest on a testing against new, independently generated data sets. What follows here is a partial test and an illustration of the ways in which the concepts might be measured and used. That return to the data suggests that the model is plausible, parsimonious, and consistent with what we know about the ways in which representatives actually make their decisions. I obviously consider its validity to be rather strongly indicated, but also obviously, a fully definitive validation would have to be done in a different fashion.

As far as the first two steps in the integrative model are concerned (Figure 26.1), the operationalization is the same as that presented in my earlier model. Since the votes were chosen partly to maximize conflict, there are no cases in these data of noncontroversial votes. As far as the second step is concerned, the congressman's field of forces includes his own specific policy attitude toward the issue under consideration, his constituency, fellow congressmen to whom he paid attention, interest groups, his staff, his party leadership, and the administration. There is no conflict among the actors in this field 47 percent of the time, and respondents voted with their fields in all these cases. Given that the votes selected were relatively high-conflict votes, the fact that the first two steps account for nearly half of these cases argues that these steps must have quite a high predictive power for legislative votes in general, since the general case is surely less conflict-ridden than these votes.

Starting with Step C, a major question of operationalization is the critical threshold of importance for each of the three important goals. What indicators would tell that a constituency interest, for instance, is sufficiently important that the congressman considers that constituency goal at Step C, rather than noticing but largely neglecting the constituency position in his decision? There is such an indicator in my data, the "importance" coding for each actor. With this coding, the congressman's comments relative to each actor were coded into four categories: (1) the actor was of no importance in the decision; (2) the actor was of minor importance; that is, the congressman noticed the actor's position, checked it, or the like, but the actor was of no greater importance; (3) the actor was of major importance; that is, whether or not the congressman ended up voting with the actor, he weighed the actor's position carefully and the actor had a major impact on his thinking; (4) the actor determined the decision, to the exclusion of other influences. The inter-coder reliability for this variable was very good.

Building on this coding, the critical thresholds of importance for the goals are operationalized as follows: for the constituency goal, the congressman passes that threshold on the decision at hand if his constituency for that decision is coded as being of major or determinative importance. If it is coded as being of minor or no importance, we consider that the threshold has not been passed, and that the constituency goal is not sufficiently important to the congressman on that decision to be involved in Step C of the model. Substantively, passing this threshold could be due to one or both of two reasons: either the constituency feeling is quite intense on the issue and any congressman would want to take account of it, or the congressman considers catering to constituency interest an important goal regardless of constituency inten-

sity. For present purposes it is not so critical which or what combination of these two reasons is responsible for the constituency being of major importance in the decision. Whatever the reason, the congressman's goal of satisfying constituents is evoked.

The constituency position, it should be noted, may not be the whole constituency, the mass public, or even a majority of the constituency. It could be these, but it could as easily be the position of a fairly narrow subset of the constituency, such as school administrators on education funding. In this connection, interest groups do not appear as a separate force in the model, since, as I have maintained elsewhere, they appear to have little impact on congressmen's voting decisions apart from their constituency connections. Thus interest groups are subsumed under constituency for present purposes, and ignored as being important in their own right.

It might be possible that a coding of "major" or "determinative" importance would be closely associated with the congressman's vote in accordance with the constituency position. If such were the case, the test of the model would not be as good as could be hoped, since passing the critical threshold would by itself imply a constituency-oriented vote, lending an artificial predictive power to the model. It turns out, however, that these apprehensions can be alleviated somewhat. Of the cases in which there is some conflict in the congressman's field, constituency is coded as being of major or determinative importance in 42. Of these 42 cases, the congressman votes with the constituency position 62 percent of the time, a performance somewhat better than chance (which is 1/2), but not dramatically better. By contrast, the model correctly predicts 93 percent of those cases. Thus, while there is naturally some association between the importance coding and the vote, it is not so strong as to negate the value of defining the critical threshold in the fashion described. The coding does not by itself produce the predictive performance.

The intra-Washington goal is treated in a similar fashion. If either the congressman's party leadership or the administration is coded as being of major or determinative importance, the congressman is considered to have passed the threshold on this decision and the goal is evoked. In addition, fellow congressmen could define the passing of the threshold on this goal, if they are coded as being of major or determinative importance, *and* if some consideration of vote-trading or intra-House power is involved. In other words, fellow congressmen do not trigger this goal, even if coded major or determinative, if the deciding legislator uses his colleagues simply to reinforce ideology, constituency, or party, or if colleagues are used in the absence of other guidance. These uses of fellow congressmen are provided for elsewhere in the model. To be relevant to the goal of intra-Washington influence, colleagues must be important for their own sakes, not because they are convenient surrogates for something else or because they are the only cues left. This supplementary coding was made by a rereading of the interview protocols in the cases involved, to see how colleagues were being used.

The goal of good public policy presents something of a problem in these data. Because the interviewing was done at the time of decision, respondents nearly always held some articulated policy attitude toward the bill or vote at hand, and voted consistent with it. But it would be very difficult, given these data, to determine the intensity or background of that attitude earlier in the process of decision. Therefore, some measure of the importance of the policy goal other than the intensity of the congressman's policy attitude toward the vote at hand is needed. Instead of trying to tap that intensity, I use here two measures of the congressman's policy position. The policy goal is considered to pass the critical threshold of importance if *either* his voting history on similar issues is coded as being of major or determinative importance in his decision, *or* his ideology as measured by Americans for Democratic Action (ADA) and Americans for Constitutional Action (ACA) scores is sufficiently extreme as to be a good guide to his decision. Some congressmen are simply considered extreme "liberals" or "conservatives," by themselves and by everyone associated with the process. If they are, I assume that

their ideology is sufficiently strong to give them considerable guidance, and to cause the congressman to pass the threshold on the policy goal. Because of a well-established voting history or a relatively extreme ideological position, in other words, he has a pretty fair notion of what constitutes "good public policy" for him in the current instance. Operationally, the ADA and ACA scores are used to form an index, in which a congressman is considered to be sufficiently extreme if either the ADA or ACA score is 90–100 or 0–10, and if the opposite score is in the opposite three deciles among my respondents. If the ADA score is zero, for instance, and the ACA score is in the upper three deciles, the congressman is considered to be a conservative; if the ADA score is 100 and the ACA score is in the bottom three deciles, for another example, the congressman is defined as liberal. Congressmen who do not meet the criteria described are considered to have a sufficiently "moderate" record that ADA-ACA position is not a guide to votes, and thus do not evoke the policy goal.

An impressionistic scanning of the members so classified confirms that those labelled the most liberal and conservative by the ADA-ACA criterion would be clearly regarded by most observers of the House as being correctly labelled. The index fails to identify some members for whom certain policy goals are clearly relevant, as, for instance, some very public doves on ABM deployment. In that sense, it may underestimate the importance of policy goals, since it discards some members for whom policy goals may be highly important. That underestimation also lowers the overall predictive performance of the model a bit. But the index does not make the other error: those who are identified as liberal or conservative are not mislabelled. As far as triggering the policy goal is concerned, the ADA-ACA index and the coding for the importance of voting history make a roughly equal contribution. Of the cases which exhibit some conflict in the field of forces in which the policy goal is evoked, the ADA-ACA index alone is responsible for that triggering in 30 cases, voting history alone in 27, and the two together in 25.

Table 26.2. *Quantitative Performance of the Integrative Model*

Step (see Figure 26.1)		Accuracy	Percentage of Cases	Cumulative Percentages
A	Non-controversial votes	–	0%	0%
B	No conflict in field	104/104 = 100%	47	47
C1	No conflict among goals	74/79 = 94%	33	80
C2–C6	Conflict among goals (from Table 26.1)	22/27 = 81%	10	90
D	Fellow congressmen	5/5 = 100%	2	92
E	Unexplained cases	$n = 7$		

Other operationalizations of the model are fairly straightforward. (1) Salience of the issue is a trichotomy (low, medium, high), as defined by the attention the issue appears to be receiving in the press, among congressmen, and among other participants in the legislative system. The model's specification of the cutting point being between high and medium salience is consistent with evidence presented elsewhere, that high-salience issues are distinctively constituency-oriented, whereas low- or medium-salience issues are less so. (2) The priority which the President places on the issue is determined from my knowledge of the administration's position and lobbying activities. In the first year of the Nixon administration, priority items tended to have to do with the budget, and these cases particularly centered on the debt limit and the surtax extension. (3) At Step D, fellow congressman importance is once again the importance coding, major or determinative constituting the criterion of entrance into that step.

The quantitative fruits of the model generation and data analysis are presented in Table 26.2, with a subset for Steps C2 through C6 more fully elaborated in Table 26.1. Overall, the model correctly predicts 92 percent of the voting decisions. Of those, only 10 percent are accounted for by Steps C2–C6, the most elaborate part of the model, which itself is not very elaborate. It seems clear that legislators' voting decisions can be understood as the workings of extremely simple decision rules, rules which are not generated in some arbitrary fashion, but in a way which is consistent with quite a rich body of previous literature on legislative voting. It must be remembered also that this particular sample of votes contains those deci-

sions which should be the hardest to predict. I deliberately selected votes which were among the most conflict-ridden of the session, which makes the high degrees of consensus (at Steps B and C1) really quite striking. One would not have expected these results, given the votes selected. Thus the model should do even better for run-of-the-mill votes. If there is as little conflict among actors and goals with these relatively "big," high-visibility votes, then there should be even less with more routine votes. I would expect, however, that for those votes, the simpler Steps A, B, C1, and D (stressing no conflict and House colleagues) would account for more of the total than these data indicate, and the more elaborate Steps C2–C6 would be resorted to even less frequently than these data indicate.

The model does specify that the congressman picks cues and votes in accordance with the specified goal. Thus far, we have only considered the percentage of *votes* predicted, without reference to whether or not the congressman also picked cues to reinforce those votes. I take it that "picking cues" here refers to choosing fellow congressmen on whom to rely according to their agreement with the goal specified in the model. Thus fellow congressmen at Step C2 should not be opposed to the constituency position, if the model is right; or at Step C6, they should not be opposed to the deciding legislator's policy position. If this factor is taken into account, we lose five cases which would otherwise be correctly predicted. That is to say, there are five cases in which the actor "fellow congressman" is opposed to a decision which was governed by the specified goal. Building this loss into the overall figures, therefore, the overall performance of the model, defined as the congressman's *both* voting as the model specifies *and* avoiding colleagues who are opposed to that vote, is 90 percent. The predictive performance, in other words, remains high.

Alternative Formulations

It may be useful to test some alternative formulations of the model, to see if this is the formulation which works best in the sense of correctly accounting for outcomes. Such an analysis would help to evaluate some plausible alternative hypotheses about the structure of the model and the place of several of the variables in it. I present here two types of alternative formulations: (1) changes in the basic structure of the model, and (2) changes in certain parts of the model.

The Basic Structure

There are three changes in the basic structure which have been tried on the data: bypassing the first consensus steps in the model, bypassing the non-consensus part of the model, and substituting one simple decision rule for the non-consensus part.

First, to bypass the first steps, we postulate that the 104 cases correctly accounted for by the consensus step (Step B) can be predicted by subsequent steps in the model (Steps C and D). In other words, we start the model running at Step C. One logical feature of the model becomes immediately clear, namely, that the only way for the goals step (Step C) to fail to predict decisions correctly is for none of the three goals to exceed their critical thresholds. If any do exceed their thresholds, then it is logically impossible in the 104 consensus cases for the goal agreement step (Step C1) not to account correctly for the outcome. If goals pass their thresholds, in other words, there is agreement among them by definition, since the original Step B filtered the cases according to the consensus criterion. Of the 104 cases at issue, then, Step C would correctly account for eighty-two. Of the remaining cases, which then reach Step D, following fellow congressmen of major importance picks up an addi-

tional nine cases. Thus Steps C and D account for 91 of the 104 cases, for an 88 percent accuracy rate; the original Step B accounted for all 104, a 100 percent accuracy rate.

Second, to bypass the nonconsensus parts of the model, we drop out Steps C2 through C6, and observe what difference it makes. In other words, if there is conflict among the evoked goals (at Step C1), the model proceeds immediately to considering the position of fellow congressmen (Step D), rather than going through the decision rules designed to sort out the goal conflict. The issues then is how many of the 27 cases originally classified as Steps C2–C6 cases are accounted for by Step D, which turns out to be 12 of the 27, or 44 percent. This compares to 22 of the 27 (81 percent) in the original formulation. As with the first reformulation, this one does not improve on the original; in fact, it performs worse.

The third basic structural reformulation, instead of bypassing the non-consensus steps (C2 through C6), substitutes a simple but plausible decision rule for them, namely that in the event of serious conflict among his goals, the legislator votes in accord with his policy position. Of the twenty-seven cases at issue, the policy goal is evoked in twenty-three, and of those twenty-three, the legislator does vote with his policy position in seventeen. Thus the hypothesized decision rule accounts for 63 percent (17/27) of the cases, compared to 81 percent (22/27) in the original model's Steps C2–C6.

Changes in Certain Parts

The last structural reformulation leads directly to some possible reformulations of parts of the model, particularly concentrating on various parts of the goals steps (Step C and substeps thereof). These changes fall into three categories: one concerned with the constituency goal, those concerned with the intra-Washington influence goal, and one which eliminates the threshold requirement at the beginning of Step C.

First, in the steps of the original model which show a conflict between constituency and other goals (C2 through C4), one could state an hypothesis that if constituency is of major importance, given the primacy of reelection to a seasoned politician, the congressman should be expected to vote with the constituency every time. That model, however, would account for only 3 of the 19 cases, whereas the model presented in Figure 26.1 accounts for 16. Thus this reformulation would represent a distinct loss of ability to account for the outcomes quantitatively.

Second, taking up reformulations having to do with the goal of intra-Washington influence, one plausible hypothesis would be that congressmen of the President's party would follow his lead. In the session under study, the hypothesis would state that when Republicans were aware of an administration position and when it played some part in their thinking, they would vote with the administration position. It turns out that when the administration was involved in Republican decisions, they voted with the administration position 68 percent of the time. By contrast, the model presented in this paper accounts for 85 percent of the same 59 cases.

Another reformulation involving intra-Washington influence would allow more than simply a president of the legislator's own party to be involved at Steps C5 and C6. Suppose, at that step in the model, that either the President of one's own party, or one's own party leadership, or colleagues within the House engaged in a logrolling exchange, could overturn one's own policy position; in other words, the entire set of evoked intra-Washington considerations could be swung into play, rather than simply a president of one's own party. It turns out that only two cases are affected by that change, and the reformulation fails to predict them correctly, whereas the original model had correctly predicted them.

The final reformulation eliminates the requirement that a goal must pass a critical threshold in order to be evoked (beginning at Step C), and then asks how the 79 cases originally disposed of at the goal consensus stage (C1) fare without that threshold requirement. Operationally, then, the goals are evoked as follows: (1) if either constituency or interest groups

are of *any* importance in the congressman's decision (rather than of major or determinative importance), then the constituency goal is evoked; (2) if either administration, party leadership, or fellow congressmen are of any importance, the goal of intra-Washington influence is evoked; (3) the policy goal threshold remains unchanged, since the ADA-ACA index must provide some sort of direction. Then because some conflict among the goals is now introduced into the seventy-nine cases that would previously have been filtered out due to the threshold requirement, we run the 79 cases through the non-consensus steps (C2 through C6) under the new conditions. The result is that Steps C2 through C6 correctly predict 62 of the 79 cases (78 percent), predict a result which does not in fact occur in 13 cases, and fails to provide a decision rule in four cases. If we allow those four cases to proceed to fellow congressmen for resolution (Step D), three of the four are correctly predicted there. Thus, by the combination of the nonconsensus and fellow congressmen steps, we have correctly accounted for 65 of the 79 cases (82 percent), whereas the original model at Step C1 accounted for seventy-nine of the 79 (94 percent).

In conclusion, after testing of several alternative formulations, it appears that the original model presented in Figure 26.1 emerges largely intact. None of the reformulations performs better in a quantitative sense, and many of them perform substantially worse. The good quantitative performance, however, does not address all of the questions which one might have about a model's usefulness. We now turn to some further questions.

A Caution about Quantitative Performance

It is appropriate to close with a caution that models of legislative voting should not be accepted solely because of their good ability to account for cases in quantitative terms. In some situations in the social sciences, a good fit to the data is regarded as a sufficient condition to accept a model, since it is difficult to predict outcomes. In other situations, such as the case of legislative voting models, a good quantitative performance is a necessary, but not sufficient condition to accept a model, since outcomes are quite easy to predict. The null hypothesis in the legislative case predicts 50 percent of the cases by itself, since if a congressman were flipping coins between "yes" and "no" in order to decide, and a random model were also flipping coins, the random model and the congressman's behavior would agree half the time. Beyond this "impressive" chance performance, quite a simple model constructed from commonplaces in the literature – e.g., some combination of party, region, constituency, and President position – would probably do quite nicely in a statistical sense. Indeed, a model which simply postulated that all congressmen vote "yea," while not theoretically interesting, would yield a fairly good prediction. As a matter of fact, most of the previous models discussed in this paper do quite nicely on their data sets, and we have become accustomed to models which predict about 85 percent of the cases. This is not to say that all possible models do well in terms of a criterion of ability to predict, as we have seen. Some models can be falsified, but that still leaves a number of models which do well.

In evaluating those remaining models of legislative voting, then, one should add to conventional criteria of statistical fit and quantitative performance, and use more conceptual and theoretical considerations. I outlined above some of these considerations, including plausibility, simplicity, political realism, and comprehensiveness. The advantages of the model presented in this paper have to do with those considerations. Our discussion attempts to use the virtues of various previous models to construct a more integrated view of legislative voting. The resulting model is quite comprehensive, and yet does not achieve this comprehensiveness at the expense of simplicity, plausibility, and realism. There is also a compelling logic to the progression protrayed, as congressmen are seen as moving from the simple to the complex, from a simple judgment about the whole environment, to a subsetting of that environment, to a further subsetting which concentrates explicitly on goals. These sorts of considerations, rather than simply an impressive ability to account for cases quantitatively, commend the model.

An instructive illustration may be the juxtaposition of the model presented here with the analysis found in *Congressmen's Voting Decisions*. I will discuss two of the types of analyses found there: the correlation analysis, which attempts to determine the influence of each of a set of actors on voting decisions, and the consensus model, which presents a process model of the decisions. Taking the correlation analysis first, in *Congressmen's Voting Decisions*, I identify six actors in the legislative system who could conceivably have an influence on a congressman's votes: the congressman's constituency, fellow congressmen, interest groups, the administration and executive branch, his party leadership, and his staff. The position of each on the issue at hand (for, against, neutral) is treated as an independent variable affecting the vote, and agreement scores, bivariate correlations, partial correlations, and stepwise regression are generated from the basic correlation model. The results are presented in great detail in the earlier work, and need not be repeated here. What is relevant to this discussion is that the multiple correlation between the six variables and the vote is .83, and that the residuals exhibit no pattern, which would lead one to suspect the adequacy of the equation. Thus the quantitative performance is good, and for some purposes, such as the ability to sort out the influence of various actors on legislative voting decisions, the analysis is quite useful.

As a model of decisional processes, however, the correlation approach does not appear to be entirely satisfying. A major point of a model such as the one discussed in this paper is that most of the time, legislators do not "weight influences" as regression, correlation, or some computer simulations portray them as doing. If legislators were to make decisions in a fashion analogous to regression, they would be required to weight each potential influence and to consider simultaneously the entire set of weighted influences. Given the severe time constraints on decision, and perhaps a general tendency for human beings to avoid thinking in such a simultaneous weighting fashion, this mode would not seem to be a plausible model of decisional processes. Furthermore, such a mode of decision is simply unnecessary on most votes. If the various possible influences agree, or the critical subsets of them agree, as they often do, then there is no need to engage in the weighting procedure that many other types of analysis require. A more minor consideration is that one would come away from the correlation analysis with the impression that fellow congressmen drive the decisions, which for a series of technical and conceptual reasons is probably not a complete model of decision, as I argue both here in this paper and elsewhere. At any rate, it is important to distinguish the objectives of a regression mode of thought from those of a process modelling approach.

The other juxtaposition is between the model presented in this paper and the earlier consensus mode of decision, which is found in *Congressmen's Voting Decisions*. The final steps of that model, unlike this current one, portray a deciding congressman as identifying the actors who were out of line with the dominant consensus in the field, and voting against them. The gain in predictive power of the model discussed here over that earlier model is trivial. What this new model does provide are important theoretical additions to the earlier work. As in the case of most of the models discussed in this paper, this integrative model does not negate or substitute for the earlier work, but rather adds to it in important ways.

To elaborate, the original consensus model in its last steps was not simply a matter of "majority rule" or mechanical counting. Somehow, there are processes at work, conceptualized earlier as "preconsensus" processes, which lead the congressman to the conclusion that these actors against which he votes are isolated, of little consequence, and capable of being safely slighted. The model presented in this paper provides a way to interpret the pattern portrayed in the consensus mode. For example, there are 19 cases in my data in which the constituency is the one actor out of line with the rest of the field and in which the congressman votes against the constituency position. In 15 of those 19, constituency is coded as being of minor importance, meaning, in terms of the model presented in this

paper, that the goal of satisfying constituents has not been evoked. The remaining four were all low-salience issues, in which the constituency interest could be overruled. Thus the operation of the model presented in this paper helps us to understand why the deciding congressmen could vote against constituency wishes in these instances. Or to take the other most numerous example, respondents voted against interest groups in 22 cases, of which 18 found constituency to be of minor importance and the remaining four found constituency opposed to the interest group position. Because interest groups are vulnerable without a constituency connection, it seems quite understandable in terms of the integrative model presented here that congressmen should find it possible to vote against an interest group when the constituency consideration is either not evoked or is opposed to the lobby position. Other examples could be discussed.

The point is that deciding congressmen are indeed voting against these actors, as the original consensus model portrays them as doing. This new model adds some further thinking about *why* they are doing so. The same could be said for other models. Thus cue-taking is decidedly taking place, and congressmen are clearly voting in ways that can be interpreted according to policy dimensions. One advantage of the new model rests not in negating previous models but in providing a more comprehensive framework within which they can all be better understood.

CONCLUSION

This paper has started with a set of models of legislative voting which at first blush have seemed to many scholars to be alternative, contradictory accounts of voting decisions. Instead of treating them as competing models, however, I have chosen to discuss them as entirely compatible with one another, each having a grasp on an important part of the whole reality. Both by a verbal discussion of the models and of their place in legislative voting decisions, and by the generation of an integrative model, I have attempted to weave the various threads of reality together in a way which is satisfying both conceptually and empirically. I have ended by relating the new model to my data on congressmen's voting decisions.

There may be a wider applicability of the key concepts presented here beyond the case of legislative voting, in the sense that wide varieties of decision-makers may use versions of a similar general approach to their decisions. Legislators, bureaucrats, judges, and others may all be thought to search for consensus in their environment, to subset that environment in the event that agreement is lacking and to search for consensus within the most critical subset, to identify their most important goals and ask if there is agreement among them, and to get into more complex decisions if these simpler rules fail them. The well-known use of standard operating procedures in bureaucracies, for example, may be due to consensus among the relevant actors in the bureaucrat's environment – his superiors, the agency clientele, his coworkers, his professional associates outside the agency –

that given SOP's are appropriate for a given class of cases. Or judges deciding on sentencing of convicted defendents, for another example, have been found to impose the sentence recommended by police, prosecutor, and probation departments if the three agree; if they do not agree, the judge must enter a more complex set of decision rules. Mass public voting behavior exhibits similar characteristics: when various important influences agree, the voting decision is made; when they do not, the voter is said to be under "cross-pressure," and the decision becomes more complicated. Space does not permit an extended discussion of the possible applications, but it is worth noting that the model presented here may represent a general decision strategy, an approach to decision-making, which is widely used. Thus this work hopefully contributes not only to further understanding of legislative behavior, but also to the general building of theory about decision processes.

CHAPTER TWENTY–SEVEN

Pivotal Politics

A Theory of U.S. Lawmaking

Keith Krehbiel

Krehbiel develops a simple, spatial model of lawmaking in the U.S. Congress. He argues that focusing on the policy positions of "pivotal" voters such as the person crucial to ending a filibuster or overriding a presidential veto, instead of divided government, is the proper way to study the causes and consequences of legislative gridlock.

Who is pivotal in U.S. lawmaking? This is a difficult question insofar as "the United States has the most intricate lawmaking system in the world." However, based on the hope that even a simple theoretical answer to a difficult question is better than no answer at all, this chapter introduces a theory of pivotal politics that is unabashedly elementary by contemporary modeling standards. The theory not only answers the question of who is pivotal in U.S. lawmaking but also generates a sizable set of empirical implications. After a brief overview of the general properties of good theories – assumptions, results, and interpretations – this chapter turns to their specific manifestations in the pivotal politics theory.

ASSUMPTIONS

Assumptions of the theory cover preferences, players, policies, procedures, and behavior.

Keith Krehbiel. 1998. "A Theory" in Keith Krehbiel, *Pivotal Politics: A Theory of U.S. Lawmaking* (University of Chicago Press), 20–48. © 1998 by The University of Chicago. All rights reserved. Published 1998.

These can be addressed in varying degrees of mathematical precision and generality. Here I opt for a relatively informal and example-based exposition.

Policy Space

Collective choice occurs via voting over proposals or policies that can be arranged on a line. That is, the *policy space is unidimensional*. It is convenient and intuitive to think of the policy space as a continuum on which liberal policies are located on the left, moderate policies are located in the center, and conservative policies are located on the right. Because the policy space is continuous, it is possible to consider policies at any point between liberal and conservative extremes. Finally, an exogenous *status quo point, q*, reflects existing policy and can be interpreted as the outcome from a prior period of decision making.

Players and Preferences

Players in the game are genetically referred to as *lawmakers* and include a president and *n* legislators in a unicameral legislature. Each player has an *ideal point* in the policy space, that is, a policy that yields greater benefits to the player than all other policies. Each player's preferences are *single-peaked*, meaning that as policies in a given direction farther and farther from an

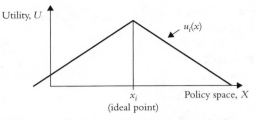

Figure 27.1. Single-peaked utility function for legislator i.

individual's ideal point are considered, utility for that player never increases. Figure 27.1 shows a simple example of one player with an ideal point x_i, and a single-peaked utility function $u_i(x)$. For convenience and spatial intuition, it is helpful further to assume that utility functions are symmetric. Therefore, for any two policies y and z in the policy space, a player always prefers that policy which is closer to his ideal point.

Procedures

In contrast to generic pure-majority-rule voting models, the capacity of politicians to enact policies in this theory is tempered by two *supermajoritarian procedures:* the executive *veto,* and the Senate's *filibuster* procedures. The U.S. Constitution confers to the president the right to veto legislation subject to a $^2/_3$ majority override by the Congress. Similarly, the Senate's Rule 22 confers to each individual the right to engage in *extended debate* (filibuster) subject to a $^3/_5$ vote to end debate (invoke cloture). Under configurations of legislative preferences to be specified, the filibuster, too, effectively raises the voting requirement for policy change.

Pivots

Webster's *New World Dictionary* defines a *pivot* as "a person or thing on or around which something turns or depends." This commonsense definition transports well into the pivotal politics modeling framework. The "something" that depends on the pivots in the theory is the collective choice, that is, the law. The focus of

the modeling exercise is to discern which of n legislators or the president is pivotal in various lawmaking situations and why.

Among the n legislators (for convenience, n is odd), two players may have unique pivotal status due to supermajoritarian procedures, even though these players possess no unique parliamentary rights. A third player, the median voter, is also singled out for baseline purposes. These are illustrated in Figure 27.2, which shows an eleven-person legislature and a liberal president. The key pivots in the most basic version of the pivotal politics theory are the *filibuster pivot* with ideal point f and the *veto pivot* with ideal point v. These are defined with reference to the president, whose ideal point is p.

If, as shown, the president is on the left (liberal) side of the median voter m, then the veto pivot is the legislator for whom his ideal point and all ideal points to his right make up exactly or just more than $^2/_3$ of the legislature. The number of ideal points to his left therefore make up no more than $^1/_3$ of the legislature. For the eleven voters in Figure 27.2, for example, the veto pivot is the fourth voter from the left. A similar definition can be given for a president on the right (conservative) side of the median voter m.

The definition of the filibuster pivot follows a similar fractional algorithm. If the president is on the left (liberal) side of the median voter m, then the filibuster pivot is the legislator for whom his ideal point and all ideal points to his left make up exactly or just more than $^3/_5$ of the legislature. The number of ideal points to his right, then, make up no more than $^2/_5$ of the legislature. For the eleven-voter case, this would be the seventh voter from the left, as shown in Figure 27.2. If the president were instead on the right (conservative) side of the median voter m,

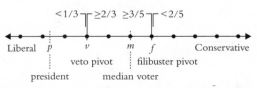

Figure 27.2. Pivotal legislators if the president is liberal.

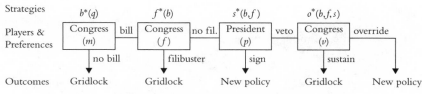

Figure 27.3. The pivotal politics model.

then the filibuster pivot will be on the opposite side of the median, likewise splitting ideal points into exact or approximate groups of $^2/_5$ and $^3/_5$.

viving policies in question – the bill, b, and the status quo, q. Thus, the model condenses a large number of individual choices into a tractable but plausible simplifying structure.

Sequence of Play

A formal version of the four-stage model is shown in Figure 27.3. First, to reflect the strictly accurate procedural fact that it takes only a simple majority to pass a bill in Congress, the median voter of the legislature moves by choosing any bill b in the policy space, or by deciding to accept the exogenous status quo point, q. Though seemingly dictatorial, this one-player choice is more appropriately interpreted as a strategic simple-majoritarian action by the median voter on behalf of all voters with ideal points to one side of m. No restrictions are placed on amendments or on who can offer them.

Second, if a bill, b, is proposed in stage 1, then the filibuster pivot with ideal point f as defined above chooses whether to mount a filibuster, which leads to a status quo outcome, or whether to let the game proceed to the next stage. This one-player choice likewise can be interpreted as a $^2/_5$ minority action even though it is modeled as an individual's strategy.

Third, if the filibuster pivot does not filibuster in stage 2, then the president with ideal point p decides whether to sign or to veto the bill.

Fourth, if the president vetoes the bill, then the veto pivot with ideal point v decides whether to sustain or to override the president's veto. As with stages 1 and 2, this unilateral action represents the behavior of a bloc of voters with identical preferences with regard to the two sur

Behavior

Players in the game are assumed to adopt strategies that maximize their utility, conditional on the expectation that all other players in future stages of the game do likewise. Players know the game, know each others' preferences, understand who is the pivotal voter in any given setting, and adopt optimal strategies accordingly.

Equilibrium and Gridlock

One analytic focal point is on the institutional basis for *gridlock*. To capture not only stalemate in government but also the sense of majority disappointment or injustice that sometimes accompanies it, *gridlock* is defined as the absence of policy change in equilibrium in *spite of the existence of a legislative majority that favors change*.

Parties

No special assumptions are made about the ability of political parties to shape individual lawmakers' decisions. This, admittedly, is a judgment that is likely to be controversial. The present aim is not to preempt or stifle controversy but rather to clarify the issue so that neutral readers can form independent judgments after a substantial amount of evidence is presented. Three preliminary observations are relevant in this regard.

RESULTS

Case 1: The Economic Stimulus Package and the Filibuster Pivot

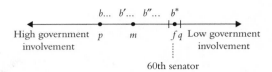

Figure 27.4. f is pivotal on the stimulus package: incremental change.

The war-room mantra for the Clinton–Gore campaign in 1992 was, "It's the economy, stupid!" Democrats campaigned aggressively and effectively on the assertion that the U.S. economy was in bad shape and that, upon the return to unified government, their party could improve it. In the meantime, Democrats alleged that Republicans "just don't get it," which, evidently, is why Democrats added the fourth word to their mantra.

Not surprisingly, an early legislative strategy in the Clinton administration was to try to capitalize on the confluence of unified government, an electoral mandate, momentum, and a honeymoon by proposing an ambitious set of programs that would infuse federal funds into the economy to jumpstart a recovery. The economic stimulus package, as it came to be called, consumed a great deal of the administration's time and effort in the early months. The original bill included high-technology purchases for the federal government, summer jobs for youths and unskilled workers, social programs for the poor, and numerous public works projects aimed at creating jobs and spurring economic development. When bundled together in a supplemental appropriations bill, these goodies came with a price tag of $16.3 billion.

After swift and smooth House passage, the ride got rough for the new administration. A divided vote in the Senate Appropriations Committee was a harbinger for the disagreements on the Senate floor. Surprisingly to some, the first obstacles were put up by Democrats, not Republicans. Fiscal conservatives (and overall moderates) such as David Boren of Oklahoma, John Breaux of Louisiana, and Richard Bryan of Nevada wanted to enact spending cuts elsewhere before appropriating money for the stimulus package. As a compromise, they proposed cutting the cost of the bill in half and coming back to the other half after the normal appropriations process had run its course. Eventually, the three B senators dropped

their demands after receiving a letter from Clinton, who pledged to propose spending cuts if Congress failed to meet the deficit reduction targets in the congressional budget resolution. But Republicans were not convinced that a stimulus package was needed, or did not view such pledges as credible, or both. Forty-two of the 43 Republicans signed a letter to Minority Leader Bob Dole promising to initiate a filibuster unless major changes to the bill were made. Several Democrats, too, continued to press for changes, including Dennis DeConcini of Arizona, Herb Kohl of Wisconsin, and Bob Graham of Florida. The threatened filibuster occurred, multiple cloture votes were taken, cloture was not invoked, and, to round up cloture votes and bill support, the bill was eventually diluted nearly beyond recognition. What had been a complex $16 billion omnibus initiative became a simple $4 billion measure to extend unemployment benefits. It passed on a voice vote.

Who was pivotal? The case can be analyzed in the pivotal politics framework to answer this question. As shown on Figure 27.4, the standard liberal–conservative spectrum can be given somewhat more precise labels pertaining to the desired level of government involvement in the economy. Liberals tend to favor high involvement (a large cash infusion); conservatives tend to favor low involvement (status quo or lower levels of cash infusion). Notwithstanding his self-proclaimed New Democrat credentials in other spheres, President Clinton clearly lay on the liberal end of this spectrum, and his initial legislative proposal reflected it. Congress, however, does not take-or-leave presidential proposals as offered, and, besides, it quickly became evident that this proposal would have been left behind – not taken – as originally offered. Thus began a long and tortuous process of diluting the bill (b, b', b'' ...). The parliamentary device that made such dilution necessary for passage of any package at all was, of course, the filibuster. A credible blocking coalition of 41 or more Republicans and moderate-to-conservative Democrats refused to vote to invoke cloture unless and until the provisions of the bill were sufficiently moderate, relative to the status quo, q, that 60 senators preferred the bill to the status quo. In the end, the scope of the package was small. The dramatic "change" that had been promised repeatedly in the election was incremental at best, and the reason it was not larger than incremental is that the supermajoritarian requirement of cloture has the effect of making f, the sixtieth percentile senator, pivotal. Given this, the equilibrium legislative proposal is the bill, b^*, which leaves the filibuster pivot, f, indifferent between the status quo, q, and the bill, b^*. Given such a bill, cloture is invoked (or the filibuster is called off because the obstructionists know their blocking coalition has been eroded), the bill is passed (by a bipartisan supermajority), and the president signs the bill (even though its content is a far cry from the initial proposal and even a substantial cry from what the median voter in the Congress wanted). In short, while this is not a case of gridlock in the sense of complete policy stalemate, it is a case of incremental change and disillusionment by moderates, attributable to supermajoritarian procedures.

Case 2: Family Leave and the Veto Pivot

As early as 1985, Democrats in Congress argued that the United States was alone among industrial nations in its failure to guarantee parents leaves of absence from their jobs in order to care for their newborns. From the mid-1980s and into the 1990s, however, Republican presidents, backed by small-business interests, argued that mandated family leave would undermine companies' competitiveness by disrupting their day-to-day operations. In the early years of this dispute, Congress threatened to act, or did act, on family leave legislation, only to see their efforts fail to come to fruition. In 1986 and 1987, for example, family leave legislation did not make it to the floor, although there was some committee activity. In 1988 and 1989, a wider assortment of committees took favorable action on family leave, but the bill languished in the Senate because of filibusters and Senate Majority Leader George Mitchell's inability to muster the requisite 60 votes to invoke cloture.

By 1990 and 1991, congressional support for the idea of family leave had increased. A key development was that moderate Republicans, such as Labor Secretary Lynn Martin and Representative Marge Roukema of New Jersey, came on board and became more assertive in giving the cause a bipartisan voice. Bipartisanship was also facilitated by the growing affinity of Republicans for family values and by considerable weakening of the family leave bill over the years. As a result, proponents obtained greater than simple-majority support in both chambers in 1991. In the Senate, Republican Kit Bond of Missouri proposed a substitute bill to the Democrats' stronger version; the substitute passed 65–32. The House then passed the bill 253–177. In spite of these seemingly comfortable majority margins, however, the bill languished in conference committee in 1991 because the vote margins were not comfortable *supermajority* margins. President Bush was clearly opposed even to the weakened legislation, so congressional leaders opted not to force Bush's hand, which had a firm grip on a veto pen.

In 1992 the conferees met and weakened further their version of the provisions of the family leave bill. The aims were twofold: obviously, to attract still broader support; less obviously (perhaps), to embarrass the reelection seeking president for being on the minority side of what was widely perceived as a majoritarian cause. So, on the eve of the Republican National Convention, the Senate passed the conference report on the bill by a voice vote. Since 65 senators had earlier voted for a stronger bill, a veto-proof majority seemed within reach. (Three of the senators who missed the earlier vote had since voiced support for the bill.) In the House, however, support seemed to be waning by the time the Congress reconvened after the convention. On September 10, the House voted 241–161 to

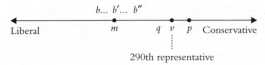

Figure 27.5. v is pivotal on the family leave bill: gridlock.

pass the conference report – about 50 votes short of that required to override Bush's certain veto.

The veto occurred on September 22. The resulting preelection rhetoric was predictably intense, and the Senate, after four years and 32 vetoes from Bush, finally overrode the president 68–31. House proponents, however, fared less well, falling 27 votes short of the $^2/_3$ mark. Thus, the status quo (and gridlock) prevailed once again.

Who was pivotal? The $^2/_3$ voter in the House, or veto pivot v, as illustrated in Figure 27.5 Similar to the case of the economic stimulus package, the history is one of fluid proposals, not take-it-or-leave-it agenda setting. Bill proponents often start with strong proposals to sharpen attention on the issues, float trial balloons, or mobilize support among more ideological legislators. Sequential proposals of this sort are not explicitly captured in the pivotal politics theory. What the theory does say, however, is that given a status quo point and a profile of preferences such as those in Figure 27.5, the veto-pivotal voter with ideal point v must be made to favor the bill or to be indifferent between the bill and the status quo for a new law to be passed. When this is not possible – as was the case in 1992 on the family leave bill and with the status quo, q – gridlock occurs.

In brief, the $^2/_3$ override provision in the Constitution makes lawmaking difficult whenever the president opposes policy changes that congressional majorities favor. In this sense, the pivotal politics theory captures the central tendency to gridlock in U.S. lawmaking.

Case 3: Family Leave and the Filibuster Pivot

Family leave was a salient election issue during the presidential campaign of 1992. On the campaign trail, Al Gore spoke often of his ability to take time off from the Senate to be with his son who was critically ill after being struck by a car. After the election, the new 103d Congress acted quickly on the new family leave bill. HR 1 passed the House 265–163 on February 3, 1993. The next day the Senate passed its own version 71–27, which the House subsequently accepted 247–152.

Although these vote margins were similar to those of the previous Congress, one thing was much different: the new president favored the bill, so a $^2/_3$ congressional majority was no longer required. Furthermore, although a $^3/_5$ majority was still required to overcome a possible filibuster in the Senate, this was not a problem insofar as the Senate had crossed that threshold in the previous year. So, on February 5 – after approximately eight years of legislative efforts – the family leave bill was signed into law. At last, gridlock was broken.

Who was pivotal? The situation is illustrated in Figure 27.6. The old veto pivot v is unimportant in light of the new president, p, who prefers any plausible leftward change in policy. Large leftward changes are still not possible, however, because of the filibuster threat. Therefore the bill, b^*, represents the optimal legislation given the $^3/_5$ senator's pivotal status. It leaves the filibuster pivot, f, indifferent between the bill and the right-of-center status quo.

Gridlock in Unified Government

In their rapid reactions to the election of Bill Clinton in 1992, journalists such as Richard Cohen hailed the new regime as a "dramatic shift from a divided government stuck in neutral to one in which a single party was operating the vehicle and had well-defined goals".

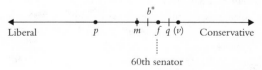

Figure 27.6. f is pivotal on the family leave bill: gridlock is broken.

In their rapid reactions to the first half of Clinton's term, however, editorial assessments even of friendly newspapers were much different. *The New York Times* put it this way: "Bill Clinton and the Democrats have failed to persuade the American people that they *[sic]* can govern as a party . . . even when [the majority party] has the keys to the Capitol and the White House." *The Washington Post* concurred: "It's back to gridlock . . . of a nasty internecine kind that makes the Bush administration seem like a checkers game by comparison." Even the public seemed to agree, with only 19 percent of respondents saying that Congress accomplished more than it does in a typical two-year period and 52 percent saying it accomplished less. Should this turnabout be surprising? A closer look of the pivotal politics theory suggests that it should not, and thus helps to explain the puzzle of gridlock in unified government.

The theory clarifies the central role the status quo plays in identifying conditions for policy change in a separation-of-powers system, but it can be criticized for two related reasons. First, the status quo is an exogenous parameter in the theory. Second, the theory is multistage but not repeated, thus it is essentially static. How does the substantive conclusion about the probable pervasiveness of gridlock change in a more dynamic setting? For example, is it empirically possible and analytically demonstrable that when divided government gives way to unified government – or, when regimes abruptly switch as in 1992 – the ostensibly rare conditions for breaking gridlock are nevertheless met?

To answer these questions and to try to shed more light on the contemporary political scene, we can conduct a simple experiment in which recent U.S. political history is viewed through the lens of the pivotal politics theory. Specifically, we begin by considering the Carter administration (unified government, left-of-center president). Then, under historically defensible suppositions about how preferences and unified/divided government regimes changed up until the Clinton administration, we identify equilibrium changes in policy over

time. The objective is to obtain a better sense of the real-world likelihood of breaking gridlock by thinking through the prior generation of otherwise exogenous status quo points.

Regime 1

Jimmy Carter was elected in 1976. Along with 292 House Democrats plus enough Senate Democrats to give his party a 61–38 majority in the upper chamber, Carter ushered in the first era of unified government since 1968.

Figure 27.7 represents major regime shifts over the subsequent two decades. The initial question is how much the hypothetical unrestricted initial distribution of status quo points q_1 for regime 1 will converge to more moderate policies after just one play of the game for any possible q. The vertical lines in Figure 27.7 represent policy trajectories that pass through specific intervals which, in effect, embody equilibrium behavior that stipulates whether and how policies change. Thus, all interval I status quo policies ($q < 2p_1 - m_1$) converge to the median m_1. Interval II status quo policies map into outcomes between Carter's ideal point p_1 and the legislative median m_1. Interval III is the gridlock interval where, by definition, policies remain unchanged and thus drop straight down. Interval IV consists of status quo points for which the filibuster constrains convergence to the median. And interval V status quos again converge fully to the legislative median.

Upon the occurrence of these events, all new policies x_1, plus old unchanged policies $q_1 = x_1$, become stable. Indeed, as noted above, gridlock in this theory is an inevitable feature of *any* administration which, with the Congress, has made one pass at the major issues of its term. The exercise also yields refined if not alternative interpretations of so-called presidential honeymoons and presidential success. Depending on starting conditions, an administration may indeed be characterized by a flurry of initial and ostensibly successful legislative activity. The prediction of this theory is that such activity inevitably drops off soon. While the drop-off makes the prior activity appear as if it were a honeymoon, the successful passage of legislation in this model is not generated by those forces

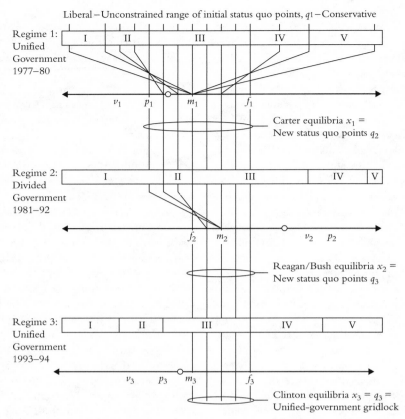

Figure 27.7. Quasidynamic properties of the theory.

identified elsewhere in the literature as central to presidential power: for example, presidential popularity, prestige, going public, persuasion, or signaling. Rather, it is a more straightforward consequence of old policies being out of equilibrium given new preferences.

Regime 2

Shown in the middle of Figure 27.7, the Reagan–Bush years marked a change not only to divided government ($p_2 > m_2$) but also to a more conservative Congress ($m_2 > m_1$). Now the theory can be applied to the divided-government Reagan–Bush years. In conjunction with the Carter regime of unified government, the Reagan–Bush regime of divided government yields a prediction about whether, which, and how the policy remnants of the Carter years will change.

Carter equilibria x_1 become Reagan–Bush status quo points q_2. The rightward shift of preferences plus the change to divided government also causes the spatial locations of the behavior-determining intervals to change. Some regime 2 status quo policies ($q_2 = x_1$) are much more liberal than the 1980s median legislator ($q_2 < 2f_2 - m_2 < m_2$) and are thus in interval I. Policy changes, but only incrementally.

Regime 3

The funneling effect of liberal policies toward the regime 2 median creates Reagan–Bush outcomes x_2 which serve as status quo points q_3 for Clinton. These are located at or near the 1980s congressional median m_2. Given the regime shift in preferences as a consequence of the 1992 election (and, in the case of the Senate, the secular loss of seats throughout the 1990s), the new median m_3 becomes more liberal than the old median m_2. Furthermore, we assume that the Clinton-regime filibuster pivot f_3 is the same as that during the Carter-regime f_1.

Piecing these observations and assumptions together, this application of the theory broadly predicts what is appropriately termed *unified-government gridlock*. All history-based status quo points lie in the unified-government gridlock interval III (p_3, f_3), thus no new policies are to be expected.

What actually happened? As always, assessments are somewhat mixed. On the positive/high-productivity side of the argument are researchers who stress that President Clinton received historically high levels of individual-vote-based congressional support and who argue that when the president announced a position on a roll call vote, his position commanded a majority of votes. On the negative/low-productivity side of the argument are observers from a broad spectrum of professions and employers. A more typical sample of wrap-ups follows.

The 103d Congress was going to be different. With one party in control of the Senate, the House, and the White House for the first time in 12 years, and a large freshman class eager to prove that Congress can get things done, it was supposed to be the end of gridlock. But barring a quick burst of activity, it will not be so. (*New York Times* op-ed, "Before Congress Quits," September 20, 1994)

The 103d Congress that began by boasting that it would break gridlock is coming to an end mired in it. (*Wall Street Journal* op-ed, "Glorious Gridlock," October 4, 1994)

With a Democrat in the White House and with Democrats firmly in control of Congress, government gridlock would end. The executive and legislative branches would work together, with a minimum of rancor. That was the prediction. That hasn't been reality. (*National Journal* cutline for Richard E. Cohen's "Some Unity!" September 25, 1993, 2290)

Finally, what about the constitutional and weak-party mechanics underlying the modal assessment of the 103d Congress and unified government?

Clearly, unified government does not provide the administration with the automatic ability to move its initiatives ahead.... The administration will appeal to party loyalty, but lacking the ability to command it, will engage in the painstaking process of assembling majorities, issue by issue, in a Congress whose members remain willing (often eager) to assert their constitutional powers. Madison lives! (Rieselbach 1993, 10, 11)

In summary, the exercise in dynamics sheds some light on recent events and provides clear answers to the two broader questions raised at the beginning of the section. How does the earlier conclusion about the probable pervasiveness of gridlock change in a more dynamic setting? It is strengthened. Any given governmental regime, unified or divided, has only so much to do that is politically feasible. Furthermore, when something can be done – that is, when status quo policies are not in the gridlock interval – that which is feasible is typically incremental. Is it, then, empirically possible and analytically demonstrable that, when divided government gives way to unified government, the ostensibly rare conditions for breaking gridlock are nevertheless met? Of course it is empirically possible for unified government to break gridlock. Indeed, this had been the hope and expectation of critics of divided government. This empirical expectation, however, has at best a weak analytic basis within the present framework, and recent events seem to provide at least a weak form of support for the theory.

CONCLUSION

The theory of pivotal politics identifies a single, conceptually tidy, necessary and sufficient condition for breaking gridlock. Policy change requires that the status quo must lie outside the gridlock interval, as defined by the president, filibuster, and veto pivots in theory and illustrated in Figure 27.7 as interval III.

More generally, the pivotal politics theory seems promising. It implies that gridlock is common but not constant, and it identifies the condition under which it will be broken. Furthermore, when gridlock is broken, it is broken by large, bipartisan coalitions – not by minimal-majority or homogeneous majority-party coalitions.

The theory has some bonus features as well. Loosely applied, it serves as a rationalizing device for one of the biggest recent surprises in U.S. politics: a unified government gridlock. Also loosely applied, it provides a sort of lens through which we can better envision other regularities: honeymoons, fast starts, and eventual fizzles within presidential terms; intraterm decreases in the number of presidential initiatives; declining presidential popularity; and frustrations of moderate legislators.

PART IX. CONGRESS AND THE PRESIDENT

CHAPTER TWENTY-EIGHT

Presidential Veto Messages

In accordance with the Constitution, the president is to return a vetoed measure to the house of origin along with a veto message containing his objections. These veto messages offer Congress valuable insight into the president's logic for vetoing a given measure and occasionally spur Congress to re-pass the measure taking into account these objections. The veto messages here are the first three messages of President George W. Bush.

MESSAGE TO THE HOUSE OF REPRESENTATIVES

May 1, 2007
TO THE HOUSE OF REPRESENTATIVES:

I am returning herewith without my approval H.R. 1591, the "U.S. Troop Readiness, Veterans' Care, Katrina Recovery, and Iraq Accountability Appropriations Act, 2007."

This legislation is objectionable because it would set an arbitrary date for beginning the withdrawal of American troops without regard to conditions on the ground; it would micromanage the commanders in the field by restricting their ability to direct the fight in Iraq; and it contains billions of dollars of spending and other provisions completely unrelated to the war.

Precipitous withdrawal from Iraq is not a plan to bring peace to the region or to make our people safer here at home. The mandated withdrawal in this bill could embolden our enemies – and confirm their belief that America will not stand behind its commitments. It could lead to a safe haven in Iraq for terrorism that could be used to attack America and freedom-loving people around the world, and is likely to unleash chaos in Iraq that could spread across the region. Ultimately, a precipitous withdrawal could increase the probability that American troops would have to one day return to Iraq – confront an even more dangerous enemy.

The micromanagement in this legislation is unacceptable because it would create a series of requirements that do not provide the flexibility needed to conduct the war. It would constrict how and where our Armed Forces could engage the enemy and defend the national interest, and would provide confusing guidance on which of our enemies the military could engage. The result would be a marked advantage for our enemies and greater danger for our troops, as well as an unprecedented interference with the judgments of those who are charged with commanding the military.

Beyond its direction of the operation of the war, the legislation is also unacceptable for including billions of dollars in spending and other provisions that are unrelated to the war, are not an emergency, or are not justified. The Congress should not use an emergency war supplemental to add billions in spending to avoid its own rules for budget discipline and the normal budget process. War supplemental funding bills should remain focused on the war and the needs of our men and women in uniform who are risking their lives to defend our freedoms and preserve our Nation's security.

Finally, this legislation is unconstitutional because it purports to direct the conduct of the operations of the war in a way that infringes upon the powers vested in the Presidency by the Constitution, including as Commander in Chief of the Armed Forces. For these reasons, I must veto this bill.

GEORGE W. BUSH
THE WHITE HOUSE,
May 1, 2007.

MESSAGE TO THE HOUSE OF REPRESENTATIVES

TO THE HOUSE OF REPRESENTATIVES:

I am returning herewith without my approval H.R. 810, the "Stem Cell Research Enhancement Act of 2005."

Like all Americans, I believe our Nation must vigorously pursue the tremendous possibilities that science offers to cure disease and improve the lives of millions. Yet, as science brings us ever closer to unlocking the secrets of human biology, it also offers temptations to manipulate human life and violate human dignity. Our conscience and history as a Nation demand that we resist this temptation. With the right scientific techniques and the right policies, we can achieve scientific progress while living up to our ethical responsibilities.

In 2001, I set forth a new policy on stem cell research that struck a balance between the needs of science and the demands of conscience. When I took office, there was no Federal funding for human embryonic stem cell research. Under the policy I announced 5 years ago, my Administration became the first to make Federal funds available for this research, but only on embryonic stem cell lines derived from embryos that had already been destroyed. My Administration has made available more than $90 million for research of these lines. This policy has allowed important research to go forward and has allowed America to continue to lead the world in embryonic stem cell research without encouraging the further destruction of living human embryos.

H.R. 810 would overturn my Administration's balanced policy on embryonic stem cell research. If this bill were to become law, American taxpayers for the first time in our history would be compelled to fund the deliberate destruction of human embryos. Crossing this line would be a grave mistake and would needlessly encourage a conflict between science and ethics that can only do damage to both and harm our Nation as a whole.

Advances in research show that stem cell science can progress in an ethical way. Since I announced my policy in 2001, my Administration has expanded funding of research into stem cells that can be drawn from children, adults, and the blood in umbilical cords with no harm to the donor, and these stem cells are currently being used in medical treatments. Science also offers the hope that we may one day enjoy the potential benefits of embryonic stem cells without destroying human life. Researchers are investigating new techniques that might allow doctors and scientists to produce stem cells just as versatile as those derived from human embryos without harming life. We must continue to explore these hopeful alternatives, so we can advance the cause of scientific research while staying true to the ideals of a decent and humane society.

I hold to the principle that we can harness the promise of technology without becoming slaves to technology and ensure that science serves the cause of humanity. If we are to find the right ways to advance ethical medical research, we must also be willing when necessary to reject the wrong ways. For that reason, I must veto this bill.

GEORGE W. BUSH
THE WHITE HOUSE,
July 19, 2006.

TO THE SENATE OF THE UNITED STATES:

I am returning herewith without my approval S. 5, the "Stem Cell Research Enhancement Act of 2007."

Once again, the Congress has sent me legislation that would compel American taxpayers, for the first time in our history, to support the deliberate destruction of human embryos.

In 2001, I announced a policy to advance stem cell research in a way that is ambitious, ethical, and effective. I became the first President to make Federal funds available for embryonic stem cell research, and my policy did this in ways that would not encourage the destruction of embryos. Since then, my Administration has made more than $130 million available for research on stem cell lines derived from embryos that had already been destroyed. We have also provided more than $3 billion for research on all forms of stem cells, including those from adult and other non-embryonic sources.

This careful approach is producing results. It has contributed to proven therapeutic treatments in thousands of patients with many different diseases. And it is opening the prospect of new discoveries that could transform lives. Researchers are now developing promising new techniques that offer the potential to produce pluripotent stem cells, without having to destroy human life – for example, by reprogramming adult cells to make them function like stem cells.

Technical innovation in this difficult area is opening up new possibilities for progress without conflict or ethical controversy. Researchers pursuing these kinds of ethically responsible advances deserve support, and there is legislation in the Congress to give them that support. Bills supporting alternative research methods achieved majority support last year in both the House and the Senate. Earlier this spring another bill supporting alternative research won overwhelming majority support in the Senate, and I call on House leaders to pass similar legislation that would authorize additional funds for ethical stem cell research. We cannot lose the opportunity to conduct research that would give hope to those suffering from terrible diseases and help move our Nation beyond the controversies over embryo destruction. I invite policymakers and scientists to come together to solve medical problems without compromising either the high aims of science or the sanctity of human life.

S. 5, like the bill I vetoed last year, would overturn today's carefully balanced policy on stem cell research. Compelling American taxpayers to support the deliberate destruction of human embryos would be a grave mistake. I will not allow our Nation to cross this moral line. For that reason, I must veto this bill.

GEORGE W. BUSH
THE WHITE HOUSE,
June 20, 2007.

CHAPTER TWENTY-NINE

Presidential Signing Statement

Signing statements are written declarations issued by the president at the time of signing legislation that indicate to Congress how he intends to direct his administration in the implementation of the law. In practice, presidents in recent history have controversially used signing statements to reject sections of statutes without vetoing the legislation in its entirety.

PRESIDENT'S STATEMENT ON SIGNING OF
EMERGENCY SUPPLEMENTAL APPROPRIATIONS
ACT FOR DEFENSE, THE GLOBAL WAR ON
TERROR, AND HURRICANE RECOVERY, 2006

Today, I have signed into law H.R. 4939, the "Emergency Supplemental Appropriations Act for Defense, the Global War on Terror, and Hurricane Recovery, 2006." The Act provides additional resources needed to fight the war on terror, help citizens of the Gulf States recover from devastating hurricanes, and protect Americans from a potential influenza pandemic.

Sections 1209 and 2202 of the Act prohibit use of certain funds appropriated in the Act to initiate new start programs unless the congressional defense committees receive advance written notice. The Supreme Court of the United States has stated that the President's authority to classify and control access to information bearing on the national security flows from the Constitution and does not depend upon a legislative grant of authority. Although the advance notice contemplated by sections 1209 and 2202 can be provided in most situations as a matter of comity, situations may arise, especially in wartime, in which the President must act promptly under his constitutional grants of executive power and authority as Commander in Chief of the Armed Forces while protecting certain extraordinarily sensitive national security information. The executive branch shall construe these sections in a manner consistent with the constitutional authority of the President.

Subsection 1304(a) of the Act amends section 550 of Public Law 109-102 to purport to require the President to consult with committees of the Congress prior to exercising authority granted to the President by section 550. Subsection 1304(b) purports to require the Secretary of State to consult such committees prior to exercising authority under that provision. Because the President's constitutional authority to supervise the unitary executive branch and take care that the laws be faithfully executed cannot be made by law subject to a requirement to consult with congressional committees or to involve them in executive decision-making, the executive branch shall construe the references in the provisions to consulting to require only notification.

The provision under the heading, "Joint Explosive Device Defeat Fund," Department of Defense-Military, that calls for the reporting to congressional committees of information that may include highly sensitive and classified national security information, will be construed consistently with the President's constitutional responsibility to control the dissemination of such information.

The executive branch shall construe the provision in the Act under the heading "Disaster Relief," Federal Emergency Management Agency, Department of Homeland Security, that purports to require the Secretary of Homeland Security to submit a housing proposal and expenditure plan for congressional committee approval as calling solely for notification, as any other construction would be inconsistent with the constitutional principles enunciated by the Supreme Court of the United States in INS v. Chadha.

Sections 7030 through 7033 of the Act, inclusive, purport to make changes in or in relation to statements of managers that accompanied various appropriations bills reported from House–Senate conferences in the past. Also, a provision in chapter 9 of the Act under the heading "Emergency Relief Program," Federal Highway Administration, Department of Transportation, purports to give binding effect to a document not presented to the President. The executive branch shall construe these provisions in a manner consistent with the bicameral passage and presentment requirements of the Constitution for the making of a law.

GEORGE W. BUSH
THE WHITE HOUSE, 2006

CHAPTER THIRTY

Veto Bargaining

Presidents and the Politics of Negative Power

Charles Cameron

Cameron examines the role of the presidential veto in the legislative process. He contends that the veto, while sparingly used, provides the president with a powerful tool for influencing legislative outcomes. Cameron develops and tests a theoretical framework in which Congress and the president bargain over policy and finds that the veto empowers the president with the ability to extract policy concessions from Congress.

INTERBRANCH BARGAINING

The separation-of-powers system was explicitly predicated on the notion of internal balance and dynamic tension among the three branches. What passes for governance in the American system is often the product of pulling and hauling, haggling and bargaining among the three branches. Though this cliché can be found in any textbook on American government, it is only recently that political scientists have placed interbranch bargaining at the center of theories of American politics.

I study a particular kind of interbranch bargaining, one in which the president looms large: veto bargaining. I study which bills get vetoed, what happens to bills after they are vetoed, how presidents use vetoes and veto threats to

Charles Cameron. 2000. "Interbranch Bargaining," "Models of Veto Bargaining," and "Testing the Models" in Charles Cameron, *Veto Bargaining: Presidents and the Politics of Negative Power* (Cambridge University Press), pp. 2–21, 83–177. Copyright © 2000. Reprinted with the permission of Cambridge University Press.

wrest policy concessions from Congress, and their success and failure in doing so. I also study the depressing effect of the veto power on Congress's legislative productivity. In other words, I study the president and the politics of "negative power" – the consequences of an institutionalized ability to say no. The research I report is often the first systematic empirical evidence on these matters. Moreover, the *way* I approach the research is also distinctive. As an analytical institutionalist, I use "rational choice theory" to study the presidency. The investigation takes us deep into the operation of the Founders' system of separated powers, a system we must live with, for better or for worse.

Are Vetoes Worth Studying?

Time and again, vetoes have bounded onto center stage in the drama of American politics.

But the existence of memorable vetoes tells us nothing about the systematic importance of the veto as an institution. This is a critical issue. Political scientists do not collect historical curios simply for their own sake; that is antiquarianism, not social science. Our interest is understanding the main currents of the separation-of-powers system. From this perspective, the presidential veto is worth studying only if it *frequently* affects the content of *significant* legislation.

Casual observation suggests this is a hard case to make. Consider the extreme rarity of vetoes. Between 1945 and 1992, Congress presented presidents with over 17,000 public general bills (i.e., bills other than private bills, so these bills have some policy import). From this flood of bills, presidents vetoed only 434. In other words, presidents in the postwar period vetoed only 25 public general bills per 1,000 passed, while 975 per 1,000 escaped unscathed. Several presidents – Kennedy and Johnson are recent examples – vetoed only a handful of bills; some nineteenth-century presidents – John Adams and Thomas Jefferson, for instance – vetoed none at all. From the perspective of simple counts, the presidential veto appears little more than a statistical fluke.

Because vetoes are rare events, can we conclude that they resemble the strike of a lightning bolt: a dramatic and memorable event, calamitous for the unfortunate target, but hardly an important factor in everyday life? *No.* Understanding why requires thinking systematically about the structural incentives embedded in the American separation of powers system.

A Bargaining Perspective on the Veto

How can a weapon that is hardly ever used shape the content of important legislation under frequently occurring circumstances? A bargaining perspective on the veto suggests a five-step answer:

1. The institutional design specified by *the Constitution almost guarantees periods when the president and Congress differ over major policy objectives.* Those periods have become a signature of contemporary American politics. We live in an age of divided government.
2. When president and Congress disagree, *the president has a strong incentive to use the veto* if Congress presses its objectives too vigorously.
3. Accordingly, *Congress will anticipate vetoes and modify the content of legislation to head them off.* The veto power will have shaped the content of legislation without actually being used. Veto threats play an important role in this process.

4. However, congressional concessions will sometimes be insufficient to satisfy the president. When that happens, *the president may use actual vetoes not only to block legislation but to shape it.* The president may veto a bill in order to extract policy concessions in a repassed version of the vetoed bill. Congress may alter and repass the bill, groping for a version the president will accept or that can beat his veto. Because this bargaining unfolds through a series of back-and-forth actions, it constitutes *sequential veto bargaining* (SVB).
5. *The true significance of veto bargaining is masked by the passage of large numbers of unimportant bills* about which the president cares little. Among the many fewer important bills in play at any given moment, the probability of vetoes is quite high and the incidence of sequential veto bargaining substantial, at least during periods of divided government.

In sum, divided government and the politics of the veto go hand in hand. Veto bargaining is an essential part of a theory of divided government.

Policy Differences between President and Congress

A good place to begin is Figure 30.1, which displays some fundamental data on the macropolitics of American political institutions. The figure shows the occurrence of divided party government from the 24th to 104th Congress, 1835 to 1996. Of course, divided government is only a rough indicator of policy differences between president and Congress, which can emerge even under unified party government. President Carter's battle with Congress over water projects supplies an example. However, policy differences are frequent and profound during divided government, even in its less conflictual periods, such as the early Eisenhower Congresses. So the data in Figure 30.1 supply an approximate lower bound on the recurrent tendency for policy divisions to emerge between president and Congress.

In the Figure 30.1, the hash marks or "rug" at 0.0 indicates each Congress in which unified

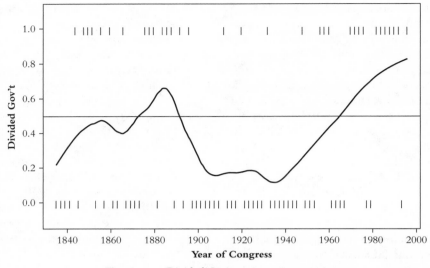

Figure 30.1. Divided Government, 1835–1996.

government prevailed. The hash marks at 1.0 show each Congress in which divided party government occurred. The undulating line is the fit from a nonparametric, locally weighted regression model of the data. Much the same effect would result from a running average of the 0–1 values but the local regression has superior statistical properties and is just as easy to interpret. Given the scoring of the data, the line indicates the estimated probability that government will be divided at each point in time. For example, the model estimates the probability of divided government at the time of the Congress of 1871–72 as 50 percent.

The regression model indicates that the great era of unified government drew to a close in the mid-1950s. A convenient watershed is the sudden appearance of a Republican president and Democratic Congress in 1955, the first such apparition since Rutherford Hayes found himself facing the 46th Congress in 1879. The model suggests that the probability of divided government continued to increase steadily throughout this new era. By the early 1960s it passed the 50 percent mark. At present, the probability of divided government is about 80 percent. Thus, we are living in the greatest period of divided government in more than a century and a half. It needs no regression model

to see that we live in the most concentrated such period since the 1880s and 1890s. One can see this simply by looking at the distribution of hash marks at 1.0.

Structural Incentives to Use the Veto

The American separation-of-powers system is rarely at war with itself. Nonetheless, the Constitution is an invitation to struggle. The checks and balances intended to stop the slide into tyranny also provide each organ with tools for bargaining over policy. In the legislative arena, the veto is the president's primary tool. The question is, Does the president have a systematic incentive to use the veto to pursue his policy goals?

A supportive piece of evidence is presidents' consistent use of the veto to further their policy objectives. Even in the earliest vetoes, before Andrew Jackson's presidency, there were clear instances in which presidents used the veto to press raw policy preferences, not merely to block laws of dubious constitutionality.

What is the source of the president's structural incentive to veto? One possibility is the public's hope that the president will counteract institutional pathologies to which Congress is particularly susceptible: "The people regard him [the president] as a check, an indispensable check, not only upon the haste and heedlessness of their representatives, the faults that the framers of the Constitution chiefly feared, but upon their tendency to yield either to pressure from any section of the constituents, or to temptations of a private nature." In modern parlance: Congress is prone to excessive pork-barreling, special interest sellouts, localistic parochialism, and sectional logrolling. The presidency is much less prone to these particular pathologies. Accordingly, a president can seek electoral advantage by using the veto to limn his own virtue against the pitch of congressional vice.

In addition, consider the strong converse of the structural incentive view: if the policy preferences of the president's electoral coalition conflict with bills passed by Congress, what incentive would restrain the veto pen? What would stop a president from pursuing his supporters' objectives even in the teeth of congressional opposition? One force might be public opinion. For example, even Roosevelt's ardent supporters found his court-packing plan hard to stomach. Thus, widespread subscription to a Whig conception of the presidency, in which the executive owes the legislature strong deference, might inhibit presidents from exercising the veto. Yet the (at least nominal) Whig Tyler was one of the greatest vetoers in history, and the decidedly Whigish William Howard Taft displayed a deft hand with the veto. The man known to his contemporaries as the "veto president" was not George Bush or even Gerald Ford. It was Grover Cleveland. A restricted notion of the office could never be maintained after Wilson and the two Roosevelts. When policy preferences differ, Congress cannot assume a compliant president. Quite the opposite.

Heading Off Vetoes

I have argued that the American Constitution sets up an institutional framework in which presidents often disagree with Congress over policy goals and have a strong incentive to use the veto. Doesn't this reasoning founder on the simple fact that presidents just don't use the veto very often (putting aside Cleveland's and FDR's vetoes of hundreds of private bills)? No. First, as I suggest later, vetoes are not as rare as they initially appear, at least under specific circumstances. But even if they were, the point would still be misdirected. Alexander Hamilton, in *Federalist 73*, explains why:

A power of this nature in the Executive [i.e., the veto] will often have a silent and unperceived, though forcible operation. When men, engaged in unjustifiable pursuits, are aware that obstructions may come from a quarter which they cannot control, they will often be restrained by the apprehension of opposition, from doing what they would with eagerness rush into, if no such external impediments were to be feared.

Hamilton is here invoking what contemporary political scientists call "the second face of power," power based on anticipated response. As has often been pointed out, actor A can influence actor B even though A takes no visible actions. The reason is that B anticipates the unpleasant response of A if B takes certain actions. Accordingly, B comports herself so as to head off A's response. It is a principle perfectly familiar from everyday life. The concept of the second face of power clearly suggests that *the veto* (a capability) can shape the content of legislation even if *vetoes* (uses of the capability) are rare.

In short, the veto does not need to be used to have an effect. Anticipation is sometimes enough. Presidents help anticipation along by making veto threats, which, somewhat amazingly, do shape legislation and head off vetoes.

Using Vetoes to Shape Legislation

There are three ways vetoes can shape legislation. First, an intransigent president can try to kill a bill. He uses the veto to force its repassage, hoping outside events derail the legislation. Second, the president can force Congress to craft a new, veto-proof version of the bill, one he may still find objectionable but nonetheless preferable to the original version. Third, the president can force Congress to rewrite the vetoed bill, offering enough concessions so he will sign the repassed bill. The president may do this even though he would have been willing to sign the first bill if it were a one-shot offer. In each of these cases the veto is a form of strategic holdout intended to shape the outcome of the interbranch bargaining. Skillful presidents can use sequential veto bargaining to impress their preferences on policy much more than static conceptions of the veto would suggest.

Each model tells a story, the story of a causal mechanism. The mechanism in the first model is the *power of anticipated response*. The model explores how the president's veto power affects the balance of power in a separation-of-powers system. The mechanism in the second model is *uncertainty*. The model shows how uncertainty tempers congressional action, allows actual vetoes to take place, and shifts the balance of power somewhat toward the president. However, this model misses an important part of the politics of the veto for it cannot explain how vetoes wrest policy concessions from Congress. The mechanism in the third model is *strategic reputation building*, the deliberate manipulation of beliefs through vetoes. This model addresses the veto and congressional policy concessions.

The Basic Model: The Second Face of Power Revisited

The Logic of Anticipation
Power can work through anticipation, so a power relationship may exist even absent visible compulsion. This idea is inherently game theoretic, so it seems natural to express it in a simple game, as shown in Figure 30.2. Though the situation is generic, I tell the story in terms of vetoes.

As shown in Figure 30.2, Congress moves first and has two choices: pass version 1 of a bill or pass a modified version, version 2. (The restriction to two choices is just to keep the example simple; in a few paragraphs I introduce a more flexible way to represent the content of bills.) The president has the next move regardless of which bill is passed. He can either veto the bill or accept it. In this tinker-toy version of

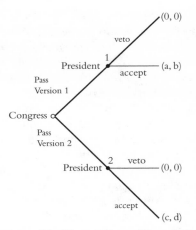

Figure 30.2. The "Second Face of Power" Game.

veto politics, neither overriding nor repassing is possible, so the game ends after the president's action. Payoffs for each player under the four possible outcomes are shown by the ordered pairs at the tips of the game tree. The first number indicates Congress's payoff, the second the president's. Because a veto enforces the status quo, I scale the payoffs so that both players value the status quo at zero. Also, to keep things interesting, assume the president and Congress potentially could agree on a bill both prefer to the status quo. However, they disagree over the best alternative. In fact, to sharpen the possible disagreement, assume the president prefers the status quo to Congress's most preferred policy. Let us say version 1 of the bill reflects Congress's preferred policy while version 2 better reflects the president's. In accord with this underlying story, then, $0 < c < a$ and $b < 0 < d$.

Will the players see an obvious way to play this game? One argument, based on the solution concept known as "subgame perfection," suggests they should. This solution concept requires each player to maximize his or her expected payoff. It requires the president to take his best possible action for *any* bill passed by Congress. And it assumes Congress can correctly anticipate the president's actions regardless of which bill is passed.

Suppose the president finds himself at the node "1." His choice at that point is either to veto version 1 of the bill, yielding a payoff of 0, or accept it, yielding the inferior payoff b. Hence, he will veto. Conversely, suppose he finds himself at the node labeled "2." Since $d > 0$ he will accept version 2 of the bill. *If Congress understands what the president will do*, then it knows that its real choice is between passing version 1 and receiving a payoff of 0, and passing version 2 and receiving a payoff of c. Hence, it will pass version 2. The president need not make an explicit veto threat nor even take any action; the truly interesting action is tasking place purely through congressional anticipation of presidential actions. Consequently, all we will see is Congress passing bills acceptable to the president and the president signing them. We might mistakely interpret this placid scene as presidential acquiescence to congressional activism! But in fact the implicit threat of a veto at node 1 compels Congress's choice of bill. This very simple model suggests how *the veto* (a capability) can shape the content of legislation even if *vetoes* (uses of the capability) are rare.

Simple as it is, the model incorporates three of the four building blocks needed to model veto bargaining: actors, sequence, and information. The actors are the president and Congress. The sequence of play is shown in Figure 30.2: Congress selects a bill, the president vetoes. (I examine much more complicated sequences shortly.) The model's information structure is extremely simple: both players know everything in the game that is worth knowing. The ability of Congress to forecast the president's actions is critical for the proposed solution to the game.

A fourth element is missing from the model, however: *policy*. Policy is central to veto bargaining. To address it, the model needs a device for representing policies. An extraordinarily useful device is the policy space.

Policy and Policy Preferences

Policy spaces are a hallmark of rational choice institutionalism. They are routinely used in models of Congress, the courts, and bureaucracy. Their use is one of the features that distinguish models of political settings from those of economic ones.

The basic idea is extremely simple and is best introduced through an example. Consider the unit interval, that is, a line whose origin is zero and whose terminus is one. Points in this unidimensional policy space could correspond to, for example, tax or tariff rates ranging from 0 to 100 percent. More generally, points on a line can represent quantities such as expenditures. In fact, points on a line can even represent more qualitative matters, such as "degree of restrictions on abortion" or "support for human rights."

Occasionally there are bills that deal only with a single ratelike quantity, for example, a routine adjustment to the minimum wage or a simple authorization. But most bills make many changes simultaneously. A literal representation of [such legislation] would require several dimensions, one for each qualitatively distinct facet. Literal representations of extremely complex legislation, by no means uncommon on Capitol Hill, would require hundreds or perhaps even thousands of dimensions.

Most models of interbranch bargaining employ only one dimension; none employs thousands. Is this justifiable? On empirical grounds, yes. Abundant empirical evidence indicates that a single dimension acounts for around 85 percent or so of the variance in roll call voting. This dimension corresponds pretty clearly to "liberalism–conservatism." In other words, most roll call voting in the House and Senate looks almost as if individual bills or amendments came labeled with a liberalism–conservatism index, and that is sufficent information for congressmen casting a yea and a nay.

I still need to define the policy preferences of the president and Congress. Again following the logic of structural incentives, I assume they have the sort of preferences conceived in decision theory. Specifically, I assume their preferences are well represented by "single-peaked" utility functions (see Figure 30.3). Experience has shown this to be a sensible modeling choice in political settings. Actors with single-peaked utility functions have most-preferred policies, with the attractiveness of other policies

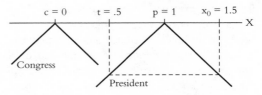

Figure 30.3. Preferences in a Spatial Setting.

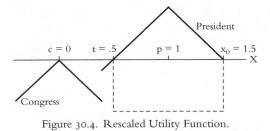

Figure 30.4. Rescaled Utility Function.

declining as they diverge more and more from the most-preferred policy. For example, you may have a preferred level of expenditures on defense policy; both underspending and over-spending are less attractive. Figure 30.3 illustrates a policy space and associated preferences. The horizontal line X is the unidimensional policy space. The vertical dimension represents "utility," the happiness (as it were) of the players. The utility of any point in the policy space to either the president or Congress can be read from their utility functions. For example, the utility to Congress of a policy located at 0 is just 0, while that of one located at 1 is -1. For any two points a and b on the line, the utility function indicates whether the actor prefers a to b or is indifferent between them.

Also shown in Figure 30.3 is a special point, x_0, the *status quo*. The status quo represents the current policy, which will continue unless the players enact a new one. Not surprisingly, the location of the status quo often has a profound effect on the nature of veto bargaining.

An important feature of single-peaked utility functions is that for any point x, there is another point x' that is *utility equivalent* to x. Of particular interest is the point utility equivalent to the status quo x_0, especially for the president.

It proves extremely helpful to rescale the president's utility function in terms of the utility equivalent points. So long as the rescaled function does not alter the preference relationship between different points on the line, the rescaled function represents the president's preferences just as well as the original one. The rescaling works as follows. Without altering its shape, slide the entire function straight upward until one end of the "tent" is anchored at x_0, the status quo (see Figure 30.4).

This utility function is constructed so the point that is utility equivalent to the status quo is always given by the point t.

The Basic Model

I can now extend the game in Figure 30.2 into a real model of the veto. The sequence of play remains the same: Congress makes a single and final take-it-or-leave-it offer of a bill with a particular ideological tenor (i.e., a given spatial location in X). The president then accepts it or vetoes it. The game ends and the players receive payoffs as specified by the utility functions. In this extremely simple model, vetoes really are bullets and are purely reactive.

The graphical device in Figure 30.5 is extremely helpful for conveying some intuition about veto bargaining in this setting. Consider all the policies the president considers as good or better than the status quo, that is, all the policies as close or closer to his ideal point than x_0. This set of policies is the president's *preferred set,* $\wp_p$. As shown in Figure 30.5, it is an interval of the line, namely $[t, x_0]$ (this notation is read: the line segment from t to x_0, inclusive). Since this is a one-shot game, the president should accept any offer in this interval, assuming all he cares about is attaining the best possible final policy. The preferred set of Congress, $\wp_c$, is defined similarly and is thus $[-x_0, x_0]$. The *intersection* of the two preferred sets, that is, $\wp_c \cap \wp_p$, is just the overlapping portions of the two preferred sets. In the figure, this is the line segment $[t, x_0]$. This set contains all the points *both* players prefer to the status quo. In voting games the intersection of the relevant preferred sets is often called the *win set*. At least under complete and perfect information (as assumed in the basic model), it seems natural to seek the outcome of

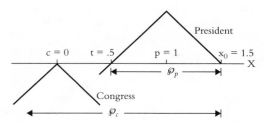

Figure 30.5. Preferred Sets in the Basic Model.

veto bargaining in the win set since Congress has no incentive to make an offer it prefers less than the status quo and the president has no incentive to accept an offer he likes less than the status quo (excluding veto overrides for the moment). All such points are found in the win set. Moreover, since Congress gets to select the bill while the president can do nothing except accept or veto, a reasonable conjecture is that Congress will pick from the win set the best possible bill from its perspective. It is not hard to deduce which bill this will be. However, I will be fairly methodical in working through this deduction.

There are three cases which are neatly characterized by the location of t. The location of t can be thought of as the president's *type*. The president's type t may take any value on a continuum, depending on the location of the status quo and the president's ideal point. But each type falls into one of three classes. The first is shown in the top panel of Figure 30.6. The critical feature of this case is that $t \leq c$ so Congress's ideal point lies in the president's preferred set. (Note that the president's ideal point p may be greater or less than c; it makes no difference so long as $t \leq c$). Accordingly, presidents of this type are willing to accept a bill located at Congress's ideal policy. Such presidents are *accommodating*. Since Congress can do no better than to offer its ideal policy, which accommodators surely accept, the solution concept specifies $x = c$ as the prediction when $t < c$.

The second case is shown in the middle panel of Figure 30.6. The defining feature of this case is that $c < t \leq x_0$. Congress's ideal point c no longer lies within the win set, here the interval $[t, x_0]$. Offering a bill at c would be futile since the president would veto it, leaving Congress with the undesirable status quo. From Congress's perspective, the best feasible policy is t, which the president would accept. Thus, the solution concept specifies $x = t$. Since presidents of the type $c < t \leq x_0$ are not accommodating but will accept some proposals [they are] *compromising*.

The final case occurs when $c < x_0 < t$, as shown in the bottom panel of the figure. In this case, the win set is composed of a single

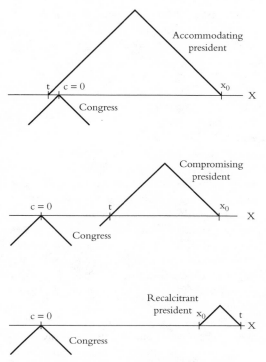

Figure 30.6. Three Cases in the Basic Model.

element, the status quo x_0. It matters naught what Congress offers; policy is deadlocked.

Veto Overrides in the Basic Model

It is extremely easy to expand the model to include the possibility of veto overrides. Simply add a third player to the game, the veto override player (the "v-player"). This player occupies a particular place within Congress: precisely two-thirds of the members have ideal points to her left (remember that I consistently assume $c = 0$ and $x_0 > 0$). Consequently, if the veto override player is exactly indifferent between a bill and the status quo, two-thirds of Congress prefers the bill and one-third prefers the status quo. As a result, veto override attempts succeed or fail according to the vote of the veto override player. If $1/3 + 1$ of congressmen lie to the right of the status quo, so does the veto override player. In this configuration, Congress cannot pass a veto-proof bill that it prefers to the status quo. But otherwise it can.

Adding the veto override player to the model is straightforward. First scale the v-player's utility function just like the president's. However, denote the point that is utility equivalent to the status quo for the override player by τ (tau) rather than t (to keep the two points distinct). The veto override player's "type" is thus given by the location of tau. Given this scaling, we can employ exactly the same analysis as in the basic game.

To see the difference imposed by a qualified rather than absolute veto, consider the following scenario: the president is compromising but just barely. But the override player is much more compromising. Imagine, for instance, Truman confronting the Republican 80th Congress over the formation of labor policy. The status quo had been set during the New Deal, establishing a policy strongly supportive of labor unions. The president was a proponent of this policy, though he was willing to put some restrictions on unions' ability to strike. But the Republican Congress, responding to a wave of strikes, was determined to clip the wings of the high-flying labor movement. Figure 30.7 represents this situation, using the basic model with veto overrides.

How much power would the two sides exercise over the outcome? The president's willingness to veto the legislation prevents the hostile Congress from passing its most preferred bill. So $x = c$ is not feasible. Instead, Congress must craft a veto-proof bill if it is to accomplish anything. Thus, the location of the veto override player is critical. Historically, the veto override player in the 80th Congress was often a moderate Democrat. According to the model, then, the Republican leadership and the bill's floor managers will try to pass a bill that makes this member indifferent between the bill and the existing policy. Therefore, they will try to place the bill exactly at τ. If the bill is located at this

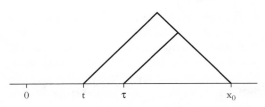

Figure 30.8. The Veto Override Player May Be Irrelevant.

strategic position, the model predicts, it will be enacted into law even over the president's veto.

This example shows how the qualified veto can shift the balance of power toward Congress, relative to an absolute veto. For if Figure 30.7 fairly represents the situation and the president had an absolute veto, he could block any move from the status quo toward Congress that went farther than t. But the qualified veto would still restrict Congress to a bill at τ rather than c.

The qualified veto does not *necessarily* reduce the power of the president, relative to an absolute veto. For example, consider Figure 30.8, which may reasonably represent the confrontation between President Clinton and the Republican 104th Congress over welfare reform and similar issues. The veto override player was, plausibly, a liberal Democrat, while the president was a more moderate Democrat. Thus, tau (the key location for an override attempt) may have been to the right of t (the key location for presidential approval). If so, Congress could craft a veto-proof bill (if $\tau \leq x_0$) but could do better by finding a bill the president would (grudgingly) sign. The model predicts the outcome here to be identical to that under an absolute veto.

Evaluating the Basic Model

The basic model is much more capacious than the elementary second face of power game. Unlike that game, it indicates the policy content of bills during veto bargaining. It identifies conditions when veto power will emerge and conditions when it won't. It specifies the factors that determine the magnitude of veto power, when it does emerge. It extends easily to study the impact of a qualified rather than an absolute veto. Most important, its elaboration of the logic of the veto seems persuasive, at least so far as it goes.

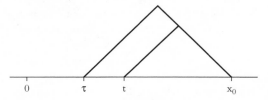

Figure 30.7. Truman Confronts the 80th Congress over Labor Legislation.

We can reject the basic model *as a model of veto bargaining* without any elaborate statistical tests at all. The problem is, the model predicts we should see no vetoes. But, of course, we do.

The way to resolve this "paradox" is to abandon the assumption of complete and perfect information. I pursue this idea in the next section.

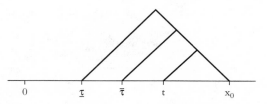

Figure 30.9. Incomplete Information about the Veto Override Player.

The Override Game

The move from the basic model – a model of the veto as a *capability* – to a model of active *veto bargaining* requires two new elements: incomplete information and repeated play.

Incomplete Information

The model introduced in this section, the override model, incorporates incomplete information by making the president and Congress somewhat uncertain about the location of the veto override player. The source of this uncertainty is the unpredictable identity of the veto override player. Although the party whips work hard to "count noses" and get their members to the floor, it is never entirely certain who will be present, and a few members may unexpectedly change their votes from what was anticipated. The ability of the president to sway undecided voters may not be clear in advance, even to himself. As a result, there can be some uncertainty about just who the critical override player will be. And consequently, there may be some doubt whether a bill is actually veto-proof.

In the previous section I introduced the notion of the veto player's "type," indicated by the location of tau, the point she finds utility equivalent to the status quo. Suppose, given the situation, there are several representatives – say, a dozen – who could be the override player, depending on who is actually present. Denote the lowest utility equivalent point among these representatives as $\underline{\tau}$ and the highest as $\overline{\tau}$. There is some probability that each of the twelve representatives with τ's between $\underline{\tau}$ and $\overline{\tau}$ could turn out to be the veto override player, but the probability that a representative with higher or lower $\overline{\tau}$ could be the key player is effectively zero. For a particular potential v-player, call the proba-

bility that he is the actual override player $f(\tau)$. The probabilities across the twelve possible "v-players" sum to one. This maneuver involves the addition of a new player, "Nature," who begins the game by drawing one of the possible veto players using these probabilities. The identity of the key player will not be revealed until the critical moment, but if the other players know the drawing probabilities – and it is assumed they do – the players can factor them into their calculations.

Even without solving the model, we can now see how an actual veto could occur. Suppose the configuration resembles the one I discussed between Truman and the 80th Congress but with a range of possible override players. This configuration is illustrated in Figure 30.9. If Congress makes a hardball offer, it would pass a bill in the interval $[\underline{\tau}, \overline{\tau}]$, since a lower offer would be futile and a higher offer needlessly accommodating. Because this interval lies outside the president's preferred set he might be inclined to veto the bill, especially since the veto player may sustain the veto (unless the offer is located at $\overline{\tau}$).

Uncertainty about τ does not necessarily imply an override attempt. In some configurations override attempts would definitely not occur. For example, if in Figure 30.9 the president's utility equivalent point t lay to the left of that of the lowest override players (i.e., if $t < \underline{\tau}$), then Congress would not need to pass a veto-proof bill. It could find a better bill (from its perspective) that the president would accept.

Dynamics

I introduce repeated play in the simplest possible way: an episode of veto bargaining can go through two iterations or rounds. Congress begins by passing a bill; the president can veto it

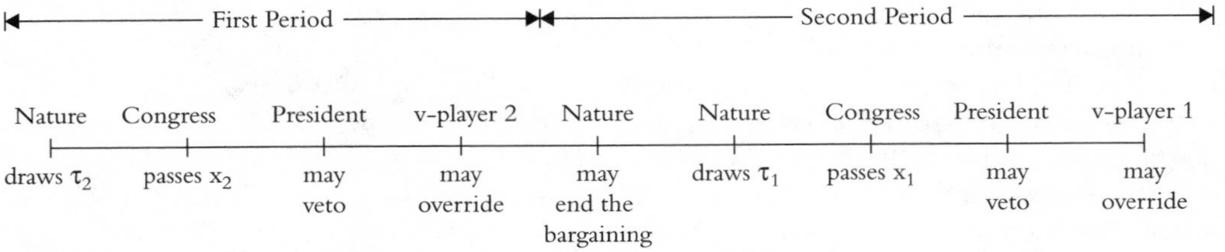

| First Period | | | | Second Period | | | | |

Nature   Congress   President   v-player 2   Nature   Nature   Congress   President   v-player 1

draws τ_2 passes x_2 may   may   may   draws τ_1 passes x_1 may   may
                              veto   override   end the   veto   override
                                                        bargaining

Figure 30.10. Sequence of Play in the Override Game.

or accept it; then the veto player can override or sustain the veto. I incorporate [the] possibility [that bargaining may break down at this point] by allowing "Nature" to terminate the bargaining, with probability q. Then, if bargaining does not break down, Congress repasses the vetoed bill, altering its content if it wishes. The president may reveto it if he chooses; and the override player again opts to sustain or override. The game terminates with the players receiving payoffs according to the policy in place at the end of the game. This sequence could be extended to any number of rounds, but two is sufficient to illustrate the impact of uncertainty on the dynamics of bargaining. Figure 30.10 shows the sequence of play, taking into account the [incomplete information manuever].

As indicated in Figure 30.10, the two-period game implies two veto override players, one in the first round and one in the second. These two need not, and probably would not, be the same person. Moreover, the first veto player wouldn't know any more about the identity of the second veto player than anyone else. She must factor this uncertainty into her override decision. Should she sustain a veto in round 1 in the hope of getting a better bill in round 2? Perhaps the new override player will sustain a veto of that better bill! She will have to calculate carefully.

Equilibrium Offers

What bills will Congress pass in the two-round game? Given the evidence, one might suspect that Congress will begin with a "tough" offer. Then, if the first bill is vetoed and the veto is sustained, Congress might make a concession. However, in the override model this intuition is incorrect.

In working out a solution to the game I again need to specify a solution concept. In this game,

the actors have beliefs about the probable location of the next τ. A sensible solution concept requires the players always to act in accord with their current beliefs. But where do the beliefs come from? A special feature of this game is that players do not learn anything about the location of the second v-player from what they observe in the first round. This follows from the fact that the two override attempts are really separate events (technically, Nature's draws are independent of one another). So beliefs about the current τ always come straight from the distribution of v-player types.

It is easiest to see what will happen in the second round (if we assume bargaining gets that far), so I begin there. Since the second bill is a take-it-or-leave-it offer, both the second veto override player and the president will act in accord with their preferred sets: the v-player will override only if the second bill is as good or better for her than the status quo, and the president will accept the bill only if it is as good or better for him than the status quo. Given the configuration in Figure 30.9, Congress need never offer a second bill greater than $\bar{\tau}$, since this bill is assuredly veto-proof. Nor will it ever make an offer lower than $\underline{\tau}$, since, if it did, the president would veto and all possible override players would sustain the president's veto. Such a low offer, though attractive to Congress, would surely fail. It is possible to calculate exactly the offer a utility-maximizing Congress would make. Taking into account the uncertainty about the location of the second veto override player, Congress's second offer will "split the difference" between the lowest possible type and the status quo, unless the status quo is quite far away, in which case it will offer a bill that is surely veto-proof (since a sustained veto would yield such an unpleasant outcome.)

Now, what will happen in the first round? The following argument supplies the intuition. Consider the veto override player. Any type who would accept the second offer will definitely accept a similar offer in the first round, since to turn it down is to risk receiving the status quo in the event of a bargaining breakdown, while gaining nothing from the risk. Conversely, any type who would reject the second offer will also reject an identical offer in the first round, since such a type prefers the status quo to the offer. In other words, type-by-type, the strategy of the first v-player must be identical to that of the second v-player. Similarly, the strategy of the president must be the same in the first round as the second round. Since the strategies of the other players are the same and Congress's information about the veto player is the same in both rounds, if x^* is the optimal offer in the second round, it must also be the optimal offer in the first round. In short, the override model predicts that *Congress passes the same bill twice; it will not make concessions.*

Sequential Veto Bargaining

Adding Presidential Reputation to the Models

A key question must be answered: what is the president's reputation *about*? What entity or variable is the subject of incomplete information? From the president's perspective, an effective reputation for "skill and will" must be such as to "induce as much uncertainty as possible about the consequences of ignoring what he [the president] wants. If he cannot make men think him bound to win, his need is to keep them from thinking they can cross him without risk, or that they can be sure what risks they run."

Consider how one builds a useful reputation in some other setting, for example when bargaining over a car or in a weekend bazaar. You try to create the impression that the merchandise is worth little to you. For example, you may feign to leave the shop when the merchant announces his opening price. You lament your limited budget. In short, you don't try to create a reputation as a "tough bargainer." You *become* a

tough bargainer by creating the impression you have a naturally low "striking price," the highest price you would possibly agree to. If the merchant believes your striking price is truly low, he will come down in price if he wants to sell.

What is the equivalent of the president's striking price in bargaining with Congress? It is the president's reservation policy, the point beyond which he will not go because he would rather veto and retain the status quo. In the spatial framework, it is exactly t, the point utility-equivalent to the status quo. The president's willingness to veto depends critically on the location of the bill relative to t. But Congress will often be somewhat uncertain where t lies. Over the course of a bargaining episode, the president may be able to turn this uncertainty to his advantage.

The Sequential Veto Bargaining Model

Much of the apparatus I developed for the override game transfers directly to sequential veto bargaining (SVB). Now, however, Congress's uncertainty concerns the president's policy preferences, which, of course, the president himself knows perfectly well. The [incomplete information] maneuver provides a method to capture Congress's uncertainty about the president's policy preferences. So at the beginning of the game let t be drawn from the interval $[\underline{t}, \bar{t}]$ using the common-knowledge distribution $F(t)$, the same uniform distribution as in the override game. The president knows his own type t, which remains fixed for the entire game, but Congress does not.

The play of the SVB game depends heavily on the location of $[\underline{t}, \bar{t}]$ relative to the override player's reservation policy and Congress's ideal point $c = 0$. For the moment assume the configuration shown in Figure 30.11, that is, $0 \leq \underline{t}$

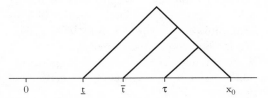

Figure 30.11. Sequential Veto Bargaining: The All Compromisers Case.

and $\overline{t} \leq \tau$. Allow the same type of dynamics as before: the game moves through two rounds of bargaining, with the possibility of a breakdown in bargaining after an initial veto.

All seems similar to the override game, except one thing: the president's true type t is fixed throughout the game, while the identity of the override player varied from round to round – a seemingly small difference but sufficient to transform the strategic situation. Whatever Congress learns about the president in the first round can and will be used in the second round. The president thus has an incentive to build a policy reputation in the first round, in order to extract a better bill in the second.

To see how this might work, picture Congress in the first round of a bargaining episode. Congress begins with a notion of the range of possible presidential preferences and so bases the content of its initial bill on its expectations about what the president might accept. Congress will not pass a bill every likely type of president would veto – such a bill would be pointless. Nor is it likely (except under special circumstances, detailed shortly) to pass a bill the president would surely sign whatever his true preferences. To do so would be to yield too much. Thus, Congress is likely to pass a tough bill but one with a reasonable chance of enactment. Suppose, though, the president vetoes the bill. How will this affect his policy reputation? If the president had been sufficiently accommodating, he would have accepted the initial bill rather than risk a breakdown and receipt of the status quo. Because the president did not accept the bill, Congress can be quite sure the president did *not* have those preferences. In other words, Congress can screen out some types of presidential preferences after seeing a veto. Given the screening, Congress will see the president as somewhat "tougher" than it did before (in the sense that his policy preferences cannot be very accommodating). The content of the second bill, if Congress gets the chance to enact it, will reflect this new understanding of the president's policy preferences. Accordingly, the second bill will incorporate policy concessions.

In the first round of bargaining the president can anticipate what Congress will offer in the second round, if he vetoes the first bill. Depending on his preferences, the president may find the second bill, if it includes concessions, more attractive than the first bill. In fact, it may be so attractive that he is willing to risk a breakdown in order to alter his policy reputation and thus extract the better bill from Congress. Such a president would engage in a *strategic veto* in the first round. But can this work if Congress knows the president has the temptation to do so?

Optimal Bills and Strategic Vetoes

By this point, the strategies of president and Congress in the second round will be familiar. Since the second bill is a take-it-or-leave-it offer, the president will veto it only if it lies outside his preferred set. Let us say that Congress, based upon its initial bill and a presidential veto, has screened out all types with t's less than a particular value, call it t_2. So in the second round, Congress believes the president's type definitely falls somewhere in the range $[t_2, \overline{t}]$. [Congress's second offer will then be] an average of the lower bound on types and the status quo, unless the status quo is quite distant [, which is exactly the form of the offer in the override game.]

Determining the president's strategy in the first round is straightforward. Call the offer in the first round x_2 (meaning, the offer occurs when two opportunities for vetoes remain) and that in the second round x_1 (meaning, only one opportunity for a veto remains). The president, seeing x_2, is able to estimate that Congress will pass x_1 in the second round in the event of a veto, as long as bargaining did not break down. Then there would be a type who is exactly indifferent between accepting the bird in the hand, x_2, and the gamble created by a veto, that is, between receiving the unattractive status quo and the quite desirable bird in the bush, x_1. Call this exactly indifferent type t_2.

Figure 30.12 illustrates such an indifferent type. He is presented the first offer, x_2, so if he accepts it he certainly has $V(x_2)$. If he rejects it, he may be offered x_1, which is more attractive. But it is a risky prospect, for with probability q he receives instead the status quo, x_0. Type t_2 is exactly indifferent between the two choices. Critically, all presidential types *lower* than t_2

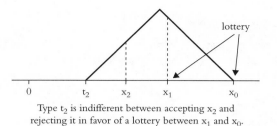

Type t_2 is indifferent between accepting x_2 and rejecting it in favor of a lottery between x_1 and x_0.

Figure 30.12. The Indifferent Type.

prefer the first offer and so accept it, while all types higher than t_2 prefer the gamble and so veto the first bill. Hence, the president's strategy in the first round is simple: accept the first bill if $t \leq t_2$ but otherwise veto. If Congress understands this strategy, and can follow the president's reasoning, then it knows that $t > t_2$ if it sees a veto in the first round.

In the SVB model, Congress makes concessions in repassed bills; there is a positive probability the president accepts each bill; and there is a positive probability no offer is accepted (unless the final offer equals $\bar{t}$) even if bargaining does not break down. In the first period, some types of president are willing to strategically veto, that is, to veto a bill they prefer to the status quo.

The process of reputation building [explains] "the new Eisenhower" of 1959. Through miscues and internal dissension, Eisenhower appeared to Congress in 1957–58 as a likely accommodator, or not a very distant compromiser, particularly in fields like education or welfare. Congress moved to take advantage of the policy opportunity. But a stunning set of vetoes in 1959 forced Congress to change its view: the president was indeed committed to a restrictive budget, low taxes, and parsimonious government. His vetoes, along with his rhetoric, recast his reputation.

Conclusion

We now have a framework for thinking about override attempts, and a framework for analyzing sequential veto bargaining.

The question remains: can the models explain the observed patterns in real veto bargaining?

TESTING THE MODELS

I use the models to generate predictions. Then I test the predictions using data. The predictions deal with three distinctively different phenomena: concessions, deadlines, and the legislative productivity of Congress.

The legislative histories often reveal concessions in successors to vetoed bills, though sometimes the record is ambiguous and hard to interpret. The prevalence of concessions supplied the starting place for the model of sequential veto bargaining. Is there additional support for the fundamental "stylized fact" targeted by the model? Beyond this, do patterns in concessions conform to the predictions of the models? In this chapter I combine data on roll call votes on initial and successor bills with estimates of legislators' preferences, derived from all roll call votes, to derive estimates of the direction and magnitude of policy concessions between successive bills in veto chains. These new data on concessions confirm the importance of concessions in veto bargaining and provide several tests of the game theoretic models.

A strong test for a model comes from predictions about a hitherto unstudied phenomenon. The bargaining models make several striking predictions about a phenomenon that political scientists have not previously studied: changes in the probability of vetoes immediately before presidential elections, a "deadline effect." Both the sequential veto bargaining model and the override model predict, first, that the probability of vetoes of important legislation should decrease immediately before a presidential election under divided government. Second, they predict that this deadline effect should be smaller for less important legislation. Finally, the sequential veto bargaining model predicts that immediately before a presidential election the probability of a veto for very important and less important bills should be the same. I present new data on deadline effects that corroborate the predictions for important and routine legislation.

Another tough test for a model is using it to gain leverage on a problem far from the model's domain of initial success. In the third section I

338 Charles Cameron

examine a phenomenon, the legislative productivity of Congress, that has received increased attention. At first glance vetoes seem likely to exert only a modest effect on the legislative productivity of Congress, since vetoes kill so few pieces of landmark legislation. Although full-blown models of legislative productivity lie outside the scope of this book, the models of interbranch bargaining imply that *anticipation* of vetoes, the "second face of power," should depress production of important bills during divided government, relative to unified government.

Concessions During Sequential Veto Bargaining

The Prediction

I examine three predictions. First, in general, the observed *direction* of concessions should reverse depending on whether the president is a Republican or a Democrat. The two configurations constitute distinctly different "regimes," in the parlance of statistics. The second prediction, derived from the override model, constitutes an exception to the first prediction: when successive bills in a chain are both clearly geared for an override attempt, observed concessions should be very small. Putting the two predictions together yields a third prediction: concessions should be larger when the bills in a chain are clearly not geared for an override attempt than when they are.

Method and Data

The Cut-Point Method for Measuring Concessions. The principal empirical difficulty in testing these predictions is finding a convincing measure of the policy content of the bills. Identifying a metric for measuring policy is no simple task.

A further problem remains even if a natural metric is clear. The problem concerns comparability across veto chains. How can one compare concessions in base-closing notification periods with concessions in raising the minimum wage?

Fortunately, common metrics emerge from multidimensional scaling of congressional roll

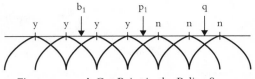

Figure 30.13. A Cut Point in the Policy Space.

call votes. Such scalings use roll call votes to place congressmen in hypothesized policy spaces. Most roll call voting is compatible with fixed positions on a single issue dimension; the dimension roughly corresponds to liberalism-conservatism (occasionally a second dimension, related to race, appears to be at play). This empirical finding suggests a way to study policy concessions during veto bargaining.

To see the logic of the method, consider Figure 30.13. The figure indicates the location of seven congressmen in an issue space. Shown for purposes of illustration are a status quo and bill, represented by points on the line. If each congressman makes a decision to vote for the bill or against it according to the indicated utility functions then there will be a cut point p in the policy space located between the bill and the status quo: all congressmen to one side of the cut point will vote in favor of the bill and all those on the other side will vote in favor of the status quo.

Now suppose the president vetoes the bill in Figure 30.13 and Congress passes a subsequent bill so the two bills form a veto chain. In practice one cannot locate either bill or the status quo in the hypothesized policy space on the basis of bill content. The status quo, however, will have remained fixed between the two bills since no legislation has passed (if one assumes that no exogenous changes occur to the status quo). Hence, *the location of the second cut point relative to the first provides a measure of the direction and magnitude of the change in content between the two bills.* This process is illustrated in Figure 30.14.

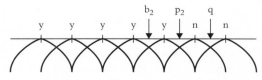

Figure 30.14. Measuring Concessions.

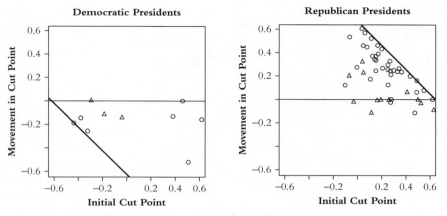

Figure 30.15. Concessions during Veto Bargaining.

Somewhat surprisingly, one need not place bills or status quos in the policy space in order to study the direction and approximate magnitude of concessions. Instead, one can measure concessions by matching roll call votes with ideology scores and locating cut points.

Data. The roll call data were matched with ideological scores for each House and Senate member, depending on the chamber in which the votes took place. For this purpose we employed "common space" NOMINATE scores.

To derive the cut points, we devised a computer program that sorts the yeas and nays in a roll call vote in ascending order of ideology scores. The program then locates the cut point or cut points that minimize the number of misclassified votes (e.g., if we assume all votes to the left of the hypothesized cut point are yeas and all to the right are nays).

Results

Figure 30.15 presents the cut point measures of concessions. In each panel, the horizontal axis indicates the location of the initial cut point. The vertical axis shows the movement in the cut point — that is, it is the value of the second cut point minus the value of the first cut point. Thus, points that lie *above* the zero line indicate a pair of bills in a veto chain with movement in the *conservative* direction between the successive bills. Points below the zero line indicate a

pair of bills in a veto chain with movement in the *liberal* direction between the successive bills. The diagonal lines show a censoring line – that is, given the initial cut point and the maximum or minimum possible value in the policy space, the line shows the largest possible movement in the subsequent cut point that could possibly be observed. Points on or abutting the diagonal line show pairs of bills in which maximal movement occurred (in other words, the vote on the second bill was unanimous). Triangles indicate pairs of bills in which not only the first but the second bill was vetoed.

The figure shows quite dramatically the regime switching predicted by the model. That is, all the veto chains that occurred during Democratic administrations lie at or below the zero line, indicating concessions in the liberal direction. Almost all the veto chains that occurred during Republican administrations lie at or above the zero line, indicating concessions in the conservative direction (all these observations come from periods of divided government). The censoring that patently affects many of the data points in the Republican regime and a few points in the Democratic regime tends to reduce the apparent size of concessions. Nonetheless, the mean concession in the Republican regime is .20 while that in the Democratic regime is −.17, a difference in means that is very highly statistically significant ($p = 0$).

Deadlines and the Probability of Vetoes

The Predictions

Why does the model predict a deadline effect? The prediction is easier to understand in the override model. It would be senseless to schedule a bill geared for an override in the final days of a Congress since the president can simply pocket-veto the bill. Such a bill must be scheduled earlier in the session; if it cannot be, the content of the bill must be altered to make presidential acceptance more likely. Since congressmen will shift such veto-prone bills from the final days of the session into the earlier period, veto rates in the later period should be lower than in the earlier period.

The sequential veto bargaining model also predicts a drop in the probability of a veto, but the mechanism is more subtle. In the SVB model, bargaining takes place in the shadow of an electoral deadline. In the last period, strategic turndowns no longer make sense for the president – there is no more value in building a reputation for the future because "the future is now." This factor makes the president more inclined to accept Congress's offers. There are two countervailing forces, however. First, Congress will anticipate the president's greater receptivity and toughen its offers, thereby increasing the probability of veto. Second, Congress can now make a real take-it-or-leave-it offer to the president, since it is the last period. This offer will be tougher than it would be absent the deadline, and may also provoke a veto. Given the presence of contending effects – greater willingness to accept offers but a greater propensity to make tougher offers – one can imagine the probability of vetoes falling, rising, or remaining the same. Securing a definite prediction requires actually solving the equations governing offers and acceptances. When one does, one finds that the model predicts tougher offers but not ones so tough they completely offset the president's greater propensity to accept bills. In other words, the probability of vetoes should *fall* in the last period.

Data

The data consist of all bills presented to the president in the congressional sessions terminating in a year of a presidential election, during divided government in the postwar period. That is, they consist of all bills presented to the president in the sessions of 1948, 1956, 1960, 1972, 1976, 1984, 1988, and 1992. During these years, Congress enacted 3,558 public laws and presidents vetoed 128 public bills. However, 15 of the vetoes were overridden. Hence, the number of bills presented to the president was $3,558 + 128 - 15 = 3671$ with an overall veto rate of $128/3671 = 3.5$ percent.

I operationalize the "final period" as the final two weeks of the sessions in question. Determining which bills were presented to the president in the last two weeks of these sessions (presented, not signed into law during that period) turns out to be surprisingly difficult. My best estimate is that 2,090 bills or 57 percent were presented to the president "early" in those sessions (before the last 2 weeks) and 1,577 bills or 43 percent were presented "late" in the sessions (during the last two weeks). These figures testify to the frenetic pace of lawmaking at the close of congressional sessions.

Results

Table 30.1 indicates the number of bills presented to the president, vetoes, and veto rates in years with divided government and presidential elections. In Table 30.1 I combine significance categories A and B in order to achieve enough observations for reliable results.

Overall, as shown in Table 30.1, the veto rate early in the congressional sessions in question was about 3 percent while that in the last two weeks of the session rose somewhat, to 5 percent – the opposite of the supposed deadline effect. In point of fact, though, the models' predictions concern deadline effects *within* and *across* significance classes. The data in the table need a closer look.

The first prediction is that, *for important legislation*, the probability of a veto should fall in the last period. For the most important legislation, levels A and B, the veto rate during the bulk of the session was 27 percent. During the last two weeks it fell to 9 percent, a decrease of 18 percentage points or two-thirds.

The model also predicts that the deadline effect – the decrease in veto rates – should be

Table 30.1. *Bills Presented, Vetoes, and Veto Rates Early Versus Late in Congressional Sessions*

Significance	Early in Session Bills Presented	Vetoes	Veto Rate	Late in Session Bills Presented	Vetoes	Veto Rate	Deadline Effect
A or B	52	14	27%	33	3	9%	18
C	163	22	13%	127	14	11%	2
D	1,875	21	1%	1,417	54	4%	−3
TOTAL	2,090	57	3%	1,577	71	5%	−2

Note: Data for congressional sessions with divided government and a presidential election (1948, 1956, 1960, 1972, 1976, 1984, 1988, and 1992). "Late" indicates last two weeks of congressional session; "early" is the remainder of the session.

larger for more important legislation than less important legislation. As indicated, the actual deadline effect for level C (routine) bills and level D (minor) bills was 2 percentage points and −3 percentage points, respectively. In other words, the deadline effect for important legislation (18 percentage points) appears much larger than that for routine and minor legislation. Simple difference of means tests (not shown) indicate only tiny chances that the deadline effect for major legislation was not larger than that for routine legislation and the deadline effect for routine legislation was not larger than the deadline effect for minor legislation.

Divided Government and Legislative Productivity

The Prediction

The relationship between the separation-of-powers models and legislative productivity is more complex than one might initially suppose. So it is worth taking some pains to lay out the prediction.

At first glance, the sequential veto bargaining model may suggest that the veto ought not to depress counts of important legislation. The reason is, vetoes are not fatal bullets but bargaining ploys, at least for important legislation. Using the data on veto chains from 1945 to 1992, one can count the number of level A (landmark) bills actually killed by presidential vetoes – that is, bills that were vetoed, not overridden, and not ultimately enacted in a successor bill in the president's administration. The number of such

bills is five, hardly enough to seriously depress overall counts of congressional production of very important legislation, even with individual Congresses.

Unfortunately, this argument is quite incomplete because it neglects the second face of power. To see the impact of the second face of power in this context, return to Figure 30.6 with its illustration of accommodating, compromising, and recalcitrant presidents. First consider the top figure, illustrating an accommodating president. Assume for the moment that the president has an absolute veto, and focus on the simple case of complete and perfect information. Given the ideal points for president and Congress shown in the figure, what set of status quos is Congress willing and able to move? The answer is, only those status quos that lie outside of the interval between the ideal points of the two players. For example, if the status quo lies to the left of c, Congress's ideal point, Congress can move the policy to its ideal point without fear of a veto. If the status quo lies to the right of the president's ideal point, Congress can move the policy to a point within the interval between the two ideal points (perhaps even to its own ideal point). But points between the two ideal points cannot be moved closer to Congress, because the president will veto such moves. Now consider the lower panel of Figure 30.6, illustrating a recalcitrant president. Again the same logic applies. What is important to note is that the set of immovable points has grown much larger, because the president's ideal is located much farther from that of Congress. Understanding this fact, Congress will not even attempt to move many status quo policies that it could easily move were the alignment like that in the top panel.

The top panel, in which the ideal points of president and Congress are relatively close, can be taken as representative of unified government. The bottom panel, where the ideal points are more distal, can be taken as representative of divided government. In either case, there are many status quo policies that cannot possibly be moved. But in the divided government scenario, the "immovable region" is far, far wider. If the legislative productivity of Congress is inversely proportional to the size of the immovable region, then legislative productivity should be lower under divided government than unified government.

In short, then, the prediction is that the number of highly significant laws produced during periods of divided government should be smaller on average than that produced during unified government, ceteris paribus. However, the direct death of bills through the veto should contribute only modestly to the decline in important bills. Instead, the reduction should be attributable to a decline in the number of very important laws passed by Congress.

Data

In the analysis that follows, I focus on just the level A bills, the bills identified by contemporary observers as legislative landmarks.

The analysis searches for an effect of divided government on legislative productivity.

Results

The model indicates that during periods of divided government, Congress produces about three fewer landmark bills per session than during periods of unified government. The effect is statistically significant.

The results should be taken with a grain of salt. Theories about the legislative productivity of Congress are in their infancy. The time series are short, better measures of the gridlock interval are needed, and the dynamic structure of the data demands a closer look. We can anticipate many changes in our understanding of legislative productivity in the years ahead. Nonetheless, *the results seem to show the second face of power in operation, exactly as predicted in the models.*

Conclusion

I began with the models and then searched for or created new data to see if predicted patterns, some quite subtle, actually exist. I used three very different data sets from three very different areas: deadline effects in vetoes, concessions during veto bargaining, and legislative productivity. Across all three data sets and across very different types of predictions, the predictions hold up. The cumulative effect of [the] investigations is to suggest that the models capture a systematic, important component of interbranch bargaining.

CHAPTER THIRTY-ONE

The Dynamics of Legislative Gridlock, 1947–1996

Sarah A. Binder

Binder explores the causes of legislative gridlock. Whereas previous scholars have concentrated primarily on divided party control between Congress and the president, Binder suggests that the distribution of policy preferences within Congress may play a more central role in causing gridlock. She finds that intrabranch party polarization and greater preference heterogeneity across the membership, as well as preference divergence between the chambers, lead to periods of decreased legislative productivity.

Although "gridlock" is said to have entered the political lexicon after the 1980 elections, stalemate is not a modern legislative invention. Indeed, in the very first *Federalist*, Alexander Hamilton complained about the "unequivocal experience of the inefficacy of the subsisting federal government" under the Articles of Confederation. Although stalemate may be endemic to American politics, no definitive account of its proportions or causes yet exists. In this article, I survey recent work, propose a new measure of gridlock, and test several alternative accounts of variation in gridlock over the last half-century.

There is no shortage of scholarship on the politics of gridlock. Most prominent is the work of Mayhew, who rejects the conventional wisdom that divided party control of Congress and the presidency dampens the legislative output of government. Subsequent work takes Mayhew as

Sarah A. Binder. 1999. "The Dynamics of Legislative Gridlock, 1947–1996" *American Political Science Review* 93(3): 519–33. Copyright © 1999 by the American Political Science Association. Reprinted with the permission of Cambridge University Press.

the point of departure, revisiting the questions he raised and researched. This project returns as well to Mayhew's work, probing in a new fashion the contours of gridlock in American national politics.

First, I build on Mayhew's null finding and offer an alternative account of variation in gridlock over time. Most important, I suggest that intrabranch friction may be more significant than interbranch conflict in contributing to policy stalemate. Second, I present a new metric of policy stalemate that measures legislative output in proportion to the policy agenda of Congress and the president. Using data from *New York Times* editorials between 1947 and 1996, I develop a Congress-by-Congress gridlock score and use it to test several hypotheses about the causes of gridlock. The results suggest the fruitfulness of developing new measures and broadening our theoretical focus in assessing the collective performance of Congress and the president.

THE STUDY OF GRIDLOCK IN POLITICS

Mayhew is the landmark study in this research tradition due to its focused theoretical perspective and the empirical rigor of its historical sweep. It also departs from much prior work by its focus on lawmaking per se, rather than the performance of any single institution. Not surprisingly, Mayhew's work has spurred a growth industry in the study of gridlock, with some refining and others challenging the nonpartisan theoretical model underlying Mayhew's empirical results and yet others using new measures to revisit the effects of divided government on lawmaking. Mayhew's null finding for the effect of divided party control on government performance has generally held up, albeit with important exceptions.

Nevertheless, there is good reason to revisit the dynamics of policy gridlock. Theoretically, Mayhew was motivated primarily by an interest in the effects of a particular independent variable, namely, divided government. Toward that end, he identified landmark laws in a two-stage process. In Sweep One, Mayhew used annual end-of-session wrap-up articles from the *New York Times* and *Washington Post* to survey contemporary judgments about the significance of Congress's work each session. In Sweep Two, Mayhew relied on policy specialists' retrospective judgments about the importance of legislation. Using the results of Sweep One to inform his selection of laws during Sweep Two, he generated a comprehensive list of landmark laws enacted each Congress between 1946 and 1990. He then tested whether the presence of divided government reduced the number of truly major laws enacted each Congress.

Although others have offered theoretical and empirical alternatives to Mayhew's contributions, no one has yet tackled both challenges simultaneously. As I argue below, no definitive account of the politics of gridlock is possible until a more robust measure has been used to test an array of competing accounts of variation in gridlock over time.

Empirical Considerations

Consider first the empirical challenge left by Mayhew's work. Essentially, he has studied the supply of federal legislation and found that the supply is more or less the same during modern unified and divided government periods. But we have no information about the demand for legislation. To be sure, Mayhew recognized this problem, but he concluded that it is "very difficult to see what a denominator for a

Congress – an agenda of potential enactments – might be. 'As demanded by the needs of the time,' perhaps? . . . That would be hopeless to administer."

Despite the obvious difficulty of developing an "agenda of potential enactments," such a measure is needed to test theories of political stalemate. Gridlock is not the inverse of legislative output. Certainly, a low level of law production may indicate a high level of political gridlock. Alternatively, it may reflect the response of a Congress and president facing a limited political agenda, in which case it may indicate a low level of gridlock. The point is that we just do not know, absent a metric of the broader political agenda. Indeed, as much was once suggested by the *New York Times*, which editorially cautioned against admiring Congress "in proportion to the volume of bills it grinds out. The only sane criterion is a comparison of its record with the problems before it."

Theoretical Considerations

Mayhew's null finding for the effect of divided government on legislative output has spurred others to develop more fine-grained theories of legislative performance. Taken together, such works suggest that party control alone cannot account for variation in the legislative performance of Congress and the president. Instead, institutional arrangements alter the strategies of legislators and presidents and thus affect the character and frequency of policy outcomes. Indeed, a recurrent theme in recent work is the effect of supermajority institutions on policy outcomes. For example, the policy preferences of supermajority "veto" players in Congress are central to explaining the dynamics of gridlock. As such, these works formalize the intuition that supermajoritarian, rather than majoritarian, models are central to legislative outcomes.

These works are important efforts to think beyond interbranch conflict. Still, institutional arrangements beyond supermajority rules clearly affect legislative outcomes. In particular, we tend to underestimate the policy consequences of the simple institutional fact of bicameralism. Recent work makes clear the need to account for bicameral features in modeling legislative outcomes.

Finally, it is important to remember that recent theoretical treatments of gridlock have been tested primarily with Mayhew's data on legislative enactments. That is, theories crafted to account for episodes of legislative stalemate have been tested with data on legislative success. But if policy gridlock is not simply the inverse of legislative output, then the empirical robustness of such theories is difficult to judge. In short, much more needs to be learned about the proportions and causes of legislative gridlock. Integrating new theoretical observations with a more robust measure of gridlock may yield new findings about its political dynamics.

THE DYNAMICS OF GRIDLOCK

Recent work on the politics of legislative productivity encourages us to think along two separable dimensions: partisan and institutional. Partisan models focus primarily on the effect of divided party control of Congress and the presidency, while institutional models emphasize the effect of supermajority rules. These works provide an important but ultimately only partial accounting of the electoral and institutional dynamics underlying gridlock in the legislative process.

The Partisan and Electoral Context

Partisan theories of legislative gridlock traditionally have centered on the effect of divided government on policy outcomes. The logic is straightforward: Unified party control of the two branches guarantees an important extra-constitutional link between the legislature and executive, which ensures common interests and shared purpose. Under unified government, shared electoral and policy motivations of the president and congressional majorities give majority party legislative leaders the incentive and capacity to use their tools and resources to pass legislation. In contrast, under divided government, differing policy and electoral interests are said to reinforce institutional rivalries between Congress and the president, which make it difficult to assemble the coherent policy majorities necessary to forge major legislation. Unified government, in this view, boosts the prospects for legislative success, while divided government makes it harder for Congress and the president to reach agreement on issues before them. Given electoral and policy differences during times of divided government, a simple divided government hypothesis follows:

HYPOTHESIS 1. *Divided party control of government increases policy gridlock, while unified control decreases gridlock.*

But elections do more than simply divide up control of the major branches of government. They also determine the distribution of policy preferences within and between the two major legislative parties. At times, partisan preferences are polarized, with most legislators at the respective ends of the underlying ideological spectrum; at other times, greater numbers of legislators stand closer to the ideological center. The number of moderate legislators is important, because it likely affects the ease with which compromises are crafted and finalized. Legislators are often likely to prefer disagreement to compromise, particularly if electoral incentives encourage the two parties to differentiate themselves. Thus, the more polarized the two parties, the greater is the incentive for them to distinguish their records and positions, and the lower is the incentive to strive for compromise and make legislative deals. If the presence of moderate legislators affects the ease of compromise, we should observe the following relationship:

HYPOTHESIS 2. *The greater the polarization of the partisan elite, the higher is the level of policy gridlock.*

Elections also affect the distribution of policy preferences across the legislature more generally, independent of the partisan alignment of preferences. Indeed, we might expect different

propensities toward gridlock in relatively homogeneous or heterogeneous legislatures. The
broader the distribution of preferences, the
greater the likelihood that legislators' goals will
be incompatible, or at least the more difficult it will be to reach a suitable compromise.
Incompatibility of goals leads to higher levels of conflict and ultimately to episodes of
"conflictual behavior." As preferences cohere
within a legislature, policy compromise should
become easier to achieve. All else equal, we
might expect the relative heterogeneity of congressional preferences to affect policy stability. In
short:

HYPOTHESIS 3. *The more cohesive legislative preferences, the lower is the level of policy gridlock.*

Finally, the timing of major electoral change
is likely to have measurable policy consequences. A unified majority at the onset of
an electoral realignment is likely to ensure legislative action, as realignments provide a basis
for relatively integrated, coherent, and effective governmental action. Even major electoral
shocks short of a realignment are likely to affect
policy stability. The argument was well stated
in a *New York Times* editorial in 1948 at the
close of the 80th Congress, the first Republican
Congress since before the New Deal:

The Republicans took control of Congress on the
basis of an obvious popular revulsion against some
of the policies of the Roosevelt–Truman administrations. There was no landslide but there was a per-
ceptible movement of the political terrain. The new
legislators certainly had a mandate to liquidate some
war measures, to loosen some New Deal controls, to
check some New Deal projects and to effect practicable economics.

The effects of such electoral shocks are likely
conditioned by the length of time a new congressional majority was in the minority. The
longer a new majority was not in control of
Congress, the more dissatisfied it is likely to
be with the status quo, and the greater is its
incentive to make changes. There is also a
strong electoral incentive for a new majority to
prove that it can govern, which further increases
the likelihood of altering the policy status
quo. The relationship between electoral shocks

and policy outcomes suggests the following
hypothesis:

HYPOTHESIS 4. *The longer a new congressional
majority has been out of power, the greater is its
dissatisfaction with the status quo, and the lower is
the level of policy gridlock.*

Elections, in short, affect legislative dynamics
in ways other than allocating party control of
Congress and the presidency. Indeed, if arguments about the effect of divided government
are primarily about the influence of electoral
and policy motivations on legislative outcomes,
then theories of gridlock need to account for
the multiple ways in which elections align policy and electoral interests within the parties and
Congress more generally.

The Institutional Context

In contrast to the partisan models, institutional
approaches suggest that structural arrangements
alter the distribution of power within Congress
and thus weaken the independent effect of party
on legislative outcomes. Institutional and partisan frameworks are commonly portrayed as
offering distinctive approaches to lawmaking
models, and the inclusion of supermajority rules
represents a break from theories more attuned to
the effects of party dynamics. Yet, despite this
distinctiveness, most recent institutional work
shares a central feature with more traditional
views of legislative productivity: Both model
legislative–executive interactions as a unicameral game.

To be sure, recent scholarship emphasizing
the effect of supermajority rules on policy
outcomes is sensitive to the distinctive procedural characteristics of the two legislative
chambers. Nevertheless, Congress tends to be
treated as a unitary actor opposing the president. Because filibusters are technically impossible under House rules and thus there is no
House filibuster pivot [scholars] argue that the
House tends to be much less of a constraint on
policy outcomes than is the Senate.

Recent formal and comparative studies of
legislatures, however, suggest that other institutional features – especially bicameralism – are

central in shaping policy outcomes. Bicameral legislatures alter the dynamics of policy change, which makes changes in the status quo more difficult than in unicameral bodies. Most important, policy stability depends on the distance between the two chambers. Movement of the critical players in a bicameral game away from each other shrinks the "winset" of the status quo – the set of all points that can defeat the status quo. Thus, as the preferences of the two chambers diverge policy stability increases, and change in the status quo becomes less likely.

The effect of chamber differences is not a recent discovery. The framers of the Constitution were careful to design two very different legislative bodies. Simply including an upper house to check the lower house was insufficient. As James Madison argued in *Federalist No. 62*, "I will barely remark, that as the improbability of sinister combinations will be *in proportion to the dissimilarity in the genius of the two bodies*, it must be politic to distinguish them from each other by every circumstance which will consist with a due harmony in all proper measures, and with the genuine principles of republican government." Madison's comments leave no doubt that the framers intended interchamber differences to come to the fore during the lawmaking process and that they expected such differences to have important policy consequences. Together, these theoretical and historical insights suggest that models of gridlock need to incorporate bicameralism. A simple bicameral hypothesis follows:

HYPOTHESIS 5. *The greater the policy distance between the House and Senate, the higher is the level of policy gridlock.*

Bicameralism is unlikely to be the sole institutional factor that shapes legislative outcomes. Supermajority rules, particularly in the Senate to limit debate, potentially restrict the ability of majorities to secure their preferred policy outcomes. The rate of death-by-filibuster has increased markedly since the middle of the twentieth century. Of course, the filibuster frequently is used to extract policy and political concessions during consideration of legislation, such that obstructionism need not kill the underlying measure. Still, an additional institutional hypothesis is worth exploring:

HYPOTHESIS 6. *The greater the threat of filibuster, the higher is the level of policy gridlock.*

To the extent that institutional arrangements mediate the effect of legislative preferences on policy outcomes, both bicameralism and supermajority rules may be central to modeling the dynamics of legislative gridlock.

The Policy Context

Partisan and institutional factors alone are unlikely to account fully for deadlock. Because different types of policies yield different patterns of politics the question is whether differences in the broader policy context affect the ease with which legislative compromise is reached. Budgetary slack and broad national trends are key features of the policy environment that can affect policy stability. The logic underpinning each factor is simple. First, the greater the surplus relative to outlays, the easier it is to accomplish legislative goals – whether these include creating new federal programs or cutting taxes. The assumption is that providing new benefits in any form is easier than cutting old ones, and providing new benefits is easier during better fiscal times. This leads us to expect:

HYPOTHESIS 7. *The greater the federal budget surplus relative to outlays, the lower is the level of policy gridlock.*

Second, prevailing national moods are said to have a significant influence on both agendas and outcomes.

One such national mood is a climate of opinion that favors governmental solutions to societal problems. Such periods may be the cause of extended periods of legislative activism. In other words, movement in public opinion – changes in global attitudes towards the role of government in society – may affect policy stability and change. Thus:

HYPOTHESIS 8. *The greater the level of public support for governmental action, the lower is the level of policy gridlock.*

Taken together, these eight hypotheses suggest a broad model of gridlock attuned to electoral, institutional, and policy correlates.

DATA AND METHOD

In this section, I present a measure of policy gridlock and a method for testing competing accounts of policy stalemate.

Dependent Variable: Measuring the Proportions of Gridlock

The definition of gridlock largely shapes how it is measured. I have in mind the [simple] idea that our primary concern should be to evaluate the success of the system in treating public problems. Gridlock reflects the relative ability of the political system to reach legislative compromises that alter the status quo. Implied here is some actually-did-pass numerator over some all-that-were-possibilities-for-passage denominator. The question is how the denominator – possibilities for passage – should be defined and operationalized. Mayhew, after giving the matter considerable thought, decided to focus exclusively on the numerator. As argued earlier, however, a denominator is crucial to an evaluation of legislative performance over time.

My approach to identifying a denominator of potential enactments [defines] the "systemic agenda" as all issues that are commonly perceived by members of the political community as meriting public attention. What needs to be measured is the proportion of the agenda that fails to be enacted in any given period, in this case each two-year Congress.

The main task is to determine what constitutes the systemic agenda. I rely on daily unsigned editorials appearing in the *New York Times* between 1947 and 1996. The choice rests on the assumption that the nation's paper of record responds to issues under consideration in Washington and highlights public problems that deserve attention. As former *Washington Post* editorial board member E. J. Dionne expressed it, an editorial writer's job is "to tack a notice up

on the board . . . to put an issue on people's radar screen." Current and former members of the *Times* editorial board concur. Their goal, they say, is to "get out in front of the news . . . jump out in front of an issue before it gets covered in the news," although they recognize that they are often "driven by the news and reacting to the news." Editorials, in short, capture issues at the much talked about stage as well as issues that may be considered the agenda of potential enactments.

From the editorial pages of the *New York Times* I extract the issues that plausibly constitute the systemic agenda, albeit the agenda of the political elite. Specifically, I coded the legislative content of each editorial that mentioned Congress, the House, or the Senate and then used the issues mentioned to compile a list of agenda items for each Congress, tallying as well the number of editorials the *Times* ran on each issue. For example, the *Times* editorialized 65 times about the successful Civil Rights Act of 1964 (which it favored) and 48 times about the Tax Reform Act of 1986 (which it favored). Eight times it discussed the failed constitutional amendment to require a balanced budget (which it opposed) in the 97th Congress (1981–82). With these lists of potential enactments for each Congress, I then determined the fate of each issue: whether it died in committee, on the Senate floor, in conference, and so on, or whether it was enacted. Gridlock scores for each Congress were then calculated as the percentage of agenda items that were not enacted by the close of that Congress.

The agenda list was smallest in the 86th Congress (1959–60), a low of 70 issues, and largest in the 99th Congress (1985–86), a peak of 160 issues. Most recently, in the 104th Congress (1995–96) the total was 118, a modest increase over the 94 issues during the Democratic 103d Congress (1993–94). Although one might expect the agenda to be significantly larger during periods of unified control, there is no significant difference in agenda size under unified and divided control: On average, unified governments have faced 107 issues, divided governments 122. Agenda size has increased steadily over time, however. It jumped sharply at the onset of the activist era starting in 1961, nearly doubling between the 86th Congress (1959–60) and the 87th (1961–62).

Because the agendas developed from the editorials include issues that the *Times* supported as well as those it opposed, the lists are not a record of liberal initiatives supported by the newspaper. Furthermore, there is no bias toward issues that ended in stalemate rather than enactment: Of the 2,899 agenda items discussed over the fifty years, exactly half were enacted. Also, the *Times* did not write more often about gridlocked issues than those clearly headed for passage. The *Times* did write significantly more often about topics that made Mayhew's list of landmark laws. On average, the *Times* editorialized nine times about the 281 issues that became landmark laws, but fewer than three times about all other issues, which suggests that the number of editorials on an issue is a valid indicator of policy importance.

My measure of gridlock seems to avoid some of the vulnerabilities that Mayhew notes about his count of landmark enactments. First, Mayhew states that his compilation of contemporary judgments ("Sweep One") "singles out one kind of legislative action and ignores others. It looks for the major direct innovative thrust . . . but it overlooks the practices and logics of the appropriations process, imaginatively placed amendments, and incrementalism by way of small bills." My editorial method, in contrast, tends to capture these smaller legislative moments, including such issues as child vaccination (enacted in the 103d) and repeal of the oleomargarine tax (enacted in the 81st after stalemating in the 80th).

Second, the editorial measure does not favor certain policy areas over others, which Mayhew considers to be a weakness of his approach. For example, my method does not slight defense weapons buildup, a policy area that tends to be overlooked by Mayhew's approach; the editorial measure detects fights over an alphabet soup of weapons production: the A-12 Avenger, the B-1 and B-2 bombers, the MX and Midgetman missiles, and so on. Third, the editorial measure is not weakened by the problem of omnibus bills in the 1980s because the agendas

Figure 31.1. Level of Policy Gridlock in Congress, 1947–1996.

for each Congress are based on particular issues, rather than final legislative packages. Finally, my method reduces the subjectivity problem, that identifying the potential significance of bills that, if passed, would have been important remains a series of judgments rather than straightforward codifications. The problem of subjectivity is reduced by relying instead on the judgments of the nation's newspaper of record to identify salient policy issues.

Figure 31.1 plots the path of gridlock over fifty years. In calculating the gridlock scores, I applied a "salience filter" to eliminate minor agenda items. I selected only those issues on which the *Times* wrote four or more editorials and then calculated the percentage of these that failed to be enacted into law by the close of Congress. The filter yields numerators (number of failed agenda items) that range from 6 to 16 per Congress and denominators (total number of agenda items) that range from 16 to 39 per Congress.

Most important, the editorial measure generates gridlock scores that comport with the received wisdom about levels of policy stalemate. Using my method, two of the three most productive congresses were the 88th (1963–64), under presidents John F. Kennedy and Lyndon Johnson, and the 89th (1965–66), the Great Society Congress under Johnson, which stalemated on only 27 percent and 29 percent of their agendas, respectively. In contrast, the two least productive were the 102d (1991–92), under President Bush, and the 103d (1993–94), under

President Clinton, which failed to resolve 65 percent and 56 percent of their agendas, respectively.

The gridlock scores also help resolve a puzzle noted by Mayhew when he compared the record of the Great Society Congress with that of the 93d (1973–74). Both produced 22 landmark laws (making them the most productive by Mayhew's count), but the 93d failed to earn much of a reputation for legislative achievement. Mayhew reasons that because of the presence of divided government under Nixon and Ford, "Journalists . . . deprived of an opportunity for a carry-out-the-mandate-script, tended to reach for a deadlock-between-institutions counterscript that probably under-reported real legislative motion." But the 89th and 93d also differed in another important way: The legislative agenda of the 93d was 40 percent larger than that of the 89th, yielding a gridlock score of 43 percent for the 93d and only 29 percent for the 89th. Journalists likely were inclined to stress legislative conflict in the divided years of the 1970s, but they also probably emphasized deadlock in the 93d because it stalemated on so much of its large agenda. Accounting for both numerators and denominators, in short, affects the interpretation of legislative performance.

Independent Variables

Electoral/Partisan Hypotheses

Hypothesis 1 (divided government) is tested with a dummy variable denoting the presence or absence of divided party control of Congress and the presidency (Divided Government coded 1, 0 otherwise).

Hypothesis 2 (party polarization) requires a measure that establishes legislators' relative ideological positions along a Left–Right spectrum. I use W-NOMINATE scores to place legislators along such a continuum and to identify "moderates": those closer to the ideological midpoint between the two party medians in each chamber than to their own party median. This produces a count of the number of conservative Democrats and liberal Republicans in each House and Senate party in each Congress, which can be aver-

aged to calculate the percentage of moderates in each chamber for every Congress. I take the mean percentage of House and Senate moderates to produce a single Percentage of Moderates for each Congress, a measure of legislator moderation over time. The lower the score, the smaller is the number of moderate legislators and the more polarized are the political parties. The resulting measure comports well with conventional wisdom about the recent disappearance of the political center, as it ranges from a high of 35 percent in the 91st Congress (1969–71) to less than 12 percent in the last two congresses.

Hypothesis 3 requires a measure of homogeneity in policy preference across the House and Senate (Ideological Heterogeneity). I average the standard deviation of the W-NOMINATE scores for each chamber in each Congress, which produces an overall measure of relative policy preference homogeneity in Congress.

Finally, Hypothesis 4 (party mandate) requires a measure of the length of time a new congressional majority has been out of power (Time Out of Majority). I count the number of congresses a new majority (controlling both the House and Senate) spent in the minority, averaging the experiences of House and Senate parties. When the new Republican majority took control in 1995, for example, Senate Republicans had been in the minority through four congresses and House Republicans through twenty, yielding a mean time out of power of twelve Congresses.

Institutional Hypotheses

Hypothesis 5 requires a measure of the relative policy space between House and Senate over time (Bicameral Distance). Again, W-NOMINATE scores are used to calculate the median score on the Left–Right dimension for each chamber in each Congress. The distance is thus measured as the absolute difference between chamber medians in each Congress. The two bodies were closest during the 98th Congress (1983–84), when boll weevil Democrats dominated the House center and Republicans controlled the Senate. They were farthest apart in the 104th Congress (1995–96), when Senate Republicans lacked enthusiasm for the House Republicans' Contract with America. Indeed, the House passed 65 percent of all the issues on the legislative agenda in the 104th, while the Senate passed only half – the greatest such gap in the past fifty years.

To test Hypothesis 6 (filibuster), I calculate the *Severity of Filibuster Threat* in each Congress. I start with the number of filibusters in each Congress to tap the extent to which this procedure is likely to limit legislative performance. Because filibusters vary in intensity and policy consequence, I next multiply the quantity in each Congress by the ideological distance between the median senator and the farthest filibuster "pivot." I assume that the greater the distance between the median and the filibuster pivot, the tougher it is to resolve policy and political differences between the majority and the filibustering minority.

Policy Hypotheses

I measure the health of the budgetary climate (*Budgetary Situation*) as the size of the federal budget surplus or deficit as a percentage of federal government outlays. To tap national sentiment, I use [an] annual measure of domestic policy mood, which is derived from opinion surveys. Higher values reflect stronger preferences for an activist federal government. I lag the *Public Mood* variable by one Congress. This cannot rule out the possibility that opinion responds to policy, but it definitely precludes the possibility of opinion responding to current policy.

RESULTS AND DISCUSSION

The results of the model are shown in Table 31.1, column 1. The model estimates show strong support for the partisan/electoral hypotheses and mixed support for the institutional and policy accounts. Most prominently, the [effect of] divided government is positive and statistically significant: Divided governments are prone to higher levels of gridlock. Although Mayhew convincingly shows that divided and unified governments do not differ in the quantity of landmark laws enacted, divided party control does appear to affect the broader ability of the political system to address major public problems. [As] many scholars have argued over the past century, deadlock is more likely when the two major parties split control of Congress.

But interbranch conflict is not the sole factor. Partisan polarization and ideological diversity both contribute to policy stalemate. The effect of party polarization is perhaps the most striking. Despite the faith of responsible party advocates in *cohesive* political parties, the results here suggest that policy change is *less* likely as the parties become more polarized and the percentage of moderate legislators shrinks. Clearly, there are limits to the power of political parties to break policy deadlock. Indeed, it appears that intense polarization can be counterproductive to fostering policy change. Still, the semblance of a party mandate matters: The longer a new congressional majority has been out of power, the lower is the level of policy gridlock under the new majority.

The magnitude of these effects can be seen by simulating expected levels of gridlock, given specified changes in the values of the independent variables. The ranges of the independent variables appear in Table 31.1, column 2, and the associated changes in gridlock appear in column 3. Of the four partisan/electoral variables, a change from unified to divided party control has the smallest effect (increasing the level of gridlock by 8%), although the range of predicted probabilities of gridlock for the four variables is relatively small. Increased ideological diversity has the greatest influence (boosting gridlock 11%), followed by the effect of a larger number of moderate legislators. As the percentage of moderates in Congress climbs from less than one-fifth to one-third of all House and Senate members, the predicted level of gridlock falls by 10 percent. Such results confirm the sentiments of the many members of Congress and observers who claim that partisan polarization limits the legislative capacity of Congress. The "incredibly shrinking middle" – as Senator John Breaux called it – seems to hamper substantially the ability of Congress and the

Table 31.1. *Determinants of Policy Gridlock, 1953–1996*

Hypothesis	Variable	(1) Coefficient (SE)	(2) Change in x (from, to)	(3) Net Change in Expected Probability of Gridlock
Partisan/Electoral	Divided government	.340* (.142)	(0, 1)	+8%
	Percentage of moderates	−.027* (.013)	(18.47, 33.67)	−10%
	Ideological diversity	6.263* (2.710)	(.47, .55)	+11%
	Time out of majority	−.177** (.049)	(0, 2)	−9%
Institutional	Bicameral distance	2.263* (.818)	(.07, .30)	+13%
	Severity of filibuster threat	.035 (.039)	(0, 7.5)	+6%
Policy	Budgetary situation	−.006 (.009)	(−19.02, −2.09)	−2%
	Public mood (lagged)	−.034* (.016)	(55.76, 65.20)	−8%
	Constant	−1.509 (1.587)		
	N	22		
	F	4.10**		
	Adjusted R^2	.5413		
	Durbin–Watson d	1.921		
	Breusch–Godfrey			
	LM test (lag 1)	.0484		
	LM test (lag 2)	1.7842		
	Portmanteau Q	15.3574		

Note: The entries in column 1 are weighted-least-squares logit estimates for grouped data (standard errors in parentheses). Time series model diagnostics based on OLS-generated residuals. *$p < .05$, **$p < .01$; one-tailed t-tests. Net change in the expected probability of gridlock is calculated as the independent variables change between the values in column 2 (i.e., between one standard deviation below and above the mean value for each of the continuous variables and between 0 and 1 for the dichotomous variable). Simulated probabilities are based on the exponential linear predictions generated by the adjust routine in Stata 6.0, and they are calculated assuming the presence of divided government (all other variables are set at their mean values).

president to reach agreement on the issues before them.

Turning to the institutional variables, the bicameral context matters greatly. Even after controlling for the effects of elections on partisan alignments, when ideological differences between the House and Senate increase, Congress finds it harder to reach agreement on pressing policy issues, and policy stalemate climbs. Indeed, bicameral differences have the greatest substantive influence on the level of gridlock: As the distance between the House and Senate increase fourfold along the Left–Right spectrum, gridlock rises by 13 percent.

This helps explain why students of Congress may have been "overly optimistic" about the prospects for governance under unified government in the 103d Congress (1993–94). Only twice before in the postwar period were the House and Senate as far apart ideologically as they were in the 103d, and the last occurrence was twenty years previously. Given the high level of partisan polarization, it is no wonder that seasoned observers concluded at the close of the 103d: "The only good news as this mud fight finally winds down is that it's hard to imagine much worse." While others have highlighted the constraining effects of supermajority

rules to account for "unified gridlock," bicameral constraints clearly help determine the level
of stalemate under unified regimes.

The results offer no support for hypothesis
[6]: The [effect of the] filibuster threat fails to
reach statistical significance.

Finally, there is mixed support for hypotheses
7 and 8. Mayhew found that major lawmaking
was significantly and substantially higher during
the activist era of the 1960s and 1970s. Substituting a measure of public opinion for Mayhew's
"activist era" dummy variable still yields statistically significant results: A ten-point jump in
public preference for activist government lowers gridlock by 8 percent. Conversely, as Mayhew also found, the budgetary situation has little
effect on the legislative record of Congress and
the president.

CONCLUSION

Unified party control of government cannot
guarantee the compromise necessary for breaking deadlock in American politics. As Mayhew
argues, looking solely at the *structural* component of the political system – the separation of
powers between Congress and the president –
tends to obscure important dynamics in American lawmaking. As the analysis here suggests,
the *pluralist* component deserves more attention. The distribution of policy views within
and across the two major political parties has
predictable and important effects on the legislative performance of Congress and the president. The temporal dimension of party politics matters as well; after long frustration as
the minority, a new majority may capitalize on
electoral mandates after gaining unified control of Congress. Intrabranch politics, it seems,
may be as important to explaining policy deadlock as the usual suspect, conflict between the
branches.

Perhaps the most important source of intrabranch disagreement is bicameralism. This
structural component, rather than the separation of power between executive and legislative branches, seems particularly relevant to
the dynamics of policy gridlock in the postwar period. To be sure, both the separation of
powers and bicameralism were central to beliefs
about the proper construction of political institutions in 1787. Still, with important recent
exceptions, the policy consequences of divided
government, not bicameralism, feature prominently in theoretical and empirical treatments
of legislative gridlock. But treating bicameral
bodies as if they were unicameral risks overlook-
ing important differences. House–Senate differences, not simply legislative–executive conflicts,
have structured patterns of gridlock in postwar
American politics.

CHAPTER THIRTY-TWO

The Politics of Shared Power
Congress and the Executive – Excerpt

Louis Fisher

Fisher examines executive–legislative relations and contends that the modern manifestastion of this relationship increasingly deviates from the theoretical notion of a strict separation of powers. Rather, Congress and the president have taken on numerous roles in the other's traditional domain. In this excerpt, Fisher explores the ways in which the president is engaged in the legislative process and members of Congress are engaged in the administration of programs.

PRESIDENT AS LEGISLATOR

To a literalist, the Constitution limits the president to two forms of legislative activity: (1) the right to recommend to Congress such measures "as he shall judge necessary and expedient" and (2) the power to veto a bill. To this list can be added the president's power (shared with the Senate) to make treaties, which the Constitution defines as part of "the supreme Law of the Land." A fourth source of influence, which has been exercised on rare occasions in the past, permits him to convene both houses or either of them. In case they disagree on the time of adjournment, the president can adjourn them "to such Time as he shall think proper."

The Supreme Court has held that in the "framework of our Constitution the President's power to see that the laws are faithfully executed

Louis Fisher. 1998. "President as Legislator" and "Congress as Administrator" in Louis Fisher, *The Politics of Shared Power: Congress and the Executive* (Texas A&M University Press), 23–105. Reprinted with permission.

refutes the idea that he is to be a lawmaker." According to this view the Constitution limits the president's functions in the lawmaking process to "the recommending of laws he thinks wise and the vetoing of laws he thinks bad." And yet superimposed upon the president's express constitutional authorities are other legislative powers either implied in the Constitution or developed by custom (often with the blessing of the courts). Some of these legislative powers are expressly delegated by Congress to the president and the executive agencies. Others result from agency regulations, presidential proclamations, and executive orders.

Express Powers

Article II of the Constitution is remarkable for its laconic treatment of presidential power. Over 60 percent of the language is devoted to the term of office, election, qualifications, removal, compensation, and oath of office. The remainder of the article describes the president's power only in general terms; the veto power is set forth in Article I.

Recommending Legislation
The Constitution requires the president "from time to time" to give Congress "Information of the State of the Union, and recommend to their Consideration such Measures as he shall judge necessary and expedient." The first presidents, George Washington and John Adams, appeared

before Congress to deliver their annual messages, but in 1801 President Thomas Jefferson discontinued that practice, preferring to submit his message in writing. More than one hundred years elapsed before President Woodrow Wilson, in 1913, revived the custom of addressing Congress in person.

In addition to the constitutional requirement for the State of the Union message, statutes direct the president to submit legislative recommendations. The two major documents transmitted to Congress each year are the budget message, prescribed by the Budget and Accounting Act of 1921, and the economic report, submitted in compliance with the Employment Act of 1946. Hundreds of other presidential reports, messages, communications, and suggestions for legislation flow to Capitol Hill in response to statutory directives. Although members of Congress periodically criticize the president for invading their legislative domain, major policy departures often await the president's initiative.

In modern times, members of Congress expect the administration to present a bill as a starting point. One committee chair reportedly advised an administration witness: "Don't expect us to start from scratch on what you people want. That's not the way we do things here – *you* draft the bills and *we* work them over."

The president's ability to recommend legislation has been simplified in recent years by a process called fast-track procedures. Under usual procedures, a presidential proposal can be ignored, buried in committee, or altered by Congress almost beyond recognition. The fast-track procedure, incorporated in the Trade Act of 1974, provides that Congress must vote on a president's proposal, either by passing it or defeating it, and it may not be amended by Congress, either in committee or on the floor. Committees must act within a specified number of days, and Congress must complete floor action within a deadline established by Congress.

The prohibition on congressional amendments, while technically correct, is lifted through informal means. Typically, the president's proposal is put in draft form and circulated within Congress and the committees of jurisdiction. If the administration is interested in having the legislation passed, it will accommodate many of the changes requested during this review process.

The Veto Power

The framers, after decisively rejecting a proposal for an absolute veto, gave the president a qualified veto, subject to an override by a two-thirds majority of each house of Congress. The Supreme Court later decided that two-thirds of a quorum present in each house, rather than of the total membership, would suffice. This is still a demanding standard, generally requiring the support of more than 60 senators and 260 to 270 House members.

Some of the Antifederalists in 1788 were deeply offended by the veto power, claiming that it was an error to allow the executive power a negative "or in fact any kind of control over the proceedings of the legislature." But Alexander Hamilton in *Federalist* 73 argued that the power was an essential instrument for protecting the president against legislative encroachments. In addition to protecting the presidency, Hamilton singled out other justifications for the veto power. It would permit the president to prevent the enactment of "improper laws" that result from haste, inadvertence, or design. James Madison also described the veto as multipurpose, available not merely to restrain Congress from encroaching on other branches but also to prevent Congress "from passing laws unwise in their principle, or incorrect in their form" and from violating the rights of the people.

The *threat* of a veto can be an effective weapon for exacting changes in a pending bill. Members of Congress who manage a bill can use the threat of a veto to eliminate unwanted amendments, claiming that such provisions invite a veto. Even entire bills are shelved in the face of presidential opposition.

The veto power today is fundamentally different from the original design. Both branches have forced changes in the system. Congress developed the practice of presenting to the president bills that had many elements, often unrelated, instead of allowing the president to consider a discrete measure. This practice became more coercive by attaching irrelevant amendments ("riders") to appropriation bills, assuming the president could not afford to veto a money bill in the closing days of a fiscal year. Congress, despite House and Senate rules to the contrary, continues to add "legislation" to appropriation bills.

The Constitution expressly recognizes a "pocket veto." Any bill not returned by the president within ten days (Sundays excluded) shall become law "unless the Congress by their Adjournment prevent its Return, in which Case it shall not be a Law." The pocket veto required several decisions by the Supreme Court to determine what conduct by Congress would "prevent" the return of a bill for legislative consideration. Although the scope of the pocket veto has been gradually restricted by these rulings, litigation has not fully resolved the constitutional dispute. Much has been left to accommodations reached by the political branches.

The veto is one of the more effective weapons in the president's arsenal. Of the 1,466 regular vetoes from Washington through Clinton, Congress has managed to override only 105. More than half of those vetoes came during the administrations of Grover Cleveland and Franklin D. Roosevelt, with the vast majority aimed at private relief bills. There have also been 1,067 pocket vetoes, with Cleveland and Roosevelt again accounting for more than half.

The threat of a presidential veto can be answered by the threat of a legislative override, producing complex results that defy statistical analysis. President Bush vetoed several bills in a row, each time escaping a congressional override. However, when he vetoed the Civil Rights Bill of 1990, Congress mounted an extensive fight to save the bill. The override vote in the Senate fell short by only one vote. Over the next year, Bush had increasing difficulty in supporting his claim that the legislation constituted a "quota" system for minorities. Congressional support solidified to the point where an override looked likely. Faced with possible defeat, Bush found a way to sign a slightly rewritten civil rights act in 1991.

This conflict underscores an important point. When the veto record is focused on nationally significant legislation (after eliminating private relief bills and minor legislation), Congress is more successful with its override efforts. A persistent Congress can win out, if not under one president, then under the next. In struggles over important bills, Congress is much more of a coequal institution.

Implied and Evolved Powers

Some constitutional scholars believe that an act of the federal government is illegal unless based upon a power enumerated in the Constitution. They take comfort in the statement of Henry Lee at the Virginia ratification convention: "When a question arises with respect to the legality of any power, exercised or assumed," the question will be, "Is it enumerated in the Constitution? . . . It is otherwise arbitrary and unconstitutional." Not only is this doctrine impractical and unrealistic, but these scholars must themselves make room for implied powers: the power of Congress to investigate, the president's power to remove executive officials, and the power of the Supreme Court to review executive and legislative actions.

The president's power as legislator expands as a result of several developments: authority delegated by Congress; the president's implied authority to issue regulations, proclamations, and executive orders; and the personal ability and institutional strength of a president to lobby for legislative proposals.

Delegated Authority

Strict interpretations of the Constitution would prohibit Congress from delegating its power to another branch. This theory finds expression in the ancient maxim *delegata potestas non potest delegari* (delegated power cannot be delegated). According to this doctrine, the power delegated by the people to Congress may not be transferred elsewhere.

Practice has not kept pace with theory, however. From an early date, the Supreme Court allowed Congress to supply general guidelines for national policy, leaving to other branches the responsibility for "filling in the details." Although time after time the Court has paid homage to the nondelegation doctrine, claiming that it would be "a breach of the National fundamental law" were Congress to transfer its legislative power to the president, the Court typically upholds the delegation in question. Delegation by Congress, said the Court in 1940, "has long been recognized as necessary in order that the exertion of legislative power does not become a futility.... The burdens of minutiae would be apt to clog the administration of the law and deprive the agency of that flexibility and dispatch which are its salient virtues."

Regulations, Proclamations, and Executive Orders

To carry out authority delegated by Congress, executive officials often issue rules and regulations that "must be received as the acts of the executive, and as such, be binding upon all within the sphere of his legal and constitutional authority." In theory, regulations are not a substitute for general policy making. That power is reserved to Congress and may be enacted only in the form of public law. While administrative regulations are entitled to respect, "the authority to prescribe rules and regulations is not the power to make laws, for no such power can be delegated by the Congress." According to the courts, a regulation that is out of harmony with a statute "is a mere nullity."

So much for general theory. Vague grants of delegated power by Congress give administrators substantial discretion to make policy. During the Senate vote in 1981 to confirm James Watt as secretary of the interior, Senator Dale Bumpers, Democrat of Arkansas, recalled that Watt had told his committee: "I believe in complying with the law." Bumpers continued: "Do you know what the law is so far as the management of the public lands is concerned? Most of the time it is whatever the Secretary of the Interior says it is."

Even when statutory language is relatively clear and specific, one provision may conflict with another in the same bill. Faced with inconsistent and perhaps contradictory congressional demands, the president and agency officials try to "harmonize" competing provisions. In 1979 a federal court ruled that the Environmental Protection Agency (EPA) acted properly by adopting a regulatory scheme that bridged conflicting provisions in the Clean Air Act. Instead of Congress resolving the policy conflict, the EPA manufactured an administrative solution.

Presidential proclamations [presidential directives with the force of law used primarily in the field of foreign affairs, for ceremonial purposes, and when directed by statute] are a second instrument of administratrative legislation. Often they are routine in nature, without legislative effect. During 1980 President Carter used proclamations to make statements for Mother's Day, Father's Day, and Salute to Learning Day. Also during that period, however, he issued proclamations that had substantive impact, including import quotas on cotton and on television parts. Several other substantive proclamations issued by Carter in 1980, imposing a fee on imported oil, were declared illegal by a federal court. The judicial decision came against a backdrop of congressional moves to strip Carter of his power to impose import fees.

In a controversial action in 1971, President Nixon issued a proclamation imposing a 10 percent surcharge on articles imported into the United States. After extensive litigation a federal court decided that although the president lacks an independent power to regulate commerce or set tariffs, and any valid proclamation had to be based on authority delegated by Congress, in this case Nixon had acted consistently with statutory authority. When a statute prescribes a particular procedure and the president follows a different course, the proclamation can be declared illegal and void.

A third form of administrative legislation is the executive order [a presidential directive with the force of law used to manage government officials and agencies]. President Franklin D. Roosevelt issued a number of executive orders in 1941 to seize industrial plants, shipbuilding companies, a cable company, a munitions plant, and approximately four thousand coal companies. Two years passed before Congress supplied statutory authority for his actions. During

World War II, President Roosevelt created several agencies by executive order, without the slightest shred of statutory support. An opponent of this practice, Senator Richard Russell, Democrat of Georgia, said he "never believed that the President of the United States was vested with one scintilla of authority to create by an Executive order an action agency of Government without the approval of the Congress of the United States." Russell successfully secured the adoption of an amendment, still in effect today, that prohibits the use of any appropriation to pay the expenses of an agency established by executive order "if the Congress has not appropriated any money specifically for such agency or instrumentality or specifically authorized the expenditure of funds by it."

The use of executive orders to eliminate employment discrimination in private industry began with President Franklin D. Roosevelt and continued with Truman, Eisenhower, Kennedy, and Johnson. These initiatives were further carried forward by President Nixon, who issued an executive order that required federal contractors to set specific goals for hiring members of minority groups (the "Philadelphia Plan"). The comptroller general concluded that the plan conflicted with the Civil Rights Act of 1964. Here the federal courts upheld the administration's action. Another executive order by Nixon attempted to rejuvenate the Subversive Activities Control Board. Congress intervened in this case to prohibit the administration from using appropriated funds to carry out the order. Senator Sam Ervin, Democrat of North Carolina, complained that board members had done little "except draw their breath and their salaries." When executive orders exceed presidential authority, the judiciary has struck them down.

OMB's Review of Agency Regulations

In response to an antiregulation mood in the 1970s, presidents from Ford to Clinton tried to create a system to monitor government regulations that impose heavy costs on businesses and consumers. The Council on Wage and Price Stability (COWPS) in the Ford White House was one effort, followed by the creation under President Carter of the Regulatory Analysis Review Group (RARG). The most ambitious attempt to centralize control over agency regulations is Executive Order 12291, issued by President Reagan in 1981. He designated the Office of Management and Budget (OMB) as the central agency to review regulations and subject them to cost–benefit analysis. The purpose was to "reduce the burdens on existing and future regulations, increase agency accountability for regulatory actions, provide for presidential oversight of the regulatory process, minimize duplication and conflict of regulations, and insure well-reasoned regulations."

By making OMB the central clearinghouse for agency regulations and arming it with a vague cost–benefit weapon, Reagan's order raised serious questions of due process. OMB could use the cost–benefit concept to delay or kill regulations the administration did not want. Moreover, OMB officials could meet privately with industry representatives to discuss pending agency rules. These ex parte contacts were contrary to the standards adopted in the Administrative Procedure Act, which calls for public "notice and comment" of proposed rules.

Although OMB was frequently criticized for its role in reviewing agency regulations, a strong congressional counterattack did not come until 1986. The House Appropriations Committee voted to cut off all funds for the office within OMB that performed regulatory review: the Office of Information and Regulatory Affairs (OIRA).

Several Senate committees were also critical of OIRA. A report issued in May 1986 by the Senate Committee on Environment and Public Works charged that the secrecy and delay imposed by OMB compromised the principles of openness and fairness required for agency rulemaking. On July 31, 1986, the Senate Governmental Affairs Committee reported a bill to reorganize OMB. Included in the bill were provisions to strengthen congressional control over OIRA by making its administrator subject to Senate advice and consent. The report also explained new procedures that would require greater disclosure of OIRA documents and activities.

Because of these developments on the Senate side, the Senate Appropriations Committee provided funding for OIRA. The continuing resolution sent to President Reagan at the end of 1986 included $5.4 million for the office. It appeared that concessions wrung from the administration made it unnecessary for Congress to enact statutory limitations on OIRA. Ambiguities in the agreement, however, led to renewed struggles between the branches. In 1989, OMB Director Richard Darman accepted new statutory language, but that fell through when White House Counsel C. Boyden Gray and White House Chief of Staff John Sununu objected that the agreement had not been brought to them.

The uncertainty over the status of OIRA created a vacuum that was soon filled by the Council on Competitiveness, chaired by Vice President Dan Quayle. President Bush created the Council in 1989 to improve U.S. competitiveness in the international market. On June 15, 1990, Bush assigned the Council responsibilities for regultory review. Critics complained that the Council operated as a conduit for industry and private interests that sided with business against the environment – the original objections leveled against OIRA. Operating within the shelter of the vice president's office, the Council was not subject to the standards of public accountability expected of OIRA. At the end of 1991, legislation (S. 1942) was introduced in Congress to establish statutory procedures for the public disclosure of all agencies that review federal regulations, but no final action was taken. In 1992, the House voted to delete funding for the salaries of staffers on the Quayle Council, using the power of the purse to punish the administration for its secrecy. However, in the face of a threatened Bush veto, the Senate restored the funds.

The Clinton administration continued to conduct centralized review of regulatory agencies but adopted reforms to avoid the insulated and secretive practices of the Reagan and Bush years. On January 21, 1993, in his first full day in office, President Clinton abolished the Council on Competitiveness and asked Vice President Al Gore to recommend new regulatory review procedures. The new procedures were incorporated in Executive Order 12866, released on September 30, 1993. If disagreements between agencies and OIRA cannot be resolved by OIRA, they may be decided by the president or the vice president. In 1996, Congress passed legislation (110 Stat. 868) that allows Congress to review and disapprove federal agency regulations. Major rules are delayed for sixty days to give Congress an opportunity to pass a joint resolution of disapproval. Joint resolutions must be presented to the president and may be vetoed.

Executive Organization and Leadership

The operations of government require constant interaction between executive and legislative leaders. Congress and the president can seldom afford to spin in separate orbits. Among the fundamental duties of the executive branch, since 1789, is the need to structure itself for a continuing dialogue with Congress on legislation, appointments, and other matters that demand close consultation and cooperation.

Initiating Legislation

The search for the source of legislation inevitably takes the traveler on a convoluted and twisted journey, full of surprises. Peel away one "source" and you discover another. The process continues to repeat itself with little hope of reaching the core. As Woodrow Wilson remarked, "Legislation unquestionably generates legislation. Every statute may be said to have a long lineage of statutes behind it."

Robert A. Dahl expressed a widely held view of legislative activity in foreign policy: "Perhaps the single most important fact about Congress and its role in foreign policy . . . is that it rarely provides the initiative." Yet other studies credit individual representatives and senators with a significant voice in shaping foreign policy. Francis O. Wilcox, writing from the perspective of chief of staff for the Senate Foreign Relations Committee from 1947 to 1955 and assistant secretary of state for international organization affairs from 1955 to 1961, concluded that "some of the most imaginative and constructive foreign policies since World War II have originated in Congress." As leading examples he cited the exchange-of-persons program, the use of surplus agricultural commodities in the foreign aid program, the International Development Association, the Peace Corps, and the U.S. Arms Control and Disarmament Agency. "Not infrequently," he noted, "an idea is born on Capitol Hill and then, when it is brought to fruition, the President receives political credit for it."

More recently, as a result of the build-up in professional staff within Congress, structural changes within the institution, and greater visibility of foreign policy issues among the public, Congress has been able and willing to assert itself on a continuous basis. Legislative actions – such as terminating the war in Vietnam, restricting presidential policy in Cyprus and Angola, enacting the War Powers Resolution in 1973 over Nixon's veto, restricting the Central Intelligence Agency, and scrutinizing arms sales – have been initiated by Congress with the assistance of outside groups and individuals. During the Reagan years, Congress consistently challenged the president's foreign policy in such areas as the Philippines, arms control, and South Africa. The Bush and Clinton administrations also witnessed strong challenges by Congress to foreign policy initiatives by the president.

Legislation is often rooted in causes that never come to light. A member of a legislator's staff, after playing a pivotal role in initiating and shaping a bill, may decide to conceal that contribution out of deference to a member or because of a self-imposed anonymity. A private organization that conceives the idea embodied in legislation, and perhaps even drafts the bill, might prefer to hide its influence in order to improve the bill's chance for passage. Further complicating the picture, an administration may allow a member of Congress to take the lead in advocating a proposal, not because the legislator conceived the idea but to avoid anticipated criticism that the executive branch is extending its power and promoting expensive programs.

Bills that "originate" in the executive branch are subsequently modified and refined by the suggestions of private groups, committee hearings and markups, and the adoption of floor amendments. Decentralization of Congress in recent years, associated with largely autonomous and well-staffed subcommittees, has produced more floor amendments and challenges to reported bills. As a result, the White House faces the prospect of substantial revisions and often radical alterations in administration bills. In the rare case when an administration bill sails through Congress with little change, this may reflect not so much the president's influence as a decision by the White House to have a draft bill cleared first by the major powers on Capitol Hill.

Executive Lobbying

Prior to World War II, presidents relied on personal assistants within the White House or the executive departments to handle contacts with Congress. The Budget Bureau, created in 1921, marked the starting point for an institutionalized liaison operation with Congress.

The Executive Office of the President (EOP), established in 1939, contained not only the Budget Bureau but other units to improve executive–legislative relations. The EOP White House Office was composed, in part, of secretaries to the president charged with the following mission: "To facilitate and maintain quick and easy communication with the Congress, the individual members of Congress, the heads of executive departments and agencies, the press, the radio, and the general public." The administrative assistants to the president were expected to bridge the gap between the branches.

Agency Initiatives

Although departments have promoted legislation throughout the history of the country, agencies in the 1930s began to realize the value of centralizing control for bill drafting in the counsel's office and assigning to someone in that office a definite responsibility for the task. Most departments had detailed someone in their organization to watch legislation, but usually on a part-time and sporadic basis. In 1934 the

Treasury Department created a legislative division with the office of the general counsel. This division was responsible for drafting departmental bills, monitoring their progress after they were introduced in Congress, and working with legislative staff in preparing amendments desired by congressional committees.

Organizing the White House, 1941–1969

During the emergency atmosphere of World War II, the task of coordinating the president's program was shared by the White House, the Budget Bureau, and the Office of War Mobilization and Reconversion. After Roosevelt's death, in 1945, Truman tried to pull the entire function back into the Budget Bureau. A small congressional liaison unit was established within the Truman White House. Two assistants were appointed in 1949. Neither had any experience in partisan politics or as congressional staff. Significant liaison responsibilities were carried out by Truman or his associates in the White House, particularly Clark Clifford and Charles S. Murphy. Senior members of the Truman White House characterized the formal liaison unit as "understaffed and relatively ineffectual. The legislative assistants attended the President's staff meetings but rarely spoke up. In the Congress they had little discretion to commit the President or to speak authoritatively for him so as to influence votes, strategy or tactics . . . the legislative assistants were primarily messengers rather than responsible political agents."

By 1953, the first year of the Eisenhower administration, a staff of senior assistants in the White House had been assigned the responsibility of legislative liaison.

The operation of the liaison staff was limited by Eisenhower's strong belief in the separation of powers doctrine and his respect for congressional prerogatives in legislative matters. But Eisenhower took seriously the promises in his party's platform and the commitments made during the campaign. In 1954 alone he made 232 specific requests for legislation to Congress.

The Kennedy administration, pledged to activist leadership, had an extensive legislative program. Kennedy's razor-thin presidential victory convinced him that a sophisticated, aggressive liaison operation with Congress was indispensable to White House objectives. The chief of the liaison unit was Larry O'Brien. The liaison unit in the Kennedy White House numbered about six full-time professionals. Compared with the Eisenhower staff, they were younger, possessed less experience in dealing with Congress, and had served in highly partisan positions before joining the administration. Several were criticized for displaying "a lack of respect for their elders in the Congress and with using crude tactics more appropriate to the rough-and-tumble of party conventions than to the political process in a coequal branch of the national government."

O'Brien's liaison unit did not try to monopolize congressional relations. Appropriations remained the responsibility of the Budget Bureau. Foreign affairs were left to the president's adviser on foreign affairs, the secretary of state, and the assistant secretary for congressional relations in the State Department (although on some issues, such as foreign aid, the White House liaison team intervened).

When President Johnson, a former Senate majority leader, entered office, he stressed the importance of the congressional liaison operation. He told cabinet members and agency heads: "There's no one more important in your department or agency than the man responsible for congressional relations. You have the responsibility to see to it that you have the best possible man available. You see to it that he's adequately staffed, and you see to it that you maintain your relationship with the Congress every day of the week." In O'Brien's estimate, Johnson's approach to congressional liaison represented a "hard-sell, arm-twisting style of operation which contrasted with Kennedy's more restrained approach."

Nixon to Clinton, 1969–1998

Nixon, like Johnson, came to the presidency with considerable congressional experience: member of the House of Representatives, senator, and vice president. And yet, more than any president before or since, he displayed a contemptuous attitude toward the legislative branch and never seemed comfortable dealing with its members.

To manage his congressional relations staff, President Nixon first turned to Bryce Harlow, veteran White House lobbyist of the Eisenhower years, and to William E. Timmons, who had served as an aide to Republican members of Congress. On December 9, 1970, Harlow resigned his post as counselor to the president. His job had been complicated by attitudes within the Nixon White House. Some senior staffers, including John D. Ehrlichman and H. R. Haldeman, had a limited understanding of Congress or the constitutional system of separated powers and little inclination to learn.

Harlow was replaced by Clark MacGregor, who had just completed ten years in the House of Representatives. Republican members of Congress praised MacGregor's appointment. On his lapel he wore a button that proclaimed: "I care about Congress." But shortly after MacGregor took office, Nixon issued a sharp attack on the 91st Congress. He said that Congress, because of its record over the previous two years, "will be remembered and remarked upon in history not so much for what it did, but for what it failed to do." The nation, he said, had watched a legislative body "that had seemingly lost the capacity to decide and the will to act."

MacGregor, objecting to this speech, extracted from Nixon a promise that future messages to Capitol Hill would first be routed through him. MacGregor believed that the tense atmosphere of confrontation tactics employed by the Nixon White House should be replaced by a more conciliatory approach. But the Nixon administration was bent on confrontation politics. MacGregor departed to make way for Timmons's hard-hitting style. On July 6, 1972, setting the tone for Nixon's reelection effort, Timmons denounced Congress as "miserable," "irresponsible," "appalling," and "cynical."

The resignations of Ehrlichman and Haldeman, on April 30, 1973, offered another opportunity to mend relations with Congress. Nixon appointed Harlow and Melvin Laird (a former member of Congress and Nixon's first secretary

of defense) to the post of White House counselor, where they were supposed to function as Nixon's "ambassadors" to Capitol Hill. Within a year, as pressure mounted for Nixon's resignation, they left the administration.

Max Friedersdorf, Timmons's deputy for House liaison, was appointed to head the liaison unit in the Ford White House. Gerald Ford had spent twenty-five years in the House of Representatives, many of them as minority leader for the Republicans. He was therefore accustomed to the give-and-take of politics. Congressional relations appeared to be off to a good start on August 12, 1974, when President Ford addressed Congress three days after he took office. In contrast to the truculent, pugnacious tone of the Nixon administration, Ford looked forward to a period of trust and harmony: "As president, within the limits of basic principles, my motto toward the Congress is communication, conciliation, compromise, and cooperation." On the whole, executive–legislative relationships improved considerably during the Ford years.

Jimmy Carter selected Frank Moore to head his congressional relations team. A native of Georgia, Moore had served as liaison with the Georgia legislature during Carter's term as governor. At no time had Moore ever worked in Washington or on Capitol Hill. Even before Carter took office, congressional Democrats began criticizing Moore's performance. Unreturned phone calls and missed meetings were part of the objections, but the complaints soon broadened to include inadequate consultation on presidential appointments and the energy program.

Some of the problems stemmed from the inexperience of Carter's liaison staff, but other factors contributed to the breakdown in executive–legislative relations. Congressional sensitivity had been heightened by the acerbity of the Nixon years, there was concern that Carter viewed Congress as little more than a national version of the Georgia legislature, and House Speaker Tip O'Neill and Senate Majority Leader Robert Byrd were much more assertive as party leaders than their predecessors, Carl Albert and Mike Mansfield. Moreover, changes in the delegate selection process at the Democratic National Convention allowed someone like Carter to win nomination with less than the usual support from Congress. Carter came in as an "outsider" and would remain one.

President Reagan's liaison team operated smoothly from the start. Friedersdorf, who had served Nixon and Ford in congressional relations, was selected to head the Reagan liaison unit. His principal assistants, Powell A. Moore (handling the Senate) and Kenneth M. Duberstein (responsible for the House), both had substantial experience on Capitol Hill.

To pass his spending and tax proposals in 1981, President Reagan used all the tools at his disposal. He invited fourteen House Democrats to Camp David for lunch, hoping to build a conservative majority in the House. He carried out his mission partly by dispatching Air Force planes to bring legislators back to D.C. for a vote.

Reagan's mastery of Congress was short-lived. By 1982 the economy had weakened, his budget policy projected massive deficits, and the Republicans lost twenty-six seats in the House. Republican legislators in both houses began to distance themselves from the president. Initially this display of independence brought threats of sanctions and reprisals from the White House.

At the end of 1986, Reagan's political fortunes sagged further after disclosure of the Iran–Contra affair. In his first year he had put together a remarkable series of legislative victories by carefully orchestrating public opinion and building a working majority in Congress. Operating through constitutional channels had been an outstanding success. Iran–Contra represented the opposite strategy. Officials within the White House and the National Security Council decided to make policy single-handedly. There would be no sharing of power with Congress. Reagan's circumvention of established procedures inflicted lasting damage on his administration.

President George Bush assembled a professional team to handle liaison operations with Congress. Frederick D. McClure, his assistant for legislative affairs, received high marks from Capitol Hill. Bush selected for his Cabinet men and women with substantial experience with the Federal Government; many of them had served as members of Congress.

Bipartisan groups of legislators were brought regularly to the White House for discussions. Unlike Reagan, Bush was prepared to discuss substantive issues without having to read from notes, held press conferences more frequently, and seemed to enjoy personal contacts with members of Congress. Bush's previous service in the House and as presiding officer of the Senate gave him a ready circle of congressional friends. After Iraq's invasion of Kuwait in August 1990, he claimed that he could take offensive action against Saddam Hussein without first obtaining authority from Congress. However, Bush decided on January 8, 1991, to seek legislative support and Congress passed the necessary legislation.

President Clinton selected Howard Paster to head the White House legislative affairs office. With substantial experience in the House, the Senate, and the private sector, Paster had a good understanding of the federal legislative process and the tools needed for success. However, a disorganized and largely inexperienced White House staff, coupled with an exceptionally heavy legislative agenda (the health bill, NAFTA, and other proposals), cast a shadow over the first year's effort. Paster left after the first session and was replaced by Patrick Griffin.

In the middle of 1994, Clinton picked OMB Director Leon Panetta to replace Thomas McLarty as White House chief of staff. The move brought order and discipline to all operations, including legislative affairs, but the White House lobbying team had less visibility and impact on Capitol Hill. High turnover within the legislative affairs office was one factor. More significant were the Republican victories in the 1994 elections, shifting the initiative for new legislation from the White House to Congress.

Conclusions

Even in the days of patronage and the spoils system, the administration of sanctions and favors by the president was time-consuming and quite likely to irritate and alienate important members of Congress. Civil service reforms and the rise of the welfare state, which automatically dispenses benefits through entitlement programs, have removed much of the leverage previously available to the White House. In addition, since members of Congress are increasingly independent of the White House in their reelection campaigns, they may vote as they please with little worry of presidential retaliation.

The president is left essentially with modest powers of persuasion, bargaining, negotiation, favors, services, flattery, appeals to national interest, and personal loyalty. Success in enlisting the support of a legislator comes at a cost, at least in time and energy; often the price is a specific benefit that the legislator wants, and expects, in return. All these tactics may fail when legislators decide that a presidential request is injurious to their constituents or contrary to their own principles and conscience.

An ambitious program to "care and feed" legislators carries a high risk. If a president extends favors to fence-sitters to secure their votes, other legislators may resent the fact that they routinely support the administration without receiving comparable assistance. Such thoughts might encourage signs of "disloyalty" until the White House takes notice and demonstrates its appreciation. A president's election rarely provides a "mandate" for the administration's program. Legislators successful in the same election usually enter office with mandates of their own, quite different from the values and objectives of the president-elect. Seldom will these legislators depend on the president's "coattail effect." Consequently, they owe the chief executive little. Two-thirds of the senators gained their seats by winning elections two to four years earlier.

Leadership from the White House will always be possible, whether Congress is centralized or decentralized. It is often argued that the decentralization of Congress in the 1970s, which took power from committee heads and dispersed it to House and Senate subcommittees, thwarted the legislative goals of Presidents Ford and Carter. They could not contact a handful of influential

committee leaders to push forward the White House program.

This is a convenient excuse, but it ignores the fact that earlier presidents complained that the *centralization* of power in Congress made it impossible to get bills past uncooperative committee heads. Legislative decentralization can be an opportunity, not an obstacle, because it opens up lines of communication. Moreover, the same congressional structure that appeared to obstruct Ford and Carter was remarkably compliant to Reagan's budgetary and tax initiatives in 1981.

It is also said that government cannot function effectively because of "divided government" (one party controlling the White House and the other party controlling Congress). But Reagan functioned well in 1981 with divided government and Carter fared poorly for four years even though his party controlled both branches. Democratic control of Congress in Clinton's first two years did not facilitate his plan to reform the nation's health system.

Part of presidential leadership consists in fashioning a broad coalition of support and remaining capable of adjusting to new circumstances and conditions. It is irresponsible to complain that conditions are not like they used to be (or not like we *thought* they used to be). A good leader makes the best of a situation that is never ideal. President Franklin D. Roosevelt once told an aide: "I am the captain of this ship, but the seas control the captain." He recognized that the strength of forces, impulses, and opinions at any given time would determine what he had to do. A skillful leader can find some margin for action in any situation.

CONGRESS AS ADMINISTRATOR

It has become customary to criticize legislators for interfering with administrative matters.

High on the list of accused congressional "meddling" are these practices: excessive detail in statutes, passage of private bills, the use of "riders" in appropriation bills to direct and confine administrative actions, statutory restrictions on personnel policies, legislative vetoes, directives in committee reports, redundant and intrusive investigations, casework demands that consume agency time, and the creation of independent commissions to perform regulatory tasks that could be carried out by existing executive departments. These congressional initiatives are criticized for undermining the unity of the presidency, violating hierarchical principles of public administration, disrupting the orderly functioning of agencies, and threatening the stability of the constitutional system. Congress is advised to confine itself to legislative duties and leave administration to the president and the executive branch.

In 1986 the Supreme Court claimed that the Constitution "does not contemplate an active role for Congress in the supervision of officers charged with the execution of the laws it enacts." According to the Court, "once Congress makes its choice in enacting legislation, its participation ends. Congress can thereafter control the execution of its enactment only indirectly – by passing new legislation." This is a caricature of Congress. The Court contradicts everything we know about the ability (and determination) of Congress to control the execution of laws through hearings, committee investigations, GAO studies, informal contacts between members of Congress and agency officials, committee subpoenas, the contempt power, and nonstatutory controls.

Members of Congress continue to participate in administration because they have learned time and again that details are the crucial building blocks of policy. No better formula for legislative impotence has ever been devised than to limit Congress to "broad policy questions" and assign "administrative details" to the executive. The administration of a program almost always involves legislative power. Congress cannot restrict itself to broad policy alone.

Constitutional Basis

Administration is not a monopoly of the executive. Congress has a legitimate role and responsibility in supervising the efforts of federal agencies. Little was said at the Philadelphia Convention concerning the president's power as administrator. Certainly the framers were keenly aware of the failings of the Continental Congress, especially its lack of administrative accountability and efficiency. Moreover delegates at the Convention warned against legislative aggrandizement. The delegates rejected the idea of a plural executive, preferring to anchor that responsibility in a single individual.

It can be argued that congressional participation in administrative matters creates a divided executive, something the framers explicitly rejected. Nevertheless, at the Convention, Roger Sherman considered the executive "nothing more than an institution for carrying the will of the Legislature into effect." Although Alexander Hamilton, Thomas Jefferson, and others had criticized the Continental Congress for meddling in administrative details, the framers were never able to distinguish clearly between legislative and executive duties.

Agencies have a direct responsibility to Congress, the body that creates them. The extent to which Congress could direct officials prompted [former Attorney General Caleb] Cushing to warn that Congress might by statute so divide the executive power as to subvert the government "and to change it into a parliamentary despotism, with a nominal executive chief utterly powerless."

Not only is the administrative process today open to congressional intervention, but parties from the private sector are invited to participate in agency decisions. The Administrative Procedure Act of 1946 requires public notice and comment in rulemaking and provides for group representation in adjudicatory proceedings. The statutory requirement for boards, committees, and task forces allows interested parties from the private sector to advise federal agencies on the implementation of laws. The Freedom of Information Act, the Sunshine Act of 1976, and funding of public participation in agency proceedings have given citizens and interest groups greater access to the administrative process.

The judiciary is another important participant in the administrative process, reviewing agency decisions to see that they conform to legislative intent, satisfy standards of procedural fairness, and meet the test of constitutionality. Courts are routinely criticized for intervening so deeply in the administrative process that they usurp the policymaking functions of Congress and the agencies.

With participation of this breadth in the administrative process, it seems anomalous to ask Congress to stay out. When members of Congress believe that an agency has departed from its statutory purpose, they are entitled, if not obligated, to express their views through individual statements on the floor, questions at committee hearings, or direct contact with agency officials. The legislative function does not cease with a bill that creates an agency. Only by monitoring the operation of a law can members uncover statutory defects and correct agency misinterpretations.

Instruments of Legislative Control

A number of express or implied constitutional powers allows Congress to direct administrative matters. Congress has the power to create an office, define its powers and duration, and determine the compensation for officials. Additional legislative guidance comes from the process of confirming presidential appointees, advisory participation in the administrative process, the investigatory and appropriation powers, private bills, casework, and nonstatutory controls.

Personnel Policies

The U.S. Code contains extraordinarily detailed instructions from Congress to cover personnel policies for agencies: examination, selection, and placement of employees; training, performance ratings, and incentive awards; classification of positions, pay rates, and travel expenses; hours of work, leave, and holidays; rights of employees; preferential points in hiring veterans; medical plans and life insurance; and restrictions on political activities by federal employees.

In creating departments, Congress may require that the appointment of certain executive officials be subject to the advice and consent of the Senate. It may stipulate the qualifications of appointees, itemizing in great detail the characteristics a president must consider before submitting a name for Senate action. Congress has the power to delegate the appointment of officers to departmental heads; it may also specify grounds for removal and impose procedural safeguards before administrators suspend or dismiss employees.

During confirmation hearings, senators have an opportunity to explore a nominee's depth of knowledge and policy commitments. Promises may be extracted at that time with regard to keeping the committees informed of proposed actions and even requiring prior approval from the committees on specific issues.

Participating as Advisers

The Constitution specifically prohibits persons from simultaneously holding federal office and serving as members of Congress. This Incompatibility Clause is one of the supporting structures of the separation of powers doctrine. Nevertheless, some statutes allow members of Congress to take part in the implementation of laws. The Trade Expansion Act of 1962 directed the president, before each negotiation, to select four representatives from the congressional tax committees to be accredited as members of the U.S. delegation. Under the Trade Act, ten members of Congress are accredited by the president as official advisers to U.S. delegations at international conferences, meetings, and negotiation sessions relating to trade agreements. The fast-track procedure in trade statutes anticipates that members of Congress will be closely involved in the negotiation process so that the president's draft-implementing bill can be handled expeditiously.

Congress appoints members of various commissions to oversee the implementation of federal policy. In 1976 Congress established a Commission on Security and Cooperation in Europe to monitor compliance with the Helsinki Agreement on human rights. Congress appoints twelve of its members to the commission. The president appoints three, drawing from the departments of State, Defense, and Commerce.

The Speaker of the House designates the chair from among the House members. As if to underscore the mixed executive–legislative nature of this commission, it is funded not from the legislative branch appropriation bill but from the State–Justice appropriation bill. The commission was reconstituted in 1985, retaining the mixed legislative–executive membership but rotating the leadership between the House and the Senate.

Investigations

The power of Congress to conduct investigations, the Supreme Court noted in 1957, "comprehends probes into departments of the Federal Government to expose corruption, inefficiency or waste."

The House of Representatives sharpens its investigative power through the use of "resolutions of inquiry." A member may introduce a resolution authorizing a committee to request the information from the heads of executive departments. All resolutions of inquiry must be reported to the House within one week after presentation. Resolutions of inquiry are answered by departmental officials, either directly or through the president. If the executive branch resists the call for certain papers, congressional committees can issue subpoenas for documents or force individuals to testify. The Court has held that the issuance of a subpoena pursuant to an authorized investigation is "an indispensible ingredient of lawmaking." If a subpoena fails to get the attention of the executive branch, Congress can invoke its contempt power to protect legislative privileges and prerogatives. Contempt proceedings produced material from Secretary of Commerce Rogers Morton during the Ford administration and from Secretary of Energy Charles W. Duncan, Jr., during the Carter administration. Similarly, the contempt power was instrumental in prying loose documents from the Reagan and Clinton administrations.

Restrictions on the investigative power generally protect private citizens rather than agency officials. Citizens are entitled to First Amendment rights of free speech and association, the Fourth Amendment right to be free of unreasonable searches and seizures, the Fifth Amendment right that protects witnesses against self-incrimination, and certain Sixth Amendment rights of due process. Committee hearings must be properly authorized; the judiciary insists that committee questions must be pertinent and directed toward a legislative purpose.

These limitations do not apply to committee inquiries into agency activities. Agencies are expected to cooperate with legislative efforts to determine the expenditure of taxpayer funds. Presidents may raise the barrier of executive privilege, claiming a constitutional right to withhold information from Congress, but such defenses are rarely employed.

The courts have added a few restrictions on congressional investigations into agency affairs. Committees may not intervene in a pending adjudicatory proceeding by focusing on the process used by agency officials to reach a decision; here the congressional interference is not in an agency's *legislative* function, but rather, in its *judicial* function." The legislative (rulemaking) function of an agency is more open to congressional inquiries than adjudicatory proceedings, but a member may not force an executive official to take into account considerations that Congress had not intended.

For the most part, however, the courts assume that agency officials possess the necessary backbone to withstand searching inquiries by congressional committees. Even when the pressure during a congressional hearing is the direct impetus for a change in agency policy, the courts treat such influence as "part of the give and take of democratic government."

Appropriations

The power of the purse allows Congress to monitor and to control the administration of programs. At the end of each appropriation bill lies a "General Provisions" section that contains dozens of limitations, riders, and restrictions on agency operations. Within each appropriation account are additional restrictions that take the form of "provisos." When Congress felt that the Legal Services Corporation had abused its powers, it resorted to an increasing number of restrictions. For example, the appropriation for fiscal 1986 provided $305.5 million subject to a long list of conditions, prohibiting the corporation from using appropriated funds to lobby the national, state, or local governments; to provide legal assistance for an alien unless certain conditions are met; to support or conduct training programs for the purpose of advocating particular public policies or encouraging political activities; or to take certain other actions proscribed by the appropriation.

Audits by the General Accounting Office (GAO) permit Congress to hold executive officers accountable for the use of public funds. The GAO has the power to disallow an expenditure, thereby making the disbursing officer liable for the funds involved in an illegal transaction.

The power of the purse cannot be protected merely through the authorization and appropriation process. Congress must monitor the *expenditure* of funds to prevent the abuse of discretionary authority by executive officials. Members of Congress find it necessary to exercise statutory and nonstatutory controls over administrative operations such as transfer of funds, reprogramming of funds, year-end buying, deficiency spending, impoundment, carry-over balances, and contractor expenses.

Very few constitutional limits operate on the appropriations power. While the flow of federal money is not "the final arbiter of constitutionally protected rights," only rarely has the judiciary placed restrictions on the power of the purse. For example, Congress may not diminish the compensation of members of the federal judiciary, since this is specifically proscribed by the Constitution. In addition, the Supreme Court, in *United States v. Lovett* (1946), declared invalid a section of an appropriation act that prohibited the payment of federal salaries to three named "subversives." The language in the statute was struck down because it represented a bill of attainder that Article II, Section 3 of the Constitution forbids.

Private Bills

Members of Congress introduce private bills to overcome injustices and inadequacies in the administrative process. The flood of private bills after the Civil War to assist constituents turned down by the Pension Bureau was particularly flagrant. President Grover Cleveland declared open season on such measures, often employing sarcastic language in his veto messages to rebuke these legislative efforts. During the 49th Congress (1885–1887) there were more than twice as many private laws as public laws: 1,031 to 434. The ratio climbed to 3-to-1 by the 56th Congress (1899–1901) – 1,498 private laws and 443 public laws. Private bills introduced in the 59th Congress (1905–1907) topped 6,000.

In an effort to reduce the private bill workload, the Legislative Reorganization Act of 1946 prohibited the consideration of any private bill or resolution (including omnibus claims or pension bills) or an amendment to any bill or resolution authorizing or directing (1) the payment of money for property damages, for personal injuries or death for suits that could be instituted under the Federal Tort Claims Act (Title IV of the 1946 act), or for a pension (other than to carry out a provision of law or treaty stipulation); (2) the construction of a bridge across a navigable stream (Title V of the act); or (3) the correction of a military or naval record.

Due to a surge in legislative activity regarding immigration from 1949 through 1955, private laws averaged more than one thousand in each Congress, but from 1971 to 1997 they fell sharply, averaging about one hundred a Congress. The number of private bills continues to decline, with only a few dozen enacted in recent Congresses.

Private bills need not be *enacted* to affect the administrative process. Whenever a senator or representative introduces an immigration bill and the judiciary committees request a report from the Immigration and Naturalization Service, a deportation is delayed until action is taken on the bill. This procedure continues to exist even after the Supreme Court declared the legislative veto unconstitutional in 1983. Although private bills are subject to abuse, they allow Congress to correct mistakes in past legislation or current administration.

Casework

Members of Congress often become aware of administrative deficiencies by attending to "casework" – that is, assisting a constituent's contact with the bureaucracy. Much of the literature on Congress refers disparagingly to casework because it supposedly diverts members from more significant matters, making them "errand runners" instead of legislators. But casework, aside from its importance for reelection, helps educate legislators on the actual workings of a law. It forces them to descend from the lofty and often abstract universe of statutes to the practical world of administration. By responding to constituent requests, legislators obtain information that allows them to perfect laws and improve agency procedures.

Nonstatutory Controls

Simple resolutions (adopted by either house) and concurrent resolutions (adopted by both houses) have been used to direct administrative action. Although these resolutions are not presented to the president and therefore escape the veto power, and are invalid under the legislative veto case of *INS v. Chadha* (1983), they can still be effective means of control. Some statutes allow committees, acting by resolutions, to direct an agency to investigate. Most resolutions are advisory only, to be accepted by agencies as a recommended course of action. They express the "sense of Congress" (or of either house) on some aspect of public policy.

Congress directs administrative action through the use of other nonstatutory controls: language placed in committee reports, instructions issued by members during committee hearings, correspondence from committee and subcommittee heads to agency officials, and various types of agreements worked out between committees and agencies. Under a philosophy of good-faith efforts by administrators, this system makes sense for both branches. Instead of locking legislative policy into a rigid statutory mold, agency officials are given substantial leeway to adjust programs throughout the year in response to changing circumstances. In return for this latitude, administrators are expected to follow the legislative policy expressed in nonstatutory directives.

In some cases the system fails. To ignore such controls invites Congress to cut agency budgets and add restrictive statutory language.

Limitations on Congress

Members of Congress have many legitimate reasons for participating in the administrative process. In some cases, however, the representative function oversteps legal boundaries and takes on the color of influence peddling, leading to indictments in the courts against members who use their legislative and oversight positions for personal gain.

This kind of activity is controlled largely by two statutes. The bribery statute (18 U.S.C. 201) is directed against public officials – including members of Congress – who seek or accept anything of value in return for an official act. The conflict-of-interest statute (18 U.S.C. 203) makes it a criminal offense for members of Congress to receive or seek compensation for services relating to any proceeding, contract, claim, or other activity of the federal government. Depending on the circumstances, members may seek immunity under the Speech or Debate Clause of the Constitution, which prohibits questioning a senator or representative for any legislative act.

The Growth of Formal Controls

Congress balances a two-pronged strategy: delegating broad grants of power to agencies while insisting on a share in overseeing programs and activities. In the case of appropriations, funds are generally granted to agencies in large, lump-sum accounts, permitting considerable agency discretion throughout the year to withhold spending in some areas (impoundment), shift funds to new programs (reprogramming), and limit the size of the agency workforce (personnel ceilings). In all three areas Congress has begun to abandon its traditional reliance on nonstatutory controls as the instrument for regulating administrative policy. Because of a breakdown in good-faith relations between the branches, over the past two decades Congress has increasingly used statutory controls.

Impoundment

Prior to 1974 several administrations impounded funds, justified either on the basis of statutory authority or on the claim that presents had inherent authority to withhold funds from obligation. Despite confrontations from time to time, the two branches managed to fashion political accommodations that were acceptable to both sides. Rarely was there a stalemate that required the courts to referee the dispute.

This informal system fell apart during the Nixon administration. Funds were withheld in a manner, quantitatively and qualitatively, that threatened Congress's power of the purse. Budgetary priorities established by Congress through the appropriation process were quickly reshuffled by administrative officials who refused to spend funds the president did not want. As a result, programs were severely curtailed and in some cases terminated. The administration assumed an adamant, even truculent, position, offering extraordinary and often bizarre legal arguments to justify the impoundments. Although the federal courts handed down dozens of decisions against the administration, the lengthy process of litigation meant that program objectives set by Congress could not be achieved.

In response to this unprecedented abuse of presidential power over expenditures, Congress stepped into the administrative process to protect its own prerogatives. The result was the Impoundment Control Act of 1974. When deciding to withhold funds, the president had to submit a report to Congress. If the withholding was temporary (a *deferral*), either house of Congress could disapprove it at any time. The funds then must be released for obligation by the agencies. If the withholding was to be permanent (a *rescission*), the president had to obtain the support of both houses within forty-five days of continuous session. Otherwise, the funds must be released. A process that traditionally had been part of "budget execution and control," and therefore within the president's realm as administrative chief, was now explicitly tied to congressional review and action.

The procedures of the Impoundment Control Act eliminated the stark confrontations between the president and Congress that characterized the Nixon years. The statute explicitly recognized the right of the president to

withhold funds but subjected executive decisions to congressional review and disapproval. This accommodation was severely shaken in 1983 when the Supreme Court struck down the legislative veto in *INS v. Chadha*. The one-house veto was no longer available to disapprove deferrals.

Especially hard hit were the housing programs. Members of Congress and urban groups responded by filing suit to invalidate the president's deferral authority. They argued that the Impoundment Act of 1974 depended on the one-house veto to check the president's deferral authority, and that when the legislative veto was declared invalid in 1983, the deferral authority disappeared as well. Congress did not intend, said the suit, that the legislative veto could ever be severed from the authority granted. If one fell, so did the other.

A federal district judge decided that the president's deferral authority under the 1974 law was no longer available. The judge concluded that the history of that statute convinced him that Congress would have preferred no statute to one without the one-house veto provision. Severing the one-house veto while allowing the president to retain impoundment authority would allow the White House to use the authority "in effect, as a 'line-item veto' (which is, of course, anathema to Congress)." That decision was upheld by an appellate court. The effect of these decisions was to limit deferrals to routine managerial actions, a policy that Congress promptly enacted into law.

Reprogramming

It is the practice of Congress to appropriate large, lump-sum amounts for general purposes.

Administrative discretion of such vast scope is narrowed by the expectation of Congress that agencies will keep faith with the itemized material they submit in their budget justifications. Agencies are expected to spend funds for the precise purposes stated in these justifications (as amended by Congress). Over the course of a fiscal year, however, officials find it desirable or necessary to depart from their original budget submissions in order to respond to unforeseen developments, new requirements, incorrect price estimates, wage-rate adjustments, and legislation enacted after appropriations. To permit these changes, Congress allows agency officials to take funds from one program and "reprogram" them to another within the same appropriation account.

The latitude for reprogramming increased dramatically after 1949, when Congress began to consolidate a number of appropriation accounts. By administering larger accounts, agency officials gained new discretionary authority to reprogram funds. To retain some semblance of control, congressional committees insisted on various types of procedures requiring agencies to notify committees of significant reprogrammings and, in some cases, to seek their prior approval.

Although these controls are nonstatutory, agencies usually feel bound by them as a means of preserving good relationships with their review committees.

Even with elaborate procedures to govern reprogramming, clearly spelled out in committee reports and agency directives, officials sometimes used reprogramming to bypass congressional control. The next step in legislative supervision was to add statutory controls.

Particularly objectionable to Congress was the Pentagon's practice of requesting funds for a program, being turned down by Congress, and then spending other appropriated funds for the rejected program. Legislation in 1974 specifically prohibited the Pentagon from asking committees for permission to reprogram funds to an item that had been previously submitted to Congress and denied. This language is repeated every year in the defense appropriation bill.

Reprogramming by domestic agencies is now scrutinized with greater care by Congress. The congressional review committees have borrowed some of the controls previously applied to the Defense Department.

Personnel Ceilings and Floors

To protect legislative priorities, members of Congress find themselves increasingly involved in monitoring personnel levels. While the Office of Management and Budget (OMB) does not actually withhold funds from agencies,

as with impoundment, OMB personnel restrictions can prevent agencies from using funds. The agencies have the money but lack the people to spend it.

Committee studies pointed out that OMB used its personnel ceilings to frustrate congressional additions to the president's budget. Congress found that even when it increased the funding of a program and funds were not withheld through the deferral-rescission process, the programs were restricted by OMB ceilings.

To discourage artificially low personnel ceilings, the House Appropriations Committee began placing the number of authorized permanent positions for each agency in committee reports. Any agency deviations from those figures were to be reported to the committee. The Senate Appropriations Committee insisted that any efforts to restrain agency spending through employment ceilings should be reported to Congress either as a deferral or a rescission.

Nonstatutory directives are usually effective. In [some cases], however, Congress [resorts] to *statutory* language to prevent the administration from using personnel ceilings to defeat congressional funding initiatives.

Members of Congress recognize that statutory specifications for personnel and total salary levels can encroach on the executive power of program management. They also realize, however, that legislators bear a responsibility for assuring sound management of the programs they have created and efficient use of taxpayer dollars. The incentive to intervene is all the greater when personnel ceilings become just another form of impoundment.

Legislative Veto

The determination of Congress to share in administrative decisions, and to do so through formal statutory controls, is reflected in the growth of "legislative vetoes." Legislative vetoes are statutory provisions that delay an administrative action, usually for sixty to ninety days, during which time Congress may approve or disapprove without further presidential involvement. Congressional action can take several forms: a one-house veto (by simple resolution of either house), a two-house veto (by concurrent resolution), a committee veto, and even a committee chair's veto. The legislative veto originated in the 1930s but proliferated in the 1970s. In *INS v. Chadha* (1983), the Supreme Court declared the legislative veto unconstitutional because it bypassed the president's veto power.

Legislative Vetoes after Chadha

Even with *Chadha*, the need for a quid pro quo between Congress and the executive branch remains. The conditions that spawned the legislative veto a half-century ago have not disappeared. Executive officials still want substantial latitude in administering delegated authority; legislators still insist on maintaining control without having to pass another law. The persistence of these legislative–executive compacts underscores the gap between the Court's decision and the operations of government. Both executive officials and legislators are finding ways to avoid the static model of separated powers advanced by the Court.

For example, it came as a surprise to some observers that Congress continued to place legislative vetoes in bills and President Reagan continued to sign the bills into law. In the sixteen months between *Chadha* and the adjournment of the 98th Congress on October 12, 1984, an additional fifty-three legislative vetoes were added to the books. During subsequent years, Congress enacted still other legislative vetoes.

[It is] a world of informal agency–committee accommodations that were solidly in place before *Chadha*. No doubt these arrangements, such as for reprogramming of funds, will continue despite the Court's strictures on the proper steps of lawmaking. Statutes after *Chadha* may rely more heavily on notification to designated committees before an agency acts. Notification does not raise a constitutional issue, since it falls within the report-and-wait category already sanctioned by prior court rulings. In an informal sense, however, notification can become a code word for committee prior approval. Few agencies will be willing to notify a committee, learn of its opposition, and proceed anyway.

The committees have many ways to retaliate, particularly with the next reauthorization or appropriation bill. *Chadha* does not affect these nonstatutory legislative vetoes. Agencies are aware of the penalties that Congress can invoke if they decide to violate understandings and working relationships with their review committees.

What is now prohibited directly by *Chadha* can be accomplished indirectly through House and Senate rules. Each house can stipulate that no funds may be appropriated for a particular purpose unless the authorizing committee has granted its approval by committee resolution. Since this procedure concerns the internal workings of Congress, the "committee veto" is directed at the appropriations committees rather than at the executive branch. To that extent it should create no problem under *Chadha*, even if this type of committee veto is the functional equivalent of the legislative veto declared invalid.

Congress retains the right to place language in an appropriations bill to deny funds for agency activities. Members of both houses find it convenient to attach legislation and limitations to the most available appropriations bill. Since a president is unlikely to veto an appropriations bill simply because it contains an offensive rider, the practical effect is at least a two-house veto. Because of accommodations and comity between the House and the Senate, the reality in many cases is a one-house veto.

Finally, Congress can use a joint resolution as a substitute for the legislative veto. It clearly meets *Chadha*'s requirement of bicameralism and presentment. Depending on the type of joint resolution, the burden shifts to Congress or the president. A joint resolution of disapproval usually weakens legislative control because it requires Congress to act and the resolution is vulnerable to the president's veto. On the other hand, a joint resolution of approval shifts the burden to the president, who would have to obtain the approval of both houses within a set number of days. The results could be ironic. For example, reorganization plans were subject to a one-house veto. If Congress selected a joint resolution of approval, and one house decided to withdraw its support or not to act at all, the practical effect is a one-house veto. Moreover, this new type of "one-house veto" would be effective by *inaction*. The previous one-house veto required Congress to act.

Chadha has not stopped Congress from placing legislative vetoes in public laws. These bills are regularly signed into law, although at times Presidents Reagan, Bush, and Clinton commented on the unconstitutionality of these provisions in light of the Court's ruling. From the day that *Chadha* was issued, on June 23, 1983, to the end of 1997, more than four hundred new legislative vetoes have been enacted into law.

Through its misreading of history, congressional procedures, and executive–legislative relations, the Supreme Court has directed the political branches to follow a lawmaking process that is impracticable and unworkable. The inevitable result is a record of noncompliance, subtle evasion, and a system of lawmaking that is now more convoluted, cumbersome, and covert than before. In many cases the Court's decision simply drives underground a set of legislative and committee vetoes that had previously operated in plain sight. No one should be misled if the number of legislative vetoes placed in statutes gradually declines over the years. Fading from view will not mean disappearance. In one form or another, legislative vetoes will remain an important technique for reconciling legislative and executive interests. Administrators want additional discretionary authority; Congress is determined to control that authority without always having to pass another public law.

Conclusions

Despite an accumulation of learned studies and reports that urge Congress to leave administrative duties to the president, legislative involvement persists from one decade to the next. The reason has to be found in something more complex than an obstinate desire on the part of members of Congress to overstep constitutional boundaries. Presidents and their supporters face continued frustration because they ignore, or try to overlook, the legitimate stake and interest of Congress in administrative matters.

When executive officials deny Congress the right to add to presidential budgetary estimates, and subsequently withhold funds or restrict programs by artifices that favor the administration's priorities over those enacted by Congress, they provoke Congress to intervene in the implementation of a statute. Out of frustration, legislators are inclined to place new restrictions in a public law, concluding that flexibility in a statute is used too often by agencies as an excuse for thwarting congressional policy.

The growth of agency and congressional staff has placed a heavy strain on traditional techniques of legislative oversight and the dependence on good-faith agency efforts. Congress now has the resources to delve more deeply into administration. As the gap between the branches widens, because of staff build-up and turnover, Congress is less able and less willing to rely on customary methods of control. Oral agreements are being replaced by committee report language, which is giving way to statutory directives.

CHAPTER THIRTY-THREE

Conscience of a Conservative

Jeffrey Rosen

In this article, appearing in the *New York Times*, Rosen interviews Jack Goldsmith, former head of the Office of Legal Counsel, and recaps the events of his short and tumultuous tenure. Goldsmith declares that a major failure of the Bush administration in the war on terror has been its unwillingness to seek congressional support. The Bush administration's "go-it-alone" attitude, in Goldsmith's view, has diminished the power of the presidency.

In the fall of 2003, Jack L. Goldsmith was widely considered one of the brightest stars in the conservative legal firmament. A 40-year-old law professor at the University of Chicago, Goldsmith had established himself, with his friend and fellow law professor John Yoo, as a leading proponent of the view that international standards of human rights should not apply in cases before U.S. courts. In recognition of their prominence, Goldsmith and Yoo had been anointed the "New Sovereigntists" by the journal *Foreign Affairs*.

Goldsmith had been hired the year before as a legal adviser to the general counsel of the Defense Department, William J. Haynes II. While at the Pentagon, Goldsmith wrote a

memo for Defense Secretary Donald Rumsfeld warning that prosecutors from the International Criminal Court might indict American officials for their actions in the war on terror. Goldsmith described this threat as "the judicialization of international politics." No one was surprised when he was hired in October 2003 to head the Office of Legal Counsel, the division of the Justice Department that advises the president on the limits of executive power. Immediately, the job put him at the center of critical debates within the Bush administration about its continuing response to 9/11 – debates about coercive interrogation, secret surveillance and the detention and trial of enemy combatants.

Nine months later, in June 2004, Goldsmith resigned. Although he refused to discuss his resignation at the time, he had led a small group of administration lawyers in a behind-the-scenes revolt against what he considered the constitutional excesses of the legal policies embraced by his White House superiors in the war on terror. During his first weeks on the job, Goldsmith had discovered that the Office of Legal Counsel had written two legal opinions – both drafted by Goldsmith's friend Yoo, who served as a deputy in the office – about the authority of the executive branch to conduct coercive interrogations. Goldsmith considered these opinions, now known as the "torture memos," to be tendentious, overly broad and legally flawed, and he fought to change them. He also found himself challenging the White House on a variety of other issues, ranging from surveillance to the trial of suspected terrorists. His efforts succeeded in bringing the Bush administration somewhat closer to what Goldsmith considered the rule of law — although at considerable cost to Goldsmith himself.

After leaving the Office of Legal Counsel, Goldsmith was uncertain about what, if anything, he should say publicly about his resignation. His silence came to be widely misinterpreted. After leaving the Justice Department, he accepted a tenured professorship at Harvard Law School, where he currently teaches. During his first weeks in Cambridge, in the fall of 2004, some of his colleagues denounced him for what they mistakenly assumed was his role in drafting the torture memos.

Now Goldsmith is speaking out. In a new book, *The Terror Presidency*, which will be published later this month, and in a series of conversations I had with him this summer, Goldsmith has recounted how, from his first weeks on the job, he fought vigorously against an expansive view of executive power championed by officials in the White House, including Alberto Gonzales, who was then the White House counsel and who recently resigned as attorney general, and David Addington, who was then Vice President Cheney's legal adviser and is now his chief of staff. Goldsmith says he is not speaking out for the money. Nor is he speaking out because he disagrees with the basic goals of the Bush administration in the war on terror. "I shared, and I still share, a lot of their concerns about what we have to do to meet the terrorist threat," he told me.

Goldsmith told me that he has decided to speak publicly about his battles at the Justice Department because he hopes that "future presidents and people inside the executive branch can learn from our mistakes." In his view, American presidents for the foreseeable future will, like George W. Bush, face enormous pressure to be aggressive and preemptive in taking measures to prevent another terrorist attack in the United States. At the same time, Goldsmith notes, everywhere the president looks, critics — as well as his own lawyers — are telling him that preemptive actions may violate international law as well as U.S. criminal law. What,

exactly, are the legal limits of executive power in the post-9/11 world? How should administration lawyers negotiate the conflict between the fear of attacks and the fear of lawsuits?

In Goldsmith's view, the Bush administration went about answering these questions in the wrong way. Instead of reaching out to Congress and the courts for support, which would have strengthened its legal hand, the administration asserted what Goldsmith considers an unnecessarily broad, "go-it-alone" view of executive power. As Goldsmith sees it, this strategy has backfired. "They embraced this vision," he says, "because they wanted to leave the presidency stronger than when they assumed office, but the approach they took achieved exactly the opposite effect. The central irony is that people whose explicit goal was to expand presidential power have diminished it."

When Goldsmith was asked, four years ago, to head the Office of Legal Counsel at the Justice Department, he jumped at the opportunity. Working for the office is one of the most prestigious jobs in government: former heads and deputies include the Supreme Court Justices William H. Rehnquist, Antonin Scalia and Samuel A. Alito Jr. The Office of Legal Counsel interprets all laws that bear on the powers of the executive branch. The opinions of the head of the office are binding, except on the rare occasions when they are reversed by the attorney general or the president.

In the post-9/11 era, the office has played a crucial role in providing legal cover to jittery bureaucrats fearful that officials in the White House, Defense and State Departments or the C.I.A. might be prosecuted for their actions in the war on terror. The Justice Department, after all, is the branch of government responsible for prosecutions, and its own prosecutors — as well as independent counsels — would be hard pressed to prosecute someone who had relied on the department's own opinions in good faith. For this reason, the office has two important powers: the power to put a brake on aggressive presidential action by saying no and, conversely, the power to dispense what Goldsmith calls "free get-out-of jail cards" by saying yes. Its opinions, he writes in his book, are the equivalent of "an advance pardon" for actions taken at the fuzzy edges of criminal laws.

In the Bush administration, however, the most important legal-policy decisions in the war on terror before Goldsmith's arrival were made not by the Office of Legal Counsel but by a self-styled "war council." This group met periodically in Gonzales's office at the White House or Haynes's office at the Pentagon. The members included Gonzales, Addington, Haynes and Yoo. These men shared a belief that the biggest obstacle to a vigorous response to the 9/11 attacks was the set of domestic and international laws that arose in the 1970s to constrain the president's powers in response to the excesses of Watergate and the Vietnam War. (The Foreign Intelligence Surveillance Act of 1978, for example, requires that executive officials get a warrant before wiretapping suspected enemies in the United States.) The head of the Office of Legal Counsel in the first years of the Bush administration, Jay Bybee, had little experience with national-security issues, and he delegated responsibility for that subject matter to Yoo, giving him the authority to draft opinions that were binding on the entire executive branch.

Yoo was a "godsend" to a White House nervous about war-crimes prosecutions, Goldsmith writes in his book, because his opinions reassured the White House that no official who relied on them could be prosecuted after the fact. But Yoo's direct access to Gonzales angered his boss, Attorney General John Ashcroft, according to Goldsmith. Ashcroft, Goldsmith says, felt that Gonzales and the war council were usurping legal-policy decisions that were properly entrusted to the attorney general, such as the creation of military commissions, which Gonzales supported and Ashcroft never liked.

The matter came to a head in the fall of 2003, when Bybee left the Office of Legal Counsel and Gonzales suggested Yoo as a candidate to lead it. Ashcroft rejected the suggestion. Yoo then recommended his friend Goldsmith to the White House as a suitable alternative. Goldsmith interviewed with Ashcroft at the Justice Department and with Gonzales and Addington at the White House. In his interview with Addington and Gonzales, Goldsmith recalls talking about the dangers of international law and the importance of military commissions. He got the job.

Several hours after Goldsmith was sworn in, on October 6, 2003, he recalls that he received a phone call from Gonzales: the White House needed to know as soon as possible whether the Fourth Geneva Convention, which describes protections that explicitly cover civilians in war zones like Iraq, also covered insurgents and terrorists. After several days of study, Goldsmith agreed with lawyers in several other federal agencies, who had concluded that the convention applied to all Iraqi civilians, including terrorists and insurgents. In a meeting with Ashcroft, Goldsmith explained his analysis, which Ashcroft accepted. Later, Goldsmith drove from the Justice Department to the White House for a meeting with Gonzales and Addington. Goldsmith remembers his deputy Patrick Philbin turning to him in the car and saying: "They're going to be really mad. They're not going to understand our decision. They've never been told no."

In his book, Goldsmith describes Addington as the "biggest presence in the room – a large man with large glasses and an imposing salt-and-pepper beard" who was "known throughout the bureaucracy as the best-informed, savviest and most conservative lawyer in the administration, someone who spoke for and acted with the full backing of the powerful vice president, and someone who crushed bureaucratic opponents." When Goldsmith presented his analysis of the Geneva Conventions at the White House, Addington, according to Goldsmith, became livid. "The president has already decided that terrorists do not receive Geneva Convention protections," Addington replied angrily, according to Goldsmith. "You cannot question his decision."

Goldsmith then explained that he agreed with the president's determination that detainees from Al Qaeda and the Taliban weren't protected under the Third Geneva Convention, which concerns the treatment of prisoners of war, but that different protections were at issue with the Fourth Geneva Convention, which concerns civilians. Addington, Goldsmith says, was not persuaded.

Months later, when Goldsmith tried to question another presidential decision, Addington expressed his views even more pointedly. "If you rule that way," Addington exclaimed in disgust, Goldsmith recalls, "the blood of the hundred thousand people who die in the next attack will be on your hands."

The conflict over the Geneva Conventions was just the beginning. About six weeks after he started work, Goldsmith became aware that there might be what he calls "potentially problematic" opinions drafted by the Office of Legal Counsel. These were the "torture memos," one of which was written in August 2002 and the other in March 2003. The August opinion defined torture as pain "equivalent in intensity to the pain accompanying serious physical injury, such as organ failure, impairment of bodily function or even death." Goldsmith concluded that this opinion defined torture far too narrowly. He also had concerns about the March 2003 opinion, the contents of which remain classified, but which dealt with the military interrogation of aliens held outside the United States.

Goldsmith told me that he objected to what he calls the "extremely broad and unnecessary analysis of the president's commander in chief power" in the memos. The August opinion, for example, boldly concluded that "any effort by Congress to regulate the interrogation of battlefield combatants would violate the Constitution's sole vesting of the Commander in Chief authority in the President." Goldsmith says he believed at the time, and still does, that "this extreme conclusion" would call into question the constitutionality of federal laws that limit interrogation, like the War Crimes Act of 1996, which prohibits grave breaches of the Geneva Conventions, and the Uniform Code of Military Justice, which prohibits cruelty and maltreatment. He also found the tone of both opinions "tendentious" rather than cautious and feared that they might be interpreted as an attempt to immunize government officials for genuinely bad acts.

Yoo has acknowledged drafting the August 2002 memo, which he says was the basis for the interrogation of Abu Zubaydah, a top Al Qaeda operative. Yoo also wrote and signed the March 2003 opinion. His friendship with Goldsmith made it especially awkward for Goldsmith to criticize the memos. "I was basically taking steps to fix the mistakes of a close friend, who I knew would be mad about it," Goldsmith told me. "We don't talk anymore, and that's one of the many sad things about my time in government."

In December 2003, Goldsmith decided that he had to withdraw the March opinion – that is, he had to tell administration officials that they could no longer rely on it. "But figuring out how to withdraw it was very tricky," he told me, "since withdrawal would frighten everyone who relied on the opinions in a very sensitive area." Goldsmith concluded that he could immediately tell the Defense Department to stop relying on the March opinion, since he was confident that it was not needed to justify the 24 interrogation techniques the department was actually using, including two called "Fear Up Harsh" and "Pride and Ego Down," which were designed to make subjects nervous without crossing the line into coercion. But the withdrawal of the August opinion was a much harder call. The August opinion provided the legal foundation for the C.I.A.'s interrogation program, Goldsmith says, which he considered much closer to the legal line.

Goldsmith, however, says he didn't have the time or resources to create a replacement opinion immediately. In his initial months on the job, his attention was focused on the more pressing matter of addressing legal issues surrounding the terrorist-surveillance program. In April 2004, however, Goldsmith's priorities were reversed when the Abu Ghraib scandal broke. Then, in June of that year, Yoo's August 2002 opinion was leaked to the media. "After the leak, there was a lot of pressure on me within the administration to stand by the opinion," Goldsmith told me, "and the problem was that I had decided six months earlier that I couldn't stand by the opinion."

A week after the leak of Yoo's August 2002 memo, Goldsmith withdrew the opinion.

Goldsmith made the decision himself, in consultation with Philbin and Deputy Attorney General James B. Comey, both of whom, Goldsmith says, agreed it was the right thing to do. He then told Ashcroft, who was, Goldsmith writes, "unbelievably magnanimous: it had happened on his watch, and he could have overruled me, and he didn't." Goldsmith was concerned, however, that the White House might overrule him. So he made a strategic decision: on the same day that he withdrew the opinion, he submitted his resignation, effectively forcing the administration to choose between accepting his decision and letting him leave quietly, or rejecting it and turning his resignation into a big news story. "If the story had come out that the U.S. government decided to stick by the controversial opinions that led the head of the Office of Legal Counsel to resign, that would have looked bad," Goldsmith told me. "The timing was designed to ensure that the decision stuck."

Again, according to Goldsmith, Addington was furious. During his brief time in office, Goldsmith had withdrawn not only the two torture opinions but also others. In the end, he says, he had withdrawn more opinions than any of his predecessors. Shortly before he resigned, Goldsmith says, Addington confronted him in Gonzales's office, pulling out of his jacket pocket a 3-by-5 card that listed the withdrawn opinions. "Since you've withdrawn so many legal opinions that the president and others have been relying on," Addington said, according to Goldsmith, "we need you to . . . let us know which [of the remaining] ones you still stand by." Goldsmith recalls that Gonzales, in his own farewell chat with him, said, "I guess those opinions really were as bad as you said."

Looking back, Goldsmith says, he criticizes but does not vilify Yoo, whom he believes wrote and defended the opinions in good faith. Praising Yoo's "knowledge, intelligence and energy," he writes in his book that "the poor quality of a handful of very important opinions is probably attributable to some combination of the fear that pervaded the executive branch, pressure from the White House and Yoo's

unusually expansive and self-confident conception of presidential power."

I have known Yoo since we were in law school together as well, and I called him for a response. "I think Jack and I had a good-faith disagreement, but I think at some level this was elevating form over substance," he said. Yoo said that in writing the torture memo, he experienced no pressure from the White House, which he described as "hands off." Instead, he said, "there was an urgency to decide so that valuable intelligence could be acquired from Abu Zubaydah, before further attacks could occur." Yoo says it is his understanding that no policies or interrogation techniques changed as a result of the withdrawal of the torture memo, noting that all policies that were legal under the withdrawn opinions are also acknowledged as legal under the opinion that eventually replaced the withdrawn ones. (That opinion was issued in December 2004, six months after Goldsmith's resignation, and was signed by Daniel Levin, his acting successor as head of the Office of Legal Counsel.)

Goldsmith puts the bulk of the responsibility for the excesses of the Office of Legal Counsel on the White House. "I probably had a hundred meetings with Gonzales, and there was only one time I was talking about a national-security issue when Addington wasn't there," Goldsmith told me. "My conflicts were all with Addington, who was a proxy for the vice president. They were very, very stressful."

During his tenure at the Office of Legal Counsel, Goldsmith also clashed with Addington over the detention and trial of suspected terrorists. In January 2004, the Supreme Court agreed to review a lower-court decision approving the detention of Yaser Hamdi, an American citizen then being held as an enemy combatant. A group of administration lawyers including Goldsmith met with Gonzales and Addington in Gonzales's office to discuss the implications of the case. "Why don't we just go to Congress and get it to sign off on the whole detention program?" Goldsmith recalls asking, reasoning that the Supreme Court would be less likely to strike down a detention program in wartime if Congress had explicitly supported it. According to Goldsmith, Addington shot down the idea.

Not long before Goldsmith left, the Supreme Court approved in June 2004, in the Hamdi case, the detention power itself but put some modest restrictions on the administration's ability to detain citizens without trial. Afterward, Gonzales, Addington, Goldsmith and others, including the deputy solicitor general, Paul Clement, met again, Goldsmith recalls, and he and Clement again proposed going to Congress to put the administration's legal strategy on a more sound footing. Once again, Goldsmith told me, the advice was ignored, and the White House continued to operate as if it assumed it could avoid a strong rebuke from the Supreme Court.

That rebuke finally arrived, however, last year in the Hamdan case, when the Supreme Court rejected the administration's claim that it could try suspected terrorists in military commissions created without Congressional approval. In a further blow to the administration, the court held that the legal protections of "common Article 3" of the Geneva Conventions, which contains minimal protections for detainees in wartime, also applied in the war against Al Qaeda. Goldsmith says he believes this ruling was "legally erroneous" but "hugely consequential." It provided detainees at Guantánamo with more rights than the administration had ever acknowledged, and it implied that the War Crimes Act might be used to prosecute administration officials for their treatment of detainees.

In debates over the detention of suspected terrorists, Goldsmith says he was struck by how Addington's efforts to expand presidential power ultimately weakened it. In September 2006, 2 months before the midterm elections, Bush eventually did ask Congress to approve his military commissions, and Congress promptly passed a law that gave him everything he asked for, authorizing many aspects of the military commissions that the Supreme Court had struck down. Although Bush had won the battle, Goldsmith sees the refusal to go to Congress earlier as the cause of an unnecessary Supreme Court defeat. "I'm not a civil libertarian, and what I did wasn't driven by concerns about civil liberties per se," he told me. "It was a disagreement about means, not ends, driven by a desire to make sure that the administration's counterterrorism policies had a firm legal foundation."

In Goldsmith's estimation, the unnecessary unilateralism of the Bush administration reached its apex in the controversy over wiretapping and secret surveillance.

He shared the White House's concern that the Foreign Intelligence Surveillance Act might prevent wiretaps on international calls involving terrorists. But Goldsmith deplored the way the White House tried to fix the problem, which was highly contemptuous of Congress and the courts. "We're one bomb away from getting rid of that obnoxious [FISA] court," Goldsmith recalls Addington telling him in February 2004.

In his book, Goldsmith claims that Addington and other top officials treated the Foreign Intelligence Surveillance Act the same way they handled other laws they objected to: "They blew through them in secret based on flimsy legal opinions that they guarded closely so no one could question the legal basis for the operations," he writes. Goldsmith's first experienced this extraordinary concealment, or "strict compartmentalization," in late 2003 when, he recalls, Addington angrily denied a request by the N.S.A.'s inspector general to see a copy of the Office of Legal Counsel's legal analysis supporting the secret surveillance program.

Goldsmith also witnessed perhaps the most well-known confrontation over the administration's aggressive tactics: the scene at Ashcroft's hospital bed on March 10, 2004, when Gonzales and Andrew Card, the White House chief of staff, visited the hospital to demand that the ailing Ashcroft approve, over Goldsmith and Comey's objections, a secret program that was about to expire. (Goldsmith refuses to identify the program, but Robert S. Mueller III, the F.B.I. director, has publicly indicated it was the terrorist surveillance program.) As he recalled it to me, Goldsmith received a call in the evening from his deputy, Philbin, telling him to go to the George Washington University Hospital immediately, since Gonzales and Card were on the way there. Goldsmith raced to the hospital, double-parked outside and walked into a dark room. Ashcroft lay with a bright light shining on him and tubes and wires coming out of his body. Suddenly, Gonzales and Card came in the room and announced that they were there in connection with the classified program. "Ashcroft, who looked like he was near death, sort of puffed up his chest," Goldsmith recalls. "All of a sudden, energy and color came into his face, and he said that he didn't appreciate them coming to visit him under those circumstances, that he had concerns about the matter they were asking about and that, in any event, he wasn't the attorney general at the moment; Jim Comey was. He actually gave a two-minute speech, and I was sure at the end of it he was going to die. It was the most amazing scene I've ever witnessed."

Goldsmith, Comey, Mueller, and other Justice Department officials were prepared to resign en masse if the White House implemented the program over their objections. Two days later, Comey had a conversation at the White House with Bush in which the president told him to do whatever was necessary to make the program legal. And in the end, the entire controversy was arguably unnecessary since the program was eventually approved by Congress and brought, at least partially, under the supervision of the FISA Court, as it could have been from the beginning. "I was sure the government was going to melt down," Goldsmith told me. "No one anticipated they were going to reverse themselves."

The heroes of Goldsmith's book – his historical models of presidential leadership in wartime – are Presidents Lincoln and Franklin D. Roosevelt. Both of them, as Arthur Schlesinger noted in his essay "War and the Constitution," "were lawyers who, while duly respecting their profession, regarded law as secondary to political leadership." In Goldsmith's view, an indifference to the political process has ultimately made Bush a less effective wartime leader than his greatest predecessors. Surprisingly, Bush, who is not a lawyer, allowed far more legalistic positions in the war on terror to be adopted in his name, without bothering to try to persuade Congress and the public that his positions were correct. "I don't know if President Bush understood how extreme some of the arguments were about executive power that some people in his administration were making," Goldsmith told me. "It's hard to know how he would know."

The Bush administration's legalistic "go-it-alone approach," Goldsmith suggests, is the antithesis of Lincoln and Roosevelt's willingness to collaborate with Congress. Bush, he argues, ignored the truism that presidential power is the power to persuade. "The Bush administration has operated on an entirely different concept of power that relies on minimal deliberation, unilateral action and legalistic defense," Goldsmith concludes in his book. "This approach largely eschews politics: the need to explain, to justify, to convince, to get people on board, to compromise."

Goldsmith says he remains convinced of the seriousness of the terrorist threat and the need to take aggressive action to combat it, but he believes, quoting his conservative Harvard Law colleague Charles Fried, that the Bush administration "badly overplayed a winning hand." In retrospect, Goldsmith told me, Bush "could have achieved all that he wanted to achieve, and put it on a firmer foundation, if he had been willing to reach out to other institutions of government." Instead, Goldsmith said, he weakened the presidency he was so determined to strengthen. "I don't think any president in the near future can have the same attitude toward executive power, because the other institutions of government won't allow it," he said softly. "The Bush administration has borrowed its power against future presidents."

PART X. CONGRESS AND THE COURTS

CHAPTER THIRTY-FOUR

Senate Voting on Supreme Court Nominees

A Neoinstitutional Model

Charles M. Cameron, Albert D. Cover, and Jeffrey A. Segal

Cameron, Cover, and Segal consider the factors that lead senators to vote for or against a president's Supreme Court nominees. They find that nominees considered to be higly qualified and closer to the policy positions of a senator's state are more likely to receive a positive vote.

Roll call voting in the U.S. Senate on nominees to the Supreme Court presents political scientists with an empirical puzzle and a theoretical challenge. The empirical puzzle stems from a curious pattern in the nomination politics of recent decades. In some cases, as shown in Table 34.1, the Senate routinely confirms the nominee. In these cases, liberal senators vote for conservative nominees and conservative senators vote for liberal nominees. For example, the most liberal members of the Senate recently voted to confirm judicial conservative Antonin Scalia. But on other occasions – including 9 of the 20 post-*Brown-v.-Board of Education* confirmations – the confirmation becomes extremely contentious. In these cases many or even most senators vote against the nominee, and voting becomes ideologically polarized. The rejection of Robert Bork illustrates this case.

We therefore face some puzzling questions: Why are some votes consensual? Why are some

Charles M. Cameron, Albert D. Cover, and Jeffrey A. Segal. 1990. "Senate Voting on Supreme Court Nominees: A Neoinstitutional Model" *American Political Science Review* 84(2): 525–34. Copyright © 1990 by the American Political Science Association. Reprinted with the permission of Cambridge University Press.

votes contentious? And what determines voting decisions in both cases? Satisfactory answers to these questions must explain the apparent switching process between the consensual and conflictual votes and the variance within the conflictual votes.

First, we discuss institutional issues in confirmation voting. Second, based on this analysis, we develop a spatial model of roll call voting on confirmations. Using newly generated data on nominees, we then test the theoretical model.

A NEOINSTITUTIONAL PERSPECTIVE ON CONFIRMATION VOTING

A neoinstitutionalist perspective suggests that votes on Supreme Court nominations depend on (1) the goals the senator pursues during the confirmation process; (2) the choices confronting the senator at each stage during the sequence of votes (or "agenda") leading to a filled vacancy on the Court; (3) the foresight the senator exercises in moving from one stage to the next in a multistage agenda; and (4) the payoffs the senator receives as a consequence of his or her choices.

With respect to motivation, we imagine senators asking themselves, "Can I use my actions during the confirmation process to gain electoral advantage? Or if I am forced to account for my votes, can they be used against me? What is the most electorally expedient action for me to have taken?" Hence, we

Table 34.1. *Nominee Margin and Vote Status*

Nominee	Year	President's Status[a]	Margin	Vote[b]
Warren	1954	strong	96-0[c]	consensual
Harlan	1955	weak	71-11	conflictual
Brennan	1957	weak	95-0[c]	consensual
Whittaker	1957	weak	96-0	consensual
Stewart	1959	weak	70-17	conflictual
White	1962	strong	100-0[c]	consensual
Goldberg	1962	strong	100-0[c]	consensual
Fortas 1	1965	strong	100-0[c]	consensual
Marshall	1967	strong	69-11	conflictual
Fortas 2	1968	weak	45-43[d]	conflictual
Burger	1969	weak	74-3	consensual
Haynsworth	1969	weak	45-55	conflictual
Carswell	1970	weak	45-51	conflictual
Blackmun	1970	weak	94-0	consensual
Powell	1971	weak	89-1	consensual
Rehnquist 1	1971	weak	68-26	conflictual
Stevens	1975	weak	98-0	consensual
O'Connor	1981	strong	99-0	consensual
Rehnquist 2	1986	strong	65-33	conflictual
Scalia	1986	strong	98-0	consensual
Bork	1987	weak	42-58	conflictual
Kennedy	1988	weak	97-0	consensual

[a] The president is labeled "strong" in a nonelection year in which the president's party controls the Senate and "weak" otherwise.

[b] A vote is labeled "conflictual" when less than 90% of the votes cast are cast on the winning side and "consensual" otherwise.

[c] Voice vote.

[d] Vote on cloture – failed to receive necessary two-thirds majority.

follow Mayhew, Fenno, and Fiorina in analyzing how the prospect of explaining behavior in Washington influences the behavior of representatives. We recognize that senators often have additional goals in mind as they make highly visible decisions. Among these goals may be furthering a vision of good public policy and enhancing power and prestige within the Senate. But a narrower focus on the electoral connection often captures much of the motivation of senators, provides a useful base line for more complex models, and offers an attractive, direct path to the statistical analysis of confirmation roll call voting.

In light of the electoral connection, a senator is likely to view roll call voting as an opportunity for position taking and credit claiming. The senator can generally expect to gain electorally (or at least not to lose electorally) from voting as constituents wish and can expect to incur losses from flouting constituents' desires, regardless of the actual outcome of a vote. In addition, to the extent that the senator's vote actually sways the outcome, the senator may claim credit for a good outcome or receive blame for a bad one.

Position taking and credit claiming must take place within the agenda of voting opportunities offered during the confirmation process. This agenda operates fairly simply. First, the president nominates a candidate; the Senate then votes on this candidate. If the nominee is approved, the process ends. If the nominee is rejected, the president nominates another candidate and the Senate votes on this candidate. The process continues until the seat is filled. In the twentieth century, the process has never proceeded past three votes and rarely past two.

As this agenda involves a potential series of votes, strategic voting is a possibility. For example, in an early stage of the agenda a senator might vote against a nominee constituents actually favor in order to create the opportunity to vote for an even better nominee at a later stage. Or a senator might vote for a nominee constituents oppose to block the confirmation of an even worse subsequent nominee.

Because strategic voting requires misrepresenting one's true motivation, it can present difficulties for senators compelled to explain roll call votes to their electorate. We have suggested elsewhere that rationally nonstrategic voting is almost always a better choice for senators than strategic voting when casting roll call votes on nominees to the Supreme Court.

A SPATIAL MODEL OF CONFIRMATION VOTING

What factors would electorally minded senators care about when judging the merits of Supreme Court nominees? Both the public record and common sense suggest that the public's principal concerns in nomination politics are the characteristics of nominees. Two characteristics in particular receive close scrutiny in hearings and in the press: (1) the nominee's professional competence and (2) the nominee's judicial philosophy. The importance of high qualifications is exemplified by the universal ridicule heaped on Senator Roman Hruska's defense of Judge G. Harold Carswell's manifest mediocrity: "Even if he [Carswell] were mediocre, there are a lot of mediocre judges and people and lawyers. They are entitled to a little representation, aren't they, and a little chance." The importance of judicial philosophy is suggested by the attacks by liberals on judicial conservative Robert Bork and those by conservatives on judicial liberals Thurgood Marshall and Abe Fortas. Ideologically proximate nominees will be attractive, poorly qualified nominees unattractive, and nominees who are both ideologically distant and poorly qualified very unattractive.

In addition, the president is not a passive bystander but an active participant in the nomination process. The president has nominated a particular person to satisfy his own constituents and possibly to further his own policy objectives. Failure to send the confirmation through the Senate harms the president's prestige, his reputation for competence, and possibly his popularity and his ability to govern. Therefore, the president is likely to bring his political resources to bear to help his nominee. In general, the president will have more political resources to deploy – and can deploy his political resources more effectively – when his party controls the Senate and when he is not in the fourth year of his term. In addition, presidential resources are not likely to affect every senator the same way. First, the president's resources will probably carry greater impact on members of his own party. Second, presidential resources are much more likely to change a senator's votes when the senator is more or less undecided on the basis of the nominee's characteristics.

Ideology can be considered a spatial characteristic; nominee qualifications and the strength of the president are nonspatial or valence characteristics of a nominee; party status is a nonspatial characteristic of a senator. Hence, define five variables, I_j, X_{ij}, U_j, S_j, and P_{ij}. I_j is a measure of nominee j's ideology, ranging from zero (a very conservative nominee) to one (a very liberal nominee). X_{ij} measures the ideal or desired ideology for nominees held by senator i's constituents at the time of nominee j, as perceived by senator i. U_j measures nominee j's (lack of) qualifications, ranging from zero (highly qualified) to one (poorly qualified). S_j and P_{ij} measure, respectively, whether the president is strong at the time of nominee j (i.e., whether the president's party controls the Senate in a nonelection year) and whether senator i is from the same party as the president at the time of nominee j.

DATA

The dependent variable consists of the 2,054 confirmation votes cast by senators from the nomination of Earl Warren to the nomination of Anthony Kennedy.

To determine perceptions of nominees' qualifications and judicial philosophy we conducted a content analysis from a source that contains comparable information on each nominee since Earl Warren, statements from newspaper editorials from the time of the nomination by the president until the vote by the Senate. We selected four of the nation's leading papers, two with a liberal stance (the *New York Times* and the *Washington Post*) and two with a more conservative outlook (the *Chicago Tribune* and the *Los Angeles Times*). We note here that the data are reliable and appear to be valid. Table 34.2 displays the ideology and qualification scores for the nominees from Earl Warren to Anthony Kennedy.

The spatial model requires a measure of senators' ideal points. Moreover, if the distance metric is to be meaningful, this measure must be comparable with that of the nominees. In the absence of a direct measure of the perceived preference of senators' constituencies about nominees' judicial philosophy, we have developed an inferential measure using senators' liberalism ratings calculated by the Americans for Democratic Action (ADA). The method we

Table 34.2. *Nominee Ideology and Qualification Scores*

Nominee	Ideology	Qualifications
Warren	.75	.74
Harlan	.88	.86
Brennan	1.00	1.00
Whittaker	.50	1.00
Stewart	.75	1.00
White	.50	.50
Goldberg	.75	.92
Fortas 1	1.00	1.00
Marshall	1.00	.84
Fortas 2	.85	.64
Burger	.12	.96
Haynsworth	.16	.34
Carswell	.04	.11
Blackmun	.12	.97
Powell	.17	1.00
Rehnquist 1	.05	.89
Stevens	.25	.96
O'Connor	.48	1.00
Rehnquist 2	.05	.40
Scalia	.00	1.00
Bork	.10	.79
Kennedy	.37	.89

Note: .00 is the most conservative and 1.00 the most liberal score possible. .00 is the least qualified and 1.00 the most qualified score possible.

employ is based on the theory of predictive mappings in the spatial theory of voting and has been discussed at some length elsewhere.

We define a variable S ("strong") which takes the value one when the president's party controls the Senate and the president is not in the fourth year of his term, zero otherwise. We define a variable P ("party"), which takes the value one when a senator is of the same party as the president, zero otherwise.

Table 34.3 provides summary statistics on the variables used in the model.

RESULTS

As the results indicate, confirmation voting is decisively affected by the ideological distance between senators and nominees. Equally important, as indicated by the virtually identical parameter estimates on the U and D terms, are the qualifications of the nominee. Overwhelmingly, however, it is the interaction of qualifications and ideology that determines the votes of senators.

As probit estimates are not readily interpretable in terms of probabilities, we provide in Table 34.4 examples of voting probabilities for varying levels of ideological distance and qualifications. Senators, even opposition senators serving with a weak president, will vote for a poorly qualified nominee if the nominee is ideologically close. They will vote for an ideologically distant nominee if the nominee is highly qualified. Ideological distance, however, becomes paramount for nominees with even moderate questions concerning their qualifications. Alternatively, we could say that qualifications become paramount for nominees of even moderate ideological distance from senators.

Additionally, presidential influence and same party status have a powerful impact on voting probabilities, especially for senators who remain undecided after examining the characteristics of the nominee. For example, in the model a switch from a weak to a strong president raises to .92 the probability of a *yes* vote from a senator who was previously undecided. Similarly, same party status raises the probability of a *yes* vote from .5 to .78.

In order to solve the puzzle of confirmation voting, a model must not only explain

Table 34.3. *Dependent and Independent Variables*

Variable	Mean	Variance	Minimum	Maximum
Vote	.850	.123	.00	1.00
Squared Euclidean distance (D)	.243	.070	.00	1.00
Lack of qualifications, $1 - Q$ (U)	.195	.063	.00	.89
Strong president (S)	.372	.234	.00	1.00
Same party status (P)	.500	.250	.00	1.00
Distance X lack of qualifications (UD)	.045	.011	.00	.89

Table 34.4. *Examples of Voting Probabilities*

Ideological Distance	Lack of Qualification (0 = most qualified, 1 = most unqualified)										
	.0	.1	.2	.3	.4	.5	.6	.7	.8	.9	1.0
.0	.96	.95	.94	.93	.91	.88	.86	.83	.80	.76	.73
.1	.95	.93	.89	.85	.79	.72	.64	.56	.47	.38	.30
.2	.94	.89	.82	.73	.61	.52	.36	.26	.14	.10	.05
.3	.93	.85	.73	.58	.41	.26	.14	.07	.03	.01	—
.4	.91	.79	.61	.41	.23	.10	.04	.01	—	—	—
.5	.89	.72	.51	.26	.10	.03	.01	—	—	—	—
.6	.86	.64	.36	.14	.04	.01	—	—	—	—	—
.7	.83	.56	.26	.07	.01	—	—	—	—	—	—
.8	.80	.47	.14	.03	—	—	—	—	—	—	—
.9	.77	.39	.10	.01	—	—	—	—	—	—	—
1.0	.73	.31	.05	—	—	—	—	—	—	—	—

Note: Examples assume a weak president and a Senator not of the president's party.

individual votes but also correctly distinguish consensual from conflictual votes. In the sample of 22 votes, 13 are consensual and 9 are conflictual. As shown in Table 34.5, the model correctly identifies all of the consensual votes.

Table 34.5. *Actual Versus Predicted* No *Votes*

Nominee	Actual	Predicted
Warren	0	0
Harlan	11	25
Brennan	0	0
Whittaker	0	0
Stewart	17	0
White	0	0
Goldberg	0	0
Fortas 1	0	0
Marshall	11	0
Fortas 2	43	36
Burger	3	0
Haynsworth	55	46
Carswell	51	53
Blackmun	0	0
Powell	1	0
Rehnquist 1	26	13
Stevens	0	0
O'Connor	0	0
Rehnquist 2	33	35
Scalia	0	0
Bork	58	29
Kennedy	0	0

Note: Mean absolute error for all votes = 4.9; for consensual votes = .2; for conflictual votes = 11.6; r actual versus predicted = .91.

It is almost as successful in identifying the conflictual votes; 7 of the 9 conflictual votes are correctly identified (78%). It fails to identify the Stewart and Marshall confirmations as conflictual; in these confirmations a group of conservative southern senators voted against the nominees. The model fails to capture the source of the senators' (apparently race-related) opposition.

The model must also account for variance in voting. On average the model misidentifies only five votes per confirmation. Within the consensual votes, however, the mean absolute error is almost zero. Within the conflictual votes, the mean absolute error is higher – 11–12 votes. The correlation between actual and predicted *no* votes is .91.

Gauging the success of the model in terms of confirmation outcomes is not a straightforward task. The vote on the Fortas nomination as chief justice was 45 *yea* and 43 *nay*, but this majority was insufficient to invoke cloture, so the nomination was defeated. Even under current rules, it is reasonable to presume that no nominee will pass with more than the 43 "nays" received by Fortas. Clarence Thomas received 48 "nays." (In fact, no nominee this century has been confirmed with more than 33 negative votes.) If we use 43 as the number of negative votes needed to ensure defeat, the model correctly predicts the outcome of every nomination except Bork's and Fortas'.

388 Charles M. Cameron, Albert D. Cover, and Jeffrey A. Segal

CONCLUSION

The model resolves the puzzle of confirmation voting straightforwardly. When a strong president nominates a highly qualified, ideologically moderate candidate, the nominee passes the Senate in a lopsided, consensual vote. Presidents have often nominated this type of candidate and consequently consensual votes have been fairly common. When presidents nominate a less well qualified, ideologically extreme candidate, especially when the president is in a weak position, then a conflictual vote is likely. Surprisingly, presidents have nominated quite a few candidates of this description, and conflictual votes occur periodically. In short, the behavior of senators emerges as sensible, predictable, and readily understandable; the real source of the puzzle in confirmation voting appears to be the behavior of presidents in choosing nominees.

Learning more about confirmation voting requires moving beyond our simple model of position taking. First, the framework assumes senators are "single-minded seekers of reelection," but we know this is not so. A more appealing framework would allow senators to trade off among competing goals in their roll call votes. In particular, to what extent do senators follow the (presumptive) desires of their constituents in confirmation votes, and to what extent do they "shirk" by voting their personal preferences? Second, future research might find it worthwhile to examine the role of interest groups in the nomination process. Finally, much more attention needs to be given to presidential selection of nominees.

In essence, we are suggesting the need to take a much more inclusive view of the nomination process. But an important issue then comes to the fore: What is properly exogenous and what is properly endogenous in the theory and models? For example, we treat the nominees' ideologies and qualifications as exogenous, but presidents presumably pick their nominees with the Senate's composition at least partly in mind. In addition, public perceptions of quality and ideology could be regarded as endogenous if interested parties can affect those perceptions. And any attempt to model interest group mobilization must confront the fact that their mobilization results from calculations by the groups and therefore must be regarded as endogenous as well. Solving these problems is likely to be the major challenge facing future analysts of confirmation voting and nomination politics more generally.

CHAPTER THIRTY–FIVE

From Abe Fortas to Zoë Baird

Why Some Presidential Nominations Fail in the Senate

Glen S. Krutz, Richard Fleisher, and Jon R. Bond

Krutz, Fleisher, and Bond explore the conditions under which presidential nominees do not gain Senate confirmation. They find that individuals who wish to see a nominee fail are more successful when they discover negative information about a nominee and manage to publicize it through the media or committee hearings in the Senate.

The U.S. Congress was designed to make legislating difficult. Fragmented power and multiple decision points afford those opposed to a bill ample opportunities to defeat it. In the Senate more than the House, members have significant parliamentary rights that allow them to delay action on legislation. Most bills introduced in Congress are ignored. Presidential proposals fare only slightly better – about one-fourth make it into law. In sum, for legislation introduced in Congress, there is a presumption of failure.

Nominations are different. Presidential nominees, even for the highest offices in the executive branch and the judiciary, typically are approved with little opposition. Although senatorial prerogatives to block action apply to nominations as well as to legislation, when the Senate receives a presidential nomination, there is a

Glen S. Krutz, Richard Fleisher, and Jon R. Bond. 1998. "From Abe Fortas to Zoë Baird: Why Some Presidential Nominations Fail in the Senate" *American Political Science Review* 92(4): 871–81. Copyright © 1998 by the American Political Science Association. Reprinted with the permission of Cambridge University Press.

presumption of success. For several reasons, the Senate by tradition defers to the president in the staffing of the government and judiciary. First, the Constitution affords the president greater authority over appointments than over legislation. Furthermore, if the Senate turns down a nominee, there is no assurance that the replacement will be less objectionable. Second, because these positions must be filled to have a well-functioning government, the Senate does not have the same leeway to ignore nominations as it does most legislative proposals. Moreover, while legislation can be amended to make it more palatable to opponents, nominees must either be accepted or rejected. Third, the president often consults with key senators before sending nominations to the Hill. Consequently, the Senate confirms all but a tiny number of presidential appointments.

Yet, some nominations run into trouble in the Senate and fail. Because of the presumption of success, explaining that failure poses an interesting question: Under what conditions does the Senate, predisposed to allow the president wide latitude in staffing the government, at times change this presumption and revert to a process more typical of its handling of legislation? We seek to answer this question with an analysis of presidential nominations from 1965 to 1994. We begin with a review of the literature, identifying gaps in our understanding of the confirmation process.

LITERATURE AND THEORETICAL FRAMEWORK

The literature provides insights about confirmation politics, but gaps remain. Much of the quantitative work has focused on nominations to the Supreme Court, analyzing senators' floor voting behavior. Such analyses do not explain the collective outcome of greatest interest to the president: success or failure. Moreover, analyzing only floor votes on Supreme Court nominees provides an incomplete understanding of confirmation politics in general, since the justices are a small and unrepresentative sample of significant presidential nominations. More important, most unsuccessful nominations fail before reaching the floor, so cases defeated by floor votes are not representative of failures.

The few studies that analyze nominations more generally cast the empirical net too wide, analyzing all nominations (tens of thousands in most Congresses). Because only a small number are salient enough for the president and Senate to take an active interest, the many routine approvals involving minor offices may distort the results.

Previous research does provide guidance for the development of a broader theoretical understanding of confirmation politics. We propose a framework based on the notion that policy entrepreneurs pursue their goals within a context of a presumption of failure for legislation and a presumption of success for nominations.

Policy Entrepreneurs and Nominations

Policy entrepreneurs are risk takers who care deeply about issues and the actions of government. Although policy entrepreneurs may come from interest groups or from the intellectual community, at some point they must enlist the active participation of members of Congress. The burden of proof differs for policy and nominations. For policy, the burden is on supporters; policy failure is most likely because it is hard to overcome the presumption of failure. For nominations, the burden is on opponents; defeat of a nominee is rare because it is hard to surmount the presumption of success.

Because of the presumption of success, supporters of nominees normally do not need to push hard to get them considered. Opponents, in contrast, face a daunting task. To change the presumption of success, opponents often use a public strategy analogous to that employed by those seeking to break up policy subsystems. Although the process does not always follow a prescribed sequence, it is useful for analytical purposes to consider two conceptually distinct phases. First, entrepreneurs portray a negative image of the nominee to provide a rationale for opposition. Second, entrepreneurs seek to expand the conflict to persuade senators to see controversy. Kingdon finds that House members go along as usual in their decision making unless they perceive controversy, in which case they seek more information and scrutinize legislation. Those opposing nominations seek to get senators into such a frame of mind. Senate rules permitting unlimited debate and the prerogative to place a "hold" on nominations allow entrepreneurs to delay action while they expand the conflict. Because of the presumption of success, entrepreneurs pick their battles carefully. Thus, we expect that a small proportion of nominations will be challenged and defeated.

Those opposed to a nominee must persuade additional senators to alter the normal presumption. The number of senators needed and the difficulty of persuading them vary at different points in the process. Defeating a nomination on the floor requires a majority to go on record against the nominee and the president. A defeat before that stage often takes less than a majority, and opponents do not always have to go public. Consequently, most failures never reach the floor. The visible floor defeats of Robert Bork and John Tower are unusual and unrepresentative of failed nominations.

We turn now to a discussion of rationales that entrepreneurs use as a basis for opposing a nominee and strategies to expand the conflict.

Rationale for Opposition

Opponents search for negative information in the nominee's background that can provide a rationale for opposition, including wrongdoing, a lack of qualifications, and ideological extremism.

The public expects government positions to be filled by ethical individuals who are qualified for the job. Credible evidence of wrongdoing provides a strong reason for opposing a nominee. Two examples of derailment due to such allegations are Abe Fortas, President Johnson's candidate for chief justice in 1968, and Zoë Baird, nominated for attorney general by President Clinton in 1993. Some government positions require special training and expertise. Although appropriate qualifications vary with the office, questions about a nominee's suitability can provide a basis for opposition. Examples include President Reagan's 1981 nomination of William Bell to head the Equal Employment Opportunity Commission and President Bush's 1989 nomination of William Lucas as assistant attorney general for civil rights.

More recently, ideological extremism has become another rationale for opposing nominations. From 1981 to 1994, senators challenged 20 cases on this ground, a fivefold increase over the four cases from 1965 to 1980. The increase in the use of wrongdoing or inadequate qualifications has been less dramatic: 15 cases from 1965 to 1980, compared to 29 from 1981 to 1994. The ideological extremism rationale was used to oppose President Reagan's nomination of Robert Bork to the Supreme Court in 1987 and President Clinton's nomination of Sheldon Hackney to head the National Endowment for the Humanities in 1993. Previous research finds that nominees' ideology affects the chances of confirmation.

Some characteristics may insulate a nominee from more intense scrutiny and increase the likelihood of confirmation, such as previous approval for a different office or former membership in the Senate or House. Opposition may be less likely if a nominee has weathered a process that failed to reveal negative information, and those with congressional experience bring political (as distinct from administrative) skill to an office. Since this skill is respected by the Senate, senators may be favorably disposed toward nominees with political and personal ties to Congress.

Expanding the Conflict in Congress

Once opponents identify a potential flaw, they exploit it by expanding the scope of conflict. In politics, how a situation (or a nominee) is perceived is often more important than objective reality. Charges of inadequate qualifications and ideological extremism are based largely on perception. Standards of wrongdoing also change over time as perceptions of what is ethical evolve, and an illegal act once considered merely a technical violation can come to be viewed as more serious. Entrepreneurs must do more than make charges about a nominee's background. They must make the case that the allegation is credible and important enough to defeat the nomination.

Two avenues for expanding conflict are (1) an internal strategy through committee hearings and (2) an external strategy that encourages scrutiny by the national media. In the rough and tumble of Washington politics, these strategies become intertwined: Revelations in a committee hearing generate additional media coverage, which leads to more hearings and tougher questioning. Therefore, separating the causal sequence is problematic, but it is useful for conceptual clarity to discuss these strategies separately. The internal strategy takes place during the confirmation hearings, which are typically low-key affairs involving the nominee and a handful of witnesses who present only positive testimony. Among the important nominations in our study, the median number of witnesses was one: solely the nominee at 52 percent of hearings; no more than four additional witnesses in 92 percent of the cases. Opponents can expand conflict by enlarging the witness list to include those who present negative testimony. This expansion is a signal to senators that the appointment deserves more attention than normal and increases the likelihood of justifying a rationale.

The external strategy expands conflict through increased media coverage, which also signals the Senate that a nomination should be closely scrutinized. Previous research finds that more intensive news coverage is associated with more controversial nominations.

Thus, opponents seek to portray a nominee in a negative light and try to expand the scope of conflict, both internally through committee hearings and externally through high media exposure. The president, however, is neither helpless nor passive in this process.

Presidential Strategies and Resources

Once a nomination becomes embattled, the president's options are limited. Going public to support a challenged nominee may draw more attention to the controversy, and presidents are constrained in how many personal appeals they can make to senators on behalf of embroiled nominees. A better strategy is to preempt the opposition. "The best point at which to manage conflict," says Schattschneider "is before it starts." The president may avoid trouble by consulting with senators to identify candidates and by screening nominees in light of past controversies. For political and policy reasons, presidents still nominate controversial individuals. When a controversial name is sent to the Senate, the president may go to extra lengths to highlight positive aspects of a nominee's experience and qualifications in an effort to preempt potential opposition.

The president's popularity with the public is a resource that may influence members of Congress. Washingtonians widely accept the view that Congress is more inclined to give presidents what they want when public support is high rather than low. Previous studies provide some empirical support for this view. Other research identifies methodological and theoretical reasons to question this relationship. Although presidential popularity may have only marginal effects on legislation, there is reason to

hypothesize that it may be more significant for nominations, since it reinforces the presumption of success. Given this presumption, opposing a nominee poses risks to entrepreneurs: (1) embarrassment and damage to reputation if the opposition is unsuccessful; (2) lost time that might have been used more effectively on a legislative initiative; and (3) possible future retribution from the president. Because high popularity reinforces the presumption of success and the risks associated with opposing a nomination, entrepreneurs may wait for another case when the president is perceived to be more vulnerable.

Political Circumstances

Entrepreneurs operate under political circumstances, some of which may be more favorable to opposing nominations than others. Circumstances that may influence the confirmation process include party control of the presidency and the Senate, timing in the president's term, and type of office involved in the nomination.

Divided Government

There are theoretical reasons to expect more failed nominations when the opposition party controls the Senate. Members of the opposition party are predisposed to disagree with the president's preferences on policy and personnel. Under divided control, there are more of these members. More important, they hold the levers of power, chairing committees and controlling the scheduling of business. Research on Supreme Court nominations finds a relationship between party control and success. But since Senate rules bestow great power on individual senators, regardless of party, this relationship may not appear in a more representative sample of nominations.

Timing

Washington time runs on the electoral calendar. Entrepreneurs may have greater difficulty challenging nominations early in the president's term. Light advises new presidents to "move it or lose it," because they are more successful in pursuing a legislative program during the honeymoon. It is also reasonable to expect the Senate to give newly elected presidents latitude in staffing the government. Conditions later in the president's term make it less difficult to challenge nominations. After the midterm elections, presidents typically have fewer members of their party in the Senate. As the presidential election approaches, opposition party senators have a greater incentive to deal the chief executive an embarrassing defeat, and a president running for reelection may become distracted with the campaign. A lame duck is in a weakened position even with senators from the same party, who know they will not have to run with this candidate at the top of the ticket.

Previous studies of judicial appointments suggest that timing influences confirmations. Ruckman and Scigliano found that Supreme Court nominations are more likely to fail late in the president's term. Richardson and Vines and Bond found that Congress is more likely to pass bills increasing the number of federal judges early in a presidential term.

Type of Office

Different offices evoke different expectations about the skills and experience needed to fill them, so this factor is likely to have a bearing on confirmations. And the Senate may be more likely to defer to the president on executive branch appointments than on appointments to the judiciary or independent regulatory agencies. Consequently, we control for type of office, but we do not have strong theoretical expectations regarding the direction of all the relationships.

RESEARCH DESIGN AND MEASURES

Units of Analysis

The unit of analysis is nominations considered by the U.S. Senate from 1965 to 1994, but not all these are appropriate to test our theory. Most presidential appointments each year are military and foreign service promotions that typically pass in large blocks with little scrutiny. Including such cases may distort the results. We need a subset of important nominations in which the president, senators, and other entrepreneurs are likely [to] take an active interest, but the sample should be broad enough to be representative. We define as important all nominations to the (1) Supreme Court; (2) U.S. Circuit Courts of Appeals; and (3) level 1, 2, and 3 positions in the Federal Executive Schedule, except "inner cabinet" positions (Defense, Justice, State, and Treasury), which also include level 4 positions. This yields a sample of 1,464 important nominations from 1965 to 1994. Supreme Court and appellate court nominations comprise the most important judicial appointments. Using the Executive Schedule identifies the top positions in the executive branch and bureaucracy.

Dependent Variable

The dependent variable is the *Outcome* of a nomination (pass = 1; fail = 0). A failed nomination is one submitted to the Senate for consideration but not confirmed. Nominations may fail at several points in the process. The Senate may reject the nominee on the floor or in committee; the president may withdraw the nomination before overt rejection; the Senate may not act because a "hold" prevents it or because time runs out at the end of the session.

Previous empirical studies of nominations focus on floor votes. As we argued above, that provides an incomplete picture because most unsuccessful nominations fail before reaching the floor. Table 35.1 presents information on the point at which nominations fail. Of the 1,464 nominations in the data set, less than 5 percent (71) failed, which suggests that even the most important cases have a presumption of success. Yet, instances of failure are sufficiently common to justify trying to identify the reasons. Of the failed nominations, more than 94 percent never reached the floor. This finding suggests that efforts to defeat a nominee are most effective during prefloor phases of the process. More than three-fourths of unsuccessful nominations (55) did not emerge from committee, so that appears to be the most critical stage; another seventeen cases failed even earlier, before committee hearings.

Table 35.1. *Point at Which Nominations Fail,*
1965–1994

Final Action	Percent	N
Floor rejection	5.6%	4
Stalled, stopped between committee and floor	11.3	8
Withdrawn after committee forwarded to chamber	5.6	4
Committee rejected by vote	16.9	12
Stalled, stopped between hearing and committee vote	19.7	14
Withdrawn before committee vote (after hearing)	16.9	12
Committee failed to consider a nomination[a]	12.7	9
Withdrawn before committee hearings[a]	11.3	8
TOTAL	100.0%	71

[a] The "Committee failed to consider a nomination" category includes cases that were not withdrawn but died because the committee never held hearings or took any action to process the nomination. The "Withdrawn before committee hearings" category includes cases withdrawn by the president or the nominee before committee hearings.

Table 35.2 shows the percentage of important nominations that passed during various administrations. Except for presidents Ford and Reagan (second term), success rates are similar across administrations. Ford's record is likely the result of the aftermath of the Watergate scandal that elevated him to the presidency without election. The decline during Reagan's second term is similar to that in Nixon's second term.

Table 35.2. *Outcome of Nominations by*
Administration, 1965–1994

Presidential Administration (Years)	% Successful	N
Johnson (1965–68)	99.0%	99
Nixon I (1969–72)	97.7	171
Nixon II (1973–74)	94.4	90
Ford (1974–76)	92.6	95
Carter (1977–80)	96.1	207
Reagan I (1981–84)	94.2	223
Reagan II (1985–88)	92.8	209
Bush (1989–92)	94.0	215
Clinton (1993–94)	96.8	155
TOTAL	95.2%	1,464

Although Clinton's 97 percent success rate during 1993–94 is above the mean of the presidents in this study, it represents the record of only two years, as opposed to four for the other presidents. This relatively high success rate does suggest, however, that the highly publicized defeats early in Clinton's first term are not representative of his record on nominations in the 103d Congress.

Success rates of recent presidents are similar to those of their predecessors, which suggests that it has not become harder to get nominees through the Senate. That is, the presumption of success on nominations prevails throughout the period of study. There is a slight divided government effect: 94 percent pass under split party control, compared to 97 percent with unified control.

Independent Variables

Nominee Factors

The nominee characteristics that entrepreneurs use as rationales for opposition are measured by four dichotomous variables (1 = yes, 0 = no) to indicate the presence or absence of a negative attribute: *Alleged Wrongdoing, Qualifications a Concern, Extreme Conservative,* and *Extreme Liberal.* Opponents alleged at least one negative attribute in about 4 percent (62) of the cases. Allegations of wrongdoing were most common (32 cases), followed by extreme conservatism (17 cases), qualifications (12 cases), and extreme liberalism (7 cases).

We also include measures of attributes that might insulate nominees from challenge: *Previously Confirmed* for another office and current or former members of the *House* or the *Senate* (1 = yes; 0 = no). About 36 percent (526) of nominees had been previously confirmed (*Marquis Who's Who,* Inc. 1969–97). Three percent (44) were former House members, and less than 1 percent (13) were former senators.

Expansion of Conflict

The measure of the *Scope and Tone of Testimony* in committee hearings is the ratio of negative to positive witnesses (number of negative witnesses/number of positive witnesses). Low key hearings with only the nominee testifying and larger hearings with only positive witnesses score zero. Such hearings are likely to lead to confirmation because no negative information is presented to challenge the presumption of success. Hearings with more negative than positive witnesses have scores greater than 1.00. Higher scores indicate greater controversy, which reduces the likelihood of confirmation. For the 1,447 cases in our data set on which hearings were held, this variable ranges from zero to 27, with a mean of .20 and a standard deviation of 1.26. The distribution, however, is highly skewed. More than 90 percent of hearings score zero (only positive witnesses), but there are six extreme outliers in which negative witnesses outnumbered positive witnesses by at least ten to one. Since we believe that the effect of adding negative witnesses is likely to increase rapidly at low values and then diminish, we transformed this variable with a square root function.

The indicator of *Media Coverage* is the number of stories in the *New York Times* (1966–95) about the nomination prior to the date of passage or failure. The scores range from zero to 93, with a mean of 1.9 and a standard deviation of 5.1. There are a few extreme values, but this variable is less skewed than the testimony variable. About 40 percent (589) of the nominees in our sample received no mention in the *New York Times*, and roughly 57 percent received between one and ten mentions. Since this variable is not highly skewed, we did not use any nonlinear transformation.

Presidential Variables

The president may attempt to preempt the opposition by publicly touting the merits of a nominee before sending the name to Capitol Hill. Our measure of *Initial Presidential Priority* is the number of column lines in the president's speech introducing the nominee. This variable ranges from zero to 203 column lines, with a mean of 19.4 and a standard deviation of 23.6. *Presidential Popularity*, a resource that might reinforce the presumption of success on nominations, is measured as the percentage approving of the way the president is handling his job in

the closest Gallup poll before the nomination passes or fails. This variable ranges from 24 percent to 87 percent, with a mean of 52 percent and a standard deviation of 11 percent.

Political Circumstances

We control for several political circumstances that might affect the fate of nominations. *Divided Government* is coded 1 if the president and the Senate majority are from different parties and 0 for unified control. About 45 percent (657) of the nominations in our sample were considered under divided government.

Four dummy variables were used to measure timing in a presidential term: *Early First Term, Late First Term, Early Second Term*, and *Late Second Term* (1 = early or late; 0 otherwise). Early is defined as the first year of the term; late is the fourth year. These variables test whether the probability of success in the first and fourth years is significantly different from that in the middle years.

Finally, we included six variables for type of office being filled to detect any differences across the categories: *Cabinet, Subcabinet, Executive Office of the President/White House, Supreme Court, Appellate Court*, or *Government Corporation/Regulatory Agency* (the excluded category). We do not have theoretical expectations about the direction of relationships for these variables.

FINDINGS

Table 35.3 presents a logit analysis of the effects of the independent variables on the confirmation process. Recall from Table 35.1 that 17 cases were withdrawn before hearings or failed because the Senate took no action. Since there were no hearings, the testimony variable is not applicable, and there is no completely satisfactory way to deal with this missing data problem. Since we have so few failures, excluding these cases from the multivariate analysis eliminates nearly one-fourth of the failures, but efforts to impute a "tone" to hearings that never occurred seem problematical. Among the various possibilities, the process of multiple imputation seems most appropriate. Although this technique is particularly appropriate for surveys,

Table 35.3. *Logit Models of the Outcome of Presidential Nominations, 1965–1994*

Independent Variables	Expected Direction	Model 1			Model 2		
		b	t	Δp	b	t	Δp
Nominee Factors							
Alleged Wrongdoing	−	−4.33***	−6.82	−.49	−4.21***	−7.05	−.49
Qualifications a Concern	−	−2.11**	−2.42	−.39	−2.05**	−2.48	−.39
Extreme Conservative	−	−2.16**	−2.41	−.40	−1.61*	−1.75	−.33
Extreme Liberal	−	−1.58	−1.32	−.33	−2.06*	−2.14	−.39
Previously Confirmed	+	1.00*	2.14	.23	.90**	2.36	.21
U.S. Senator	+	−.91	−1.33		−.08	−.05	
U.S. House Member	+	.28	.25		−.26	−.31	
Expansion of Conflict							
Scope and Tone of Testimony	−	−1.15***	−4.19	−.15 (−.26)	−1.06***	−4.20	−.14 (−.24)
Media Coverage	−	−.06*	−2.05	−.10 (−.18)	−.05*	−1.99	−.09 (−.16)
Presidential Resources							
Initial Presidential Priority	+	.02*	1.88	.20 (.29)	.02*	1.72	.16 (.23)
Presidential Popularity	+	.04*	1.87	.43 (.45)	.04**	2.75	.44 (.46)
Political Circumstances							
Divided Government	−	.26	.66		−.43	−1.30	
Early First Term	+	−.14	−.23		−.47	−.93	
Late First Term	−	−1.40**	−2.65	−.30	−1.67***	−3.96	−.34
Early Second Term	+	−.67	−1.06		−.48	−.81	
Late Second Term	−	−1.48**	−2.40	−.31	−1.19*	−2.20	−.27
Type of Office							
Cabinet		3.83**	2.97	.48	3.54**	2.89	.47
Subcabinet		.13	1.17		.03	.05	
EOP/White House		1.50	1.08		1.31	1.05	
Supreme Court		.64	.40		.53	.35	
Appellate Court		.65	1.01		−.30	−.55	
Constant		1.93*	2.00	.37	1.88*	2.18	.37
N of cases		1,447			1,464		
Likelihood ratio test (21 d.f.)		187.181***			210.032***		
Percent correctly predicted		97.3			96.1		
Percent in modal category		96.3 (pass)			95.2 (pass)		
Proportional reduction in error		.27			.19		

Note: The dependent variable is coded 1 if the nomination passed and 0 if it failed. $*p \leq .05$, $**p \leq .01$, $***p \leq .001$, one-tailed; two-tailed tests were used for type of office and the constant.

it can be used to deal with missing data in non-survey designs. Thus, we estimate the model two ways. Model 1 reports estimates without the 17 failures that had no hearings ($n = 1,447$), while Model 2 reports estimates with hearing values imputed for these failures ($n = 1,464$). The results of both models support our expectations about negative information and the expansion of conflict.

All the rationales that entrepreneurs use to portray a nominee in a negative light – alleged wrongdoing, lack of qualifications, and ideological extremism – significantly reduce the chances that the nomination will be confirmed. To see substantive effects, we present the change in probability of success under different values of the independent variables. Charges of not being qualified or ideological extremism

reduce the probability of confirmation by at least one-third; alleged wrongdoing has the strongest effect, cutting the chances of success nearly in half.

Background characteristics that might insulate nominees from challenge have less influence. Those who have weathered a previous confirmation tend to be successful, but the marginal increase in the probability of success is only about 20 percent. Former members of Congress do not receive more favorable treatment in the Senate than nominees without congressional ties.

The models also show that both internal and external strategies to expand conflict significantly reduce the probability of confirmation. Hearings with 1.5 times more negative than positive witnesses (one standard deviation above the mean) reduce the chances by 15 percent (at two standard deviations above the mean, the odds drop another 10 percent). If media coverage increases to six stories, the probability of confirmation declines 10 percent.

Presidential resources enhance the probability of confirmation. Efforts to preempt potential opposition by signaling that a nomination is a high priority increase the chance of success about 20 percent. Presidential popularity has a stronger influence. If public approval is one standard deviation above the mean (about eleven points), the positive effect on the probability of success is about 40 percent, a similar magnitude to the detrimental effects of negative nominee factors. The strong association with public approval suggests that entrepreneurs may be reluctant to assume the risks of trying to change the presumption of success on nominations when the president is extremely popular. This result stands in sharp contrast to previous findings indicating that public approval of the president has a marginal influence on legislative success in Congress.

Political circumstances have mixed effects. Contrary to studies of Supreme Court nominations, we find no significant independent effect of divided party control, which suggests that nominations of justices are not representative of nominations in general. Given Senate rules that bestow significant power on individuals, it is not surprising that once opponents provide a rationale and expand the conflict, they can challenge nominations about as effectively under unified as under divided control. Consistent with previous studies, nominations are more likely to fail late in the president's term.

Finally, among the various types of offices, only cabinet nominations are treated differently: Nominees to head these departments are more likely to be confirmed than nominees to other offices. This result may reflect a tendency to allow the president leeway in forming his government.

CONCLUSION

In a legislative system designed to block initiatives, nominations pose a puzzle. In contrast to legislation, most nominations – even the most important cases selected for this study – pass without challenge. Our model attempts to explain why, given the presumption of success, some nominations fail. Our theoretical framework is based on the notion that policy entrepreneurs pursue their goals within the context of this presumption. If no controversy arises around a nomination, senators, committees, and the chamber go along with the president and confirm the nominee. The aim of opposition entrepreneurs, therefore, is to alter the presumption. They want senators to see controversy and to scrutinize nominees closely. We suggest that entrepreneurs accomplish this through a two-part strategy: (1) Identify negative information about a nominee to provide a rationale for changing the presumption, and (2) expand the conflict internally through committee hearings and externally in the mass media.

Our analysis of important nominations from 1965 to 1994 tends to support this theory. Less than 5 percent of these nominations failed. Ninety-four percent of failures were rejected or withdrawn before reaching the floor, which suggests that opponents are most effective during the prefloor stages of the process. Allegations of wrongdoing, concerns about qualifications, and ideological extremism all provide a rationale to defeat a nomination. Expansion of the conflict, as indicated by a disproportionate number of negative witnesses at the hearings and considerable coverage in the national press, also reduces the likelihood of confirmation. And nominations made late in the president's term are more likely to fail. High presidential approval and extra efforts to tout the candidate's qualifications in the president's speech announcing the nomination increase the chances of success. In addition, nominees who have been previously confirmed for another office and especially the cabinet are more likely to pass than others. Contrary to previous research, divided government has no independent effect on the fate of nominations.

These findings suggest at least two implications for our understanding of politics in Congress. First, our model's presumptions of failure for legislation and success for nominations is a useful way to think about policymaking in Congress. The tasks and strategies of policy entrepreneurs vary with these presumptions. On legislation, supporters struggle to get the proposal noticed and considered. On nominations, it is opponents who must struggle to get the attention of others. If they succeed in portraying a nominee negatively, then the president is constrained in how to help a nomination through.

Second, previous studies of floor voting focus on Supreme Court appointments and provide an incomplete understanding of confirmation politics in general. The justices represent only a fraction of the nominees to important offices that the president must get confirmed in the Senate. And defeats on the floor are a small and unrepresentative sample of the relatively rare failures. Our analysis of a broader, more representative sample of important nominations confirms some previous findings and suggests that others should not be generalized beyond the Supreme Court context.

PART XI. CONGRESS, LOBBYISTS, AND INTEREST GROUPS

CHAPTER THIRTY-SIX

Buying Time

Moneyed Interests and the Mobilization of Bias in Congressional Committees

Richard L. Hall and Frank W. Wayman

Hall and Wayman examine the effects of campaign contributions on legislative behavior. Unlike previous literature, which primarily concentrated on voting behavior, the authors examine the relationship between moneyed interests and members' legislative participation. They find that group expenditures are more likely to have an effect in committee than on the floor, and contributions significantly encourage legislative involvement.

At least since Madison railed about the mischiefs of faction, critics of U.S. political institutions have worried about the influence of organized interests in national policymaking. In this century, one of the most eloquent critics of the interest group system was E. E. Schattschneider, who warned of the inequalities between private, organized, and upper-class groups on the one hand and public, unorganized, and lower-class groups on the other. The pressure system, he argued, "mobilized bias" in national policymaking in favor of the former, against the interests of the latter, and hence against the interests of U.S. democracy. Such concerns have hardly abated thirty years since the publication of Schattschneider's essay. In particular, the precipitous growth in the number and financial strength of political action committees has refu-

Richard L. Hall and Frank W. Wayman. 1990. "Buying Time: Moneyed Interests and the Mobilization of Bias in Congressional Committees" *American Political Science Review* 84(3): 797–820. Copyright © 1990 by the American Political Science Association. Reprinted with the permission of Cambridge University Press.

eled the charge that moneyed interests dominate the policy making process.

Despite the claims of the institutional critics and the growing public concern over PACs during the last decade, the scientific evidence that political money matters in legislative decision making is surprisingly weak. Considerable research on members' voting decisions offers little support for the popular view that PAC money permits interests to buy or rent votes on matters that affect them. Based on an examination of 120 PACs in 10 issue areas over four congresses, one recent study concludes flatly that PAC contributions do not affect members' voting patterns. Another study, designed to explore the "upper bounds" of PAC influence on House roll calls, emphasizes "the relative inability of PACs to determine congressional voting." On the whole, then, this literature certainly leads one to a more sanguine view of moneyed interests and congressional politics than one gets from the popular commentaries. Does money matter?

Our approach to this question is two-pronged. In the first two sections, we revisit the question by developing a theoretical account of the constrained exchange between legislator and donor quite different from the one evident in the substantial literature cited above. In particular, we adopt the premise that PACs are rational actors, seeking to maximize their influence on the legislative outcomes that affect their affiliates; but we take issue with the standard account of PAC rationality. Our approach does not lead us to predict a strong causal relationship between PAC money and floor votes. House members and interest group representatives are viewed as parties to an implicit cooperative agreement, but the constraints on member behavior and the rational calculations of group representatives limit the extent to which votes become the currency of exchange. Instead, we advance two hypotheses about the effect of money on congressional decision making.

First, we suggest that in looking for the effects of money in Congress, one must look more to the politics of committee decision making than those of the floor. This view, of course, is neither original nor remarkable. Students of Congress have long contended that interest group influence flourishes at the committee level, and recent students of PAC influence invariably advocate that work move in this direction. To date, however, systematic studies of PACs and committee decision making have been altogether rare. We focus here at the committee level and emphasize the theoretical reasons for doing so.

Second, and more importantly, our account of the member–donor exchange leads us to focus on the *participation* of particular members, not on their votes. This variable, we believe, is a crucial but largely neglected element of congressional decision making. It is especially important in any analysis of interest group influence in a decentralized Congress. If money does not necessarily buy votes or change minds, in other words, it can buy members' time. The intended effect is to mobilize bias in congressional committee decision making.

We then develop and estimate a model of committee participation that permits a direct test of whether moneyed interests do mobilize bias in committee decision making. Analyzing data from three House committees on three distinct issues, we find that they do. In the final section we briefly discuss the implications of the findings for our understanding of money, interest groups, and representation in Congress.

THE RATIONAL PAC REVISITED

The interdependencies of legislators and moneyed interests have been widely discussed by political scientists and widely lamented by critics of pluralism. The basis for political exchange is clear. Each depends at least partially on the other to promote its goals. Interest groups seek, among other things, favorable action on legislation that will affect them; members of Congress seek financial and political support from particular groups. Like the relationship between legislators and bureaucrats, however, the relationship between legislators and interest groups is one of *implicit* exchange: the actors "trade speculatively and on credit." Contributions are marked somewhere in the invisible ledger, and a group's political strategists presumably can use them to their momentary legislative ends.

This account of the legislator–interest group relationship underpins the now considerable literature on contributions and roll call voting. The working hypothesis is that contributions influence legislative outcomes by "purchasing" the votes of particular members or, less directly, by serving as "investments" that will pay dividends in legislative support at some later date. The scientific evidence that such effects appear only infrequently may be cause for relief among critics of the system, but it is puzzling to theorists of institutional behavior. Why should PACs flourish, both in number and financial strength, when their legislative efficacy is so low? The payoffs would appear inadequate to sustain the cooperative relationship.

One possible explanation is that PACs raise and disburse money with local congressional elections, not specific legislative ends, in mind. Wright argues, in fact, that the decentralized nature of most PAC organizations inclines them to do just that. But this account simply moves the issue of PAC rationality to a second, institutional level. Why would PACs organize in this way? Wright suggests that the typical national PAC office permits local officials substantial discretion because it wants to encourage them to continue raising funds. But the organization's fund-raising and disbursement, presumably, are intended for some more ultimate purpose, namely, to increase the net political benefits associated with governmental action (or inaction) on issues that affect it. On the whole, using money solely to affect election outcomes is not likely to be a rational means to this end.

The probability that any single group's contribution will affect the outcome of a congressional election – in which a wide range of more powerful forces are at work – is almost certainly slight. In the aggregate it might affect the organization's political support within Congress by only a member or two. While organizational arrangements may create some inefficiency in the way PACs employ funds to promote their political ends, one should still expect to find systematic patterns of allocation that are driven by legislative considerations, even among PACs that are highly decentralized (and especially among those that are not). Indeed, there is growing evidence that this is the case.

If the principal value of contributions lies in their potential to affect floor roll calls, however, a second puzzle appears. One would expect to find contribution strategies that favor the swing legislators in anticipated floor battles, since these are the cases where the marginal utility in votes purchased per dollar spent is likely to be greatest. Money allocated to almost certain supporters (or almost certain opponents) should be counted as irrational behavior, evidence of scarce resources wasted. In fact, however, the evidence suggests that such "misallocations" systematically occur. The Business-Industry Political Action Committee (BIPAC) and the National Chamber of Commerce give overwhelmingly to conservative Republicans. Labor PACs such as the AFL-CIO's Committee on Political Education give overwhelmingly to incumbent Democrats loyal to labor's agenda. Oil PACs give to conservative incumbents regardless of party and to friends regardless of ideology. In general, PACs are prone to reward their friends – even when their friends are not in danger of defeat. On the whole, it would seem that if, as Schattschneider said, moneyed interests sing with an upper-class accent, they also spend a good deal of effort singing to the choir.

One oft-mentioned solution to these puzzles is that contributions buy not votes but "access" to members and their staffs. But this solution only provokes a second query: If money buys access, what does access buy? Presumably, it gives the representatives of contributing groups important opportunities to directly lobby and potentially persuade legislators to the group's point of view. In this scenario the language of *access* may serve symbolically to launder the money going from group to roll call vote, but the effect of the group on the vote should still appear in systematic analysis. As we note above, it does not.

THE RATIONAL PAC REVISED

The literature on PAC contribution strategies and members' roll call voting behavior thus suggests two puzzles. First, if group strategists are reasonably rational, why would they continue to allocate scarce resources to efforts where the expected political benefits are so low? Second, if PAC allocation strategies are designed to influence members' votes, why do they contribute so heavily to their strongest supporters and occasionally to their strongest opponents? Is it the case that PACs are systematically irrational and, by extension, that claims about the influence of money on legislative process almost certainly exaggerated? We believe that the premise of rationality need not be rejected but that theoretical work in this area requires a more complete account of rational PAC behavior. Simply put, interest group resources are intended to accomplish something different from, and more than, influencing elections or buying votes. Specifically, we argue that PAC money should be allocated in order to *mobilize* legislative support and *demobilize* opposition, particularly at the most important points in the legislative process.

This argument turns directly on what we already know about the nature of legislators' voting decisions from a very rich literature. The simple but important point is that a number of powerful factors exist that predispose a member to vote a certain way, among them party leaders, ideology, constituency, and the position of the administration. Moreover, members' votes on particular issues are also constrained by their past voting histories. Members attach some value to consistency, independent of the other factors that influence their voting behavior. A third and related point is that the public, recorded nature of the vote may itself limit the member's discretion: a risk-averse member may fear the appearance of impropriety in supporting major campaign contributors in the absence of some other, legitimate force pushing her in the same direction. Finally, the dichotomous nature of the vote acts as a constraint. Money must not only affect members' attitudes at the margin but do so enough to push them over the threshold between *nay* and *yea*. In short, the limits on member responsiveness to messages wrapped in money are substantial, perhaps overwhelming, at least insofar as floor voting is concerned.

Of course, almost all studies of PAC contributions and roll calls acknowledge the importance of such factors and build them into their statistical models of the voting decision. But it is also important to consider the implications of these findings for the vote-buying hypothesis itself. Interest group strategists tend to be astute-enough observers of the legislative process to appreciate the powerful constraints that shape members' voting behavior. To the extent that this is true the rational PAC should expect little in the way of marginal benefits in votes bought for dollars spent, especially when individual PAC contributions are limited by the Federal Election Campaign Act to ten thousand dollars – a slight fraction of the cost of the average House race. Individual votes, that is, simply aren't easy to change; and even if some are changed, the utility of the votes purchased depends on their net cumulative effect in turning a potentially losing coalition into a winning one. For the rational PAC manager, the expected marginal utility approximates zero in most every case. All other things being equal, scarce resources should be allocated heavily elsewhere and to other purposes.

How, then, should the strategic PAC distribute its resources? The first principle derives from the larger literature on interest group influence in Congress. Well aware of the decentralized nature of congressional decision making, interest groups recognize that resources allocated at the committee stage are more efficiently spent. Interest group preferences incorporated there have a strong chance of surviving as the bill moves through subsequent stages in the sequence, while provisions not in the committee vehicle are difficult to attach later. Second,

the nature of the committee assignment process increases the probability that organized interests will find a sympathetic audience at the committee or subcommittee stage. Members seek and often receive positions that will permit them to promote the interests that, in turn, help them to get reelected. Finally, the less public, often informal nature of committee decision making suggests that members' responsiveness to campaign donors will receive less scrutiny. In short, groups will strategically allocate their resources with the knowledge that investments in the politics of the appropriate committee or subcommittee are likely to pay higher dividends than investments made elsewhere. Indeed, this principle is especially important in the House, where the sheer size of the chamber's membership, the greater importance of the committee stage, and the frequent restrictions on floor participation recommend a more targeted strategy.

If PACs concentrate at the committee level, what, specifically, do they hope to gain there? Purchasing votes is one possibility; and, in fact, the rationale for allocating campaign money to buy votes in committee is somewhat stronger than for vote-buying on the floor. But even within committee, PACs still tend to give to their strongest supporters. In addition, committee votes, like floor votes, are dichotomous decisions. And despite the lower visibility of committee decision making, the factors of constituency, ideology, party, and administration are almost certainly at work. In fact, while research on PACs and committee voting is just now beginning to emerge, there is little evidence that contributions influence voting in committee any more than they do voting on the floor.

The alternative hypothesis that we test here is that political money alters members' patterns of legislative involvement. The object of a rational PAC allocation strategy is not simply the *direction* of legislators' preferences but the *vigor* with which those preferences are promoted in the decision making process. Such strategies should take the form of inducing sympathetic members to get actively involved in a variety of activities that directly affect the shape of committee legislation: authoring or blocking a legislative vehicle; negotiating compromises behind the scenes, especially at the staff level; offering friendly amendments or actively opposing unfriendly ones; lobbying colleagues; planning strategy; and last and sometimes least, showing up to vote in favor of the interest group's position.

Several arguments support this view. First, participation is crucial to determining legislative outcomes; and voting is perhaps the least important of the various ways in which committee members participate. Second, while members' voting choices are highly constrained, how they allocate their time, staff, and political capital is much more discretionary. At any given moment, each member confronts a wide range of opportunities and demands, the response to any subset of which will serve one or more professional goals. To be sure, the member must choose among them. Legislative resources are scarce, and their allocation to one activity results in other beneficial opportunities forgone. But for the most part, the purposive legislator is free to choose among the abundant alternatives with only modest constraints imposed by constituents, colleagues, or other actors. Hence, the member's level of involvement is something that a strategic PAC can reasonably expect to affect. The contribution need not weigh so heavily in a member's mind that it changes his or her position in any material way; it need only weigh heavily enough to command some increment of legislative resources.

A third advantage of this view is that it explains the ostensibly anomalous tendency of PACs to contribute so heavily to members who are almost certain to win reelection and almost certain to support the group's point of view. Such behavior now appears quite rational. It is precisely one's supporters that one wants to mobilize: the more likely certain members are to support the group, the more active it should want them to be. Furthermore, this view of purposive PACs makes sense of the evidence that PACs sometimes contribute to members who will almost certainly oppose them and whose involvement in an issue stands to do the group harm. The PAC may have no hope of changing the opponent's mind, but it may, at the margin

at least, diminish the intensity with which the member pursues policies that the organization does not like. The intent of the money, then, is not persuasion but demobilization: "We know you can't support us, but please don't actively oppose us." However, we should not expect the demobilizing effect of money to be nearly so strong as the mobilizing effect. The message provided through contributions to one's supporters is widely perceived as a legitimate one: in asking for help, the group is encouraging members to do precisely what they would do were resources plentiful. In contrast, contributions to opponents are meant to encourage them to go against their predispositions: the implicit message is to "take a walk" on an issue that they may care about. In short, the expected effects are not symmetric; the mobilization hypothesis is on stronger theoretical ground.

A final advantage of the view of rational action employed here is that it renders the matter of access more comprehensible. We have already noted that according to the standard account of PAC behavior, the importance that both legislators and lobbyists attach to the money–access connection makes little sense, given the evidence that money has little ultimate effect on votes. In light of the theory sketched here, however, access becomes an important, proximate goal of the interest group pursuing a legislative agenda. Access is central to stimulating agency. It gives the group the opportunity to let otherwise sympathetic members (and their staff) know that some issue or upcoming activity is important to them. The ideal response they seek is not simply "I'll support you on this" but "What can I do to help?" Perhaps, more importantly, access refers to the reciprocal efforts of the group. It is the pipeline through which the group effectively subsidizes the considerable time and information costs associated with their supporters' participation in the matters the group cares about. As various accounts reveal, group representatives often serve as "service bureaus" or adjuncts to congressional staff. They provide technical information and policy analysis; they provide political intelligence; they draft legislation and craft amendments; they even write speeches or talking points that

their supporters can employ in efforts on their
behalf. Such subsidies to the "congressman-
as-enterprise" do not necessarily persuade, but
they should affect the patterns of activity and
abdication that have a direct bearing on legislative deliberations and outcomes.

THE DATA: MONEY AND MOBILIZATION
ON THREE COMMITTEES

The data for this investigation are drawn from
staff interviews and markup records of three
House committees on three issues: (1) the Dairy
Stabilization Act, considered by the Agriculture
Committee in 1982; (2) the Job Training Part-
nership Act (JTPA), considered by Education
and Labor in 1982; and (3) the Natural Gas
Market Policy Act, considered by Energy and
Commerce during 1983–84.

Several features of these cases make them particularly appropriate for exploring the effects of
money on the participation of committee members. First, all were highly significant pieces of
legislation, the stakes of each measuring in the
billions of dollars. At issue in the Natural Gas
Market Policy Act was the deregulation of natural gas prices, a proposal that would transfer billions of dollars from one region to another, from
consumer to industry, and within the industry from interstate pipelines and distributors to
the major natural gas producers. Annual spending on the Job Training Partnership Act was
expected at the time of its passage to be in the
four-to-five-billion-dollar range, and it replaced
one of the most important domestic programs
of the 1970s. While more narrow than these in
scope, the Dairy Stabilization Act also entailed
significant economic effects. The principal purpose of the act was to adjust the scheduled support price for milk downward by as much as a
dollar per hundredweight over two years, creating budget savings of 4.2 billion dollars for fiscal
years 1983–85 and decreasing the profitability of
milk production by as much as 30 percent for
the typical dairy farmer. In each case, then,
evidence of the influence of PAC money on
congressional decision making can hardly be
counted narrow or trivial. The deliberations

in each case bore in significant ways on major
interests, both public and private.

A second feature relevant to this investigation follows from the economic importance
attached to these issues. All three were salient
among actors other than the private groups
immediately affected, a feature that the considerable research on roll call voting suggests
should depress the effect of PAC contributions
on congressional decision making.

Finally, each of the policy areas we examine here has received the attention of previous
scholars studying PAC contributions and floor
roll calls; and in each case the effects of PAC
money were found to be slight.

At two levels, then, past research indicates
that our selection of cases is biased against our
argument. It suggests that high salience issues
should exhibit little PAC influence on legislative behavior, yet each of the cases here commanded the attention of a wide range of political actors. Second, past research suggests that we
will find little PAC influence in precisely these
three policy areas. Should we find support for
the hypothesis that money mobilizes support (or
demobilizes opposition) at the committee level,
we should be on reasonably solid ground to conclude that (1) the results of this exploration are
apt to generalize to other committees and other
issues and (2) the null results of past research
are more likely to be artifacts of the legislative
behavior and the legislative stage studied than
evidence that moneyed interests do not matter
in congressional decision making.

THE MODEL

The model of participation we use to test
for the hypothesized effects begins from the
same motivational premise that we employed
in our discussion of PAC contribution behavior. Members of Congress are purposive actors
who allocate their time, staff, and other legislative resources in such a way as to advance
certain personal goals or interests. There are
several goals that commonly figure in these
calculations. The one most prominently cited in
the literature on legislative behavior is reelection

or, more generally, service to the district; but we report elsewhere that the relevance of any particular goal to a member's participation depends directly on the nature of the issue and the legislative context. Any particular issue may evoke several goals simultaneously or may evoke none at all. In the latter case, a member is simply uninterested, the expected benefits of participation slight; in the former, the level of interest is intense, the expected benefits of participation high.

In the three cases under study here, in fact, several goals were probably at work in the resource allocation decisions of most committee members. But the goal most consistently evident in staff interviews, markup debates, and secondary accounts of the three bills was promoting or protecting district interests. For the purposes of this analysis, then, we adopt the simpler and more tractable motivational assumption common to most models of legislative behavior. In deciding whether and to what extent to participate on a particular issue, the member estimates both the expected benefits and expected costs, where benefits are a direct function of the issue's economic relevance to the district.

If the interests of one's constituents motivate a member to become involved, the costs of participation are also important and highly variable: resources are scarce, and the allocation to one activity results in other profitable opportunities forgone. Several factors affect the resources available to particular members on particular issues. First, assignment to the subcommittee of jurisdiction provides members both with greater formal opportunities to participate and access to an earlier stage of the sequential process. It also gives the member greater access to staff and to lines of communication with other interested actors both on and off the committee. For similar reasons, a committee or subcommittee leadership position subsidizes participation even more. The greater staff allocations that these positions bestow, the procedural control over the agenda, and the central place in the committee communication network diminish the time and information costs associated with meaningful involvement in the issue at hand. Finally, freshman status tends to increase the

information costs and diminish the opportunities or resources a member enjoys for any particular bill.

The variable of greatest interest in this investigation, however, is the level of contributions each member receives from PACs interested in the issue at hand. To what degree, that is, does money affect members' decisions regarding whether and to what extent they will participate in the committee deliberations? Two points require emphasis here. First, the foregoing discussion suggests that the effects of money on participation should not be simply linear. The positive effect of contributions on participation should be contingent on probable support; this is the mobilization hypothesis. To the extent that contributions are given to probable opponents, on the other hand, they should diminish participation; this is the demobilization hypothesis.

Second, contributions may well be related to other activities that moneyed interests employ to further their legislative aims, making it difficult to isolate the effects of any particular part of their effort. For instance, it may be the case that those groups that organize PACs for the purpose of channeling money to candidates are also the most active in developing grass roots campaigns or direct lobbying efforts. While there is evidence to suggest that the correlation among these activities is modest for the cases under study here, our data on interest group activity are limited to political action committee campaign contributions. Hence, while our model tests for the effect that money has on committee behavior, one might more accurately characterize our results as capturing the effect of the several resources that moneyed interests employ.

The dependent variable is the participation of member i on bill j, where participation refers to a member's activity both during formal committee markups and committee action behind the scenes. Our data on activity are drawn from two sources: semistructured interviews with both the majority and minority staffers assigned to cover each bill and the largely unpublished but meticulously kept committee and subcommittee markup records. The summary measure of participation that we use for the purposes of this exploration is a simple scale score [based on] six activities: attendance; voting participation; speaking; offering amendments during committee markups; role in authoring the legislative vehicle or an amendment in the nature of a substitute; and negotiating behind the scenes at either the member or the staff level. The measurement of the independent variables, in turn, follows directly from the preceding discussion. Members' institutional positions and status are measured with dichotomous variables that are set at zero except as the following conditions hold: subcommittee membership takes a value of one if a member sat on the subcommittee with jurisdiction over the bill; leadership position takes a value of one if a member was chair or ranking minority member of either the full or subcommittee; and freshman status takes a value of one for members in their first term in the House.

In measuring the relevance of each issue to committee members' districts, we assume that relevance is primarily economic in nature. In the natural gas case, this takes two quite different forms: total district-level natural gas production and the economic effect of gas price increases on residential consumers in the member's district, which we measure using industry data on natural gas price increases and census data regarding congressional district natural gas use. If high production and high inflation capture dimensions of intradistrict salience, however, the presence of both at once should produce intradistrict conflict. The member is torn between two significant economic interests, and activity on behalf of one may alienate the other. As intradistrict conflict increases, in any case, the expected benefits of activity on the issue should diminish, ceteris paribus. In the natural gas case, then, intradistrict conflict occurs as the production and inflation variables both approach their upper limits. We measure this condition as the product of two terms: "high production" is the extent to which natural gas production in the district exceeds the mean district production for all members of the committee; similarly, "high inflation" is the extent to which the district inflationary effect exceeds the mean for all committee members. When either

district gas production or inflationary effect is below the committee mean, then, intradistrict conflict is zero.

In the other two cases the measurement of district interest is uncomplicated by potential conflicts within members' geographic constituencies. In the dairy stabilization case district relevance is directly related to the importance of dairy farming, measured simply by the total number of dairy cows in the member's district as reported by the United States Department of Agriculture biennial census. Given that milk prices were not a salient consumer issue per se and that the Dairy Stabilization Act was not likely to affect retail prices in any significant way, we do not assume a more general public concern with this issue. For the Job Training Partnership Act, likewise, district relevance is directly related to the importance of federal jobs programs in addressing structural unemployment, which we measure as the current level of CETA expenditures in the member's district. This variable not only taps the district-specific economic benefits of clients of the expiring job training program but (given that CETA allocations were directly tied to local unemployment rates), also captures the severity of structural unemployment in the district.

Consistent with the preceding theoretical discussion, we estimate the effect of group expenditures on participation by including pairs of interactions between group contributions (measured as the amount contributed during the two-year election cycle prior to committee action) and indicators of probable support or opposition. For each case, the exact specification of the interactions is straightforward. In the dairy stabilization case, we measure probable support or opposition using the ratings of the National Farmers' Union (NFU), an organization that strongly supports federal intervention in the agricultural economy to control supply and support the commodity prices paid to farmers. Given that we expect very different effects for contributions on the behavior of likely supporters and opponents, however, the model requires two separate interactions: *Money to supporters* is the product of contributions and the members distance from the mean NFU score where the member's rating is greater than the mean; the money-support term is zero otherwise. *Money to opponents* is the product of contributions and the members distance from the mean NFU score, where the member's rating is less than the mean; the money-opposition term is zero otherwise. Following the theoretical reasoning of the last section, then, the expected effect on participation is positive for money to supporters. The expected effect is negative for money to opponents in each case.

Any attempt to model the effect of contribution activity on legislative behavior cannot assume that a particular industry is necessarily unified; however, one segment of an industry may have different interests and work in ways that offset some other segment. In the case of the federal dairy legislation, no such split within the industry was apparent among the principal actors, thus permitting the fairly simple specification described above. But in general – and in the natural gas case in particular – an industry may not be so easily simplified. While the gas producers were by far the most visible and most vigorous among the corporate actors and gave by far the most money in campaign contributions among energy PACs, the natural gas industry was seriously divided, a feature that we attempt to capture. The alignments were by no means perfect, but the principal issues at stake in the legislation before House Energy and Commerce pitted the major gas producers and intrastate pipelines against the interstate pipelines and distributors. As a result, different segments of the industry were likely to target different members to serve as legislative agents and identify different members as their likely opponents. Our first task therefore was to distinguish the various energy PACs according to the principal business activities of their affiliates. Using the detailed descriptions of individual companies provided by Moody's Investor Service, we classified each affiliate according to its principal interests in the natural gas area. We then divided the contributions a member received according to whether they came from producers or intrastate pipelines on the one hand and interstates or distributors on the other. The measure of contributions that we employ,

then, is the producer-intrastate contributions minus the interstate-distributor contributions, the value of which was positive in almost every case.

The operationalization of the interactions tapping the net producer-intrastate effects, in turn, was handled in a fashion analogous to the dairy stabilization case. In the natural gas case, however, members' Americans for Democratic Action (ADA) scores were more appropriate as an indicator of likely support or opposition. For the producer-intrastate segment of the gas industry at least, the issue of greatest concern was the extent to which the government continued its intervention in the natural gas market by controlling the price of old gas. The ADA score should tap members' historical tendency to support such federal interventions quite well. *Money to supporters*, then, is the product of net producer-intrastate contributions and the member's distance from the mean ADA score where the member's rating is less than the mean; the money-support term is zero otherwise; and *money to opponents* is the product of contributions and the member's distance from the mean ADA score where the member's rating is greater than the mean; the money-opposition term is zero otherwise.

Unlike the dairy and natural gas cases, finally, the job training bill did not involve issues specific to a particular industry. The organized interests most concerned with CETA and its prospective replacement were the national labor unions: public service employment and training programs were at the top of labor's agenda, especially in 1982, when unemployment was approaching postwar records. Moreover, labor unions were one of the single largest categories of contributors to congressional campaigns and gave to five-sixths of the members of House Education and Labor. It is the effect of these contributions on committee behavior with which we are primarily concerned. This is not to say, however, that labor unions were the only groups interested in mobilizing support on this bill. On the business side, national business associations generally opposed any public service employment provisions and favored an expanded role for private industry councils so

that federally subsidized training would be tailored to meet the changing needs of the private sector. As in the natural gas case, we thus
employ a net contributions variable, which takes
the value of the member's total labor contributions less the total contributions received from
national business organizations. As in the other
two cases, likewise, the indicator of probable
support or opposition was constructed using
the appropriate group rating, in this case, the
AFL-CIO's Committee on Political Education
(COPE) score. *Money to supporters*, then, is
the product of net labor contributions and the
member's distance from the mean COPE score,
where the member's rating is greater than the
mean; and *money to opponents* is the product of
contributions and the member's distance from
the mean COPE score where the member's rating is less than the mean.

RESULTS AND INTERPRETATIONS

The analysis provides solid support for the principal hypothesis of this study, that moneyed
interests mobilize bias in committee decision
making.

This finding is clear for all three cases.
The campaign contributions that dairy industry PACs gave to their likely supporters significantly increased their participation, even when
we controlled for the importance of the issue
to individual members' districts, whether they
sat on the subcommittee of jurisdiction, and
whether they held a leadership position. When
dairy PACs did give to their probable opponents, moreover, there is some evidence that
the contributions diminished participation. In
short, the more money a supporter received
from the dairy PACs and the stronger the member's support, the more likely he or she was to
allocate time and effort on the industry's behalf
(e.g., work behind the scenes, speak on the
group's behalf, attach amendments to the committee vehicle, as well as show up and vote at
committee markups). Alternatively, money may
have diminished the intensity of the opposition.
The effect of money on decision making in
the House Agriculture Committee, then, was

to encourage industry supporters to be active
and, if anything, to encourage industry opponents to abdicate.

The results of the job training case are also
clear, and the specific estimates are striking in
their similarity to the dairy stabilization case.
The contributions that labor groups made to
their supporters had a substantial, statistically
significant effect on participation during Education and Labor deliberations. Remarkably,
the [impact of] the money support variable is
almost identical in size to the dairy stabilization model despite the fact that the two cases
are drawn from different committees with qualitatively different jurisdictions and policy environments. In each case, a change in the money
support variable from its minimum to its maximum value moves a member approximately
one-fourth of the way along the participation
scale. In both cases, likewise, this [effect] is
greater than that for subcommittee membership, a variable generally considered central to
understanding participation in the postreform
House. As in the dairy stabilization case, finally,
the Education and Labor bill provides some support for the demobilization hypothesis.

The results regarding moneyed interests and
mobilization are only slightly less compelling in
the natural gas case, a case complicated both by
divisions within the industry and the apparent
importance of both organized and unorganized
interests. As we note above, such conditions are
likely to mitigate the efficacy of interest group
efforts, and they complicate the measurement
of anticipated support and opposition. Still, the
mobilization hypothesis finds strong support in
the behavior of Energy and Commerce members. While the size of the [effect of] the money
support variable is somewhat smaller than for
the other two cases, it is still substantial. A
change in the money support variable from
its minimum to its maximum moves a Commerce Committee member approximately one-
sixth of the way along the participation scale. By
way of illustration, this amounts to the difference between Minnesota Representative Gerry
Sikorski, who did little more than faithfully
attend and vote during formal markups, and
Alabama Representative Richard Shelby, whose

staff participated in behind-the-scenes negotiations and who offered two substantive amendments during subcommittee markup, both of which passed.

Finally, the demobilization hypothesis is not supported in the natural gas case. The foundation for the demobilization hypothesis being theoretically weaker, however, the null result here, as well as the weak results in the dairy and job training cases, are not altogether surprising. The theoretically stronger hypothesis, that money mobilizes a pro-PAC bias at the committee level, is confirmed in all three.

For the most part, the other variables in the model also perform as predicted and suggest interesting implications for the politics of representation in a decentralized Congress. The relevance of an issue to the member's district enhances member participation in two cases, providing evidence that Agriculture and Commerce members purposively allocate their legislative time and resources to promote the interests of their constituencies. On House Agriculture, the more important dairy farming was to the member's district, the more likely he or she was to participate in committee deliberations. Likewise, the greater the presence of natural gas production in the district, the more likely the Energy and Commerce member was to participate in deliberations on the Natural Gas Market Policy Act. Indeed, a change in gas production from its minimum to its maximum corresponds to a 32 percent change along the participation scale, the difference between simply showing up and being a major player on the bill. By comparison, however, the effect of natural gas price increases on district consumers appears smaller by half. And the importance of structural unemployment and program spending in the districts of Education and Labor members had at best a slight effect on their involvement in the Job Training Partnership Act.

Pending better measurement of unorganized constituents' interest at the district level, of course, we cannot draw unqualified conclusions regarding their importance in shaping committee behavior. Should such patterns hold up under subsequent analysis, however, the implications for member responsiveness to industry

interests and industry money relative to more general constituency concerns would be several and important. If members allocate their scarce legislative time and resources with district interests in mind, they perceive their districts in terms of different constituencies; and these perceptions affect their behavior as representatives. In part, the results presented here suggest that organized economic interests within districts figure more prominently in the psychology of representation than the diffuse and unorganized interests of rank-and-file voters. Such was the charge that Schattschneider made thirty years ago, one which critics of pluralism have echoed repeatedly since.

At the same time, however, the findings in the natural gas case also suggest that the preferences of unorganized interests sometimes constrain the responsiveness of members to organized groups. Even if members are inclined to respond to producer interests, in short, this tendency is mitigated when consumer interests are also high.

Finally, most of the variables that tap members' institutional positions prove to be strong determinants of committee participation. While the [effect of] freshman status [decreases participation], both subcommittee membership and leadership position [increase participation in a substantively large manner]. Even on issues that are widely perceived among the committee membership to be important, issues where the organized interests in the policy environment are themselves active, the opportunities and resources provided by formal institutional position are major factors in determining who makes the laws at the committee stage.

CONCLUSION

We have elaborated a theory of the member–group exchange relationship that comprehends the general patterns of PAC contributions reported in the literature. House members and interest group representatives are parties to an implicit cooperative agreement, but the constraints on member behavior and the rational calculations of group strategists limit the extent to which votes become the basis for exchange. This view suggests expectations about the effects of money on congressional decision making quite different from the ones that motivate the substantial research on the subject. We should find little causal connection between contributions and votes, especially on the floor – an expectation generally supported, although not adequately explained, in the literature. We should expect to find an important connection between contributions and the legislative involvement of sympathetic members, especially in committee – a relationship that empirical research to date has altogether ignored.

In order to test this view of moneyed interests and congressional decision making, we investigated the participation of House members on three issues in three committees. In each case, we found solid support for our principal hypothesis: moneyed interests are able to mobilize legislators already predisposed to support the group's position. Conversely, money that a group contributes to its likely opponents has either a negligible or negative effect on their participation. While previous research on these same issues provided little evidence that PAC money purchased members' votes, it apparently did buy the marginal time, energy, and legislative resources that committee participation requires. Moreover, we found evidence that (organized) producer interests figured more prominently than (unorganized) consumer interests in the participation decisions of House committee members. Such findings suggest several implications for our understanding of political money, interest groups, and the legislative process.

The first and most important implication is that moneyed interests *do* affect the decision-making processes of Congress, an implication that one does not easily derive from the existing political science literature on contributions. In fact, it matters most at that stage of the legislative process that matters most and for a form of legislative behavior likely to have a direct bearing on outcomes. Only a small fraction of the decisions that shape a bill ever go to a vote, either in committee or on the floor. The vast majority are made in authoring a legislative

vehicle, formulating amendments, negotiating specific provisions or report language behind the scenes, developing legislative strategy, and in other activities that require substantial time, information, and energy on the part of member and staff. While such efforts by no means guarantee that a particular member will influence the final outcome, they are usually a precondition for such influence.

A second and related implication of this investigation, then, is that empirical research should expand its view of the legislative purposes of political money and the other group resources that may accompany it. We focus here on committee participation; but the more general implication is that group expenditures may do much more than buy votes, or they may buy votes under certain conditions and affect other forms of legislative behavior under others. Such a suggestion, of course, usually appears in the various studies that examine the relationship between contributions and floor roll calls, but it needs to be elevated from the status of footnote or parenthetic remark to a central element of future research designs. Even for a small set of issues and a single group, the legislative strategies available are several, sometimes mixed. To speculate beyond the research reported here, for instance, we believe groups allocate their various resources (1) to mobilize strong supporters not only in House committees but also on the Senate floor, in dealings with executive agencies, and in various other decision-making forums relevant to the group's interests; (2) to demobilize strong opponents; and (3) to effect the support of swing legislators. We require greater knowledge of the frequency and efficacy of such strategies, in any case, before we denigrate the role of moneyed interests in Congress, especially when the overwhelming weight of the evidence provided by Washington journalists and political insiders suggests that they matter a great deal.

Finally, the argument presented here provides a very different slant on the role of interest groups as purveyors of information in the deliberations of representative assemblies. A common defense of group lobbying activity, in fact, is that it provides ideas and information although its effect on member preferences is slight. Members (and their staff) tend to consume information selectively, relying on sources with whom they already agree and discounting sources with whom they usually disagree. The view that we have advanced here suggests that while this may in fact describe how such information is used, it does not render it inconsequential. In light of the extraordinary demands on each congressional office, information − gathering it; analyzing it; turning it into speeches, amendments, and bills; using it to develop legislative strategy − can be very costly. Such costs, more than anything, limit the extent to which a nominal member will be a meaningful player in the decision-making process on a particular bill. At the very least, then, money-induced activity will distort the "representativeness of deliberations," a standard that democratic theorists since John Stuart Mill have used to evaluate the legitimacy of legislative assemblies. But it may also affect the "representativeness of decisions." By selectively subsidizing the information costs

associated with participation, groups affect the *intensity* with which their positions are promoted by their legislative agents. In short, not all preferences weigh equally in legislative deliberations; and the resources of moneyed interests at least partly determine the weights.

The extent to which such efforts are damaging to representative government, as Schattschneider claimed, depends in part on the balance of interests and resources apparent in the relevant set of groups that are organized for political action. On any given issue, the efforts of one interest to mobilize supporters in Congress may be at least partially offset by the efforts of some competing group to mobilize its own supporters; indeed, there is some evidence that such countervailing efforts occurred in the natural gas case. But for those who believe that money is an illegitimate resource in such efforts − that pluralism requires something more than a competition among moneyed interests − the results of this study can only be disturbing.

CHAPTER THIRTY-SEVEN

"Legislative Lobbying" – Excerpt

John Wright

Wright offers a theoretical account of interest group influence in Congress. He contends that interest groups gain influence by offering members of Congress a valuable resource – information. Through the strategic presentation of information, interest groups have the potential to spur sympathetic members to legislative action and opponents to inaction.

Organizations attempt to influence legislative decisions through a broad range of activities. These include efforts at cultivating and maintaining good working relationships with legislators; engaging in public relations and advertising campaigns; organizing and mobilizing constituents at the grassroots; making campaign contributions; researching policy issues; gathering information about legislators' voting intentions and the legislative agenda; testifying before congressional committees; and communicating directly with legislators, their personal staff, or committee staff. All of these activities constitute what is generally referred to as *lobbying*. It is through these various lobbying activities that organized interests acquire and transmit information to legislators.

The argument [here] is that interest groups achieve influence in the legislative process by strategically providing information to change or reinforce legislators' beliefs about legislative

John Wright. 1996. "Legislative Lobbying" in John Wright, *Interest Groups and Congress: Lobbying, Contributions, and Influence* (Allyn & Bacon), 75–113. Copyright © 2003 by Pearson Education, Inc. Reprinted by permission.

outcomes, the operational effects of policies, and the electoral ramifications of their actions. The key components of this argument are developed in four sections. The first discusses the two fundamental goals of all interest groups – access and influence. A distinction is drawn between access and influence that highlights the differences between how lobbyists *position* themselves to present information and how they *persuade* legislators through the presentation of information. The second section identifies the major sources of uncertainty in the legislative process. It explains how uncertainty makes it difficult for representatives to achieve their legislative and political goals and, consequently, why legislators seek information. The third section describes how groups specialize in the types of information legislators seek, and the fourth describes how interest groups strategically use information to achieve influence.

THE OBJECTIVES OF ORGANIZED INTERESTS: ACCESS AND INFLUENCE

All lobbying begins with access. Access is absolutely critical to any successful lobbying campaign and, along with influence, is one of the principal objectives of organized interests. Yet, exactly what access is and how it differs from influence is seldom made clear by the politicians, journalists, and academics who frequently talk and write about access and influence. Unfortunately, when the concepts are used interchangeably, as they often are, typical explanations for access – for example, making campaign contributions or hiring high-profile lobbyists in Washington – can incorrectly be construed as explanations for influence. Some clarification is needed.

Access

The concept of access is one of the most ubiquitous, and also one of the most ambiguous, in all of the lobbying literature. To some, access means nothing more than establishing contact with a member of Congress or a staff person. One specific measure of access in this sense is the number of minutes a member of Congress spends in his or her office with representatives from organized interests. To others, however, access means not only establishing contact but also achieving influence – getting legislators or staff to give serious consideration to particular arguments, perhaps even to act on them. Another scholar notes at least four meanings of the term *access:* (1) convincing a policy maker to listen to arguments; (2) establishing a "regular relationship" with a policymaker for the exchange of information; (3) becoming "institutionalized" into the policy process by, for example, acquiring formal representation on governing boards of agencies; and (4) gaining influence.

One way to conceptualize the differences between access and influence is to imagine a continuum ranging from no access on one end to influence on the other. Such a continuum for any given interest group and legislator is depicted graphically in Figure 37.1. Although the divisions on this continuum are arbitrarily located, they represent qualitatively different relationships between a legislator and group. At the far left of the continuum is the lobbyist who has no access whatsoever with a given legislator. A lobbyist with no access is one who is unable, or else makes no effort, to communicate with the legislator in any fashion – either through social interaction, staff contacts, personal business meetings, or telephone or fax communica-

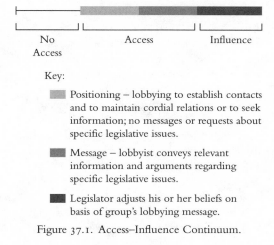

Key:

[image] Positioning – lobbying to establish contacts and to maintain cordial relations or to seek information; no messages or requests about specific legislative issues.

[image] Message – lobbyist conveys relevant information and arguments regarding specific legislative issues.

[image] Legislator adjusts his or her beliefs on basis of group's lobbying message.

Figure 37.1. Access–Influence Continuum.

tions. Lobbyists sometimes fail to achieve access, or else choose not to seek it, because they are not well known individually or employed by a well known group, because the lobbyist's group is one with which the legislator does not wish to be associated for political reasons, or because they are perceived as unreliable or untrustworthy.

Access to legislators can be achieved at two different levels. The first and most basic level of access is represented by the most lightly shaded region in Figure 37.1. At this level, lobbyists try to *position* themselves favorably in order to send a particular message or make a specific appeal at some later time. Positioning involves efforts to attain recognition as a regular participant or "player" in a policy area, to establish cordial working relationships with legislators, and generally to demonstrate that one has something worthwhile to say. Groups and their lobbyists position themselves by opening Washington offices, inviting legislators to social functions, assisting them with constituency requests for information, and making campaign contributions. The distinguishing feature of contacts at this basic level is that they are very generalized. Lobbyists may discuss broad policy interests of the organization, but the objective of access at this level is not to try and persuade the legislator to support or oppose any particular legislative issues. The purpose instead is simply to establish visibility and good relations with legislators through professional and social courtesies.

Being favorably positioned with a legislator can be beneficial to an organization even if it leads to no specific legislative favors or victories. Interest groups routinely seek information about bills that might be introduced, the scheduling of hearings or votes, and the policy positions of legislators. Gathering information about the political process is a large part of what lobbyists do, and those lobbyists who are favorably positioned with legislators are most likely to acquire this information.

A second level of access is depicted in Figure 37.1 by the second most heavily shaded region. Access at this level is much more specific in nature than access at the first level. Here access typically involves a scheduled meeting with the legislator or staff person, and it is at this time that the lobbyist conveys a specific *message* designed to gain the legislator's support. Relative to the first level of lobbying, this second level constitutes a relatively small part of the overall process.

Although the cost to the legislator of granting either type of access is not trivial, it is still relatively low. While it is true that legislators have enormous demands on their time, it is also true that Congress is by design an accessible institution. Each member commands a large personal staff and usually several district offices. Legislators frequently assign staff, and occasionally even interns, to meet with lobbyists. Moreover, most meetings with lobbyists are short, as lobbyists usually understand the constraints on a legislator's time. Somewhat surprisingly, a survey of 92 House members from the 95th Congress revealed that the average legislator spends only 37 minutes each week in face-to-face contact with representatives of organized groups. Based on a reported average week of 54 hours of work, meetings with lobbyists consume only 1 percent of the average legislator's time. Clearly, the popular image of representatives having their offices overrun with lobbyists is more fiction than fact.

, One reason that legislators do not spend more of their time in face-to-face meetings with lobbyists is that there are numerous other ways for organized interests to present information to members of Congress. Organizations write letters, stage demonstrations, present their case to the media, and participate in committee hearings. Naturally, lobbyists prefer face-to-face meetings in order to ensure that their messages are presented and interpreted accurately, but getting messages delivered is not the ultimate concern of lobbyists. Their main problem is getting legislators to consider their arguments carefully and to give weight to their claims.

Influence

Even before talking to lobbyists, legislators usually have fairly well-formed beliefs about whether proposed policies will be economically efficient, socially equitable, and politically viable. They also generally have well-formed beliefs about the importance of these policies to their constituents and the likely electoral consequences of the positions they take. Importantly, however, legislators may *revise* their beliefs when new information becomes available. Ultimately, interest groups hope to determine legislators' policy stands, but to do so they must first manipulate the beliefs that determine legislators' policy preferences and their perceptions of the electoral implications of the positions they take. The purpose of a lobbying message is to introduce information that will alter or affect these beliefs. Sometimes legislators dismiss lobbyists' claims, but other times they accept the claims and adjust their beliefs accordingly.

The point at which access ends and influence begins is the point at which legislators adjust their beliefs on the basis of lobbying information. This point is depicted in Figure 37.1 by the darkly shaded region. Upon receiving lobbying information, legislators can either dismiss it, in which case they are not influenced, or revise their beliefs, in which case they are influenced. Thus, lobbying information can affect legislators' beliefs in two basic ways: it can *maintain* or *reinforce* their beliefs – that is, prevent their beliefs from changing in response to alternative information; or information can alter the *direction* of legislators' beliefs held prior to any lobbying – that is, change their beliefs about whether a policy will work as claimed or whether their constituents support or oppose a given proposal.

Influence differs from access, therefore, in that access implies only that lobbyists are in a *position* to affect legislators' beliefs, not that beliefs have actually been altered, maintained, or reinforced. Since influence involves the impact of lobbying information on beliefs, not behavior, influence will not always be readily observable. Legislators may change their beliefs without altering their policy preferences or their perceptions of their constituents' preferences. Consequently, the distinction between access and influence is much easier to make at a conceptual level than at an empirical one, and this may explain why access is frequently taken as the standard measure of a lobbyist's success. Relative to influence, access is tangible. Interest groups can easily be observed making campaign contributions, playing golf with legislators, participating in congressional hearings, and so forth, and thus any apparent influence that lobbyists achieve is often attributed to these sorts of activities.

That new information can change the way legislators think and, therefore, act presumes that legislators are often uncertain about what course of action to take. This assumption is critical to an information-based explanation of interest group influence, for unless legislators are uncertain about what to do, there is no need for them to seek the counsel of professional lobbyists. Hence, it is important to establish clearly the various sources of uncertainty in legislative decision making.

THE UNCERTAINTY OF LEGISLATIVE DECISION MAKING

Legislators are motivated by three basic goals: reelection, good public policy, and influence within the legislature. To most Americans, the success of legislators in making good public policy or achieving legislative success is not as apparent as their success in getting reelected. Nonetheless, many legislators do espouse these as central goals. The three goals are interdependent: legislators must have some influence within the legislature if they are to enact good policies, and they must hold onto their jobs in order to pursue their legislative objectives. The attainment of these goals is complicated by the fact that legislators cannot be certain about how voters will react to their policy decisions, how policies will actually work once implemented, or what kinds of political complications might arise during the legislative process.

There are, then, at least three important sources of uncertainty that affect legislators' decisions. Perhaps the most important of these is uncertainty about *reelection*. Legislators must know which issues are important to their constituents and which positions to take on those issues. Legislators who seriously misjudge the direction or intensity of constituents' preferences often experience stiff electoral competition and sometimes even defeat. The *legislative process* is a second important source of uncertainty. Questions about how other legislators will react to a bill, what kinds of trade-offs will be necessary to gain majority support, and what kinds of procedural roadblocks lie ahead can weigh importantly into legislators' decisions about what actions to take. Uncertainty about the legislative process is of particular concern to those legislators whose primary goal is influence within the legislature. A third source of uncertainty concerns *policy performance*. The technical and substantive aspects of policy proposals must be fully understood in order to determine whether a policy will truly produce the outcomes that are intended. Uncertainty about policy performance affects all legislators seeking to make good public policy.

Uncertainty about Reelection

Legislators must constantly evaluate the electoral ramifications of the positions they take. They must discern the prevailing direction of opinion among constituents, and they must assess whether or not the position they take will become an issue during the next election campaign. Although most constituents pay little attention to what Congress is doing, there is always a possibility that they will *become* attentive. Latent preferences among inattentive constituents "can quickly be transformed into intense and very real opinions with enormous political repercussions."

Given the high reelection rate for members of Congress, it is not immediately clear that uncertainty about reelection is one of their main concerns. More than 90 percent of incumbent members of the U.S. House of Representatives seeking reelection have won in 21 of the 24 congressional elections since 1950. Moreover, more than 70 percent of all incumbents seeking reelection have won with 60 percent of the vote or more on average over the past twenty elections. With these success rates, how can members of Congress be uncertain about reelection?

The answer is that these statistics are not appropriate indicators of uncertainty. Reelection rates are statistical averages, but uncertainty must be measured by variation around these averages. It is the variation around the reelection rates that indicates the tendency for incumbents to win easily in one election but then to either lose or win by a small margin in the next. The *variance* in interelection vote swings for incumbents not only is surprisingly high but also has been increasing over the years. In other words, even though incumbents have been winning at high rates on average over the years, the probability that incumbents' vote margins will deviate from what they were in the last election has also been increasing. Electorates, it seems, have become more volatile over time.

One in every six incumbents who won with 63 percent of the vote in 1988, for example, would be expected to win with just under 55 percent of the vote in 1990. Also, one in every six incumbents who won with 58 percent or less of the vote in 1988 would be expected to lose in 1990. Thus, it is with some regularity that incumbents win very easily in one election and marginally in the next or that they make a solid showing in one election and lose in the next. To make the point more specifically, 15 U.S. House incumbents were defeated in 1990; yet, these same 15 won election in 1988 with an average of 61.4 percent of the vote. Similarly, the 17 House incumbents who were defeated

in 1992 won in 1990 with an average of 64.1 percent of the vote. The 36 House incumbents who lost in 1994 won with an average of 55 percent of the vote in 1992.

Uncertainty about the Legislative Process and Policy Performance

To realize their policy objectives, legislators must ensure that their favored proposals not only receive legislative support but also that the contents of their proposals lead to the desired outcomes. They must deal with the variability of the legislative process *and* with questions about how policies will actually perform once implemented.

Legislators who take or share responsibility for managing a bill must confront a host of difficult questions. What are the personal and political agendas of other lawmakers? How will national economic or political factors affect the viability of the bill? How much interest group support or opposition does the bill have or is it likely to have? Is there majority support in committee or on the floor? If not, how can a majority coalition be fashioned? How should the bill be handled procedurally in the House and in the Senate? Should it be rolled into and buried in an omnibus bill? Should it be considered under a suspension of the rules in the House, or can it be tabled in the Senate? Questions such as these have no quick and easy answers.

Even legislators who have no responsibility for managing a bill must still confront difficult questions about the bill's legislative life. Will the bill proceed far enough into the legislative process that it will demand their attention? If the bill gains the attention of constituents or relevant interest groups, will it be stalled in committee or will it require a roll call vote? When will it be necessary to stake out a position? Most legislators simply do not have the time or the resources to answer these questions for each bill that comes before them.

In their quest to make good public policy, legislators must also judge whether a bill will produce desirable economic, social, or environmental outcomes. What outcomes legislators judge desirable or undesirable depend, of course, on their individual ideological predilections, but, even so, it is often difficult to ascertain whether policies will actually operate consistently with those predilections. Bureaucratic agencies, for example, must be given specific enough instructions to carry out policies as designed yet have sufficient flexibility to respond to unforeseen economic or political circumstances. Policies must also be designed to anticipate demographic changes and legal loopholes or challenges that could affect the distribution of benefits or costs.

Accurately forecasting the impact of policy proposals is a constant challenge for professional policy analysts. In early 1993, for example, the country's leading economic experts disagreed over the likely consequences of President Clinton's budget proposal. Some thought his proposed tax increases would stifle the emerging economic recovery at the time, while others thought that increased consumer confidence and lower interest rates resulting from a smaller federal budget deficit would offset the dampening effects of the tax increases. President Clinton's health care reform proposals in 1993 offer another example of uncertainty over policy performance, as experts disagreed about whether a plan of "managed competition" would produce significant savings in comparison to a market-based approach. Even a study by the Congressional Budget Office was unable to conclude that one approach would clearly lead to greater savings than another. Debate over ratification of the North American Free Trade Agreement (NAFTA) during the fall of 1993 provides yet another example of policy uncertainty. What the net economic benefits or costs to the nation from NAFTA would be were unclear. While there was general agreement that some American jobs would be lost if NAFTA was enacted, it was unclear whether removing trade barriers would stimulate the economy sufficiently to offset those losses.

Uncertainty about policy performance and electoral circumstances are often connected. If one does not know the operational effects of policies, for example, it may be difficult to judge the electoral ramifications. However, even when the operational effects are known with certainty, the electoral consequences may not be. A legislator might know that by voting in favor of stronger pollution controls on industries in his or her district will cost 300 jobs, but to know the electoral consequences of these job losses requires additional information. To assess the electoral implications, one must know how well organized the unemployed workers are and to what extent they will hold the legislator responsible for their job losses at election time. Conversely, even when legislators have little or no uncertainty about electoral consequences, they may still not know which decision is economically most efficient or socially most equitable.

Legislators do not necessarily encounter uncertainty about reelection, the legislative process, and policy performance on each and every bill that comes before them. They may be absolutely sure that some bills will or will not become salient, that constituents will rebel or remain silent in response to their positions on others, and that some bills will never produce the effects that are intended. Yet, it seems likely that legislators encounter at least one and perhaps several kinds of uncertainty for many of the issues on which they must take positions. Since the existence of any uncertainty is potentially an obstacle to the achievement of representatives' legislative and political goals, their demand for good political and policy information is quite high. Predictably, interest groups specialize in the kinds of information legislators need most. The specialized information they acquire is probably their most valuable asset in their quest to influence legislators' policy choices.

THE INFORMATION SPECIALTIES OF
ORGANIZED INTERESTS

Interest groups specialize in three basic types of information. They collect and disseminate information about the status and prospect of bills under active consideration; they provide information about the electoral implications of legislators' support for or in opposition to those bills; and they analyze and report on the likely economic, social, or environmental consequences of proposed policies. It is no coincidence that these three types of information correspond to the three types of uncertainty that beset lawmakers. The informational relationship between legislators and lobbyists has a marketlike quality to it: legislators demand information to reduce uncertainty, and lobbyists supply it.

The special role that interest groups play in the acquisition and transmission of information is recognized by representatives, lobbyists, and academics alike. Former representative Tony Coelho once remarked that lobbyists sometimes "know more about the subject than the staff or the committee members. The Cotton Council will be writing legislation for the cotton industry in the cotton subcommittee." Representative Michael Synar expressed concern about the power that interest groups can wield on the basis of their expertise: "They have become such a dominant force in politics, financially and information-wise. They have better grassroots organizations than most congressmen." Lobbyists understand their informational roles quite well. One lobbyist explained: "A good lobbyist is simply an extension of a congressional member's staff . . . if they want information and they trust you, they'll call *you* for that information."

While there is widespread agreement that interest groups have useful information to offer legislators, it is not entirely clear how groups actually acquire their information. If the acquisition of information is easy or relatively costless, then information provides little strategic advantage for groups, for legislators can acquire the same information without relying on interest groups. Consequently, for information to be a source of influence for groups, it must be the case that information is scarce *and* that groups can acquire or provide it more efficiently than members of Congress, political parties, or private individuals.

Constituency Preferences and Reelection

Short of holding a special election, the only way representatives or interest group leaders can

really be sure of the extent to which voters are concerned about a particular issue, and the extent to which it might eventually affect their voting decisions at election time, is to observe the extent to which constituents are willing to register their concerns through some costly political activity. Costly political activities include writing letters or sending telegrams to members of Congress, calling representatives' offices, raising money, contributing money, passing out leaflets, registering others to vote, attending informational meetings, writing editorial letters to local newspapers, and so forth. Political activities that are costly to undertake require voters to put their money where their mouth is, so to speak, and thus costly activities are the best indicators of the electoral significance of voters' preferences. Not all expressions of political preference are costly, however, and those that are not yield little information. Consider opinion polls, for example. Since virtually no effort is required for poll respondents to tell an interviewer that they care about an issue very strongly, or even that a representative's position on that issue will determine their vote, there is no necessary reason to believe that respondents in public opinion polls will back up their rhetoric with action.

Much more informative than opinion polls are grassroots lobbying campaigns in which groups mobilize citizens to write or call their members of Congress and engage in other costly activities. The principal value of grassroots mobilization, and one of the reasons that grassroots campaigning has become increasingly common and important, is that it *simulates* electoral mobilization. Grassroots lobbying campaigns and election campaigns typically employ some of the same basic technology. Political consultants "have been active in equipping PACs and single-issue groups with the tools of the new campaign technology – survey research and polling, sophisticated television and radio advertising, and direct mail for fund-raising and voter persuasion." If these techniques fail to mobilize voters to phone or write their representatives on an important congressional issue, then it is also unlikely that these same techniques will succeed in mobilizing voters over the same issue at election time.

Practically speaking, lobbyists and other group officials do not always develop precise estimates of the effects of organizational effort on the success of grassroots campaigns. They do, however, gauge the overall spontaneity of grassroots campaigns, and this information has considerable value because of its scarcity. Since organizations are not required to disclose publicly how much they spend overall on grassroots mobilization, it is difficult for outsiders, even legislators, to judge accurately the spontaneity of the effort. Legislators observe the actual output of the mobilization campaign – the number of letters, telegrams, phone calls, and so forth – but without information about the group's actual expenditure of time and money, they cannot be certain how easy or difficult it was for the group to mobilize constituents. This is information legislators would like to have, however, as spontaneous constituency reaction is often much more compelling politically than constituency reaction that is forced or manufactured, even if both result in the same number of letters and phone calls. Many representatives place much greater weight on original, hand-written letters than on form letters, postcards, or other mass-produced mail. Thus, it is not always the total volume of mail that counts, but the ease or difficulty in generating responses that is important, and in this regard interest groups have a distinct informational advantage over legislators.

Interest groups not only provide important electoral information to members of Congress, but they also *create* it. In addition to mobilizing citizens to contact their representatives, organizations also monitor, evaluate, and even shape perceptions of how well incumbents are doing their jobs. Many organizations tabulate and publicize voting scores for legislators as a way of alerting and informing constituents about the voting trends of their representatives. Some organizations encourage their members to write editorials for local newspapers in the district, criticizing or praising their representatives. Other organizations actively recruit candidates to run against incumbents. Groups that participate in these activities, especially groups with politically active members in a representative's district, tend to know the political trends in the district because they create the trends. For this reason, representatives often make it a point to meet with officials or members of politically organized groups when they visit their districts.

Most importantly, though, to make credible claims about electoral consequences, groups must recruit members and activists, invest in mobilization technology such as direct mail, or perhaps even form a political action committee. These are all costly investments and commitments, which serve to differentiate groups with credible electoral information from those without credible information. Think tanks and policy institutes, for example, can make credible claims about the economic or social ramifications of various policy choices, but lacking mass memberships, such organizations cannot credibly make claims about the electoral ramifications of policy choices.

Legislative Process and Policy Performance

Lobbyists can acquire a great deal of institution-specific information through regular contacts with legislators. In the normal course of establishing and maintaining access to legislators, they may learn about the scheduling of hearings, markups, floor debates, and votes; procedural strategies that committee or subcommittee chairmen will employ in markup sessions; positions that legislators have taken or are thinking about taking; and amendments that other legislators or groups might offer. In short, by simply making their routine legislative rounds – lunch or dinner, golf, or a chance meeting in the hallway – lobbyists learn about what legislators are thinking and planning on doing. It is for this reason that access is of critical importance to lobbyists, for it is primarily through access that they gather information about the legislative process.

One piece of information that lobbyists collect systematically is information on legislators' voting predispositions on particular bills. To make efficient decisions about how to allocate their lobbying efforts, organizations must keep track of legislators' positions, monitoring constantly changes in their expected support or opposition. Lobbyists assemble their head counts from analysis of prior voting patterns, from personal meetings and conversations with legislators and their staffs, and from secondary reports by other organizations or legislators. The ability to conduct a thorough head count, and a reputation for conducting accurate ones, is an important informational resource for lobbyists.

Lobbyists who accumulate information about legislators' positions and plans gain an important informational advantage in the legislative process. In a large body like the U.S. House of Representatives with its 435 members, it is not always easy for legislators to know what their colleagues are thinking or planning. Lobbyists, particularly those who have broad access, can play an important role in facilitating the exchange and dissemination of information throughout the legislature. Lobbyists obviously do not have a monopoly on such information, but a large portion of their job is devoted to acquiring it, and many seem to do so with relative efficiency. Their knowledge about what legislators are planning and thinking is an important resource that can be used to shape perceptions about the viability of various policy options.

Like electoral information, information about the legislative process that is easy to acquire is of little value. The lobbyists with the most valuable legislative information are typically those who are best known for their ability to obtain access and to understand the legislative process. It is no accident that the lobbying profession is full of people who earlier had careers as legislative or committee staffers, or who were elected representatives. These are individuals who have invested significant portions of their lives in developing the skills needed to understand the legislative process and to know where and how to acquire information. Lawyer-lobbyists, or "hired guns," earn high salaries precisely because of their reputations for being able to gain access to key decision makers. Their ability to gain access broadly to key members of Congress virtually assures that they have valuable legislative information to share.

A group's expertise about policy performance – the economic, social, or environmental consequences of existing policies as well as proposed policies – derives from two basic sources. One is the organization's professional research staff. For example, the National Association of Realtors employs professional economists to assess the impact of tax policies and other economic policies on the real estate market; the Environmental Defense Fund employs engineers to assess the impact of various land use policies on the environment; and the National Association of Life Underwriters employs accountants and legal experts to monitor the complex and arcane tax laws relating to insurance companies. The second source of technical information, although not available to all organizations, is the group's rank-and-file membership. Individual group members, whether insurance agents, farmers, small and large businesses, or elderly citizens, are the ones who are affected economically and socially by tax laws, welfare programs, and other public policies. Individuals directly involved with government programs and policies are a natural and credible firsthand source of information about how existing policies are actually working or not working, and it is for this reason that organizations often call upon their members to testify at congressional hearings and to submit written comments to congressional committees.

Not all organizations claiming policy expertise have members to draw upon as a source of expertise. Organizations such as the Food Research and Action Center, the National Women's Law Center, the Health Research Group, and the Children's Defense Fund have no dues-paying members. Sometimes called staff groups, these organizations are funded largely by foundation grants, proceeds from publications and conferences, and private donations. Lacking a large membership base, these organizations and others like them achieve their reputations for technical expertise because of their singular focus, their professional staffs, and their research orientation. Naturally, these organizations are much better known for their technical expertise than for their political expertise. These organizations often gain considerable policy expertise through their participation before the courts or administrative agencies.

In general, whether information is about reelection, policy outcomes, or the legislative process, the only expedient information in lobbying is information that is difficult and costly to acquire. The costliness, or scarcity, of information, tends to screen organizations that do not have the resources to acquire relevant information out of the lobbying game. If the informational costs of lobbying are too low, legislators cannot distinguish between good information and bad information, as all groups will appear informed. Any organization can claim to be an expert if the costs of becoming an expert are relatively low, but as the costs to interest groups of acquiring information increase, legislators can begin to distinguish between the organizations that truly have the capability of acquiring the relevant information and those that do not.

THE STRATEGIC USE OF INFORMATION

The preceding sections have emphasized the uncertainty of legislative decision making and the ability of organized interests to acquire and transmit information through lobbying activities. What remains is to discuss how groups strategically use their information to achieve their legislative objectives. As discussed earlier, legislators hold prior beliefs – prior to any lobbying, that is – about how policies work or about the electoral ramifications of their positions and support for bills. These beliefs are usually predicated on experience with similar bills or on general knowledge about their constituencies. Legislators stake out their a priori policy positions on the basis of these beliefs. The strategic objectives of lobbying are to change legislators' beliefs, and hence positions, or else to prevent these beliefs from being changed, by presenting accurate, or sometimes misleading information.

Groups' lobbying strategies can be characterized generally as either *proactive* or *counteractive*. Under a proactive strategy, a group presents information in an effort to *change* a legislator's policy position; under a counteractive strategy,

it presents information in an effort to *prevent* an opposing group from changing the legislator's position. Groups use proactive strategies, therefore, for legislators whose a priori policy positions are opposite their own, and they use counteractive strategies for legislators whose a priori positions are the same as their own.

When a group chooses its lobbying strategy, it must anticipate what opposing groups will do. A group will use a counteractive strategy only when it anticipates that an opposing group will lobby proactively and, if not countered, successfully. In the event that no potentially successful proactive effort is expected, it makes little sense for a group to expend valuable resources lobbying a legislator whose a priori agrees with the group's position. Similarly, a group will use a proactive strategy only when it anticipates that it will not encounter a successful counteractive effort.

The notion that interest groups will strategically attempt to *change* a legislator's position is alien to the model of interest group politics that became popular during the 1960s. The argument here is that groups will actively and strategically attempt to change the beliefs of legislators who *disagree* with them, and that groups will lobby their friends only in an effort to counter the efforts of groups employing proactive strategies.

Misrepresentation as a Lobbying Strategy

One common feature of [contentious lobbying] cases is [the frequency with which] disputes about the accuracy of the information presented by one side or the other [arise]. The existence of such disputes is an essential and predictable feature of an information-based theory of interest group lobbying. Indeed, if there were no conflicts over the veracity of lobbying information, then one could explain interest group behavior simply in terms of "service bureaus" or as extended staff for legislators. Legislators could always trust lobbyists, and lobbyists would never violate this trust, even if they could get away with it and gain important economic and political benefits. Moreover, one should never find lobbying messages from opposing groups to be in conflict. If lobbyists are always telling the entire truth and if lobbyists are well informed, then there should be no disagreement in the information they present. Thus, disputes about the veracity of lobbying information or other evidence of misrepresentation of the facts pose a substantial challenge to the traditional view of interest group politics.

Some might question the extent to which groups deliberately attempt to mislead legislators. After all, a reputation for accuracy is frequently noted as one of the essential qualities of a successful lobbyist. Yet, lobbyists who always divulge everything they know, who do not provide information selectively so as to present their case in the most favorable light, and who refuse to play up the amount of grassroots support for their position may miss important strategic opportunities to exercise influence. This is not to say the lobbyists regularly abuse whatever confidence legislators have in them; nevertheless, the *possibility* of misrepresentation by interest groups, especially in the transmission of information about political strength, is very real.

Examples of misrepresentation are common. One alleged instance in 1993 involved the Student Loan Funding Corporation (SLFC), which manages the secondary market for student loans. The SLFC opposed President Clinton's proposal for revamping the student loan program, because under the president's proposal the program was to be administered directly by the federal government, which would have eliminated the need for a secondary market. Although the SLFC has no individual dues-paying members, it clearly understood the importance of demonstrating broad political support in legislators' constituencies. Consequently, the organization spent $25,000 on advertising directed at college students in Ohio, encouraging them to call their senators through an 800 number. Senator Paul Simon, sponsor of the direct loan program in the Senate, criticized the lobbying effort as a "sham," even though the SLFC claimed it did not attempt to disguise the source of the grassroots response. Evidently, what upset Simon and others was the implication that

grassroots opposition to the president's proposal was spontaneous and independent when in fact it was not.

One can surely uncover many other examples of misleading claims – or at least allegations of misleading claims – in lobbying campaigns both past and present. Perhaps more important than the actual number of such instances, however, is the fact that some of these cases appear to involve deliberate misrepresentation. Groups do sometimes knowingly and strategically encourage or allow legislators to believe information that does not perfectly represent the facts. This should not be too surprising whenever the political stakes are high.

Misrepresentation can be an important source of interest group influence. It is unclear, however, whether exaggeration is as common and widespread [as some suggest], and exactly when groups elect to employ a strategy of misrepresentation. One very important consideration in the strategic decision to misrepresent the facts is the likelihood of being discovered and punished, for as the possibility of discovery increases, the likelihood of successful misrepresentation decreases. Ultimately, the likelihood of discovery depends on the legislator's ability to verify the lobbying claims made by groups.

Checking Misrepresentation

Legislators have numerous sources they can turn to for information about the legislative or political outlook on any given issue, and the possibility that they will turn to these sources provides a strong inducement for lobbyists to report information accurately. To appreciate the importance of legislators' own resources for encouraging groups to provide accurate information, suppose for the moment that legislators could never determine when lobbyists were telling the truth and when they were not, so that all groups could misrepresent the facts with impunity. Under these conditions, legislators could never trust any information provided by groups. In fact, in a world where all lobbying information was unreliable, legislators would have no reason to listen to groups, for groups could never be relied upon to provide accurate information. However, if legislators never believed anything they heard from interest groups, interest groups would have little incentive to lobby. Their claims would always fall on deaf ears, and thus there would be no reason to incur the costs of lobbying.

Yet, interest groups do lobby, and they lobby extensively. This fact alone suggests that some reliable information must be transmitted through lobbying. Evidently, legislators trust lobbyists – at least some of the time – and thus it follows that legislators must have some way of determining when lobbyists are misrepresenting the facts. What makes informational lobbying possible, then, is that legislators have sources of their own, independent of groups, that they can turn to for information.

Of the three basic types of information provided by interest groups – information about the legislative process, information about the policy process, and information about the political situation in the constituency – the easiest for legislators to verify is information about the legislative process. Legislators talk to other legislators, and members of their staffs talk to members of other staffs. Legislators can also turn to the party whips for head counts or other information about levels of support or opposition within the chamber. Although relying on lobbyists for some of this information may be a convenient shortcut, legislators do not have to rely entirely on lobbyists to learn when hearings or votes might be scheduled, what amendments or rules might be proposed, and other information relevant to the legislative process. When necessary, they can acquire the relevant information through their own resources and use it to verify what lobbyists tell them.

Some electoral information is also within the reach of legislators. Members of Congress have budgets for essentially an unlimited number of trips back to their districts each year, and most visit their constituencies every weekend. They also have ample allowances for district offices and staff – the average House member employs six to eight staff persons in the district; the average senator employs roughly 12 – and these resources help them keep abreast of political situations in the district even when they are in Washington. Supplementing these travel and staff benefits is 15,000 minutes of long-distance telephone time from Washington to the district each year. All of these resources help legislators stay in touch with their districts, and even though they cannot simulate electoral mobilization as effectively as interest groups can through grassroots campaigns, they can and do gain a good sense of where their constituents stand on most issues.

Legislators also have various resources to draw upon to understand the operational effects of policies. Not to be underestimated is their own experience and expertise in specific policy areas. The House Ways and Means Committee, for example, regularly deals with accounting and tax rules for corporations, and the House Agriculture Committee writes a major farm bill every five years. Through repeated exposure to complex issues, legislators often acquire sufficient expertise that they do not have to rely on lobbyists to understand how "nonrecourse loans" work, for example, or how tax rules apply to capital gains arising from the conversion of "C corporations" to "S corporations."

In addition, legislators can turn to their own personal staff and to committee staffs for technical expertise, and when more intensive study or analysis of a particular problem is called for, they can turn to the Congressional Research Service, the Congressional Budget Office, the General Accounting Office, and the Office of Technology Assessment. These agencies can provide general reference assistance or conduct analytical studies in areas such as economics, education, environmental policy, and foreign affairs. Reports from these agencies often play an important role in buttressing or refuting arguments and claims of competing interests.

Despite the considerable array of resources available to legislators, the acquisition of any kind of information is still costly. Representatives cannot travel to the district prior to each and every important vote, and there are only so many hours they and their staff can spend on the telephone each day speaking with constituents or colleagues. The resources of committee staff and the research agencies are also limited, and studies cannot always be generated as quickly as they are needed. The significance of the informational resources available to legislators, therefore, is not that they satisfy all of their informational needs all of the time, but that they make it possible for legislators occasionally to *verify* information from organized interests.

When legislators have their own resources for verifying lobbyists' claims, the proclivity for lobbyists to provide misleading information is greatly reduced, for it is always possible that inaccurate information will be discovered and the fabricator revealed. Legislators can then punish the fabricator in a variety of ways. They can vote against the group on subsequent issues, they can deny access, and they can use their contacts with the media to generate negative publicity for the group.

[It is true,] then, that interest groups sometimes exaggerate the facts, but [it would be] incorrect [to assert that interest groups'] "claims are not subject to verification." To the contrary, it is the fact that interest groups' claims *are* subject to verification that makes them potentially useful to legislators, and thus potentially influential.

Lobbying and Influence in American Politics

While there can be no denying that groups do occasionally present misleading information or else knowingly allow legislators to base their decisions on misleading information, groups are limited in their ability to manipulate legislators' beliefs with inaccurate information. Legislators themselves can verify lobbying information by relying on advisors and their own experience, and opposing groups can always counter with accurate information. Interest group influence in American politics, therefore, takes a rather subtle form. Influence derives as much, or even perhaps more, from counteractive lobbying – that is, preventing an opposing group from changing a legislator's position – than from proactive lobbying.

Preventing legislators from changing their positions, however, is just as important a form of influence as *persuading* them to change. Were it not for the fact that groups lobby counteractively, legislators would surely change their positions in response to lobbying much more often than they do, and they would also surely be misled by groups much more often than they are. There is a bit of irony in all of this: the possibility and threat of successful proactive lobbying inspires counteractive lobbying, which in turn reduces the effectiveness of proactive lobbying. Still, proactive lobbying is sometimes successful, and thus the possibility of proactive lobbying is always present.

Finally, it is worth emphasizing once again that one source of interest group influence in American politics is the possibility that facts will be misrepresented. Groups do sometimes achieve influence by knowingly misrepresenting the facts, but this is not the only route to influence. A more common route is that groups present accurate information in order to discourage opponents from presenting inaccurate information. The possibility that misrepresentation will be successful, however, is what motivates both proactive and counteractive lobbying efforts, and thus interest group influence cannot be understood and explained apart from misrepresentation. Although deliberate misrepresentation may not occur all that often in American politics, the threat of misrepresentation is always present, and so is interest group influence.

PART XII. CONGRESS AND BUDGET POLITICS

CHAPTER THIRTY-EIGHT

Appropriations in the Republican Era

Diana Evans

At one time, the House Committee on Appropriations was one of the two or three most powerful committees in Congress. Evans provides an insightful analysis of the declining power of the committee over federal spending during the period 1995 to 2000, years of Republican control of the House. Discretionary spending increased greatly during the period, as did the use of earmarks to target the favored projects of individual legislators.

The appropriations process in Congress has undergone significant change in the past twelve years. The Republican era, especially in the House of Representatives, transformed the politics of appropriations from its traditional bipartisanship to a far more partisan, even rancorous politics than was depicted by Richard F. Fenno in his classic study of the appropriations committees in the 1950s and 1960s, *The Power of the Purse*. Fenno found a highly unified House Appropriations Committee in which partisanship was played down in favor of intracommittee integration, expertise, professionalism, and compromise; the shared policy goal was guardianship of the Treasury.

This relatively peaceful state of affairs was not to last forever; indeed, it began to slip within a few years. Both the congressional budget process instituted in 1974 and the growing polarization of the congressional parties contributed to the shift. Not surprisingly, scholars found an

Diana Evans. 2007. "Appropriations in the Republican Era" *Extensions*, spring 2007, 9–14. Copyright 2007. Carl Albert Congressional Research and Studies Center, University of Oklahoma. All rights reserved.

increase in partisanship on both the House and Senate appropriations committees in the post-reform era. Nevertheless, the House Appropriations Committee in particular continued to exhibit a degree of bipartisanship and independence unusual on the Hill in the 1980s.

Although partisanship in the House and Senate appropriations process was on the rise on the eve of the 104th Congress, it is difficult to overstate the importance of the institutional and normative changes imposed on the appropriations process by the new Republican majority in the House. The story of the House Appropriations Committee between 1995 and 2006 is a story of progressive decline in committee autonomy and bipartisanship as the new majority leadership of the House took aim at precisely those features. While Newt Gingrich and his lieutenants engaged in a broad strategy to bring all committees in the House under their control, the Appropriations Committee was particularly important in that effort. The leadership aimed to use the appropriations process to cut the federal budget and replace Democratic spending priorities with their own. Just as importantly, they intended to use appropriations bills to change the direction of public policy in scores of policy areas despite a House rule against including substantive legislation in appropriations bills.

Appropriations bills are considered "must-pass," and Republicans gambled that a Democratic president would not veto those bills just to eliminate the legislative provisions that congressional Republicans inserted into them. On the other hand, Clinton would, it was thought, be far more likely to veto authorization bills that contained such policy changes. Thus, appropriations bills were to be vehicles for passage of a wide range of Republican priorities over the ineffectual objections of the president. Clearly the committee could not retain its bipartisanship and accomplish the objectives of the majority party.

The story of how the new Republican leaders went about this campaign and their mixed success has been recounted in a number of scholarly and journalistic works, so I will summarize briefly here. I will also discuss the more limited changes in the Senate appropriations process. Then I will examine trends in discretionary spending (the portion of the budget controlled by the appropriations committees) as well as the growth in earmarks, or pork barrel benefits, in appropriations bills.

THE DECLINE OF APPROPRIATIONS COMMITTEE INDEPENDENCE IN THE HOUSE

In an early signal of his intentions toward the committee, Gingrich personally chose Robert Livingston (R–La.) as chair, leapfrogging four members with more seniority. The most senior of Republicans on the committee, Joseph McDade, was then under indictment on corruption charges. Also bypassed were John Myers (Ind.), C.S. Bill Young (Fla.) and Ralph Regula (Ohio). Gingrich perceived Livingston to be sufficiently conservative and the most loyal of the senior committee Republicans. In violating seniority to choose him, Gingrich signaled both his determination to impose discipline on committee chairs and the potential rewards for members' loyalty.

Livingston was then allowed to choose the 13 subcommittee chairs (known as cardinals in recognition of their power over large expanses of federal spending). However, prospective cardinals were required to meet individually with Gingrich and sign a letter promising to adhere to the Contract with America as a condition of appointment. This was seen as a signal that

Gingrich intended to exert direct pressure on the cardinals despite their having been formally appointed by Livingston. Gingrich also appointed seven freshmen, a group that was particularly loyal to him, to the committee.

Among the other key changes imposed on the House Appropriations Committee were the following:

- At the beginning of the 104th Congress, the Republican Conference imposed six-year term limits on the cardinals, as they had done with full committee chairs.
- With respect to substantive policy, control of limitation amendments was transferred to the majority leader from subcommittee chairs, who normally floor-manage – and protect – their subcommittees' bills. This change effectively destroyed the ability of the cardinals to block limitation amendments and control the content of their bills.
- The 104th Congress gave the president a line-item veto over appropriations, mandatory spending bills, and narrow tax provisions. Clinton used this power a number of times before the Supreme Court declared it unconstitutional in 1998. Had this power stood, it would have done some damage to the power of the appropriations committees, although some have argued that they easily could have found mechanisms by which to avoid the veto.
- In 2003 Republican conservatives, angry over perceived overspending by the committee, further consolidated leadership control over the cardinals, instituting a requirement that they be chosen by the leadership-controlled Steering Committee rather than by the full committee chair.
- In 2005, majority leader Tom DeLay pushed through a major reorganization of Appropriations subcommittee jurisdictions, reducing the number of subcommittees from 13 to 10. The reorganization was intended to ease the leaders' promotion of Republican policy and spending priorities.

Not surprisingly, these changes introduced considerable tension into the functioning of the House Appropriations Committee. Livingston, who was both a loyal partisan soldier and a long-time senior appropriator, was apparently torn between the norms and traditions of the committee and the goals of his caucus. He declined to fire key staff members who had formerly worked for the Democratic majority; he needed their expertise. Predictably, that decision provoked considerable unhappiness in the Republican Conference, whose more militant members saw the committee as part of the problem of excessive spending and pork-based logrolling that traditionally got things done in the appropriations process.

The Senate Appropriations Committee, by comparison, experienced relatively few changes. Although Republicans imposed term limits on their full committee chairs, they did not move to impose the same degree of party control over them, not surprising given the individualism of the Senate. Nor did they violate seniority in choosing the Appropriations Committee chair. As a consequence, they got a chair who was not conservative enough for many in the increasingly conservative Republican conference. Indeed, Mark Hatfield (Ore.) was one of the most moderate Republicans in the Senate. When he cast a critical vote against the Republicans' balanced budget amendment to the Constitution (part of the House Republicans' Contract with America), many of his conservative colleagues demanded that he be stripped of his chair. Majority leader Robert Dole declined to do so, but the impulse to punish Hatfield was seen as a warning signal of reduced willingness of some junior senators to tolerate the accommodationist style of the Appropriations Committee.

Nevertheless, floor amendments to appropriations bills became more partisan in the 104th Congress: hostile amendments against appropriations bills were more likely to be offered by minority party members, especially those on the reporting subcommittee, in the 104th Congress than in the 103rd. And the committee assumed a sharper partisan edge when the chairmanship was assumed by Ted Stevens at the beginning in the 105th Congress. As *CQ Weekly* observed, "Stevens, though he possesses a fiercely independent streak, appears more willing than Hatfield to serve as a vehicle for the leadership."

Early in the 104th Congress, the combined effects of the House's political and procedural changes were quickly felt, as the Appropriations Committee proposed roughly $17 billion in recissions for the current year's (FY 1995) spending; the Senate reduced the size of the recissions, playing its preform era role of appeals court for aggrieved interests. The cuts were targeted systematically at Democratic programs, including social benefits, the environment, and funding for the arts, as Republicans sought to move public policy and spending priorities to the right.

The effort of the House Republican leadership to use appropriations to force through changes in public policy gathered steam as the Appropriations Committee took up the FY 1996 spending bills. The leadership pressured committee leaders to include a large number of legislative provisions in their bills. At Gingrich's behest, the Rules Committee then wrote special rules for those bills waiving points of order against those otherwise impermissible legislative provisions.

For its part, the Senate simply did not enforce its rule against legislation in appropriations bills at all between 1995 and 1999, resulting in large amounts of legislative language in appropriations bills throughout that period. Nevertheless, the Senate along with President Clinton resisted many of the conservative legislative provisions in the House bills; indeed, many were ultimately were removed in conference committee.

Yet many conflicts with the White House were not resolved. Thus, Clinton vetoed four appropriations bills in 1995 partly over the legislative provisions, including measures to prohibit federal agencies from spending appropriated funds to enforce environmental laws and regulations; other legislative language imposed additional restrictions on abortions, among many other limitations in those bills. Other disputes included funding cuts to programs favored by Clinton and congressional Democrats.

Finally, many conservative Republicans hoped to use the confrontation to force Clinton to agree to a balanced budget plan. The resulting impasse famously led to shutdowns of large swaths of the federal government on two separate occasions. The subsequent beating administered to congressional Republicans in the opinion polls helped Clinton to win many, though not all, of the policy and funding battles.

By contrast with that bloody battle, Congress finished all of the following year's (FY 1997) spending bills on time, in the process giving Clinton much of what he wanted as Republican legislators raced home to try to save their seats.

In 1997 Congress negotiated with Clinton a budget balancing agreement which helped to produce a balanced budget the very next year, with surpluses projected into the future. However, the abundance of revenue did not end the struggles over spending priorities and policy riders. Indeed, for the remainder of the 1990s the appropriations process was characterized by intense conflict and negotiations between congressional leaders and the White House. Such high-level negotiations necessarily diminished the power and autonomy of the appropriations committee chairs.

The use of the appropriations process by the House Republican leadership to move spending priorities and public policy to the right resulted, ultimately, in enormous difficulty in passing appropriations bills. The House struggled with the Senate and with Clinton, who, with his now-credible threats of vetoes and government shutdowns, fought to protect programs supported by Democrats. The appropriators themselves ignored spending caps in 1999 and 2000 to push their own priorities, but Republican appropriators complained every year about Clinton's endgame victories on appropriations bills, as the committees in both houses surrendered to many of his demands as the end of each fiscal year passed without passage of all of the 13 appropriations bills. The resulting need to pass multiple continuing resolutions and, ultimately, an omnibus appropriations bill elevated the role of congressional leaders at the expense of the appropriators as party leaders took control of the process of bicameral and interbranch negotiations.

In 2001, with the White House and both houses of Congress in Republican hands (Democratic control of the Senate spanned the months between June 2001 and January 2003), the early power equation between Congress and the new Republican president was altered by the terrorist attacks of September 11, 2001. That crisis led to a remarkable but temporary renewal of bipartisan and bicameral cooperation in the passage of all thirteen appropriations bills.

However, it was not long before the pattern of interbranch conflict resumed. The surplus rapidly evaporated, and disputes emerged between Congress and the president over spending priorities. For example, the FY 2003 omnibus appropriations bills included drought relief for farmers and increased spending on education, both policies that the president opposed. Moreover, Bush was perceived by conservative Republicans as having little interest in reducing spending overall, although his relative spending priorities among programs were far more compatible than Clinton's with their own preferences.

Yet, in the House, Republican leaders worked with the Bush administration to impose White House spending and policy priorities, often over the objections of the House Appropriations Committee and the Senate. Perhaps the rawest exercise of administration power through House leaders came on legislative provisions on appropriations bills, two of which overturned administration rules such as FCC media ownership rules and pro-business changes in rules on overtime pay. Those legislative provisions overturning Bush administration rules passed both houses of Congress. Nevertheless, they were removed in conference by the maneuvering of administration officials and the House leaders who helped them get their way.

By this time, conflict between House appropriators and the leadership had become chronic. For example, in 2002, *CQ Weekly* reported that appropriators were once again pursuing a "time-tested strategy," underfunding the most popular domestic programs and delaying their progress so that Republican leaders would be forced to exceed budget limits in order to end the session. Meanwhile, in the Senate, Appropriations chair Robert Byrd, with Stevens's

Table 38.1. *Changes in Federal Discretionary Spending, 1981–2005**

Fiscal Years	Change in Total Discretionary Spending (billions)	Percent Change Total	Change in Defense Spending (billions)	Percent Change in Defense Spending	Change in Non-Defense Spending (billions)	Percent Change in Non-Defense Spending
1981–1985	93.2	14.1	122.3	33.2	−29.1	−9.9
1985–1989	15.2	2.0	14.0	2.8	1.2	0.5
1989–1993	−40.8	−5.3	−80.6	−15.9	39.7	15.0
1993–1997	63.2	−8.7	−70.7	−16.7	7.6	2.5
1997–2001	50.2	7.5	8.6	2.4	41.4	13.3
2001–2005	252.5	35.3	170.2	47.0	82.1	23.2
1965–1969	141.9	29.4	116.6	33.8	25.3	18.5

* Figures are calculated from CBO historical tables in constant 2005 dollars.

backing, moved to boost spending over budget limits in defiance of both the House and the president.

Over the past 12 years, continuing resolutions and omnibus appropriations bills became the rule rather than the exception. 1996 was the only year of the past twelve in which all appropriations bills were passed by the October 1 start of the fiscal year. Even then, four of the most controversial bills (those typically including the most policy riders) had to be folded into an omnibus with the defense appropriations bill in order to make the deadline.

The following year, 1997, there was no omnibus bill, but only four of the thirteen appropriations bills passed by the beginning of the new fiscal year. After that, Congress was compelled to pass omnibus appropriations bills, all of them late, in every calendar year but 2001 and 2005. The most complete breakdown in the process since 1995 occurred in 2006, when Congress passed only two stand-alone appropriations bills, those for the Defense and Homeland Security departments. The remaining 2006 bills (for FY 2007) were combined into an omnibus and passed by the new Democratic-controlled Congress on February 14, 2007.

OVERALL DISCRETIONARY SPENDING

The George W. Bush administration and the Republican-controlled Congress were derided by liberals and conservatives alike as being the biggest-spending government in recent history. That claim is easily assessed. Most federal spending (currently just under two-thirds) is mandatory, the outlays based mostly on entitlements. Those amounts cannot be changed without changing the underlying law. The spending controlled by the appropriations committees is discretionary spending; it is typically broken into defense and nondefense spending. The total amount available to the appropriations committees is set by the annual budget resolution's Section 302(a) allocations. This amount is subdivided by the committee and distributed to appropriations subcommittees for specific appropriations; these amounts are known as Section 302(b) allocations.

Table 38.1 shows the changes in discretionary outlays in billions of dollars and in percentages by administration since the first Reagan administration. The figures on which the table is based were taken from the Congressional Budget Office's "Historical Budget Data," and the figures are in constant 2005 dollars (http://www.cbo.gov/budget/historical.shtml). To save space, I have not presented the actual dollar amounts. Rather, I have calculated the changes in outlays using as the first year in a sequence the outlays that an administration "inherited" from the previous administration (in some cases from itself if the president served two terms). The last year in the sequence consists of the discretionary outlays during the fiscal year that began during an administration's final year. Thus, for Reagan, the sequence starts in FY 1981 (Carter's final fiscal year) and ends in FY 1985, as Fiscal 1985 spending was set in 1984, the final year of Reagan's first term. Likewise, the second sequence begins with FY 1985. This approach allows a comparison of changes in spending that occurred during a particular administration relative to the one that preceded it. In this table I have ignored overall spending and revenues, so nothing can be inferred about the level of the surplus or deficit.

The table shows that over the last 25 years, although discretionary spending has normally increased over the course of a presidential administration, it declined during George H.W. Bush's presidency and Clinton's first term. These real spending reductions reflect the impact of the 1990 Budget Enforcement Act (BEA), in effect from 1991 through 2002; the first drop in spending during the first Bush administration occurred for FY 1991. Not surprisingly, spending increased during Clinton's second term, as the Republican Congress and the administration both enjoyed the fruits of the surpluses that their balanced budget agreement created and fought over how those surpluses should be used. They increasingly resolved the conflict by ignoring the spending caps set under the BEA.

During George W. Bush's first term, discretionary spending increased by the highest percentage of the past 25 years – 35.3 percent – even as the surpluses of the late 1990s turned into the large deficits of the twenty-first century. In fact, although I do not include all of the results here, the increase during the G.W. Bush administration outpaced that of any comparable period since 1962, the first year included in CBO's historical table. Even Lyndon Johnson and his large Democratic congressional majorities boosted discretionary spending by less (29.4%) during Johnson's one full term in office (1965–1969). These years included a war (Vietnam) as well as the massive social spending of the War on Poverty. The greatest share of the increase from FY 2002 to FY 2005 occurred, not surprisingly, in defense spending, which increased 47 percent; yet nondefense spending also rose at a faster-than-usual pace, increasing by 23.2 percent

during that period, the largest increase in over 40 years.

WAS IT THE PORK BARREL?

Critics of Congress often attribute this rapid recent growth in spending to an unfettered appetite for pork in Congress. No wonder: the number of earmarks in appropriations bills increased at a rapid pace beginning a year after the Republican majority took over. *The Pig Book*, an annual compilation of pork in appropriations bills published by Citizens Against Government Waste (http://www.cagw.org/site/PageServer?pagename=reports_pigbook2004), shows that between FY 1996 and FY 2006, the number of projects increased by a dramatic 940 percent. However, the increase in the cost of earmarks during that period was much less – 80 percent in constant dollars. While this is a substantial increase, it is clear that members of Congress have sought to profit electorally by dividing up a somewhat larger pork pie into a great many more pieces.

To make the data comparable to Table 38.1, during the second period of decline in discretionary spending shown (1993–1997), the cost of earmarks nearly doubled, increasing by 97.5 percent (not shown in the table), thus compensating members for some of the cuts during those years. The increase leveled off somewhat during the second Clinton term, with an increase of 15.4 percent. However, earmarking shot up by 33.4 percent during Bush's first term. The latter increase was slightly less than the overall increase in discretionary spending, but in the previous two periods, earmarking increased at a higher pace than discretionary spending (CAGW's data only go back to 1991). During this period (1993–2005), pork barrel benefits have not exceeded 2.5 percent of the budget. However, as a percentage of discretionary spending they have grown from 1.1 percent in 1993 to 2.5 percent in 2005. During the period of the largest spending increase, 2001–2005, the earmarks so generously handed out by the appropriations committees contributed to the growth in discretionary spending, but they are not responsible for a disproportionate share of that growth.

CONCLUSION

The appropriations process changed dramatically during the 12 years of nearly constant Republican control of Congress, mostly as a result of changes in the House, where Republican leaders experienced some success in imposing their own (and their caucus's) policy and spending preferences on the Appropriations Committee. The result was a reduction in that committee's bipartisanship, autonomy, and expertise as well as increased conflict with the Senate and, in the George W. Bush administration, growth of presidential influence as House leaders played the role of agents of the administration in the appropriations process. Over that time there was a decline in regular order in passing appropriations bills, as for three years in a row (2002–2004 inclusive), a majority of appropriations bills were passed in a massive omnibus bill. Another ironic outcome was a massive increase in spending not only to fuel the wars in Afghanistan and Iraq, but also in the nondefense arena under Republican-controlled government.

If the goal of such spending increases was merely electoral self-preservation, as many critics argued, it has to be judged a failure. Indeed, one could argue that it backfired as Republicans surrendered any claim to be the party of fiscal responsibility, reducing the cost to fiscally conservative voters of flinging them out of office. The question is whether the House Appropriations Committee will recover any of its traditions under the new Democratic majority. The Democrats have already realigned their subcommittees, resulting in 12 subcommittees in each house; that may reduce House–Senate conflict and speed the passage of appropriations bills. However, Democrats have imposed their own term limits on committee chairs, one of many signals that conditional party government exists under Democrats as it did in the Republican era. This pattern suggests at least some degree of majority party control over the appropriations process.

Congress also agreed to reform the earmarking process in that members' sponsorship of an earmark will now be made public. However, that reform is arguably little more than cosmetic, as it applies only to earmarks given to entities in individual members' states or districts. That is precisely the sort of earmark for which members are more than happy to claim credit with their constituents. The earmarks that have raised ethical concerns are those slipped in for private interests such as defense contractors at the behest of lobbyists who are then alleged to reciprocate with campaign contributions to the member. Those need not be revealed. If earmarking declines, it is unlikely to be because of earmark reform.

CHAPTER THIRTY-NINE

Pet Projects' Veil Is Only Partly Lifted

Lawmakers Find Other Paths to Special-Interest Funding

John Solomon and Jeffrey H. Birnbaum

Earmarking – designating money for specific projects in bills or committee reports – was made more transparent by new rules adopted in 2007. *Washington Post* writers Solomon and Birnbaum report on legislators' continuing practice of lobbying executive agencies on behalf of projects to be built in their districts and states. When the lobbying originates with legislators whose support is critical to an agency, the pressure on the agency is considerable and, at least in appearance, circumvents the new rules. Agencies that yield to the pressure gain no additional budget, at least not immediately, but they reduce the funding available for other projects and activities while complying with the wishes of important legislators.

Rep. Rahm Emanuel was extremely proud when the House passed a major spending bill early this year that contained not a single special-interest project. "This is an earmark-free bill," the Illinois Democrat jubilantly declared on Feb. 1.

A week later, however, he and 18 other Illinois lawmakers signed a letter to the Energy Department to "express our strong support" for a bio-energy project at the University of Illinois. Emanuel also sent his own letter to the department seeking "support and assistance in securing" $500,000 for Children's Memorial Hospital in Chicago and $750,000 for the Illinois Institute of Technology.

John Solomon and Jeffrey H. Birnbaum. 2007. "Pet Projects' Veil Is Only Partly Lifted: Lawmakers Find Other Paths to Special-Interest Funding" *Washington Post*, September 9, 2007. © 2007, *The Washington Post*. Reprinted with permission.

Such requests for specific institutions are commonly known as earmarks. But Emanuel, a member of the Democratic House leadership, declines to call them that. "Letter-writing is not an earmark," he said in an interview.

In the wake of last year's controversy over the Alaskan "bridge to nowhere" and other notorious legislated programs, Democrats in Congress have made "earmark" into an epithet – the E-word that they are reluctant to say aloud. But the taboo has not stopped either Democrats or Republicans from continuing to seek these expenditures while calling them something else.

Members of Congress are now resorting to less obvious tactics that allow them to get money to favored beneficiaries without acknowledging support for what others consider to be earmarks:

- Lawmakers are holding hearings meant to cajole or pressure executive branch officials into providing money for their pet projects – even when those agencies already have rejected the requests.
- Congressional chairmen are writing favored projects into their committees' spending bills, exploiting a loophole in the rules that enables those expenditures to avoid being counted, and therefore disclosed overtly, as earmarks.
- Like Emanuel, a growing number of lawmakers are asking executive branch officials to use their authority to send tax dollars into congressional districts or states, effectively financing projects they desire but do

not wish to accomplish with specific, and highly public, legislation.

Government watchdog groups and a few dissident lawmakers have noticed these sleights of hand and have begun to complain. They say the approach deceives the public about how many special spending projects are being handed out, noting that lawmakers' contacts with agencies usually are conducted out of public view. *The Washington Post* learned of Emanuel's requests by filing a Freedom of Information Act request.

"Going to agencies outside the congressional process avoids any measure of transparency or accountability," said Ellen Miller of the nonpartisan Sunlight Foundation. "Earmarks remain and are just called by a different name."

So tainted is the word that lawmakers now tend to eschew it, using a more antiseptic phrase instead: "congressionally directed spending."

"They are trying to change the whole vernacular so that earmarks aren't earmarks anymore," said Steve Ellis, vice president of Taxpayers for Common Sense.

To be sure, Ellis and Miller have lauded recent changes in the rules that govern special-interest spending. Congress has agreed to prohibit the once-common practice of dropping unaired, anonymously backed projects into House and Senate spending bills. In addition, expenditures identified as earmarks must be both clearly explained and publicly linked to their authors.

Congress appears to have reduced its hunger for earmarks this year. Member-disclosed earmarks passed by the House have fallen to about 6,000, with a cost of $8.5 billion – less than half the number and total amount of two years ago, Taxpayers for Common Sense estimated.

But more legislating lies ahead, especially in the Senate, and "things don't tend to get smaller," Ellis said.

What's more, plenty of projects slip through the new disclosure requirements and cannot be easily accounted for. Programs inserted into spending bills at the request of executive branch officials, for example, are generally not considered earmarks, so lawmakers often try to persuade agency officials to request the pet projects they want – thus avoiding that pejorative label.

In addition, if projects are included in legislation by the primary author of a spending bill – usually the chairman of a committee – those projects do not have to be as clearly marked as other earmarks. This is because formal earmarks are requested by members; if they appear in the starting-point bill, they are not considered earmarks.

Rep. Jeff Flake (R-Ariz.) confronted David R. Obey (D-Wis.), chairman of the House Appropriations Committee, on the House floor in March over this practice, noting that a spending bill then under debate contained $35 million for a risk-mitigation program at a federal space-exploration facility, even though the measure had been certified to contain no earmarks.

"We have passed some good rules with regard to earmark reform and transparency," Flake said. "But we have found a way around them already." Obey said that the provision was not an earmark under the rules. "An earmark is something that is requested by an individual member," Obey said. "This item was not requested by any individual member; it was put in the bill by me."

Two months later, Obey again rebuffed Flake when Flake pointed out that a supposedly earmark-free bill on the House floor contained an allocation of $8.7 million to ward off floods in New York. The provision was not called an earmark, Flake noted, but Rep. Nita M. Lowey (D-N.Y.) put out a news release applauding the provision and its potential benefit to her district.

Other lawmakers have ginned up support for narrow spending proposals through hearings. Two subcommittees of the House Science and Technology Committee pressed Energy Department officials in hearings this year, for example, about the department's decision to end its funding for the Savannah River Ecology Laboratory, near Aiken, S.C.

Energy officials offered the committee written proof that there was an agreement between the administration, Congress, and the lab to end its funding after 2007, but lawmakers still demanded more money.

"The Savannah River Ecology Lab served the Department of Energy, the communities affected by the site and the nation for more than 50 years," Rep. Brad Miller (D-N.C.) said at a hearing last month. "It was, by any financial measure, a very inexpensive lab to operate. It would be hard to find a better return on investment anywhere in the federal science complex."

Rep. Nick Lampson (D-Tex.) added: "There is simply no reason for DOE to discontinue funding. There are funds available. There is work to be done."

The tongue-lashing did not persuade the department to cough up the money, however, so Rep. Bart Gordon (D-Tenn.), chairman of the full committee, added a new threat. Gordon told the department's chief financial officer in a letter that he would not approve funding that the department requested for a bioenergy lab unless it allocated $2 million to help keep the ecology lab afloat.

"We have received no follow-up from DOE to the letter as yet," said Alisha Prather, the committee's spokeswoman.

Other lawmakers do not play as roughly to get the money they want. Sometimes they just write a letter and then make a phone call.

Emanuel, who is chairman of the House Democratic Caucus and was a major proponent of making earmarks in spending bills more transparent, said he followed up his letters with a call to Energy Secretary Samuel W. Bodman.

"I'm on bended knee," he said of the call. "I have to go to an executive in another party and ask for resources, but the people in my district elected me to fight for these things."

Energy Department spokeswoman Megan Barnett said Emanuel's requests have not been funded. "We regularly hear from members of Congress for support on various projects, and this year was no different. We look at each of these projects on the merits," she said.

Emanuel defended his requests as "a good public investment" and added: "If I think it is good, I'm going to use all the tools to fight for it, whether it is an earmark, letter-writing or lighting myself on fire. I may even go on a hunger strike."

But he declined to say whether he and other lawmakers ought to disclose their private contacts with federal agencies when they seek money for projects. "Let me just say that I'm a big believer in transparency," Emanuel said.

PART XIII. FURTHER READINGS
ON CONGRESSIONAL POLITICS

CHAPTER FORTY

Introduction to the Spatial Theory of Legislating

Steven S. Smith, Jason M. Roberts, and Ryan J. Vander Wielen

The editors include this appendix from their text-book, *The American Congress*, to provide an intro-duction to the spatial theory of legislative politics. Spatial theory views legislators' policy positions as locations in geometric space and exploits basic geom-etry to characterize expected policy outcomes. The technique is widely used by scholars of politics to study elections and bureaucratic, judicial, and legisla-tive decision making.

Much of congressional politics has geomet-ric characteristics. When we speak of most Democrats as liberals, most Republicans as con-servatives, and some legislators as moderates, we have in mind an ideological or policy spec-trum – a line or dimension – along which we can place legislators. In recent Congresses, the parties have been sharply divided, with very little overlap between the parties. Figure 40.1 illustrates this for the 109th Congress (2005–2006) for senators. Using a statistical technique, senators were scored on the basis of their over-all voting record in the Congress. Democrats and Republicans were concentrated on oppo-site sides of the spectrum, creating one of the most polarized Senates in history.

Legislators' policy positions also can be repre-sented in two or more dimensions, when appro-

priate. In Figure 40.2, senators' policy positions are identified in two dimensions for a debate on an immigration reform bill in 2006. Their locations are identified with the help of a sta-tistical analysis of their votes on about three dozen amendments and other motions that were considered on the Senate floor. The most sig-nificant issue during the debate concerned the standards for allowing illegal immigrants to gain legal entry to the United States. Senators who opposed special arrangements for reentry lined up on the far right, while senators who favored standards that would ease reentry for work or citizenship were located on the left (the hori-zontal dimension). Other issues, such as the ceil-ing on the number of legal immigrants allowed, were debated, too, and sometimes divided sen-ators differently than the votes related to the treatment of current illegal immigrants (the ver-tical dimension). Democrats tended to favor both standards that facilitated reentry and larger quotas, while Republicans were split on reentry standards and tended to favor smaller quotas.

BASIC CONCEPTS FOR ANALYZING A LEGISLATIVE BODY

Political scientists have taken advantage of geo-metric representations to develop spatial theo-ries of legislative politics. The theories provide a way to conceptualize the location of legislators, policy alternatives, and policy outcomes. Like all scientific theories, spatial theories are based

Steven S. Smith, Jason M. Roberts, and Ryan J. Van-der Wielen. 2007. "Introduction to the Spatial Theory of Legislating" in Steven S. Smith, Jason M. Roberts, and Ryan J. Vander Wielen, *American Congress*, 5th ed. (Cambridge University Press), 387–98. Copyright © 2007. Reprinted with the permission of Cambridge University Press.

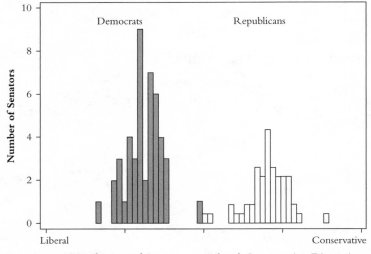

Figure 40.1. Distribution of Senators on Liberal-Conservative Dimension, 2005–2006 (Democrats on left; Republicans on right). *Source:* Optimal Classification scores; www.voteview.com.

on assumptions that allow us to draw inferences about expected behavior. With a few assumptions about legislators, the policy space, and the rules governing decisions, we can deduce remarkably useful and usually intuitive propositions about the location of legislative outcomes. Nonintuitive predictions are particularly useful because they often yield insights that even the close observer of legislative politics might overlook.

PREFERENCES AND THE POLICY SPACE

Spatial theories assume the legislators, presidents, and other players have preferences about

policy outcomes. Preferences may reflect personal beliefs or political influences. The preferences are assumed to be consistent. For example, if a legislator prefers policy A over policy B and also prefers B over C, then she favors A over C (transitive preferences, we say). When a legislator's preferences are depicted geometrically, as in the figures, it is usually assumed that alternatives that are closer to the legislator's ideal point are preferred to more distant points (a Euclidean policy space, we say). Furthermore, it is assumed that each legislator chooses a strategy that she believes will yield the best possible outcome – that is, minimizes the distance between her ideal point and the outcome.

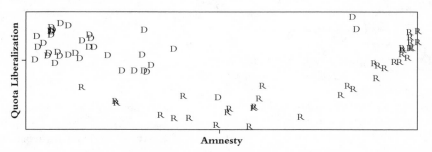

Figure 40.2. Senators' Policy Positions on 2006 Immigration Bill in Two Dimensions (Democrats, D; Republicans, R). *Source:* Optimal Classification scores on Senate votes related to S2611, 109th Congress.

A   B   C   D   E

Median

Figure 40.3. Illustration of the Median Voter Theorem.

SIMPLE MAJORITY RULE AND THE MEDIAN VOTER THEOREM

Spatial theorists define "institutions" as a set of rules that govern decision making. Rules may concern who has the right to participate, the "weight" that each participant has in determining the outcome, the way in which policy proposals are constructed, the order in which policy proposals are considered, the standard for a final decision, and so on. Here, we assume that each legislator has the right to cast one vote and, to begin, that a simple majority of legislators is required for a proposal to be adopted.

In Figure 40.3, a small legislature with five legislators is illustrated. With a simple majority decision rule, a winning majority will always include legislator C. As the median legislator, C can join two other legislators – to the left with A and B, to the right with D and E, or in the middle with B and D – to form a three-vote majority. Of course, larger majorities could form, but they will always include C. A spatial theorist would say that C is pivotal – C must be included in a majority and so can demand that the outcome be located at her ideal point. The *median voter theorem*, which we will not formally prove here, provides that if C's position is adopted it cannot be defeated by another proposal. A corollary is that if two alternatives are presented, a majority will always prefer the alternative closer to the median legislator.

The median voter theorem means that when a median exists we can predict the outcome by knowing only the median legislator's ideal point. Spatial theorists refer to the stable prediction of the median outcome as an *equilibrium*. When a new legislature is elected, a new median location would lead us to predict a change in the outcome. That is, a new equilibrium is expected.

MULTIDIMENSIONAL SPACES AND THE CHAOS THEOREM

A multidimensional policy space, such as the one in Figure 40.4, creates important complications for predicting legislative outcomes. No legislator is the median on both dimensions. C is the median on the amnesty dimension but E is the median on the quota liberalization dimension. What is the expected outcome? In fact, political scientists have demonstrated mathematically that in most cases there is no single predicted outcome, no equilibrium, as there is in the unidimensional case.

A thought experiment will demonstrate an important point. Let us assume that current policy is located at x_1. Legislator B might propose a policy at x_2 and would win the support of A and C, both of whom are closer to x_1 than to x_2 and so would join B to form a majority to vote for x_2 and defeat x_1. But then D might offer x_3 and win the support of A and E. This process can continue indefinitely with a new majority of three forming at each step. If the rules allow a continuous flow of new proposals, there is no single outcome that cannot be defeated by some other proposal. This illustrates the *chaos theorem*. The theorem provides that, as a general rule, we cannot expect a stable outcome from simple majority rule in two (or more) dimensions.

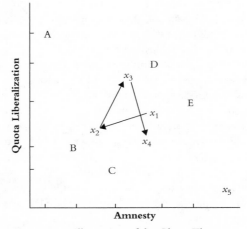

Figure 40.4. Illustration of the Chaos Theorem.

AGENDA SETTING, STRUCTURE-INDUCED
EQUILIBRIA, AND POLITICAL POWER

The chaos result – or majority rule cycling –
may seem surprising. Legislatures regularly
make final decisions without endless cycling
through proposals. Why that is the case is the
subject of a vast literature in political science. We
do not want to review the complexities here, but
three important points about legislative politics
need to be understood.

First, legislative rules may not allow multidimensional proposals or may limit the number
of proposals that may be considered. Such rules
would limit the range of possible outcomes and
make those outcomes more predictable. If only
unidimensional proposals may be considered,
the median voter theorem applies and majority rule chaos is avoided. Theorists use the label
structure-induced equilibria for constraints on outcomes that are imposed by the rules. Thus, even
if legislators' preferences are multidimensional,
the rules may generate median outcomes by
either limiting the range of proposals that are
allowed or imposing unidimensionality on the
proposals that may be considered.

Second, special influence over the agenda,
either granted under the rules or gained through
informal means, may control the alternatives
subject to a vote and further limit the possible outcomes. A Speaker or presiding officer
may be able to limit who is recognized to offer a
motion. A coalition of legislators, such as members of the majority party, may agree to support
only those proposals that a majority of the coalition endorses, thus limiting the set of proposals
that can win majority support.

Three, introducing a proposal that creates a
new dimension can transform a situation that
would produce a median outcome into one
with no predictable outcome. A legislator who
dislikes the median outcome might be motivated to offer a proposal on an issue that divides
his colleagues in a new way in order to avoid the
certain, but undesirable outcome. The original
median legislator would be motivated to create
an agenda that prevents the proposal on the new
issue from being considered.

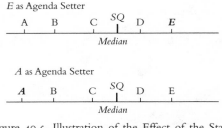

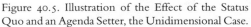

Figure 40.5. Illustration of the Effect of the Status
Quo and an Agenda Setter, the Unidimensional Case.

In practice, then, rules and legislative strategies can contract or expand the range of possible
outcomes. Real politics is often played in this
way. Political scientists have studied many of the
consequences of a variety of rules and strategies,
but continue to pursue research on the relationship between rules, strategies, and outcomes.

THE STATUS QUO AND AGENDA SETTING

A legislature often inherits policy from past legislatures. In most cases, the inherited policy,
which we call the *status quo* (SQ), remains in
place until a new policy is adopted. That is, the
SQ is the default outcome if it is not defeated
by a new proposal. The set of proposals that can
defeat the SQ is called the *win set of SQ*. When
there are no proposals that can defeat the SQ,
we say that the win set is empty and predict that
the outcome will remain at SQ.

The effect of the SQ on legislative strategies is
important and intuitive. In Figure 40.5, five legislators are arrayed on a single dimension. In the
figure's top panel, let's assume that no proposal
can be considered unless legislator E approves,
but if a proposal is offered it can be amended.
E, of course, wants the outcome at her own
ideal point and might make a proposal there.
However, A, B, or C might offer an amendment to move the outcome away from E and
to the other side of SQ. Such an amendment
would win a majority and E would be worse off
than if he left the policy at SQ. Consequently,
we would expect E to refuse to make an initial proposal. In this case, the agenda setter, E,
protects the status quo. In contrast, in the lower

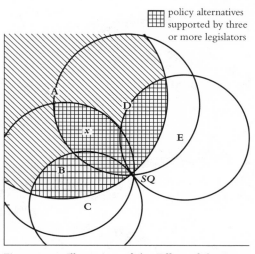

policy alternatives supported by three or more legislators

Figure 40.6. Illustration of the Effect of the Status Quo and an Agenda Setter, the Multidimensional Case.

panel in Figure 40.5, legislator A is the agenda setter. Because A prefers the median's position over the *SQ*, A is willing to allow the legislature to consider a proposal and have it amended to C, the expected outcome.

Thus, the location of the status quo relative to the median determines the agenda setter's strategy. With the same agenda setter and median, different issues can generate different outcomes – the median or the *SQ*.

The same logic applies to the multidimensional case, as in Figure 40.6. Legislators will support a proposal that improves on the status quo, *SQ*. In the figure, these *preferred-to* sets are denoted by the partial or full circles. For example, within the shaded circle centered on legislator A is the preferred-to set for A. The double shaded areas are the sets of locations preferred by at least three of the five legislators over *SQ*. Because points in the double shaded areas attract majority support for a proposal over the *SQ*, they define the win set of *SQ*. A large number of locations will not defeat *SQ* so majority rule narrowed the possible outcomes considerably. But, in this two-dimensional space, the win set includes a wide range of possibilities, many of which are less preferred to the *SQ* by one or two of the legislators. A, B, and D might agree

to an outcome at *x*, which would make C and E worse off than leaving the policy at *SQ*.

BICAMERALISM, SEPARATION OF POWERS, AGENCY DECISIONS, AND LEGISLATIVE OUTCOMES

Bicameralism

In the previous section, we considered a single legislative body. Congress and many other legislatures are bicameral, and usually require that a majority of each chamber approve legislation before it is sent to the president or chief executive. Spatially, this means that we must consider the relationship between the outcomes in the two chambers.

In unidimensional space, shown in Figure 40.7, the outcome would be negotiated between the House and Senate medians. If both medians favor some of the same proposals over *SQ*, as they do in the top panel, they will negotiate an outcome among the range of proposals that they both prefer to *SQ*. If *SQ* falls between the two medians so that each house median prefers *SQ* to anything the other house would prefer to *SQ*, as in the figure's lower panel, the houses will not agree to a new policy and the outcome will be *SQ*.

In multidimensional space, as depicted in Figure 40.6, we would define the bicameral win set as the intersection of the win sets in the two houses. We do not show that situation here. The overlap in the win sets for the two houses can be very small or very large. Little overlap greatly narrows the range of possible outcomes. Large

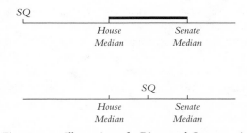

Figure 40.7. Illustration of a Bicameral Outcome in One Dimension.

overlap creates the possibility that a conference committee charged with finding compromise legislation will be able to exercise great discretion in determining the location of the final bill and still be able to attract majority support in both houses for the final version.

THE PRESIDENT AND THE VETO

Under the Constitution, the president may veto legislation and a veto can be overridden only with the support of a two-thirds majority in each house of Congress. The threshold of a two-thirds majority in each house makes it necessary to appeal to more legislators than the requirement of a simple majority for initial approval of legislation. In our five-legislators illustrations, this means attracting the support of four of the five legislators (three of five would be less than the two-thirds required).

The president will veto any legislation that makes him worse off than SQ. In one dimension, several possibilities arise. In Figure 40.8, the president's ideal point is P and the House and Senate medians are M_H and M_S, respectively. The two houses of Congress negotiate a bill at B somewhere between their medians. The president prefers SQ to B so he vetoes the bill. Both House and Senate medians would like to override the veto but they must gain the support of two thirds of their colleagues. V_H and V_S are the *veto pivots*. That is, they are the legislators who are the leftmost members of the two-thirds majority that is required to override a veto. Without their support for the bill over the SQ, the veto cannot be overridden. In this case, V_H prefers SQ to B and so votes against the override. SQ is the outcome. Thus, the general rule is that a presidential veto will kill a bill whenever at least one of the veto pivots is on the same side of SQ as the president.

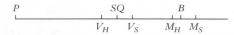

Figure 40.8. Illustration of Upholding a Presidential Veto, in One Dimension.

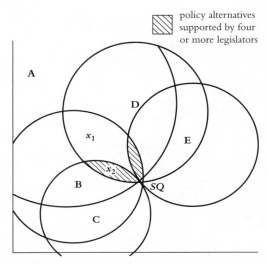

Figure 40.9. Location of Veto Override Coalitions, the Multidimensional Case.

Other scenarios are easy to understand without illustration. Whenever the chamber medians are on the same side of SQ as the president, the president will sign the bill with a veto. Whenever V_H and V_S are on the same side of SQ opposite the president (not shown), the two houses of Congress can override the veto of the president.

As always, the multidimensional case is more complicated but it is still easy to visualize. In Figure 40.9, there are two regions in which four of the five legislators of one house would favor the bill over the SQ. Consequently, a veto would be overridden any time the president vetoes a bill that is located in those regions. The bill also would have to be located in similar regions in the other house for both houses to override a president's veto. A bill that is located in the *veto win set of SQ* is one for which a veto can be overridden in both houses.

Plainly, the two-thirds majority requirement for a veto override shrinks the region of bill locations that can survive a veto to one that is smaller than the region of bill locations that can receive simple majority support in both houses. The implication is that the threat of a veto requires more careful negotiations within Congress and may have implications for legislators who win and lose. In Figure 40.9, for example, the bill at x_2 survives a veto but a bill at x_1 does not, although both would receive simple majority support. But the outcome at x_2 is less favorable to legislators A and D and more favorable to B and C.

AGENCY DECISIONS

Political scientists often think of executive branch agencies as having policy preferences of their own. Staffed by people who have personal or professional experience in a policy field, agencies are likely to devise rules and regulations that implement law in a manner that reflects their own preferences. Congress and presidents may seek to control the independence of agencies, but agency officials know that it may not be easy for Congress and the president to enact new legislation to place additional constraints on them. After all, new legislation requires the approval of the House, Senate, and president, or, in the case of a veto, a two-thirds majority in both houses. This is a high threshold. If a House majority, Senate majority, or president favors the direction an agency is taking, it can block legislation that would place new constraints in statute.

The strategic setting of agency decision making can be treated spatially, as we do in Figure 40.10. To simplify, we characterize the House and Senate as having specific locations in multidimensional space just as the president does. If an agency took action to move a policy from a_1 (the current policy) to a_2, the Senate would like the move and block any effort by the House to enact legislation to require that the policy be returned to a_1. In this case, the agency, knowing that the Senate will protect its move, is free to shift policy without fear that the law will be changed. In contrast, if the agency sought to move policy as far as a_3, all three of the policy-making institutions would be better off by enacting legislation located on the line between S and P.

These scenarios demonstrate that the autonomy of an agency is limited to the range of policy moves that will not generate a new law. The farther apart the House, Senate, and president, the greater the discretion the agency enjoys. In

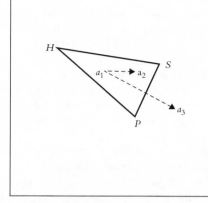

Figure 40.10. Illustration of Agency Discretion, in Multidimensional Space.

fact, the triangle formed by the House, Senate, and president defines the limits of agency discretion. Any move that yields policy inside or to the edge of the triangle will be defended by at least one of the House, Senate, or president. Any move outside of the triangle will stimulate new legislation.

ADVANCED THEORY AND THE LIMITS OF SPATIAL THEORY

We have presented a rudimentary introduction to the spatial theory of legislative politics. Political scientists have extended the theory in many directions. They have developed additional theory on the conditions that limit the range of possible outcomes under majority rule, explored the effect of agenda control rules that advantage parties or committees, and considered the effects of different assumptions about legislators' preferences and decision rules. We encourage our readers to pursue these important subjects elsewhere.

Spatial theory is not the ultimate theory of legislative politics. The spatial theorist assumes that legislators' policy preferences are known and invariant and theorizes only about how they motivate strategies. The determinants of legislators' policy preferences are beyond the scope of spatial theory.

The effects of nonpolicy motivations, such as the desire for reelection or to serve in the majority party, also are beyond the scope of spatial theory. Such motivations may be the overriding consideration in some circumstances. A legislator whose bill is rejected by the House of Representatives might be seen as a loser by some observers, but she may benefit from favorable press coverage and an appreciative home constituency for putting up a good fight. A legislative majority that fails to override a presidential veto may use the issue in a campaign to get more fellow partisans elected in the next Congress. Winning and losing in politics is sometimes hard to judge, at least in the short term.

Nevertheless, spatial theory is a powerful tool for predicting behavior and legislative outcomes. It often establishes a baseline expectation for outcomes against which the effects of other considerations can be measured. We can better judge the effects of persuasion by party leaders or presidents once we have a prediction for the outcome expected on the basis of legislators' prior policy preferences. It also shows that policy preferences and parliamentary rules often do not yield very specific predictions and define sometimes large ranges of possible outcomes that can be influenced by other political forces at work. Most important, spatial theory yields important insights about the effects of institutions – the rules of the game – that are so transparent in legislative decision making.

CHAPTER FORTY-ONE

The Institutional Foundations of Committee Power

Kenneth A. Shepsle and Barry R. Weingast

Using spatial theory, Shepsle and Weingast argue that the power of congressional standing committees rests on their domination of conference committees. Members of the committees originating legislation dominate conference committee delegations and know that the parent houses must approve or disapprove of conference reports without amendment. This system gives committee members an opportunity to overturn changes in committee bills that were approved on the floor and creates a disincentive for legislators to offer amendments to committee bills in the first place. This conference power is called an *ex post veto* because it follows floor action.

Legislative committees have fascinated scholars and reformers for more than a century. Differences of opinion concerning the role of committees persist, but there is a substantial consensus on a number of stylized facts:

Committees are "gatekeepers" in their respective jurisdictions.
Committees are repositories of policy expertise.
Committees are policy incubators.
Committees possess disproportionate control over the agenda in their policy domains.
Committees are deferred to, and that deference is reciprocated.

Kenneth A. Shepsle and Barry R. Weingast. 1987. "The Institutional Foundations of Committee Power" *American Political Science Review* 81(1): 85–101. Copyright © 1987 by the American Political Science Association. Reprinted with the permission of Cambridge University Press.

There is, however, a troublesome quality to this consensus. The items in this list (and there could undoubtedly be more) describe or label committee power, but they do not explain it. Explanations of these empirical regularities require a theory. In the case of each of these stylized facts, that is, a theory is needed to determine why things are done this way. In many cases it is insufficient to refer to institutional rules because many of the practices alluded to above either are not embodied in the rules at all or have evolved from them only slowly. It is therefore necessary to begin the theoretical analysis from first principles.

There is an added advantage to a theory that begins with first principles: although formulated to accommodate some stylized facts, such a theory will yield new implications so that it may be employed as a discovery procedure. Consider some anomalies that the theory we formulate below can explain:

In a bicameral system, how is it possible that change in the composition of a committee or a majority in *one* chamber is sufficient to lead to policy change?
Why are explicit procedures in the House of Representatives to diminish the gatekeeping monopoly of committees (specifically the discharge petition) rarely employed; and when they are employed, why do they rarely result in law?
How is it that committees maintain their influence over policy change when, once

they "open the gates" by bringing forth a proposal, majorities can work their will in ways potentially unacceptable to the proposing committee?

Why do members appear to defer to committees, even to the point of defeating amendments to committee proposals that have clear majority support?

In our view, the explanation of committee power resides in the rules governing the sequence of proposing, amending, and especially of vetoing in the legislative process. We demonstrate a surprisingly important role for the last stage of the legislative process, the conference procedure, in which bicameral differences are resolved. The ex post adjustment power conferred on committees in this forum provides them with subtle yet powerful means to affect the voting and proposing power of other members on the floor during the earlier legislative stages. Indeed, we show that the deference given committees on the floor is a natural consequence of the ex post adjustment powers wielded by committees in conference.

In the first section of this paper we briefly describe some alternative theoretical explanations of committee power. In each instance, we make explicit what we regard as the kernel of truth it contains, but we also point out crucial missing elements that ultimately render it incomplete. We provide the basic concepts of our own explanatory framework in the second section. In the next two sections, we develop the logic of committee enforcement emphasizing the importance of the manner in which the various stages of legislative deliberation are sequenced. In the fifth and sixth sections we provide both theoretical and empirical detail on the institutionalization of enforcement in the conference committee procedure. In the last section we pull our arguments together and address some extensions and applications.

THEORETICAL FOUNDATIONS
OF COMMITTEE POWER

We may describe the foundation of committee power as consisting of gatekeeping, informa-

tion advantage, and proposal power. Underlying these is a system of deference and reciprocity, according to which legislators defer to committee members by granting them extraordinary and differential powers in their respective policy jurisdictions.

What is amazing about these foundations of committee power is that nowhere are they carved in granite. Committees, as an empirical matter, are veto groups that may choose to keep the gates closed on a particular bill. But parliamentary majorities have recourse to mechanisms by which to pry the gates open, the discharge petition being only the most obvious. Why, then, do parliamentary majorities only rarely resort to such mechanisms? That is, why does the system of deference to committee veto judgments survive?

The question of survival also arises concerning information advantage and proposal power. As empirical matters, these are robust regularities. Yet the Speaker of a contemporary Congress is relatively free to break any alleged monopoly of proposal power held by committees through his right of recognition in House proceedings, his referral powers, his control of the Rules Committee, and his power to create ad hoc and select committees for specific purposes. Likewise, the contributions to information and expertise from the lobbyist denizens of Washington's "K Street Corridor" and an expanded congressional staff system mitigate the alleged informational advantages of committees.

Several reasons may be put forward to explain how a cooperative system of reciprocated deference is nevertheless sustained. The first and least persuasive is that no one ever has any reason to challenge it. The committee system and its division of labor, it might be alleged, are so successful in parceling work that anyone interested in a particular subject easily obtains membership on the committee that deals with it. Under these circumstances, deference becomes self-enforcing because there are no incentives to upset the applecart. Needless to say, this explanation denies or ignores interdependence among policy areas, fiscal dependencies, and the prospect that some issues — trade, energy, and health, for example — are not amenable to a neat division-of-labor arrangement because their incidences are both substantial and pervasive.

A second, related rationale to explain deference is not so sweeping. It suggests that while the matching up of work with interested members through committee assignments is not perfect, it is nevertheless sufficient to discourage violations of reciprocity. This view argues that the long-term advantages of deference outweigh the occasional short-term disappointments and so serve to maintain the system.

To sum up, the argument for deference to committees claims that the benefits to be secured by violating deference and challenging a committee are either small (as in the first rationale) or not worth the costs (as in the second rationale). We believe this argument is incomplete and that its premises are not always plausible. There are, first of all, too many opportunities in which it *is* worthwhile to oppose (or to be seen to oppose) committee positions. Second, the terms of deference to committees are extremely vague. Third, the behavioral forms violations may take range from minor opposition (say, going on record as having some doubts about a committee bill) to major revolt (introducing a "killer" amendment or initiating a discharge petition). In short, the concepts of reciprocity and deference are at best convenient terms of discourse. Their very vagueness, combined with what we believe are frequent and compelling occasions in which a legislator will not wish to honor them, greatly reduces the power of self-enforcement as an explanation of committee power.

The puzzle of committee power remains. The idea of deference as a form of self-enforcing ex ante institutional bargain among legislators cannot account for the disproportionate influence of committees in their respective jurisdictions because it cannot explain away the temptations to defect from the bargain. To be persuasive, deference must be sustained by more explicit enforcement mechanisms. We discuss three such mechanisms that committees employ to bolster their institutional influence: (1) punishment; (2) ex ante defensive behavior; and (3) ex post defensive behavior.

A committee may discourage opposition to its actions (or nonactions) by developing a reputation for punishing those who oppose it. The current chairman of the House Ways and Means Committee, a Chicago machine Democrat who knows how to keep score, was once reported to have said of a particularly obstructionist colleague, "I wouldn't support anything he wanted, even if the deal was for everlasting happiness" (personal interview). There is also the now classic story of the efforts by Senator James Buckley of New York to reduce the scale of the nefarious Omnibus Rivers and Harbors Bill. With the "help" of the Chairman of the Senate Public Works Committee, Buckley's assault on the pork barrel produced only one result — the striking of a project for the state of New York. These anecdotes aside, it would appear that the capacity to punish and the general use of a tit-for-tat strategy by the committee provide precisely the basis for the emergence of the cooperative relationship between a committee and the rest of the parent chamber.

This explanation, in our view, is most convincing in the distributive politics realm in which the committee's bills are (1) of significance to a substantial number of legislators; (2) disaggregatable by legislator; and (3) introduced on a regular basis. The first condition requires that there be some prospect for punishing any given legislator in a manner that the legislator and his or her district cannot ignore — a condition not met by some highly specialized committees like Agriculture or Merchant Marines and Fisheries. The second requires that the means to punish be available so that threats are credible. The third requires that occasions to punish be readily available. For many committees, punishment of this sort is available only in blunt form, if it is available at all.

A committee may induce cooperative, deferential behavior not only by (threats of) ex post punishment but also by ex ante accommodation. Surely a committee tries, when putting a proposal together, to anticipate what will pass in the parent chamber. Similarly, it will weigh reactions to its killing a bill before actually doing so. Such anticipatory behavior, however, is hardly a basis for committee power but rather is an indication of its limitations. There are other noncommittee groups that share veto power with a committee and may use that power against committee proposals. Majorities may "veto" committee bills by voting them down. The Rules Committee in the House may refuse to grant a rule for a committee bill, thereby scuttling it. The Speaker may use his power to schedule legislation and to control debate in ways detrimental to the prospects of a committee bill. A small group of senators in the U.S. Senate may engage in filibuster and other forms of obstruction. Any individual senator may refuse unanimous consent to procedures that would expedite passage of a committee bill. In short, veto groups are pervasive in legislatures; committees are but one example. Consequently, ex ante defensive behavior by committees, necessary though it may be owing to the existence of other veto groups, cannot be regarded as an influence mechanism; rather it constitutes a recognition of the influence of others.

We acknowledge a role for ex post punishment and ex ante defensive behavior. But neither strikes us as an entirely satisfactory enforcement mechanism because the conditions for the use of punishment are not met in all circumstances and ex ante defensive behavior accommodates the interests of others rather than enforcing a committee's own desires. There is, however, a third mechanism with which a committee maintains its dominance as veto group and primary policy proposer in its jurisdiction: ex post defensive behavior. We believe this to be the most potent enforcement mechanism and the least understood or appreciated.

Suppose a committee possessed an *ex post veto*. Suppose that, having molded a bill and reported it to its chamber and having allowed its chamber to "work its will," a committee could then determine whether or not to allow the bill (as amended, if amended) to become law (or, in a bicameral setting, to be transmitted to the other chamber). *The ex post veto, we assert, is sufficient to make gatekeeping and proposal power effective, even though their effectiveness appears to most observers to be the product of nothing more than informal reciprocity arrangements.*

Consider gatekeeping first. Suppose that some legislative majority could, by a discharge petition or some other bullyboy tactic, threaten to pry the gates open. If there were an ex post committee veto, then (aside from symbolic position taking) there would be little point to this sort of exercise. The ex post veto would ensure that changes in the status quo adverse to the interests of a decisive committee majority could be denied final passage. Indeed, the history of the discharge petition suggests precisely this. Even on those relatively rare occasions when a discharge petition obtained the necessary support (218 signatories), the bill of which the committee was discharged almost never became law.

Now consider proposal power. Imagine a major amendment to a committee proposal favored by a chamber majority but opposed by a committee majority. The amendment might or might not pass, but surely even its most ardent proponents would have to consider whether the amendment were distasteful enough to the committee to trigger an ex post veto. The existence of an ex post veto would encourage the amendment proponents to work out a deal in advance with the committee, would lead to a pattern in which most successful amendments were supported by a committee majority as well as a chamber majority and, in those few instances where anticipation did not discourage amendments obnoxious to the committee, would trigger such a veto.

In the remainder of this paper, we explore in an analytical fashion the ex post veto as the enforcement mechanism that allows reciprocity and deference to work smoothly. Although our model is abstract and thus is consistent with any number of different operational forms of an ex post veto, we argue that the conference procedure, in which differences in legislation between the chambers of a bicameral legislature are resolved, provides the kind of forum in which committees get a "second crack" at a bill. We believe this kind of ex post enforcement mechanism clarifies and explains why various forms of cooperation work in legislatures such as the U.S. Congress despite their transparent fragility and vulnerability.

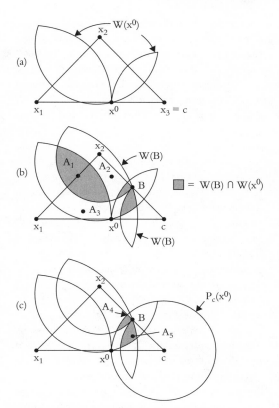

Figure 41.1. Effect of Ex Post Veto.

ROLLING THE COMMITTEE: LIMITATIONS OF GATEKEEPING AND INITIATION POWER

To provide more precise intuition, we develop an example that illustrates committee power under various proposal and veto conditions. Figure 41.1a presents a three-person legislature, operating in a two-dimensional jurisdiction by majority rule. Agent 3 has various committee powers. The points x_1, x_2, and x_3 are agent ideal points and, to simplify the figure, we place the status quo, x^0, on the 1–3 contract locus; our argument does not depend on this feature. The set $W(x^0)$ consists of two "petals" that are composed of the points preferred to x^0 by the floor majorities $\{1,2\}$ and $\{2,3\}$, respectively.

Ex ante veto power alone is strictly a defensive tool. If x^0 lies close to x_3, then the committee can prevent subsequent change by blocking any proposal. Figure 41.1b has the same setup as in Figure 41.1a, along with various

motions – B, A_1, A_2, A_3. We have also identified both $W(x^0)$ and $W(B)$. At x^0 a motion like $A_1 \in W(x^0)$ will be vetoed by the committee (thereby frustrating the preferences of a majority) since A_1 is less preferred than x^0. Should the committee bring forth a motion like B (since $B \in P_c[x^0]$), it forgoes any future influence on the course of events. Once the gates are opened with the motion B, amendments like A_1 are in order and, in this example, $A_1 \in W(B) \cap W(x^0)$. Thus, any point in the shaded region of Figure 41.1b, like A_1, could result since all such points defeat both B and x^0 in majority contests. (We assume here the *amendment procedure*, according to which an agenda consisting of x^0, some bill B, and amendments $A_1, \ldots, A_t$ are voted in pairwise fashion in reverse order with the losing alternative deleted.) In sum, the ex ante veto – the power to bring motions to the floor or bottle them up – is a defensive tool and, while it might be valuable to the committee because of its potential threat value, it cannot assure very much for the committee.

Joining monopoly initiation powers to the ex ante veto does not improve matters much for the committee. Initiation power allows the committee to propose points like $B \in P_c(x^0)$. But such bills, once proposed, take on a life of their own over which the committee has little subsequent control. Indeed, as we have just seen, B is vulnerable to an amendment like A_1 since A_1 can beat $B(A_1 \in W(B))$, and then it can defeat the status quo ($A_1 \in W(x^0)$). Since $A_1 \in P_c(x^0)$, a committee proposal can lead to a decline in committee welfare precisely because the committee has no future control once it opens the gates.

We have shown how limited gatekeeping and initiation power are as instruments of committee control. The former is essentially negative and the latter provides no guarantees unless expanded to proscribe all amendments to or modifications of committee proposals (closed-rule environment). Inasmuch as we rarely encounter legislatures, empirically, that prohibit modifications of committee proposals altogether, we are left with the conclusion that committee power is essentially negative. Any attempt by the committee to promote positive changes in an open-rule environment invariably results in the possibility of a decline in committee welfare. Once the committee opens the gates, it risks getting rolled on the floor.

EX POST VETO POWER

Suppose now that a committee possessed ex post veto power in addition to gatekeeping and initiation powers. Once it has opened the gates and made a proposal and after the legislature has worked its will, either accepting the proposal or modifying it in some germane fashion, the committee now may either sanction the final product or restore the status quo, x^o. A committee with an ex post veto possesses the power to protect itself against welfare-reducing changes in the status quo. The ex post veto shares with the ex ante veto this defensive property. But because of its position in the sequence of decision making, the ex post veto confers offensive capabilities as well. Coming last in the sequence, it affects prior beliefs and behavior of other agents.

In Figure 41.1b suppose that committee bill B stimulates the floor amendment A_1. As noted earlier, $A_1 \in W(B) \cap W(x^o)$, with Member 1 and Member 2 preferring it both to B and to x^o. However, $A_1 \in P_c(x^o)$ so that, with the ex post veto, if A_1 passes, then the committee will veto it and reinstate x^o. A vote for A_1, then, is in reality a vote to maintain the status quo. But both members 2 and 3 prefer B to x^o. Thus, despite a nominal preference for A_1 over B, Member 2 finds the prospect of an ex post veto a credible threat and joins with Member 3 in defeating all amendments like A_1. In short, while an agent like 1 has every incentive to move an amendment like A_1 against B, sophisticated calculation induced by ex post veto power leads Member 2 to depart from a nominal preference for A_1 and vote against it.

The ex post veto ensures that the final outcome will either be x^o or an element of $P_c(x^o)$. It therefore protects a committee from being rolled on the floor. One would expect, as a consequence of ex post veto power, that many amendments nominally supported by legislative majorities will not pass on the floor if they are opposed by a committee majority. Such is the case for all amendments in the one shaded petal of Figure 41.1b containing A_1. Opposed by the committee, such amendments will be voted down by sophisticated majorities.

The ex post veto does not protect against amendments in the shaded regions containing A_4 and A_5 (see Figure 41.1c) because the veto threat is no longer credible there. In these instances, the final outcome is still superior to x^o in the committee's preferences. The committee may bluster, but it will not veto. Thus, some amendments (like A_4) will pass despite committee opposition, and others (like A_5) will pass with committee support. These amendments turn out to be non-problematical for committees, as we show in the next section.

There is one aspect of behavior induced by credible threats of ex post veto (such as the case of A_1) that bears further discussion. As we related in the introductory section, much is made in the congressional literature of a system of reciprocated deference. But why is deference practiced at all? Is deference unqualified and honored always and everywhere? Our predictions provide a more discriminating explanation of this aspect of deference (or the appearance of it) than does the more traditional lore. In the case of an amendment like A_1, Member 2 may *appear* to defer to the committee by voting against the amendment despite a sincere preference for it; indeed, Member 2 may rationalize his or her own behavior in this way. Thus, one might wish to *label* this behavior *deference. But it should be clear that it is deference to the ex post veto power of the committee, not deference to expertise or an instance of reciprocal cooperation.* In the absence of an ex post veto, we would not always expect to see deference by Member 2; rather, if the committee opened the gates in the first place, we would expect to see members 1 and 2 support an amendment like A_1. *Likewise, even with an ex post veto, there are some amendments to a committee bill (even some opposed by the committee) for which no deference at all will be observed.* An amendment like A_4, for example, will find majority support and no deference because the veto threat is not credible here. In our view deference is endogenous, is not everywhere applicable, and is most usefully thought of as a reflection of the strategic character of a situation.

INSTITUTIONALIZATION OF THE EX POST VETO: CONFERENCE COMMITTEES

In the United States Congress, as in most state legislatures, a bill must pass both chambers of the legislature in precisely the same form before it may be sent to the chief executive for his signature. Should a bill pass in different forms in the two chambers, a process is set in motion to reconcile differences. After the second chamber has acted on a bill, the first chamber may "concur" in the second chamber's amendments. If, instead, the first chamber "disagrees" with the second chamber's amendments (or concurs in those amendments with further amendments of its own), then the second chamber may "recede" from its original amendments (or concur in the first chamber's new amendments). Or it may, in turn, concur in the first chamber's new amendments with its own new amendments, putting the ball back in the first chamber's court. Although this process, known as *messaging between the chambers*, cannot continue indefinitely, the bill can be sent back and forth several more times in the hope that one of the chambers will accept the final position of the other. However, once a stage of disagreement is reached in which one chamber "insists" on its version of the bill and the other chamber disagrees, then one chamber requests a conference, and the other chamber accepts. While as many as three-fourths of all public laws manage to avoid the conference stage, nearly all major bills – appropriations, revenue, and important authorizations – end up in conference.

There is now a considerable body of rules and commentary on conference proceedings. Conferees of each chamber (also called *managers*) are appointed by the presiding officer; these appointments come principally from the committees of jurisdiction at the suggestion of those committees' chairpersons (some evidence is provided below). Occasionally an additional conferee is appointed to represent a particular

amendment that the presiding officer (in the House) believes will not otherwise be fairly represented (like A_1 in Figure 41.1); but even in this exceptional case, the views of the committee chairpersons are dominant. The conferees from each chamber seek to resolve differences in the respective versions of the bill, and an agreement is said to be reached when a majority of *each* delegation signs the conference report. If both sign, the report and accompanying bill containing the agreement are brought back to each chamber to be voted up or down (no amendments are in order). That is, the conference report is considered under a closed rule as a take-it-or-leave-it proposal.

The conference procedure, described in simplified fashion in the preceding two paragraphs, thus does two things. First, it institutionalizes the ex post veto and, as described in the previous sections, gives credibility to the committee during floor deliberations in its chamber. Second, to the extent that there is some discretion on the part of conferees on the terms to which they may agree (discussed later), the take-it-or-leave-it treatment of conference reports confers additional ex post adjustment power on the committee. It is to this latter consideration that we now proceed.

We begin with the jurisdiction X, which we assume is common to both the House and the Senate, and the status quo $x^o \in X$. Four sets in X are of interest:

1. $W_H(x^o)$: win set of x^o in House
2. $W_s(x^o)$: win set of x^o in Senate
3. $P_H(x^o)$: preferred-to set of x^o of House committee
4. $P_s(x^o)$: preferred-to set of x^o of Senate committee

We have already seen from Figure 41.1 that the final outcome must be an element of $W_H(x^o)$. House majorities constrain changes in x^o. Likewise, in the Senate $W_s(x^o)$ is a constraint set. To pass, therefore, the conference outcome must be an element of $F(x^o) = W_H(x^o) \cap W_s(x^o)$. The status quo, x^o, may be imposed by either conference delegation (which we assume to be the relevant legislative committee in each chamber) if a proposed settlement is not an element of

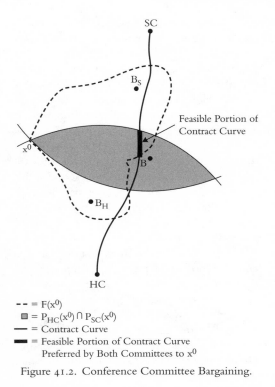

Figure 41.2. Conference Committee Bargaining.

- - - = F(x⁰)
■ = $P_{HC}(x^0) \cap P_{SC}(x^0)$
— = Contract Curve
▬ = Feasible Portion of Contract Curve
Preferred by Both Committees to x⁰

Senate committee ideal points (*HC* and *SC*, respectively), and the committee contract locus ($P_H[x] \cap P_s[x] = \emptyset$). The latter curve is heavily shaded where it has common intersection with $F(x^0) \cap P_H(x^0) \cap P_s(x^0)$. Also, we have indicated the bills, B_H and B_s, which have passed the respective chambers in different forms, necessitating the conference.

The respective conferees take $F(x^0)$ as a constraint and seek a negotiated settlement, say B^*, consistent with that constraint. This normally requires a compromise in which the preferences of each chamber (as reflected in B_H and B_s respectively) are to some degree sacrificed. Indeed, in Figure 41.2, the committees sacrifice as well, agreeing on an outcome less preferred to them than their respective chamber's bills. Different configurations of preferences, however, need not have this property.

one of their preferred–to sets, that is, $P_H(x^0)$ or $P_s(x^0)$, respectively. Thus, we have as a necessary condition for a change in x^0 the following set inequality:

$$F(x^0) \cap P_H(x^0) \cap P_s(x^0) \neq \emptyset.$$

The ex post veto power of a committee follows from the fact that it represents its chamber in conference proceedings and may refuse to agree to a conference settlement. If the preferences for change of the House and Senate committees, for instance, fail to intersect ($P_H(x^0) \cap P_s(x^0) = \emptyset$), then any proposed change will be vetoed by one of them. Similarly, if changes preferred in common by the two delegations fail to intersect the feasible set, $F(x^0)$, then no alteration of x^0 is possible.

We are not yet in a position to model conference proceedings explicitly, but on the basis of the set inequality above, there are some additional points to be made about the opportunities the conference mechanism presents to committees. Assume, then, that the set inequality holds. In Figure 41.2 we depict x^0, $F(x^0)$, House and

COMMITTEE DOMINANCE
OF THE CONFERENCE

In order for committees of jurisdiction to possess an ex post veto, they must dominate conference committee delegations. On the basis of the reports of early students of the subject (unfortunately, without much in the way of supporting evidence), such dominance has been the case for more than a century. We do not present a full-blown empirical analysis here, but in order to give some veracity to our claims we have examined all conferences listed in the Congressional Information Service's Annual Abstracts of Congressional Records and Legislative Histories for 1981, 1982, and 1983.

Before reporting our evidence we note that a consequence of the 1970s reforms in the House and of the loose germaneness restrictions in the Senate is that many pieces of legislation are the handiwork of several committees in each chamber. A House bill, for example, might be amended in a nongermane manner by the Senate. Conferees are drawn from the committees of original jurisdiction plus additional conferees to deal (only) with the nongermane Senate amendment. Alternatively, it is occasionally the case in the House that the Speaker partitions

Table 41.1. *Conference Committee Composition*

Type of Conference	Number of Conferees Not on Germane Committee					
	1981		1982		1983	
	House	Senate	House	Senate	House	Senate
Budget[a]	0 (15)	0 (12)	0 (15)	0 (10)	0 (15)	0 (8)
		[2]		[3]		[1]
Appropriations[b]	0 (168)	0 (187)	0 (155)	0 (187)	0 (225)	1 (219)
		[12]		[11]		[8]
All others	2 (190)	3 (155)	3 (399)	3 (276)	2 (206)	0 (126)
		[17]		[38]		[16]

Note: Cell entries give total number of conferees *not* from the committee of jurisdiction for each conference type. In parentheses are the total number of conferees. In brackets are the number of conferences.

[a] Neither the Omnibus Budget Reconciliation Act of 1981 nor the Omnibus Budget Reconciliation Act of 1982 is included here. Each was an exceptional situation involving an unusually large number of conferees.

[b] Does not include omnibus supplemental appropriations or continuing resolutions.

Source: Congressional Index Service, 1981–83.

a bill into parts and commits these to different committees for hearings and markup according to their respective jurisdictions; in the Senate, multiple referral may occur by unanimous consent. Again, conferees from all relevant committees make up the delegation.

In Table 41.1 we present evidence on conference committee composition for the conferences held from 1981 through 1983. For each year, by chamber and type of legislation, we report the number of conferees who were *not* members of the committee(s) of jurisdiction. The data are crystal clear in their message. On only one occasion in the three years, was a member – not sitting on the Appropriations Committee of either chamber – a conferee for an appropriations bill. On only a handful of occasions (fewer than 1% in the House; about 1% in the Senate) were noncommittee members conferees for legislative committee bills. And finally, on budget resolutions only members of the two budget committees were conferees.

A further perusal of the data on which Table 41.1 is based yields additional impressions, though we will not attach any quantitative weight to them here. First, it is almost always the case that the chairperson and the ranking minority member of the full committee from which the bill originated serve on the conference. Second, it is extremely rare for a conference to produce an agreement to which these two persons are not signatories; it happens on occasion (for example, Chairman Hatfield did not sign several Appropriations conference reports), but we hesitate to draw any conclusions from these events for they are likely to involve contextual details that are not available without in-depth study of the particular cases. Third, there is considerable evidence that, in addition to full committee chair and ranking minority member, the subcommittees responsible for the bill dominate the conference delegation (see below for some additional details).

Committee dominance at the conference stage is perhaps the most complete and certainly the most obvious in our data in the area of appropriations. Moreover, the decentralization to the subcommittee level within each appropriations committee is clearly evident at the conference stage as well. In Table 41.2 we display the evidence for this claim for all appropriations measures (omnibus bills excepted) in 1981, 1982, and 1983. Subcommittee autonomy is said to be complete in conference if all the members (and only all the members) serve as managers. Subcommittees are dominant when

Table 41.2. *Subcommittee Autonomy in Conference: Appropriations Committees*

	Senate Autonomy		
House Autonomy	Complete	Dominant	Partial
Complete	18	3	2
Dominant	2	1	0
Partial	0	0	0

Key:
  Complete: The conference delegation was identical to the subcommittee membership.
  Dominant: Either one subcommittee member was deleted, or one nonsubcommittee member was added to the conference delegation.
  Partial: Subcommittee representation was neither complete nor dominant.

Note: Table includes Appropriations conferences in 1981, 1982, and 1983 exclusive of omnibus supplemental appropriations or continuing resolutions.

either one subcommittee member was excluded from the conference or a nonsubcommittee member was included. Since the former circumstance may often arise with no political weight attached (e.g., a Senator is out of town; a Representative is ill) and the latter occurred on only a single occasion, most of the dominant autonomy occurrences are hardly different from their complete autonomy counterparts. Finally, partial autonomy arises when more than one subcommittee member is deleted from conference. As the evidence suggests, subcommittees of both appropriations committees not only take full responsibility within their respective chambers for marking up appropriations measures and managing them on the floor but the same

(relatively small) group of legislators meets year after year to hammer out a final compromise.

As a final bit of empirical corroboration, we have taken a sample of conferences by legislative committees from the 1981–83 period to see the extent to which the subcommittee autonomy evidenced in the appropriations realm carries over to other types of legislation. The results appear in Table 41.3. Of the 71 legislative committee conferences from the 1981–83 period, we examined the composition of 27 to see the extent to which the subcommittee of jurisdiction dominated the conference delegation. The evidence of subcommittee influence here, while not as overwhelming as in the appropriations realm, is nevertheless considerable. In both chambers subcommittee members dominate the conference delegations. In the House they constitute about 90 percent of the conferees; in the Senate, nearly 80 percent of the conferees. More importantly, the median case is one in which the conference delegation is drawn entirely from the subcommittee of jurisdiction.

DISCUSSION

We have sought to offer a more discriminating notion of committee veto power, to embed it in a decision-making sequence, and thereby to provide a firmer explanatory foundation for committee power than has been provided heretofore. Our theoretical examples and the accompanying figures illustrate the

Table 41.3. *Subcommittee Autonomy in Conference: Legislative Committees*

House and Subcommittee Membership	On Conference	Off Conference
House Members		
On subcommittee	210	248
Off subcommittee	25	720
Senators		
On subcommittee	136	72
Off subcommittee	35	204

Note: The populations are the committees of jurisdiction. The first row of each panel gives the number of subcommittee members on and off the conference delegation. The second row gives the number of nonsubcommittee members (but on the full committee) on and off the conference delegation.

methodological tools and suggest the lines of what is a fairly general argument. Of central importance is the role of sequence. It matters, for example, whether veto power comes first (as in gatekeeping) or at the penultimate stage (as in conference proceedings). An undiscriminating treatment of committee agenda power that fails to distinguish between different sequential properties of that power is often misleading.

In emphasizing sequence and explicit enforcement arrangements, we do not intend to deprecate the ideas of self-enforcing agreements, implicit cooperation, and deference that have constituted traditional stock-in-trade explanations for committee power. Surely, all of these operate. Moreover, our focus on ex post enforcement is in no way inconsistent with the fact that many participants might themselves explain their behavior as essentially deferential. It would not surprise us to find most legislators saying, "Sure, I let those people over on Education and Labor do pretty much what they think is reasonable. And they do the same for us on Armed Services. That's the way things are done around here." We would only claim that "deference" labels a behavioral regularity; it does not explain it. The theoretical question of interest is why that behavior is an equilibrium. We have, in effect, sought to give deference a rational basis by embedding it in the strategic realities produced by the sequence of decision making.

In our analytical approach to legislative institutions, we have focused on the locus and sequence of agenda power. In characterizing legislative decision making in terms of who may make proposals (motions, amendments), and in what order, and who may exercise veto power and in what order, we wish to emphasize that these features are not merely the minutiae of parliamentarians. Rather, they provide the building blocks from which legislative institutions are constructed. The results presented here and by others elsewhere show that different mixes of these institutional building blocks lead to different outcomes and, correspondingly, to significantly different political behavior.

In the context of the committee system in the U.S. Congress, we showed that proposal power and ex ante veto power are insufficient to the task of institutionalizing an effective division-of-labor arrangement. In the absence of some form of ex post veto power, committee proposals are vulnerable to alteration and, because of this, committees have agenda control in only a very truncated form. It is unlikely, in our view, that such a shaky foundation would induce individuals to invest institutional careers in the committees on which they serve.

CHAPTER FORTY–TWO

The Return to Equilibrium

Controlling Legislative Agendas

Gerald S. Strom

Gaining a stable, predictable outcome in a legislature operating under majority rule is not guaranteed. Strom reviews the agenda-setting mechanisms and other processes that limit amendments and narrow the range of possible outcomes. Important features of Congress, particularly in the House of Representatives, limit the range of options considered and often bias outcomes. Among other things, Strom questions the conclusions of Shepsle and Weingast in the previous selection about the effectiveness of conference committees as a source of committee power.

The spatial theory of simple majority rule in a multidimensional issue space implies that the chaotic disequilibrium situations are a common occurrence. This creates an empirical puzzle because in most real-world decision-making situations, neither chaos nor disequilibrium is frequently observed. Although there may be some unperceived chaotic and disequilibrium situations, decision-making institutions like Congress do not usually appear to wander randomly through issue spaces, nor are decisions, once made, easily overturned. Experimental outcomes in largely unstructured cases also do not appear to be randomly scattered across the issue space. This lack of agreement between theory and practice has led to attempts

Gerald S. Strom. 1990. "The Return to Equilibrium: Controlling Legislative Agendas" in Gerald S. Strom, *The Logic of Lawmaking: A Spatial Theory Approach* (Johns Hopkins University Press), 76–91. © 1990 The Johns Hopkins University Press. Reprinted with permission of The Johns Hopkins University Press.

to explain why there is so much stability in real-world decision processes. Short of assuming that all decisions are made in a unidimensional space in which Black's theorem produces an equilibrium at the median, three kinds of answers to this question are possible. (1) One singles out a set of decision makers and gives them special powers to manipulate the agenda of the legislative process. (2) Simple majority rule is replaced by a form of restricted majority rule in which a set of institutional structures and rules restricts the possible outcomes and simultaneously induces stability in decision-making processes. (3) One can replace the assumption of sincere voting with a form of sophisticated voting over fixed or anticipated agendas.

In this chapter, the first of these answers will be explored. In particular, it will be shown that the existence of agenda control can induce stability in legislative decision making. However, there is a price for this method because, as will be seen, the existence of agenda control can substantially benefit those having such control at the expense of other legislators.

AGENDA CONTROL THEORIES

One possible way of explaining the empirical regularities of the legislative process in Congress and similar legislatures is that a particular legislator or set of legislators has control of the agenda. Those having such control can dictate which alternatives are considered and in which order. As an example of how this can work, consider again the classic paradox of voting in which there is a three-person legislature with the legislators having the following preference orders for outcomes X, Y, and Z:

Legislator A: $X > Y > Z$

Legislator B: $Y > Z > X$

Legislator C: $Z > X > Y$

The social preference ordering here is intransitive with X preferred to Y, Y preferred to Z, and Z preferred to X. However, if legislator A has agenda control, he or she can arrange for an order of voting in which the first vote is between Y and Z so that Y wins and eliminates the only outcome that can defeat X. The second vote will then be between Y and X, and X will win, which is legislator A's most preferred outcome.

Alternatively, consider the same case with legislator B rather than A having agenda control. B's most preferred outcome is Y, and from the preference orders, he or she can see that Y can defeat Z and Z can defeat X. By setting up an agenda in which the first vote is between X and Z, Z will win and eliminate X so that on the second vote, Y will defeat Z and become the social choice. Thus, both legislators A and B were able to manipulate the agenda so that their most preferred outcome became the social choice; it can also be seen that legislator C could manipulate the agenda to yield Z as the social choice.

In the examples above, the legislator with agenda control was able to exploit the fact that the social preference order was intransitive. Consider now the case in which the three legislators have the following preference orders:

Legislator A: $X > Y > Z$

Legislator B: $Y > X > Z$

Legislator C: $Z > Y > X$

It can be seen here that the social preference order is $Y > X > Z$, which is transitive, and Y is the Condorcet winning alternative. It can also be seen that there is no way to structure an agenda to prevent Y from being the outcome.

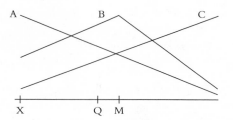

Figure 42.1. Agenda Control in the Case of Three Legislators with Single-Peaked Preferences in a Unidimensional Issue Space.

Y will defeat whatever alternative it is put against; so in this case, agenda control cannot be used to manipulate the outcome.

In the examples above, there was only a discrete set of alternatives, and each was required to enter the voting at some stage. Theoretically, however, spatial models of legislative decision making allow for a potentially infinite number of alternatives, and not all of them are required to enter the decision-making process. In this more general context, can agenda control be used to manipulate outcomes?

Consider first the case in which there is a unidimensional issue space, and all the legislators have single-peaked preferences. An example of such a case for a three-person legislature is given in Figure 42.1. It can be seen in this figure that the median preference peak is defined by the preference curve of legislator B so that the point labeled M is the Condorcet winning alternative. This implies that M can defeat any of the other alternatives; for this reason, if M enters the agenda at any stage, it will be the outcome. However, will M enter the agenda if one of the legislators has agenda control?

Before answering this question, an important question of legislative procedure must be addressed. In the cases in which there were only a relatively few discrete alternatives and each was required to enter the agenda, the issue of how the decision-making process ends did not arise because it was implicit that it did so when all the alternatives had entered the agenda. In the current case, however, in which there is a potentially infinite number of alternatives and not all of them must enter the agenda, it is unclear at what point the decision process ends and an outcome is chosen.

Real legislatures like Congress deal with this problem in two ways. First, only a fixed number of alternatives can be proposed. Thus, as seen earlier, the House allows only five alternatives: an original bill, an amendment to this bill, an amendment to the amendment, a substitute amendment, and an amendment to the substitute. Alternatively, legislative rules allow for a call of the previous question, which, if adopted, prohibits the offering of additional alternatives.

Because the latter of these two rules is somewhat less restrictive of the power of an agenda setter than is the former, it will be assumed in the following examples that the legislator with monopoly agenda control also has the exclusive right to call the previous question and end the decision-making process. With this rule, the decision-making process operates in the following way. The agenda setter offers an initial alternative that is immediately put against the implicit status quo motion. Whichever of these wins on this first vote then becomes the extant status quo, and further alternatives can then be proposed until the previous question is moved and adopted. The last adopted motion then becomes the outcome.

Consider now the case in Figure 42.1 in which legislator A has monopoly control of the agenda. This legislator would most prefer the outcome X, where his or her preference curve has its peak. However, under the rules, the first vote must be between the implicit status quo Q and an alternative that A proposes. If legislator A proposes X, it will lose on the first vote to Q because a majority of preference curves rises toward Q in the X–Q interval. More generally, it can be seen that Q will defeat any alternative located to its left, so the only alternatives that can defeat Q are those located to its right. However, only the agenda setter can propose alternatives, and legislator A prefers Q to any of the alternatives to its right. Thus, in this case, Q must be the final outcome.

The fact that Q is the final outcome in this case is significant because it is not the Condorcet winner. By exploiting agenda control,

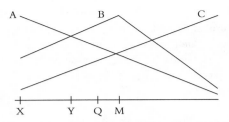

Figure 42.2. Agenda Control in the Case of Three Legislators with Single-Peaked Preferences in a Unidimensional Issue Space.

legislator A was able to prevent the adoption of M, which would otherwise have been selected. This implies that when agenda control exists in a unidimensional issue space, Condorcet winning alternatives may not be adopted.

Consider now the case illustrated in Figure 42.2, which is identical to that in Figure 42.1 except that the location of Q has been altered. Again, it can be seen that legislator A's most preferred alternative X cannot be selected because a majority of B and C prefers Q to X. It can also be seen that a majority of A and B prefers outcomes to the left of Q, and if A proposes one of these, it will defeat Q. In fact, A would have an incentive to propose the left-most alternative that can defeat Q in order to get an outcome as close to his or her most preferred outcome. Thus, in the case of Figure 42.2, agenda setter A would have an incentive to propose the alternative Y, which is just slightly preferred by legislator B to Q. Legislators A and B will then vote for Y against Q, after which A will call the previous question. It will also pass, making Y the outcome.

Again, in this case, it can be seen that agenda control by a legislator has resulted in an outcome different from the Condorcet winner. More generally, it is straightforward to show that the only times the Condorcet alternative will be chosen are when the legislator with the median preference peak has agenda control or when the positions labeled M and Y coincide. *A priori* for a relatively large legislature, the probability of either of these conditions existing is relatively small so that in realistic cases, it is unlikely that a Condorcet winning outcome, if one exists, will be selected.

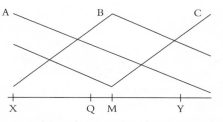

Figure 42.3. Agenda Control in the Case of Three Legislators with Non–Single-Peaked Preferences in a Unidimensional Issue Space.

As a final unidimensional example, consider the case illustrated in Figure 42.3. In contrast to the cases above in which all the preference curves were single peaked, the preferences in Figure 42.3 are such that they cannot simultaneously be represented by single-peaked curves. Consequently, a Condorcet winning alternative does not exist in this case. Thus, the alternative M, which is under the median preference peak, cannot defeat all other alternatives, and in particular, it cannot defeat any position to the left of itself because two preference curves are rising as one moves left of M.

As in the earlier examples, assume that legislator A has agenda control. Under the procedural rules used earlier, the first motion that A makes will be put against the status quo motion Q. For legislator A, getting his or her most preferred outcome in this case is simple. By noting that two of the preference curves are rising toward X in the Q–X interval, A knows that by proposing X, it will defeat Q. If A then proposes the previous question so that no additional alternatives can be considered, it will also pass with the support of A and B so that X will become the final outcome.

In the case above, legislator A was able to exploit agenda control to achieve his or her most preferred outcome in a single step. However, this is not always possible when an intransitive social preference order exists. For example, if legislator B in Figure 42.3 had been the agenda controller instead of A, B could not have achieved outcome M by simply proposing it because both A and C prefer Q to M. Notice, however, that a majority of A and C prefers X to M, a majority of C and B prefers

Y to X, and a majority of B and A prefers M to Y. Thus, B could first propose X, then Y, and finally M. Each of these alternatives defeats the previous motion; if B then calls the previous question, the final outcome will be M, B's most preferred outcome.

The previous two examples illustrate how an agenda controller, in a case of intransitive social preferences, was able to exploit this power to achieve his or her most preferred outcome. It should be noted, however, that it does not follow that an agenda controller can always do this in the unidimensional situation. One instance of this is when there is a cycle among a set of alternatives, including Q, and when any of the alternatives in this cycle defeats all others. For example, if there is a cycle among alternatives R, Q, and S such that $R > Q > S > R$ and each of these three alternatives defeats all others, an agenda setter cannot achieve his or her most preferred outcome if it is not one of the three in the cycle.

Thus, the existence of agenda control in a case of socially intransitive unidimensional preferences does not imply that the controller's most preferred outcome is selected. As the examples here have also shown, however, agenda control is a significant power that allows the legislator having it to manipulate outcomes to his or her advantage.

Up to this point, agenda control has been considered only in a unidimensional issue space. To see what happens in a multidimensional space, consider Figure 42.4. As in the earlier examples, this is a three-person legislature deciding on a two-dimensional issue. The ideal points of the three legislators are labeled with

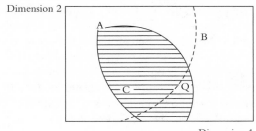

Figure 42.4. Agenda Control in a Two-Dimensional Issue Space.

letters *A* through *C*, and it is assumed that they have circular indifference curves. As is typical of multidimensional decision making, it can be seen in the figure that social preference order is intransitive so that no equilibrium (or Condorcet outcome) exists. Here, the question is which alternative will be selected if one of the legislators has monopoly control of the agenda.

In examining this question, it is assumed that the legislature operates under the same procedural rules as above with the agenda setter having the exclusive right to call the previous question. Further, it is again assumed here that legislator A has agenda control. The questions, then, are what is the extent to which A can use agenda control to manipulate outcomes, and, in particular, can A achieve an outcome corresponding to his or her ideal point?

Note first in Figure 42.4 that the status quo position *Q* will defeat *A*'s ideal point. In fact, any alternative in the shaded area is preferred by a majority to alternative *A*. Thus, legislator A cannot propose any of these and achieve alternative *A*. However, note that the alternatives corresponding to B's ideal point would lose to A's ideal point. Also note that legislator A prefers *B* to *Q* (shown by the dashed indifference curve). Thus, if A first proposes alternative *B*, it will defeat *Q*. Legislator A can then propose *A* against *B*, and *A* will defeat *B*. A call of the previous question will then pass (with A and C supporting it), and the final outcome will be A's ideal point.

In the case of a multidimensional issue space, this result is not extraordinary. A monopoly agenda setter in a multidimensional issue space can manipulate the agenda to produce any outcome in the whole issue space. In some cases, this may require a relatively long agenda, but that does not detract from the fact that when [an] equilibrium does not exist, a monopoly agenda setter can always achieve his or her ideal point as the outcome.

A major implication of both the unidimensional and multidimensional examples of agenda control is that the existence of such control generally appears to make a majority of legislators worse off than they would have been in the absence of such control. Thus, in the

unidimensional cases in which a Condorcet winning alternative existed, the fact that this alternative was not the final outcome implies that a majority would have achieved more utility if agenda control had not existed and the Condorcet alternative had been chosen. Similarly, a majority of *B* and *C* in Figure 42.4 would have preferred any outcome in the shaded area, including *Q*, to the outcome legislator A was able to achieve using agenda control.

The fact that majorities of legislators are generally made worse off by the existence of agenda control raises the serious question of why they would allow such control to exist. Agenda control imposed on a legislature from the outside (e.g., by a constitution) would not make this an important problem, but generally such an imposition is not made. The U.S. Constitution, for example, explicitly states that the chambers of Congress have the right to establish their own procedural rules. From this it would follow that formal agenda control derived from legislative rules would exist either in very limited forms or not at all.

With one major exception, there is empirical support in Congress for [the] conclusion that legislators have little incentive to grant agenda control to either individuals or groups. The exception to this conclusion is the gatekeeping power of congressional committees which allows them to prevent legislation from being considered by their full chambers. The other two instances of agenda control in Congress are the closed rule in the House, which prohibits amendments to committee bills, and the closed rule for bills reported by a conference committee. As will be shown below, neither of these appears to be a significant form of agenda control.

Consider first the gatekeeping power of congressional committees. In both the House and Senate, all bills, when introduced, are immediately referred to a standing committee for initial consideration. For most bills, this is the end of their sojourn through the legislative process because committees generally do not consider most of the bills referred to them. In the 99th Congress (1985–86), for example, there were 5,743 bills introduced and referred to committee in the House, but only 599 were eventually considered and reported by House committees. Thus, during this congress, committees effectively killed 90 percent of the bills referred to them.

There are rules in both the House and Senate which allow the full chamber to discharge a committee from consideration of a bill so that it can be considered by the full chamber. Such rules are seldom invoked, however, and even when they are, it is unlikely that the bill will become a law. In fact, between 1910 and 1984, House committees were only discharged of 26 bills, and of these, only 20 became public law.

The facts that all bills are initially referred to a committee and that committees are seldom discharged from their consideration of a bill are potentially substantial forms of agenda control. In theoretical terms, however, it is unclear why such powers would be granted. It should be noted that since committees fail to report 90 percent of the bills sent to them, their gatekeeping power is vastly overstated. Many of the unreported bills are duplicates of other bills, and many more would not receive majority support in the full chamber if they were reported. In addition, a full chamber majority always has the option of discharging a committee if the members of the majority really want to act on a bill. Therefore, although the existence of gatekeeping must be considered an exception to [the] conclusion, it is not too significant an exception because many of the instances in which it is used are consistent with the preferences of full chamber majorities who have the option of discharging a committee.

Note also that committee gatekeeping is a negative power: it only allows committees to prevent the passage of bills that a committee majority prefers not to pass. As such, gatekeeping cannot explain the apparent success of committees in having their reported bills passed by their full chambers in largely unaltered form. Generally, about 90 percent of reported bills are eventually passed by the full chamber, and many of those that do not pass die not from outright rejection but from the lack of time, as they are pending action at the time Congress adjourns.

Moreover, the floor seldom makes any major change in reported bills. Amendments to bills in the full chamber are generally minor ones that do not substantially alter the main provisions of the bill as reported from committee. If an agenda control is to be a valid explanation for the stability and general predictability of legislative decision making, it must also explain these apparent empirical instances in Congress.

One form of agenda control which would explain the success of committees in Congress is the closed rule prohibiting amendments to a bill reported from a committee. In this case, the committee reporting a bill has complete agenda control. With a closed rule, the full chamber is faced with a choice between only two alternatives: the reported bill and the status quo.

For several reasons, it does not appear that closed rules for committee bills can explain the empirical regularities observed in Congress. First, closed rules are only possible in the House so they cannot explain the success of Senate committees. Moreover, the success of House and Senate committees in their respective chambers is nearly identical. Moreover, closed rules are seldom used in the House. In the 97th and 98th Congresses (1981–82 and 1983–84), for example, no closed rules were issued, and in the 99th Congress (1985–86), only one was issued. Modified open and modified closed rules also restrict amendments and are more commonly used, but again their use cannot generally explain committee success in the Senate, which has no such rules. It would thus appear that the use of formal amendment control regulations like the closed rule cannot explain the empirical regularities observed in Congress.

An alternative form of agenda control in Congress is the closed rule on bills reported from a conference committee. This form of agenda control explains the apparent success of congressional committees in getting their recommendations adopted by the full Congress. The membership of conference committees is made up exclusively or almost exclusively from the committees that reported the bill in each chamber. This fact along with the closed rule suggested that committees can generally discard any full chamber amendment with which they disagree. For example, if a committee reports a bill B to the full chamber, and it is then amended over committee objections to B', the committee can change it back to B in conference. Further, because conference bills cannot be amended, the full chamber cannot change the bill back to B' again. Moreover, because committees have this power, there will be a reluctance on the part of full chamber legislators to push amendments opposed by the committee because even though they might win in the first round, they will lose in the last.

Although it is an interesting suggestion, there are many problems with the *ex post* veto theory as an explanation for committee power. One major problem is that the House and Senate have alternatives to conference committees for resolving their differences. For example, a chamber can simply accept the bill as passed by the other chamber; or a chamber can amend the bill as passed by the other chamber, and send it back for either acceptance or further amendment in the other chamber. By repeating this process until a bill acceptable to both chambers is found, a conference can be avoided. Moreover, the use of such procedures is not the exception but the norm. During the 98th Congress (1983–84), for example, 86.4 percent of bills were passed with no conference; 5.4 percent were passed with some combination of a conference and rules restricting the outcome of a conference; and only 8.2 percent of differences between the chambers were resolved exclusively by a conference.

It could be argued, however, that it is not the actual occurrence of a conference but the threat of one which limits full chamber amendments. The argument is that members do not offer amendments to committee bills because they think a conference may be likely and that in the conference, the conferees from the committee will eliminate their amendment. However, what this argument ignores is that the decision of whether or not to go to conference is made by the full chamber, not by the committee. If a full chamber committee supports an amendment against the wishes of a committee majority, this same majority can also refuse to request a conference and explore alternative ways of

resolving the differences between the chambers. As noted earlier, in the full chamber, a committee majority or even a unanimous committee constitutes less than 10 percent of the full membership so that any threat of a conference by this small minority need not be taken seriously. Full chambers only need send bills to conference when they feel they can trust the committee conferees to follow the wishes of a full chamber majority.

For these basic reasons, major problems exist for the *ex post* veto theory of committee power. It may explain some cases, but it cannot explain the 85 percent and more of instances in which no conference was needed. More importantly, it cannot explain the key situation in which the preferences of a committee majority are different from the preferences of a full chamber majority because it is the latter, not the former, which decides which bills go to conference.

In these three instances of congressional agenda control, the ability to affect the agenda was derived from formal rules. Thus, committee gatekeeping, the closed rule in the House, and the closed rule for conference bills are all powers granted by the rules of the House and/or Senate. Moreover, consistent with [the] conclusion that legislators would have little incentive to grant agenda control powers, these formal grants, with the exception of committee gatekeeping, do not appear to be very important, and they cannot explain committee success in Congress. Nevertheless, that formal agenda control does not exist as a significant power in most cases does not imply that some other form of agenda control may exist which will explain both the stability of congressional outcomes and the success of congressional committees.

One form that informal agenda control can take derives from a "political failure in the agenda formation process" induced by the costs of formulating and proposing alternatives. Some costs, for example, are entailed in calculating what the content of an agenda alternative should be, drafting the alternative, and then constructing arguments to convince others why they should support the new proposal. In a congressional context, this argument suggests that committees are successful in the full chamber because of the costs involved in formulating and passing alternatives to proposed committee bills. When a congressional committee brings a bill to the full chamber, the floor managers of the bill can and generally do make a strong case that the committee members have worked hard and extensively studied the issues involved. From this work and from the knowledge they have gained, the committee members argue that they have put together a legislative package that the nonexperts in the rest of the chamber should not only support but also not change by offering amendments. Such amendments, the committee will argue, are not derived from the knowledge and expertise available to the committee and therefore may have unknown or unanticipated consequences that will interfere with, or even totally thwart, the basic purpose of the legislation.

As used by congressional committees, this is a normative argument implying that noncommittee members *should* not offer amendments to committee bills. However, committees do not need to rely solely upon such a norm because if the norm is violated, committees often have available extensive facts and other data to construct a strong case against the adoption of any proposed amendment. To combat these arguments, amendment proposers need to construct alternative arguments that often require an independent set of facts. As a consequence, offering a potentially successful amendment is not a costless task; beyond the activities of formulating, drafting, and proposing an amendment, it also must be supported by argument and data. The formulation of arguments and the acquisition of relevant data, however, can be difficult, expensive, and time consuming. By thus raising the costs of proposing amendments, congressional committees attempt to discourage them, and to the extent that they are successful in limiting the number of alternatives considered, they can control the full chamber agenda and thereby win the unamended passage of their bills.

As stated, this argument implies that congressional committees have a significant amount of proposal power because of their ability to control the decision-making agenda. Moreover, this control derives from the induced costs of

formulating and proposing alternatives. In these terms, the earlier noted success of congressional committees in having their bills passed in the full chamber is not a function of any formal rules but rather of informal mechanisms exploited by committees – in particular here, their expertise and informational advantages.

Note as well that a similar kind of argument can be made to explain the gatekeeping power of congressional committees. If committees are the main repository of knowledge and expertise in a policy area, the normative argument would be that committees should not be discharged of their consideration of a bill because to do so may result in the passage of a seriously flawed law. However, committees also have the resources to construct strong arguments against their being discharged, and, as above, this raises the costs for those who might propose a discharge petition. Consequently, relatively few discharge petitions would be expected, and the gatekeeping power of congressional committees would seldom be challenged.

Is such an agenda control explanation based upon the costs of formulating alternatives valid for the proposal and gatekeeping power of congressional committees? From close observers of congressional committees, there is some evidence that it may be so. In his analysis of the House Appropriations Committee, Fenno noted that "Subcommittee spokesmen defend their recommendations on the grounds that the subcommittee specialists have a more informed understanding of the subject matter than anyone else. On this basis, they appeal for a vote of confidence from their fellow Members."

Similarly, Fleisher and Bond have shown that the single most significant factor explaining the success or failure of amendments to committee bills in both chambers of Congress was the unity of the committee. When committees were united in either support of or opposition to a proposed amendment, the committee position won almost every time; however, when there was division on the committee, the position consistent with that of a committee majority was much less likely to prevail. In the terms used above, this suggests that when the self-proclaimed committee experts are in agreement they win; but when there is disagreement among them, it is less likely that any of them will carry the full chamber.

Also consistent with the costs-of-amendments explanation of congressional committee success are the results presented by Smith. He looked at amending activity in the House between 1955 and 1986 and found that although the members of any given committee constitute less than 10 percent of the membership of the House, committee members generated about half of all floor amendments. This disproportionate offering of amendments by committee members is consistent with the costs hypothesis because if there are costs to proposing full chamber amendments in the House, presumably these would be less for committee members who have the expertise gained through participation in committee hearings and mark-up sessions and who also have access to the information generated by the committee.

These observations and data suggest that the costs-of-amendments hypothesis may have some validity in explaining both the apparent stability of congressional outcomes and the success of congressional committees in their full chambers. There is additional evidence, however, which suggests that this hypothesis may be somewhat of an artifact of a more fundamental reason for congressional committee success. The more fundamental reason for committee success appears to be that committees anticipate what outcomes a majority in the full chamber will accept and do not report bills that conflict in any serious way with these anticipations.

Committee success in Congress, in other words, does not appear to be a situation in which a committee majority forces its will on a reluctant majority in the full chamber because it is so costly for the latter to formulate, offer, and pass amendments to committee bills. Rather, it appears that committees report bills at, or close to a position favored by a full chamber majority so that the only changes generally considered in the full chamber are marginal adjustments, and the benefits derived from these adjustments will often not be worth the costs of making adjustments.

CONCLUSIONS

It has been seen in this chapter that agenda control can be a significant power that not only induces stability in legislative decision making but does so to the benefit of those exercising this power. For this reason, it is not likely that legislators will grant anyone formal control of the agenda. As seen above, it does not appear that formal regulations like the closed rule in the House or the rule prohibiting amendments to conference bills can explain the apparent stability of congressional outcomes or the success of congressional committees in their full chambers. Also, it does not appear that informal cost constraints on the offering of amendments are a basic explanation of committee success. In general, committees are not successful when they oppose full chamber majorities. When a reported bill differs significantly from a position favored by a full chamber majority, the costs of formulating, offering, and passing an amendment will not constrain this majority. In these terms, the success of committees in Congress is largely explained by the fact that committees develop expectations about what positions a full chamber majority will support and report a bill that accords with these expectations.

It would thus appear that agenda control explanations are not very successful or fundamental in accounting for the success of congressional committees or the stability of congressional outcomes.